Trypillia Mega-Sites and European Prehistory
4100-3400 BCE

Edited by Johannes Müller, Knut Rassmann and Mykhailo Videiko

Themes in Contemporary Archaeology

Series Editors:

Professor Kristian Kristiansen, *University of Gothenburg, Sweden*
Professor Eszter Banffy, *German Archaeological Institute, Frankfurt, Germany*
Professor Cyprian Broodbank, *University of Cambridge, UK*

Themes in Contemporary Archaeology provides cutting edge summaries of areas of debate in current archaeological enquiry, with a particular emphasis on European archaeology. The series has a broad coverage, encompassing all periods and archaeological disciplines from theoretical debate to statistical analysis and three-dimensional imaging. The multi-author volumes are based on selected sessions from the well-regarded annual conference of the European Association of Archaeologists.

Published Volumes:
Volume 1: Assembling Çatalhöyük

The European Association of Archaeologists (EAA) is the association for all professional archaeologists of Europe and beyond. The EAA has around 2200 members from 60 countries world-wide working in prehistory, classical, medieval, and later archaeology.

The EAA aims

- to promote the development of archaeological research and the exchange of archaeological information
- to promote the management and interpretation of the European archaeological heritage
- to promote proper ethical and scientific standards for archaeological work
- to promote the interests of professional archaeologists in Europe
- to promote co-operation with other organisations with similar aims.

Trypillia Mega-Sites and European Prehistory 4100–3400 BCE

Edited by Johannes Müller, Knut Rassmann and Mykhailo Videiko

LONDON AND NEW YORK

First published 2016
by Routledge
2 Park Square, Milton Park, Abingdon, Oxon OX14 4RN

and by Routledge
711 Third Avenue, New York, NY 10017

Routledge is an imprint of the Taylor & Francis Group, an informa business

© European Association of Archaeologists 2016

The rights of Johannes Müller, Knut Rassmann and Mykhailo Videiko to be identified as the authors of the editorial material, and of the authors for their individual chapters, has been asserted in accordance with sections 77 and 78 of the Copyright, Designs and Patents Act 1988.

All rights reserved. No part of this book may be reprinted or reproduced or utilised in any form or by any electronic, mechanical, or other means, now known or hereafter invented, including photocopying and recording, or in any information storage or retrieval system, without permission in writing from the publishers.

Trademark notice: Product or corporate names may be trademarks or registered trademarks, and are used only for identification and explanation without intent to infringe.

British Library Cataloguing in Publication Data
A catalogue record for this book is available from the British Library

Library of Congress Cataloging in Publication Data
A catalog record for this book has been requested

ISBN: 978-1-910-52602-6 (hbk)
ISBN: 978-1-315-63073-1 (ebk)

ISSN: 2056-6174
e-ISSN: 2057-1011

Typeset in ACaslonPro-Regular 10.5/12.5
by Techset Composition India (P) Ltd, Bangalore and Chennai, India

Statements in this volume reflect the views of the authors, and not necessarily those of the Association, editors or publisher.

Printed and bound in the UK by Charlesworth Press, Wakefield

Contents

List of Contributors	vii
List of Figures and Tables	ix
Preface	xvii

	Introduction *Johannes Müller and Knut Rassmann*	1
	Framing the Mega-Sites	
CHAPTER 1	**Demography and Social Agglomeration: Trypillia in a European Perspective** *Johannes Müller*	7
CHAPTER 2	**Research on Different Scales: 120 Years Trypillian Large Sites Research** *Mykhailo Videiko and Knut Rassmann*	17
	Mega-Sites	
CHAPTER 3	**The New Challenge for Site Plans and Geophysics: Revealing the Settlement Structure of Giant Settlements by Means of Geomagnetic Survey** *Knut Rassmann, Aleksey Korvin-Piotrovskiy, Mykhailo Videiko and Johannes Müller*	29
CHAPTER 4	**Copper Age Settlements in Moldova: Insights into a Complex Phenomenon from Recent Geomagnetic Surveys** *Knut Rassmann, Patrick Mertl, Hans-Ulrich Voss, Veaceslav Bicbaiev and Alexandru Popa and Sergiu Musteață*	55
CHAPTER 5	**Maidanetske: New Facts of a Mega-Site** *Johannes Müller and Mykhailo Videiko*	71
CHAPTER 6	**Nebelivka: From Magnetic Prospection to New Features of Mega-Sites** *Nataliia Burdo and Mykhailo Videiko*	95
CHAPTER 7	**Nebelivka: Assembly Houses, Ditches, and Social Structure** *John Chapman, Bisserka Gaydarska and Duncan Hale*	117
CHAPTER 8	**Chronology and Demography: How Many People Lived in a Mega-Site?** *Johannes Müller, Robert Hofmann, Lennart Brandtstätter, René Ohlrau and Mykhailo Videiko*	133
	Economies, Social Structure and Ideologies	
CHAPTER 9	**The Natural Background: Forest, Forest Steppe or Steppe Environment** *Wiebke Kirleis and Stefan Dreibrodt*	171
CHAPTER 10	**Demography Reloaded** *Aleksandr Diachenko*	181
CHAPTER 11	**Trypillian Subsistence Economy: Animal and Plant Exploitation** *Wiebke Kirleis and Marta Dal Corso*	195
CHAPTER 12	**Living on the Edge? Carrying Capacities of Trypillian Settlements in the Buh-Dnipro Interfluve** *René Ohlrau, Marta Dal Corso, Wiebke Kirleis and Johannes Müller*	207
CHAPTER 13	**Pottery Kilns in Trypillian Settlements. Tracing the Division of Labour and the Social Organization of Copper Age Communities** *Aleksey Korvin-Piotrovskiy, Robert Hofmann, Knut Rassmann, Mykhailo Yu Videiko and Lennart Brandtstätter*	221
CHAPTER 14	**From Domestic Households to Mega-Structures: Proto-Urbanism?** *Johannes Müller, Robert Hofmann and René Ohlrau*	253

Crisis, Collapse, Transformation?

CHAPTER 15 **Small is Beautiful: A Democratic Perspective?** 269
Aleksandr Diachenko

CHAPTER 16 **Trypillia and Uruk** 281
Johannes Müller and Susan Pollock

Mega-Sites and Mega-Cities: From Past to Present

CHAPTER 17 **Low-density Agrarian Cities: A Principle of the Past and the Present** 289
John Chapman and Bisserka Gaydarska

CHAPTER 18 **Human Structure Social Space: What We Can Learn From Trypillia** 301
Johannes Müller

Index of Places 305
René Ohlrau

Index of Subjects 309
René Ohlrau

List of Contributors

Veaceslav Bicbaev
National Museum of History of Moldova, Republic of Moldova

Lennart Brandstätter
*Institut für Ur- und Frühgeschichte
Christian-Albrechts-Universität zu Kiel, Germany*

Nataliia Burdo
*Institute of Archaeology
National Academy of Science of Ukraine, Ukraine*

John Chapman
*Department of Archaeology
Durham University, UK*

Marta Dal Corso
*Institut für Ur- und Frühgeschichte,
Christian-Albrechts-Universität zu Kiel, Germany*

Aleksandr Diachenko
*Institute of Archaeology
National Academy of Science of Ukraine, Ukraine*

Stefan Dreibrodt
*Institut für Ökosystemforschung
Christian-Albrechts-Universität zu Kiel, Germany*

Bisserka Gaydarska
*Department of Archaeology
Durham University, UK*

Duncan Hale
*Department of Archaeology
Durham University, UK*

Robert Hofmann
*Institut für Ur- und Frühgeschichte
Christian-Albrechts-Universität zu Kiel, Germany*

Wiebke Kirleis
*Institut für Ur- und Frühgeschichte
Christian-Albrechts-Universität zu Kiel, Germany*

Aleksey Korvin-Piotrovskiy
*Institute of Archaeology
National Academy of Science of Ukraine, Ukraine*

Patrick Mertl
Mainz, Germany

Johannes Müller
*Institut für Ur- und Frühgeschichte
Christian-Albrechts-Universität zu Kiel, Germany*

Sergiu Musteață
*History Department
"Ion Creanga" State University, Republic of Moldova*

René Ohlrau
*Institut für Ur- und Frühgeschichte
Christian-Albrechts-Universität zu Kiel, Germany*

Susan Pollock
*Institut für Vorderasiatische Archäologie
Freie Universität Berlin, Germany*

Alexandru Popa
*Nationalmuseum der Ostkarpaten
Judetul Covasna, Rumänien*

Knut Rassmann
*Römisch-Germanische Kommission
Deutsches Archäologisches Institut, Germany*

Mykhailo Videiko
*Institute of Archaeology
National Academy of Science of Ukraine, Ukraine*

Hans-Ulrich Voss
*Römisch-Germanische Kommission
Deutsches Archäologisches Institut, Germany*

List of Figures and Tables

FIGURES

0.1 Trypillia mega-sites in the period 4100–3600 BCE in the Southern Buh-Dnipro Interfluve are the main focus of this book. The area of interest is marked on the map. *Source*: Institute UFG Kiel, K. Winter. — 2

0.2 Chronological chart on the development of societies in South East Europe and Trypillia. — 2

0.3 The distribution of Trypillia B1 sites (kernel density; KDE radius 30 km). *Source*: K. Rassmann/K. Winter (Frankfurt/Kiel) — 3

0.4 The distribution of Trypillia C1 sites (kernel density; KDE radius 30 km). *Source*: K. Rassmann/K. Winter (Frankfurt/Kiel). — 4

0.5 Recent use of a sledge for transport purposes in Siberia (*photo:* J. Oelker, TAZ). — 4

1.1 Sites mentioned in the text: Late Neolithic Okolište (5200–4600 BC), Chalcolithic Vinča (5500–4600 BCE), Maidanetske (3900–3700 BCE), and Valencina (3600–2300 BCE), and Iron Age Heuneburg (600 BC). *Source*: Institute UFG Kiel, K. Winter. — 8

1.2 Large settlements and mega-sites in the Uman region. All sites belong to the Volodymyrivska–Tomashivska local group of Trypillia B2/C1. The largest mega-sites are Nebelivka, Dobrovody, Taljanky, and Maidanetske. *Source*: Institute UFG Kiel, R. Ohlrau. — 8

1.3 A comparison between the largest settlement agglomerations in the Near East and Europe displays huge differences: while in Mesopotamia cities are already known from the Early Bronze Age onwards, in most other regions comparable settlement sizes start no earlier than after 1500 BC. An exception is the development of North Pontic Trypillian sites (Müller, forthcoming). *Source*: Institute UFG Kiel, K. Winter/J. Müller. — 9

1.4 The chronology of Trypillia. Besides the main periodization and phasing, the Trypillia regional groups display characteristic inventories with sub-phases. The main mega-sites are indicated in *italics* (after Kruts, 2012; Menotti, 2012; Ryzhov, 2012; Wechler, 1994; Diachenko, 2012; Kadrow, 2013). — 10

1.5 Okolište, the Visoko basin and the reconstruction of local and regional late Neolithic mobility. (a) The site of Okolište; (b) The Visoko basin with domestic sites and arable land (hatched); (c) Estimated population densities in the late Neolithic Middle Danubian area and Bosnia (isolines, person/km²) and suggested herding activities of the Visoko communities into unpopulated mountain ranges (arrows); (d) The estimated herding area of late Neolithic Butmir agricultural core areas; (e) The percentage of late Neolithic impressed pottery (isolines, %/site); (f) The boundary between arrowheads (Adriatic) and sling shots (Danubian) in the Neretva-Bosna area (*source*: H. Dieterich, Kiel). — 11

1.6 In Late Neolithic Okolište, part-time specializations within the direct neighbourhoods depict a community organized on 'equal terms'. In spite of this, some economically and demographically productive households stood out. *Source*: Institute UFG Kiel, K. Winter/J. Müller. — 12

1.7 Absolute population values, and values for Agrarian population, in Europe (a) and relative population values in Europe and the near East (b) from 6500 to 1500 BC. The numbers indicate the technological innovations and social changes described in the text. *Source*: Institute UFG Kiel, K. Winter/J. Müller (after Müller, 2013a). — 14

2.1 Petreni (Moldova). Ceramic of the Trypillia Culture from the excavations in 1902 und 1903 (Stern 1907, table 10). — 18

2.2 Large site near Volodymyrivka, BII stage (1) plan after T. Passek, 1949; (2) plan after K. Shyshkin (1985); (3 and 4) excavations of clusters of houses, 1947. — 18

2.3 Plans of Trypillia large sites (aerial photographs) after K. Shyshkin (1985) (1) Sushkivka, stage CI; (2) Chychyrkozivka, stage CI; (3) Fedorivka (Mykhailivka), stage BII; (4) Dobrovody, stage CI; (5) Kosenivka, stage CII. — 20

2.4 Cucuteni-Trypillia large sites in Moldova (aerial photographs), after K. Shyshkin and V. Bicbaev. (1) Stolniceni-I; (2) Sofia V; (3) Brynzeni VIII; (4) Petreni. — 21

2.5 Magnetometer M27. This instrument was used by Dudkin in Maidanetske and Taljanky (*photo*: M. Videiko). — 22

2.6 Maidanetske (Uman district). An isoline-interpolation of the survey data by Dudkin (b). V. Dudkin by using the M-27 on the survey Maidanetske in 1971 (a) (Videiko, 2005). — 22

2.7 Maidanetske (Uman district). (a) Interpretation of aerial photograph (Shyshkin, 1973). (b) First synthesis of geomagnetic data and aerial photograph (Shmaglij, 1978). (c) Final geomagnetic map of Dudkin's surveys from 1971 to 1974 (Videiko, 2005). — 23

2.8 Taljanky (Uman district). (a) Final geomagnetic map of Dudkin's surveys (Kruts, 2001). (b) Interpretation of aerial photograph (Shyshkin, 1973). — 23

2.9 Plans of large Trypillia sites: (1 and 2) Yatranivka, BII stage; (3 and 4) Glybochok ((1 and 3) aerial photographs by K. Shyshkin; (2 and 4) geomagnetic survey by V. Dudkin). — 24

2.10 Maidanetske, excavations of clusters of houses, 1986–1987 by M. Shmaglij, M. Videiko, and N. Burdo. — 25

3.1 Geomagnetic survey on settlements of Trypillia-Cucuteni groups by the Romano-Germanic-Commission in cooperation with the University Kiel with the year of the campaign. Additionally mapped: the former Ukrainian survey (Koshelev, 2005) and the survey in Nebelivka (Durham University). (1) Kolomyjshchyna, (2) Stajky (ur. Charkove), (3) Vasylyshyn Jar (Grebeny), (4) Vynogradne (Grebeni), (5) Jancha 1, (6) Jancha 2, (7) Popova Levada, (8) Kuriache Polé (Jushky), (9) Grygorivka (ur. Chatyšce), (10) Rzyshchiv (Homyne), (11) Jushky (ur. Zhuravka), (12) Konovka (Ukraine), (13) Brinzeni Ostrov (14) Trifaneshty, (15) Putineshty, (16) Ivanovka, (17) Starye Raduliani II, (18) Glavan 1, (19) Glavan (Sofija 2a), (20) Lamojna 1, (20) Lamojna 2, (21) Petreni, (22) Mogylna 2, (22) Mogylna 3, (23) Glybochok, (24) Fedorivka (Mychajlivka), (25) Jatranivka, (26) Jampil´, (27) Moshuriv 1 (früh), (27) Moshuriv 1 (spät), (28) Maidanetske, (29) Taljanky, (30) Vilkhvets, (31) Ochiul Alb, (32) Cobani, (33) Horodka, (34) Ruginoasa, (35) Rapa Morii, (36) Prohezesti, (37) Apolianka, (38) Dobrovody, (39) Nebelivka, (40) Singerei. — 30

3.2 The 16-channel magnetometer (SENSYS MAGNETO®-MX ARCH) during a survey campaign in Taljanky in 2012 (*photo*: M. Videiko). — 30

3.3 V. Kruts accompanying the 2011 and 2012 Taljanky surveys. The equipment transport trailer is visible in the background. — 31

3.4 Overview of a spatial analysis of the geomagnetic data. — 31

3.5	(a) Taljanky (Cherkasy Oblast). Overview of the topographical location of the site. (b) Overview of the survey area with the other sites (i.e. Maidanetske, Apolianka, and Dobrovody). All sites are located at the southern edges of plateaus bordered by small streams. The features marked here represent geomagnetic signatures of houses.	32
3.6	Taljanky (Cherkasy Oblast). (a) Geomagnetic map of Dudkin's 1983–1985 survey (Koshchelev, 2004: 305). (b) Overview of the 2011–2012 geomagnetic survey.	33
3.7	Taljanky (Cherkasy Oblast). Overview of the northern part of the settlement with its $c.$ 610 houses. The red circle marks a likely square.	33
3.8	Taljanky (Cherkasy Oblast). Magnetic anomalies in the southern part of the settlement. (a) Houses with different orientations and sizes, pits, and linear structures (alleys). (b) Gap between two house rows, linear structures, and prominent alleys.	34
3.9	Taljanky (Cherkasy Oblast). Magnetic anomalies and houses with prominent positions in front of the entrance area in the southern part of the settlement. Kilns are marked by red Ks. (a) Row of medium-sized burnt houses (70–80 m^2). (b) Entrance area with linear anomaly (trackway) and houses of different sizes and states of preservation: (1) Unburnt or badly preserved houses; (2) large, poorly preserved building. (c) Row of burnt houses and unburnt or badly preserved houses in front of the entrance.	35
3.10	Taljanky (Cherkasy Oblast). Magnetic anomalies and burnt and unburnt houses in the north-western part of the settlement. (a) Burnt houses and circular anomalies (pits refilled with burnt daub?) northeast of the pits to unburnt (?) houses. (b) House rows with different orientations.	35
3.11	Taljanky (Cherkasy Oblast). Magnetic anomalies in the north-western part of the settlement. (a) Area with unregularly distributed small anomalies indicating excavation trenches from the campaigns which took place between 2001 and 2014. (b) House rows with different lengths and numbers of houses.	36
3.12	Taljanky (Cherkasy Oblast). Variation of house sizes in the northern part of the settlement area.	36
3.13	Histogram of the house sizes on Cucuteni-Trypillian sites in Moldova and Ukraine (Petreni, Singerei, Ochiul Alb, Cobani–Moldova; Apolianka, Maidanetske, Taljanky, and Dobrovody). The columns have a width of 10 m each. At Dobrovody, one value above 250 m^2 was omitted.	37
3.14	Choropleth map of house sizes in Taljanky, Maidanetske, and Petreni. The tiles comprise 10,000 m^2 each and show the median of the sizes of all houses per tile.	38
3.15	Taljanky (Cherkasy Oblast). Overview of the around 1550 houses detected and the results of house density estimated by kernel density. The KDE was based on bi-weighted interpolation with a 40 m radius and the centroids of reconstructed houses. The selected 12 m isoline includes more than ninety per cent of the houses. The KDE visualizes the house groups, which can be used for the spatial separation of house groups. As a second category, pottery kilns were also mapped. A re-evaluation of the anomalies allowed for the identification of seventy-four kilns.	38
3.16	Maidanetske (Cherkasy Oblast). (a) Overview of the topographical situation around the site. (b) Overview of the geomagnetic survey area ($c.$ 150 ha) with a detail of the northern area.	40
3.17	Maidanetske (Cherkasy Oblast). Overview of the geomagnetic survey in the north-western part of the settlement.	40
3.18	Maidanetske (Cherkasy Oblast). Overview of the geomagnetic survey in the western part of the settlement.	41
3.19	Maidanetske (Cherkasy Oblast). Overview of the geomagnetic survey in the northern part of the settlement with the highest density of buildings.	41
3.20	Maidanetske (Cherkasy Oblast). Overview of the geomagnetic survey in the south-western part of the settlement with the highest density of buildings.	42
3.21	Maidanetske (Cherkasy Oblast). Overview of the nine special buildings. The geomagnetic data reveal differences in size and preservation, likely the result of their construction and spatial context in relation to the house rows.	43
3.22	Maidanetske (Cherkasy Oblast). Details from the north-western part of the settlement. (1) Rows of heavily burnt houses and a line of less burnt or badly preserved houses. (2) Houses of different sizes and pits. The pits likely mark the back sides of the houses.	44
3.23	Maidanetske (Cherkasy Oblast). Details from the northern part of the settlement. (1) Heavily burnt large houses and a row of pits in an adjacent area north of the houses. (2) House rows framing a linear structure (alleys) and a square with a building in the centre. (3) A second court-like situation that is enclosed by house rows. (4) House rows and a special building close to the excavated kiln and a second unexcavated one (marked by red Ks).	45
3.24	Maidanetske (Cherkasy Oblast). Details from the central part of the settlement. (1) Small houses with different orientations. The small circular anomalies in the north might indicate the house rows of an earlier phase that have a different preservation state. (2) An area without any indication of archaeological features in the central part of the settlement. (3) Houses with differing states of preservation and a special building. (4) Houses of different sizes, preservations, and orientations, as well as circular anomalies (likely pits).	46
3.25	Maidanetske (Cherkasy Oblast). Interpretation of the geomagnetic house anomalies as a result of the recent surveys. The anomalies detected by Dudkin's survey are shown for the western settlement area.	47
3.26	Maidanetske (Cherkasy Oblast). Kernel density estimation of the 1870 house anomalies from recent surveys and the re-digitized 490 from Dudkin's map (after Videiko, 2005). KDE was based on bi-weighted interpolation, 40 m radius, and on the centroids of reconstructed houses. The selected 5 m KDE isoline includes more than eighty per cent of the houses. The KDE visualizes a settlement structure that was divided into sectors. With the inclusion of pottery kilns and special buildings, two other categories are mapped. A re-evaluation of the anomalies identified 18 as kilns, which is a remarkable lower number than at Taljanky (74).	48
3.27	Distribution of large houses (>140 m^2). (a) Taljanky (b) Maidanetske.	48
3.28	Dobrovody (Cherkasy Oblast). (a) Overview of the local topography surrounding the site. (b) Overview of the 23.5 ha geomagnetic survey area.	49
3.29	Dobrovody (Cherkasy Oblast). Details from the northern survey area. (1) House row and special building (260 m^2). (2) A large building (540 m^2) inside the northern house ring. (3) A special building (size 160 m^2) situated in a gap between house rows, a particularity that was often observed in Taljanky and Maidanetske. (4) Rows of small houses and groups of less burnt or badly preserved small houses.	49

3.30	Dobrovody (Cherkasy Oblast). Comparison of the recent survey with Dudkin's earlier results (after Videiko, 2005). (a) Dudkin's survey and the interpolation with aerial photographs. (b) Location of the recent survey (map based on Google Earth). (c) Interpretation of the geomagnetic survey.	50
3.31	Apolianka (Cherkasy Oblast). Overview of the topographical situation around the site.	51
3.32	Apolianka (Cherkasy Oblast). (a) Central area of the geomagnetic survey with concentrically orientated houses and a second group of NE–SE-oriented large buildings in the north-eastern part. (b) Interpretation of the geomagnetic data and house sizes.	52
3.33	Boxplots of the house sizes on Cucuteni-Trypillian sites in Moldova and Ukraine (Petreni, Singerei, Ochiul Alb, Cobani–Moldova; Apolianka, Maidanetske, Taljanky, and Dobrovody–Ukraine). The boxes comprise fifty per cent of the data, the whisker comprises eighty per cent with outliers.	52
3.34	Boxplot of the house sizes of larger settlements of the late Cucuteni-Trypillia Culture (Singerei, Petreni–Moldova; Maidanetske, Taljanky, and Dobrovody–Ukraine). The boxes comprise fifty per cent of the data, the whisker comprises eighty per cent without outliers.	53
4.1	Survey in 2009 in Horodka (district). Alexandru Popa and Klaus Baltes using the 5-channel-system.	56
4.2	Sîngerei (district Sîngerei). View from the North to the settlement on the promontory adjacent to the reservoir.	56
4.3	Sîngerei (district Sîngerei). The topography around the site and an overview of the survey area (DEM SRTM 30 × 30 m).	57
4.4	Sîngerei (district Sîngerei). An overview of the geomagnetic survey and large house structure in the northern settlement.	57
4.5	Sîngerei (district Sîngerei). An overview of the geomagnetic survey on the southern promontory and details of the central part of the Cucuteni-Trypillian settlement.	58
4.6	Sîngerei (district Sîngerei). Interpretation of the geomagnetic data from the Cucuteni-Trypillian settlement.	59
4.7	Petreni (district Drochia). View from the central part of the settlement to the North.	60
4.8	Petreni (district Drochia). (a) The topography around the site. (b) Overview of the survey area (DEM SRTM 30 × 30 m).	60
4.9	Petreni (district Drochia). Overview of the geomagnetic data from the 2010 and 2011 campaigns. The red circle marks the remains of former excavations.	61
4.10	Petreni (district Drochia). Details of the geomagnetic data. (a) Excavation area of Stern 1902–1903. (b) Special building in the centre of the settlement. (c) Two ditches and burnt houses in the southern part of the settlement. (d) Special building with an axial orientation and in isolated position.	62
4.11	Petreni (district Drochia). KDE-based estimation (r 20 m) of the house centroids.	62
4.12	Petreni (district Drochia). Interpretation of the geomagnetic data.	63
4.13	Cobani (district Glodeni). View from the plateau to the northwest.	65
4.14	Cobani (district Glodeni). View to the stone quarry on the south-eastern part of the promontory.	65
4.15	Cobani (district Glodeni). The topographical location around the site and an overview of the survey area (DEM SRTM 30 × 30 m).	66
4.16	Cobani (district Glodeni). (a) Geomagnetic map. (b) Interpretation of the geomagnetic data.	66
4.17	Ochiul Alb (district Drochia). View from the South to the site.	67
4.18	Ochiul Alb (district Drochia). The topographical location around site and an overview of the survey area (DEM SRTM 30 × 30 m).	67
4.19	Ochiul Alb (district Drochia). (a) Geomagnetic map. (b) Interpretation of the geomagnetic data.	68
5.1	Location of the mega-site Maidanetske. Beside the canyon system of the small rivers, the location of three mega-sites at approximately 15 km distance from each other is visible (Dobrovody, Taljanky, and Maidanetske). The features represent the geomagnetic features of the sites.	72
5.2	Maidanetske, plan according to magnetic prospection 1971–1974 and 2011–2012. Objects explored 1972–2014 marked by letters and numbers.	73
5.3	Maidanetske, details: (1) traces of ditch and clusters of houses; (2) large building structure between the rows of houses; (3) traces of ditches and clusters of houses; (4) central part, excavations 2014 (tr.80 and 92); (5) pit 60 and houses around; (6) pit 50 and house 12 ('И'); (7) remains of house 12 ('И'), explored at 1984.	75
5.4	Maidanetske, 2013: (1–7) house 44; (8) pit 52; (1) general view; (2) profile; (3) remains of clay bench; (4) pottery under the upper layer; (5) clay construction on the upper layer of daub; (6) platform of oven, partly covered by the upper layer of daub; (7) floor and pottery on top; (8) profile of pit 52 (*graphics* figure 4.2 and 4.8: R. Hofmann).	77
5.5	Maidanetske, 2014: house 54: (1) general view; (2) pottery on the lower layer of daub; (3) pottery near remains of house; (4) part of lower layer, (a) remains of round structure; (5) goblet, found under the burnt clay platform; (6) clay elevation on ground floor, under the lower layer of daub.	78
5.6	Maidanetske, 2013: pit 50: (1) top of burnt daub layer; (2) profile; (3) group of animal bones and pottery on top of the backfilling; (4) pottery; (5) plan of group; (6) view of burnt layer; (7) plan of burnt daub; (8) profile of the pit; (9) profile (*graphics* 6.5; 6.7, and 6.9: R. Hofmann).	80
5.7	Maidanetske, 2014: documentation of the features of the top layer of house 54 (*graphics*: S. Terna).	81
5.8	Maidanetske, 2014: documentation of the orientation of daub imprints of the top layer of house 54 (*graphics*: S. Terna).	82
5.9	Maidanetske, 2014: documentation of the features of the first floor of house 54 (*graphics*: S. Terna).	83
5.10	Maidanetske, 2014: documentation of the orientation of daub imprints of the first floor of house 54 (*graphics*: S. Terna).	84
5.11	Maidanetske, 2014: documentation of the features of the ground floor of house 54 (*graphics*: S. Terna).	85
5.12	Maidanetske, 2013: pit 60: (1) at the beginning of excavations; (2 and 3) view at excavations; (4 and 5) profiles; (6) general profile; (7) pottery from pit 60; (8) samples of daub from pit 60: (a) fragment of elevation, (b) daub with imprints of wooden constructions (*graphics*: R. Hofmann).	87
5.13	Maidanetske, 2013: pottery from different objects, Tomashivka group, phase 3 (*photo:* S. Jagiolla).	88
5.14	Maidanetske, 2014: trench 80: excavations of kiln: (1–6) the upper layer; (7–8) middle layer.	89

5.15	Maidanetske, 2014: trench 80: excavations of kiln and pits: (1–3) kiln, lower layer; (4–8) pits: (4) general situation at final stage of excavations; (5 and 6) filling and profile of the pit across from the upper kiln; (7) pit opposite to kiln of middle and lower layers; (8) group of artefacts in the pit.	90
5.16	Model of depositional activities related to pit 60. Judging by the ^{14}C-dates a part of a house was deposited in the pit in the 39th century BCE.	91
6.1	Nebelivka, Trypillia BII site: (1) plan after K. Shyshkin, superimposed on the satellite image; (2) pottery from the 1981 field survey by M. Shmaglij.	96
6.2	Nebelivka 2014, excavations of a ditch in the northern part of the site: (1) trench 8 from helicopter (*photo* by Boiko & Boiko), (A) marks the trench according to the geomagnetic prospection; (B) displays the real edges of the ditch; (C) the bottom of ditch; (2 and 3) the profiles of ditch.	97
6.3	Nebelivka 2014, excavations of the ditch in the southern part of the site: (1) trench 10; (A) marks the context as detected by the geomagnetic prospection; (C) displays traces of ditches in the profile; (D) other pits; (2) explored part of the ditch	98
6.4	Nebelivka 2014, excavations in the kiln area: (1) trench 9 at the beginning of the excavations; (2) trench 9—in view from helicopter close to the final stage of explorations (*photo* by Boiko & Boiko).	99
6.5	Nebelivka 2014, excavations in the kiln area: (1) kiln, covered by waste; (2) kiln after being cleaned from waste; (3) materials, including part of a figurine, found inside the channels of the kiln; (4) heavily burnt wall of the channel, enlarged; (5) kiln after being cleaned from waste; (6) reconstructed cover of the channels; (7) use of covers (reconstruction); (8) kiln and pit at the final stage of excavation; (9) fragment of a figurine in the pit near the kiln.	100
6.6	Nebelivka 2014, excavations in the kiln area: (1) plan of trench 9 at the beginning of the excavations; (2) kiln (3) profile of the pit.	101
6.7	Nebelivka 2009, excavations of burnt house A9: (1) general view from E; (2) N part of house remains; (3) imprints of wood on daub and on the surface below it; (4) platform from the oven/fireplace; (5) elevation/altar under the daub layer; (6 and 7) fragmented binocular vessels.	102
6.8	Nebelivka 2013, excavations of burnt house B17: (1) general view from SW; (2) part of platform from the oven/fireplace and traces of ploughing; (3) remains of an altar under the daub; (4) fragment of a wall-painting; (5) fragment of an altar; (6) edges of a decorated dolly tub; (7) part of a profile with two layers of burnt daub.	103
6.9	Nebelivka 2014, excavations of 'probable houses' in trench 5: (1) part of house 1, distribution of daub and pottery; (2) plan of trench 5 (after V. Rud).	104
6.10	Nebelivka 2012, excavations of dwelling B5—'mega-structure': (1) W part of trench with traces of ploughing (A), the direction of plough-marks is identical to the present-day orientation of the crops in the field; (2) W part of the trench with clearly visible black fill from the top part of the pit near dwelling B5 ((1 and 2)—*photo* by M. Household); (3) profile with remains of dwelling B5 and the ploughing layer above; (4) remains of altar 2 in the profile.	105
6.11	Nebelivka 2012, excavations of dwelling B5—'mega-structure': (1) the remains at the first stage of the excavations; (2) reconstruction of the frame system based on imprints ((1 and 2)—*photo* by M. Household); (3)—part of a deposition with traces of a timber construction; (4) reconstruction of the destruction process; (5) sample of daub with visible layers; (6) daub with imprints of round timber construction and cord connection.	106
6.12	Nebelivka 2012, excavations of dwelling B5—'mega-structure': (1) remains of a cross-like altar; (2) reconstructed decoration of the altar (after S. Fedorov); (3) profile of the altar 1 with multiple layers (renewals); (4) podium on the lower layer of daub, partly buried under the upper layer of daub; (5) clay dolly tub with a millstone; (6) remains of a threshold and decoration from the doorframe; (7) remains of the 1.7-m wide threshold at the eastern entrance.	107
6.13	Nebelivka 2013, excavations of pit B17/1: (1) pit and house B17, view from W; (2) layer of finds on the edge of the pit; (3) figurine between the fragments of pottery; (4) part of the profile at the deepest part of pit B17/1; (5) layer of finds on the edge of the pit, view from SW; (6) edge of pit B17/1 and profile from E.	108
6.14	Nebelivka, reconstruction of investigated features: (1) frame construction of dwelling B5; (2) dwelling B5, plan of the ground floor; (3) dwelling B5, plan of the first floor; (4) dwelling B5, reconstructed as a temple (3D by M. M. Videiko); (5) profile of kiln; (6) profile of palisade.	109
7.1	Plan of the Nebelivka mega-site, showing quarters and perimeter ditch (*source*: Y. Beadnell).	118
7.2	Trench 4, showing location of northern ditch section (*photo*: J. Chapman) (EAA 5).	118
7.3	Northern ditch section (*photo*: J. Chapman).	119
7.4	Drawing of northern ditch profile (*source*: V. Cherubini and D. Miller).	120
7.5	Trench 10, showing location of ditches (*photo*: J. Chapman).	120
7.6	Section across southern ditch (*photo*: J. Chapman).	120
7.7	Kite photograph of mega-structure during excavation (*source*: M. Household).	121
7.8	Kite photograph of unburnt part of the mega-structure during excavation (*source*: M. Household).	121
7.9	Phase 2 construction daub, mega-structure (*source*: B. Gayadarska & M. Nebbia).	122
7.10	Fired clay slots to support walls, West wall, mega-structure.	122
7.11	Reconstruction of the mega-structure, Durham view (*source*: St. Johnston).	123
7.12	Fired clay treshold, from East (*photo*: M. Videiko).	124
7.13	The largest of the Raised Areas, from South East (*photo*: John Chapman).	124
7.14	Fired clay bin, from South (*photo*: M. Videiko).	125
7.15	Miniature vessel with graphite decoration: rim diameter 4 cm (*photo*: modified from M. Videiko).	125
7.16	Destruction daub, Phase 3A (*source*: B. Gayadarska & M. Nebbia).	126
7.17	Destruction daub, Phase 3B (*source*: B. Gayadarska & M. Nebbia).	126
7.18	Pottery distribution, Phases 2–4 (*source*: E. Caswell).	127

7.19	Gold hair—ornament, mega-structure (*photo:* M. Videiko).	127
7.20	Fired clay cones, mega-structure (*photo:* M. Videiko).	128
7.21	Spacings between Assembly Houses, Nebelivka (*source:* J. Chapman).	129
8.1	Maidanetske, SSW part of the settlement. The nine house rings, the excavation trenches and the numbers of the houses that were test-trenched or fully excavated (house 44). Pits 50, 52, and 60 are located in trenches with the same numbers. ^{14}C-data are available from nearly all features (see text).	135
8.2	The short profile of house 44. The layers are described in the text, the location of the ^{14}C-samples that date *termini ad quem* are marked (*graphics*: R. Hofmann, UFG Kiel).	161
8.3	Modelling of ^{14}C-dates from Maidanetske. The sequential calibration of 6 groups of dates, which are related to different houses and pits, indicates the most probable chronological timeframe for the features. While for house 44, pit 50, and pit 60 the stratigraphic order of the samples could be integrated in the calculation, in all other cases phases were indicated by ^{14}C-dates of non-stratigraphic order. The median of each boundary calculation was used to display the most probable range for the dates in relation to their spatial order (cf. Müller *et al.*, 2014; Bronk Ramsey, 2009; Reimer *et al.*, 2013).	161
8.4	The chronology of Trypillia. Besides the main periodization and phasing, the Trypillia regional groups display characteristic inventories with sub-phases. The main mega-sites are indicated in *italics* (after Diachenko, 2012; Kadrow, 2013; Kruts, 2012; Menotti, 2012; Ryzhov, 2012; Wechler, 1994). The radiometric data describe the chronological value also of CI-sub-phases.	165
8.5	CA of ceramic shapes and ornamentation types of the Volodymyrivska-Nebelivska-Tomahivska local group sub-phases that were developed by Ryzhov (1999). The typological sequence displays a continuum with a normal distribution of the types that were analysed. The absolute chronological duration of Nebelivka, Taljanky, and Maidanetske, which is based on the available ^{14}C-data, confirms the chronological relevance of the sub-phases, but also indicates the contemporaneity of styles (*graphics*: L. Brandtstätter/J. Müller, UFG Kiel).	166
8.6	CA of ceramic shapes and ornamentation types of the Volodymyrivska-Nebelivska-Tomahivska local group sub-phases (BII/CI T 1–3) that were developed by Ryzhov (1999). In addition, inventories of the 2013 Maidanetske excavation are added. The ^{14}C-dates indicate chronological tendencies (*graphics*: L. Brandtstätter/J. Müller, UFG Kiel).	167
9.1	Natural vegetation: the distribution of forest, forest steppe, and true bunch grass steppe in the western Pontic plant region (after Bundesamt für Naturschutz, 2004).	172
9.2	On-site pollen spectra (Trenches 51, 52, 60, 71, 72, 73, and 75), excavation campaign Maidanetske 2013. Percentage values based on the terrestrial pollen sum (*analyses*: C. Floors/W. Dörfler).	173
9.3	The charcoal assemblages from pit fills (Trenches 50, 52, and 60), excavation campaign Maidanetske 2013 (*analysis*: V. Robin, Kiel).	174
9.4	(a) Cf. *Stipa* (feathergrass), charred awn fragments, sample 51182_12; (b) Modern *Stipa ucrainica*, Botanical Garden, Halle University, Germany (*photo*: S. Jagiolla/W. Kirleis).	174
9.5	Summary of palaeo-ecological and palaeoclimatological reconstructions for the wider region. (a) Pedo-lithogenic cycles reconstructed by Sycheva (2006). S1–S4 represent regional phases of slope stability and soil formation, interrupted by erosive phases. Temperature and precipitation estimates are reconstructed from the record of soils and sediments. (b) Reconstruction of Lake Balquash lake level from Kremenetski (1997) (radiocarbon ages recalibrated). (c) Reconstruction of paleo-precipitation based on the magnetic properties of soils buried by burial mounds from Demkin *et al.* (2014). (d) Holocene palaeoclimatic summary of pollen diagrams given by Gerasimenko (1997) (radiocarbon ages recalibrated).	175
9.6	Maidanetske; stratigraphy of Trench 70. (a) Scaled drawing with age data. fBw: buried cambic horizon, fAh: buried humus surface horizon, M1-3: colluvial layers (M: lat. migrare). (b) Number and colour of krotovina fills from different horizons and layers.	177
10.1	Population estimates for SV-1 of the Volodymyrivsko-Tomashivska line of the WTC. (a) All sites; (b) largest settlements.	186
11.1	Map of Trypillia sites with charred botanical macro-remains differentiated according to phases A–C.	196
11.2	The main phytolith morphotypes in the assemblages from Maidanetske 2013 give indications of Pooideae ((a) rondel, (b) trapeziform), Panicoideae ((c) bilobate), and pooid cereal chaff ((d) dendritic long cell) (*photos:* M. Dal Corso).	201
11.3	The phytolith single cells assemblage from the 2013 excavation campaign in Maidanetske according to archaeological context.	202
11.4	The silica skeleton assemblage from the 2013 excavation campaign in Maidanetske according to archaeological context in % on the sum of phytoliths and skeletons.	202
Plate	Charred macro-remains from Maidanetske *(photos:* S. Jagiolla/W. Kirleis) (1) *Pisum sativum* (pea), sample 51647, house context. (2) *Hordeum vulgare* (barley), sample 600191, refuse pit. (3) *Panicum miliaceum* (broomcorn millet), sample 51182, house context. (4) *Triticum monococcum* (einkorn), sample 60079, refuse pit. (5) *Triticum monococcum* (einkorn), glume bases, sample 60165, refuse pit. (6) *Triticum monococcum/dicoccon* (einkorn/emmer), glume base, sample 60165, refuse pit. (7) *Triticum dicoccon* (emmer), glume bases, sample 60165, refuse pit. (8) *Galium aparine* (cleavers), sample 60145, refuse pit. (9) *Setaria viridis* (green foxtail), sample 51182, house context.	203
12.1	Distribution map of Trypillian sites in the Buh-Dnipro interfluve considered in this model. The names of the settlements are provided in Table 5.	212
12.2	Modelled land-use for sites in the Southern Buh-Dnipro interfluve. Trypillia BII (Volodymyrivska 1–Nebelivska 1).	217
12.3	Modelled land-use for sites in the Southern Buh-Dnipro interfluve and remains of former land-use from previous stage. Trypillia BII-C1 (Nebelivska 2–Tomashivska 2).	217

12.4	Modelled land-use for sites in the Southern Buh-Dnipro interfluve and remains of former land-use from previous stage. Trypillia C1 (Tomashivska 2–4).	218
12.5	Woodland use and recovery during the final stage of mega-sites.	218
13.1	The distribution of kilns in Southeast and Eastern Europe and their absolute dating in 500-year increments. The size of the points represents the number of kilns per site. The values are displayed in List 1.	222
13.2	Taljanky (Talne district). Overview of the geomagnetic survey.	225
13.3	Taljanky (Talne district). Kiln C. Comparison of the excavated kiln and the geomagnetic data. Visible are the differences regarding the size of the geomagnetic anomaly and the real size of the kiln. The 20 nT line correlates with the size of the kiln.	226
13.4	Taljanky (Talne district). Overview on the northern part of the settlement with detailed plans of the excavation areas with pottery kilns A, B, and D in the first, and kiln C in the second.	227
13.5	Taljanky (Talne district). Schematic map of the excavation area of kilns in the northern area of the settlement. Houses and pits are drawn in idealized form.	228
13.6	Taljanky (Talne district). Kiln A. View from the South.	229
13.7	Taljanky (Talne district). Kiln A. View from the southeast.	229
13.8	Taljanky (Talne district). Kiln A. View from the East.	230
13.9	Taljanky (Talne district). Kiln A. View from the northeast.	230
13.10	Taljanky (Talne district). Kiln A. View from the North.	231
13.11	Taljanky (Talne district). Kiln A. View from the northwest.	231
13.12	Taljanky (Talne district). Kiln A. After uncovering.	232
13.13	Taljanky (Talne district). Kiln A. View from the West.	233
13.14	Taljanky (Talne district). Kiln B. View from the South.	233
13.15	Taljanky (Talne district). Kiln B. View from the East.	234
13.16	Taljanky (Talne district). Kiln B. View from the East.	234
13.17	Taljanky (Talne district). Kiln B. View from the South.	235
13.18	Taljanky (Talne district). Kiln B. View from the West.	235
13.19	Taljanky (Talne district). Kiln B, View from the North.	236
13.20	Taljanky (Talne district). Kiln C. Upper level with pottery remains.	237
13.21	Taljanky (Talne district). Kiln C. View from the South.	238
13.22	Taljanky (Talne district). Kiln C. View from the West.	238
13.23	Taljanky (Talne district). Kiln C. View from the West.	239
13.24	Taljanky (Talne district). Kiln C. View from the East.	239
13.25	Taljanky (Talne district). Kiln C. Burned ground under the kiln.	240
13.26	Taljanky (Talne district). Kiln D.	240
13.27	Taljanky (Talne district). Kiln D.	241
13.28	Taljanky (Talne district). Kiln D.	241
13.29	Taljanky (Talne district). Compilation of the ground plans of the four pottery kilns which were excavated in Talianki in 2013 and 2014.	242
13.30	Maidanetske (Talne district). Schematic map of the excavation area of the kilns in trench 80. Houses are drawn in an idealized form. Some of the pits were used for the deposition of misfired pottery and other production remains, as the two pits close to pottery kiln T80 indicate.	243
13.31	Maidanetske (Talne district). Pottery kiln in trench 80. Plan of the three construction phases of the pottery kiln.	244
13.32	Maidanetske (Talne district). Pottery kiln in trench 80. Photogrammetric picture of construction phase 1 remains.	245
13.33	Maidanetske (Talne district). Pottery kiln in trench 80. Section 28 through the first construction phase of the kiln. Large vessel fragments are integrated into the internal partition of the kiln basement.	246
13.34	Maidanetske (Talne district). Pottery kiln in trench 80, northern part of construction phase 1 with rounded ends of the channels. (a) Partition wall, rounded on the upper edge; (b) flat bedding on top of the outer wall; (c) bedding at the outer wall, sloped towards the centre of the kiln.	246
13.35	Maidanetske (Talne district). Pottery kiln in trench 80. 3D-model of construction phase 2 remains.	247
13.36	Maidanetske (Talne district). Pottery kiln in trench 80. 3D-model of construction phase 3 remains.	247
13.37	Maidanetske (Talne district). Pottery kiln in trench 80. Flat bedding at the outer side of construction phase 3.	248
13.38	Overview of the calculation of the production and consumption of pottery, in respect to the archaeological data and specific uncertainties in the excavation record.	248
13.39	Schematic map of the location of kilns in the settlements of Maidanetske and Taljanky (both Talne district) and Petreni (district Drochia, Moldova). The identification of the pottery kilns is based on the geomagnetic data. Five such anomalies at Maidanetske and Taljanky were correctly proven to be kilns by excavation in 2013 and 2014.	249
13.40	Schematic map of the location of kilns in the settlements of Maidanetske and Taljanky (both Talne district) and Petreni (district Drochia, Moldova) in relation to the size of houses. The house size is calculated based on the median in 100 × 100 m raster cells.	249
13.41	First attempt at a schematic reconstruction of the pottery kilns from Maidanetske and Taljanky: (a) firebox with three channels (here: longitudinal section); (b) grate (platform) or mobile covering of round clay slabs; (c) firing chamber; (d) fire or loading pit; (e) loading mouth. The tunnel-like loading mouth of the kiln which is displayed in the reconstruction is not proven in the archaeological record. The same is true for the shape of the fire chamber above the grate.	250
14.1	Maidanetske house 44 displays a typical *ploschchadka* with internal divisions into several features that are known from most domestic Trypillian C1 houses (cf. Chernovol, 2012). *Source:* R. Hofmann/J. Müller/K. Winter, UFG Kiel.	254
14.2	Artefact distributions on the ground floor, on the main floor, and in the vicinity of house 44 display different spatial patterns that aid in the reconstruction of activity areas within and around the house. *Source:* R. Hofmann/K. Winter, UFG Kiel.	255

14.3	Maidanetske house 44 with reconstructed activity areas. Source: R. Hofmann/J. Müller/K. Winter, UFG Kiel.	257
14.4	Scheme of the house place organisation. *Source:* J. Müller/K. Winter, UFG Kiel.	258
14.5	Differences in the reconstructed demand on arable land, using the floor size of houses in Taljanky for population estimations, and the reconstructed use of arable land using the number of millstones per house as a proxy for the amount of cereal processing (cf. Müller *et al.*, in print). The number of millstones and loom-weights implies a division into three categories of houses: with many millstones, with millstones and loom-weights, and without both. *Source*: J. Müller/K. Winter, UFG Kiel.	260
14.6	The typological dissimilarities and similarities between houses in the southeastern house-ring of Maidanetske are expressed in the amount of shared ornamentation types and in the eigenvector value of the first eigenvector of a correspondence analyses on pottery decoration (Brandtstätter, in print; Tkachuk & Melnik, 2005). *Source*: K. Winter, UFG Kiel.	261
14.7	The reconstruction of house clusters by the average distance between neighbouring houses. *Source*: R. Ohlrau, UFG Kiel.	262
14.8	View-shed analysis of the Y-space at Maidanetske. The visibility increases from blue to red (number of cell connectivity). Megastructures are mainly placed in the 'public' space or blocking radial accesses to the central space. *Source*: R. Ohlrau, K. Winter, UFG Kiel.	264
14.9	Reconstruction of quarters in Maidanetske by mapping nearest distances of houses to mega-structures. Clusters of kilns are also associated with these quarters. *Source*: R. Ohlrau, K. Winter, UFG Kiel.	266
14.10	The model of decision-making processes in a mega-site. *Source*: J. Müller/K. Winter, UFG Kiel.	267
15.1	The WTC settlements between the Dniester and the Dnipro. Landscapes: (a) forest-steppe upland dissected landscapes; (b) loess upland terrace landscapes; (c) floodplain landscapes; (d) pine forest terraces; and (e) northern steppe upland and slope landscapes. Settlements: (1) Chechelnytska local group; (2) Serednobugza local group; (3) Volodymyrivska local group; (4) Nebelivska local group; (5) Tomashivska local group; and (6) Kosenivska local group and Kocherzhyntsi-Shulgivka type. Settlements concerned in this study: (1) Tomashivka; (2) Dobrovody; (3) Maidanetske; (4) Nebelivka; (5) Fedorivka; (6) Glybochok; (7) Vi'lkhovets 1; (8) Chychyrkozivka; and (9) Vasylkiv.	270
15.2	The ETC settlements (1–5) and the Western Trypillia sites outside the Southern Bug and Dnipro interfluve (6) that were considered in this study. (1) Chapaivka, (2) Trypillia, ur. Lypove, (3) Veselyj Kut, (4) Onopriivka, (5) Vi'lkhovets 2, and (6) Mayaky.	271
15.3	The Horodişte-Folteşti–Tripolye CII sites (after Dergachev, 2000). (1) Fortified settlements, (2) probably fortified settlements, (3) settlements with toponymy related to fortifications, and (4) fortified and probably fortified settlements with toponymy related to fortifications.	275
16.1	Areas of intensive settlement surveys in Southern Mesopotamia and neighbouring regions (from Pollock, 1999: 55, figure 3.8).	282
17.1	Trajectories of high-density to low-density urban sites (*source*: Fletcher, n.d.).	290
17.2	Worldwide distribution of low-density urban sites: (1) Cahokia; (2) Stonehenge; (3) Mont Beuvray; (4) Trypillia mega-sites (Nebelivka); (5) Ile Ife; (6) Great Zimbabwe; (7) Co Loa; (8) Angkor Wat; (9) Chaco Canyon; (10) Manaus (Amazonia); (11) Longshan group (*source*: B. Gayadarska).	291
17.3	Settlement sizes by Trypillia phase (*source*: J. Chapman).	292
17.4	The Nebelivka house-burning experiment: the two-storeyed house, showing the south wall and door after 1 hour 30 minutes of burning (*photo*: M. Nebbia).	293
17.5	A possible communal cooking feature, from the South (*photo*: M. Yu. Videiko).	295
18.1	Pit 50 from the mega-site Maidanetske. Two cattle skulls, many bones, and various pots were deposited before the infilling of huge masses of daub began. The assemblage perhaps displays the remains of a feast with a subsequent ritual deposition, as is also known from other areas of Europe in the 38th century BCE (*photo*: Institute UFG).	303
18.2	A vision of the deliberate destruction of a mega-site, archaeological excavations, and a modern city (*photo*: J. Müller, wall painting/photograph in the Legedzine museum).	303

TABLES

2.1	Large-scale geomagnetic surveys under the direction of V. Dudkin 1971–1995	24
3.1	Statistical data on Cucuteni-Trypillia houses based on geomagnetic data	46
5.1	Value data objects between the old and new plans	72
5.2	The main excavated features of the excavation campaigns 2013–2014 with preliminary publications	76
List 1	The Maidanetske houses, key data	74
6.1	Nebelivka, British–Ukrainian investigations 2009, 2012–2014	96
6.2	Excavations of dwellings in Nebelivka: 2009–2014	109
8.1	Population estimations for Maidanetske based on estimated maximal and minimal areas per person and estimated maximal and minimal numbers of contemporary houses (2297 houses: burnt houses; 2968: burnt and unburnt houses; 2633 houses: average between bot values).	164
List 1	Maidanetske ^{14}C-dates.	136
List 2	Cucuteni-Trypillia ^{14}C-dates	143
10.1	Estimation of the average family size based upon sex–age structure of people buried in Vykhvatyntsi cemetery	182
10.2	Number of burnt and the so-called 'unburnt and/or eroded dwellings' at the recently prospected settlements (after Chapman et al., 2014; Rassmann et al., 2014)	183
10.3	Population estimates for the settlements	184
10.4	Relative chronology of sites considered in this study	185
10.5	Population estimates for the settlement clusters	186
10.6	Density of dwellings at the largest settlements	188
11.1	(Belongs to Figure 1) Compilation of charred and mineralized botanical remains from Trypillian sites. n=single finds, nnn=numerous finds	198
12.1	Estimated total and contemporary population sizes of Maidanetske and Taljanky	208
12.2	Calculation of crops demand, assuming them to cover the seventy-seven per cent of kilocalories in the diet	209
12.3	Comparison of estimations regarding demanded hectare of arable land per capita per year	209
12.4	Herd composition per household used in this model, after Kruts et al. (2001, 85)	209
12.5	Required land for the subsistence economy of Trypillian settlements in the Southern Buh-Dnipro interfluve by variables discussed in the text	211
List 1	Uman region resource demands (for reference)	213
List 1	List of Southeast European and North Pontic Neolithic, and Chalcolithic kilns	223
14.1	Statistics for buildings in the clusters at Maidanetske (Ohlrau, 2014)	263
14.2	Statistics on mega-structure areas in relation to house groups and kilns. The division into four spatial classes A–D represents one of the possible models for the organization of Maidanetske (Ohlrau, 2014)	265
17.1	Basic quantitative variables for four Trypillia mega-sites	294

Preface

Research on the Trypillia phenomenon has a long and intensive history, starting already at the end of the nineteenth century with the systematic excavations of Vikentiy Khvoika near the village of Trypillia. Both the multicultural climate within the main towns and cities of the North Pontic area, as well as the inspired regional and local research, are responsible for early archaeological work that identified these tremendous archives of unique societies. This constellation led to a wide perspective on the Trypillian phenomena as visible, for example, in the early publication of Ernst von Stern in 1907. He discussed the Trypillian phenomena in the context of the archaeological archives of Southeast and Central Europe, and compared, for example, Trypillian development with that of the Bosnian Butmir.

After decades of intense research by Soviet archaeologists, further methodological breakthroughs were achieved in the 1970s by research teams with very sophisticated approaches: aerial photography and geomagnetic survey were developed and applied, together with target excavations, on a scale that was not reached by any Western archaeology at that time: The identification of mega-sites with more than 2000 houses and concentric house rings was conducted under the direction of V. P. Dudkin. Related to these breakthroughs, recent developments are merely a follow-up to this research: During the last decade, new modern geomagnetic devices, new radiometric dating, and scientific analyses have aided in disentangling Trypillia social practices.

Besides many others, four European on-going research projects in recent years have especially expanded the information on particular phenomena of Late Trypillia: the Kyiv–Frankfurt–Kiel team on geomagnetic surveys, a Kyiv team on the Taljanky mega-site, a Kyiv–Durham team on the mega-site Nebelivka, and a Kyiv–Kiel team on Maidanetske. They disentangle the environmental conditions, plus the organization and development of the Trypillia mega-sites in the period 4100–3600 BCE in the Southern Buh-Dnipro Interfluve.

The archives, which were unravelled for the first time in the 1970s, yield excellent information on different analytical scales: from the reconstruction of local events, to the general question of proto-urbanism that is relevant for worldwide archaeology and anthropology. The social practices for developing population agglomerations of probably more than 10,000 persons are the phenomenon which forms the central aspect of this book: How and why did these agglomerations develop, and what kind of societies do they represent? With the presentation of new geophysical site plans, new contextual analyses on Late Trypillia houses, improved chronological resolution, and new discourses on kilns and mega-structures we hope to contribute to a wider European perspective: What caused prehistory in this region to develop in such a non-evolutionary way and so differently to other areas of the world, where population agglomerations like those detected in Late Trypillia led to the development of oppressive kingdoms and states?

The recent burst of new fieldwork on Trypillia mega-sites led to a lively debate including divergent opinions on this extraordinary phenomenon. These positions differ on the size of the estimated site populations, the proportion of the site occupied at the same time, the question of permanent vs. seasonal occupations of houses, the level of hierarchical complexity and, most interestingly if paradoxically, the attribution of the mega-site phenomenon to rural, proto-urban, or urban attributes. The debate well captured in this volume, will surely frame the theoretical and methodological agenda of Trypillia mega-site archaeology for the next decade.

This book would not have been possible without the tremendous job done by Nicole Taylor and Karin Winter from the Johanna-Mestorf Academy, Kiel and the Institute of Prehistoric and Protohistoric Archaeology, Kiel on the editing of the English texts and the graphics. Both of them carried the main burden of the editing. Aleksandr Diachenko from the National Academy of Science of Ukraine Kyiv also helped immensely, both in transliteration as well as content-related questions. We wish to thank them for their extremely valuable help.

This book is the outcome of a research project of the Graduate School 'Human Development in Landscapes', which also financed the editing. The whole book-project is linked to the joint work of the Institute of Archaeology of the National Academy of Science of Ukraine in Kyiv, the Romano-German-Commission of the German Archaeological Institute in Frankfurt, and the Christian-Albrechts-University

© European Association of Archaeologists 2016

in Kiel. The German partners are very grateful for the possibility to be integrated as guests in this extraordinary Trypillia research opportunity.

We dedicate this volume to Volodymyr Kruts, who was the main driver of Ukrainian Trypillia research for many decades. The fieldwork which he conducted and published, as part of a huge project on the mega-site of Taljanky, forms the main basis for all new inquiries. We will keep him in our memory, both as a promoter of our geomagnetic surveys and excavations, as well as an extremely knowledgeable partner in the discussion of Trypillia topics.

Johannes Müller, Knut Rassmann, Mykhailo Videiko

Introduction

Johannes Müller and Knut Rassmann

During the last decade, tremendous changes have taken place in the study of European prehistory. The elaboration of field activities, including huge geomagnetic surveys and advances in excavation documentation, has made it possible to reconstruct social space and environment on different spatial scales. Furthermore, advances in dating methodology and other scientific analyses made the linkage between material culture and archaeological features much easier. Both the reconstruction of environmental and societal processes and also the detection of the ideological perception of environs and societies have made huge advances. This is also true for the phenomenon of Trypillia societies in the North Pontic forest-steppe and steppe area.

The theme of this book focuses on a special development: the agglomeration of demographic, economic, and societal resources in the so-called mega-sites that belong to Late Trypillia (*c.* 4100–3600 BCE) mainly in the Southern Buh-Dnipro interfluve (Figure 1). We define 'mega-sites' on the one hand, in a technical way, as sites that are larger than *c.* 150 hectares in size and whose highly structured settlement layout implies some kind of planning (and thus contemporary existence) of most of the involved structures. On the other hand, we also define them as sites which, in comparison to other contemporary sites, are at least 10 times larger than the next smaller ones.

When we deal with the many aspects of these mega-sites in respect to the environment, the organization of social space, the reconstruction of daily life, political institutions, and site histories, we should bear in mind that mega-sites are only one step in a centuries-long development, which started no later than *c.* 4800 BCE in the North Pontic region (Figure 2).

Besides many differences in the development of material culture throughout the Trypillia phenomenon, in principle the features and ornamentation of objects could be traced to a tradition starting around the start of Early Trypillia (Trypillia A; Figure 2). Despite the lack of proper scientific dating approaches and spatial analyses, the typological similarities in pottery design, for example, as well as the similarities in the early settlement ground plans, indicate the link to Cucuteni and Pre-Cucuteni of the Carpathian regions. As the many successful synchronizations of Cucuteni and Trypillia chronologies link Cucuteni/Trypillia to 'one cultural complex', the starting point of this development has to be sought in the West: Precucuteni dates as early as around 5200 BCE.

Thus, Cucuteni-Trypillia links the South East European developments with the North Pontic Space. In principle, the development of the Late Neolithic with Vinča A starts in the central Carpathian Basin around 5500 BCE, some centuries after the first neolithization processes introduced the 'neolithic' to a mosaic of Balkan landscapes. The creation of villages with communal activities is characteristic for this period of innovation. The transition to Vinča B around 5200 BCE marks the transition to more elaborated ceramic designs from settlement developments. Furthermore, the development of copper metallurgy enhances changes within the societies. Settlement mounds, which were already known from the Aegean area and Anatolia in the Early Neolithic, became one of a number of settlement types in the Central Balkans and Carpathian Basin around 5300 BCE. The Late Neolithic/Early Chalcolithic is characterized by the concentration of houses in an increasingly denser arrangement, as well as by flat land settlements, which sometimes surround tell sites. Vinča C1 (*c.* 5050 BCE) and different cultural groups in Transylvania and Serbia experiment with new settlement patterns, namely concentric and radial orientations of houses within domestic sites (Iclod and Burdos–recent investigation by R. Hofmann, CAU Kiel).

As early as around 5200 BCE, communities which are labelled 'Pre-Cucuteni' in East Carpathian regions develop several new typological elements. Obviously this is the point of departure for the development of new ideas and new principles, mainly in respect to the organization of social space. Based on the basic chronological charts of Schmidt (1932) for Cucuteni, and Passek (1949) for Trypillia, the synchronization shows significant Trypillia sites at the latest around 4800 BCE in the Western area of their distribution. One of the earliest known sites with a concentric settlement pattern is Bernashivka in the Dniestr region of Ukraine. Around 4600 BCE a new impetus of influences and perhaps mobile groups led to the acculturation of areas east of the Trypillia A development. Trypillia B (Figure 3) is linked to an enlargement of the settlements.

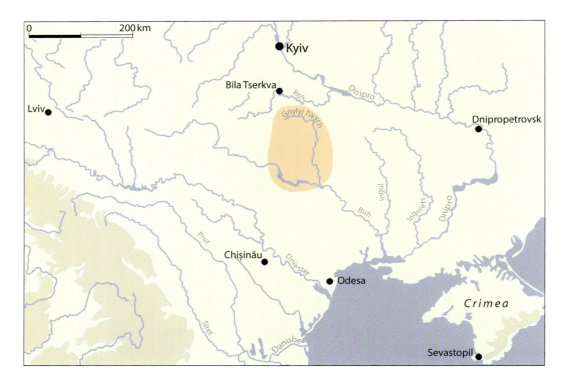

Figure 1. Trypillia mega-sites in the period 4100–3600 BCE in the Southern Buh-Dnipro Interfluve are the main focus of this book. The area of interest is marked on the map. Source: Institute UFG Kiel, K. Winter.

BCE	Carpathian Basin		Central Balkan	East Balkan	Lower Danube	Prut-Dniester	Buh-Dnipro	BCE
3100								3100
3200	Baden		Cotofeni I/II	Ezero A	Jamnaja	Hurodistea-Foltesti		3200
3300							Trypillia C2	3300
3400	Boleraz		Cernavodă III	Cernavodă III	Cernavodă III			3400
3500								3500
3600	Proto-Boleraz					Cucuteni B		3600
3700	Hunyadihalom		Salcuta-Krivodol IV		Hotnica		Trypillia C1	3700
3800								3800
3900	Bodrogkeresztúr	Balaton				Cucuteni AB	Trypillia B2	3900
4000								4000
4100							Trypillia B1/B2	4100
4200	Tiszapolgár		Krivodol III Salcuta		Krivodol			4200
4300		Sopot IV	Bubanj Hum			Cucuteni A	Trypillia B1	4300
4400				Karanovo VI	Gumelniţa			4400
4500					Varna			4500
4600	Tisza III	Sopot III	Vinča D					4600
4700	Tisza II	Herpály		Karanovo V		Precucuteni	Trypillia A	4700
4800								4800
4900	Tisza I		Vinča C	Marica	Boian			4900
5000		Sopot II			Hamangija			5000
5100	Szakálhát / Bükk		Vinča B	Karanovo IV				5100
5200		Sopot I		Karanovo III-IV			Buh-Dniester	5200

Figure 2. Chronological chart on the development of societies in South East Europe and Trypillia.

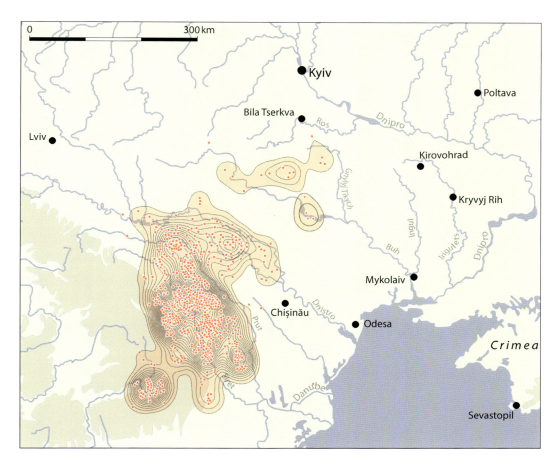

Figure 3. The distribution of Trypillia B1 sites (kernel density; KDE radius 30 km). Source: K. Rassmann/K. Winter (Frankfurt/Kiel).

Elaborated painted pottery is now also produced in the eastern areas of the distribution. The ever denser agglomeration of settlement sites, besides additional new small sites, is observed.

In Southeast Europe we observe the development of metallurgical production, as well as demographic and social processes, which lead to the concentration of people in the tells, on the one hand, and to the accumulation of wealth in certain settlements and graveyards, on the other hand. As described by so many archaeologists, metallurgical products reached from the Balkans further east–best represented by the Trypillia B hoard from Karbuna. E.N Chernych's reconstruction of the Eurasian Metallurgical Circle still describes the general network of production and exchange within a supra-regional setting.

We have to bear in mind that during all these developments, which lasted centuries in both the western and eastern parts of the Trypillia landscape, the earliest Trypillia A settlements were already present in the eastern area. Thus, not only mobility between different regional groups, but also internal developments in each Trypillia region, are responsible for the new and different social patterns that we observe in the archaeological remains of social practices.

From a technological point of view, immense technological changes are visible within the Trypillia world during middle Trypillia. While a decrease in the use of copper is obvious, which has to be linked to the downfall of metallurgical societies in the eastern Balkans, the development of new traction-devices probably had a huge impact on the societies (Figure 5). Within the steppe landscape the cattle-drawn sledge, as documented from terracotta models, made access to arable land and the transport of raw materials easier. The importance of weaving, represented by loom weight clusters in Trypillia B2/C1 houses, and the appearance of 3-channelled pottery kilns mark further technological changes in the societies that, in the long run, changed both economic and social daily life to a certain degree. Some of these innovations were internal creations (e.g. the sledge), whereas others were introduced from other regions (e.g. the advances in weaving). These main aspects might be related to the appearance of mega-sites around 4100 BCE (Figure 4).

These demographic agglomeration processes in the North Pontic Area, which are not known from any other European prehistoric society, happen during a time when the eastern part of Southeast Europe did not produce extraordinary archaeological remains. For

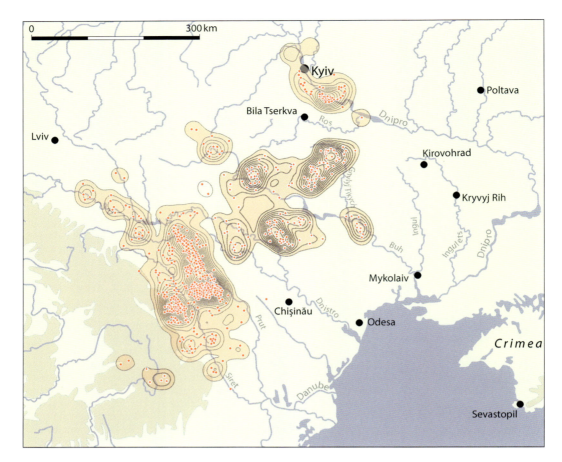

Figure 4. The distribution of Trypillia C1 sites (kernel density; KDE radius 30km. Source: K. Rassmann/K. Winter (Frankfurt/Kiel).

centuries after 4100 BCE we do not recognize huge sites in the Eastern Balkan area or in the Carpathian regions. Nevertheless, the roots for the Trypillia concentric settlement design with such huge population agglomerations might be found in the Central Balkans. The rise of large settlements with a population size of up to 2,000 inhabitants in the Central Balkans obviously accelerated the creation of social, technical, and cultural innovation. The central sites acted as power containers in conjunction with their surroundings, in a similar sense to how Giddens (1984, 195) formulated the role of cities. In this way, we can take the evidence for metal production in the Vinča sites Plocnik and Belovode as signs for the anchoring of early metallurgy in large sites.

By Trypillia C, the concentration of people, the optimization of communication and knowledge transfer, the increasing social competition etc. led perhaps to a more differentiated division of labour; more in a sense of the constitution of societies and the stabilization of intergroup relationships. With larger population sizes, people have to manage the higher vulnerability of higher complexity. The reaction the changes in the political environment as well as to changes in the natural environment requires the ability to adapt them. Above all, the limitations of non-literate societies might be visible in the processes involved in the rise and decline of Trypillian mega-sites. As a consequence, Trypillian mega-sites ceased after Trypillia C1 and both a reduction in settlement sizes, as well as a general regionalization, took place. Thus, the use of terms like ruralization and urbanization, or even proto-urbanization, as valid terms for Trypillian sites should be reviewed again at the end of this volume.

This volume will frame the 'mega-site question' in the first two chapters, by placing 'Trypillia in a

Figure 5. Recent use of a sledge for transport purposes in Siberia (photo: J. Oelker, TAZ).

European perspective' and outlining the research history of the Trypillia phenomenon, which is necessary for understanding the results of recent research on Trypillia.

In 'Framing the mega-site' the next chapters deal with structures, settlement ground plans, chronologies, and population densities of individual mega-sites, but also with newly discovered features like kilns and mega-structures. The vivid discussion on the interpretation both of single contexts as well as of structural approaches describes the inspiring interpretation of the Trypillia phenomenon. The new quality of research will be obvious: from single structures to geomagnetic plans, which for the first time allow the scaling of contextual observations, for example.

'Economies, social structures and ideologies' are the content of the next few chapters. The natural background and changes in the environment will be dealt with, and a general approach to demography and the reconstruction of subsistence economies will enhance a model of land-use and carrying capacities. Traces of supra-household organizations will be dealt with, again with the example of the newly discovered kilns. Last but not least, different scales of political institutions in Trypillia mega-sites are developed related to the question of proto-urbanism.

The reasons for, and consequences of, 'transformations' will be addressed in respect to the period after the mega-sites, but also in respect to their principal differences to the other, more or less contemporary, demographic agglomeration process–the South Mesopotamian development. Lastly, after the deconstruction of ideas about the development of 'urban' landscapes in the North Pontic area, two contributions try to identify the role which Trypillian mega-sites played in a world-historical perspective: Addressing a model of 'low density agrarian cities' and general aspects of the organization of social space in changing environments.

This volume combines the general approach to the organization of social space in a changing environment with detailed analyses and discussions of newly discovered features. Both social anthropological and archaeological questions are combined with new scientific field work.

References

Giddens, A. 1984. *The Constitution of Society, Outline of the Theory of Structuration*. Cambridge: Polity Press.

Passek, T.S. 1949. *Periodozatsiya tripolskikh poselenij (III–II tys. do n.e.). Materialy i issledovaniya po archeologii SSSR*, 10. Пассек, Т.С. 1949. Периодизация трипольских поселений III–II тыс. до н.э. Материалы и исследования по археологии СССР, 10.

Schmidt, H. 1932. *Cucuteni in der oberen Moldau, Rumänien: die befestigte Siedlung mit bemalter Keramik von der Steinkupferzeit bis in die vollentwickelte Bronzezeit*. Berlin: W. de Gruyter.

CHAPTER 1

Demography and Social Agglomeration: Trypillia in a European Perspective

JOHANNES MÜLLER

Since the discovery of Trypillia mega-sites in the 1970s, their huge size and the issue of their social organization has been the major aspect of research. The development of these huge sites, which took place around 4100–3500 BCE especially in the Uman region, is comparable in its structural reasoning with other processes of population concentration in prehistoric Europe, and closely linked to social processes. Thus, an evaluation of demographic and social processes in Europe may aid in judgements about the mega-sites.

SOCIAL STRUCTURES, SETTLEMENT PATTERNS, AND DEMOGRAPHY

The social constitution of a society, and the role which an individual may play in it, depends on many factors. One of the most formative aspects in this sense is the size of the local residential unit that takes the communal decisions and the density of the population within a reachable area: demographic reconstructions of past societies are one of the most challenging questions in archaeological research. Despite the difficult task of reconstructing group sizes, village and proto-urban populations, and the population values of demographic processes, archaeological investigations need to tackle this field of research; addressing questions concerning group size and population densities involved in political systems. The possibility to mobilize people for either communal activities or individual power structures, to organize the exchange of items, and to create identities depends on such population sizes.

The Trypillia development in Ukraine and Moldova is one such example. As the Trypillian societies began around 5000 BCE with small sites of typical late Neolithic and early Chalcolithic appearance, further changes within the settlement system and the efforts of the growing population were finalized in the foundation of mega-sites: agglomerations of up to *c.* 3000 houses that are unknown in other areas of Europe at this time and worldwide only known from contemporary Mesopotamian proto-cities. As this is the case (Figures 1–3), the inquiry into the triggers, constitution, meaning, and detectable end of these mega-sites is of general interest for world prehistory.

In general, our 'laboratory' of research, and with that also the spatial and chronological frame of this book, is a local development in one spatially and chronologically defined area: the Tomashivska group of the Trypillia development, in which the biggest cluster of mega-sites within the Trypillia development appears (Figures 2–4). Nebelivka, Dobrovody, Taljanky, and Maidanetske have been the main sites of scientific interest during the last decades, and the challenge of understanding the triggers for the construction of such agglomerated sites, but also for the reasons behind their decline, is one of the goals of different international research projects going on in the region.

Very much linked to the reconstruction of population sizes is the reconstruction of settlement patterns. Dispersed and agglomerated population distributions in the landscape effect the means of control or non-control of people. In a dense space of a sub-urban settlement, 1000 people are much easier to control than the same number of people in a diffuse distribution of single farmsteads over a huge area. The density of a demographic unit influences power structures, the costs for the mobilization of people for economic activities, and the necessity of establishing institutions for the regulation of societal affairs. Clearly, the dense agglomeration of people in a restricted space enables forms of economic activities, political organization, and social control which have not been systematically considered in prior archaeological research. New forms of labour division and specialization are closely linked to the maintenance of man power in such demographic units.

AGGLOMERATION, SOCIAL CONTROL, AND THE MAINTENANCE OF HUGE STRUCTURES: TWO EXAMPLES FROM EUROPEAN PREHISTORY

In Neolithic and Chalcolithic Europe, population agglomerations of more than 1000 inhabitants are exceptional, and linked to special environmental or

© European Association of Archaeologists 2016

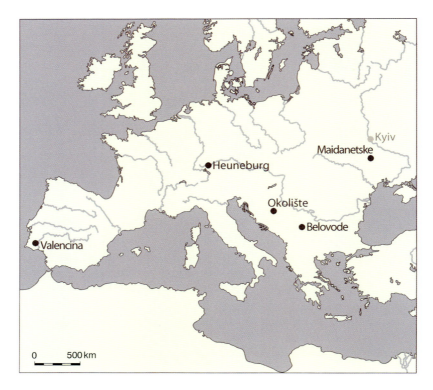

Figure 1. Sites mentioned in the text: Late Neolithic Okolište (5200–4600 BC), Chalcolithic Belovode (5500–4600 BCE), Maidanetske (3900–3700 BCE), and Valencina (3600–2300 BCE), and Iron Age Heuneburg (600 BC). Source: Institute UFG Kiel, Karin Winter.

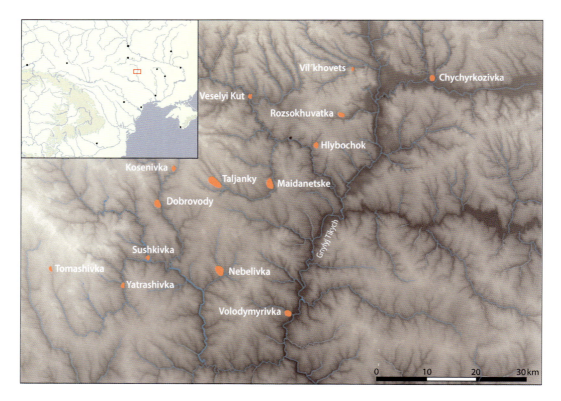

Figure 2. Large settlements and mega-sites in the Uman region. All sites belong to the Volodymyrivska–Tomashivska local group of Trypillia B2/C1. The largest mega-sites are Nebelivka, Dobrovody, Taljanky, and Maidanetske. Source: Institute UFG Kiel, René Ohlrau.

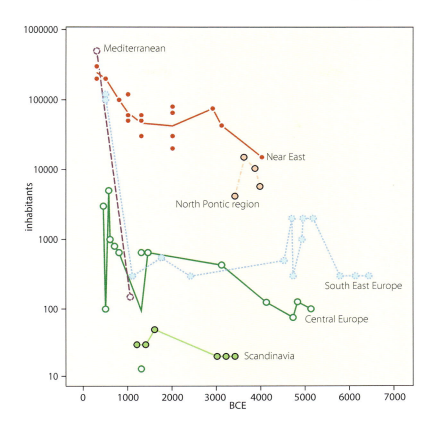

Figure 3. A comparison between the largest settlement agglomerations in the Near East and Europe displays huge differences: while in Mesopotamia cities are already known from the Early Bronze Age onwards, in most other regions comparable settlement sizes start no earlier than after 1500 BC. An exception is the development of North Pontic Trypillian sites (Müller, forthcoming). Source: Institute UFG Kiel, Karin Winter/Johannes Müller.

social conditions within the development of social space or the environment. Regions discussed as candidates for 'mega-sites', with the huge size that is known from Trypillia B2/C1, were the Late Chalcolithic Iberian Guadalquivir region and the Central Balkan Vinča region. Since in the first case a huge production and distribution centre exists 3200–2300 BCE, e.g. at Valencina de la Concepción (Nocete, 2014), the probability of the contemporaneity of discussed contexts is not clear. Most probably, a huge site existed there over 1000 years. Recent research on the Vinča sites, like Belovedo, that were handled as candidates for mega-sites indicated that they represent the agglomeration of smaller sites of different phases in one place (Rassmann et al., forthcoming). In consequence, only Trypillian mega-sites remain as sites with more than 10,000 inhabitants in Neolithic or Chalcolithic Europe. Nevertheless, there are developments of population agglomerations in different periods of European prehistory (cf. Figure 3) which can be compared structurally with the development of huger population agglomerations. It is worth, in a general approach, dealing with reasons for this in well-analysed examples before we 'dive' into deeper waters with Trypillia sites.

While in Central Europe, no other evidence for such a kind of agglomeration exists before the Urnfield societies, in Southeast Europe different examples of proto-urban developments are already known for the Neolithic and the Chalcolithic. Until now, one of the best investigated regions is the Late Neolithic of Central Bosnia (5200–4600 BCE). The longstanding investigations in this area describe a development of agglomerated and diverse settlement patterns, which could be associated with social changes within the society.

The investigated test area, the Visoko basin, measures about 150 km² in size, and is located on the Upper Bosna, 35 km northeast of the Bosnian capital Sarajevo. Fieldwork was undertaken by Kiel University, RGK Frankfurt, and the National Museum of Sarajevo from 2002 to 2008. A multidisciplinary team was able to reconstruct the environment, the settlement pattern, and economic and social developments (cc. Müller et al., 2011; Hofmann, 2013; Müller et al., 2013). After the first Neolithic communities had settled in the area, starting at approximately 5900 BC, the 7 ha large settlement of Okolište was planned and constructed around 5200 BC at the most fertile place, and along the communication line of the

BCE	Trypillia period	Trypillia phase	Trypillia local group	Subphase of local group		Associated sites
3350–3600	late	C II	Kosenivska (K)	K2/K3 (C II/1)		Vilkhovets 1 Kosherzhyntsi-Shulgivka
				K1 (C II/1)		Apolianka Kosenivka
3600–3850		C I	Tomashivska (T)	T4		Tomashivka Rakhny Sobovi
				T3	Stage 2	*Maidanetske*
					Stage 1	*Taljanky*
				T2		*Dobrovody* Yatranivka 1
				T1		Sushkivka
3750–4100	middle	B II	Nebelivska (N)	N2	Stage 2	
					Stage 1	Glybochok Yampil Khrystynivka 1
				N1		*Nebelivka* Kryvi Kolina
			Volodymyrivska (V)	V late		Volodymyrivka Peregonivka
				V early		Fedorivka
4100–4200		B I/B II				
4200–4600	early	B I				
4600–4800		A				

Figure 4. The chronology of Trypillia. Besides the main periodization and phasing, the Trypillia regional groups display characteristic inventories with sub-phases. The main mega-sites are indicated in italics *(after Kruts, 2012; Menotti, 2012; Ryzhov, 2012; Wechler, 1994; Diachenko, 2012; Diachenko and Menotti, 2012; Kadrow, 2013).*

Bosna-Neretva route, which linked the Adriatic with the Danube via different Butmir settlement areas ('*Siedlungskammern*'). A deliberate enclosure encompassed the domestic space; small long houses existed and a population of no less than 2000 people was agglomerated at the site (Figure 5). The size of the site contrasts with what is generally known from the Late Neolithic or Early Chalcolithic of Southeast Europe. The 'normal' settlement size measures less than 2.5 ha; probably no more than 200 people living together in one space. While the size of Okolište is extraordinary in terms of demographic concentration, the economy is not. Subsistence practices hint to the usual Neolithic economy, with cattle breeding and cereal production. The main difference to other, smaller domestic sites, both in the Visoko basin and in most other Butmir sites, lies in the enclosed space and the concentration of ritual activities at the site. Anthropomorphic and zoomorphic figurines, which are interpreted as signs of ritual practices, are concentrated at Okolište.

The reason for the demographic agglomeration at Okolište is as yet unclear. The enclosure, probably used as a fortification, as well as the geometric settlement arrangement, hints at a clear construction plan: Not the steady agglomeration of people, but a planned space right from the beginning, involving conscious decisions by a larger acting group of communities.

This site was in use for around ten generations, but the occupied space was already reduced in size after some decades. The carrying capacity of the area was probably reached, and a reduction in population size reflects a process which reduced conflicts with other villages. Within Okolište, a specialization of households is visible. Besides household difference with respect to general productivity, e.g. in processing cereals, differing specializations can also be observed between households: some were engaged in woodworking, others in fur production or in weaving. However, no spatial differentiation between craftsman-quarters could be determined. Instead, different part-time specializations within the direct neighbourhoods describe a community, organized on 'equal terms' (Figure 6). In spite of this, some economically and demographically productive households stood out.

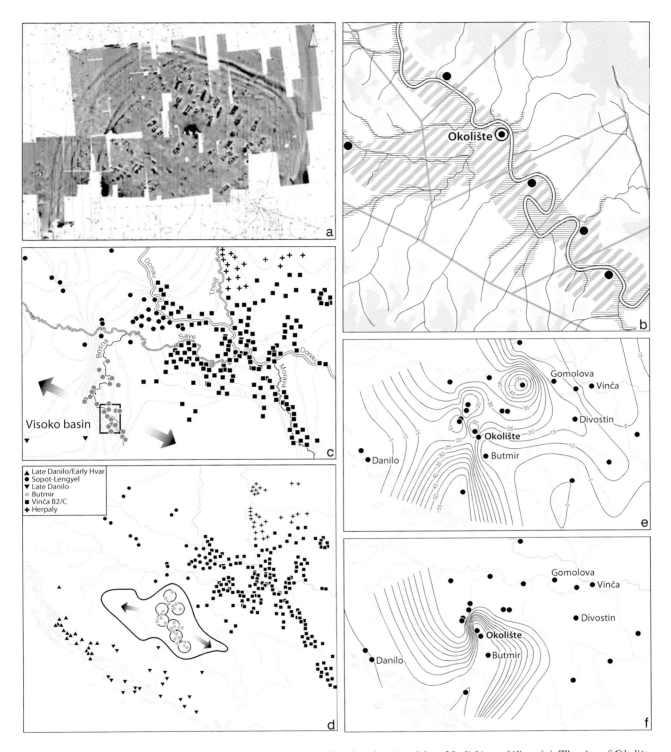

Figure 5. Okolište, the Visoko basin and the reconstruction of local and regional late Neolithic mobility. (a) The site of Okolište; (b) The Visoko basin with domestic sites and arable land (hatched); (c) Estimated population densities in the late Neolithic Middle Danubian area and Bosnia (isolines, person/km^2) and suggested herding activities of the Visoko communities into unpopulated mountain ranges (arrows); (d) The estimated herding area of late Neolithic Butmir agricultural core areas; (e) The percentage of late Neolithic impressed pottery (isolines, %/site); (f) The boundary between arrowheads (Adriatic) and sling shots (Danubian) in the Neretva-Bosna area (source: Holger Dieterich, Kiel).

Presumably, the role of these families within the village led to the destruction of these big households around 4900 BC. The size of the site was reduced rather abruptly to a normally sized village, the enclosure was no longer in use, and further dispersed sites were established at other places in the Visoko basin or in the near surroundings. Both the hierarchical settlement system and the huge concentration of people in

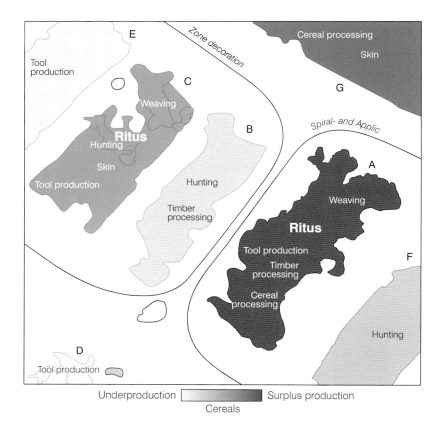

Figure 6. In Late Neolithic Okolište, part-time specializations within the direct neighbourhoods depict a community organized on 'equal terms'. In spite of this, some economically and demographically productive households stood out. Source: Institute UFG Kiel, Karin Winter/Johannes Müller.

one place had collapsed, probably due to social and not environmental changes. There seems to be an overall link between population concentrations, the increased opportunity to control people, and demographic development.

Besides comparable processes in other Southeast European tell-societies, in which newly rising social inequalities are assumed to be responsible for their collapse (Windler *et al.*, 2012), another fascinating development of early demographic agglomerations is seen in the Central European Late Hallstatt constitution.

In Central Europe, the huge defended hill forts (*Fürstensitze*) appeared as a new quality of population agglomeration, especially if we consider the population reconstruction of *c.* 5000 inhabitants at the Heuneburg (Ha D1) and the 3000 of the Ehrenbürg in contrast to the general pattern of single farmsteads or small hamlets with populations of about ten to twenty inhabitants (Müller-Scheessel, 2007). Nevertheless, it is quite clear that the carrying capacity of the surroundings was not reached (e.g. the 6 km territory around the Heuneburg could have fed 9000 people (Fischer *et al.*, 2010)). The average population of about 1.5 inhabitants/km² also did not indicate a general shift from Bronze Age or Neolithic conditions. If we consider the difference in size between normal and agglomerated settlements of the Hallstatt period, the question arises of whether at other times in European prehistory such agglomeration processes also occurred.

The discussion of the function and history of the Heuneburg is especially linked to the question about what triggered the agglomeration of so many people in one place. A common interpretation underlines that both the conglomeration of normal farmsteads (*Gehöfte*) on the fortified promontory and the quarters of farmsteads in the large lower settlement areas (*Außensiedlung*), are linked to a kind of flat stratification (cf. Kurz, 2010: 251 ff.: 'Big Men system'). The agglomeration of about 5000 people ceased around 540/530 BC with the destruction of the adobe wall (*Lehmziegelmauer*) and the farmsteads in both the upper and lower settlement areas. Social tension probably existed in the ruling families and between these families and the 'others' (Kurz, 2010: 253). As a consequence, most of the farmsteads in the surrounding quarters of the fortified part of the Heuneburg were abandoned; the inhabitants dispersed in the surroundings, and a new kind of settlement structure of newly, but differently ruling 'chiefs' made the Heuneburg and richly equipped and marked burials (*Prunkgräber*) on original areas of the *Außensiedlung* into symbols of their power. In spite of the new kind of power structures, which lasted only for two to three generations, social control over the huge number of people in one place, which existed before 540/530 BC, did not persist. The change might be the result of an attempt by the families of the *Außensiedlung* to limit access to the social control which had developed in the huge site. These instabilities contributed to the unsustainable development of the proto-urban settlements of Late Hallstatt/Early La Tène cultures.

Decision-Making and the Course of European Prehistory

In consequence, the questions concerning population size ('How many are we?') and population densities ('How agglomerated do we live together?') are linked to the character of both the political and social institutions of societies, with the resultant questions about how many decision-making institutions are necessary (discussed as early as Johnson, 1982) and how many persons can be mobilized for communal activities (e.g. Roscoe, 2012). Population sizes and densities are also linked to the economic formation of a society, i.e. how specialization is organized within a society. The trigonal relationship between demography, economy, and social constitution is responsible for the political formation of a society.

On a historical scale, the reconstruction of population values and densities allows a diachronic comparison. In European prehistory, one of the main research issues deals with the question of whether, across the immense variability of societal formations (hunter–gatherer communities, specialized foragers, settled horticulturalists, early agriculturalists, complex farming societies with early chiefdoms or urbanized societies, and the first kingdoms), the development of 'denser' structures with a concurrent rise in the complexity of the social formation represents a linear process, or whether certain structures are repeatedly known at different times in different societies, while the technological and demographic premises of these societies did not alter dramatically. Until now, there are interpretations in favour of an oscillation between complex and less complex structures, at least during Central European prehistory until the La Tène period (Müller, 2005; Zimmermann, 2012), and those in favour of a social evolution from small and not complicated to big and complicated societies (Otto, 1981; Grünert, 1982; Johnson and Earle, 2000). In the scope of this volume, the question is posed, of whether centralization processes of Late Trypillia could be compared to the observed patterns or not.

In general, different studies on the size of the largest sites during different time periods (Figure 3) indicate the extraordinary role of Trypillia mega-sites in a European and Near Eastern context. While prior to 1500 BCE in the Mediterranean, South East Europe, Central Europe, and Scandinavia population agglomerations in settlements vary between 50 and 5000 inhabitants, only in the Near East larger are population agglomerations known. The exceptional role of the North Pontic mega-sites is already obvious at this stage. In general, processes of agglomeration and dispersion could be seen all over Europe and even the mega-sites of the Tomashivska region represent only one stage of a general agglomeration that was followed by a disaggregation.

Nevertheless, the processes of agglomeration and dispersion should also be linked to a broader reconstruction of population development: Did agglomerations of larger population groups correlate with periods of demographic growth? Did they result from detectable economic or technological changes? Or could they, in fact, be a result of internal or external social developments? For that reason, a short look at the general population developments in Europe might be helpful.

General Demographic Development in Europe

Until today, many archaeologists, geographers, and demographers have dealt with the question of population densities in Europe and the Near East. More than 150 studies have been published, in which the absolute densities in core areas of development (i.e. highly populated, agriculturally used settlement basins) or global population densities (both core areas and less settled or uninhabited areas of the regions) are reconstructed (compare Müller, 2013a; Müller, 2013b). At least, ten different methods have been employed, not resulting in *a priori* different results. On a continental and sub-continental scale, the average curves of the manifold reconstructions were used to produce relative and absolute population curves. The advantage of this inquiry is that the local and regional estimations of archaeologists, who have huge expertise regarding the respective features and local conditions, could easily be implemented for general studies. The results are quite striking (Figure 7). In absolute terms, a population increase from *c.* 1 million inhabitants around 6500 BC, to 8 million around 2000 BC, and 14 million around 1500 BC was reconstructed. While a steep exponential growth of the European population with fluctuations is visible, the relative population density (Figure 7b) displays a smooth, more or less linear, increase from

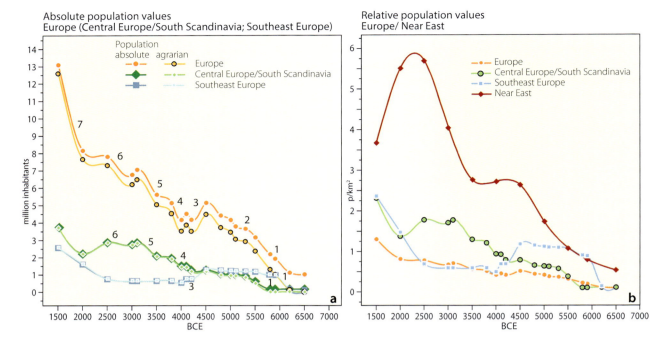

Figure 7. Absolute population values, and values for Agrarian population, in Europe (a) and relative population values in Europe and the near East (b) from 6500 to 1500 BC. The numbers indicate the technological innovations and social changes described in the text. Source: Institute UFG Kiel, Karin Winter/Johannes Müller (after Müller, 2013a).

0.5 to 1.5 inhabitants/km² (except the steep rise in densities after 2000 BC). In conclusion, the highest increase rate in the long term is linked to a colonization or acculturation of increasingly larger areas (from 1 million km² around 6000 BC to 5 million km² around 2000 BC).

Nevertheless, fluctuations in the curve might be due to significant changes in technologies. The shifts in population dynamics are, in my opinion, due to technological and social changes within the societies (cf. numbers Figure 7a):

1. The establishment of horticultural and agricultural practices in many regions of Europe (Bánffy, 2000; Lüning, 2000; cf. Guilaine, 2007; Müller, 2009b; Kozłowski and Raczky, 2010) was responsible for the population increase from c. 6500 to 5500 BC.
2. The immense development of the Southeast European Early Chalcolithic, with the introduction of new technologies such as copper melting, mining and new crops, as well as the social concentration of people in core areas of power (e.g. Hansen, 2010; Hofmann et al., 2012), was responsible for population peaks from c. 5500 to 4500 BC.
3. A decline in population was linked to the termination of many of these core areas and the change from stable, agglomerated settlement patterns to dispersed organizations of social space after c. 4500 BC (e.g. Parkinson, 2006; Windler et al., 2012).
4. The neolithization of Northern and Northwestern Europe (probably with new forms of slash-and-burn agriculture; Schier, 2009; Feeser et al., 2012) was also one of the causes for the observed population increase.
5. The introduction of the plough and developing technologies (e.g. the introduction of the wheel) (cf. Mischka, 2011) might also be the cause of rising population figures from c. 3500 to 3000 BCE.
6. The establishment of sub-continental value systems, such as the Corded Ware and Bell Beaker phenomena (Furholt, 2004; Czebreszuk and Szmyt, 2003), in contrast to regional identities, might have triggered different reactions in different areas, leading to fluctuating population levels.
7. The introduction of Bronze Age ideologies, including bronze as a technology, triggered the spread of Neolithic and Bronze Age societies to vast areas of Europe (e.g. Earle and Kristiansen, 2011). A major population increase is observed in both the already settled and in new areas of interest.

In consequence, increases and decreases of populations were, apart from the general growth tendency, depend on economic and social changes. The introduction of new technologies was often linked to changes in the social organization of societies, and thus connected to the variable organization of social space.

Within such a frame, we have to consider that the decisions and processes leading to a dispersed or agglomerated settlement pattern, and the concentration of populations in settlement areas, large villages, or the first cities, is not deliberate: The more densely a population is concentrated, the farther the transport paths of subsistence products and the return transport distances of tools to the surrounding places are to the more densely populated places. As a result, the development of the costs of transport is essential to the options of how highly agglomerated people live together (cf. Fujita *et al.*, 2001: 68, figure 5.4). Nevertheless, even if the costs of transport are as low as possible to allow an agglomeration of people, the political framework of a society may still leave the possibility open, not to agglomerate: A disperse settlement pattern could be viewed, for example, as a desired decision in order to lower the influence of power structures on daily life (Vansina, 1978). In respect to Trypillia mega-sites, the introduction of new transport techniques like the oxen-drawn sledges, which are documented as ceramic models since mainly Trypillia phase B2, probably enabled the agglomeration of many people by reducing the time-investment to reach, for example, arable land. Nevertheless, the decision to agglomerate in mega-sites was possible because of technological changes, but it was still a conscious political decision by huge groups of people that we have to disentangle.

Demographic Development and Social Control

Indications of a growing population in Europe, and variations of this growth, are not linked to a clear pattern in the agglomeration of people in core areas or in domestic sites. The foundation of the 3000-inhabitant site of Okolište (around 5200 BC) is not linked to an immense general population increase in the Balkans; the same is probably true for the >10,000-inhabitant Trypillian sites around 3800 BCE and for the 5000-inhabitant site of Heuneburg around 600 BC (Figure 7). The intention to create such huge sites is based on economic and social decisions made by communities. A concentration of people in one place enables social control over them, which might entail a control regime within a stratified or a more egalitarian society. The social models that are proposed for Okolište or the Heuneburg involve social disruption and competition between internal groups of the society as one reason (of perhaps a combination of different reasons) for the reduction in population size. As we are confronted with processes not necessarily known from historical or ethnographical records, a new term is useful—*social agglomeration-control* ('*agglo-control*')—which highlights prehistoric centralization processes as triggers of social control in non-literate societies. This could also be used for the Late Trypillia development.

References

Bánffy, E. 2000. The Late Starčevo and the Earliest Linear Pottery Groups in Western Transdanubia. *Documenta Praehistorica*, 27: 173–185.

Czebreszuk, J. & Szmyt, M. 2003. *The Northeast Frontier of Bell Beakers: Proceedings of the Symposium Held at the Adam Mickiewicz University, Poznaàn (Poland), 26–29 May 2002*. Oxford, England: Archaeopress.

Diachenko, A. 2012. Settlement System of West Tripolye Culture in the Southern Bug and Dnieper Interfluve. Formation Problems. In: F. Menotti & A. Korvin-Piotrovskiy, eds. *The Tripolye Culture Giant-Settlements in Ukraine*. Oxford: Oxbow Books, pp. 116–38.

Diachenko, A. & Menotti, F. 2012. The Gravity Model: Monitoring the Formation and Development of the Tripolye Culture Giant-Settlements in Ukraine. *Journal of Archaeological Science*, 39: 2810–17.

Earle, T. & Kristiansen, K. eds. 2011. *Organizing Bronze Age Societies*. Cambridge: Cambridge University Press.

Feeser, I., Dörfler, W., Averdieck, F.-R. & Wiethold, J. 2012. New Insight into Regional and Local Land-use and Vegetation Patterns in Eastern Schleswig-Holstein during the Neolithic. In: M. Hinz & J. Müller, eds. *Siedlung, Grabenwerk, Grosssteingrab Studien zu Gesellschaft, Wirtschaft und Umwelt der Trichterbechergruppen im nördlichen Mitteleuropa*. Bonn: Habelt, pp. 159–91.

Fischer, E., Rösch, M., Sillmann, M., Ehrmann, O., Liese-Kleiber, H., Voigt, R., Stobbe, A.K., Arie, J., Stephan, E., Schatz, K. & Posluschny, A. 2010. Landnutzung im Umkreis der Zentralorte Hohenasperg, Heuneburg und Ipf. In: D. Krausse, ed. *'Fürstensitze' und Zentralorte der frühen Kelten*. Stuttgart: Theiss, pp. 195–266.

Fujita, M., Krugman, P. & Venables, A.J. 2001. *The Spatial Economy. Cities, Regions, and International Trade*. Cambridge/London: MIT Press.

Furholt, M. 2004. Enstehungsprozesse der Schnurkeramik und das Konzept eines Einheitshorizontes. *Archäologisches Korrespondenzblatt*, 34: 479–98.

Grünert, H. ed. 1982. *Geschichte der Urgesellschaft*. Berlin: VEB Deutscher Verlag der Wissenschaften.

Guilaine, J. 2007. Die Ausbreitung der neolithischen Lebensweise im Mittelmeerraum. In: C. Lichter, ed. *Vor 12000 Jahren in Anatolien: Die ältesten Monumente der Menschheit*. Stuttgart: Theiss, pp. 166–76.

Hansen, S. 2010. *Leben auf dem Tell als soziale Praxis (Symposium Berlin 2007)*. Bonn: Habelt.

Hofmann, R. 2013. *Okolište 2 - Spätneolithische Keramik und Siedlungsentwicklung in Zentralbosnien*. Universitätsforschungen zur prähistorischen Archäologie 234. Habelt: Bonn.

Hofmann, R., Mötz, K. & Müller, J. eds. 2012. *Tells: Social and Environmental Space (Proceedings of the International Workshop 'Socio-Environmental Dynamics over the Last 12,000 Years: The Creation of Landscapes II' 14th-18th March 2011 in Kiel)*. Bonn: Habelt.

Johnson, G. A. 1982. Organizational Structure and Scalar Stress. In: C. Renfrew, M. Rowlands & B.A. Segraves, eds. *Theory and Explanation in Archaeology: The Southampton Conference*. London: Academic Press, pp. 389–421.

Johnson, A. W. & Earle, T. K. 2000. *The Evolution of Human Societies: From Foraging Group to Agrarian State*. Stanford, CA: Stanford University Press.

Kadrow, S. 2013. Werteba Site in Bilcze Zlote: Recent Research and Analyses. In: S. Kadrow, ed. *Bilce Zlote. Materials from the Werteba and the Ogród sites*. Kraków: Muzeum Aechaeologiczne Krakow, pp. 13–21.

Kozłowski, J. K. & Raczky, P. eds. 2010. *Neolithization of the Carpathian Basin: Northernmost Distribution of the Starčevo/Körös Culture*. Kraków: Polska Akademia Umiejętności.

Kruts, V. 2012. Giant-Settlements of Tripolye Culture. In: F. Menotti & A. Korvin-Piotrovskiy, eds. *The Tripolye Culture Giant-Settlements in Ukraine*. Oxford: Oxbow Books, pp. 70–78.

Kurz, S. 2010. Zur Genese und Entwicklung der Heuneburg in der späten Hallstattzeit, In: D. Krausse, ed. *"Fürstensitze" und Zentralorte der frühen Kelten*. Stuttgart: Theiss, pp. 239–256.

Lüning, J. 2000. *Steinzeitliche Bauern in Deutschland. Die Landwirtschaft im Neolithikum*. Bonn: Habelt.

Menotti, F. 2012. Introduction. In: F. Menotti & A. Korvin-Piotrovskiy, eds. *The Tripolye Culture Giant-Settlements in Ukraine*. Oxford: Oxbow Books, pp. 1–5.

Mischka, D. 2011. The Neolithic Burial Sequence at Flintbek LA 3, North Germany, and its Cart Tracks: A Precise Chronology. *Antiquity*, 85(329): 742–58.

Müller, J. 2005. Geschlecht und Alter in ur- und frühgeschichtlichen Gesellschaften: Konsequenzen. In: J. Müller, ed. *Alter und Geschlecht in ur- und frühgeschichtlichen Gesellschaften*. Bonn: Habelt, pp. 189–94.

Müller, J. 2009b. Die Jungsteinzeit (6000–2000 v. Chr.). In: S. von Schnurbein, ed. *Atlas der Vorgeschichte Europa von den ersten Menschen bis Christi Geburt*. Stuttgart: Theiss, pp. 60–107.

Müller, J., forthcoming. *Produktion, Konsumtion, Distribution in Neolithikum und Chalkolithikum Mittel- und Südosteuropas: die Entwicklung sozialer Differenzen*, Bonn: Habelt.

Müller, J., Hofmann, R., Müller-Scheessel, N. & Rassmann, K. 2011. Zur sozialen Organisation einer spätneolithischen Gesellschaft in Südosteuropa (5200–4400 v.Chr.). In: S. Hansen & J. Müller, eds. *Sozialarchäologische Perspektiven: Gesellschaftlicher Wandel 5000–1500 v. Chr. zwischen Atlantik und Kaukasus (Tagung Kiel 2007)*. Mainz: von Zabern, pp. 81–106.

Müller, J. 2013a. 8 Million Neolithic Europeans: Social Demography and Social Archaeology on the Scope of Change–from the Near East to Scandinavia. In: K. Kristiansen & J. Turek, eds. *Paradigm Change*. Oxford: Oxbow.

Müller, J. 2013b. Demographic Traces of Technological Innovation, Social Change and Mobility: From 1 to 8 million Europeans 6000–2000 BCE. In: S. Kadrow, ed. *Festschrift Kruk*. Cracauw/Bonn: Habelt.

Müller, J., Rassmann, K. & Hofmann, R. 2013. *Okolište 1- Untersuchungen einer spätneolithischen Siedlungskammer in Zentralbosnien*. Universitätsforschungen zur prähistorischen Archäologie 228. Habelt: Bonn.

Müller-Scheessel, N. 2007. Bestattungsplätze für die oberen Zehntausend? Berechnungen der hallstattzeitlichen Bevölkerung Süddeutschlands. In: P. Trebsche, I. Balzer, C. Eggl, J. K. Koch, H. Nortmann & J. Wiethold, eds. *Die unteren Zehntausend - auf der Suche nach den Unterschichten der Eisenzeit*. Langenweissbach: Beier & Beran, pp. 1–10.

Nocete, F. 2014. Southern Iberia in the 4th and 3rd Millennia Cal. BC. In: M. Almagro-Gorbea, ed. *Iberia. Protohistory of the far West of Europe: from Neolithic to Roman conquest*. Burgos: Universidad de Burgos, pp. 83–94.

Otto, K.-H. 1981. *Deutschland in der Epoche der Urgesellschaft*. Berlin: VEB Deutscher Verlag der Wissenschaften.

Parkinson, W.A. 2006. *The Social Organization of Early Copper Age tribes on the Great Hungarian Plain*. Oxford: Oxbow.

Rassmann, K., Scholz, R., Mertl, P., Radloff, K., Pendic, J. & Jablankovic, A. forthcoming. Belovode– Geomagnetic data as a proxy for the reconstruction of house numbers, population size and the internal spatial structure of Copper Age settlements. In: M. Radvojevć & Th. Rehren, eds. *Rise of Early Eurepean Metallurgy*. London: UCL.

Roscoe, P. 2012. Before Elites: The Political Capacities of Big Men. In: T. L. Kienlin & A. Zimmermann, eds. *Beyond Elites Alternatives to Hierarchical Systems in Modelling Social Formations Universitätsforschungen zur prähistorischen Archäologie*. Bonn: Habelt, pp. 41–54.

Ryzhov, S. N. 2012. Relative Chronology of the Giant-settlement Period BII-CI. In: F. Menotti & A. Korvin-Piotrovskiy, eds. *The Tripolye Culture Giant-Settlements in Ukraine*. Oxford: Oxbow Books, pp. 139–168.

Schier, W. 2009. Extensiver Brandfeldbau und die Ausbreitung der neolithischen Wirtschaftsweise in Mitteleuropa und Südskandinavien am Ende des 5. Jahrtausends v. Chr. *Prähistorische Zeitschrift*, 84:15–43.

Vansina, J. 1978. *The Children of Woot: A History of the Kuba People*. Madison: University of Wisconsin Press.

Wechler, K.-P. 1994. Zur Chronologie der Tripolje-Cucuteni-Kultur aufgrund von ^{14}C–Datierungen. *Zeitschrift für Archäologie*, 28: 7–21.

Windler, A., Thiele, R. & Müller, J. 2012. Increasing Inequality in Chalcolithic Southeast Europe: The Case of Durankulak. *Journal of Archaeological Science*, 40(1): 204–210. DOI information: 10.1016/j.jas.2012.08.017.

Zimmermann, A. 2012. Cultural Cycles in Central Europe during the Holocene. *Quaternary International*, 274: 251–258.

CHAPTER 2

Research on Different Scales: 120 Years of Trypillian Large Sites Research

Mykhailo Videiko and Knut Rassmann

The last four decades of studies into the Trypillia Culture were marked by intensive investigations of the large settlements—the so-called mega-sites—which cover areas of tens and hundreds of hectares. For the first time in the history of Trypillia Culture studies, a comprehensive method combining aerial survey, geomagnetic survey, traditional excavations, and field survey was applied. It was a welcome escape out of the stalemate, where the researchers were both physically and financially restricted in their investigations of such an intriguing phenomenon of the Copper Age Prehistory. Combined investigations have now become the standard model for studies of Neolithic and Eneolithic sites all over the Europe. These innovative developments in the archaeological field have led to a pressing need to report in full on the experience and results of such comprehensive studies of the Trypillia Culture 'mega-sites'.

The Beginning of the Investigations

One of the first individuals who mentioned the large size of Trypillia sites was Vikentij Khvoika. He noted that one of the sites, which he explored in 1899 near the village of Trypillia, was roundish and had 'two versty in diameter' (Khvoika, 1901: 793, 795)—i.e. more than 2.1 km, which means c. 350 ha square. The actual size of the cape on which the site is located is less than 1 × 1 km.

Inspired by the presentation on these investigations at the All-Russian Archaeological Conference in Kyiv in 1899, Ernst von Stern started his research on the site in Petreni, Moldova in former Bessarabia (Häusler, 1985). His excavations, which took place in 1902 and 1903, revealed the remains of several houses and a large amount of pottery remains (Figure 1). Stern interpreted the burnt buildings as 'houses of the dead' and the vessels as urns (Stern, 1907: 62; 1921: 161 f.). This interpretation as evidence for a cremation tradition was later intensively not only discussed the Russian literature but also criticized by, among others, by the famous German archeologist Carl Schuchhardt (1920: 515).

This controversial discussion, as a footnote to the research, illustrates wide international interest in the remarkable research on Trypillian sites. Despite great successes in settlement archaeology since the late 1930s, there was no further continuation of the international perspective on the Trypillian phenomena.

Milestone: Settlement Archeology— Large-Scale Research

During the first half of the twentieth century, excavations started at many large sites, including Volodymyrivka, Maidanetske, Bilyj Kamin, Sushkivka, Popudnia, Kolodyste, producing rich finds—painted pottery, numerous figurines, as well as hitherto unknown clay models of houses from Sushkivka and Popudnia (Videiko, 2002: 11–21). At that time, only a few archaeologists had mentioned their size as something unusual. The majority of researchers mainly focused on the more common research problems at hand, attempting to reconstruct the architecture of houses based on their remains, and offering periodization and chronology of the site and local features of the culture.

The best known of these Trypillian large sites at that time was Volodymyrivka, located on the Syniukha River. The first report, based on field survey, was published by T. Passek in 1949, which included the discovery of around 200 houses, situated in a 72 haectare area. In a very ambitious excavation programme, more than twenty-seven structures were explored, including separate buildings and clusters of burnt houses (Passek, 1949b) (Figure 2). T. Passek recognized Volodymyrivka as typical of B-II stage 'patrimonial villages' (Passek, 1949a: 108).

During this period, only a handful of scientists speculated on Volodymyrivka as a special place in the Trypillia Culture social system. In 1947, V. Petrov, who worked in the 1930s at Volodymyrivka, believed that the existence of such a large settlement was evidence of the transformation of rural settlements into cities (Petrov, 1992: 18). However, in 1965 S. Bibikov

© European Association of Archaeologists 2016.

18   Trypillia Mega-Sites and European Prehistory

Figure 1. Petreni (Moldova). Ceramic of the Trypillia Culture from the excavations in 1902 und 1903 (Stern 1907, table 10).

Figure 2. Large site near Volodymyrivka, BII stage (1) plan after T. Passek, 1949b; (2) plan after K.V. Shyshkin (1985); (3 and 4) excavations of clusters of houses, 1947.

wrote about 'centers based on clan systems'. He regarded the sites as places of interactions between the 'Trypillian tribes' and he supposed that Volodymyrivka was one of these centres. (Bibikov, 1965: 58).

Crucial for the archaeological research at this stage was a perspective that did not focus on certain parts of the settlements, but rather took the whole site and its surroundings into account. This research design is visible within some projects, like the sophisticated sampling strategy of Kruts in Chapaevka (Kruts, 1977: 166; figure 4).

From Field-Walking to Aerial Photography

The main problem of researching these large settlements is their location within modern agricultural lands, which are of restricted availability for detailed research. As a result, archaeologists have occasionally mapped several independent settlements within an area, which were in fact actually one large continuous settlement site. The large Trypillia large sites were initially discovered with the help of aerial photography in the 1960s by Konstantin Shyshkin, a military topographer who studied data from the territory of Ukraine (Shyshkin, 1973).

Shyshkin first published maps and plans for Trypillia Culture sites in 1973 (Shyshkin, 1973) (Figures 3 and 4). The total number of sites identified through aerial photography was around 250 (Shyshkin, 1973: рис. 1). Verification of a selection of these settlements was performed through field-walking, undertaken by K. Shyshkin and V. Stefanovych at the end of the 1960s. In 1985, K. Shyshkin published settlement-plans of twenty-seven sites, including (but not limited to) Taljanky, Maidanetske, Dobrovody, Nebelivka, Glybochok, Yatranivka, Volodymyrivka, and Kosenivka (Shyshkin, 1973: 1985) (Figure 3).

The field verification of these plans had already started in the 1970s, when expeditions were organized by archaeologists from Moscow (Shtiglits, 1971: 236) and Kyiv separately. Both expeditions visited the site near Maidanetske (which was estimated at 200 ha) and confirmed its size. Mykola Shmaglij presented the plans of the settlement, which included data from K. Shyshkin, a field-walking campaign in 1971, and a small-scale geomagnetic survey by Valerij Dudkin (carried out in 1971) (Figure 7c).

Additionally, aerial photographs of Trypillia settlements in Moldova were analysed. The Petreni settlement plan, first published in 1981 by Vsevolod Markevich (Markevich, 1981: рис. 14) became the most famous. Verification of these images, provided by K. Shyshkin, was carried out by Viacheslav Bicbaev, who published several plans (Bicbaev, 2007: 14, рис. 3), including the largest sites—Stolnicheni I (almost 100 ha), Brinzeni (65–80 ha) (Figure 3), Sophia-V (almost 38 ha), and Sophia II le Gavan (37 ha).

The experience gained by working with the results of aerial surveys showed that this method enables one to determine the size and rough outline of settlements, but only very generally. Producing more detailed results requires the use of other methods of research.

Maidanetske: At the Beginning of the Methodological 'Revolution'

By the beginning of the 1970s, a first solution about 'what to do' with mega-sites was found. Aerial photography and field-walking became the first step, and was organized by Mykola Shmaglij at Maidanetske, a Trypillia CI site of around 200 ha. These two methods were supplemented with archaeological excavations and large-scale geomagnetic survey. The first results of this programme were described in 1973 (Shmaglij et al., 1973). In 1971, Valerij Dudkin started with geomagnetic survey on Maidanetske, using M-23 and M-27 (Figures 5 and 6, Table 1) magnetometers in a 4 × 4 m grid (Dudkin, 1978). The grid resolution proved sufficient for detecting the remains of burnt houses. The resulting plan of the site, finished in 1974, included nearly 180 ha of the total 200 ha—except for obstructing elements like roads, forest lines, and parts that are located under the current village of Maidanetske (Figure 7c). Through this application of geophysics, 1575 anomalies were detected that are interpreted as the magnetic response of burnt houses, which vary in size. The houses are located in four elliptical rows, with streets dividing the rows and sections within these rows. Centrally located within these elliptical rows is a big open area devoid of structures (Shmaglij, 1980). A further large site at Taljanky was studied between 1983 and 1986, also by V. Dudkin. A total of 232 ha were studied of the supposed 450 ha identified by aerial photography (Figure 8). This plan became a starting point for studies of this, the largest site (eventually estimated at 340 ha) of the known Trypillia Culture mega-sites. For a long time, it was the site with the largest area of any Copper Age site studied by geomagnetic survey. For this survey, more sensitive ММП-203 magnetometers were used, but the grid, which has proved its general worth for surveys, remained the same —4 × 4 m.

Both plans generally confirmed the data from aerial photography, presented by K. Shyshkin for this site, but produced much more interesting details. For the first time, it became possible to count the number of houses at a Trypillia Culture site without excavations

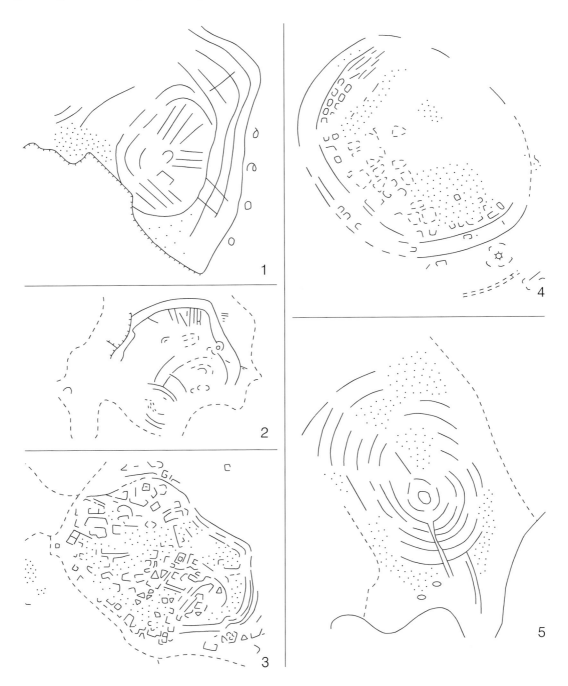

Figure 3. Plans of Trypillia large sites (aerial photographs) after K. Shyshkin (1985) (1) Sushkivka, stage CI; (2) Chychyrkozivka, stage CI; (3) Fedorivka (Mykhailivka), stage BII; (4) Dobrovody, stage CI; (5) Kosenivka, stage CII.

and, therefore, produce detailed plans while saving time and resources. It was estimated that when excavating ten houses a year, archaeologists would have first created the same plan of Maidanetske after more than a hundred years of investigations (Shmaglij *et al.*, 1973).

The main aims of the archaeological excavations that were started in 1972 on the Maidanetske settlement were verification of the geomagnetic survey; studies of architecture and households; the relative, absolute; and internal chronology of the site. The first excavation campaign confirmed the position of geomagnetic house anomalies on V. Dudkin's maps with an accuracy of ±1 m. A new approach was devised to great advantage in comparison with the conventional approach to finding houses; the researchers used cross-shaped test trenches. It proved more efficient to dig based on this plan, than using traditional cross of test-trenches. The best results were produced by investigations of household 'B' in 1972, which was recognized not as a singular household, but as part of a cluster of houses (Figure 6).

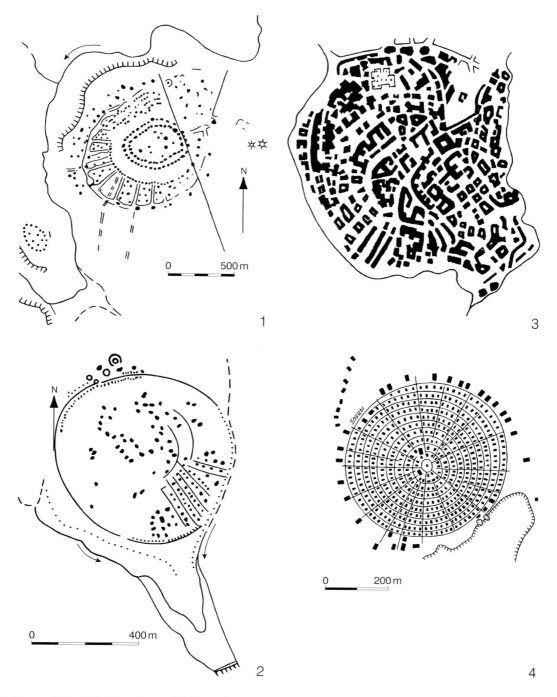

Figure 4. Cucuteni-Trypillia large sites in Moldova (aerial photographs), after K. Shyshkin and V. Bicbaev. (1) Stolniceni-I; (2) Sofia V; (3) Brynzeni VIII; (4) Petreni.

Studies by Konstantin Zinkovsky on the architecture of these houses offered new insights and dramatically changed the view of these structures. The remains of the burnt houses, comprising burnt clay with imprints of wood, were associated with clay 'platforms' for a long time. These platforms were thought to have been created using fire in order to create a solid base. However, Zinkovsky recognized the burnt clay platforms as the remains of the ceilings of burnt houses (cf. Korvin-Piotrovskiy *et al.*, 2012; Shatilo, 2014).

The ultimate reconstructions by Zinkovsky produced two-storied house plans containing several rooms.

The concept was later elaborated by Kruts and confirmed by experiments on house construction and their experimental destruction (Kruts, 1989, 2003; Kruts *et al.*, 2001).

The combination of aerial photography and geomagnetic survey on this scale was an innovation in settlement archaeology. It is remarkable that the Ukrainian archaeologists already implemented a research

One of the most impressive achievements of the initial phase of the study of mega-sites was large-scale geomagnetic survey under the direction of V. Dudkin (Table 1). There were three stages to this process. The first was undertaken at Maidanetske (1971–1974), with a research methodology that was tested at this stage and later used without significant changes over the next 2 decades. The second stage involved surveys of such settlements as Taljanky, Talne 2, Moshuriv, Pischana, and Kosenivka in the 1980s. The third, a geomagnetic survey programme between 1992 and 1995, delivered plans of five large settlements: Glybochok, Yatranivka, Yampil, Vilhovets 1, and Fedorivka (Figure 9). At this stage, V. Dudkin used the same ММП-203 magnetometer, but the grid was 3 × 3 m (Dudkin, 2007: 57–70). Archaeologists received plans of the nine mega-sites and two small Trypillia villages from the Uman region.

The survey served as the first step to optimize the excavation strategy. Thanks to the precise geomagnetic maps, a large number of Copper age houses were excavated. Archaeological excavations were accompanied by a wide range of interdisciplinary methods, including archaezoological studies (Zhuravlev, 2008), archaeobotanical studies (cf. Kirleis and Dal Corso, 2016), and ^{14}C-dates (Wechler, 1994).

Figure 5. Magnetometer M27. This instrument was used by Dudkin in Maidanetske and Taljanky (photo: M. Videiko).

design with geomagnetic survey in the 1970s as the backbone to solve a clearly defined scientific problem (Figure 9). The situation in other European countries was quite different, as Neubauer (2001: 29) has described. After an ambitious beginning of geomagnetic research in the 1960s, the following decade showed a stagnation in geophysical research. In stark contrast, a systematic research programme was instigated and realized for nearly three decades in Moldova and the Ukraine.

Trypillia Expedition 1981–1991

One of the largest projects of all explorations of mega-sites took place over ten seasons and was organized by the Institute of Archaeology of the Ukrainian Academy of Sciences. At the outset, two years of wide field survey was organized, which provided important

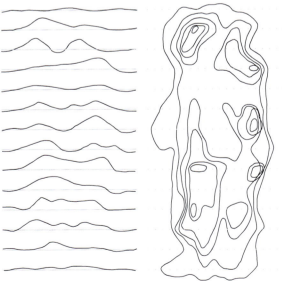

Figure 6. Maidanetske (Uman district). An isoline-interpolation of the survey data by Dudkin (b). V Dudkin by using the M-27 on the survey Maidanetske in 1971 (a) (Videiko, 2005).

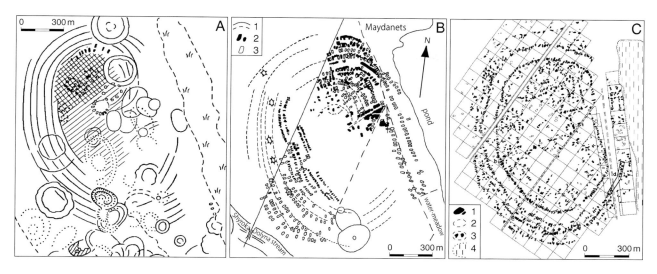

Figure 7. Maidanetske (Uman district). (a) Interpretation of aerial photograph (Shyshkin, 1973). (b) First synthesis of geomagnetic data and aerial photograph (Shmaglij et al., 1973). (c) Final geomagnetic map of Dudkin's surveys from 1971 to 1974 (Videiko, 2005).

information on other Trypillia settlements in the Uman region. Chief of expedition Ivan Artemenko explored a few kurgans from the Early Bronze Age in the area of the mega-sites and the surrounding areas. After ten years of investigations, this area became one of the best explored territories of the Cucuteni-Trypillia cultural unit. Excavations also took place: Taljanky, CI stage, 340 ha (by Volodymyr Kruts and Sergij Ryzhov); Dobrovody, CI stage, 200–250 ha and Kosenivka, early CII stage, almost 70 ha (Tamara Movsha); Veselyj Kut, BI-BII stage, 150 ha (Olena Tsvek); and excavations continued at Maidanetske (Mykola Shmaglij, Mykhailo Videiko, Nataliya Burdo).

Rescue excavations in 1990 took place on the small sites Talne-2 and Talne-3, both contemporary with Maidanetske (Videiko, 1991: 11–12; Kruts and Videiko, 1991: 31–32). Two houses were excavated by V. Kruts and S. Ryzhov at Chychyrkozivka (CI stage, 200 ha) and Pischana (BII stage, 20 ha). Across all of these sites from 1981 to 1991, the remains of around seventy burnt houses and more than twenty other objects were explored. A large programme of archaeomagnetic dating was carried out by F. Zagnij, which established a 1400-year relative chronology from period BI to CI (Kruts, 2008: table 3).

The results of the research were summarized in 1990–1991 at two field workshops, and in 1993 at an international conference in Taljanky. It was the first public discussion about the character and reasons for the emergence of mega-sites (Shmaglij and Videiko, 1990; Zbenovich, 1996), their architecture (Kruts, 1990; Markevich, 1990), their chronology—including internal chronology (Shmaglij and Videiko, 1990b; Ryzhov, 1990), their social and spatial organization

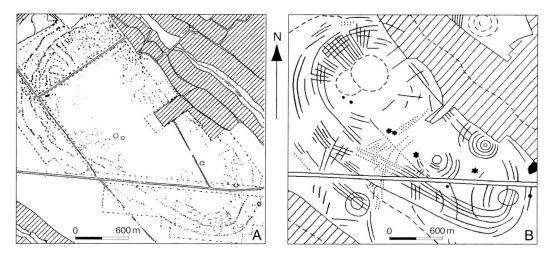

Figure 8. Taljanky (Uman district). (a) Final geomagnetic map of Dudkin's surveys (Kruts et al., 2001). (b) Interpretation of aerial photograph (Shyshkin, 1973).

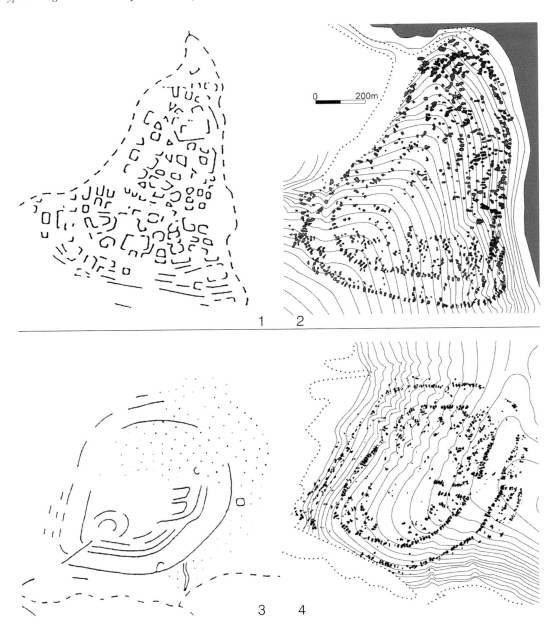

Figure 9. Plans of large Trypillia sites: (1 and 2) Yatranivka, BII stage; (3 and 4) Glybochok ((1 and 3) aerial photographs by K. Shyshkin; (2 and 4) geomagnetic survey by V. Dudkin).

Table 1 Large-scale geomagnetic surveys under the direction of V. Dudkin 1971–1995

No	Name of site	Year	Supposed square, ha	Surveyed, ha	Trypillia stage
1	Maidanetske	1971–1974	200–250	180,2	CI
2	Taljanky	1983–1986	400–450 (341.5?)	232	CI
3	Pischana	1989	16.3*	~10	BII
4	Vilkhovets 1	1993	110–117.8*	116	CII
5	Yatranivka	1994–1995	60	~60	BII
6	Glybochok	1994–1995	100*	114	BII
7	Fedorivka	1993	35***	~39	BII
8	Yampil	1994–1995	~40–36.7*	~32	BII
9	Kosenivka	Before 199	62.8*	~70?	CII
	All	1971–1995		~853.2	BII-CII

(Videiko, 1990), and their economy (Zhuravlev, 2008).

At the beginning of 1990s, progress on investigations was interrupted after the collapse of USSR. From this time, all projects related to large sites were usually limited to the study of separate settlements at a local rather than a global scale. Only the Taljanky expedition survived and investigations continued on this, the largest known, mega-site (cf. Kruts, 2008).

THE PROBLEM OF CHRONOLOGY AND MICRO-CHRONOLOGY OF MEGA-SITES

The single most important research question is whether the hundreds and thousands of houses across these mega-sites were contemporary or not—in many respects, this is the same question that emerged at the beginning of the excavations in the 1970s. At that time, archaeological approaches offered two ways to address this: typological seriation of pottery and archaeomagnetic or ^{14}C dating. The general duration of the BII and CI periods according to archaeomagnetic dating was around 600–700 years.

The first step to a more precise chronology of mega-sites was offered by S. Kruts and V. Ryzhov, who developed the first scale of relative chronology of sites in this region based on studies of pottery. They divided the BII stage into three phases[1] and CI into four phases (Kruts and Ryzhov, 1985). This periodization was supported by other archaeologists and became generally accepted by specialists who studied the Trypillia Culture.

Taking into account the relative chronology proposed for the BII and CI stages on the basis of archaeomagnetic dating, the duration of each phase was around 100 years. It followed that archaeologists had to identify differences in ceramic complexes for a time interval of less than 100 years. Such a division, of course, needs a solid statistical base.

At the end of the 1980s, when several dozens of houses were explored at Taljanky and Maidanetske, it became possible to try to separate some 'earlier' and 'later' houses and pits. This work resulted in two small articles, the conclusions of which were similar:

- most of houses at Taljanky and Maidanetske were burnt at the same time (Shmaglij and Videiko, 1990b; Ryzhov, 1990: 83–90)
- there was a probability that some houses were erected earlier (Ryzhov, 1990: 89–90).

These conclusions were also supported by a few facts from the real stratigraphy discovered at Maidanetske when several pits were covered by later houses or filled with the remains of burnt houses.

[1] Now this amount has increased to 5.

Figure 10. Maidanetske, excavations of clusters of houses, 1986–1987 by M. Shmaglij, M. Videiko, and N. Burdo.

Before the last investigations, there were only forty-five known ^{14}C dates (these results were from different laboratories) for large sites starting from BI period Berezivka up to CII stage Vilkhovets 1. For such sites as Taljanky, 11 dates were known; for Vilkhovets 1, 13 dates in total. However, their standard deviation was problematic in that it ranged from ±29–33 up to ±80–90 years. So, it remained problematic to use these dates, not only for the internal chronology of mega-sites, but also for simple correlations between stages or phases of the Trypillia culture.

THE LAST DECADE BEFORE THE REVIEW

In 2000, Taljanky was the last place where investigations of mega-sites continued in Ukraine (cf., e.g. Kruts, 2008). At this time, a lot of publications appeared that presented data from excavations at Taljanky (e.g. Eduard Ovchynnykow collected a lot of data from field surveys and explored a few large (50–100 ha) sites, such as Valiava and Kvitky, also from the BII and CI periods, located far to the East of the Uman region (Ovchinnikow, 2015). Rescue excavations were conducted at Sharyn, a 34 ha large site from the early CII stage close to Uman. In 2004, a complete list of Trypillia Culture sites in Ukraine was published, detailing more than 2000 sites, and, collecting data about all of the known large sites from the Dniester to the Dnipro river (Videiko et al., 2004) a further list of 139 Trypillia sites starting from 10 ha up to 340 ha was also published (Videiko, 2007).

Unsurprisingly, an international conference was hosted in Taljanky on this phenomenon, first in 2003 and also in 2011. Topics discussed included the origin and development of large settlements (Kruts, 2003: 71–73; Burdo, 2003: 14–17), their values, their place in ancient European history (Videiko, 2003), and the material culture and economy of settlements (Nikolova and Pashkevich, 2003: 89–95; Gaydarska, 2003: 212–6). The first conference became the starting point for future project 'Early urbanism in Europe?: the case of the Trypillia mega-sites', large-scale geomagnetic surveys by the RGK, and further excavations in Maidanetske.

Different investigations were carried out, including archaezoological (Zhuravlov, 2008), archaeobotanical studies and ^{14}C-datings (Telegin et al., 2003; Wechler, 1994).

Despite limited resources, the Ukrainian archaeologists continued their ambitious research on the giant settlements (Videiko, 2002). The publications reflected a wide analytical perspective on the archaeological data. Starting with descriptive excavation reports and subsequent demographical calculations (Kruts et al., 2001), precise typo-chronological studies (Ryzhov, 1990), and comprehensive modelling of settlement data (Diachenko, 2012; Diachenko and Menotti, 2012), the researchers contributed to a sophisticated research strategy.

New international projects between Ukrainian, German, and British archaeologists will build on, add to, and re-evaluate the results produced thus far using high-resolution geophysics and large-scale survey strategies based on elaborate interdisciplinary sampling strategies. The combination of different research traditions is a promising constellation which will have a positive effect on further developing archaeological strategies.

REFERENCES

Bibikov, S.N. 1965. Hoziajstvenno-ekonomicheskij kompleksa razvitogo Tripolja. *Sovertskaya Archeologiya*, 1: 48–62. Бибиков, С. Н. 1965. Хозяйственно-экономический комплекс развитого Триполья. Советская археология 1: 48–62.

Bicbaev, V.M. 2007. 'Bashni Petren' (ot archeologicheskoj interpretatsii aerofotosnimkov k rekonstuktsii zhizni tripolskih poselenij). *Tyragetia*, I(XVI)/1: 9–26. Бикбаев, В. М. 2007. «Башни» Петрен (от археологической интерпретации аэрофотоснимков к реконструкции жизни трипільських поселений). Tyragetia 1 (XVI)/1: 9–26.

Burdo, N.B. 2003. Sakralnyj aspect arhitektury triposkih protogorodov. In: O.G. Korvin-Piotrovskiy, V.O. Kruts & S.M. Ryzhov, eds. *Trypilski poselennia-giganty. Materialy mizhnarodnoi konferentsii*. Kyiv: Korvin-press, pp. 18–21. Бурдо, Н. Б. 2003. Сакральный аспект архитектуры трипольских протогородов. В сб.: О.Г.Корвин-Пиотровский, В.О. Круц і С.М. Рижов, ред. Трипільські поселення-гіганти. Матеріали міжнародної конференції. Київ: Корвин-пресс, с. 18–21.

Burdo, N.B. 2008. *Sakralnyj svit trypilskoi tsyvilizatsii*. Kyiv: Nash chas. Бурдо, Н. Б. 2008. Сакральний світ трипільської цивілізації. Київ: Наш час.

Diachenko, A. & Menotti, F. 2012. The Gravity Model: Monitoring the Formation and Development of the Tripolye Culture Giant-Settlements in Ukraine. *Journal of Archaeological Science*, 39: 2810–17.

Dudkin, V.P. 1978. Goefizicheskaya razvedka krupnyh tripolskih poselenij. In: V.F. Gening, ed. *Ispolzovanie metodov estestvennyh nauk v archeologii*. Kiev: Naukova dumka, pp. 35–45. Дудкин, В. П. 1978. Геофизическая разведка крупных трипольских поселений. В: Генинг, В. Ф, отв. ред. Использование методов естественных наук в археологии. Киев: Наукова думка, pp. 35–45.

Dudkin, V.P. 2007. Magnitometrychni doslishennia poselen trypilskoi tsyvilizatsii. In: S. Kot & M. Videiko, eds. *Trypilska kultura. Poshuky. Vidkryttia. Svitovyj kontekst*. Kyiv: Spadshchyna LTD, pp. 57–70. Дудкин, В. П. 2007. Магнітометричні дослідження поселень трипільської цивілізації. В: Кот, С. & Відейко, М., ред. Трипільська культура. Пошуки. Відкриття. Світовий контекст. Київ: «Спадщина» ЛТД, с. 57–70.

Gaydarska, B. 2003. Application of GIS in Settlement Archaeology: An Integrated Approach to Prehistoric Subsistence Strategies. In: O. Korvin-Piotrovsky, V. Kruts & S. M. Ryzhov, eds. *Tripolian Settlement-Giants. The International Symposium Materials*. Kyiv: Institute of Archaeology, pp. 212–5.

Häusler, A. 1985. Ernst von Stern, Archäologe in Odessa und Halle zum 125. Geburtstag. *Ethnogr.-Arch. Zeitschrift*, 25: 683–95.

Khvoika, V. 1901 The Stone Age of the Middle Dnieper region. In *Proceedings of the 11th Archaeological Convention in Kiev in 1899*. Vol. 1.: 737–812. Moscow: Moscow Archaeological Society Press (in Russian).

Kirleis, W. & Dal Corso, M. 2016. Trypillian Subsistence Economy: Animal and Plant Exploitation. In: J. Müller, K. Rassmann & M. Videiko, eds. *Trypillia Mega-Sites and European Prehistory: 4100–3400 BCE*. London and New York: Routledge, pp. 195–205.

Korvin-Piotrovskiy, A.G., Chabanyuk, V. & Shatilo, L. 2012. Tripolian House Construction: Concepts and Experiments. In: F. Menotti & A. Korvin-Piotrovskiy, eds. *The Tripolye Culture Giant-Settlements in Ukraine: Formation, Development and Decline*. Oxbow Books: Oxford, pp. 210–29.

Kruts, V.A. 1977. *Pozdnetripolskie pamyatniki Srednego Podneprovja*. Kiev: Naukova dumka. Круц, В. О., 1977. Позднетриполские памятники Среднего Поднепровья. Киев: Наукова думка.

Kruts, V.A. 1989. Kistorii naseleniya tripolskoj kultury v mezhdurechje Yuzhnogo Buga I Dnepra. In: S. S. Berezanskaya, ed. *Pervobytnaya archeologiya: Materialy i issledovaniya*. Kiev: Naukova dumka, pp. 117–32.

Круц, В. А. 1989. К истории населения трипольской культуры в междуречье Южного Буга и Днепра. В сб.: Березанская, С. С., ред. Первобытная археология: Материалы и исследования. Киев: Наукова думка, pp. 117–32.

Kruts, V.A. 1990. Planirovka poseleniya u s. Taljanki i nekotorye voprosy tripolskogo domostroitelstva. In: V. G. Zbenovich, ed. *Rannezemledelcheskie poseleniya-giganty tripolskoj kultury na Ukraine. Tezisy dokladov pervogo polevogo seminara*, Taljanki: Instytut archeologii AN of the USSRpp, pp. 43–47. Круц, В. А. 1990. Планировка поселения у с. Тальянки и некоторые вопросы трипольского домостроительства. В: *Раннеземледельческие поселения-гиганты трипольской культуры на Украине. Тезисы докладвпервого полевого семинара*. Тальянки: Институт археологии АН УССР, с. 43–47.

Kruts, V.A. 2003. Tripolskie ploshchadki – rezultat ritualnogo sozzheniya domov. In: O.G. Korvin-Piotrovskiy, V.O. Kruts & S.M. Ryzhov, eds. *Trypilski poselennya-giganty. Materialy mizhnarodnoi konferentsii*. Kyiv: Korvin-pres, pp. 74–76. Круц, В. А. 2003. Трипольские площадки – результат ритуального сожжения домов. В: Круц, В. А., Корвин-Пиотровский, А. Г. & Рыжов, С. Н., ред. *Трипільські поселення-гіганти. Матеріали міжнародної конференції*. Київ: Корвин-пресс, с. 74–76.

Kruts, V.A. 2008. Giant-Settlement of Talianki. In: A. Korvin-Piotrovkiy & F. Menotti, eds. *Tripolye Culture in Ukraine: The Giant-Settlement of Talianki*. Kiev: Institute of Archaeology of the NASU, pp. 57–70.

Kruts, V.A. & Ryzhov, S.M. 1985. Fazy rozvytku pamjatok tomashivsko-sushkivskoi grupy. *Archeologiya*, 52: 45–56. Круц, В. О. і Рижов, С. М. 1985. Фази розвитку пам'яток томашівсько-сушківської груп. Археологія 52: 45–56.

Kruts, V.A. & Videiko, M.Yu. 1991. Raskopki talnovskogo otryada Tripolskoj ekspeditsii. In: S.D. Kryzhitskij, ed. *Archeologichni doslidzhennya na Ukraini u 1990 r.* Kyiv: Verlag, pp. 31–32. Круц, В. А. & Видейко, М. Ю. 1991 Раскопки тальновского отряда Трипольской экспедиции.–В сб.: Крижицький, С. Д., ред. *Археологічні дослідження на Україні у 1990 р.* Київ: Verlag, с. 31–32.

Kruts, V.A., Korvin-Piotrovskiy, A.G. & Ryzhov, S.N. 2001. *Talianki – Giant-Settlement of the Tripolian Culture. Investigations in 2001*. Kiev: Institute of Archaeology of the NASU.

Markevich, V.I. 1981. *Pozdnetripolskie plemena Severnoj Moldavii*. Kishinev: Shtiintsa. Маркевич, В.И. 1981. *Позднетрипольские племена Северной Молдавии*. Кишинев: Штиинца.

Markevich, V.I. 1990. Domostroitelstvo Plemen Kultury Tripolye – Cucuteni. In: V.G. Zbenovich, ed. *Rannezemledelcheskie poseleniya-giganty tripolskoj kultury na Ukraine. Tezisy dokladov pervogo polevogo seminara*. Taljanki: Institute of Archeology of AS of the USSR, pp. 47–51. Маркевич, В. И. 1990. Домостроительство племен культуры Триполье-Кукутень. В: *Раннеземледельческие поселения-гиганты трипольской культуры на Украине: Тез. докл. I полевого семинара*. Тальянки: Институт археологии АН СССР, pp. 47–51.

Neubauer, W. 2001. Magnetische Prospektion in der Archäologie. *Mitt. Prähist. Kommission 44*. Wien: Verlag der Österreichischen Akademie der Wissenschaften.

Nikolova, A.V. & Pashkevich, G.A. 2003. K voprosu ob urovne razvitiya zamledeliya tripolskoj kultury. In: O. G. Korvin-Piotrovskiy, V. O. Kruts & S. M. Ryzhov, eds. *Trypilski poselennya-giganty. Matrialy mizhnarodnoi konferentsii*. Kyiv: Korvin-pres, pp. 89–95. Николова, А. В. & Пашкевич, Г. А. 2003. К вопросу об уровне земледелия трипольской культуры. У зб.: В.О. Круц, О.Г. Корвін-Піотровський і С.М. Рижов, ред. *Трипільські поселення-гіганти. Матеріали міжнародної конференції*. Київ: Корвин-прес, с. 89–95.

Ovchynnykov, E.V. 2015. Rozpysna keramika z megastruktury na trypilskomu poselenni Nebelivka. In: M. Yu. Videiko, J. Chapman, I.A. Kozyr & V.V. Sobchuk, eds. *Na shidnij mezhi Staroi Evropy*. Materialy Mizhnarodnoi konferentsii, Kirovograd, Nebelivka 12–14 tarvnia 2015 roku. Kirovograd, pp. 35–37. Овчинников, Е.В. 2015. Розписна кераміка з мегаструктури трипільського поселення Небелівка. У зб.: М.Ю. Відейко, Дж. Чепмен, І.А. Козир і В.В. Собчук, ред: На східній межі Старої Європи. Матеріали міжнародної наукової конференції, Кіровоград, Небелівка, 12–14 травня 2015 року. – Кіровоград, с. 35–37. In: M. Videiko, J. Chapman, I. Kozir, V. Sobchuk, eds. At the eastern frontiers of Old Europe. Proceedings of the International Conference in Kirovograd and Nebelivka, May 12–14 2015. Kirovograd, museum: pp 35–37.

Passek, T.S. 1949a. *Periodizatsiya tripolskih poselenij III-II tys. do n.e. Materialy i issledovakiya po archeologii* SSSR 10. Пассек, Т. С. 1949а. *Периодизация трипольских поселений. Материалы и исследования по археологи СССР*. Выпуск 10.

Passek, T.S. 1949b. Tripolskoe Poselenie Vladimirovka. *Kratkie soobshcheniya Instituta istorii materialnoj kultury*, 26: 47–56. Пассек, Т. С. 1949б. Трипольское поселение Владимировка. В: Краткие сообщения Института истории материальной культуры 26: 47–56.

Petrov, V. 1992. *Pohodzhennia ukrainskogo narodu*. Kyiv Петров, В. 1992. Походження українського народу. Київ: Verlag.

Ryzhov, S.N. 1990. Microchrnologiya tripolskogo poseleniya u s. Taljanki. In: V.G. Zbenovich, ed. *Rannezemledelcheskie poseleniya-giganty tripolskoj kultury na Ukraine. Tezisy dokladov pervogo polevogo seminara*. Taljanki: Institute of Archaeology of the AS of the USSR, pp. 83–90. Рыжов, С. Н. 1990. Микрохронология трипольского поселения у с. Тальянки. В кн.: Раннеземледельческие поселения-гиганты трипольской культуры на Украине: Тез. докл. І полевого семинара. – Тальянки: Институт археологии Ан СССР, с. 83–90.

Schuchhardt, C. 1920. Die Anfänge der Leichen-verbrennung. *Sitzungsberichte der Preußischen Akademie der Wissenschaften* 26 (Berlin) 515.

Shatilo, L. 2014. Reconstruction of the Roof Shape of Eneolithic Houses in South-Eastern Europe on the Example of Tripolian Buildings. Sources and Problems. In: G. Dumitroaia, C. Preoteasa & N. Ciprian-Dorin, eds. *Cucuteni Culture within the European Neo-Eneolithic Context*, Editura Constantin Matasa: Piatra-Neamt, pp. 113–16.

Shmaglij, N.M. 1980. Krupnye tripolskie poseleniya v mezhdurechje Dnepra i Yuzhnogo Buga. In: I.I. Artemenko, ed. *Pervobytnaya archeologiya poiski i nahodki*. Kiev: Naukova Dumka, pp. 198–203. Шмаглий, Н. М. 1980. Крупные трипольские поселения в междуречье Днепра и Южного Буга. В сб.: Артеменко, И. И. ред. Первобытная археологи: поиски и находки. Киев: Наукова думка, с. 198–203.

Shmaglij, N.M. & Videiko, M.Yu. 1990a. Krupnye tripolskie poseleniya i problema rannih from urbanizatsii. In: V.G. Zbenovich, ed. *Rannezemledelcheskie poseleniya-giganty tripolskoj kultury na Ukraine. Tezisy dokladov pervogo polevogo seminara*. Kiev: Institute of Archaeology of the AS of the USSR, pp. 12–16. Шмаглий, Н. М. и Видейко, М.Ю. 1990а. Крупные трипольские поселения и проблема ранних форм урбанизации. В сб.: В.Г. Збенович, ред. *Раннеземледельческие поселения-гиганты трипольской культуры на Украине. Тезисы докладов первого полевого семинара*. Киев: Институт археологии АН УССР, с. 12–16.

Shmaglij, N.M. & Videiko, M.Yu. 1990b. Mikrochornologiya poseleniya Maidanetskoe. In: V.G. Zbenovich, ed. *Rannezemledelcheskie poseleniya-giganty tripolskoj kultury na Ukraine. Tezisy dokladov pervogo polevogo seminara*. Kiev: Institute of Archaeology of the AS of the USSR, pp. 91–94. Шмаглий, Н. М. и Видейко, М. Ю. 1990б. Микрохронология поселения Майданецкое. В сб.: В.Г. Збенович, ред. Раннеземледельческие поселения-гиганты трипольской культуры на Украине. Тезисы докладов первого полевого семинара. Киев: Институт археологии АН УССР, с. 91–94.

Shmaglij, M.M. & Videiko, M. Yu. 1992. Trypilski poselennya na Cherkashchyni. *Archeologiya*, 3: 124–130. Шмаглій, М. М. і Відейко, М. Ю. 1992. Трипільські поселення на Черкащині. Археологія 3: 124–130.

Shmaglij, M.M., Dudkin, V.P. & Zinkovskiy, K.V. 1973. Pro kompleksne vyvchennya trypilskyh poselen. *Archeologiya*, 10: 23–31. Шмаглій, М. М., Дудкін, В.П. і Зіньковський, К.В. 1973. Про комплексне вивчення трипільських поселень. Археологія. 10: 23–31.

Shtiglits, M.S. 1971. Razvedki tripolskih pamiatnikov rajone Umani. In: *Archeologicheskie otkrytiya v SSSR 1970g.*: 236. Штиглиц, М. С. 1971. Разведки трипольских памятников в районе Умани. Археологические открытия в СССР 1970 г: 236.

Shyshkin, K.V. 1973. Z praktyky deshyfruvannya aerofotoznimkiv u archeologichnyh tsilyah. *Archeologiya*, 19: 32–41. Шишкін, К. В. 1973. З практики дешифрування аерофотоэнімків у археологічних цілях. Археологія 19: 32–41.

Shyshkin, K.V. 1985. Planuvannia trypilskyh poselen za danymy aerofotozjomky. *Archeologiya*, 52: 72–77. Шишкін, К.В. 1985. Планування трипільських поселень за даними аерофотозийомки. Археологія, 52: 72–77.

Stern, V.E. 1907. Die „prämykenische Kultur' in Süd-Russland. Bericht über die Ausgrabungen in Petreni 1902 und 3. 13. *Archeologičeskogo Cezda v Jekaterinoslav*, 1905: 1–95.

Stern, V. E. 1921. Die Leichenverbrennung in der prämykenischen Kultur Südrußlands. In: *Festschrift Adalberg Bezzenberger*. Göttingen: Vandenhoeck & Rupprecht, pp. 16–166.

Telegin, D.Ya., Lillie, M., Potekhina, I.D & Kovaliukh, M.M. 2003. Settlement and Economy in Neolithic Ukraine: A New Chronology. *Antiquity* 77: 456–470.

Videiko, Y.M. 1990. Zhilishhno-hozjajstvennye kompleksy poselenija Majdaneckoe i voprosy ih interpretacii. In: V. G. Zbenovich, ed. *Rannezemledelcheskie poseleniyagiganty tripolskoj kultury na Ukraine. Tezisy dokladov pervogo polevogo seminara*, Taljanki: Instytut archeologii AN of the USSR, pp. 115–120. Видейко М.Ю. 1990. Жилищно-хозяйственные комплексы поселения Майданецкое и вопросы их интерпретации. In: Збенович 1990. Раннеземледельческие поселения-гиганты трипольской культуры на Украине. Тезисы докладвпервого полевого семинара. Тальянки: Институт археологии АН УССР. 115–120.

Videiko, M.Yu. 1991. Doslidzhennya piznotrypilskogo poselennya Talne 3. In: S.D. Kryzhytskiy, ed. *Archeologichni doslidzhennya na Ukraini u 1990 r.* Kyiv, pp. 11–12. Видейко, М. Ю. 1991. Дослідження пізньотрипільського поселення Тальне-3. В сб.: Крижицький, С. Д., ред. Археологічні дослідження на Україні у 1990 р. – Київ: Verlag с. 11–12.

Videiko, M.Yu. 2002. *Trypilski protomista: istoriya doslidzen*. Kyiv: Akademperiodyka. Відейко, М.Ю. 2002. Трипільські протоміста. Історія досліджень. – Київ: Академперіодика.

Videiko, M.Yu. 2003. Processes of Urbanization in Old Europe and Trypillya Culture Proto-Cities. In: O. G. Korvin-Piotrovkiy, V.O. Kruts & S.M. Ryzhov, eds. *Tripolian Settlement-Giants. The International Symposium Materials*. Kyiv: Korvin-pres, pp. 256–261.

Videiko, M.Yu. 2005. Looking for Trypillya Culture Proto-Cities. Author's edition. Kiev.

Videiko, M.Yu. 2007. Contours and Contents of the Ghost: Trypillia Culture Proto-Cities. *Memoria Antiquitatis*, 24: 251–276.

Videiko, M.Yu., Videiko, M.M., Kochkin, I.T., Kvitnytskyj, M.V., Pichkur, E.V., Ovchynnykov, E.V. & Polishchuk, L.Yu. 2004. Archeologichni pamjatky na terytorii Ukrainy. Reestr. In: M.Yu. Videiko, ed. *Entsyklopediya trypilskoi tsyvilizatsii. Tom 1*. Kyiv: Ukrpoligrafmedia, pp. 563–699. Відейко, М. Ю., Відейко, М. М., Кочкін, І. Т., Квітницький, М. В., Пічкур, Є. В., Овчинников, Е. В. і Поліщук, Л. Ю.2004. Археологічні пам'ятки на території України. Реєстр. В: Відейко, М. Ю., ред. Енциклопедія трипільської цивілізації. Том 1. Київ: Укрполіграфмедіа, с. 563–699.

Wechler, K.-P. 1994. Zur Chronologie der Tripolje-Cucuteni-Kultur aufgrund von ^{14}C-Datierungen. *Zeitschrift für Archäologie*, 28: 7–21.

Zbenovich, G., ed. 1990, Rannezemledelcheskie poseleniyagiganty tripolskoj kultury na Ukraine. *Tezisy dokladov pervogo polevogo seminara*, Taljanki: Instytut archeologii AN of the USSR, В.Г. Збенович 1990. Раннеземледельческие поселения-гиганты трипольской культуры на Украине. Тезисы докладвпервого полевого семинара. Тальянки: Институт археологии АН УССР.

Zhuravlev, O.P. 2008. *Tvarynnytstvo ta myslyvstvo u trypilskyh plemen na terytorii Ukrainy*. Kyiv: Shlyah. Журавльов, О. П. 2008. Тваринництво та мисливство у трипільських племен на території України.–Київ: Шлях.

CHAPTER 3

The New Challenge for Site Plans and Geophysics: Revealing the Settlement Structure of Giant Settlements by Means of Geomagnetic Survey

Knut Rassmann, Aleksey Korvin-Piotrovskiy, Mykhailo Videiko and Johannes Müller

During three campaigns in 2011, 2012, and 2014, a combined team from the RGK Frankfurt a.M. and the CAU Kiel engaged in geomagnetic surveys on Copper Age settlements in the Talne district, Cherkasy Oblast of Ukraine. This paper focuses on the results of those surveys and outlines the perspectives for reconstructing the size and spatial structure of the settlements. It based on the sites of Taljanky, Maidanetske, and Apolianka on representative data and on the information gleaned from Drobrovody (at which a large portion of the site is covered by the modern village). These various geomagnetic surveys delivered excellent data for areas of more than 4 km². In addition, long term, ongoing excavations at Taljanky and Maidanetske revealed numerous settlement remains. All in all, these sites provided excellent prerequisites for survey campaigns, including rich comparative excavation data (useful for understanding and interpreting geomagnetic anomalies) as well as the geomagnetic data itself. The latter can be used to interpolate information from unexcavated areas in order to estimate the size of settlements and investigate their internal structures.

Technical Equipment and Data Processing

Our survey was conducted by means of a 16-channel magnetometer (SENSYS MAGNETO®-MX ARCH). The 16-channel magnetometer is mounted on a vehicle-drawn cart (Figures 1 and 2). The gradiometers were set at 0.25 m intervals on a 4 m wide sensor frame, itself set at right angles to a 6 m long tow bar. With speeds ranging ~12–16 km per hour and a sample rate of twenty readings per second, the system provided xyz data on a mesh of 0.25 m by approximately 0.3 m.

MAGNETO®-MX compact 16-channel data acquisition electronics with 20 Hz sampling frequency was used for data acquisition with Trimble RTK-DGPS georeferencing (base/rover combination). The DGPS of 5-channel system was based on a Leica DGPS (1000). Data acquisition was accomplished with RTK fix and RTK float positional accuracy (±0.02/±0.02 m).

Data Processing

The use of this new generation of geomagnetic instruments enables us to prospect large areas in relatively short time periods (Figure 2). The first challenge, however, is to analyse the data produced within an appropriate time frame. The second difficulty involves the production of reliable data in order to facilitate the straightforward comparison of different sites. The work can be accomplished only through close cooperation with our respective project partners. For the recent project, the wealth of experience possessed by our Ukrainian partner was an excellent assist in reading the geomagnetic data. Volodymyr Kruts, in particular, contributed a great deal to our regular evening discussions in 2011 (Figure 3). In order to succeed, discussion and interpretation must be placed on equal footing. To this end, one must always work with the same data and software tools. Only the first level of survey was completed with commercial software. In the later stages of analysis, we used open source software to facilitate such cooperations.

The SENSYS MonMX, DLMGPS, and MAGNETO®-ARCH software package was used for data acquisition, primary data processing, interpolation, and export. Each track contains the measurements produced by the five or sixteen channels and the DGPS data and was saved separately (e.g. in Maidanetske 165 ha, 1136 tracks, of a length of 412 km). The tracks recorded by SENSYS MonMX were then imported into the DLMGPS software. To check the data in the field, we used MAGNETO®-ARCH for initial geomagnetic map imaging. For more detailed interpolation, we used OASIS montaj. In order to export the data

© European Association of Archaeologists 2016

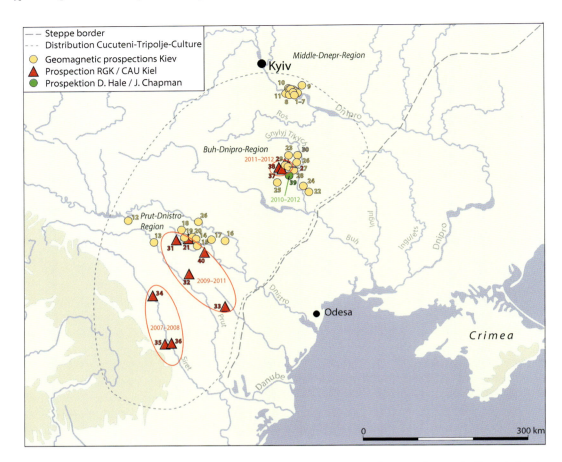

Figure 1. Geomagnetic survey on settlements of Trypillia-Cucuteni groups by the Romano-Germanic-Commission in cooperation with the University Kiel with the year of the campaign. Additionally mapped: the former Ukrainian survey (Koshelev, 2004) and the survey in Nebelivka (Durham University). (1) Kolomyjshchyna, (2) Stajky (ur. Charkove), (3) Vasylyshyn Jar (Grebeny), (4) Vynogradne (Grebeni), (5) Jancha 1, (6) Jancha 2, (7) Popova Levada, (8) Kuriache Polé (Jushky), (9) Grygorivka (ur. Chatyśce), (10) Rzyshchiv (Homyne), (11) Jushky (ur. Zhuravka), (12) Konovka (Ukraine), (13) Brinzeni Ostrov, (14) Trifaneshty, (15) Putineshty, (16) Ivanovka, (17) Starye Raduliani II, (18) Glavan 1, (19) Glavan (Sofija 2a), (20) Lamojna 1, (20) Lamojna 2, (21) Petreni, (22) Mogylna 2, (22) Mogylna 3, (23) Glybochok, (24) Fedorivka (Mychajlivka), (25) Jatranivka, (26) Jampiĺ, (27) Moshuriv 1 (früh), (27) Moshuriv 1 (spät), (28) Maidanetske, (29) Taljanky, (30) Vilkhovets, (31) Ochiul Alb, (32) Cobani, (33) Horodka, (34) Ruginoasa, (35) Rapa Morii, (36) Prohezesti, (37) Apolianka, (38) Dobrovody, (39) Nebelivka, (40) Singerei.

from DLMGPS to Oasis montaj, a simple text file was produced which contained the vertical gradient (z) as nanotesla values and the measured track and number of the probes in the following manner:

x-Coordinate	y-Coordinate	nT	Track file	Probe number
36319139.039	5407912.165	20.1	Tal123.prm	1
36319138.820	5407912.045	12.5	Tal123.prm	2

Post-processing, however, was completed with Oasis montaj 8. This differs from our former workflow based on GRASS-based rfill.gap algorithm (Darvill et al., 2013: 88). The use of Oasis montage 8 opens more options for the post-processing of the data. The results were exported as a Surfer 7 file (which can be easily imported into GIS software). The use of Surfer 7 files enables the user to modify threshold, colour scale and (in combination with the rich choice of available raster and vector tools) to produce spatial

Figure 2. The 16-channel magnetometer (SENSYS MAGNETO®-MX ARCH) during a survey campaign in Taljanky in 2012 (photo: M. Videiko).

Figure 3. V. Kruts accompanying the 2011 and 2012 Taljanky surveys. The equipment transport trailer is visible in the background.

analysis of the data. This further processing was done in QGIS 2.6. Each digitized anomaly was assigned an ID number for further analytical steps. This last is especially important when features are added to the specific ID, albeit on different layers (e.g. electromagnetic data and aerial photography).

Methodological remarks

The closer integration of the geomagnetic survey in the archaeological practice (especially the fact that archaeologists organized and realized the survey, the data processing and the following GIS-based interpretation) finally led to a deeper understanding of geomagnetic data and its archaeological background. An excellent example is the pushing of geophysical survey and remote sensing by prehistorians like M. Doneus or W. Neubauer from the LBI, or the successful surveys on LBK settlements by the University Cologne or by the 'Human Development in Landscape' graduate school at the Christian Albrechts University in Kiel.

The highly informative survey data of the Copper Age settlement in Eastern Europe demonstrate the potential for a contextual interpretation of the archaeological data.

Our interpretation starts with the classification of single geomagnetic features as outlined in Figure 4 (e.g. houses, special buildings, pits, workshops, fortifications, and alleys). The classification of the features is qualified by the comparative use of excavation date. The advantage of prospecting on Trypillian sites is the availability of a rich amount of excavation data such as was present at the sites in Taljanky and Maidanetske (where nearly ninety houses were excavated).

The identification of archaeological objects continued in the contextual analyses. Thus, it became clear that superordinate structures (like house cluster) were also used as fortifications and alleys. This analytical

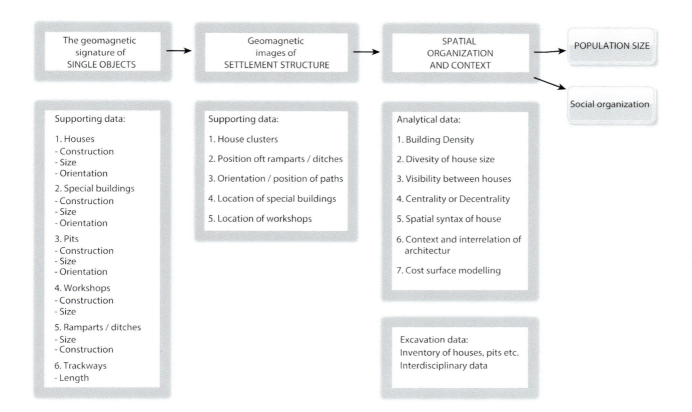

Figure 4. Overview of a spatial analysis of the geomagnetic data.

step considers the location and orientation of these elements. In a final step, the elements were used in a spatial analysis. GIS provides a range of tools for analysing the architectural density and the visibility between houses for the modelling of private and public space. The centrality or remoteness of buildings can be calculated and used by Network analysis as well as other agent-based models. In combination with archaeological and natural scientific data, spatial data can be used for more complex reconstructions of population size and social organization (Müller et al., 2013; Nowaczinski et al., 2013; Trebsche et al., 2010).

Overview of the Magnetic Data

Taljanky (Oblast Cherkassy)

With an area of approximately 320 ha, Taljanky is the largest Copper Age settlement in Europe. Taljanky is located in the southern part of a Chernozem plateau that is bordered by the Taljanka River to the East and a small watercourse in confluence with the site on the settlement's southeast edge (Figure 5).

By taking aerial photographs the detection of the extraordinary size of the settlement was effectuated' in the early 1970s (Dudkin, 1978) and large-scale geomagnetic surveys (Dudkin, 1978; Koshelev, 2004). The Dudkin's survey between 1983 and 1986 covered an area of 232 ha (Figure 6a; Koshelev, 2004: 305 f.). An excavation programme under the direction of V.O. Kruts, A.G. Korvin-Piotrovskiy, V.V. Chabanyuk, and L.A. Shatilo was carried out from 1981 to 1999. In the 2012 excavation campaign, house no. 47 was excavated (Kruts et al., 2013b: 10ff.).

These recent geomagnetic surveys were conducted by the RGK Frankfurt a.M., Kyiv Academy, and CAU Kiel (Kruts et al., 2011, 2013a). Within the new geomagnetic survey (which covered 195 ha), c. sixty per cent of the settlement area was surveyed. The building density in Taljanky is different (Figure 6b). In the surveys in central part of the settlement (which measured c. 140 ha), no indication of house buildings was found. To put this fact into perspective, only 170 ha of the whole 340 ha was settled. Of this settled area, seventy per cent was covered by the magnetic survey. That means that our surveys are representative and can be used to draw some general conclusions concerning total house numbers and to reconstruct the general structures present at the site.

The recent surveys revealed 1370 burnt houses and 221 unburnt or poorly preserved houses as well as 1871 pits and 74 circular anomalies (interpreted as pottery kilns), 10 larger houses in prominent positions in entrance areas' linear anomalies that can be classified as trackways, and the indications of two heavily eroded kurgans.

Geomagnetic Signatures of Single Objects

1. A total of 1335 burnt rectangular houses are distributed in loosely ovoid concentric rings and in

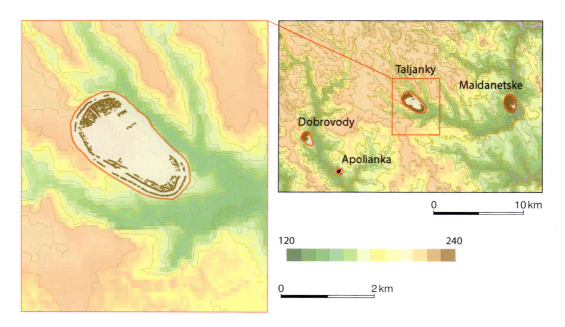

Figure 5. (a) Taljanky (Cherkasy Oblast). Overview of the topographical location of the site. (b) Overview of the survey area with the other sites (i.e. Maidanetske, Apolianka, and Dobrovody). All sites are located at the southern edges of plateaus bordered by small streams. The features marked here represent geomagnetic signatures of houses.

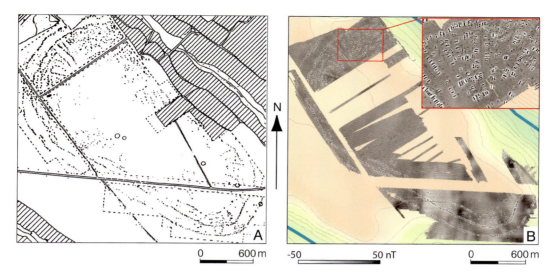

Figure 6. Taljanky (Cherkasy Oblast). (a) Geomagnetic map of Dudkin's 1983–1985 survey (Koshelev, 2004: 305). (b) Overview of the 2011–2012 geomagnetic survey.

axial and rows (Figure 6b). However, while the general pattern of the burned houses is similar, if we analyse the objects in detail, each house-anomaly differs in shape. The interpolation map shows variations of c. 15–60 nT caused by massive layers of burnt clay (Figures 7–11). The presence of massive layers of burnt clay can be explained by the specific architecture of Trypillian houses (Kruts et al., 2001: 71 figure 60). A small number of houses show lower values between 15 nT while some of those areas with nT value >15 measure less than 10 m^2. (Figures 9b 1–2 and 11b). The variation of nT values indicates a difference in the location and thickness of the accumulated burnt clay. The varying thickness of house remains is less an indication of different domestic architectures than it shows variations in the intensity of house destruction by fire or differences in the preservation of the archaeological layer. Around 220 structures are visible. They could be identified either by geomagnetic features or even by the layout of the pits which align with the houses. Their special distribution is similar to that of the burnt houses. The size of the burnt houses varies. In the northern settlement, the largest houses are located in the outer rings, whereas the central part is occupied by smaller houses (Figure 12). To sum up the geomagnetic map, 1335 burnt and 220 unburnt or poorly preserved houses can be identified.

2. The pits were detected by the recent surveys. Their signatures are less clear than those of the houses (Figure 9a and c). A sum of 1871 pits of different sizes could be identified in the survey. In most cases, they were spatially bound to the houses and appear on the outer or inner gables of said structures (Figures 9–11). Their diameter varies from 4

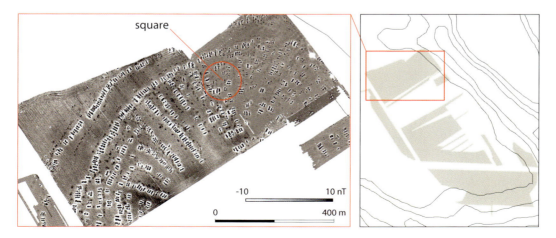

Figure 7. Taljanky (Cherkasy Oblast). Overview of the northern part of the settlement with its c. 610 houses. The red circle marks a likely square.

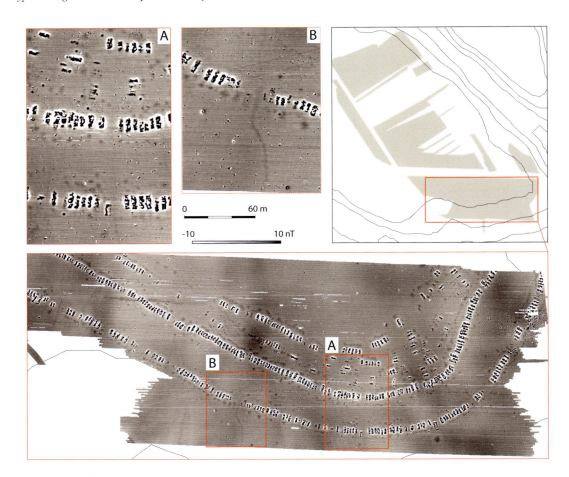

Figure 8. Taljanky (Cherkasy Oblast). Magnetic anomalies in the southern part of the settlement. (a) Houses with different orientations and sizes, pits, and linear structures (alleys). (b) Gap between two house rows, linear structures, and prominent alleys.

to 7 m. The low nT values and the size argue for their use as clay extraction pits.

3. Mega-structures such as in Maidanetske are unknown in Taljanky. However, larger houses similar to those found in Maidanetske are present (Figure 13). A small number of larger house are situated in separate positions. They are located in front of gaps (Figure 9b and c) or behind the circular house rows in an axial orientation (Figure 10b, mark by red 1). There is an overlapping with another house in axial orientation. This might indicate two settlement phases.

4. A sum of seventy-four circular structures with high nT values were identified as possible kilns (Figure 9b and c). Three of these were already excavated in 2013; a fourth in 2014 (see Korvin-Piotrovskiy et al., 2016). This number increased based on a re-evaluation of the geomagnetic data.

5. Seven elongated geomagnetic features radially oriented to the main outer ring and leading away from the site can be interpreted as tracks. If we consider the other empty spaces within the house rings, approximately eight gateways could be identified in the south at regular distances of about 250 m each (Figures 8 and 9b).

6. The geomagnetic features of two kurgans in the central area were also identified. Even if the kurgans are probably of later date than the latest domestic occupation, their special position seems to take a central spot in the south which could perhaps have been linked to the track system present at the centre of the site (Kruts et al., 2013a: 95, figure 4)

7. A rectangular enclosure in the north is not in line with the general layout of houses or other features in that area and might belong to a different period (Kruts et al., 2013a: 96).

HOUSES, SPECIAL BUILDINGS, KILNS, AND TRACKWAYS IN THE CONTEXT OF THE SETTLEMENT LAYOUT

The described single features are embedded in a highly visible spatial context. Houses are grouped in rows with circular and axial orientations. In the northwest settlement, house rows formed around courtyard-like situations (Figure 7). The size of the houses varies. The diverse structures can be observed as described above in the northern area of the site

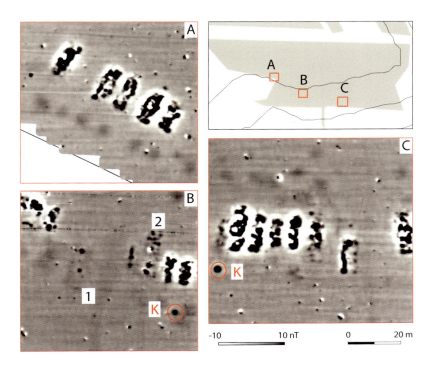

Figure 9. Taljanky (Cherkasy Oblast). Magnetic anomalies and houses with prominent positions in front of the entrance area in the southern part of the settlement. Kilns are marked by red Ks. (a) Row of medium-sized burnt houses (70–80 m^2). (b) Entrance area with linear anomaly (trackway) and houses of different sizes and states of preservation: (1) Unburnt or badly preserved houses; (2) large, poorly preserved building. (c) Row of burnt houses and unburnt or badly preserved houses in front of the entrance.

(Figure 12) as well as throughout the whole of the settlement (Figure 14). The detailed view available in the northern sector seems to indicate the presence of size variation within the house rows (Figure 12).

Larger buildings in prominent positions are visible inside the house groups (Figure 9) placed in front of gaps between the house rows. For the most part, they were not heavily burnt or unburnt? (Figure 9a).

Figure 10. Taljanky (Cherkasy Oblast). Magnetic anomalies and burnt and unburnt houses in the north-western part of the settlement. (a) Burnt houses and circular anomalies (pits refilled with burnt daub?) northeast of the pits to unburnt (?) houses. (b) House rows with different orientations.

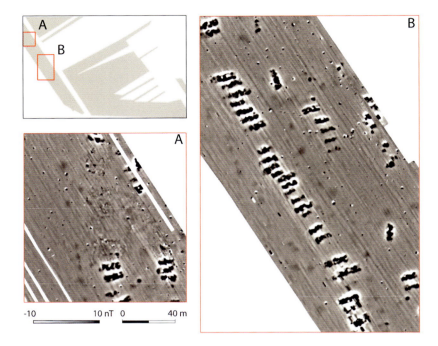

Figure 11. Taljanky (Cherkasy Oblast). Magnetic anomalies in the north-western part of the settlement. (a) Area with unregularly distributed small anomalies indicating excavation trenches from the campaigns which took place between 2001 and 2017. (b) House rows with different lengths and numbers of houses.

The number 74 kiln-like anomaly is a central issue for analysing the division of labour in the settlement (see Korvin-Piotrovskiy et al., 2016). The kilns are widely distributed without indications of centralization (Figure 15). In comparison with a Kernel density estimation of building density, there is a tendency for the kilns to be located along the periphery of areas with higher densities (Figure 15).

Streets and paths are the central structuring element in cities as well as in villages. The potential trackways in Taljanky are located in the southern periphery of the settlement. They are oriented towards gaps between the house rows and they correlate with the location of prominent larger buildings (Figures 8 and 9)

Quantification and Settlement Layout

An understanding of the revealed settlement layout needs a structural perspective for the data. The descriptions above underline the central elements for the structure of the settlement. They can be briefly summarized as follows:

1. circularly oriented house rows;
2. axially oriented house rows;
3. gouses placed in courtyard-like layouts;
4. larger buildings in separate positions in front of gaps;
5. variation in house sizes within the rows and the regularly distributed larger buildings;

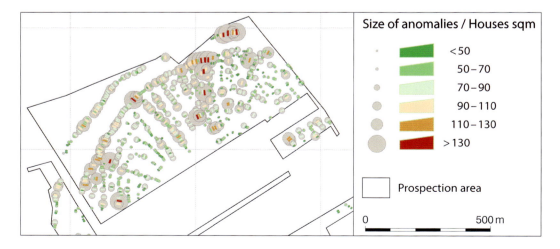

Figure 12. Taljanky (Cherkasy Oblast). Variation of house sizes in the northern part of the settlement area.

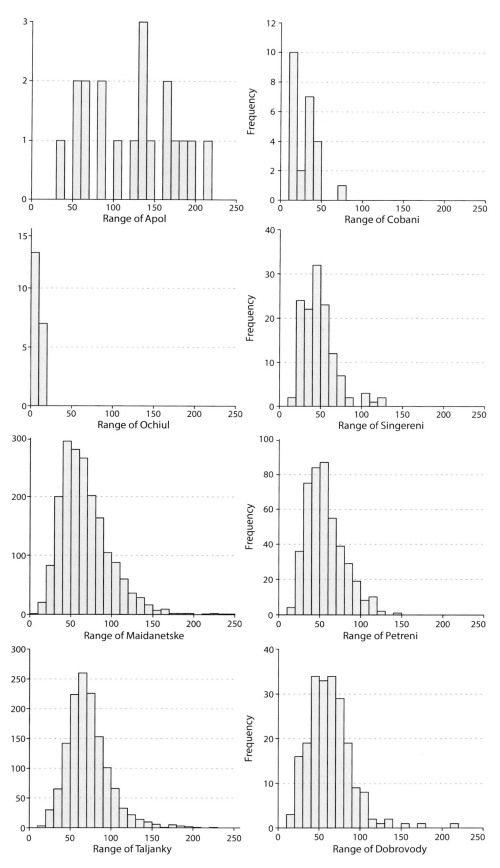

Figure 13. Histogram of the house sizes on Cucuteni-Trypillian sites in Moldova and Ukraine (Petreni, Singerei, Ochiul Alb, Cobani–Moldova; Apolianka, Maidanetske, Taljanky, and Dobrovody). The columns have a width of 10 m each. At Dobrovody, one value above 250 m^2 was omitted.

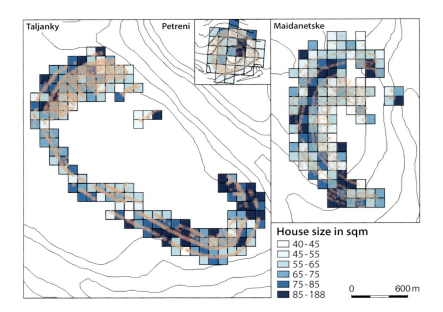

Figure 14. Choropleth map of house sizes in Taljanky, Maidanetske, and Petreni. The tiles comprise 10,000 m² each and show the median of the sizes of all houses per tile.

6. location and orientation of trackways;
7. gaps between house rows (entrance areas?);
8. gaps in the interrelation with axial house rows;
9. position of workshops.

In addition to these qualitative features, their distributions are valuable for GIS-based spatial analysis for the calculation of building density (Figures 14 and 15) and intervisibility or agent-based models (Kruts, 2013b; Ohlrau, 2014). Building density is crucial to the overall analysis of the settlement. Starting with the calculation of house-centroids, the points were used for the kernel density estimations. In this way, the settled area can be measured as an area with higher

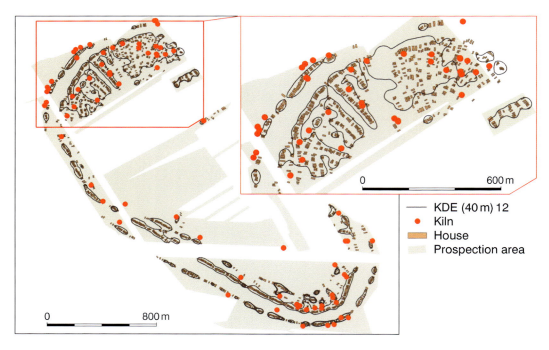

Figure 15. Taljanky (Cherkasy Oblast). Overview of the around 1550 houses detected and the results of house density estimated by kernel density. The KDE was based on bi-weighted interpolation with a 40 m radius and the centroids of reconstructed houses. The selected 12 m isoline includes more than ninety per cent of the houses. The KDE visualizes the house groups, which can be used for the spatial separation of house groups. As a second category, pottery kilns were also mapped. A re-evaluation of the anomalies allowed for the identification of seventy-four kilns.

density (Figure 15). In comparison with spatial analysis of house size, the relation between building density and house size can be analysed (Figures 14 and 15). It is obvious that areas with the highest densities of houses and what were mostly smaller houses and kilns are closer to areas with smaller houses.

Besides the house size, their diversity is a further potential indicator for the rise of social differentiation. In the northern settlement area, a wide variation in house size is apparent. They seem not distinctive in the areas with lower building density in the northeast area, while greater diversity is visible in the northwest (Figure 12).

The general settlement layout is defined by three loosely ovoid concentric rings lined gable by gable and oriented on a radial axis to the central clear space. The overall settlement plan indicates differences in spatial order. The northern area has a main ring of two parallel house rows at a distance of 100–150 m and further rings of lesser distance (50 m?). The huge inner empty space is obviously settled at the northern and southern fringe by clusters of houses that are well structured in the western part but which become more irregular to the east.

The southern area is dominated by house rows. These are less axial rows than those in the northwest. Building density is lower. The distance between the outer ring in the north and south is nearly 2.5 km. Even initial analysis revealed differences between the settlements, which shall be analysed in greater detail in our forthcoming investigation. For a deeper understanding of these structures, a more detailed internal chronology for the crucial spatial element is needed. It can be realized by a synthesis of valuable typochronological studies and a series of ^{14}C-dates. Ceramic inventories of nearly fifty excavated houses provide a promising basis for this work.

SPATIAL ORGANIZATION AND POPULATION SIZE

The number of houses is a proxy for the calculation of population size in numerous papers (e.g. Diachenko 2016; see also more references to the former research in this volume). Another option would be to calculate the settled area and to use the size of house groups as proxy for the reconstruction (Rassman *et al.*, 2016). Some indications in Petreni (see Rassmann *et al.*, 2016) or Vinča sites suggest that house groups occupy areas below 4000 m². For one house group, a population size of forty to sixty (mean 50) persons can be calculated. We can see similar structures in Taljanky, Maidanetske, and Dobrovody. The KDE-calculated settled area in Taljanky occupies 70 ha. The selected isoline enclosed houses are revealed in our geomagnetic data. When this number is added to the 0.4 ha estimated for one house group, a maximum of 200 house groups can be calculated, which yields a sum of around 10,000 residents.

MAIDANETSKE (OBLAST CHERKASY)

General information about the site

Ten kilometers from Taljanky as the crow flies, the mega-site of Maidanetske is situated on a Chernozem high plateau (Müller and Videiko, 2016) (Figure 5). The Taljanka River marks the western border of the settled area. The site itself is situated at the confluence of a small watercourse with the Taljanka River 170–190 m a.s.l.

The site has a long research history. The first excavations by G. Bzuvenglinsky took place in the 1920s, although unfortunately both documentation and excavated material are lost. After the analysis of aerial photographs by K.V. Shyshkin (Shyshkin, 1973), the first full geomagnetic plan was executed by V.P. Dudkin from 1972 to 1974 (Dudkin, 1978). Dudkin's plans confirmed the results already obtained by aerial photography (Videiko and Rassmann, 2016). In field campaigns that began in 1971 and ended in 1998, several houses were excavated by Ukrainian teams. In 2012 and 2013, the new geomagnetic surveys were conducted. Excavation started in 2013 with the publication of preliminary results in 2014 (Müller *et al.*, 2014; Müller and Videiko, 2016).

As per the reconstruction made by means of aerial photography, the site measured 200 ha overall, of which *c.* 80 ha is constructed space.[1] In the recent geomagnetic survey, 165 ha was surveyed, of which *c.* 120 ha exhibits built structures (Figures 16-24). So far, our survey data cover nearly 74 per cent of the settlement; the settled area comprises 79 ha (Figure 25). The DEM (Figure 16) visualizes the erosion risk (a factor only relevant for the eastern area close to the Taljanka River). For this area, no data from the recent survey are available. Here Dudkin's survey can be used to bridge this gap. In other settlement areas, the erosion effect is minimal (this is evidenced by the geomagnetic data). Therefore, the revealed geomagnetic features are representative of Trypillia occupation.

GEOMAGNETIC SIGNATURES OF SINGLE OBJECTS

As was the case with the presentation of the survey results in Taljanky, the geomagnetic features of the

---

[1] The size of the constructed area depends on the way in which it is calculated. To minimize the subjectivity factor, we use a kernel density estimation. The settled area is defined by the KDE-Line that enclosed ninety-five per cent of the settlement's houses.

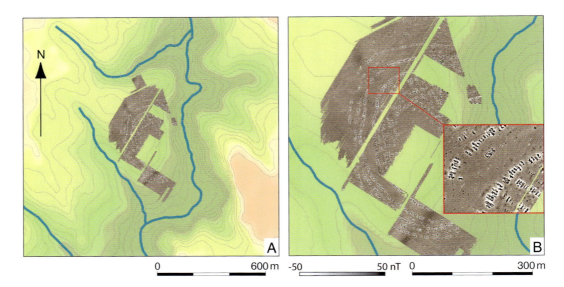

Figure 16. *Maidanetske (Cherkasy Oblast). (a) Overview of the topographical situation around the site. (b) Overview of the geomagnetic survey area (c. 150 ha) with a detail of the northern area.*

new survey could be divided into several categories (houses, pits, special buildings, and pottery kilns):

1. As was the case at Taljanky, the geomagnetics revealed 1493 burnt rectangular houses (Figures 16–24). These features are similar to those in Taljanky. At 67 m^2, the size of the house structures is a little smaller than at Taljanky with 72 m^2 (Table 1). Besides these differences, the relation between large and smaller buildings is the same as in Taljanky (Figure 13). In comparison with the 220 unburnt houses, the 415 less burnt or even eroded houses are remarkably higher. They are arranged in a similar layout to the burnt houses (Figure 21(1)). How these anomalies should be interpreted should remain an open question. The row of eleven houses in Figure 22(1) might be an example of a social group which did not practise the ritual of burning down their houses.

2. To sum up, the total number of detected houses in Maidanetske counts some 1717 examples. In relation to the *c.* seventy per cent of the site covered by the survey, we can interpolate the total number at *c.* 2100. It is a little smaller than other estimations, but is nonetheless higher than our estimation for Taljanky (at 1950; Rassmann *et al.*, 2014).

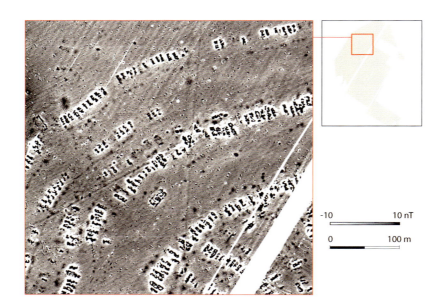

Figure 17. *Maidanetske (Cherkasy Oblast). Overview of the geomagnetic survey in the north-western part of the settlement.*

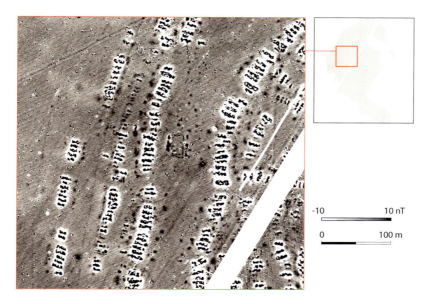

Figure 18. Maidanetske (Cherkasy Oblast). Overview of the geomagnetic survey in the western part of the settlement.

3. A further difference between Maidanetske and Taljanky involved the fact that we detected less pits (1537) than houses (1717). As was at the case at Taljanky, the pits are associated with house rows and thus also form concentric pit alignments in accordance with the width of the houses (Figures 17–24) in the empty spaces, probably demarcating houses that are not visible in the geomagnetic plan seldom in loose context outside or inside the settlement. Pits are of very different sizes and represent different functions and depositional processes that are similar to the pits present at other sites, like Taljanky and Dobrovody.

4. Nine special buildings can be characterized by their extraordinary size and significant spatial positions within otherwise mainly empty house rings (Figure 16: 25). They vary in size from 120 to 400 m² as well as in their state of preservation and mode of construction. It has to be emphasized that large houses of similar size are also known from Taljanky. There is only one exception within the large construction ('mega-structure') rule. At 400 m² (Figure 21(3)), that building is exceptional, even for Maidanetske. The distribution of the nine special buildings in Maidanetske is nevertheless regular (Figure 21).

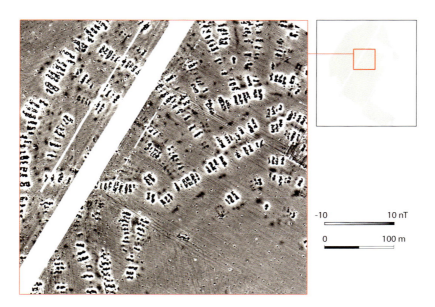

Figure 19. Maidanetske (Cherkasy Oblast). Overview of the geomagnetic survey in the northern part of the settlement with the highest density of buildings.

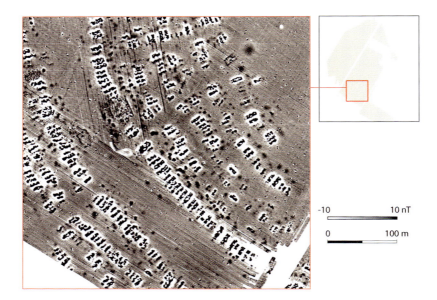

Figure 20. Maidanetske (Cherkasy Oblast). Overview of the geomagnetic survey in the south-western part of the settlement with the highest density of buildings.

5. What both sites also have in common is the occurrence of kilns. Two signatures were selected in 2013 and 2014. In one case (2013), the circular anomaly was a pit filled with burnt daub and garbage and the second case (2014) involved a pottery kiln (Figure 23(4)–Korvin-Piotrovskiy *et al.*, 2016). The feature set for detecting pottery kilns was specified with our excavation experience from Maidanetske and then applied to the Taljanky dataset. The likelihood of classifying an anomaly as a kiln should now be higher than fifty per cent. Based on the geomagnetic data, twenty kilns were identified.

Houses, Special Buildings, Kilns, and Ditches in Relation to Settlement Layout

Houses are grouped in rows with circular and axial orientations. The houses are more densely grouped than at Taljanky. The spatial pattern inside the inner ring is similar to that in the northern area in Taljanky (Figure 7: 25).

As was the case at the latter site, the size of the houses varied over the settlement areas. In the central area inside the inner house ring, houses were small. However, the size increased in the outer rings. A map of houses larger than 140 m² shows two groups of large buildings in the second ring. One groups in the northeast and another in the southwest (Figure 27). Once again, this constellation echoes that present at Taljanky. Excepting these two groups, the other large houses at Maidanetske were placed in house rows within the neighbourhood of smaller buildings. They are regularly distributed in the inner house ring. There might be a structural correlation between the distribution of the special buildings in the space between house rings 1 and 2 and the large house buildings in house ring 1 (Figure 12: 27).

As was mentioned above, the number of kilns at Maidanetske (20) is smaller than the seventy-four present at Taljanky. In contrast to Taljanky, the Maidanetske kilns were more closely concentrated. There are five groups; only two kilns are located isolated Figure 27.

In the northern and western settlement areas, two linear anomalies (ditch?) are detected (Figure 17, Müller and Videiko, 2016). They are less significant, the signatures are nevertheless an indication of the settlement having been either enclosed or open (provided that this structure has a more symbolic meaning than a functional importance).

Quantification and Settlement Layout

The calculation of the house buildings follows the workflow described above by KDE of the house-centroids (Figure 26). The map visualizes a general spatial pattern of the settlement that follows two well-known structural elements of which the first are the ovoid house rings. Only the inner and the adjacent outer rings enclosed the whole settlement if we interpolate from our survey data. The other outer rings are made of rather bowlike segments with different lengths ranging from 600 to 800 m (Figure 26). The second elements are defined by the axially oriented house rows and alley-like zones. This pie-like sectoral

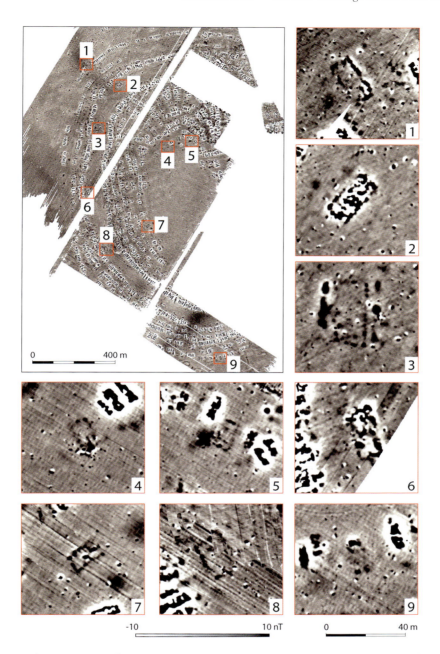

Figure 21. Maidanetske (Cherkasy Oblast). Overview of the nine special buildings. The geomagnetic data reveal differences in size and preservation, likely the result of their construction and spatial context in relation to the house rows.

division might be visible in the KDE map. This spatial pattern might be confirmed by mapping the special buildings and the kiln-clusters in relation to the larger houses (Figure 27).

What remains unknown is the function of the centrally located oval space which measures 26 ha. No significant features were detected by the geomagnetic survey. Once again, the situation is similar to that present at Taljanky. However, it has to take into account the fact that only fifty per cent of this area was covered by the recent survey and the prominent central part contained no information. The settlement layout in Petreni (Moldova, Rassmann *et al.*, 2016) is somewhat similar. A crucial point here is the location of the largest building in the centre of the settlement.

The spatial deciphering of the geomagnetic features should generally take the chronology of houses and their unclarified contemporaneity into account (Müller *et al.* 2016a; 2016b.)

Spatial Organization and Population Size

As with the reconstruction for Taljanky, we calculate an independent alternative to the use of houses for the

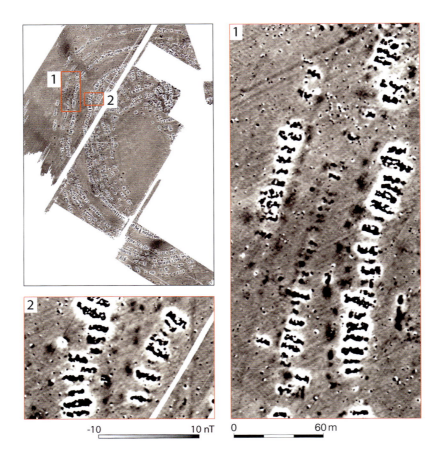

Figure 22. Maidanetske (Cherkasy Oblast). Details from the north-western part of the settlement. (1) Rows of heavily burnt houses and a line of less burnt or badly preserved houses. (2) Houses of different sizes and pits. The pits likely mark the back sides of the houses.

reconstruction of population: on average, one house group was placed on approximately 0.4 ha of settled area. The calculated dense settled area by KDE is 79 ha within our total 164 of prospected area. We have to take into account the fact that our survey covered around seventy per cent of the settlement. Because of this, we should therefore raise our estimate of the dense settled area from the 79 ha measured to an estimated 112 ha. This would be enough space for 282 groups of 50 persons each, giving a total number of 14,100 residents. Despite the smaller size of the settlement, Maidanetske seems to have had a higher population than Taljanky's estimated 10,000 residents.

Dobrovody (Oblast Cherkassy)

General information about the site

To the west of the modern village of Dobrovody (180–210 m a.s.l.) is situated yet another large Trypillian settlement. Like Taljanky, the site of Dobrovody is located on the southern edge of a Chernozem plateau (Figure 5). Despite the fact that only a small part of the settlement was prospected, the Hnizdechna stream in the east and a smaller confluence to the west form natural limits for the size of the settlement.

Approximately fifty per cent of the Trypillian site is covered by the recent village and their cemetery. Despite this restriction, Dobrovody is a promising site worthy of further investigation. The first geomagnetic surveys and excavations on site were conducted by M. M. Shmaglij and T. Movsha from 1974 to 1984 (Movsha, 1985a, 1985b). In 2012 and 2013, geomagnetic surveys were carried out at the northern and western central areas of the site. While subterranean artificial pipes, masts, and heavy dipoles impede the interpretation of the geomagnetic features in the south, the surveyed area to the north is not contaminated.

Within the *c.* 19 ha that was surveyed, four concentric house rows associated with pits at the outer and the inner sides of the concentric house chains as well as possible tracks and special buildings were discovered (Figures 28–30). Based on geomagnetic features within the surveyed area, 240 houses, *c.* 178 pits, 8 kilns, and 4 special buildings (<180 m^2) were identified.

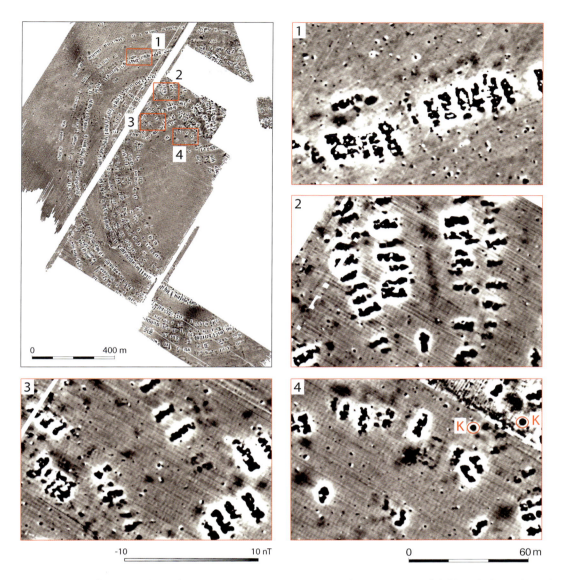

Figure 23. Maidanetske (Cherkasy Oblast). Details from the northern part of the settlement. (1) Heavily burnt large houses and a row of pits in an adjacent area north of the houses. (2) House rows framing a linear structure (alleys) and a square with a building in the centre. (3) A second court-like situation that is enclosed by house rows. (4) House rows and a special building close to the excavated kiln and a second unexcavated one (marked by red Ks).

When the results of aerial photography, geomagnetic surveys, small excavations, and field walking are taken into account, the site seems to measure around 170 ha. To date, only the settled area *c.* 7 per cent of the inner area enclosed by ring 1 and fifteen per cent of the area between rings 3 and 4 has been surveyed.

Geomagnetic signatures of single objects

1. Despite the small survey area of 19 ha, 255 houses anomalies were detected. They have the characteristic signatures known from Maidanetske and Taljanky. A small number of approximately 10 per cent of the houses are unburnt or poorly preserved (Figure 29).
2. The number of pits is a bit lower than that of the houses, similar to that situated at Taljanky. They are positioned on the gable side of the houses, in the outer row (no. 4), for the other rows mainly directed to the inner site.
3. Four houses or rectangular enclosures are labelled 'special buildings' and are oriented towards the concentric axes (Figures 29 and 30). Three of these are characterized by prominent *wall foundations*, which might indicate the demarcation of open spaces rather than roofed areas (Figure 29(1–2)). The fourth is classified as a special building based on its size (>180 m^2) and its separate position in

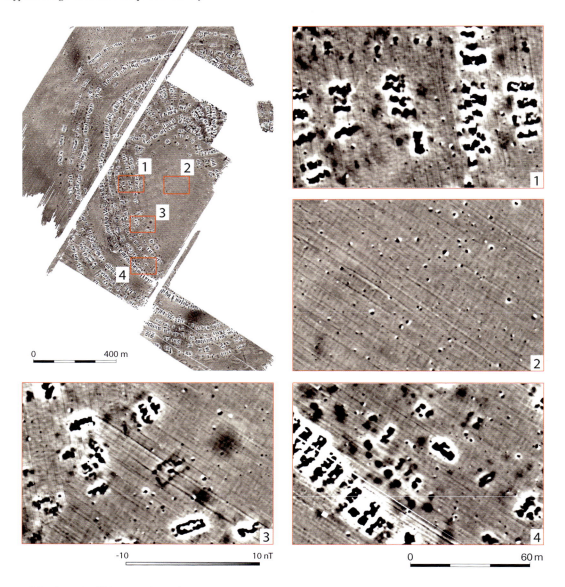

Figure 24. Maidanetske (Cherkasy Oblast). Details from the central part of the settlement. (1) Small houses with different orientations. The small circular anomalies in the north might indicate the house rows of an earlier phase that have a different preservation state. (2) An area without any indication of archaeological features in the central part of the settlement. (3) Houses with differing states of preservation and a special building. (4) Houses of different sizes, preservations, and orientations, as well as circular anomalies (likely pits).

Table 1. Statistical data on Cucuteni-Trypillia houses based on geomagnetic data

	Apol	Cobani	Ochiul	Singereni	Petreni	Majdanetskoje	Taljanki	Dobrovody
Mean	122,133	29,1333	9,7335	48,3068	56,484	67,1427	71,9307	64,4829
Median	131,69	29,75	8,95	44,705	53,8	61,65	68,6181	60,7847
Variance	2936,21	234,601	16,5066	429,742	499,693	907,131	681,278	1483,05
Std. Dev.	54,1868	15,3167	4,06283	20,7302	22,3538	30,1186	26,1013	38,5104
Std. Err.	12,4313	3,1265	0,908476	1,81816	1,05494	0,696117	0,705698	2,63869
Skewness	0,0147032	1,19745	1,08992	1,4232	0,808443	1,2088	1,22579	5,69061
Minimum	30,2	10,9	5,05	18,6	17,2	8,7	15,2745	10,3521
Maximum	217,8	76,7	18,89	124,96	140,1	244,6	228,953	461,797
Sum	2320,53	699,2	194,67	6279,88	25361,3	125691	98401,1	13734,9
N	19	24	20	130	449	1872	1368	213

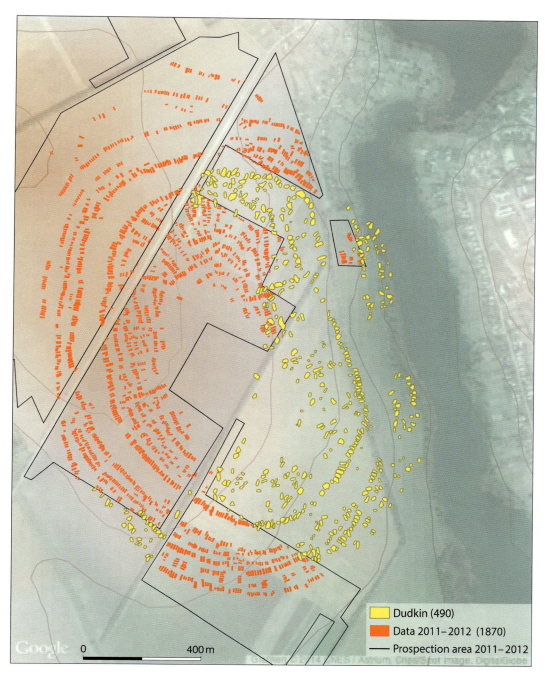

Figure 25. Maidanetske (Cherkasy Oblast). Interpretation of the geomagnetic house anomalies as a result of the recent surveys. The anomalies detected by Dudkin's survey are shown for the western settlement area.

the same manner as the three other special buildings.
4. Eight circular anomalies might indicate kilns. The ratio of houses to kiln is 1:30, a scale similar to that present at Taljanky (1:21).

Houses, special buildings, kilns, and ditches in relation to settlement layout

The observation area is too small for the extraction of an idea of the site's general layout. Nonetheless, some conclusions can be drawn when placed in context with our data from Taljanky and Maidanetske. The houses are grouped into radial and axial rows. The size of the houses in the northern area varies. The diversity in house sizes in the central part is significantly smaller than in northern circuits 3 and 4. This tendency is the same as in the central area in Maidanetske and northern area in Taljanky. The smaller houses in the central area have radial and axial orientations.

As mentioned above, four special buildings are located in the typical orientation outside the radial

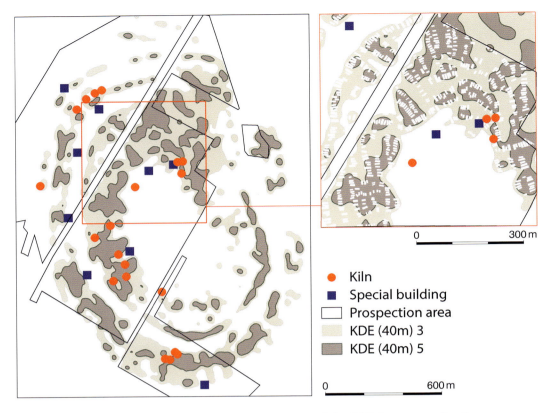

Figure 26. Maidanetske (Cherkasy Oblast). Kernel density estimation of the 1870 house anomalies from recent surveys and the re-digitized 490 from Dudkin's map (after Videiko, 2005). KDE was based on bi-weighted interpolation, 40 m radius, and on the centroids of reconstructed houses. The selected 5 m KDE isoline includes more than eighty per cent of the houses. The KDE visualizes a settlement structure that was divided into sectors. With the inclusion of pottery kilns and special buildings, two other categories are mapped. A re-evaluation of the anomalies identified 18 as kilns, which is a remarkable lower number than at Taljanky (74).

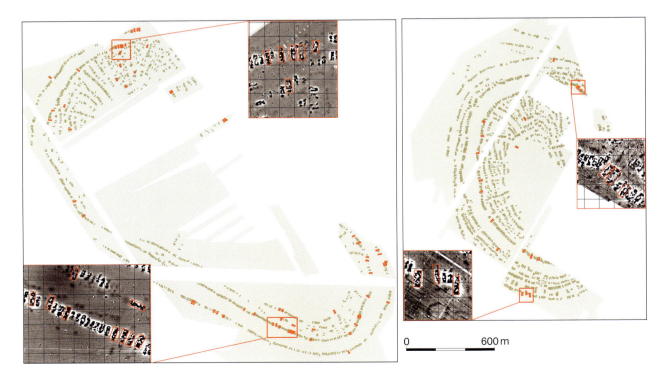

Figure 27. Distribution of large houses (>140 m^2). (a) Taljanky (b) Maidanetske.

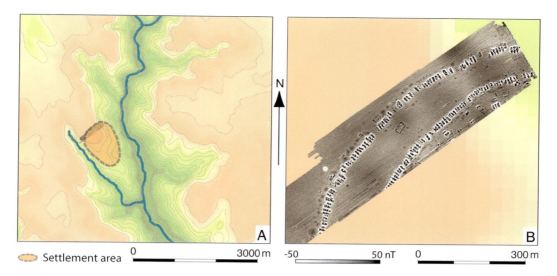

Figure 28. Dobrovody (Cherkasy Oblast). (a) Overview of the local topography surrounding the site. (b) Overview of the 23.5 ha geomagnetic survey area.

house rows. At 1:60, their ratio to the standard houses is similar to that in Petreni (Rassmann *et al.*, 2016) and remarkably lower than that in Maidanetske (1:200). If we compare the number of larger houses (>120 m²) in Taljanky and Maidanetske and their distribution, the pattern in Taljanky and Dobrovody is nearly the same (Figure 27).

The biggest building is positioned within the main ring and seems to be spatially linked to a second special building that was built at the outer side of the main ring. The third special building that was only partly documented is found at the outer row of the main ring. The first mentioned building possesses three pits at each long side, a particular feature also known from the

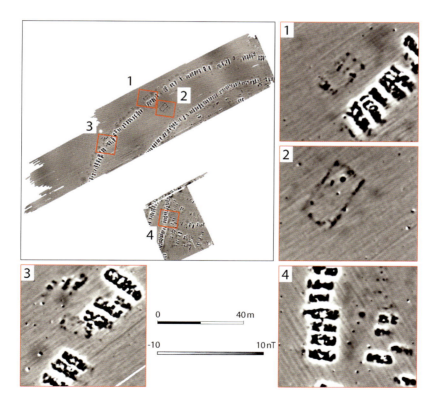

Figure 29. Dobrovody (Cherkasy Oblast). Details from the northern survey area. (1) House row and special building (260 m²). (2) A large building (540 m²) inside the northern house ring. (3) A special building (size 160 m²) situated in a gap between house rows, a particularity that was often observed in Taljanky and Maidanetske. (4) Rows of small houses and groups of less burnt or badly preserved small houses.

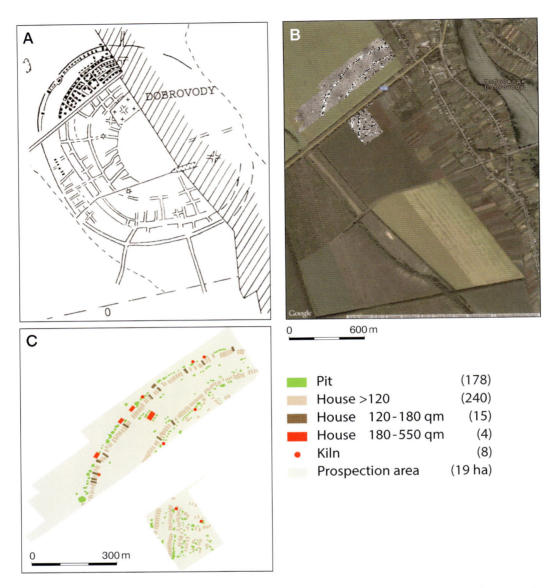

Figure 30. Dobrovody (Cherkasy Oblast). Comparison of the recent survey with Dudkin's earlier results (after Videiko, 2005). (a) Dudkin's survey and the interpolation with aerial photographs. (b) Location of the recent survey (map based on Google Earth). (c) Interpretation of the geomagnetic survey.

special buildings in Maidanetske. At the two other buildings, the pits are extraordinarily large in comparison with the other pits present on site.

Eight kilns are widely distributed throughout the settlement without indications for the clustering present in Maidanetske (Figure 30).

QUANTIFICATION AND SETTLEMENT LAYOUT

The general settlement layout consists of four radial rings (Figure 30). We assume that all the rings are detected in our observation windows. The distance between the two outer house rows (3–4) is about 100 ±50 m. The existence of further outer rings (such as in Maidanetske) cannot be excluded. However, especially in the northwest survey area with its lack of any indication for building in the outer areas by ring no. 4, the general picture argues against this presumption.

The distance between the two inner house rows (1–2) is smaller (50±20 m). If the outer circuits and 1–2 are contemporary, the distance between rows 2–3 would be about 100 m. While the space between 3 and 4 and 1 and 2 obviously seems to be empty, the space between 2 and 3 and inside 1 seems to be filled with other pits and houses.

As mentioned above, the small survey in the centre of the site revealed an area within smaller houses. Within the house circuits, houses are positioned with parallel gables on a concentric axis; houses within the built space between rows are positioned with parallel gables either on concentric or on radial axes. At 64 m², the mean of all houses is a little lower than in Maidanetske (67 m²) and Taljanky (71 m²). The location of larger houses in the outer ring is similar to that in Taljanky. In Maidanetske, in contrast, the houses are located mainly on the inner circuit.

With the exception of the special buildings that resemble those from Maidanetske, the spatial pattern here shows more similarities to Taljanky including the relationship between kilns and houses, the relationship between larger houses and smaller houses and the widely distributed large houses.

Spatial Organization and Population Size

The survey area covered a small part of the settlement. Taking the data from former surveys into account (Figure 30), *c.* fifteen per cent of the settlement area was surveyed. An interpolation of our data leads to an estimation of 1500 houses, 25 special buildings, and 53 kilns. However, the database is too small to formulate an accurate calculation of the settled area inside the 150 ha settlement space.

To get comparable data for the number of house groups, we calculated the densely settled areas by KDE as in Taljanky and Maidanetske. To account for the unevenly populated area where the survey took place, we calculated the outer area between ring 3 and ring 4 and the inner area separately. The outer area includes 65 ha of which 10 ha (*c.* fifteen per cent) was prospected. The inner settlement area enclosed by ring 3 measures 80 ha including the unbuilt area of 30 ha in the centre. Here, 7 ha (*c.* 7 per cent) of the *c.* 50 ha settled area has been prospected. The total area calculated by KDE for the whole settlement is 65 ha (twenty-seven for the outer ring; thirty-eight for the inner ring). That means that there was space for 163 superordinate house groups (0.4 ha per group) which leads to a total number of 8150 residents.

The estimations of the population size based on the KDE calculation are valuable as alternative method to the house number-based reconstruction (Müller *et al.*, 2016a). As was found with other categories of data, Dobrovody (8000 residents) and Taljanky (10,000 residents) are similar whereas Maidanetske had with a much larger population of 14,100 residents.

Apolianka (Oblast Cherkassy)

General remarks on the site

A further Trypillia site is situated on the Chernozem plain to the east of the southern terraces of the Hnizdechna River near Apolianka at a slight elevation (180–200 m a.s.l.). As such, the topographical situation is similar to the other Trypillian sites (Figures 5 and 31).

Field-walking on site clearly verified signs of erosion. Ploughing has unfortunately already reached house features that were indicated by daub and artefact scatters on the surface.

The geomagnetic survey covered a total of 39 ha. The geomagnetic features later demonstrated that some of the houses were damaged by erosion. Furthermore, a recently destroyed garage was placed on the site.

The houses are oriented differently. In the central part, houses are circularly orientated but are far less dense than on the giant settlement. In the adjacent northeast area are two large buildings (*c.* 280–400 m²) which are likely younger and date to the Cherniakhiv Culture.

Geomagnetic signatures of single objects

1. The houses vary in size, construction, and preservation (Figure 32). The size of the thirteen houses in the concentric order measures between 116 and 342 m². The majority are larger and measure around 180 m², which marks a clear difference from the giant settlement (Figures 13, 32, and 33). The separately located houses in the east (422 and 274 m², respectively) are much larger. They are most likely younger than the Trypillian houses.
2. On the settlement, a small number of less characteristic pits are visible (Figure 32).

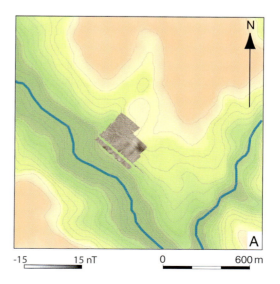

Figure 31. *Apolianka (Cherkasy Oblast). Overview of the topographical situation around the site.*

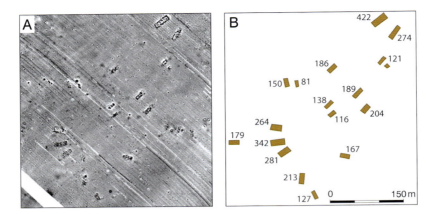

Figure 32. Apolianka (Cherkasy Oblast). (a) Central area of the geomagnetic survey with concentrically orientated houses and a second group of NE–SE-oriented large buildings in the north-eastern part. (b) Interpretation of the geomagnetic data and house sizes.

3. In contrast to the mega-sites, special buildings did not appear in the survey (which probably covered most of the settlement).

Quantification and settlement layout

The size of the settlement appears is remarkably smaller than those of the other sites. The thirteen houses in the central part correspond with our estimations on the principal house groups defining the lowest organization of Copper Age settlements. The differences between the houses are much more pronounced than at the other surveyed sites. Moreover, a clear association between pits and houses is not present. The site of Apolianka dates in the final stage of the Trypillian Culture subsequent to Maidanetske. It is tempting to interpret the extensive use of space in Apolianka as a counter reaction to the restriction of spatial access at the giant settlements.

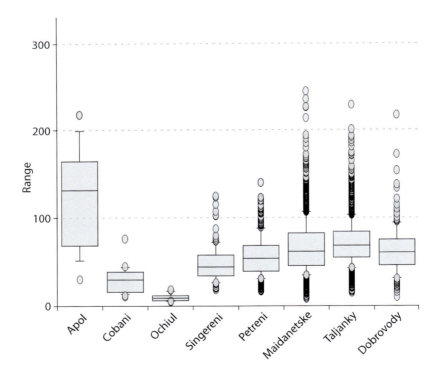

Figure 33. Boxplots of the house sizes on Cucuteni–Trypillian sites in Moldova and Ukraine (Petreni, Singerei, Ochiul Alb, Cobani–Moldova; Apolianka, Maidanetske, Taljanky, and Dobrovody–Ukraine). The boxes comprise fifty per cent of the data, the whisker comprises eighty per cent with outliers.

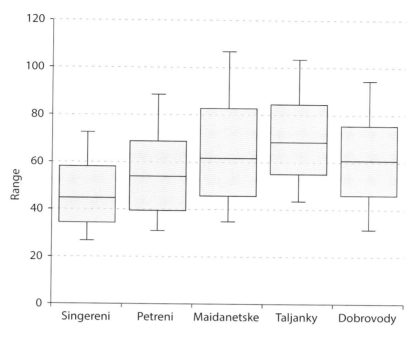

Figure 34. Boxplot of the house sizes of larger settlements of the late Cucuteni-Trypillia Culture (Singerei, Petreni–Moldova; Maidanetske, Taljanky, and Dobrovody–Ukraine). The boxes comprise fifty per cent of the data, the whisker comprises eighty per cent without outliers.

Conclusion

In two geomagnetic campaigns in 2011 and 2012, over 4 km² was prospected.

In contrast to the geomagnetic surveys that took place before 2005, those which were post-2005 utilized geomagnetic devices with high resolutions that also detected pits, kilns, track ways, and other features besides the known 'large' structures.

The rich amount of data revealed around 3600 houses arranged in a clear spatial layout. They are a valuable to compare different parameter as the house size from site to site (Figures 33 and 34).

The principle of concentric house rings around an inner space is visible at each site.

The data indicating the similarities and differences between the large settlements in Taljanky, Maidanetske, and Dobrovody. What seems to be crucial are the relationships between large houses and standard houses, houses and kilns, and special buildings and standard houses. They are the same in Dobrovody and Taljanky, whereas in Maidanetske fewer kilns and large houses are visible. A further difference between Dobrovody and Taljanky in relation to Maidanetske is the non-hierarchical wider distribution of kilns and large houses. The latter are much more concentrated in Maidanetske.

The distribution of kilns and large houses are valuable for structuring the settlement.

Besides the subsidiary house groups presumably accorded 0.4 ha per six to twenty houses (Rassmann et al., 2016, 64), we have indications for superordinate house groups visible in the results of kernel density estimation and the occurrence of large and special buildings and kilns. These principal house groups are larger in Maidanetske (100–200 houses) than in Taljanky and Dobrovody (50–80 houses).

We interpret this pattern as an indication for increasing centralization and hierarchy in Maidanetske. The differences between Taljanky and Dobrovody on the one hand and Maidanetske on the other hand indicate the higher likelihood of differences in the social organization and the size of political groups inside the giant settlement.

The estimations of the population size based on the KDE calculation are valuable as alternative method to the house number-based reconstruction (Müller et al., 2016a). The new results for Dobrovody (8000 residents) and Taljanky (10,000 residents) are similar whereas Maidanetske had a much larger population (14,100 residents).

The limitations of our geomagnetic data mainly involve chronological uncertainties. These problems anticipated our recent research. The first series of ¹⁴C-dates in Maidanetske form the first step in solving this issue. The new German–Ukrainian research is a promising means of evaluating the first spatial analysis in the light of field work results. The models and analysis presented here mark only the beginning of a new stage in the spatial analysis of Trypillian settlements.

References

Darvill, T., Lüth, F., Rassmann, K., Fischer, A. & Winkelmann, K. 2013. Stonehenge, Wiltshire, UK: High Resolution Geophysical Surveys in the Surrounding Landscape, 2011. *European Journal of Archaeology*, 16(1): 63–93.

Diachenko, A. 2016. Demography Reloaded. In: J. Müller, K. Rassmann & M. Videiko, eds. *Trypillia Mega-Sites and European Prehistory: 4100–3400 BCE*. London and New York: Routledge, pp. 181–194.

Dudkin, V.P. 1978. Geofizicheskaya razvedka krupnyh tripolskih poselenij. In: V.F. Gening ed. *Ispolzovanie metodov estestvennyh nauk v arheologii*. Kyiv: Naukova Dumka, pp. 35–45. Дудкин, В.П. 1978. Геофизическая разведка крупных трипольских поселений. В сб.: В.Ф. Генинг, ред. Использование методов естественных наук в археологии. Киев: Наукова думка, с. 35–45.

Korvin-Piotrovskiy, A., Hofmann, R., Rassmann, K., Videiko, M. & Brandstetter, L. 2016. Pottery Kilns in Trypillian Settlements. Tracing the Division of Labor and the Social Organization of Copper Age Communities. In: J. Müller, K. Rassmann & M. Videiko eds. *Trypillia Mega-Sites and European Prehistory: 4100–3400 BCE*. London and New York: Routledge, pp. 221–252.

Koshelev, I.N. 2004. *Pamyatniki tripolskoj kultury po dannym magnitnoy sjemki*. Kiev Authors edition. Кошелев, И. Н. 2004. Памятники трипольской культуры по данным магнитной съемки. Киев: Verlag. - http://ukrknyga.at.ua/load/0-0-1-1916-20.

Kruts, V.A., Korvin-Piotrovskiy, A.G., Chabanyuk, V.V. & Shatilo, L.A. 2013a. *Talianki-Settlement-Giant of the Tripolian Culture Investigations in 2012*. Kyiv: Archaeological Institute Kyiv.

Kruts, V.A., Korvin-Piotrovskiy, A.G., Mischka, C., Ohlrau, R., Windler, A. & Rassmann, K. 2013b. Talianki 2012: The Geomagnetic Prospection. In: A. G. Korvin-Piotrovskiy & K. Rassmann eds. *Settlement Giants of the Tripolian Culture. Investigations in 2012*. Kyiv: Archaeological Institute Kyiv, pp. 85–103.

Kruts, V., Korvin-Piotrovskiy, A., Peters, D. & Rassmann, K. 2011. Talianki Reloaded: Geomagnetic Prospection Three Decades after V. P. Dudkin's work. In: A. G. Korvin-Piotrovskiy & F. Menotti eds. *Settlement Giants of the Tripolian Culture. Investigations in 2011*. Kyiv: Archaeological Institute Kyiv, pp. 60–85.

Kruts, V.A., Korvin-Piotrovskiy, A.G. & Ryzhov, S.N. 2001. *Talianki–Giant-Settlement of the Tripolian Culture. Investigations in 2001*. Kiev: Archaeological Institute Kyiv.

Müller, J., Rassmann, K. & Hofmann, R. 2013. Okolište 1–Untersuchungen einer spätneolithischen Siedlungskammer in Zentralbosnien. Bonn. Habelt-Verlag.

Müller, J., Hofmann, R., Rassmann, K., Mischka, C., Videyko, M. & Burdo, N.B. 2014b. Maydanetskoe: Investigations, Based on Updated Plan (Майданецкое: исследования по обновленному плану поселения). *Stratum Plus*, 2: 285–302.

Müller, J. & Videiko, M. 2016. Maidanetske: New Facts of a Mega-Site. In: J. Müller, K. Rassmann & M. Videiko, eds. *Trypillia Mega-Sites and European Prehistory: 4100–3400 BCE*. London and New York: Routledge, pp. 71–94.

Müller, J., Hofmann, R., Brandtstätter, L., Ohlrau, R. & Videiko, M. 2016a. Chronology and Demography: How Many People Lived in a Mega-Site? In: J. Müller, K. Rassmann & M. Videiko, eds. *Trypillia Mega-Sites and European Prehistory: 4100–3400 BCE*. London and New York: Routledge, pp. 133–169.

Müller, J., Hofmann, R. & Ohlrau, R. 2016b. From Domestic Households to Mega-Structures: Proto-Urbanism? In: J. Müller, K. Rassmann & M. Videiko, eds. *Trypillia Mega-Sites and European Prehistory: 4100–3400 BCE*. London and New York: Routledge, pp. 253–268.

Movsha, T.G. 1985a. Srednij i pozdnij etap tripolskoj kultury. In: I.I. Artemenko ed. *Arheologiya Ukrainskoj SSR*. Kiev, pp. 206–63. Мовша, Т.Г. 1985А. Средний и поздний этап трипольской культуры. В кн.: И.И. Артеменко, ред. Археология Украинской ССР. Kiev, с. 206–63.

Movsha, T.G. 1985b. Vzaemovidnosyny Trypillia-Cucuteni z synhronnymy kuluramy Tsentralnoi Evropy. *Arheologiya*, 51:22–31. Мовша, Т.Г. 1985b. Взаємовідносини Трипілля-Кукутень з синхронними культурами Центральної Європи. Археологія, 51: 22–31.

Nowaczinski, E., Schukraft, G., Rassmann, K., Hecht, S., Texier, F., Eitel, B. & Bubenzer, O. 2013. Geophysical–Geochemical Reconstruction of Ancient Population Size–the Early Bronze Age Settlement of Fidvár (Slovakia). *Archaeological Prospection*, 20:267–83.

Ohlrau, R. 2014. *Tripolje Großsiedlungen. Geomagnetische Prospektion und architektursoziologische Perspektiven*. unpub. MA Thesis. CAU Kiel.

Rassmann, K., Ohlrau, R., Hofmann, R., Mischka, C., Burdo, N., Videjko, M.Y. & Müller, J. 2014. High Precision Tripolye Settlement Plans, Demographic Estimations and Settlement Organization. *Journal of Neolithic Archaeology*, 16: 96–134.

Rassmann, K., Mertl, P., Voss, H.-U., Bicbaev, V., Popa, A. & Musteață, S. 2016. Copper Age Settlements in Moldova: Insights into a Complex Phenomenon from Recent Geomagnetic Surveys. In: J. Müller, K. Rassmann & M. Videiko, eds. *Trypillia Mega-Sites and European Prehistory: 4100–3400 BCE*. London and New York: Routledge, pp. 55–69.

Shyshkin, K.V. 1973. Z praktyky deshyfruvannya aerofotoznimkiv u archeologichnyh tsilyah. *Arheologiya*, 19:32–41. Шишкин, К. В. 1973. З практики дешифрування аерофотознімків у археологічних цілях. Археологія 19: 32–41.

Shmaglij, N. & Videjko, M. 2003. Maidanetskoe - A Tripolian Proto-City. *Stratum Plus*, 2:44–140. Шмаглий, Н.М. и Видейко, М.Ю. 2003. Майданецкое – трипольскийпротогород. StratumPlus, 2: 44–140.

Trebsche, P., Müller-Scheeßel, N. & Reinhold, S. eds. 2010. *Der gebaute Raum. Bausteine einer Architektursoziologie vormoderner Gesellschaften*. Tübinger Archäologische Taschenbücher 7. Waxmann: Münster.

Videiko, M. & Rassmann, K. 2016. Research on Different Scales: 120 Years Trypillian Large Sites Research. In: J. Müller, K. Rassmann & M. Videiko, eds. *Trypillia Mega-Sites and European Prehistory: 4100–3400 BCE*. London and New York: Routledge, pp. 17–28.

CHAPTER 4

Copper Age settlements in Moldova: Insights into a Complex Phenomenon from Recent Geomagnetic Surveys

KNUT RASSMANN, PATRICK MERTL, HANS-ULRICH VOSS, VEACESLAV BICBAEV, ALEXANDRU POPA AND SERGIU MUSTEAȚĂ

INTRODUCTION

The Prut–Dniester region is characterized by a multi-faceted cultural pattern during many archaeological periods. The diverse settlement landscape in the Copper Age reflects the specific situation in the region, with cultural influences from the Carpathians (Chernysh, 1982; Markevich, 1981), the Buh-Dnipro interfluve and the northern Pontic area, as visible in the medium-sized settlement of Petreni. Between 2009 and 2011 the Romano-Germanic Commission, in cooperation with Moldavian partners from the National Museum of Archaeology and History of Moldova and the State Pedagogical University (Ion Creanga) in Chișinău, conducted three geomagnetic surveys and field surveys on Copper Age sites and settlements of the younger Sântana de Mureș Culture (Popa *et al.*, 2010). Our first survey campaign in autumn 2009 was conducted with a 5-channel magnetometer (SENSYS MAGNETO®-MX ARCH). Its intention was the sampling of appropriate sites for forthcoming surveys with the larger 16-channel magnetometer (SENSYS MAGNETO®-MX ARCH). Therefore, the surveyed areas from 2009 measured only 1–2 ha on average but were representative enough to clarify the research goals (Figure 1). In comparison with Petreni, the other sites surveyed in 2009 were rather small. Horodca, Ochiul Alb, and Cobani date from the earlier stage of the Cucuteni-Tripolje Culture. Not surprisingly, the most promising data stem from Petreni, well known because of the remarkable aerial photographs and the reconstruction by Markevich (1981: figure 14). In consequence, in 2010, the survey was continued at Petreni, and the fourth site Sîngerei was added. Sîngerei is only dated by surface finds from the Sântana de Mureș and Cucuteni-Trypillian Cultures (Cucuteni-Trypillian B1/2). The survey in Moldova contributed to our knowledge of settlements of different sizes and stages of the Cucuteni-Trypillian Culture. Apart from the excellent results in Petreni, the unravelling of its connection to the smaller sites is essential to understand the rise of the large complex settlements and their relations to the settlement system in the surrounding landscape, an aspect that should be the focus of the forthcoming research.

OVERVIEW OF THE MAGNETIC DATA

Sîngerei (district Sîngerei)

General information on the site
"The Cucuteni-Trypillian-site (B1/2) Sîngerei is located 5 km north of the modern city and 15 km southeast of the city of Balti (Figures 2–3). The Copper Age settlement is situated at the southern corner of a triangular plateau at heights of 110–140 m a.s.l. The south-eastern border is marked by a recent water reservoir.

The surface of the southern plateau is scattered with ceramic finds of the Cucuteni-Trypillian Culture, whereas in the north, surface finds of the Sântana de Mureș Culture dominate. Through field walking, small areas with a high density of ceramic founds were recorded, which can be interpreted as house places destroyed by erosion.

The survey area covered the complete settlement area with its 22 ha and detected 130 house anomalies (Figure 4). The chronology of the anomalies, however, remains unclear. The comparison with the ceramic distribution makes it likely that the majority of the anomalies belong to the Cucuteni-Trypillian Culture. The most northern building is 28 m long and likely dates to the Sântana de Mureș Culture, as can be inferred from its size and is also indicated by surface finds (Figure 4).

Geomagnetic signatures of single objects
1. The survey revealed 130 house of sizes between 20 and 130 m^2 (Figure 5). They are smaller than in Petreni (56.5 m^2) and the giant settlements in

Figure 1. Survey in 2009 in Horodka (district). Alexandru Popa and Klaus Baltes using the 5-channel-system.

the Uman region (Taljanky 72 m^2, Maidanetske 67 m^2, and Dobrovody 64 m^2). The preservation of houses is likely worse than in Petreni or the mega-sites in the Uman region. The house anomalies precisely reflect the shape of the houses. In some cases, the foundations of the house walls are visible (Figure 5 C). The detrimental preservation of houses correlates with the erosion on the slope and is unlikely related to differences in the practice of burning down houses.

2. In the surveyed area, around 160 pits were detected. The largest number was found outside the

Figure 2. Singerei (district Singerei). View from the North to the settlement on the promontory adjacent to the reservoir.

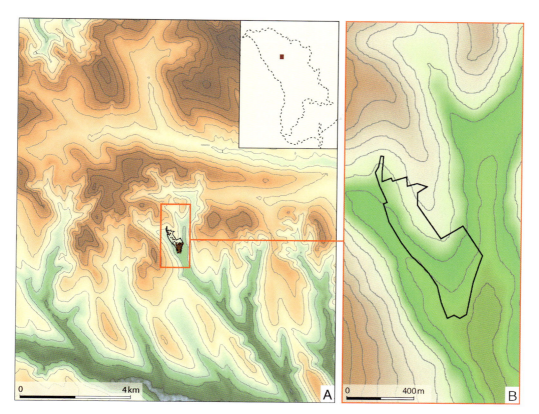

Figure 3. Singerei (district Singerei). The topography around the site and an overview of the survey area (DEM SRTM 30 × 30 m).

Cucuteni-Trypillian settlement in the northern area. As mentioned above, there is only one large building which belongs to the Sântana de Mureş Culture. At the southern periphery, a cluster of settlement pits is visible (Figure 4). Their diameter varies between 1 and 3 m. The pronounced

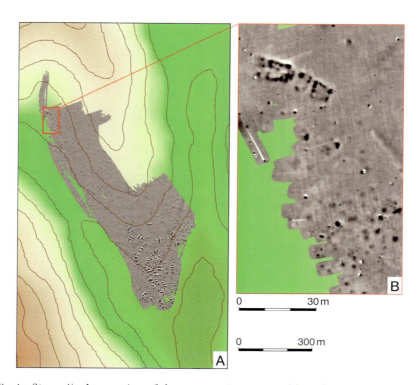

Figure 4. Singerei (district Singerei). An overview of the geomagnetic survey and large house structure in the northern settlement.

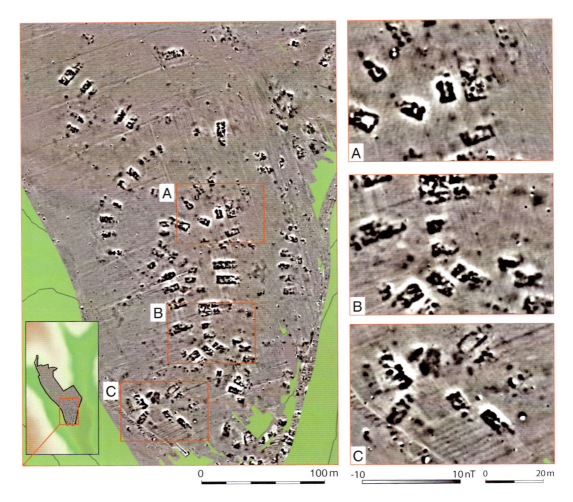

Figure 5. Singerei (district Singerei). An overview of the geomagnetic survey on the southern promontory and details of the central part of the Cucuteni-Trypillian settlement.

geomagnetic contrast indicates a refilling with settlement garbage.

On the southern part of the plateau–the area of the houses of the Cucuteni-Trypillian Culture–the pits vary in size and magnetic contrast; these are indications for differences in their primary function or in their secondary refilling.

3. Special buildings, pottery kilns, and ditches. In the geomagnetic data, we did not find any indications for separated special buildings, ditches, or kilns.

Houses in the context of the settlement layout

A clear general spatial layout is only partly visible. In the central area, two arch-shaped house rows are observable. The outer one completely encloses the central part of the settlement. Other house rows are organized linearly. The orientation of the rows varies. The arch-shaped outer row no. 1 follows the typical Trypillian layout (Figure 6). Only in the western area are the houses regularly distributed, whereas in the North and East, the reconstruction of the rows remains somewhat uncertain.

The differing orientations seen in the spatial pattern of house rows indicate several chronological settlement phases.

Quantification, settlement layout, and population size

Without excavation data, any reconstruction must be preliminary. The house rows and clusters consist of seven to eleven houses, except for the largest central group with thirty houses, which might consist of two to three smaller house groups. So far, the number of subsidiary house groups can be estimated as between eight and ten. The total size of the Copper Age settlement is 9 ha, with a densely settled area of 5 ha. The area was calculated using kernel density estimation (KDE) with the same workflow as used for Taljanky, Maidanetske, and Dobrovody (Rassmann *et al.*, 2016). By estimating an area per house group of 0.4 ha twelve subsidiary house groups might have existed. Based on this calculation, the total population size can be estimated at a scale of 400–600 residents.

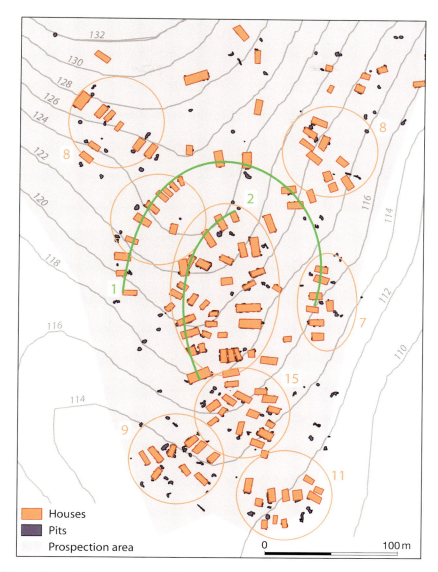

Figure 6. Singerei (district Singerei). Interpretation of the geomagnetic data from the Cucuteni-Trypillian settlement.

Petreni I (district Drochia)

General information on the site

The late Cucuteni-Trypillian (C1) site of Petreni is situated on a small West–East-orientated Chernozem promontory (Figures 7–8) 1 km East of the modern village of Sofia, at a height of 110–140 m a.s.l. The village of Petreni is located 5 km to the East (Figure 6). The site is located almost exactly in the middle of a plateau between the rivers Kubolta and Raut. The plateau is incised by a large number of small streams (Figure 8).

The excavation in Petreni by Ernst von Stern marked the beginning of research on the Cucuteni-Trypillian Culture in Moldova (see Videiko and Rassmann, 2016). During two campaigns, Stern excavated at eight locations inside the settlement (Stern, 1907: 39). Three of them are located in the centre of the settlement, two in the southern area, and two in the western part.

The excavation areas are partly visible in the geomagnetic data (Figure 12). Stern (1907: 15) describes the size of the houses excavated as a maximum of 14 m in length and 5–8 m in width.

In 1944, a further excavation by Vlad Sirra took place, but without any publication. With the help of aerial photographs, Shyshkin (1973) reconstructed settlement features, which were later used by Markevich (1981) to reconstruct a general settlement layout. In the light of recent geomagnetic data, he might have overstretched the information provided by the aerial photographs, but the number of houses is of the same magnitude as our interpretation. Based on the recent geomagnetic survey, joint excavation projects of the German Archaeological Institute and the National Archaeology and History Museum Chisinau started in

Figure 7. Petreni (district Drochia). View from the central part of the settlement to the North.

2011 (Uhl, 2014). Considering the rich house inventories published by Stern (1907), the settlement can be dated to the first phase of stage C1 of the Cucuteni-Trypillian Culture (Movsha, 1984; Sorochin, 2004). Markevich (1981: 67) used the inventories to define a 'Petreni' group. Based on the recent geomagnetic data, the settlement measured *c.* 25 ha, including areas outside the ditches, where the kilns and uncharacteristic geomagnetic anomalies (known as ash places) are situated. The area within the outer ditch measures 22 ha. The survey revealed 457 houses, 8 special buildings, 21 kilns, and 320 pits.

When interpreting these observations, we have to take the erosion on the southern rim of the promontory into account. This affects approximately 4–6 ha of the settlement area. Therefore, the outer ditch might have

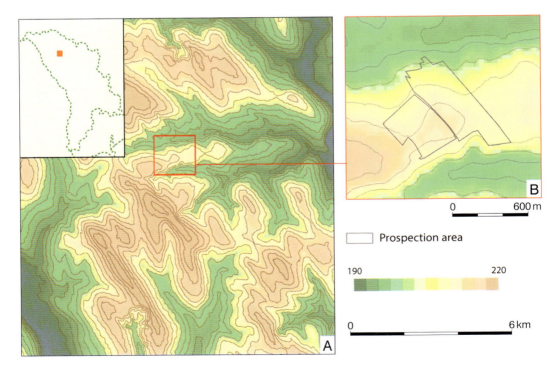

Figure 8. Petreni (district Drochia). (a) The topography around the site. (b) Overview of the survey area (DEM SRTM 30 × 30 m).

Figure 9. Petreni (district Drochia). Overview of the geomagnetic data from the 2010 and 2011 campaigns. The red circle marks the remains of former excavations.

originally enclosed 26 ha and–to take the outer area with uncharacteristic geomagnetic anomalies (known as ash places) into account–around 30–34 ha.

Geomagnetic signatures of single objects (Figures 9–10)

1. The survey revealed 457 houses, a number close to Markevic's (1981) 500 houses in his general settlement reconstruction. The houses are, with a mean of 56 m^2, slightly larger than in Sîngerei (48 m^2), but clearly smaller than at Dobrovody (64 m^2), Maidanetske (67 m^2), and Taljanky (71 m^2). Only 139 houses measure more than 64 m^2 (mean size at Dobrovody). These larger houses are concentrated in the northern settlement and in the inner circuit. Nearly all house anomalies are characterized by high nT values, suggesting a massive layer of burnt daub. Clear cues for unburnt houses have not been found. Some house anomalies indicate traces of erosion and detrimental preservation.
2. The 320 pits vary in size from a diameter of less than 1–5 m. The largest was perhaps originally used for the extraction of clay. Their high contrast suggests refilling with garbage and burnt daub.
3. A small number of eight special buildings are revealed in the survey. Two are located in the central area, four in the space outside the inner house rows, and two in the outer house area (Figure 14). The building in the centre is by far the largest, with an area of nearly 300 m^2. The mean of the other houses is *c.* 200 m^2. Except for the two houses in the outer house area, the other buildings are located separately, a spatial pattern which we know from Dobrovody, Maidanetske (Rassmann *et al.*, 2016), and Nebelivka (Videiko *et al.*, 2015).
4. Outside the ditches, at the periphery of the settlement, circular anomalies are regularly distributed. The anomalies show the same distribution patterns as the excavated pottery kilns in Taljanky and Maidanetske. Besides the outer situated kilns, we found some anomalies inside the settlement (Figure 14). As at Taljanky, Dobrovody, and Maidanetske, the kilns are in the Neighbourhood of smaller houses. In the excavation report of E. Stern from 1902 to 1903, an indistinct hint to the excavation of a kiln is found (Stern, 1907: 56 ff.; Ellis, 1984: 124; Markevic, 1981). Besides these indications, it is obvious that the kiln anomalies have to be verified by future fieldwork.

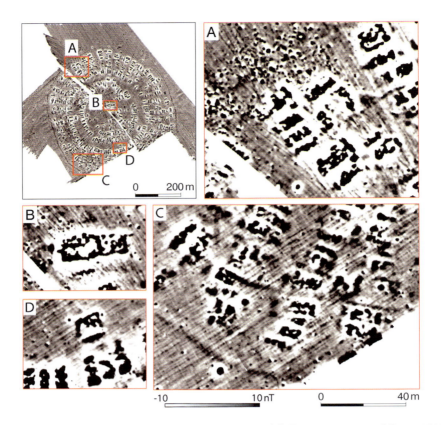

Figure 10. Petreni (district Drochia). Details of the geomagnetic data. (a) Excavation area of Stern 1902–1903. (b) Special building in the centre of the settlement. (c) Two ditches and burnt houses in the southern part of the settlement. (d) Special building with an axial orientation and in isolated position.

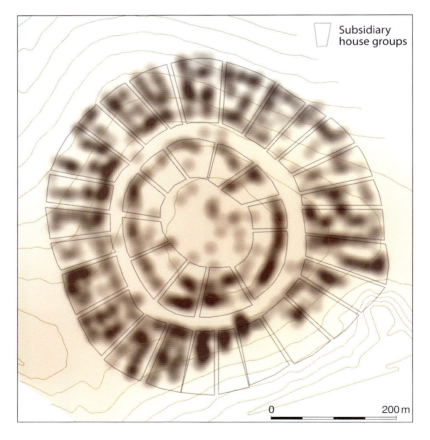

Figure 11. Petreni (district Drochia). KDE-based estimation (r 20 m) of the house centroids.

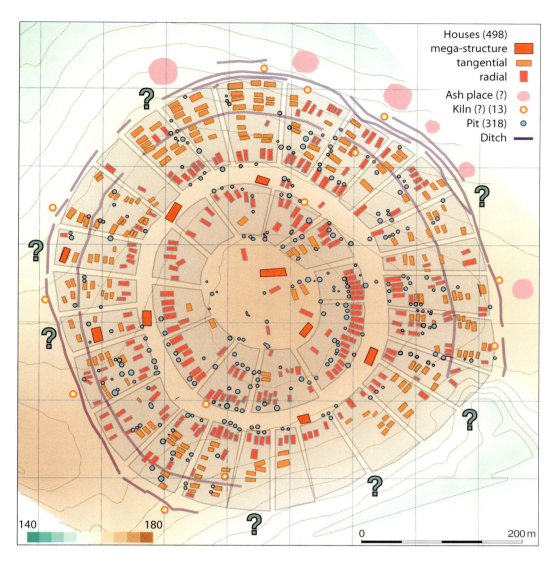

Figure 12. Petreni (district Drochia). Interpretation of the geomagnetic data.

5. Two ditches enclose the settlement. The outer ditch marks the limit of the settlement. A second ditch at a distance of *c.* 50 m to the centre is superposed with burnt houses. The signatures of the ditches are rather less significant. The width of the anomalies is *c.* 2 m. Along in the outer ditch entrances are visible in some places, which correlate with alleys between houses.
6. Already in the aerial photograph, some larger circular anomalies were visible in the periphery of the settlement. Their magnetic contrast is rather low and their diameter is around 20 m. This pattern is so far unknown from other sites. Their circular distribution around the settlement indicates at least a structural connection.

Houses, special buildings, kilns, and ditches in the context of the settlement layout

The majority of houses (247) are radially orientated, with fewer (209) located axially. The circular layout is the most eye-catching spatial structure. Approximately twenty-six house groups define an outer house area. An inner house circuit encloses the central settlement area, and at a distance of *c.* 35 m a second circuit defines a baseline for the *c.* 26 radially orientated house groups.

Between the radial houses are gaps that seem to be alleys, with some alleys continuing to the centre of the settlement. This can, for example, be seen in the structure that follows the orientation of the special buildings in the centre to the West.

The special building in the middle of the settlement is, at nearly 300 m^2, by far the largest. The mean area of the seven other large houses is *c.* 200 m^2. Two large houses are in radial house groups, five are in the common pattern, as at Maidanetske and Dobrovody (Rassmann *et al.*, 2016), situated in the empty space between circular house rows (Figure 12). The two houses that are part of the radial rows are 'standard houses' rather than special buildings. Their classification has to consider the context of the settlement layout more than size, and shape of the anomaly.

As mentioned above, the kilns are distributed on the periphery of the settlement (Figure 12). Their distribution seems remarkably consistent. However, there is now direct correlation to the special buildings or other large houses. The kilns are in the Neighbourhood of rather small houses (Korvin-Piotrovskiy *et al.*, 2016). Gaps in the distribution at the southern periphery can be explained by the erosion of around 4 ha of settlement area. The absence of kilns in the North is an effect of the excavation of Stern (1907). The placement of kilns at the periphery is observed at Taljanky (Korvin-Piotrovskiy *et al.*, 2016), but not in this consistent pattern.

The two ditches are valuable indicators for at least two settlement phases. In the south-eastern area, the inner ditch is superposed with several burnt houses with different orientations; a constellation which reflects the variation of house orientations in the younger settlement phase. The distribution of the kilns outside the ditches might imply a more symbolic meaning of the ditch, rather than serving a real purpose as fortification.

Quantification and settlement layout

A valuable parameter for quantification is the size of the houses and the density of buildings.

For the latter, we can calculate the house centroids as the basis for KDE.

The KDE-map reflects house clusters of similar size (Figure 11). It seems reasonable to understand these subsidiary house groups as a basic element to structuring settlements. The size of the subsidiary house groups varies in number (six to twenty-one houses, with a mean of 13.5 houses) and area (0.3–0.6 ha, with a mean of 0.45 ha). There are some uncertainties in defining the subsidiary house groups but reconstruction based on KDE appears to be a viable approximation. Thus far, we can calculate a total of thirty-nine house groups. The reconstruction of the number of contemporary houses is crucial for the estimation of the population size. For our first reconstruction, we have calculated twelve houses and a total of fifty residents, as in the reconstruction for Dobrovody, Maidanetske, and Taljanky (Rassmann *et al.*, 2016). That leads us to a total number of *c.* 2000 residents for a Copper Age settlement of 25 ha; a population size reached in the final stage of the settlement. In an earlier stage, marked by the inner ditch, the settlement likely consisted of a smaller number of subsidiary house groups.

To compare the reconstruction with the mega-sites in the Uman district, the size of the closer settled area (KDE r 40 m) is 18 ha there. Using the generalized size of 0.4 ha per house group, we get forty-eight house groups. The comparison between the KDE-based calculation and the more in-depth picture from the detailed settlement layout reflects a tendency for a slight overestimation of the number of house groups in the KDE-based calculation by a factor of nearly eighteen per cent.

Besides the around thirty-nine subsidiary house groups, the number of other elements, like special buildings, is much smaller. A small number of alleys cross the settlement from the outer rim to the centre. To take this feature into account, larger groups might be defined, consisting of three to six house groups. The nine large principal house groups are correlated with kilns and special buildings. So far, the contextualized perspective on the geomagnetic data has delivered indications for structural units on different levels: houses, subsidiary house groups, and principal house groups.

The crucial problem is the chronological differentiation of the features from the geomagnetic record. A small auger programme revealed a house structure settlement layer until the depth of 1.1 m in the centre of the settlement. The accumulation of this settlement layer is not reflected by the geomagnetic data in this area, but the digital elevation model provides some indications (Figure 8). A detailed understanding of the spatial layout of the settlement through time can be gained by future excavations

COBANI (DISTRICT GLODENI)

General remarks on the site (Trypillia B1)

The settlement of Cobani is located on the northern area of a Chernozem promontory, 1 km east of the modern village and *c.* 0.8 km north of the street from Cobani to Glodeni (Figures 13, 15). Parts of the promontory are damaged, largely by a modern stone quarry, which is already close to the southern border of the settlement (Figure 14).

The topographical situation is like a hillfort. The need for a protected settlement is reflected by the double ditch in close proximity to the modern stone quarry, which was previously revealed by aerial photography analysed by Bikbaev (2007). These two ditches plus a third were revealed by the geomagnetic survey. The settlement is briefly mentioned by Ketraru (1987: 154–55).

On the basis of surface finds, the settlement can be dated to stage B1 of the Trypillian Culture. The survey in 2009 covered an area of 1.5 ha. The survey area crossed the central part of the promontory. The area enclosed by the double ditch covers 4.5 ha. Nearly, thirty per cent of the settlement was surveyed.

Figure 13. Cobani (district Glodeni). View from the plateau to the northwest.

The data are representative for the central part of the settlement. Besides three ditches, twenty-four houses were revealed. With a mean area of 29 m^2, their size is remarkably small when compared with Petreni and Sîngerei. The variation in house size and the three ditches indicates more than one settlement phase. A continuation of the survey is planned for 2015.

OCHIUL ALB (DISTRICT DROCHIA)

General remarks on the site (Trypillia B2)

The topographical location of the settlement is different from the aforementioned sites, which are situated on a promontory protected by the specifics of the local

Figure 14. Cobani (district Glodeni). View to the stone quarry on the south-eastern part of the promontory.

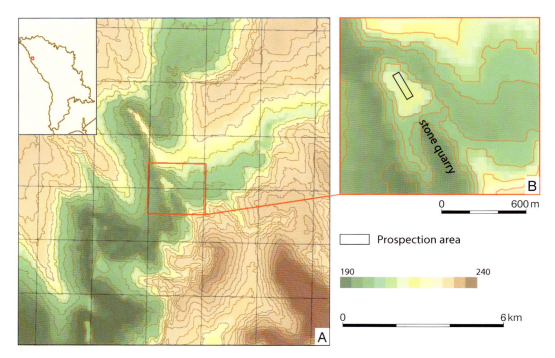

Figure 15. Cobani (district Glodeni). The topographical location around the site and an overview of the survey area (DEM SRTM 30 × 30 m).

terrain (Figures 17–18). Only on the southern rim is the access to the Chernozem-plateau restricted by steep slopes.

The settlement is located 2.5 km southwest of the modern village. The settlement was discovered by V. Bikbaev through aerial photographs in 1991 which indicate ditches, enclosing an area of 3.2 ha. Inside this area, around thirty cropmarks might represent floor-plans of houses. Only 0.5 ha was surveyed in 2009 (Figure 19). The survey confirmed the circular ditch seen in the aerial photographs. The arch-shaped ditch segment has a width of 2 m.

Inside the survey area, twenty small house anomalies with a mean area of 10 m² were detected.

The largest house anomaly indicates a size of 20 m². A small number of pits (just twenty) are visible, with diameters around 2 m. Their contrast on the geomagnetic plan is varying. Seven of them are likely refilled with settlement garbage or burnt daub.

These data are valuable for planning the further surveys which are scheduled for summer 2015. A more detailed description of the data will follow in the final publication of the complete geomagnetic data.

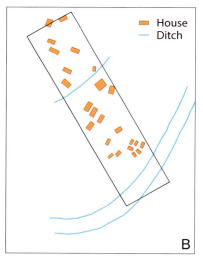

Figure 16. Cobani (district Glodeni). (a) Geomagnetic map. (b) Interpretation of the geomagnetic data.

Figure 17. Ochiul Alb (district Drochia). View from the South to the site.

Conclusion

The geomagnetic survey in Moldova marked the second stage of a large-scale settlement research programme of the Romano-Germanic Commission and Kiel University after its first phase in Romania. The survey revealed the excellent research potential of the sites in Moldova. They are valuable due to their well-preserved houses and other settlement features. In contrast to our research in the Uman region, the sites here are more varied in their size and spatial structure, a constellation which has to be verified by further research.

The remarkably detailed data from Petreni deliver precise insights into the settlement layout of a Copper Age settlement. However, a deeper understanding

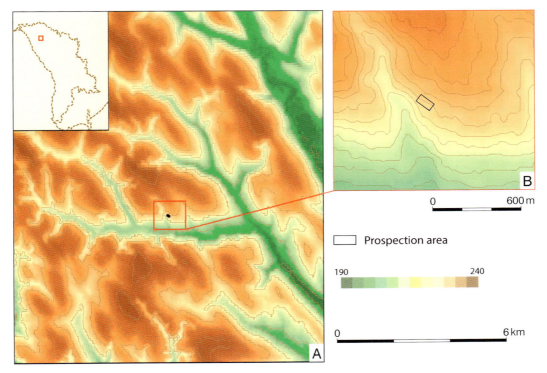

Figure 18. Ochiul Alb (district Drochia). The topographical location around site and an overview of the survey area (DEM SRTM 30 × 30 m).

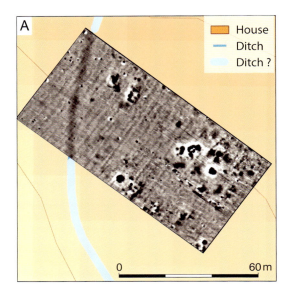 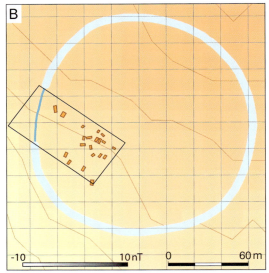

Figure 19. Ochiul Alb (district Drochia). (a) Geomagnetic map. (b) Interpretation of the geomagnetic data.

of the site requires more reliable data from its surroundings.

Acknowledgements

We would like to thank our Moldavian colleagues Sergej Agulnikov, Gennadi Sîrbu, Victor Dron, and the volunteer Klaus Baltes (Frankfurt a. M.) for supporting us on the surveys in 2009 and 2010.

References

Bicbaev, V. 2007. "Bashni" Petren (ot archeologicheskoj interpretatsii aerofotosnimkov k rekonstruktsii zhizni kukuten-tripolskih poselenij. *Tyragetia I (XVI)*, nr. I:9–26. Бикбаев, В, 2007, «Башни Петрен» (от археологической интерпретации аэрофотоснимков к реконструкции жизни кукутень-трипольских поселений), in: TyragetiaI (XVI) nr.I: 9–26.

Chernysh, E.K. 1982. Eneolit Pravoberezhnoj Ukrainy i Moldavii. In: V.M. Masson & N.Ya. Merpert eds. *Eneolit SSSR*. Moscow: Nauka, pp. 165–320. Черныш 1982: Черныш, Е. К. 1982. Энеолит Правобережной Украины и Молдавии. В кн.: В.А. Массон и Н.Я. Мерперт, ред. Энеолит СССР. Москва: Наука, с. 165–320.

Ellis, L. 1984. *The Cucuteni-Tripolye-Culture: Study in Technology and the Origins of Complex Societies*. BAR Intern. Ser. 217. Oxford: BAR.

Ketraru, N.A. 1987. Svod pamyatnkikov istorii i kultury MSSR. Severnaya zona. *Kishinev*, 154–5.

Korvin-Piotrovskiy, A., Hofmann, R., Rassmann, K., Videiko, M.Y. & Brandtstätter, L. 2016. Pottery Kilns in Trypillian Settlements. Tracing the Division of Labour and the Social Organization of Copper Age Communities. In: J. Müller, K. Rassmann & M. Videiko, eds. *Trypillia Mega-Sites and European Prehistory: 4100–3400 BCE*. London and New York: Routledge, pp. 221–252.

Markevich, V.I. 1973. *Pamyatniki epohi neolita i eneolita. Archeologicheskaya karta MSSR*. Kishinev. Маркевич, В. И. 1973. Памятники эпохи неолита и энеолита. Археологическая карта МССР. Кишинев: Verlag.

Markevich, V.I. 1981. *Pozdnetripolskie plemena Severnoj Moldavii*. Kishinev: Shtiinta. Маркевич, В.И. 1981. Позднетрипольские племена Северной Молдавии. Кишинев: Штиинца.

Movsha, T.G. 1984. Petrenska regionalna grupa trypilskoi kultury. *Archeologiya*, 45: 10–23. Мовша 1984: Т. Г. Мовша, Петренська регіональна група трипільської культури. *Археологія* 45: 10–23.

Popa, A., Musteaþă, S., Bicbaev, V., Rassmann, K., Munteanu, O., Posticǎ, G.I. & Sârbu, G. 2010. Consideraþii privind sondajele geofzice din anul 2009 în Republica Moldova. *Revista Arheologicã (Chisinău) Serie nouă VI*, 1, 2010: 171–9.

Rassmann, K., Korvin-Piotrovskiy, A., Videiko, M. & Müller, J. 2016. The New Challenge for Site Plans and Geophysics: Revealing the Settlement Structure of Giant Settlements by Means of Geomagnetic Survey. In: J. Müller, K. Rassmann & M. Videiko, eds. *Trypillia Mega-Sites and European Prehistory: 4100-3400 BCE*. London and New York: Routledge, pp. 29–54.

Shyshkin, K.V. 1973. Z praktyky deshyfruvannya aerofotznimkiv u archeologichnyh tsilyah. *Archeologiya*, 19: 32–41. Шишкін, К. В. 1973. З практики дешифрування аерофотознімків у археологічних цілях. Археологія, 19: 32–41.

Sorochin, V. 2004. Aşezarea cucuteniană de la Petreni, jud. Bălţi. Un secol de la descoperire. *Memoria Antiqvitatis XXIII*, 2004: 253–64.

Stern, E. 1904. Predvaritelnoe soobshchenie o raskopkah v imenii Petreny v Beltskom uezde Bessarabskoj gubernii. *Zapiski Odesskogo Obshchestva Istorii i drevnostej*, XXV: 69–72. Штерн, Э. 1904, Предварительное сообщение о раскопках в имении Петрены в Бельцком уезде Бессарабской губернии. Записки Одесского общества Истории и древностей XXV: 69–72.

Stern, E. 1906. Die prämykenische Kultur in Süd-Russland: Die Ausgrabungen in Petreny, im

Bielzer Kreise des Gouvernements Bessarabien, 1902 und 1903. Moskau: G. Lissner and D. Sobko.

Stern, E. 1907. Doistoricheskaya grecheskaya kultura na Yuge Rossii. In: Trudy XIII Archeologicheskogo sjezda v Ekaterinoslave v 1905g. Tom I. Moscow, *c.* 9–94. Штерн, Э. 1907 Доисторическая греческая культура на юге России. Труды XIII AC в Екатеринославе в 1905 г. т.I, Москва, *с.* 9–94.

Uhl, R. 2014. Petreni, Republik Moldau. Die Arbeiten der Jahre 2012 Und 2013. *Forschungsberichte des DAI 2014*, 2(DAI): 78–81.

Videiko, M.Y., Chapman, J., Burdo, N.B., Gaydarska, B., Ţerna, S.V., Rud, V.S. & Kiosak, D.V. 2015. Kompleksnye issledovaniya sooruzhenij, proizvodstvennyh kompleksov i ostatkov postroek na tripolskom poselenii u s. *Nebelevka. Stratum Plus*, 2: 147–70. Видейко, М.Ю., Чэпмен, Дж., Бурдо, Н.Б., Гайдарска, Б., Церна, С., Рудь В. и Киосак, Д. 2015а. Комплексные исследования оборонительных сооружений, производственных комплексов и остатков построек на трипольском поселении у села Небелевка – Complex Investigations of Defensive Systems, Production Complexes and Remains of Constructions on the Tripolye Site near the Village of Nebelevka. Stratum Plus, 2: 147–70.

Videiko, M. & Rassmann, K. 2016. Research on Different Scales: 120 Years Trypillian Large Sites Research. In: J. Müller, K. Rassmann & M. Videiko, eds. *Trypillia Mega-Sites and European Prehistory: 4100-3400 BCE*. London and New York: Routledge, pp. 17–28.

CHAPTER 5

Maidanetske: New Facts of a Mega-Site

JOHANNES MÜLLER AND MYKHAILO VIDEIKO

INTRODUCTION

The mega-site Maidanetske (48°80′37″ N, 30°68′17″ E, 180–150 m a.s.l.) is located in central Ukraine at the border between the oblasts of Cherkasy and Kirovohrad. The mega-site is situated West of the Taljanka River and West of the village Maidanetske on the Chernozem high plateau. The site itself is positioned at the confluence of a small watercourse with the Taljanka River, 170–190 m NHN (Figure 1). *c.* 10 km downstream the Taljanka River the mega-site Taljanky and *c.* 20 km downstream the mega-site Dobrovody are placed in similar environmental locations. The Taljanka River drains into the Girskyj Tikych River to the East. The Girskyj Tikych River is a tributary of the Southern Buh River flowing into the Black Sea.

The site has a long research history. The first excavations by G. Bezvenglinsky (Videiko, 2012: 107) took place in the 1920s, but both the documentation and the material are lost. After analyses of aerial photographs by Shyshkin (1973), the first full geomagnetic plan was conducted by V.P. Dudkin from 1972 to 1974 (Dudkin, 1978). Dudkin's plans confirmed the results already obtained by aerial photography. In field campaigns that started in 1971, several houses were excavated by Ukrainian teams until 1998 (Shmaglij and Videjko, 2003). In 2011–2013, a new geomagnetic survey was conducted and excavations started in 2013, with the publication of preliminary results in 2014 (Burdo *et al.*, 2012; Müller *et al.*, 2014; Rassmann *et al.*, 2014; Videiko *et al.*, 2014, 2015).

By means of the new geomagnetic prospection, many previously unknown objects were discovered, such as a few new rings and trackways, the remains of enclosures (three lines of ditches or palisades), large special buildings–'mega-structures' (approximately 8), and traces of pottery kilns. This was supplemented by data about 1537 pits of various types and *c.* 3000 ordinary buildings, much more than considered before (Table 1). In 2013 and 2014, the geophysical plan of the site enabled the interdisciplinary Ukrainian–German excavation team to focus on different questions on the character and function of different features.

Target excavations of main archaeological features were conducted to enable the reconstruction of the primary contexts (e.g. the evaluation of a house or a pit), including their stratigraphy and duration, function, and economy. The excavations resulted in the documentation of the archive in respect to depositional processes, architectural features, material culture, and archaeozoological and archaeobotanical remains. The reconstruction of social practices that were associated with the structures was possible through detailed scientific, typological, and spatial analyses of the linkage between material objects, macro-remains, and features (Müller *et al.*, in print). Test sondages in similar archaeological categories were conducted to gather, for example, samples for dating. Test sondages, which focus on geomagnetic features from houses in the concentric house rings, could help in dating the concentric house rings (see Müller *et al.*, 2016). Thus, the combination of target excavations and test sondages was used as a strategy to deal with the huge mass of features in a manageable field strategy. A new series of C14 dates provided the opportunity to start discussion of the possibility of studying the internal chronology of settlement, using such dates. Correlation of these data with evidence from stratigraphy and pottery assemblages made it possible to determine the specific stages in the history of settlement (Müller *et al.*, 2016). Furthermore, geoarchaeological studies established a model of the vegetation and soil development of the site (see Kirleis and Dreibrodt, 2016).

In this article, we present a short overview of the most interesting new features from the new geophysical survey and the excavations.

THE SETTLEMENT PLAN

The overall size of the site (reconstructed from aerial photography) measures 200 ha, of which 174 ha is built space. In 1971–1974, 180 ha was surveyed (Shmaglij, 1980: figure 1). In the new geomagnetic survey, 150 ha was surveyed of which 112 ha exhibits built structures (Figure 1). (Rassmann *et al.*, 2014: figure 22a). The combination of Dudkin's plan (Dudkin, 1978) with the new plan permitted us to calibrate the old results with the new (Ohlrau, 2014; Rassmann *et al.*, 2014). It became clear that Dudkin

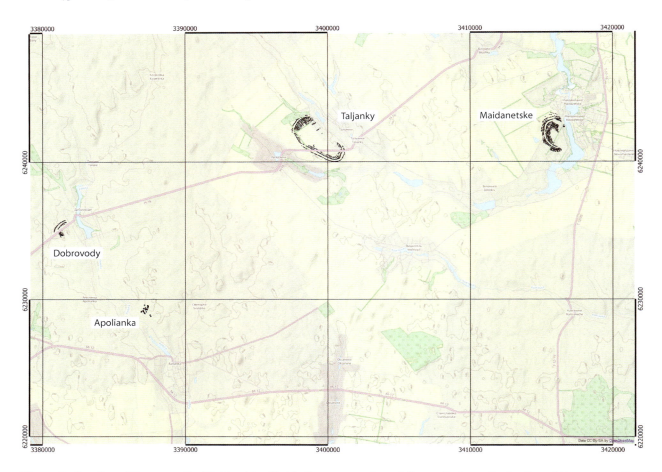

Figure 1. Location of the mega-site Maidanetske. Beside the canyon system of the small rivers, the location of three mega-sites at approximately 15 km distance from each other is visible (Dobrovody, Taljanky, and Maidanetske). The features represent the geomagnetic features of the sites.

identified more or less half of the geomagnetic structures that were identified in the same areas by the new survey, even one-quarter of the unburnt houses. In consequence, the total arrive at 2300 burnt and about 670 unburnt house structures at Maidanetske (Table 1 and Figure 2). Of these, forty-three were excavated during the field 1971–1998 campaigns, and two in the 2013–2014 campaigns (List 1).

In principle, Maidanetske houses are organized in nine concentric house rings around a central open space (cf. section geomagnetic results). They form empty rings between the rows, usually 20–30 m in width. An exception is one main ring with a distance of up to 100 m between the neighbouring house rows. To the South and to the North of the site, the aforementioned ditches are visible, partly overlapping with pits. Additionally, houses that are not organized in concentric rings form quarters to the North and South of the central open space. Most of the houses are associated with one pit. Besides the houses pits are the most numerous features of the site. 'House places' are defined as the space for house-associated pits, the space in the vicinity of a house and the house itself. Special buildings (labelled as mega-structures) are positioned radially oriented to the centre–mostly within the gateways of the settlement–or on a

Table 1. Value data objects between the old and new plans

Objects	Plan 1971–1974 (180 ha)	Plan 2011–2012 (~70 per cent of site)
Burnt houses	1575	1493
Less burnt houses	—	415
Mega-structures special buildings	—	9
Pits	—	1537
Probable kilns	—	12
Ditches	—	3
Total amount	1575	3469

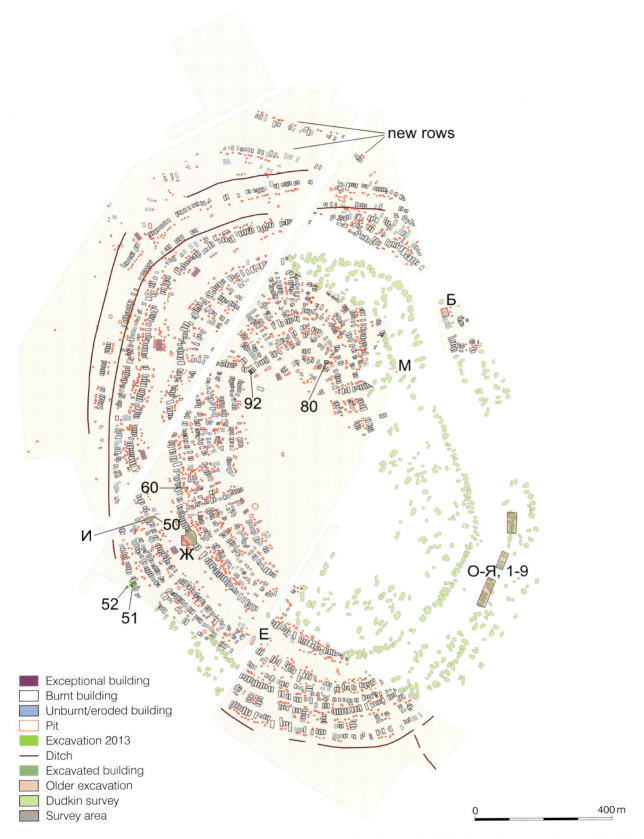

Figure 2. Maidanetske, plan according to magnetic prospection 1971–1974 and 2011–2012. Objects explored 1972–2014 marked by letters and numbers.

List 1. The Maidanetske houses, key data

Name	House	Transliteration	Width	Length
Б	1	B	6	12
Б	2	B	4	14
Б	3	B	5	14
Е-1	4	je-1	5	11
Е-2	5	je-2	3	10
Ж-1	6	sh-1	4,5	12
Ж-2	7	sh-2	15	11,5
Ж-3	8	sh-3	6	16
Ж-4	9	sh-4	5	14
З-1	10	s-1	5	14
З-2	11	s-2	5	14
И	12	I	9	21
К	13	K	4	9
Л	14	L	4,5	10
М	15	M	7	24
О	16	O	4,3	12,6
П	17	P	10	15
Р	18	R	1,2	15,6
С	19	Ss	4,2	10,4
Т	20	T	4	10
У	21	U	4,5	14
Ф	22	F	4,6	11
Ы	23	Y	4,5	10
Х	24	Ch	4,2	10,8
Э	25	E	4,5	14,5
Ц	26	Z	4	11
Ч	27	Tsch	3,5	10
Ш	28	Sch	4,4	10,5
Щ	29	Schtsch	3,8	10
Ю	30	Ju	5	13,5
Я-1	31	ja-1	4,3	14
Я-2	32	ja-2	3,2	11,5
1	33	1	4,2	14,6
2	34	2	4,5	10,7
3	35	3	4,3	10,5
пл.3	36	pl3	3,5	13
4	37	4	4–4,8	15,6
5	38	5	4	?
6	39	6	5	10
7	40	7	4	?
8	41	8	5	?
9	42	9	5	14
10	43	10	4,4	?
51	44		5	15
71	45		4	10
72	46		5	12
73a	47		5	15
73b	48		5	15
74	49			
75	50		4	13
76	51		4	12
77	52			
79	53			
92	54		4,1	7,2

concentric axis, mainly within the main ring of the site. They are characterized by wall trenches (*Wandgräbchen*). The spatial position of the four western special buildings in the main ring might at least indicate a distance of about 250 m from each other.

In addition to Dudkin's plan, two lines of gable parallel houses with associated pits are also displayed at the northern fringe of the site. Their orientation differs from the other concentric rows (Figure 2). They obviously represent a different phase of the settlement.

In contrast to the research carried out until 1998, the newly discovered features are ditches, mega-structures, and kilns (Figure 3). These features were confirmed by plans of several Trypillia B2 and C1 phases large sites–from Petreni and Dobrovody to Nebelivka (Rassmann *et al.*, 2014: figures 31, 33a, 38, 39; Chapman *et al.*, 2014: figures 3, 20; see Rassmann *et al.*, 2016; Chapman, 2016). They are 'the' newly discovered common features of the majority of mega-sites. Some of these previously unknown objects are now explored and they also expand our picture of the organization of mega-sites (see Rassmann *et al.*, 2016; Müller *et al.*, 2016).

The 2013–2014 Excavations

During the excavation campaigns in 2013 and 2014, on the one hand two *ploschchadki*, five pits, and three kilns were excavated; on the other hand, test trenches were conducted at nine further houses to gain, for example, samples for dating purposes (see Müller *et al.*, 2016). The results were published in preliminary reports (Table 2). Information was gained about three house places and further pits and kilns that are not directly associated with a house.

Houses

To add relevant data to the model of a Trypillia domestic house place, investigations were carried at three locations. At house place 44, the house and the associated pit were excavated; at house place 54, the house; and at house place 12, a pit that belongs to house 12, which was excavated already in 1984.

House place 44

House 44 (trench 51) is located in the outer row of houses (row 1), in the southernwest part of the site (Figure 2). The size of burnt daub deposition is nearly 5 × 17 m, oriented by the long side to the central part of site. Preserved are two layers of daub (with an abundant admixture of plant remains) with imprints

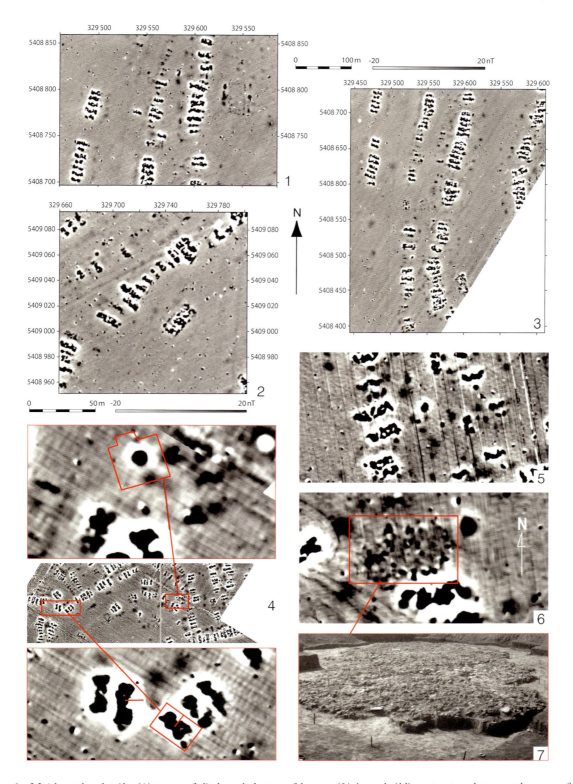

Figure 3. *Maidanetske, details: (1) traces of ditch and clusters of houses; (2) large building structure between the rows of houses; (3) traces of ditches and clusters of houses; (4) central part, excavations 2014 (tr.80 and 92); (5) pit 60 and houses around; (6) pit 50 and house 12 ('И'); (7) remains of house 12 ('И'), explored at 1984.*

of chipped wood on the bottom (Figure 4, 1 and 2). The main direction of imprints was perpendicular to the long axis of the building, but several were along this axis. Pottery was found between the layers of daub and also under the lower layer (Figure 5, 3 and 4; cf. also Müller *et al.*, 2016).

After the upper layer was removed, some features from the interior were discovered on the lower layer of

Table 2. The main excavated features of the excavation campaigns 2013–2014 with preliminary publications

Objects	Trench. No. (year)	Total number of objects explored	Publications
Burnt house	51 (2013), 92 (2014)	2	Відейко та ін. 2014; Мюллер и др. 2014
Pit	50,52,60 (all 2013), 80 (2) (2014)	5	Відейко та ін. 2014; Мюллер и др. 2014
Kiln	80 (3) (2014)	3	Відейко та ін. 2015
2013–2014		10	Відейко та ін. 2015

daub, including a 2 × 2 m base of the oven and the remains of a clay bench (Figure 4, 3). Also, many pieces of the large 'pythos' close to the clay bench were found. Part of the upper layer was covered by a 3–4 cm layer of daub without plant admixture (Figure 4, 7). At northeastern part of the ruins was a place with several pieces of well-preserved plaster from the walls or ceiling.

Around the *ploschchadki*, a depression with a dark fill, which included fragments of pottery, animal bones (nearly 150), and a few stones (Figure 4, 2) was documented. This depression probably developed when some of the surrounding loess was used for plastering the walls and other constructions of this house.

In trench 52 lies a pit, which is part of house place 44, located 9 m southwest of house 43. It was a geomagnetic feature of 5 m diameter and up to 10 nT, which indicated a pit-like structure (1.5 m deep; 4.6 m top diameter). The pit was buried under a colluvium (0.8 m thick) and appeared with a diameter of 4.6 m (Figure 4, 8). The infilling was a homogenous black-brown sediment without daub. A further sedimentological division was not possible. 1.5 m deeper (at 169.9 m a.s.l.) the base of the pit was reached; still roundish with a diameter of 1.2 m. At least 9.2 m^3 soil was extracted during the Chalcolithic; because of erosional processes, we could reckon with 10 m^2. Different estimations of soil conditions and the character of burnt daub showed that the extracted clay would have been enough for the construction of house 44 (Müller *et al.*, in print).

The artefact density of the pit was very low; the few finds, including animal bones, and daub, were concentrated on the base of the pit and near its borders. Ceramics, if identifiable, belong to a biconical vessel and a bowl (Trypillia C1, Tomashivska group, and phase T3).

The ^{14}C-dates from these objects belong to the deeper part of the pit (cp. Müller *et al.*, 2016). Two of them represent *termini post quem* (possible old wood effect–60190 and 60347 *Quercus*), the two others *termini ad quem* (Poz-60292 4920 ± 40 bp (bos) from spit 1e (3713–3651 cal BC) and Poz-60296 4955 ± 35 bp from spit 1f (bone of a large mammal): 3775–3695 cal BC). Thus, the depositional processes probably took place in the 38th century BCE. Accordingly, there is a high probability that pit 52 existed contemporarily with house 44. It possibly originated as an extraction pit for building purposes.

House place 54

House 54 (trench 92) is located in the northeastern sector of the central part of the site, and is part of a cluster of at least three small buildings (within 2–2.5 m one from another), at the edges of the free area inside the settlement (Figure 3, 4).

The size of the *ploschchadki* is 4 × 11 m (including a collapsed wall to the southeast), oriented by its long side to the centre of Maidanetske (Figure 5). Preserved are two layers of daub (with an abundant admixture of plant remains) with imprints of chipped wood on bottom. The top layer is preserved only in some parts, and it is clearly visible that it was partly destroyed by ploughing (Figure 5, 4). The main direction of the wood imprints was across the long axis of the building, but several were along this axis. Pottery was found between the layers of daub and also under the lower layer (Figure 5, 2).

The majority of bowls, goblets, and biconical vessels were located on the lower layer along the length of one side of the house remains. On the same layer, two features from the interior were discovered: a 2 × 2 m platform from an oven or fireplace, and pieces from a destroyed round clay elevation with traces of red paint on it; a possible altar (Figure 5, 4a). Another similar fragmented elevation, with traces of incised decoration and red paint, was preserved under the lower layer of burnt daub (Figure 5, 6). A small goblet and half of a bowl from this layer were deposited 1.2 m from this elevation, at a depth of 0.18 m (Figure 5, 5). A lot of pottery and animal bones were also found around the remains of this house.

Both houses were similar in construction and the features of their interior. It is possible to reconstruct them as two-storeyed buildings with living space on the second floor (see below). Both houses were used for domestic purposes and the daily activities of a household community. The separation into a ground floor (mainly for storing instruments and special resources) and a second floor for food processing and consumption, and perhaps also house rituals, indicates a clear spatial pattern of activities. Tool production also took place in the direct vicinity of the house. The

Figure 4. Maidanetske, 2013: (1–7) house 44; (8) pit 52; (1) general view; (2) profile; (3) remains of clay bench; (4) pottery under the upper layer; (5) clay construction on the upper layer of daub; (6) platform of oven, partly covered by the upper layer of daub; (7) floor and pottery on top; (8) profile of pit 52 (graphics figure 4, 2 and 4, 8: Robert Hofmann).

Figure 5. *Maidanetske, 2014: house 54: (1) general view; (2) pottery on the lower layer of daub; (3) pottery near remains of house; (4) part of lower layer, (a) remains of round structure; (5) goblet, found under the burnt clay platform; (6) clay elevation on ground floor, under the lower layer of daub.*

waste management seems to be clear (cf. contribution Müller et al., 2016).

Houseplace 12

Pit 50 (trench 50) is located between the central and second rows of houses in the southeast sector of the site, close to household 'И' (house 12) from row 4 (Figure 3, 6 and 7). This household was explored in 1984 and was one of the largest in this area: 9 × 21 m with a few rooms on two levels, which possibly played a special role in the social life of some small community located in this part of the site (Shmaglij and Videiko, 2005: 62, 63). It is interesting that two pits are clearly visible on the geomagnetic plan, located close to each short side of this dwelling (Figure 3, 6); they obviously belong to the house place of 'И' (house 12).

Beneath the top layer of black soil (0.7 m), the rectangular pit 50 (3.85 × 3.4 m; 178.4 m a.s.l.) with rounded corners became visible, which represents the archaeological remains of the oval geomagnetic feature with the strength of 20 nT. The pit was dug into the loess soil, which is disturbed with a lot of krotovinas (Figure 6, 1 and 2). The loess soil was composed of a buried humus horizon (fA_1) and the fBw horizon. This pit was 0.8–1.2 m deep and the bottom of the pit was oval and slightly inclined, 3.9 × 3.0 m in size. After the pit had been dug out, a huge fire, which made the soil extremely reddish, burnt on the bottom of the pit (Figure 6, 6 and 7). The deepest infilling was grey-brown and followed by a similar infilling, with some daub additionally mixed in. On top of this layer, two cattle skulls, many bones, and different pots were deposited (Figure 6, 2–5), before the infilling of huge masses of daub started, which became less frequent in the top parts of this infilling. The infilling on top of the described artefact concentration was just debris, of which the daub pieces were sorted; with bigger ones at the bottom and smaller ones on top (Figure 6, 9).

All ceramics belong, from a typochronological point of view, to Trypillia C1, Tomashivska group, and phase T3. As there is no typological difference between the assemblages of the different infillings, this might underline that after the deposition of the first infilling with the cattle skulls, the second infilling of the whole pit took place in a very short event (Figure 6, 6).

A careful context analysis of the seven radiometric samples of the pit indicates a high probability that the first infilling took place in the 39th century BCE, and the second infilling in the 38th century BCE (see Müller et al., 2016).

In any case, it is clear that this pit was in use for a long time and these activities were connected with household 'И'. A representative collection of pottery from this house belongs to the Trypillia C1, Tomashivska group, and phase 3, similar to that of the pit (Figure 6, 4 and 13).

An account of the two-storeyed house

One of the main issues in the interpretation of discovered Trypillian house features is 'whether the Tripolye dwellings of the giant-settlements were one- or two-storey houses' (Korvin-Piotrovski et al., 2012; Menotti, 2012: 255). In the case of house 54, the documentation technique that was mainly developed by Stanislav Terna (cf. Ursu and Terna, 2014) clearly confirmed the existence of a two-storeyed house. In principle, three different layers were identified on the excavation. The first layer of daub pieces, partly disturbed by agrarian activities, covered a second layer with horizontal daub pieces, and daub pieces of different installations on top. The first layer (Figures 7 and 8) indicates two different orientations of the plank-imprints: (1) oriented with the short side of the house in the inner part of two areas; (2) oriented with the long side of the construction in an area to the southwest. In principle, we interpret the remains in the northern parts of the roof, but in the southwestern area as the parts of a collapsed wall. Thus, we could talk of a house that has a height of at least 3.5 m. The second layer of burnt daub (Figures 9 and 10) indicates an orientation of the plank-imprints with the broad side of the house. Furthermore, installations are visible like the aforementioned 2 × 2 m base of an oven and the round platform in the northwestern part of the house. Additionally, the distribution of ceramics near the

southwestern wall could hint to a line of ceramics near the wall, which is known from other houses as existing on a small bench, which is missing in case of house 54. The third layer beneath the floor is indicated by pieces of burnt clay and the distribution of many artefacts, including ceramics and querns (Figure 11).

In principle, we would interpret the whole structure as the remains of planks from the roof and the remainder of a collapsed wall, installations and the burnt clay screed of the second floor, as well as the artefact layer on the ground floor. The house is quite small (7.2 × 4.1 m) without a division into rooms. If we calculate a height of c. 2 m for the top floor, and a height of c. 0.5 m for a rounded roof (Shatilo, 2014), then probably only 1 m is left for the ground floor. With such a reconstruction, the ground floor could serve primarily for the deposition of objects and not for residential purposes.

Further pits and kilns

Pit 60: a deposited dwelling

Pit 60 (trench 60) is located in the southeast sector of the site, in the almost innermost row of houses (row 5) (Figure 2, 5). This pit had an extraordinarily high magnetic flux density of 50 nT. The pit was

Figure 6. Maidanetske, 2013: pit 50: (1) top of burnt daub layer; (2) profile; (3) group of animal bones and pottery on top of the backfilling; (4) pottery; (5) plan of group; (6) view of burnt layer; (7) plan of burnt daub; (8) profile of the pit; (9) profile (graphics 6.5; 6.7, and 6.9: Robert Hofmann).

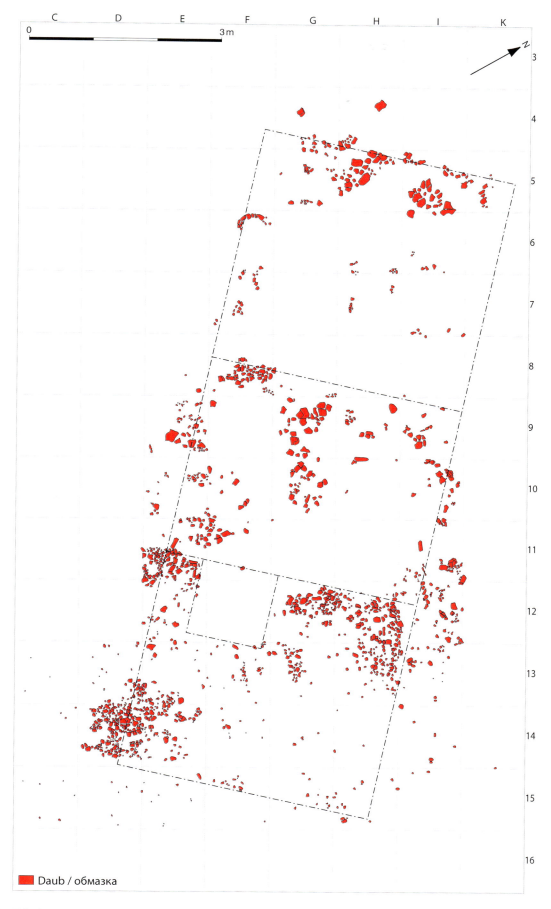

Figure 7. Maidanetske, 2014: documentation of the features of the top layer of house 54 (graphics: Stanislav Terna).

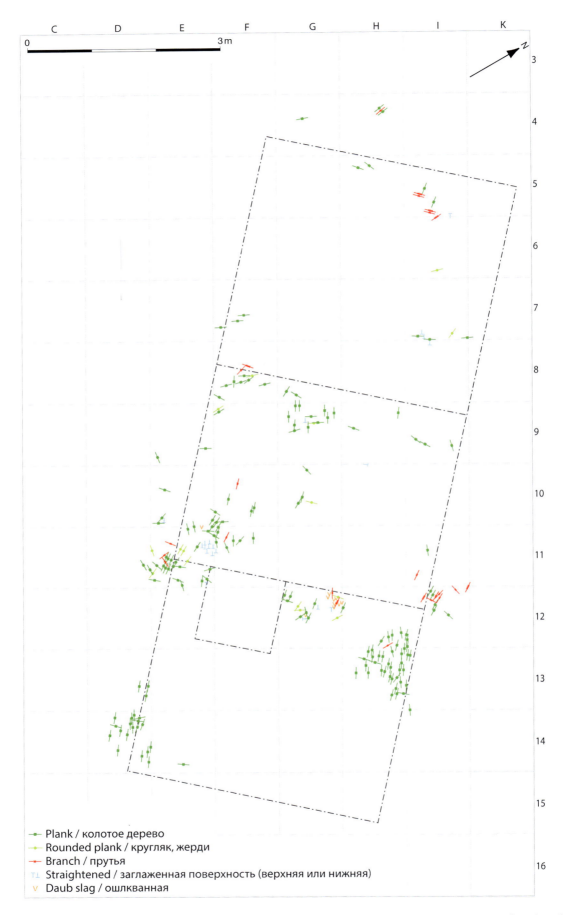

Figure 8. Maidanetske, 2014: documentation of the orientation of daub imprints of the top layer of house 54 (graphics: Stanislav Terna).

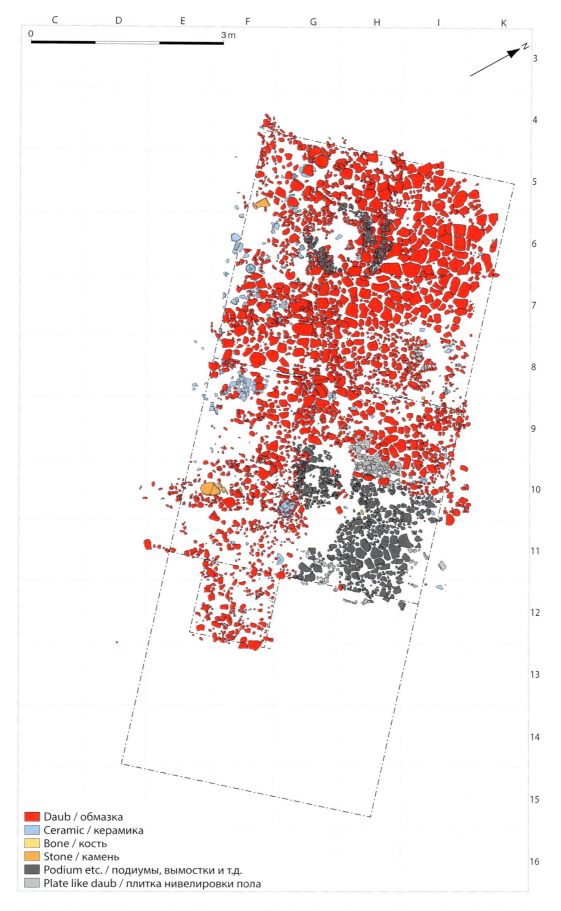

Figure 9 Maidanetske, 2014: documentation of the features of the first floor of house 54 (graphics: Stanislav Terna).

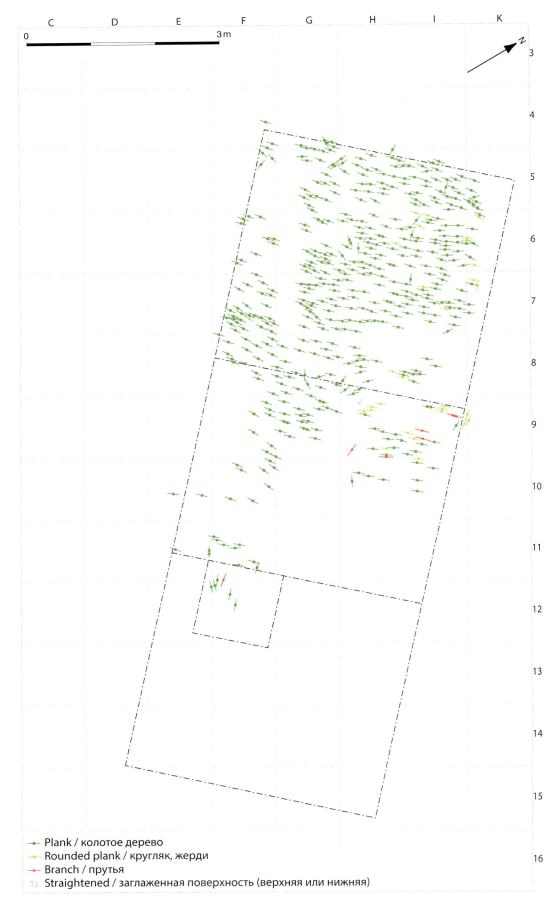

Figure 10. *Maidanetske, 2014: documentation of the orientation of daub imprints of the first floor of house 54 (graphics: Stanislav Terna).*

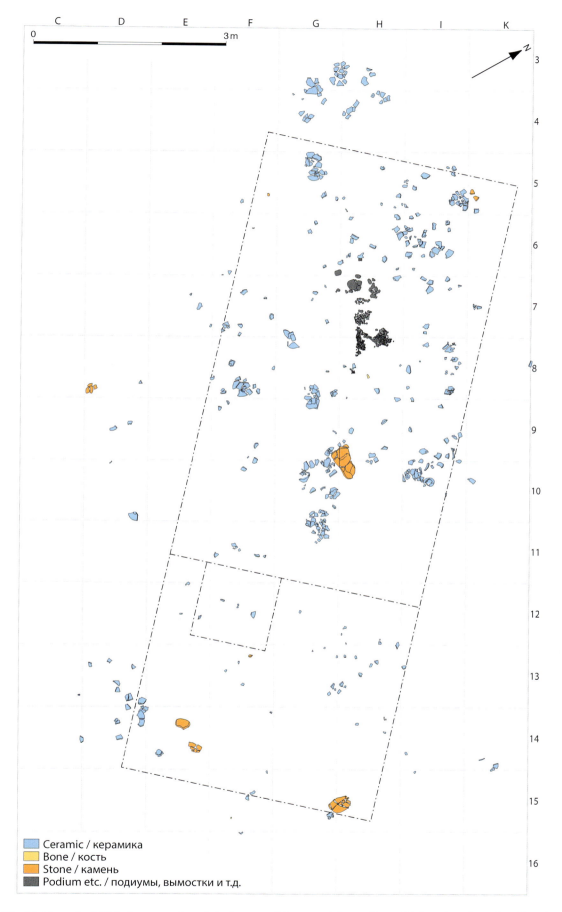

Figure 11. Maidanetske, 2014: documentation of the features of the ground floor of house 54 (graphics: Stanislav Terna).

filled by an immense mass of daub, which caused kiln-like anomalies (Figure 12, 1–6).

Beneath the 0.5 m thick Chernozem of the top soil (180.7 m a.s.l.), a cluster of daub measuring *c.* 5 m diameter became visible, which formed the top of the oval pit (Figure 12). The 1.5 m deep pit changed in its deeper parts into a rectangular form (4 m [N-S] ×3.5 m [O-W]) with rounded edges. The base, reached at 178.7 m depth, was quite uneven (Figure 12, 6). The pit is the result of a series of three or four cuts and infillings. These separate pits had rounded bottoms and smoothed walls, and were obviously refilled very suddenly. The substrate of each of these sub-pits was, in general, very loose and ashy, but in every case enriched with unsorted daub pieces. The top layers showed a more humic character; the bottom layers a strong infiltration with daub.

Among the pieces of burnt daub were clearly visible details from a burnt house: daub with plant admixture and imprints of wood, fragments of walls or floors with remains of paintings, pieces of clay platforms (Figure 6, 8). Between these daub pieces were numerous fragments of painted pottery (Figure 12, 7), animal bones (102), stone, pieces of flint, and a fragment of a human figurine, giving the impression of domestic waste. Obviously, the remains of a dwelling were deposited inside the large pit.

The five radiometric dates indicate that the oldest phase dates to the 39th century BCE, the second phase to the turn of the 39th/38th century BCE, and the last phase to the 38th century BCE (Müller *et al.*, 2016). In principle, the pit is a depositional place for daub from destroyed houses. If this is the case, the oldest phase probably has to be associated with the oldest phase of the settlement. The duration of the occupation of the area under discussion (parts of ring 5 or 6) lasted until the thirty-eighth century, judging from the youngest ^{14}C-dates.

The complex biography of pits 50 and 60 could be explained by non-daily, probably ritual activities.

The kiln area

A kiln area (trench 80), which included the remains of three pottery kilns one above the other and two pits, is located at northeastern side of the central part of the site (Figure 3, 4).[1] It was detected as a large nT anomaly. 15 m northeast a similarly strong anomaly was located; possibly another kiln. The remains of object 80 became visible at a depth of 0.6 m from the recent surface. It means that cultural layers around were never disturbed by ploughing (Figure 14, 1).

The top part of the kiln is represented by the remains of two partly destroyed substructure constructions and damaged foundations of surrounding walls.

This object was probably near 1.8 × 1.8 m in size (Figure 9, 1–6). The construction is similar to kilns from Taljanky (Kruts *et al.*, 2014; Korvin-Piotrovskiy *et al.*, 2016). The remains of the kiln were covered by fragments of destroyed constructions and heavily burnt pottery. A horizon, which was contemporary with the last activities in this space, was marked by fragments of heavily burnt pottery scattered around (Figure 14, 1 and 2). After cleaning the kiln of remains, it became visible that the level of cultural remains contemporary with the use of this device was visibly lower. This means that the kiln was not in use for some time before the whole settlement was abandoned. The channels of the kiln were 20 × 20 cm in size. The bottom of the kiln channels and substructure walls were plastered with fireproof clay. This kiln was oriented with its fireplace to the East with some slight deviation. Opposite the fireplace, at a 1 m distance, began a large pit, which partly cut the cultural layer of the previous period (Figure 14, 4–6). This pit was partly explored and its base at a depth almost 1 m from the Trypillia horizon. Its filling included a large number of fragments of pottery (most with traces of heavy secondary burning), broken details from the kiln, and small stones which were in layers full of ashes.

After cleaning the remains of this kiln, several details of an object below, which were previously covered by the destruction layer and damaged plaster from the bottom of the kiln, also became visible. After removing the details from the upper kiln, the remains of a previous furnace were discovered. Only certain elements were preserved: 8–10 cm of the base, some lower parts of the dome of the kiln, and plaster from the substructure foundation (Figure 14, 7 and 8). Three channels were 22–25 cm wide; 2–5 cm more than for the previously described object. This kiln was oriented with the fireplace to the South with some deviation. The working surface of this object was marked by a horizon with scattered sherds.

The first kiln was buried under the remains of two devices, described below (Figure 15, 1–4). Partly preserved substructures were built from clay with inclusions of large fragments of painted pottery. It is interesting that parts of the same forms of pottery were included in the construction; bowl opposite bowl, pot opposite pot. Some large fragments were used for the foundation of the fireplace in front of the kiln, which was also oriented to the South with some deviation. The size of the channels is as follows: 30–32 cm width and up to 20 cm height. Substructures were constructed on a 10–12 cm clay platform, for which the usual clay with fireproof plastering on top was used. This kiln was placed in a roundish 1.8 m pit with 10–15 cm depth (Figure 15, 3). This pit was probably part of a larger depression, located 1–1.2 m

---
[1] More details about this and other kilns see Korvin-Piotrovkiy *et al.*, 2016.

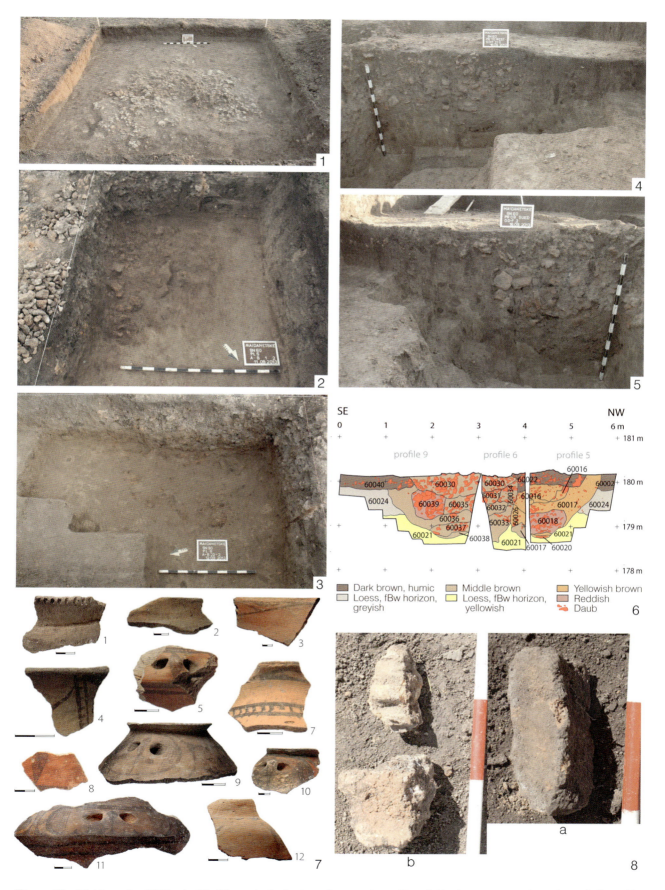

Figure 12. Maidanetske, 2013: pit 60: (1) at the beginning of excavations; (2 and 3) view at excavations; (4 and 5) profiles; (6) general profile; (7) pottery from pit 60; (8) samples of daub from pit 60: (a) fragment of elevation, (b) daub with imprints of wooden constructions (graphics: Robert Hofmann).

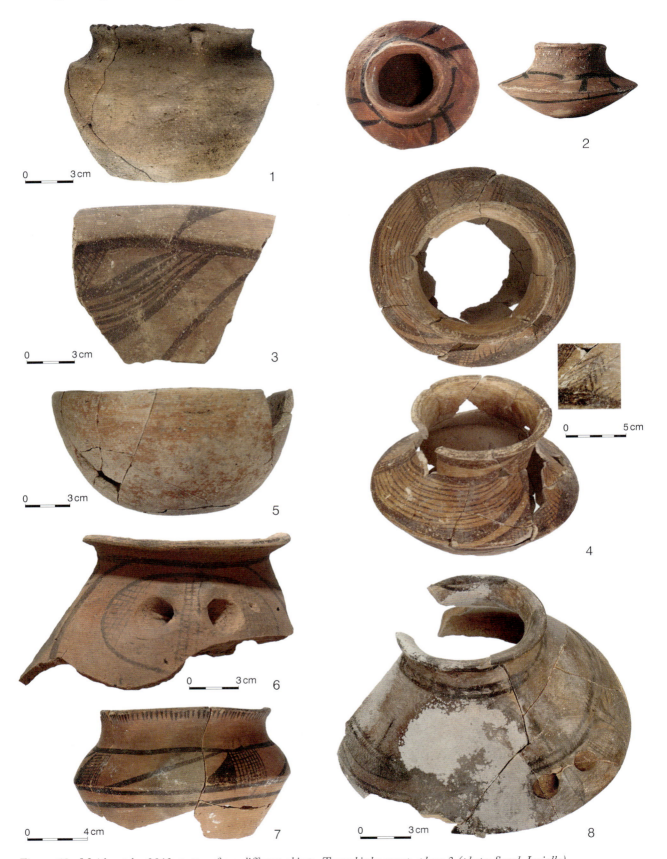

Figure 13. Maidanetske, 2013: pottery from different objects, Tomashivka group, phase 3 (photo: Sarah Jagiolla).

Figure 14. *Maidanetske, 2014: trench 80: excavations of kiln: (1–6) the upper layer; (7–8) middle layer.*

away from the fireplace. This horizon also was marked by the deposition of numerous fragments of pottery on the surface.

The pit, located opposite the fireplaces of first two kilns, consisted of some parts which started at a different depth, including a horizon of the last kiln

Figure 15. Maidanetske, 2014: trench 80: excavations of kiln and pits: (1–3) kiln, lower layer; (4–8) pits: (4) general situation at final stage of excavations; (5 and 6) filling and profile of the pit across from the upper kiln; (7) pit opposite to kiln of middle and lower layers; (8) group of artefacts in the pit.

(Figure 15, 4 and 7). It means that it was in use during the whole period of activities at this place. The fill of this pit was partially different and included not only fragmented pottery and parts of the kiln, but also pieces of burnt daub from the construction of a house, numerous animal bones, a complete hoe made of deer horn, and a complete goblet. The last two objects were deposited with animal bones and fragmented pottery (Figure 15, 8).

This kilns are similar to objects explored in 2013/2014 at Taljanky (Kruts *et al.*, 2014: figure 1; Korvin-Piotrovskiy *et al.*, 2016) and Nebelivka (Videiko *et al.*, 2015: figure 1). The difference is in small details and the fact that the kiln at Maidanetske was reconstructed and repaired a few times. The stratigraphy demonstrated a long history of activities at this place, related not only to pottery production, but also to some rituals.

Carbon Dating

The series of thirty-five radiocarbon dates from Maidanetske, which were obtained after the 2013 season, can provide information about the chronological relevance of different features. For the first time, it was possible to gain dates from all of the different rings of a Trypillia settlement and from pits (cf. Müller *et al.*, 2016).

First, the radiocarbon dates display statistically identical dates for all houses which were dated. They support the model of a contemporary existence around 3800/3600 BCE. Furthermore, all other dated structures were abandoned in a similar timespan. In consequence, burnt material from the houses and the upper fill of the pits now represent the latest settlement event: the time at which (most of) the site burnt down. The close vicinity and the full burning of whole houses, resulting in nearly rectangular remains of daub, was obviously a deliberate act.

Second, in contrast to most of the houses, these remains represent the latest stage of development; the pits contain different stages of infilling that represent longer histories of the place. Evidence from pits 50 and 60 confirms that the earliest activities already took place around 3900 cal BC at the latest. As pit 60 demonstrates sophisticated waste management, with burnt daub sorted and deposited according to its sizes in different infillings of one pit; obviously most of the damaged material was taken away. This hypothesis could explain the small amount of daub.

In consequence, around 3700 cal BCE most of the settlement existed contemporarily. Both pits and houses were in use. The typochronological estimation of the excavated assemblages places Maidanetske in the final stage of Trypillia C1/T3 of the Tomashivska group which is in accordance with the interval 3800/3600 BCE.

Interpretation and Conclusion

The remains of the two houses are interpreted as normal domestic households with different kinds of activities; subsistence and otherwise. Their material remains display clear signs of a spatial order of activity zones within the house place (cf. Müller *et al.*, 2016), and their archaeobotanical and archaeozoological remains clear patterns of subsistence organization (cf. Kirleis and Dreibrodt, 2016; Kirleis and dal Corso, 2016). Nevertheless, clear differences are visible between house 44 and house 54. House 54 has a floor size of only *c.* 30 m², is a single-room dwelling, and has only two basic installations—an oven and an 'altar'. House 44 is more than double the size (floor size: *c.* 75 m²), a two-room dwelling, and has several installations. In our opinion, social differences are responsible for such divergent architectural settings, indicating at least different economic power between households.

The deposition of daub in the lower parts of pit 60 seems to indicate a conscious decision to clear older remains of houses from the top soil or any living area

Figure 16. Model of depositional activities related to pit 60. Judging by the ^{14}C-dates a part of a house was deposited in the pit in the 39th century BCE.

of the surrounding. The deposition might indicate the burying of at least part of a house, as no other remains of a half-destroyed house or similar had been found in the ground. Figure 16 displays a model of depositional activities related to pit 60. Judging by the ^{14}C-dates part of a house was deposited in the pit in the 39th century BCE, while in a second stage, in the 38th century BCE, the pit was used for a house; of which the remains are also visible in the burnt *ploschchadki*. If such an interpretation would be valid, the higher nT values of a group of pits in the southwestern area of the site could be interpreted as the remains of the oldest settlement in Maidanetske that is 'stored' in the pits.

In principle, the 2013–2014 excavation indicates, on the one hand, the daily processes within a single household of specific economic power; on the other hand ritual activities, which are linked to festivities and intentional depositions of special purpose. These differences are detected not only in different contexts and the reconstruction of depositional processes, but also in material culture: pits whose fills are interpreted as 'ritual' yield more bowls as tools for the consumption of food (Brandtstätter, in prep.).

REFERENCES

Brandtstätter, L. in prep. Die Keramik aus Maidanetske im Tripolje-Zusammenhang. *Journal of Neolithic Archaeology*.

Burdo, N.B., Videiko, M.Yu., Chabaniuk, V.V., Rassmann, K., Gauss, R., Peters, D. & Lutz, F. 2012. Shirokomashtabnaja geomagnitnaja sjemka v Maidanetskom: sovremennye technicheskie reshenija v izuchenii tripolskih mega-poselenij. *Stratum Plus*, 2:265–86. Бурдо, Н.Б., Видейко, М.Ю., Чабанюк, В. В. Рассманн, К., Гаусс, Р., Петерс, Д. и Лютц, Ф. 2012. Широкомасштабная геомагнитная съемка в Майданецком: современные технические решения в изучении трипольских мега-поселений. Stratum Plus 2: 265–86.

Chapman, J., Gaydarska, B. & Hale, D. 2016. Nebelivka: Assembly Houses, Ditches, and Social Structure. In: J. Müller, K. Rassmann & M. Videiko, eds. *Trypillia Mega-Sites and European Prehistory: 4100–3400 BCE*. London and New York: Routledge, pp. 117–132.

Chapman, J., Videiko, M., Gaydarska, B., Burdo, N. & Hale, D. 2014. Architectural Differentiation on a Trypillia Mega-Site: Preliminary Report on the Excavation of a Mega-Structure at Nebelivka, Ukraine. *Journal of Neolithic Archaeology*, 16: 135–57.

Dudkin, V.P. 1978. Geofizicheskaya razvedka krupnyh tripolskih poselenij. In: V.F. Gening, ed. *Ispolzovanie metodov estestvennyh nauk v arheologii*. Kyiv: Academy Kyiv, pp. 35–45. Дудкин В.П. Геофизическаяразв едка крупных трипольских поселений. В сб.: В.Ф. Генинг, ред. Использование методовестествен ных наук в археологии. Киев: ИА НАНУ, с. 35–45.

Kirleis, W. & Dal Corso, M. 2016. Trypillian Subsistence Economy: Animal and Plant Exploitation. In: J. Müller, K. Rassmann & M. Videiko, eds. *Trypillia Mega-Sites and European Prehistory: 4100–3400 BCE*. London and New York: Routledge, pp. 195–206.

Kirleis, W. & Dreibrodt, S. 2016. The Natural Background: Forest, Forest Steppe or Steppe Environment. In: J. Müller, K. Rassmann & M. Videiko, eds. *Trypillia Mega-Sites and European Prehistory: 4100–3400 BCE*. London and New York: Routledge, pp. 171–180.

Korvin-Piotrovskiy, A.G., Chabanyuk, V. & Shatilo, L. 2012. Tripolian House Construction: Concepts and Experiments. In: F. Menotti & A. Korvin-Piotrovskiy, eds. *The Tripolye Culture Giant-Settlements in Ukraine: Formation, Development and Decline*. Oxford: Oxbow Books, pp. 210–29.

Korvin-Piotrovskiy, A., Hofmann, R., Rassmann, K., Videiko, M. & Brandtstätter, L. 2016. Pottery Kilns in Trypillian Settlements. Tracing the Division of Labour and the Social Organization of Copper Age Communities. In: J. Müller, K. Rassmann & M. Videiko, eds. *Trypillia Mega-Sites and European Prehistory: 4100–3400 BCE*. London and New York: Routledge, pp. 221–252.

Kruts, V., Korvin-Piotrovsky, A. & Rassmann, K. 2014. New discovery of the kilns in the Tripollian giant-settlement Talianki. In: G. Dumitroaja, C. Preoteasa & C.-D. Nicola, eds. *Cucuteni Culture within the European Neo-Eneolithic Context*. Piatra-Neamt: Editura Constantin Matasa, 117–21.

Menotti, F. 2012. Epilogue. In: F. Menotti & A. Korvin-Piotrovskiy, eds. *The Tripolye Culture Giant-Settlements in Ukraine: Formation, Development and Decline*. Oxford: Oxbow Books, pp. 254–5.

Müller, J., Hofmann, R., Brandtstätter, L., Ohlrau, R. & Videiko, M. 2016. Chronology and Demography: How Many People Lived in a Mega-Site? In: J. Müller, K. Rassmann & M. Videiko, eds. *Trypillia Mega-Sites and European Prehistory: 4100–3400 BCE*. London and New York: Routledge, pp. 133–169.

Müller, J., Hofmann, R., Kirleis, W., Ohlrau, R., Brandtstätter, L., Dal Corso, M., Out, V., Rassmann, K. & Videko, M. in print. Maidanetske 2013. *New Excavations at a Trypillia Megasite*. Studien zur Archäologie in Ostmitteleuropa. Bonn: Habelt.

Müller, J., Hofmann, R., Rassmann, K., Mischka, C., Videyko, M. & Burdo, N.B. 2014. Maydanetskoe: Investigations, Based on Updated Plan (Майданецкое: исследования по обновленному плану поселения). *Stratum Plus*, 2: 285–302.

Ohlrau, R. 2014. Tripolje Großsiedlungen. Geomagnetische Prospektion und architektursoziologische Perspektiven. Unpublished Master's thesis, Kiel University.

Rassmann, K., Korvin-Piotrovskiy, A., Videiko, M. & Müller, J. 2016. The New Challenge for Site Plans and Geophysics: Revealing the Settlement Structure of Giant Settlements by Means of Geomagnetic Survey. In: J. Müller, K. Rassmann & M. Videiko, eds. *Trypillia Mega-Sites and European Prehistory: 4100–3400 BCE*. London and New York: Routledge, pp. 29–54.

Rassmann, K., Ohlrau, R., Hofmann, R., Mischka, C., Burdo, N., Videjko, M.Y. & Muller, J. 2014. High Precision Tripolye Settlement Plans, Demographic Estimations and Settlement Organization. *Journal of Neolithic Archaeology*, 16: 96–134.

Shatilo, L. 2014. Reconstruction of the roof shape of neolithic houses in South-Eastern Europe on the example of Tripolian buildings. Sources and problems. In: G. Dumitroaia, C. Preoteasa & N. Ciprian-Dorin, eds. *Cucuteni Culture within the European Neo-Eneolthic Context*. Piatra-Neamt: Editura Constantin Matasa, pp. 113–16.

Shmaglij, N. & Videjko, M. 2003. Maidanetskoe - Aa Tripolian Proto-City. *Stratum Plus*, 2: 44–140. Шмаглий, Н.М. и Видейко, М.Ю. 2003. Майданецкое – трипольский протогород. *Stratum Plus*, 2: 44–140.

Shmaglij, N.M. 1980. Krupnye tripolskie poseleniya v mezhdurechye Dnepra i Yuzhnogo Buga. In: I. I. Artemenko, ed. *Pervobytnaya archeologiya: Poiski i nahodki*. Kiev: Naukova Dumka, pp. 198–203. Шмаглий, Н.М. 1980. Крупные трипольские поселения в междуречье Днепра и Южного Буга. В сб. И.И. Артеменко, ред. *Первобытная археология: поиски и находки*. Киев: Наукова думка, с. 198–203.

Shmaglij, N.M. & Videiko, M.Yu. 2005. *Maidanetskoe – tripolskij protogorod*. Kiev: Institute of Archaeology of the NASU. Шмаглий, Н.М. и Видейко, М.Ю. 2005. Майданецкое – трипольский протогород. Киев: Институт археологии НАНУ.

Shyshkin, K.V. 1973. Z praktyky deshyfruvannya aerofotoznimkiv u arheologicnyh tsiliah. *Arheologiya*, 10: 32–41. Шишкін, К.В. 1973. З практики дешифрування аерофотознімків у археологічних цілях. *Археологія*, 10: 32–41.

Ursu, C.-E. & Terna, S. 2014. Building No. 3 / 2013 discovered at Baia - In Muchie (Suceava County), initial data. In: G. Dumitroaia, C. Preoteasa & N. Ciprian-Dorin, eds. *Cucuteni Culture within the European Neo-Eneolthic Context*. Piatra-Neamt: Editura Constantin Matasa, pp. 98–104.

Videiko, M.Y. 2012. Kompleksnoe izuchenie krupnykh poselenij Tripolskoj kultury: 1971–2011. *Stratum Plus*, 2: 225–63. Комплексное изучение крупных поселений Трипольской культуры: 1971–2011. *Stratum Plus*, 2: 225–63.

Videiko, M., Burdo, N., Müller, J., Hofmann, R., Rassmann, K. & Mischka, C. 2014. Vidnovlennia kompleksnyh doslidzen na velykomy poselenni bilia s. Maidanetskogo. In: D. Kozak, ed. *Archeologichni vidkryttia v Ukraini 2013 roku*. Kyiv, pp. 266–7. Відейко, М.Ю., Бурдо, Н.Б., Мюллер, Й., Хоффманн, Р., Рассманн, К. і Мішка, К. 2014. Відновлення комплексних досліджень на великому поселенні біля с. Майданецького. В зб.: Д. Козак, ред. *Археологічні відкриття в Україні 2013 року*. Київ, 266–67.

Videiko, M.Yu., Müller, J., Burdo, N.B., Hofmann, R. & Tserna, S. 2015. Doslidzhennia u tsentralnij chastyni Maidanetskogo. *Archaeologiya*, 1: 71–78. Відейко, М.Ю., Мюллер, Й., Бурдо, Н.Б., Хоффманн, Р. і Церна, С. 2015. Дослідження у центральній частині Майданецького. *Археологія* 1: 71–78.

CHAPTER 6

Nebelivka: From Magnetic Prospection to New Features of Mega-Sites

NATALIIA BURDO AND MYKHAILO VIDEIKO

The international project at Nebelivka included three field seasons, funded by grants obtained by Prof. John Chapman (Durham University, UK).[1] The Institute of Archaeology of NAS Ukraine, for its part, has provided researchers, obtained the necessary permits for excavations, organized the storage of finds and worked with them, and worked on the field reports. The Kirovohrad region provided administrative support, plus cooperation with the Vynnychenko University and the Kirovohrad Museum of Natural History.

This site was discovered in the 1960s by Vasyl Stefanovych; later K. Shyshkin recognized it as a mega-site of around 300 ha and published a plan, based on aerial photos (Figure 1, 1) (Shyshkin, 1985). Field prospection, organized by Mykola Shmaglij in 1981 gave the possibility to attribute it to the BII stage of the Trypillia Culture (Shmaglij and Videiko, 1992) (Figure 1, 2). Later, Sergij Ryzhov distinguished a local Nebelivka group with two phases. Nebelivka was the largest site from the first phase of this group. This local group was followed by the Tomashivka local group from CI stage (Ryzhov, 1993: 101–14).

Excavations at Nebelivka started with a plan of the site, created by specialists from Durham University (Hale et al., 2010; Chapman et al., 2014a, 2014b). It was an important task to check new kinds of anomalies and their relations to archaeological objects. Between these objects were some features which had never explored before: traces of ditches, the remains of huge dwellings ('mega-structures'), pottery kilns, 'possibly burnt houses'. On the other hand, a lot of anomalies from pits were discovered, which promised other data, which are interesting from different points of view.

After four field seasons (2009, 2012–2014) at Nebelivka, fifteen features had been investigated (Table 1). As of May 2015, the results of research were published over thirty papers (Videiko, 2015: 9–10) and about twenty reports presented at the conference in Kirovograd on 13th–14th May. This, incidentally, means that not only have the main preliminary results of this research been published, but also that the exciting process of its interpretation has begun.

DITCH OR PALISADE?

Traces of the ditch were detected around the site as a line 3–4-m wide. The depth of this feature, detected by coring, was assumed as up to 4 m (Figure 2, 1). Two small sections of this structure were explored: one at the North and one at the South (Figures 2 and 3). The former revealed one line of anomalies, and the second revealed three lines of anomalies. According to predictions from the prospection and coring data, the northern ditch was cut by 4-m wide trench.

The traces of the ditch were clearly visible in profile (Figure 2, 2–3). This ditch was 3–4-m wide on top and 0.4–0.6 m at the bottom. The depth, estimated from the ancient horizon, was around 0.8–0.7 m. The dark fill of this depression was the mixed soil, rather than the fill of an open ditch. In this fill and around it, a few small fragments of pottery and burnt daub were found.

The southern ditches were explored with a trench 2-m wide. The traces of these features were not so clearly visible, but the trench was located close to places determined by geomagnetic prospection (Figure 3, 1). Only one thing was clear—they were not as deep as those in the North and they were no wider than 1 m. The features were located on a slope, so it is possible that the top part of soil here was damaged by erosion (Figure 3). Explorations in both trenches confirmed the presence of the ditch, but revealed it to be smaller than previously supposed.

There are two points of view on this feature. The first—it was a small ditch, some symbolic border/enclosure of the settlement (J. Chapman). The second—it was a ditch, which was made for the construction of palisades (M. Videiko) (Figure 14, 6). The character of its fill (mixed soil) supports the latter view.

---

[1] Arts and Humanities Research Council (AHRC) Grant No. AH/I025867: 2012–2016; investigations of 'mega-structures' from National Geographic Society, Grant No. 2012/211

Figure 1. *Nebelivka, Trypillia BII site: (1) plan after K. Shyshkin, superimposed on the satellite image; (2) pottery from the 1981 field survey by M. Shmaglij.*

In the case of an open ditch-enclosure, all profiles would have shown clear traces of sediments. At Nebelivka in any case, sediments were recorded. Absence of traces of pillars indicates that they may have been disposed of at the moment of leaving the settlement. This does not preclude the mixed soil in the ditch filling.

A similar feature was explored by Natalja Skakun at Bodaky, a Trypillia BII flint workshop site at Ternopil domain. This ditch had a 2-m width and a 0.6–0.7-m depth, plus a triangular profile with a black fill (Videiko et al., 2005: 14, figures 25–28, 35). The same kind of anomalies are well known from investigations in Central and Northern Europe, where excavations confirmed the existence of palisades (Raczky and Anders, 2012: figures 7 and 14; Turek, 2012: 185, 201).

Investigations of Kiln Area

After discovery in 2013 of the remains of three pottery kilns at Taljanky, where they were detected by

Table 1. *Nebelivka, British–Ukrainian investigations 2009, 2012–2014*

Objects from geomagnetic plan	Tr. No, Year, team explored	Total number of objects explored	Bibliography
Burnt house	1 (2009, U) 3 (2013, U)	2	Chapman et al. (2010), Chapman & Videiko (2011), Videiko et al. (2013a, 2013b, 2014a); Videiko (2015)
Probable house	5(2014,U)	1	Videiko et al. (2015), Rud (2015)
'Mega-structure'	2 (2012 B,U)	1	Burdo (2014a, 2014b, 2014c), Burdo & Videiko (2014a), Chapman et al. (2014c), Fedorov (2015), Gaydarska (2015), Korvin-Piotrovskiy (2015), Shevchenko (2015), Videiko et al. (2014), Videiko (2014), Videiko & Burdo (2015a, 2015b)
Pit	1 (A9); 4(B5)3 (near B17 and B18, 2013 U),4 (2013–14 B); 8 (2014, U)	9	Videiko et al. (2014a, 2014b, 2015)
Kiln	8 (2014, U)	1	Videiko et al. (2015)
Ditch/palisade	9,10 (2014, U)	1	Videiko et al. (2015)
2009–2014		15	

B: British team; U: Ukrainian team.

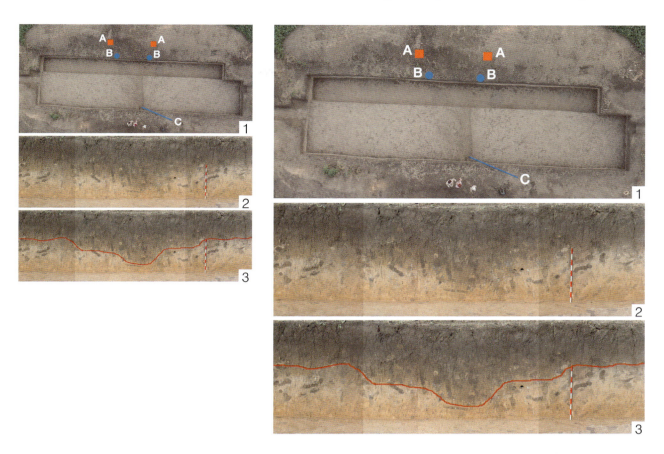

Figure 2. Nebelivka 2014, excavations of a ditch in the northern part of the site: (1) trench 8 from helicopter (photo by Boiko and Boiko), (A) marks the trench according to the geomagnetic prospection; (B) displays the real edges of the ditch; (C) the bottom of ditch; (2 and 3) the profiles of ditch.

geomagnetic prospection in 2012 (Kruts *et al.*, 2014), the three similar anomalies were proposed for further investigations at Nebelivka. Two of them were modern features with numerous iron items, but one feature appeared consistent with remains of the Trypillia Culture period (Figures 4–6). The strong anomaly, nearly 2 m in diameter, corresponded with an abandoned pottery kiln. Another, not so strong, but 5 × 4 m-sized feature corresponded with a pit, located near the feature assumed to be a kiln. This group of anomalies is situated in the southerneast sector of the central part of the site. They are at the end of one of the radial 'streets'. From the point of view of the Durham team, the function of this object is controversial. The Ukrainian team, however, basing their interpretation on the excavations of the Taljanky kilns (Kruts *et al.*, 2014), determined this object to be a pottery kiln (Figure 14, 5).

The remains of the kiln, represented by a 2 × 2 m clay platform with four walls, formed one construction, created from the same material on top (Figures 4, 2 and 5, 1, 2, and 5). Three channels between them were up to 0.2–0.25-m wide. The walls, 0.25–0.3-m high, were rounded on top with a surface which was heavy burnt. The use of only fire-proof plastering preserved it from destruction (Figure 5, 4). Inside the walls, some stones were visible (Figures 5, 5 and 6, 2). At the edges of the platform, some traces of plastering on its dome were preserved. The fireplace of this kiln was northwest-oriented and faced towards the pit located 1.2 m away from it.

Remains of the kiln were buried under a layer of broken clay constructions, which had a green colour and were probably used to cover the channels during the burning process. They were mixed with soil, fragments of pottery, and animal bones. A fragment of a clay human figurine also was found inside one of the channels (Figure 6, 2). The surface around this feature was covered with numerous fragments of broken channel covers and fragments of pottery (Figure 4, 1). This pottery does not have traces of secondary burning, as was the case for the Taljanky kilns (see Kruts *et al.*, 2014). There are some finds of fragmented pottery, which were mixed in with the surface of clay covers.

The pit which was discovered by geomagnetic prospection close to the remains of the kiln was only partly explored. It was large feature, filled with

Figure 3. Nebelivka 2014, excavations of the ditch in the southern part of the site: (1) trench 10; (A) marks the context as detected by the geomagnetic prospection; (C) displays traces of ditches in the profile; (D) other pits; (2) explored part of the ditch.

numerous fragments of pottery (without traces of secondary burning), animal bones, broken covers of kiln channels, stones, and a few flint tools, distributed across four layers (Figure 6, 3). Starting from the top part of the pit (0.4–0.6 m from the contemporary surface), thirty-one fragments from thirty human figurines and two fragmented animal figurines were found. The depth of the pit was up to 1.4 m from ancient surface. At the deepest part, sediments that appeared after the heavy rains were clear visible.

The aforementioned finds, especially the broken clay covers of channels, were probably connected with the activities related to the pottery kiln. However, it looks like this feature was abandoned some time before people left the settlement. For some time, this place was used for rubbish (broken covers, pottery, and bones) and some rituals, in which numerous clay human and animal figurines were used. The nearest kiln-like anomaly we can see lies 10–15 m to the West of the explored area. A similar grouping of kilns fwas noted through geomagnetic prospection at Maidanetske and Taljanky, and in the latter case it was also confirmed by excavations (Videiko *et al.*, 2015).

Dwellings: Households and Temple

In 2009–2014, the remains of six dwellings were explored, four completely and two partly (Figures 9–13). They represent three kinds of anomalies shown

Figure 4. Nebelivka 2014, excavations in the kiln area: (1) trench 9 at the beginning of the excavations; (2) trench 9—in view from helicopter close to the final stage of explorations (photo by Boiko and Boiko).

on the plan of Nebelivka: burnt houses, 'probable houses', and 'mega-structures'. The second and the third groups of features at Trypillia sites were excavated here for the first time.

Burnt houses

This kind of remains is represented by rectangular depositions of burnt daub pieces of different size with a thickness from 5–10 cm up to 30–40 cm in different parts (houses A9, B17, and B18). In these depositions, sometimes details of interior, clay-like platforms from ovens or fireplaces, altars, bins, thresholds, and other features, are visible (Table 2). At Nebelivka, the remains of burnt houses usually had two or more layers of daub with imprints of wooden constructions.

The top layer in most cases was destroyed by ploughing, because the depth of deposition started from 0.2 m below the modern surface (Figures 7, 1 and 8, 1–2). This level is associated with the remains of a garret, sometimes overlapping a fragment of a wall that fell inside or outside the building. The remains of the overlying garret are identifiable in this case by tree imprints on daub, which are oriented across the long axis of the building. Fragments of walls are identifiable by wood imprints along the long axis of building and prints of sticks, but also by the remains of clay plastering with traces of paint and wall-painting, especially at house B17 (Figure 8, 4).

The lower layer of daub was associated with the ceiling of the first floor and the second floor. Imprints of wood in this layer are usually across the long axis of the building. The thickness of the plaster ranges from 5–8 to 10–14 cm; it was usually applied in two or three layers of 3–4 cm each. This surface was covered with a layer of clay that is stained with red paint. Preservation of this paint is usually poor, but it was present in most of the remains of houses (Table 2).

Open fires or stoves were used for heating. Their remains are presented by massive platforms of clay 20–40-cm thick and around 2 × 2 m in size (Figures 7, 4 and 8, 2). These platforms were built on the lower layer of plaster coating to the right of the entrance. The edifice used vertical supports to support the overlapping load; their imprints were recorded during the excavation of buildings A9 and B17.

Figure 5. Nebelivka 2014, excavations in the kiln area: (1) kiln, covered by waste; (2) kiln after being cleaned from waste; (3) materials, including part of a figurine, found inside the channels of the kiln; (4) heavily burnt wall of the channel, enlarged; (5) kiln after being cleaned from waste; (6) reconstructed cover of the channels; (7) use of covers (reconstruction); (8) kiln and pit at the final stage of excavation; (9) fragment of a figurine in the pit near the kiln.

Altars were discovered at houses A9 (2) and B17 (3) on both layers: on the ground and first floors. They consist of two to three well-burnt layers of small, clay, tile-like fragments 2–3-cm thick (Figures 7, 5 and 8, 3 and 5). At house B17, altars were decorated with incised lines and red paint. The fragmented

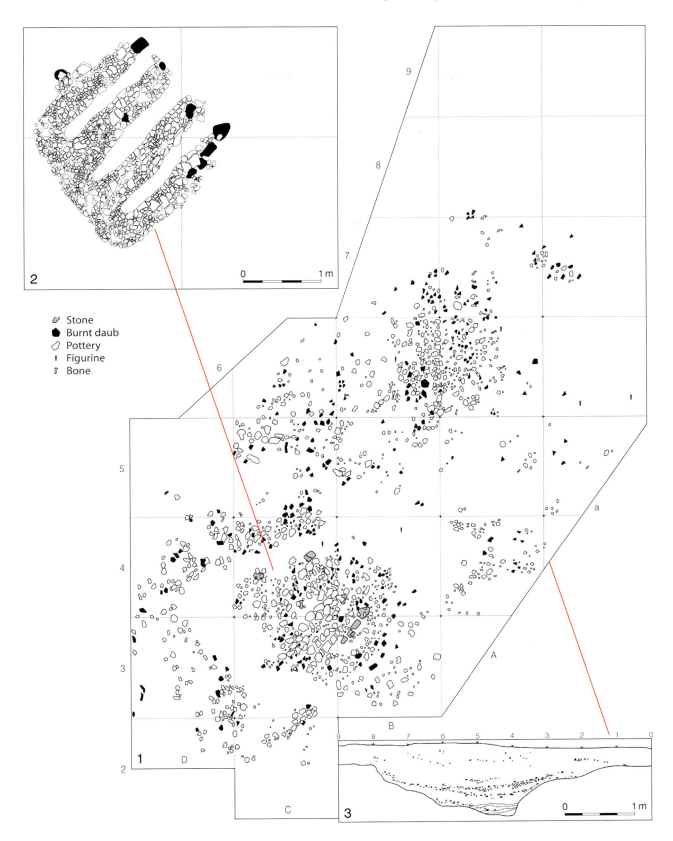

Figure 6. Nebelivka 2014, excavations in the kiln area: (1) plan of trench 9 at the beginning of the excavations; (2) kiln; (3) profile of the pit.

Figure 7. Nebelivka 2009, excavations of burnt house A9: (1) general view from E; (2) N part of house remains; (3) imprints of wood on daub and on the surface below it; (4) platform from the oven/fireplace; (5) elevation/altar under the daub layer; (6 and 7) fragmented binocular vessels.

Figure 8. Nebelivka 2013, excavations of burnt house B17: (1) general view from SW; (2) part of platform from the oven/fireplace and traces of ploughing; (3) remains of an altar under the daub; (4) fragment of a wall-painting; (5) fragment of an altar; (6) edges of a decorated dolly tub; (7) part of a profile with two layers of burnt daub.

edges of this construction were rounded, reminiscent of the details of cross-like altars, known from former excavations at Trypillia sites and ceramic models of buildings.

Finds of pottery (complete vessels) were associated with the lower layer and the space under it. From house A9 originate five bowls, six small goblets, four small vessels, five large vessels, one 'kitchen' pot, and three binocular vessels. From house B17, we have four bowls, two large goblets (one with a handle), four large vessels, and two 'kitchen' pots. In both cases, we see the absence of some categories of vessels

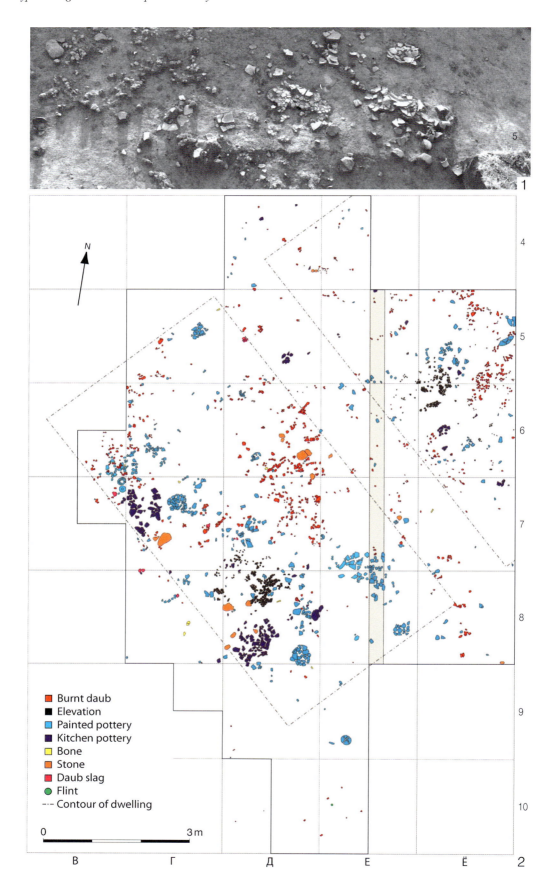

Figure 9. Nebelivka 2014, excavations of 'probable houses' in trench 5: (1) part of house 1, distribution of daub and pottery; (2) plan of trench 5 (after V. Rud).

Figure 10. Nebelivka 2012, excavations of dwelling B5—'mega-structure': (1) W part of trench with traces of ploughing (A), the direction of plough-marks is identical to the present-day orientation of the crops in the field; (2) W part of the trench with clearly visible black fill from the top part of the pit near dwelling B5 ((1 and 2)—photo by Mark Household); (3) profile with remains of dwelling B5 and the ploughing layer above; (4) remains of altar 2 in the profile.

known from Nebelivka pits, including big storage vessels.

A lot of fragments of pottery, mainly small ones (up to 30–40 per 2 × 2 m grid), were deposited around the remains of houses. They were accompanied by fragments of animal bones. In all profiles, it is clearly visible that around burnt houses a cultural layer up to 30-cm thick formed, which is absent under the burnt daub[2]. This means that loess soil was used in the period when the houses were constructed. This layer is also visible as geomagnetic anomalies around the

---

[2] A similar situation was documented at Maidanetske—see Müller & Videiko, 2015, Figure 3, 2.

Figure 11. *Nebelivka 2012, excavations of dwelling B5—'mega-structure': (1) the remains at the first stage of the excavations; (2) reconstruction of the frame system based on imprints ((1 and 2)—photo by Mark Household); (3)—part of a deposition with traces of a timber construction; (4) reconstruction of the destruction process; (5) sample of daub with visible layers; (6) daub with imprints of round timber construction and cord connection.*

explored house and many other burnt houses at Nebelivka.

House A9 is an example of the usual two-storeyed family dwelling with a fireplace on the first floor. House B17 is larger and had a more sophisticated interior with two fireplaces on the first floor and three altars, two of them on ground floor. The owner was likely linked to the temple[3] located at a distance of 30 m, which might explain the size and unusual interior of this house.

---

[3]Mega-structure, dwelling B5.

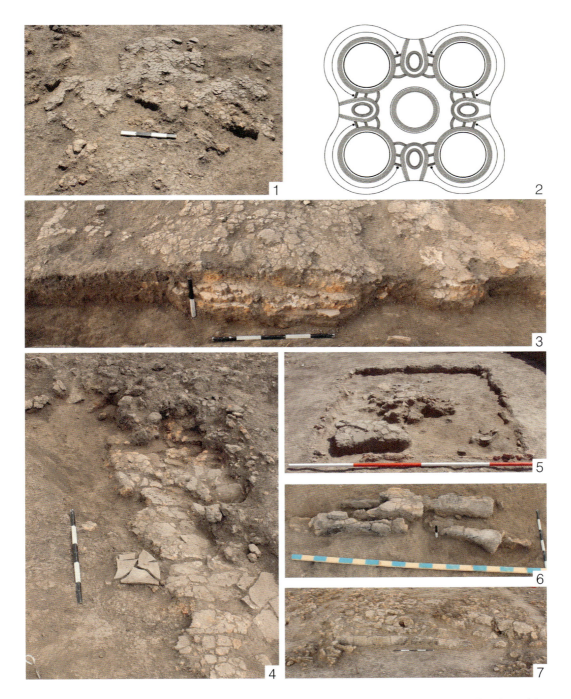

Figure 12. Nebelivka 2012, excavations of dwelling B5—'mega-structure': (1) remains of a cross-like altar; (2) reconstructed decoration of the altar (after S. Fedorov); (3) profile of the altar 1 with multiple layers (renewals); (4) podium on the lower layer of daub, partly buried under the upper layer of daub; (5) clay dolly tub with a millstone; (6) remains of a threshold and decoration from the doorframe; (7) remains of the 1.7-m wide threshold at the eastern entrance.

'Probable houses' (trench 5/2014)

Anomalies, named as 'probable houses', were numbered up to twenty-one per cent of the remains of houses at Nebelivka (Rud, 2015: 26). In 2013, part of such a feature was explored with a 1 × 4 m test-pit in the outer row of houses, when some broken pots and small fragments of burnt daub were found. In the 2014 season, the larger area here was investigated (Rud, 2015; Videiko *et al.*, 2015). The remains of dwellings were discovered at a depth of 0.4–0.5 m from the contemporary surface. They formed close to rectangular structures, created by small fragments of burnt daub, broken pottery, including different kinds

Figure 13. Nebelivka 2013, excavations of pit B17/1: (1) pit and house B17, view from W; (2) layer of finds on the edge of the pit; (3) figurine between the fragments of pottery; (4) part of the profile at the deepest part of pit B17/1; (5) layer of finds on the edge of the pit, view from SW; (6) edge of pit B17/1 and profile from E.

of vessels, stones, and clay platforms on the ground floor—destroyed elements of the interior (Figure 9).

From house 1 originate no less than nineteen items: a bowl, a semi-spherical bowl, six goblets, seven bi-conical vessels, a pear-like vessel, a pot, and two 'kitchen pots'—no less than from the normal (and larger) houses A9 and B17, as described before. The situation with storage vessels is the same.

The character of pottery burning, its distribution and deposition, the amount of burnt daub (with admixture of plants), and pieces of slag-like daub provided clear evidence that these two features in this

Table 2. Excavations of dwellings in Nebelivka: 2009–2014

Dwelling/year of excavation	Size, m	No. of floors	Oven/fireplace	Dolly tub	Altar	Podium	Painted floor/walls	Pit
A9/2009	5–6 × 18	2	1	–	2?	1?	+	1
B5/2012	20–24 × 66	2	1	1	7	1	+	3
B17/2013	5.5–8 × 24	2	2	–	3	–	+	1
B18/2013	? × 20	2	1	–	–	–	+	1
1/2014	4.3 × 8.2	2	1?	–	–	–	–	–
2/2014	c. 4 × 8	2	1?	–	–	–	–	–

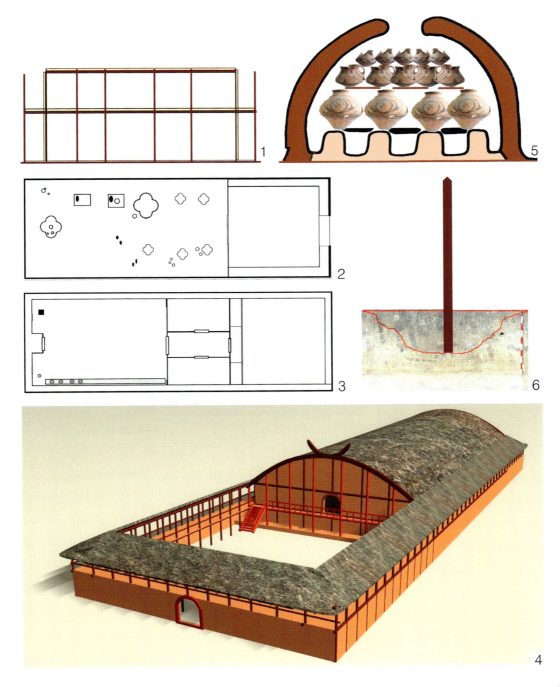

Figure 14. Nebelivka, reconstruction of investigated features: (1) frame construction of dwelling B5; (2) dwelling B5, plan of the ground floor; (3) dwelling B5, plan of the first floor; (4) dwelling B5, reconstructed as a temple (3D by M. M. Videiko); (5) profile of kiln; (6) profile of palisade.

area were burnt, as occurred to other houses to the left and to the right of this place. It is possible to suppose that the amount of burnt daub in such a case depends on

(a) the amount of clay used for construction of the house;
(b) the process of burning, different here from the surroundings. The last feature is similar to central part of the mega-structure (dwelling B5) investigated in 2012.

There is no reason now to examine all the remains of this type of building as objects left without burning or as some different phase of site development.

Mega-structure: temple

Interpretations of this object now have an impressive bibliography, which rapidly increased last year with the appearance of three (or more?) possible reconstructions (Chapman et al., 2014b; Gaydarska, 2015; Korvin-Piotrovskiy, 2015; Videiko and Burdo, 2015a).

Excavations confirmed the size and configuration of the structure (Figure 11, 1). It consisted of burnt daub with imprints of wood, which are usually recognized as the remains of burnt houses (Shevchenko, 2015). The remains of some elements, such as clay platforms, started at 0.2–0.4 m below the surface. Traces of ploughing were cleaned by the Durham team in the western part of the trench at a depth of 0.4–0.5 m from the modern surface during the second week of excavations (Figure 10, 1). The same traces were visible on the eastern side of the trench. This means that a lot of objects were destroyed or removed (for example, pieces from a binocular vessel which was on the altar elevation) by ploughing, which partly changed the picture of mega-structure destruction which we documented in 2012 (Figure 10, 3–4). It means that we can speak about finds and features *in situ* only starting from depth of more than 0.5 m from the contemporary surface.

Dwelling B5 diverged from the normal houses mainly in its size and also in some elements of design. The first circumstance gives us the possibility to work with these remains according to the conventional procedure of investigations, documenting, and interpretation of dwellings remains from Trypillia sites (Chapman et al., 2014a, 2014b, 2014c : tables 1 and 4).

The remains of the structure were oriented almost West-East along its long side. They consisted of two parts: an accumulation of burnt daub fragments (western part, nearly 20–24 × 38–40 m) and an area partly surrounded by narrow (1–1.5 m) lines of burnt daub fragments (eastern part, nearly 20 × 20 m) (Figure 11, 1). In the western part, two layers of burnt daub were investigated, associated with the plastering of wooden constructions which belonged to overlapping structures of the loft (upper layer) and the level ceiling (lower layer). Both layers of daub had imprints of different wooden constructions. Examination of all imprints gave the evidence for the reconstruction of the wooden skeleton of the structure (Figure 11, 2–6).

On the upper layer, only imprints of planks were found. The direction of most imprints was South–North, which means perpendicular to the long side of the structure, as is usually the case when exploring Trypillia Culture dwellings. These imprints are associated with 3.5–4-m planks up to 10-cm thick. They were enough to hold 5–7 cm of plaster made from clay mixed with straw. The construction of the loft ceiling was perhaps supported by the same system of frame construction as the level ceiling (see below).

The lower layer demonstrated not only imprints of planks, but also of the numerous round beams which belonged to a sophisticated frame construction (Figures 11, 2 and 14, 1). In many cases, the location of beams was well visible after the cleaning of the upper layer. This was possible because the plaster was broken exactly along the line of beams (Figure 11, 3–4). The discovery of these lines gave us a picture of the horizontal frame construction. All imprints which were detected here belonged to round beams 20–25 cm in diameter. On some daub pieces, imprints of ropes were also visible, which were used to fasten these beams to other parts of the frame, probably to poles (Figure 11, 6).

The horizontal frame consisted of 3.5 × 4–4 × 4 (4.5) m sections (Figure 11, 2). Such a size is comparable with the width of usual Cucuteni-Trypillia dwellings (4–5.5 m). As such, it was possible to cover each frame with 3.5–4.5-m planks. It was a nice solution for creating an impressive structure 20-m wide and 38-m long. The long sides were created from eleven to twelve such sections, for the short side up to six. It means that this construction also included up to ninety-one (7 × 13) poles, which also supported the frames of the loft construction.

Such a strong construction of a frame would have created a good foundation for the first floor rooms. The plan of this part of the 'mega-structure' (Figure 14, 4) is based on the finds of the remains of thresholds and the location of such details of the interior as a long elevation or podium (nearly 18 × 0.4 m) (Figure 12, 4) and the round elevation (up to 2 m in diameter). Such elements of the interior are usual and well known for smaller Cucuteni-Trypillia dwellings; in case of Nebelivka structure, only the size was different. All aforementioned objects were associated with the lower layer of burnt daub.

On the eastern side, a 1.7-m wide threshold located exactly in the middle of structure (Figure 12, 7). It was based on a beam from the front frame of the construction. To the left and to the right, postholes from vertical poles were visible. The eastern entrance is also located in the middle of the frame. The remains of the next two thresholds are located on both sides of the next (the second) frame to the West (Figure 12, 6). It means that here were entrances to two large rooms, opening onto an around 4-m wide and up to 12-m corridor, at the end of which the fourth, 2.2-m wide, threshold was found. Here was entrance to the largest room with the long podium under the southern wall. It was attached to the wall, which was clearly seen in a few places. All rooms, especially the largest, were divided by rows of frame construction poles.

The last threshold is located in the middle of the western side, also based on the beam of frame construction. Here was a western wall of the central hall of the structure. At this part of structure, but in front of this wall, a round elevation was also located, associated with a fireplace, as is usual for Cucuteni-Trypillia house construction and size. It means that there was a room here, suitable for year-round occupation; the only one in this structure.

From three sides, the lodges of the first floor were surrounded by an open gallery, associated with a daub horizon of the ceiling, which extended out 1.5 m from the line of the walls. This gallery construction was continued at the eastern end of the mega-structure, where its remains were represented by 1–1.5 m lines of burnt daub with imprints of wood on the bottom (Figures 10, 1 and 14, 2–5).

The ground floor level was marked by the remains of seven fired-clay platforms of different sizes, but with the same construction. One of them was cross-like in form (4.3 × 4.3 m) and located on the axis of symmetry close to the western side of structure. The other six are situated close to the eastern side in two equal groups (three in each), to the left and to the right to axis of symmetry (Figure 14, 2). Under the northern wall, the remains of two bins with stones inside were discovered. The placement of all features was coordinated with the location of posts which divided the space of the ground floor. The floor was levelled and covered by brown clay plaster (up to 6-cm thick) which was not burnt.

The yard, located on the eastern side, was nearly 20 × 20 m in size and surrounded by a gallery, maybe with an external wall. No traces of an entrance were found, but it is possible that it was opposite the entrance to the first floor. In the area of the yard (near 400 m^2), only approximately hundred fragments of pottery and animal bones were found. This demonstrated a big difference with the cultural layer around other three sides of the structure, where over 1500 such finds were found. It is visible on kite images that the colour of this place was black, like the top fill of the pit (Figure 10, 2). Unfortunately, we were unable to investigate most of this place.

It is also interesting that there is a 0.4 m difference between the levels of the yard and the ground floor, which means that this part of the mega-structure possibly stood on a slight elevation. Maybe this feature appeared because there is a small slope here which was necessary to level out in the process of erection of the mega-structure. This feature possibly also had some symbolical significance.

We have no direct evidence about the construction of the roof. It is possible to suppose that it looks like those on pottery models of houses, which were found on sites of the Nebelivka group: arched (probably from rush mats) with conventional bull horns over the pediment.

Platforms 1–7 could possibly be recognized as altars. Cross-like altars with painted surfaces and incised decoration are well known from excavations at Volodymyrivka, Maidanetske, and other BII–CI sites in this region, as well as from the pottery models of dwellings found in this region. Altars/platforms 1 and 2 stand out due to their size, which is two to three times greater than usual. Altar/platform 5 demonstrated a nice sample of decoration by paint and incised lines after restoration, which was done first time for this kind of feature (Figure 12, 1 and 2). The system of ornament is similar to the decoration of the large storage vessels. The altars were repaired several times: first—up to seven to eight times, second—three to four times, the others—two to three times. Each layer was burnt during use (Figure 11, 5). Near the second altar, fragments of binocular vessels were found; on the first altar—a large broken pot and two bowls. Platform 8 from the first floor was recognized as the remains of a fireplace, partly destroyed in the centre. Near this fireplace, two broken pots were found. A clay dolly tub was located close to platform 2 (Figure 12, 5). The bottom was partly burnt. On it remained some clay construction (in the central part) and a large granite millstone. A broken pot was found in the corner. The corners of the bin were probably decorated with some modelled features which were not preserved. From the second bin, located near the first to the West, only a piece of its corner and few pieces of its wall were preserved. In its vicinity were also found pieces of the large millstones. Such bins are known from excavations of Cucuteni-Trypillia sites, but usually the largest were not as large as this one. Ritual milling and production of bread was a usual thing for sanctuaries.

All other features related to the first floor of a mega-structure. Clay thresholds are situated at two entrances at the East and West. The eastern threshold

(1.7-m wide) is twice as large as the thresholds usually known from excavations of Trypillia dwellings. Nearby, part of clay arch was found, which probably decorated the frame of this door. The central threshold to the largest room was 2.2-m wide. Such doors are comparable with the width of entrances to temples from Mesopotamia. Near the one threshold, the remains of clay decoration from the doorframe were found (Figure 12, 6).

The podium with three large storage vessels was located under the southern wall in the largest room on the first floor. Here were also several of the usual painted vessels and bowls. The podium surface was painted in white, while storage vessels were painted in red. The volume of each vessel was around fifty litres and they were probably used for the storage of grain. On the surface of the podium, numerous burnt bones of lamb, associated with sacrifice, were also found. The floors and walls of all rooms on the first floor were decorated with red paint, which created a ceremonial atmosphere.

On the ground floor of the mega-structure were concentrated all of the altars and bins, which were used for rituals and sacrifices. Its square, free of platforms and bins, was around 600 m^2, which is enough space for a few hundred people. Gardens previously had an area of around 300 m^2, with available space for 200–300 people at one time. The division of the first floor into rooms decreased the potential number of visitors. It is likely that the two rooms around corridor were used for storage. In the southern room were found a large pot, two bowls, and twenty-two small pots around them. The small room on the first floor with a fireplace was the only one in this dwelling which would have been suitable for year-round occupation and/or cooking.

The area of the Nebelivka mega-structure included elements usual for ancient temples: sacred places for sacrifice (altars/platforms), an open-air yard enclosed on all sides in front of the entrance from the East, rooms for storage and ceremonies for some people on the first floor, a small living room for personnel. Some elements of the interior, such as altars 1 and 2, the bins, the podium, and the thresholds at the main entrances, were created similar to those of the usual houses, only two to three times larger (Figure 14, 4).

The Nebelivka mega-structure is located in the internal row of houses, but it probably was built before it, since the orientation of the nearest dwellings was changed to include B5 in the planning system. At Nebelivka, only one construction of such a size was discovered. Its construction, planning, interior details, as well as also its size and location within the settlement (at one of the highest points) distinguished it from other dwellings at this site. We have all the motives and enough evidence to determine it to be a central temple for the whole village community.

Pits: The 'Dairy' of the Ancient Households and Craft

The number of anomalies interpreted at Nebelivka as ancient pits is the same or great than the number of anomalies from houses. In 2009–2014, three kinds of these features were investigated: those related to households (6), those linked to building activities (2), and a kiln (1). Pits of the first group were studied in trenches 3 (near houses B17 and B18) and 4 (close to the external row of houses in the southern-west part of site). To this group possibly belonged the feature located to the West of the houses B5 and A9. All pits were large in size and were only partly explored.

Pit B17/1 started close to remains of a house and continued to the border of the trench, which was at a distance of 14 m (Figure 13, 1). The contours at the upper part were identified by a spread of numerous fragments of pottery and animal bones. Some fragments of clay human figurines were also found. Starting from 0.8 to 1.2 from the contemporary surface in some places, this find formed a continuous layer with some groups of material (Figure 13, 2, 3, and 5). This layer marked the pit slope, which was not too steep at this part. Only close to centre (at a depth of up to 1.6–1.7 m) did it become deeper, ending nearly 3 m from surface.

The final black soil fill of the pit, which was more predominant in the central part of the pit, was very visible in both profiles (Figure 13, 1 and 6). This means that at the time when house B17 was abandoned, this pit was only partly filled by waste and natural sediments. This fill was also clearly visible in profile and included over 8000 fragments of pottery, 2000 animal bones, destroyed burnt clay platforms, some flint tools, and seventeen fragments of human figurines. These finds created a 15–20-cm layer on the sides of pit, which was the most intense on the side closest to dwelling B17. Some figurines were deposited inside piles of bones and fragments of dishes. In the lower part of the pit were two 2–3 cm layers of charcoal, separated by a layer of yellow clay sediments. The same sediments, which included fragmented pottery, bones, and figurines, were also present at the base of the pit (Figure 13, 4).

The fills of other pits of this type, which were only partly explored (pit B18/1—with a 2-m trench, in trench 4—only the central part to some depth), were similar, including the Chernozem on top, figurines, charcoal, and clay sediments at the bottom.

Under the remains of dwelling B5 two pits were explored, which appeared at the time when mega-structure was created. They were relatively small with a depth of around 1–1.2 m from the floor of the building. Pit 1, close to platform 2, had a fill composed of pieces of 'chocolate clay' on its base, which was used for levelling the surface of the ground floor. The rest of the pit was filled with loess soil with a few fragments of pottery on top. In pit 2, located close to the platform/altar on other side of the dwelling, were also only a few fragments of pottery. At the time of use of the mega-structure, both pits were not visible on the surface of the ground floor.

All aforementioned pits were important sources for different kinds of clay, which was used for plastering walls and floors, and probably appeared at the time when dwellings were created. Later, most of them were used not only for 'waste' deposition, but also for some rituals. There is a difference between pottery assemblages of pits of type 1 and related houses. For example, in pits large storage and pear-like vessels were deposited, which are totally absent in the explored houses. Further studies of these assemblages may be important not only for the reconstruction of everyday life, but also for some details of the ritual of abandoning houses at Trypillia sites.

SUMMARY

During four seasons at Nebelivka, several objects were investigated which changed the image of mega-sites. They were large public buildings ('mega-structure'), fortifications (symbolic ditch or real palisade), and a kiln (Figure 14). This 'triad' marked such well-known features of urbanization, as monumental architecture and developed craft, which as some people still believe, were totally absent in Trypillia (see, for example, Tolochko, 2015: 32). Magnetic prospection discovered not only one large building, but also an impressive system of more than ten smaller objects, which later became common features for other mega-sites, like Dobrovody, Petreni, and Maidanetske. The kiln explored at Nebelivka is now the earliest of eight similar devices, discovered in 2013–2014 at Trypillia sites in Ukraine[4]. The characteristics of the furnace put a stop to long discussions of whether there was a developed craft economy at large sites or not. Investigations of the households, which included houses and pits, were important for the reconstruction of different aspects of life at the large sites. New data obtained during excavations in Nebelivka substantially complemented data from large Trypillia settlements.

REFERENCES

Belenko, M.M. 2010. Kremjanyj material z poselennia Nebelivka. *Archeologiya i davnia istoriya Ukrainy*, 3:15–17. Беленко М.М. 2010 Крем'яний матеріал з поселення Небелівка, *Археологія та давня історія України*, 3: 15–17.

Boiko, O. & Boiko, S. 2015. Dosvid vyvchennia pamjatok trypilskoi kultury metodamy aerophotozjomky. In: M. Yu. Videiko, J. Chapman, I.A. Kozyr & V.V. Sobchuk, eds. *Na shidnij mezhi Staroi Evropy. Materialy Mizhnarodnoi konferentsii, Kirovograd, Nebelivka 12–14 tarvnia 2015 roku*. Kirovograd, pp. 38–39. Бойко, О. і Бойко, С. 2015ю Досвід вивчення пам'яток трипільської культури методами аерофотозйомки. У зб.: М.Ю. Відейко, Дж. Чепмен, І.А. Козир і В.В. Собчук, ред. *На східній межі Старої Європи. Матеріали міжнародної наукової конференції, Кіровоград, Небелівка, 12–14 травня 2015 року*. Кіровоград, с. 38–39. In: M. Videiko, J. Chapman, I. Kozir, V. Sobchuk, eds. *At the eastern frontiers of Old Europe. Proceedings of the International Conference in Kirovograd and Nebelivka, May 12–14 2015*. Kirovograd, museum, pp. 38–39.

Burdo, N. 2014a. Anthropomorphic Plastic Art of Trypillia Culture: Dialectic of Similarities and Differences. In: C.-E. Ursu & S. Țerna, eds. *Anthropomorphism and Symbolic Behaviour in the Neolithic and Copper Age Communities of South-Eastern Europe*. Suceava: Karl A. Romstorfer, pp. 303–64.

Burdo, N. & Videiko, M. 2014a. The Temple on the Trypillia Mega-site of Nebelivka. In: N. Başgelen, Ö. Yilmaz & D. Mazlum, eds. 20th Annual Meeting of the European Association of Archaeologists 10–14 September 2014 Istanbul – Turkey. *Abstracts*. Istanbul: Archaeology & Art Publications Tur. San. ve Tic. Ltd Șt, p. 411.

Burdo, N.B. 2014b. Interior of the Nebelivka Temple. In: G. Dumitroaia, C. Preoteasa & C.-D. Nicola, eds. Cucuteni Culture within the European Neo-Eneolithic Context: International Colloquium Cucuteni – 130: abstracts: Piatra-Neamț, 15–17 octombrie 2014. Piatra-Neamț: 'Constantin Matasă', pp. 79–82.

Burdo, N.B. 2014c. Antopomorphni figurky trypilskogo poselennia Nebelivka. *Archeologiya i davnia istoriya Ukrainy*, 1 (12):79–83. Бурдо, Н.Б. 2014. Антропоморфні фігурки трипільського поселення Небелівка. *Археологія і давня історія України*, 1 (12): 79–83.

Burdo, N.B. 2015. Antropomorfna plastyka z Nebelivky. In: M.Yu. Videiko, J. Chapman, I.A. Kozyr & V. V. Sobchuk, eds. *Na shidnij mezhi Staroi Evropy. Materialy Mizhnarodnoi konferentsii, Kirovograd, Nebelivka 12–14 tarvnia 2015 roku*. Kirovograd, pp. 29–32. Бурдо, Н.Б. 2015. Антропоморфна пластика з Небелівки. У зб.: М.Ю. Відейко, Дж. Чепмен, І.А. Козир і В.В. Собчук, ред. *На східній межі Старої Європи. Матеріали міжнародної наукової конференції, Кіровоград, Небелівка, 12–14 травня 2015 року*.Кіровоград, с. 29–32. In: A. Diachenko, F. Menotti, S. Ryzhov, K. Bunyatyan and S. Kadrow, eds. *The Cucuteni–Trypillia Cultural Complex and its*

---

[4] See more details about new discovered kilns: Korvin-Piotrovskij, 2015.

Neighbours. Essays in Memory of Volodymyr Kruts. Kiev 'Astrolabe', pp. 29–32.

Chapman, J. 2014a. Settlement Planning at the Trypillia Mega-Site of Nebelivka – Improvisation and Adaptation. In: N. Başgelen, Ö. Yilmaz & D. Mazlum, eds. *20th Annual Meeting of the European Association of Archaeologists 10–14 September 2014 Istanbul - Turkey. Abstracts of the oral and the poster presentations*. Istanbul: Archaeology & Art Publications Tur. San. ve Tic. Ltd Şt, p. 408.

Chapman, J. 2014b. Settlement Planning of the Trypillia Mega-Site of Nebelivka. In: G. Dumitroaia, C. Preoteasa & C.-D. Nicola, eds. *Cucuteni Culture within the European Neo-Eneolithic Context: International Colloquium Cucuteni – 130: abstracts*. Piatra-Neamţ, 15–17 octombrie 2014. Piatra-Neamţ: 'Constantin Matasă', p. 74.

Chapman, J. 2015a. Burn or Bury? Mortuary Alternatives in the Neolithic and Chalcolithic of Central and Eastern Europe. In: A. Diachenko, F. Menotti, S. Ryzhov, K. Bunyatyan & S. Kadrow, eds. *The Cucuteni–Trypillia Cultural Complex and its Neighbours. Essays in Memory of Volodymyr Kruts*. Kiev: 'Astrolabe', pp. 259–78. У зБ: Дяченко, О., Менотті, Ф., Рижов, С., Бунятян, К і Кадров, С., ред. *Культурний комплекс Кукутень-Трипілля та його сусіди. Збірка наукових праць пам'яті В. О. Круца.* – Київ: Астролябія, с. 259–78.

Chapman, J. 2015b. Early Urbanism in Europe? The Case of the Trypillia mega-sites: Introduction to the Project. В: На східній межі Старої Європи. Матеріали міжнародної наукової конференції, Кіровоград, Небелівка, 12–14 травня 2015: року. – Кіровоград, с. 6. In: M. Videiko, J. Chapman, I. Kozir & V. Sobchuk, eds. *At the Eastern Frontiers of Old Europe. Proceedings of the International Conference in Kirovograd and Nebelivka, May 12–14 2015*. Kirovograd, Museum, p. 6.

Chapman, J., Gaydarska, B., Villis, R., Svann, N., Burdo, N.B., Kotova, N.S., Belenko, M. & Videiko, M.Yu. 2010. Doslidzennia na posilenni trypilskoi kultury bilia s. Nebelivka 2009 roku. In: D. Kozak, ed. *Archeologichni doslidzhennia v Ukraini 2009 roku*. Kyiv-Lutsk, pp. 458–60. Чапмен, Дж., Гейдарська, Б., Вілліс, Р. Сванн, Н., Бурдо, Н. Б. Котова, Н. С., Беленко, М. і Відейко, М. Ю. 2010. Дослідження на поселенні трипільської культури біля с. Небелівка 2009 р. У зб.: Д. Козак Д.,ред. *Археологічні дослідження в Україні 2009*. Київ-Луцькб с. 458–60.

Chapman, J. & Videiko, M. 2011. The Tripillia Culture Mega-Site Near Nebelivka: Summer 2009 Season. *Praehistorica (Prague)*, XXIX: 79–94.

Chapman, J., Videiko, M., Gaydarska, B., Burdo, N. & Hale, D. 2014c. Architectural Differentiation on a Trypillia Mega-Site: Preliminary Report on the Excavation of a Mega-Structure at Nebelivka, Ukraine. *Journal of Neolithic Archaeology*, 16: 135–57.

Chapman, J., Videiko, M., Gaydarska, B., Burdo, N., Hale, D., Villis, R., Swann, N., Thomas, N., Edwards, P., Blair, A., Hayes, A., Nebbia, M. & Rud, V. 2014a. The planning of the earliest European proto-towns: a new geophysical plan of the Trypillia mega-site of Nebelivka, Kirovograd Domain, Ukraine, Antiquity Project Gallery, Volume 88, Issue 339 [accessed 02 June 2015]. Available at http://antiquity.ac.uk/projgall/chapman339/.

Chapman, J., Videiko, M., Hale, D., Gaydarska, B., Burdo, N., Rassmann, K., Mischka, C., Müller, J., Korvin-Piotrovskiy, A. & Kruts, V. 2014b. The Second Phase of the Trypillia Mega-Site Methodological Revolution: A New Research Agenda. *European Journal of Archaeology*, 17 (3): 369–406.

Fedorov, S. 2015. Protses restavratsii hrestopodibnoi vymostky z poselennia Nebelivka. In: M.Yu. Videiko, J. Chapman, I.A. Kozyr & V.V. Sobchuk, eds. *Na shidnij mezhi Staroi Evropy. Materialy Mizhnarodnoi konferentsii, Kirovograd, Nebelivka 12–14 tarvnia 2015 roku*. Kirovograd, pp. 45–46. Федоров С. 2015. (Кіровоградський обласний краєзнавчий музей) Процес реставрації хрестоподібної вимостки з поселення Небелівка. У зб.: М.Ю. Відейко, Дж. Чепмен, І.А. Козир і В.В. Собчук, ред. *На східній межі Старої Європи. Матеріали міжнародної наукової конференції, Кіровоград, Небелівка, 12–14 травня 2015 року*. Кіровоград, с. 45–46. In: M. Videiko, J. Chapman, I. Kozir, V. Sobchuk, eds. *At the eastern frontiers of Old Europe. Proceedings of the International Conference in Kirovograd and Nebelivka, May 12–14 2015*. Kirovograd, museum: pp. 45–46.

Gaydarska, B. 2015. The Nebelivka Megastructure – An Alternative View. In: M.Yu. Videiko, J. Chapman, I. A. Kozyr & V.V. Sobchuk, eds. *Na shidnij mezhi Staroi Evropy. Materialy Mizhnarodnoi konferentsii, Kirovograd, Nebelivka 12–14 tarvnia 2015 roku*. Kirovograd, p. 16. In: M. Videiko, J. Chapman, I. Kozir, V. Sobchuk, eds. At the eastern frontiers of Old Europe. Proceedings of the International Conference in Kirovograd and Nebelivka, 12–14 May 2015. Kirovograd, museum: 16.

Hale, D., Chapman, J., Swann, N., Videiko, M. & Villis, R. 2010. Early Urbanism in Europe? Geophysical Survey at Nebelivka, Ukraine. In: Recent Work in Archaeological Geophysics. 15th December 2010. Abstracts. London: The Geological Society, pp. 35–36.

Kiosak, D.V. 2015a. Vyroby z kremenu poselennia Nebelivka (za materialamy rozkopok 2014 roku). *Archeologiya*, 1: 61–70. Кіосак, Д. В. 2015а. Вироби з кременю поселення Небелівка (за матеріалами розкопок 2014 року), Археологія, 1: 61–70.

Kiosak, D.V. 2015b. Kremenevyj Inventor Nebelivskogo Poselennia-Giganta Z Rozkopok 2014 roku. In: M. Yu. Videiko, J. Chapman, I.A. Kozyr & V.V. Sobchuk, eds. *Na shidnij mezhi Staroi Evropy. Materialy Mizhnarodnoi konferentsii, Kirovograd, Nebelivka 12–14 tarvnia 2015 roku*. Kirovograd, pp. 32–34. Кіосак, Д. В. 2015b. Кременевий інвентар небелівського поселення-гіганта з розкопок 2014 року. У зб.: М. Ю. Відейко, Дж. Чепмен, І.А. Козир і В.В. Собчук, ред. *На східній межі Старої Європи. Матеріали міжнародної наукової конференції, Кіровоград, Небелівка, 12–14 травня 2015 року*. Кіровоград, с. 32–34. In: M. Videiko, J. Chapman, I. Kozir, V. Sobchuk, eds. *At the eastern frontiers of Old Europe. Proceedings of the International Conference in Kirovograd and Nebelivka, 12–14 May 2015*. Kirovograd, museum: 32–34.

Korvin-Piotrovskiy, A.G. 2015. 'Megastruktury' na poseleniyah-gigantah tripolskoj kultury: varianty interpretatsij. In: M.Yu. Videiko, J. Chapman, I.A. Kozyr & V.V. Sobchuk, eds. *Na shidnij mezhi Staroi Evropy. Materialy Mizhnarodnoi konferentsii, Kirovograd, Nebelivka 12–14 tarvnia 2015 roku*. Kirovograd, pp.

19–20. Корвин-Пиотровский, А.Г. 2015. «Мегаструктуры» на поселениях гигантах трипольской культуры: варианты интерпретаций. У зб.: М.Ю. Відейко, Дж. Чепмен, І.А. Козир і В.В. Собчук, ред. *На східній межі Старої Європи. Матеріали міжнародної наукової конференції, Кіровоград, Небелівка, 12–14 травня 2015 року.* Кіровоград, с. 19–20. In: M. Videiko, J. Chapman, I. Kozir, V. Sobchuk, eds. *At the eastern frontiers of Old Europe. Proceedings of the International Conference in Kirovograd and Nebelivka, May 12–14 2015.* Kirovograd, museum: 19–20.

Kruts, V., Korvin-Piotrovskiy, A. & Rassmann, K. 2014. New Discovery of the Kilns in the Tripolian Giant-Settlement Talianki. In: G. Dumitroaia, C. Preoteasa & C.-D. Nicola, eds. Cucuteni Culture within the European Neo-Eneolithic Context: International Colloquium Cucuteni – 130: abstracts. Piatra-Neamţ, 15–17 octombrie 2014. Piatra-Neamţ: 'Constantin Matasă', pp. 117–23.

Ovchynnykov, E.V. 2015. Rozpysna keramika z megastruktury na trypilskomu poselenni Nebelivka. In: M. Yu. Videiko, J. Chapman, I.A. Kozyr & V.V. Sobchuk, eds. *Na shidnij mezhi Staroi Evropy. Materialy Mizhnarodnoi konferentsii, Kirovograd, Nebelivka 12–14 tarvnia 2015 roku.* Kirovograd, pp. 35–37. Овчинников, Е.В. 2015. Розписна кераміка з мегаструктури трипільського поселення Небелівка. У зб.: М.Ю. Відейко, Дж. Чепмен, І.А. Козир і В.В. Собчук, ред: *На східній межі Старої Європи. Матеріали міжнародної наукової конференції, Кіровоград, Небелівка, 12–14 травня 2015 року.* – Кіровоград, с. 35–37. In: M. Videiko, J. Chapman, I. Kozir, V. Sobchuk, eds. *At the eastern frontiers of Old Europe. Proceedings of the International Conference in Kirovograd and Nebelivka, May 12–14 2015.* Kirovograd, museum: pp. 35–37.

Pashkevych, G.O. 2015. Rezultaty paleobotanichnogo analizu z rozkopok megastruktury na poselenni bila s. Nebelivka. In: M.Yu. Videiko, J. Chapman, I.A. Kozyr & V.V. Sobchuk, eds. *Na shidnij mezhi Staroi Evropy. Materialy Mizhnarodnoi konferentsii, Kirovograd, Nebelivka 12–14 tarvnia 2015 roku.* Kirovograd, р. 44. Пашкевич Г. О. 2015. Результати палеоетноботанічного аналізу залишків рослин з розкопок мегаструктури на поселенні біля с. Небелівка. У зб.: М.Ю. Відейко, Дж. Чепмен, І.А. Козир і В.В. Собчук, ред. *На східній межі Старої Європи. Матеріали міжнародної наукової конференції, Кіровоград, Небелівка, 12–14 травня 2015 року.* Кіровоград, с. 44. In: M. Videiko, J. Chapman, I. Kozir, V. Sobchuk, eds. *At the eastern frontiers of Old Europe. Proceedings of the International Conference in Kirovograd and Nebelivka, May 12–14 2015.* Kirovograd, museum: p. 44.

Raczky, P. & Anders, A. 2012. Neolithic Enclosures in Eastern Hungary and their Survival into the Copper Age. In: F. Bertemes & H. Meller, eds. *Neolithische Kreisgrabenanlagen in Europa - Neolithic Circular Enclosures in Europe: Internationale Arbeitstagung vom 7. bis 9. Mai 2004 in Goseck.* Tagungen des Landesmuseums für Vorgeschichte Halle 8. Halle (Saale): Landesmuseum für Vorgeschichte Halle (Saale), pp. 271–309.

Rud, V. 2015. Doslidzhennia zalyshkiv zhytel na rozkopi 5 poselennia Nebelivka. In: M.Yu. Videiko, J. Chapman, I.A. Kozyr & V.V. Sobchuk, eds. *Na shidnij mezhi Staroi Evropy. Materialy Mizhnarodnoi konferentsii, Kirovograd, Nebelivka 12–14 tarvnia 2015 roku.* Kirovograd, pp. 26–27. Рудь, В. 2015. Дослідження залишків жител на розкопі 5 поселення Небелівка. У зб.: М.Ю. Відейко, Дж. Чепмен, І.А. Козир і В.В. Собчук, ред. *На східній межі Старої Європи. Матеріали міжнародної наукової конференції, Кіровоград, Небелівка, 12–14 травня 2015 року.* Кіровоград, с. 26–27. In: M. Videiko, J. Chapman, I. Kozir, V. Sobchuk, eds. *At the eastern frontiers of Old Europe. Proceedings of the International Conference in Kirovograd and Nebelivka, 12–14 May 2015.* Kirovograd, museum, pp. 26–27.

Ryzhov, S.M. 1993. Nebelivka grupa pamjatok trypilskoi kultury. *Archeologiya*, 3: 101–14. Рижов С.М. 1993. Небелівська група пам'яток трипільської культури, *Археологія*, 3: 101–14.

Shevchenko, N.A. 2015. Issledovanie materialov drevnego hrama tripolskogo poseleniya v s. Nebelevka Arhangelskogo rajona Kirovogradskoj oblasti (tehnologicheskij aspekt). In: M.Yu. Videiko, J. Chapman, I. A. Kozyr & V.V. Sobchuk, eds. *Na shidnij mezhi Staroi Evropy. Materialy Mizhnarodnoi konferentsii, Kirovograd, Nebelivka 12–14 tarvnia 2015 roku.* Kirovograd, pp. 40–43. Шевченко, Н.А. 2015. Исследование материалов древнего храма трипольского поселения в с. Небелевка Архангельского района Кировоградской области (технологический аспект): У зб.: М.Ю. Відейко, Дж. Чепмен, І.А. Козир і В.В. Собчук, ред. *На східній межі Старої Європи. Матеріали міжнародної наукової конференції, Кіровоград, Небелівка, 12–14 травня 2015: року.* Кіровоградб с. 40–43. In: M. Videiko, J. Chapman, I. Kozir, V. Sobchuk, eds. *At the eastern frontiers of Old Europe. Proceedings of the International Conference in Kirovograd and Nebelivka, May 12–14 2015.* Kirovograd, museum: pp. 40–43.

Shmaglij, M.M. & Videiko, M.Y. 1992. Trypilski poselennia na Cherkashchyni. *Archeologiya*, 3: 124–30. Шмаглій М.М. і Відейко М.Ю. 1992. Трипільські поселення на Черкащині. Археологія, 3: 124–30.

Shyshkin, K.V. 1985. Planuvannia trypilskyh poselen za danymy aerofotozjomky. *Archeologiya*, 52: 72–77. Шишкін, К.В. 1985. Планування трипільських поселень за даними аерофотозйомки. *Археологія*, 52: 72–77.

Skakun, N.N., Tsvek, E.V., Kruts, V.A., Mateva, V.I., Korvin-Piotrovskiy, A.G., Samzun, A. & Yakovleva, L. M. 2005. *Archeologicheskie issledovaniya tripolskogo poseleniya Bodaki v 2005 godu.* Kiev: Sankt-Peterburg. Скакун, Н. Н., Цвек, Е. В,, Круц, В. А., Матева, Б. И., Корвин-Пиотровский, А. Г., Самзун, А. и Яковлева, Л. М. 2005. *Археологические исследования трипольського поселения Бодаки в 2005 г.* Киев-Санкт-Петербург.

Tolochko, P. 2015. Tripolye: kultura i etnos. In: A. Diachenko, F. Menotti, S. Ryzhov, K. Bunyatyan & S. Kadrow, eds. *The Cucuteni-Tripolye Cultural Complex and its Neighbours: Essays in Memory of Volodymyr Kruts.* Lviv: Astrolabe, pp. 27–35. Толочко, П. 2015. Триполье: культура и этнос. In: A. Diachenko, F. Menotti, S. Ryzhov, K. Bunyatyan and S. Kadrow, eds. *The Cucuteni–Trypillia Cultural Complex and its Neighbours. Essays in Memory of Volodymyr Kruts.* Kiev 'Astrolabe', pp. 27–34.

Turek, J. 2012. The Neolithic Enclosures in Transition. In: A. Gibson, ed. *Enclosing the Neolithic. Recent studies in Britain and Europe.* BAR International Series, 2440. Oxford: Archaeopress, pp. 185–201.

Videiko, M. 2014. Reconstruction of Nebelivka Mega-Structure. In: G. Dumitroaia, C. Preoteasa & C.-D. Nicola, eds. *Cucuteni Culture within the European Neo-Eneolithic Context: International Colloquium Cucuteni – 130: abstracts.* Piatra-Neamț, 15–17 octombrie 2014. Piatra-Neamț: 'Constantin Matasă', pp. 75–78.

Videiko, M., Chapman, J., Burdo, N., Gaydarska, B., Ignatova, S., Ivanova, S. & Rud, V. 2014a. Prodovzhennia doslidzen na trypilskomu poselenni etapu BII bilia s. Nebelivka. In: D. Kozak, ed. *Archaeologichni vidkryttia v Ukraini 2013 roku.* Kyiv, pp. 161–62. Відейко, М., Чапмен Дж., Бурдо Н., Гейдарська Б., Ігнатова С., Іванова С., Рудь В. 2014a. Продовження досліджень на трипільському поселенні етапу ВІІ біля с. Небелівка: *Археологічні відкриття в Україні 2013 р.* Київ: с. 161–162.

Videiko, M., Chapman, J., Burdo, N., Gaydarska, B., Ignatova, S., Ivanova, S. & Rud, V. 2014b. Issledovaniya po proektu 'Ranniaja urbanizatsija v Evrope? Tripolskie megaposeleniya'. *Tyragetia*, VIII [XXIII], Nr. 1: 107–44. Видейко, М., Чапмен, Дж., Бурдо, Н., Гейдарська, Б., Игнатова, С., Иванова, С. и Рудь, В. 2014. Исследования по проекту «Ранняя урбанизация в Европе? трипольские мегапоселения, *Tyragetia*, VIII [XXIII], Nr.1:107–44.

Videiko, M., Chapman, J., Gaydarska, B., Burdo, N., Ovchinnikov, E., Pashkevich, G. & Shevchenko, N. 2013a. Issledovaniya megastruktory na psoelenii tripolskoj kultury u s. *Nebelevka v 2012 godu. Tyragetia*, VII [XXII], Nr. 1: 97–124. Видейко, М., Чапмен, Дж., Гейдарская, Б., Бурдо, Н., Овчинников, Э., Пашкевич, Г. и Шевченко, Н. 2013. Исследования мегаструктуры на поселении трипольской культуры у с. Небелевка в 2012 году, *Tyragetia*, VII [XXII], Nr. 1: 97–124.

Videiko, M., Chapman, J., Gaydarska, B., Burdo, N., Ovchynnykov, E., Pashkevych, G. & Shevchenko, N. 2013b. Doslidzennia na poselenni trypilskoi kultury bilia s. Nebelivka. In: D. Kozak, ed. *Archeologichni doslidzennia v Ukraini.* Kyiv-Lutsk, p. 209. Відейко, М., Чапмен, Дж., Гейдарська, Б., Бурдо, Н., Овчинников, Е., Пашкевич, Г. і Шевченко, Н. Дослідження на поселенні трипільської культури біля с. Небелівка. У зб.: Д. Козак, ред. Археологічні дослідження в Україні. Київ-Луцьк, с. 209.

Videiko, M., Chapman, J. & Nebbia, M. 2014b. Razvedki vokrug poseleniya Nebelivka. In: D. Kozak, ed. *Archeologichni vidkryttia v Ukraini 2013 roku.* Kyiv, p. 163. Відейко, М., Чапмен, Дж. и Неббия М. 2014b. Разведки вокруг поселения Небелевка. У зб.: Д. Козак, ред. *Археологічні відкриття в Україні 2013 р.* Київ:, с. 163.

Videiko, M.Yu. 2015. Doslidzennia mizhnarodnoi ekspedytsii 2012–2014 rr. u Nebelivtsi: rezultaty ta perspektyvy. In: M.Yu. Videiko, J. Chapman, I. A. Kozyr & V.V. Sobchuk, eds. *Na shidnij mezhi Staroi Evropy. Materialy Mizhnarodnoi konferentsii, Kirovograd, Nebelivka 12–14 tarvnia 2015 roku.* Kirovograd, pp. 7–11. Відейко, М. Ю. 2015. Дослідження міжнародної експедиції 2012–2014 років у Небелівці: результати та перспективи.У зб.: М.Ю. Відейко, Дж. Чепмен, І.А. Козир і В.В. Собчук, ред. *На східній межі Старої Європи. Матеріали міжнародної наукової конференції, Кіровоград, Небелівка, 12–14 травня 2015 року.* Кіровоград, с. 7–11. In: M. Videiko, J. Chapman, I. Kozir, V. Sobchuk, eds. *At the eastern frontiers of Old Europe. Proceedings of the International Conference in Kirovograd and Nebelivka, May 12–14 2015.* Kirovograd, museum, pp. 7–11.

Videiko, M.Yu. & Burdo, N.B. 2015a. Megastruktura: hram na trypilskomu poselenni bilia s. Nebelivka. In: A. Diachenko, F. Menotti, S. Ryzhov, K. Bunyatyan & S. Kadrow, eds. *The Cucuteni-Tripolye Cultural Complex and its Neighbours: Essays in Memory of Volodymyr Kruts.* Lviv: Astrolabe, pp. 209–336. Відейко, М. Ю. і Бурдо, Н. Б. 2015a. «Мегаструктура» - храм з трипільського послення біля с. Небелівка. In: A. Diachenko, F. Menotti, S. Ryzhov, K. Bunyatyan and S. Kadrow, eds. *The Cucuteni–Trypillia Cultural Complex and its Neighbours. Essays in Memory of Volodymyr Kruts.* Kiev: Astrolabe, pp. 209–336.

Videiko, M.Yu. & Burdo, N.B. 2015b. Rekonstruktsiya ta interpretatsiya mega-struktury na poselenni Nebelivka. In: M.Yu. Videiko, J. Chapman, I.A. Kozyr & V. V. Sobchuk, eds. *Na shidnij mezhi Staroi Evropy. Materialy Mizhnarodnoi konferentsii, Kirovograd, Nebelivka 12–14 tarvnia 2015 roku.* Kirovograd, pp. 21–25. Відейко, М.Ю. і Бурдо, Н.Б. 2015b. Реконструкція та інтерпретація мега-структури на поселенні небелівка. Узб.: М.Ю. Відейко, Дж. Чепмен, І.А. Козир і В.В. Собчук, ред. *На східній межі Старої Європи. Матеріали міжнародної наукової конференції, Кіровоград, Небелівка, 12–14 травня 2015: року.* Кіровоград, с. 21–25. In: M. Videiko, J. Chapman, I. Kozir, V. Sobchuk, eds. *At the eastern frontiers of Old Europe. Proceedings of the International Conference in Kirovograd and Nebelivka, May 12–14 2015.* Kirovograd, museum, pp. 21–25.

Videiko, M.Yu., Chapman, J., Burdo, N.B., Gaydarska, B., Tserna, S.V., Rud, V.S. & Kiosak, D.V. 2015. Komplexsnye issledovaniya oboronitelnyh sooruzhenij, proizvodstvennyh kompleksov i ostatkov postroek na tripolskom poselenii u s. *Nebelevka, Stratum Plus,* 2: 147–70. Видейко, М. Ю., Чепмэн, Дж., Бурдо, Н. Б., Гайдарска, Б., Церна, С. В., Рудь, В. С. иКиосак Д. В. 2015. Комплексные исследования оборонительных сооружений, производственных комплексов и остатков построек на трипольском поселении у села Небелевка, *Stratum Plus,* 2, pp. 147–70.

Yakubenko, O.O. & Videiko, M.Yu. 2015. Trypilske poselennia bilia s. Volodymyrivka i volodymyrivska localna grupa. In: M.Yu. Videiko, J. Chapman, I.A. Kozyr & V. V. Sobchuk, eds. *Na shidnij mezhi Staroi Evropy. Materialy Mizhnarodnoi konferentsii, Kirovograd, Nebelivka 12–14 tarvnia 2015 roku.* Kirovograd, pp. 82–85. Якубенко, О.О. і Відейко, М. Ю. 2015. Трипільське поселення біля села Володимирівка і володимирівська група пам'яток. У зб.: М.Ю. Відейко, Дж. Чепмен, І.А. Козир і В.В. Собчук, ред. *На східній межі Старої Європи. Матеріали міжнародної наукової конференції, Кіровоград, Небелівка, 12–14 травня 2015 року.* Кіровоград, с. 82–85. In: M. Videiko, J. Chapman, I. Kozir, V. Sobchuk, eds. *At the eastern frontiers of Old Europe. Proceedings of the International Conference in Kirovograd and Nebelivka, May 12–14 2015.* Kirovograd, museum, pp. 82–85.

CHAPTER 7

Nebelivka: Assembly Houses, Ditches, and Social Structure

John Chapman, Bisserka Gaydarska and Duncan Hale

Introduction

The great German aerial archaeologist Otto Braasch once remarked that 'Europe was half-blind' (Braasch, 1995: 109). What Braasch meant was that the extensive prohibition on flying and the use of satellite images during the Warsaw Pact period (1945–1989) prevented our knowledge of the full distribution of sites of all periods which showed up regularly as soil-marks or crop-marks in Western Europe but had never been identified in Eastern Europe. Moreover, ground-based geophysical prospection was also rare in that period. A hurricane of recent research projects addressing these issues has proved that Braasch was correct, through the discovery of thousands of new sites and monuments and the production of hundreds of new geophysical plans (Becker, 1996; Braasch, 1996; Fröhlich, 1997; Goyda, 2006; Mischka, 2010, 2012; Popa et al., 2010). One part of this story concerns the Trypillia mega-sites of Ukraine.

One of the rare exceptions to the prohibition on remote sensing projects in the Cold War period was the Ukrainian-led first methodological revolution of the late 1960s and the 1970s, which led to the discovery of the Trypillia mega-sites (Videiko, 2013; Chapman et al., 2014; see Videiko and Rassmann, 2016). This research defined five basic design principles of the mega-sites: (1) at least two, and possibly as many as four, principal concentric circuits of structures; (2) an open space in the centre of the site, inside the inner circuit; (3) an open space between the two circuits, constituting a buffer zone of varying widths; (4) the construction of some structures inside the inner circuit; and (5) the construction of some structures outside the outer circuit.

However, it was not until the second revolution of the 2000s–2010s that two important new classes of anomaly were discovered (Chapman et al., 2014). The first was a form of structure much larger than the usual dwelling house; the second was the perimeter boundary. These new features were important because they demonstrated that some Trypillia communities were concerned to define the outer limits of their settlements—to distinguish 'inside' from 'outside' (Harding et al., 2006) and that there were architectural materializations of the means of integrating the dozens or hundreds of people who contributed their labour to communal building projects. In this account, we shall discuss perimeter boundaries from the sites of Nebelivka and Maidanetske, before considering the Assembly Houses of the mega-sites. As regards the latter, there is a major anomaly in social and spatial organization, which we flag up for future research attention.

Perimeter Boundaries

The current geophysical plots of Taljanky and Dobrovody (Rassmann et al., 2014) fail to show any form of perimeter boundary, despite the potential length of c. 4 km at Taljanky (Rassmann et al., 2014: figure 9a) and c. 0.8 km at Dobrovody (Rassmann et al., 2014: figure 31) available for geophysical investigation. On this basis, we may assume that the communities at these sites had decided not to construct such a boundary. This negative decision is of great interest and we shall return to the possible reasons later (below, see p. 129).

At Nebelivka, the perimeter of the site covers a linear distance of c. 5.9 km, of which seventy-three per cent (c. 4.3 km) was available for geophysical investigation (Chapman et al., 2014a) (Figure 1). The geophysical plot shows a single ditch over much of the available perimeter, specifically at the edge of Quarters D–L on the North, West, and South sides of the settlement. Erosion down the steeper slope of the East side probably removed traces of the ditch on the edge of Quarters B and C although fragments of a ditch-type anomaly also survived there. There was little opportunity to investigate the outer part of the settlement in Quarters N and A, while no ditch-type anomaly was noted in Quarter M. A series of parallel linear anomalies in Quarters K–M probably represent later trackways. Setting aside the perimeter of Quarters N–C, there are seven well-defined gaps in the

© European Association of Archaeologists 2016

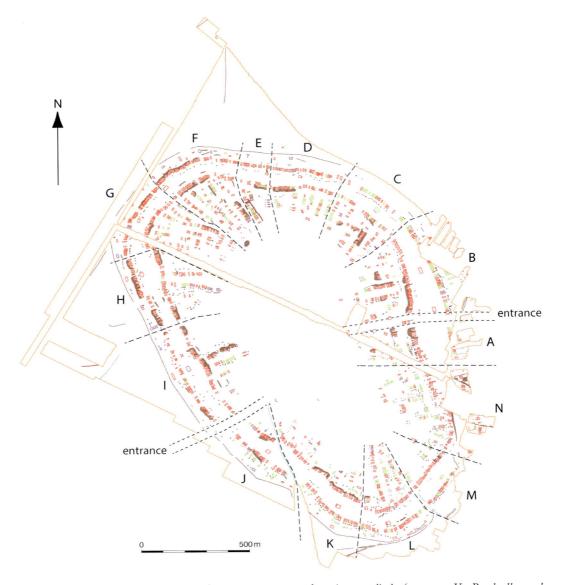

Figure 1. *Plan of the Nebelivka mega-site, showing quarters and perimeter ditch* (SOURCE*: Y. Beadnell, re-drawn from ASUD plan*).

perimeter ditch in Quarters F–J, with the width of the smallest gap being 12 m and the largest 55 m. Since there were no geological or pedological reasons to cause the magnetometry to miss existing stretches of ditch in these Quarters, we can assume that these gaps were genuine and thus resemble the kind of porous perimeter boundary well known to British prehistorians in the class of monument known as the 'causewayed enclosure' (aka 'interrupted ditch enclosure': Whittle *et al.*, 1999; Mercer, 2006).

The initial excavations of sections across the northern part of the perimeter ditch (Sonda 4, in Quarter F) and its southern part (Sonda 10, in Quarter L) were accomplished by the Ukrainian side using large trenches (Sonda 4: 22 × 5 m; Sonda 10: 15 × 2 m) ambitiously. In both trenches, the geophysical plans proved accurate guides of the location of the ditches

Figure 2. *Trench 4, showing location of northern ditch section (photo: J. Chapman).*

Figure 3. Northern ditch section (photo: J. Chapman).

but in neither trench were the ditches as deep as they had been expected (Figures 2–4). Trypillia sherds were recorded from the middle and upper fill of the northern ditch but not in the lowest fill; no animal bones were recovered from within the ditch. The width of the northern ditch segment was *c.* 2 m, while there was considerable debate about the depth of the northern ditch exposure (Figure 4 - Ditch A, with two possible ditch lines), with different views recorded on the section drawing. While the greatest depth was believed to be 3 m, the majority view is that the ditch was 1.50 m deep from the base of the Chernozem A horizon. Snail-rich bulk samples from the ditch fill indicated a distinctive habitat which persisted for some time—for example; an open, gradually infilling ditch, mainly dry, but holding significant pockets of moisture, with thick/long grasses and other herbaceous plants, perhaps sparse trees, but in a landscape dominated by short grassland. Thus, the debate over whether this shallow ditch contained a palisade has been settled in favour of the lack of a palisade—an interpretation confirmed by the lack of post-holes visible to document this kind of feature. Unfortunately, the ditch was too shallow for the preservation of pollen.

Sonda 10 was laid out across an area in which three parallel ditch sections were indicated by the geophysical plot. Each ditch was recognizable but their depths were less than the shallowest interpretation of the northern ditch segment, in no case exceeding 1 m in depth (Figures 5 and 6). Trypillia sherds were found in the middle fill of the southernmost ditch and loosely associated with the northernmost ditch. One animal bone sample was recovered from the southern ditch section for AMS dating.[1] Unfortunately, the ditches were too shallow for the preservation of pollen.

The interim conclusion is that the shallowness of the ditch in the northern and southern areas was not commensurate with a defensive ditch but, rather, a marker of an enclosed space. The interruptions in the ditch in the West side of the settlement also make a defensive function improbable, as has long been argued for the European causewayed enclosures (Smith, 1965; Andersen, 1997).

The investigations at Maidanetske also identified possible ditches within the geophysical ground plan (Müller *et al.*, in print; Rassmann *et al.*, 2014). As at Nebelivka, obviously there were repeated interruptions to both the inner and the outer ditch, suggesting the likelihood of a symbolic enclosure line rather than a serious defensive structure (Rassmann *et al.*, 2014: figure 22a).

Thus, we have an interesting situation in that the earliest mega-site (Nebelivka: Phase BII) has a single ditch without a palisade and there is variation between the later mega-sites, with the smallest and the largest sites lacking a perimeter boundary. What do these differences mean?

The concept of a perimeter boundary is usually taken to imply a pre-existing plan with an idea of where to place the boundary and what to build inside it or outside it. But such a plan may have been formulated in a very general way in the case of the mega-sites' interrupted ditch enclosures, where an area for settlement could have been pre-defined by the high land between two or three streams. Moreover, a new stretch of ditch could have been added to the general 'perimeter line' sometime after an earlier stretch of ditch had been dug without disturbing the overall plan. Lack of excavation at both mega-sites precludes us from telling whether the long, uninterrupted ditch sections were dug in one method or in many stretches by different work groups (cf. Whittle *et al.*, 1999). But all other aspects of the Nebelivka plan suggest that the actual building project was rather loosely related to the original design concept (Chapman and Gaydarska, in press).

The presence of ditch segments ranging in length from 20 m to several hundred metres meant a major communal effort, bringing together everyone from the adjacent Quarter to forge a new identity by common labour. The fact that the perimeter ditch was incomplete for much of the life of the mega-site made little difference to the inhabitants, since the local purpose was symbolic—the creation of a vertical dimension which created an 'inside' and an 'outside', as well as practical—the creation of a garden space between the ditch and the outer house circuit. There were two principal reasons why these boundaries could not have possessed defensive power—the large number of gaps in the ditch(es) and the impossibility of manning the entire ditch circuit in the face of attack (for other reasons, see Neustupný, 2006: 2).

The decisions taken at Taljanky and Dobrovody not to construct a perimeter ditch around their mega-site suggest alternative routes to communal integration rather than the lack of power to organize such a major

---

[1] The AMS date falls within the range of AMS dates for the Trypillia occupation.

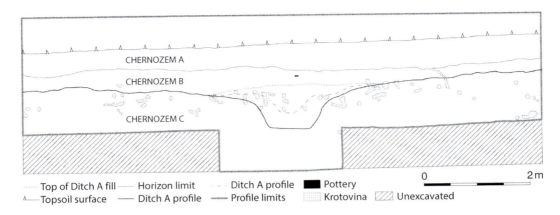

Figure 4. Drawing of northern ditch profile (V. Cherubini and D. Miller).

undertaking. Close co-operation between houses in Neighbourhoods would have perhaps vitiated the need for further communal integration, as well as denying the need for vertical expression of symbolic difference by dint of the existing one- and two-storeyed houses. But the absence of Assembly Houses at Taljanky on top of the absence of a perimeter ditch indicates a question-mark over a communal approach to social integration (see below, p. 129).

Assembly Houses

During the 2009 summer field season of the Durham–Kyiv team, the creation of a plot of 15 ha of the mega-site of Nebelivka, Kirovograd Domain, led to the identification of all of the major, and well-known, features of a mega-site plan but in much greater detail than before, as well as a number of new features (Hale *et al.*, 2010; Chapman *et al.*, 2014). The most striking finds comprised the identification of three magnetic anomalies which we have interpreted as burnt structures much larger than the 'usual' anomalies interpreted as burnt houses (Figure 1). The largest of these formed an anomaly 66-m long and 22-m wide, with most of the western half strongly burnt and the remaining, eastern part unburnt but enclosed. It was oriented East-West and carefully placed in the wide break between the two concentric rings of houses, in an area devoid of other structures. This mega-structure is currently the largest structure known from the Trypillia-Cucuteni group; the *prima facie* interpretation would be that such large buildings were some kind of 'public' building, performing integrative functions for several parts of the Nebelivka mega-site. It has been argued elsewhere that this kind of structure contributes to a better understanding of Fletcher's (1995) conundrum of the mega-sites' anomalous position in his global settlement model—the lack of any integrating structures in sites that transcended his 100 ha interaction limit. Since these anomalies represented very rare buildings, it was decided to explore the largest example through excavation in summer 2012. The preliminary description of the mega-structure has been presented elsewhere (Chapman *et al.*, 2014b), with an account of the drastically differing interpretations of the Kyiv and Durham sides. In this

Figure 5. Trench 10, showing location of ditches (photo: J. Chapman).

Figure 6. Section across southern ditch (photo: J. Chapman).

Figure 7. Kite photo of burnt part of mega-structure during excavation (source: M. Household).

Figure 8. Kite photograph of unburnt part of the mega-structure during excavation (source: M. Household).

account, we shall simply summarize the Durham view before making an assessment of the meaning of such mega-structures for overall mega-site settlement order.

The excavation of the largest of the three large structures identified in the geophysical investigations in summer 2009 at Nebelivka (Chapman and Videiko, 2011) took place over eight weeks in the summer of 2012.[2] The large bi-partite structure (Figure 7) covered an area of 1200 m², with 800 m² represented by burnt remains. The stratigraphy of the mega-structure can be divided into four phases: Phase 1—pre-mega-structure; Phase 2—use of mega-structure; Phase 3—deposits representing the destruction of the mega-structure; and Phase 4—the soil fill above the destruction deposits.

The mega-structure was divided into two large areas—an unburnt area and a burnt area. In the former, there were relatively few features, which could not be differentiated into earlier or later phases. In contrast, the latter was defined primarily by a mass of burnt daub normally interpreted as the remains of the deliberate burning of the structure. The unpicking of the sequence of construction remains and destruction debris proved to be the principal challenge in the excavation.

Unburnt area (Figure 8): according to the 2009 geophysical investigations, the eastern half of the mega-structure was defined by linear anomalies suggestive of burnt walls or ditches filled with daub. The removal of the upper 50–60 cm of soil deposit in this area[3] revealed no traces of internal or external features at all but, at a depth of 0.50 m, traces of linear daub scatters were identified on the South and North sides, defining an area 30 m in length and 22 m in width. Excavation to a greater depth also confirmed no obvious ditch profiles in the excavated sections. There were also no traces of ditches in the eastern most sector of this area. However, the absence of any traces of ditches adjacent to the daub scatters may have been caused by removal through over-excavation. Preliminary sorting of all artefact types recovered in this area indicates a much lower level of discard than in the burnt areas.

Burnt area: Phase 1— this phase comprises all of the contexts found from what appears to pre-date the construction of the mega-structure. There are currently three contexts indicating prior deposition in the

---

[2]In the eight-week period, the Kyiv side prepared the site by stripping topsoil in Week 0, there was a joint six-week excavation by a large part of the Durham and Kyiv sides (Weeks 1–6) and a final week after the departure of the Durham side, conducted solely by the Kyiv side (Week 7). This division of working times has led to a certain variation in the methods of excavation favoured by each side, which should be taken into account in the final interpretation of finds and, especially, the comparison of finds excavated in Weeks 1–6 and Week 7. The Durham system of single-context recording allowed for sub-divisions in any of the Phases, perhaps most significantly in the case of Phase 2. The Kyiv team was also fully committed to Total Station (henceforth 'TSt') 3-D recording of architectural details and finds, although less so to the single-context recording that is part-and-parcel of TSt recording.

[3]A programme of laboratory phosphate analysis is being undertaken by Mr Ed Treasure to ascertain the extent of phosphate variation both within the unburnt area and between the unburnt area and samples within the burnt mega-structure.

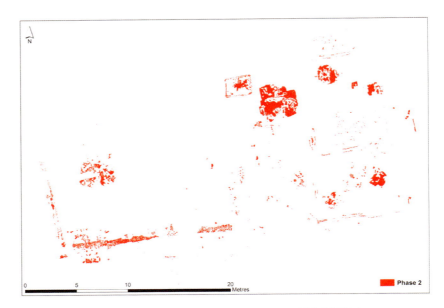

Figure 9. Phase 2 construction daub, mega-structure (source: B. Gaydarska and M. Nebbia).

area subsequently covered by the mega-structure: a fill beneath the level of the base of the podium, a foundation deposit under a Raised Area and a post-hole below the central open area. In addition, there are several instances of contexts outside the burnt area of the mega-structure which may date to Phase 1.

Burnt area: Phase 2—the construction of the mega-structure (Figure 9): the digitization of all the construction daub shows the overall features of Phase 2 of the mega-structure. Linear daub concentrations indicated the place of walls—whether external or internal. While part of the West wall revealed clear fired clay 'slots' which would have supported vertical planks (Figure 10), other parts consisted of narrow, patchy daub deposits. The East wall showed an intensive concentration of daub. It remains doubtful that a

Figure 10. Fired clay slots to support walls, West wall, mega-structure.

Figure 11. Reconstruction of the mega-structure, Durham view (source: C. Unwin and S. Johnston).

roof or roofs covered the whole of the mega-structure. The eastern end is by far the most densely structured, with a series of partitions, including one with a dark-fired clay threshold, which would have formed five or six small 'rooms'. These spaces could conceivably have been roofed. In comparison with the East end, the central part had fewer partitions—perhaps two from the South wall and one from the North wall. Its relatively open nature means that it is hard to imagine that the central area was roofed over. The West end differs from the other areas, with an open area stretching towards the equally open central area and a series of contrasting spaces along the western wall—a long, thin 'room' and two small square rooms. There may have been a lean-to roof covering the rooms linked to the West wall. A reconstruction of the mega-structure according to the Durham view shows these features (Figure 11).

The digitization of the construction daub excavation data confirms the interior features[4] shown in the kite photograph taken during excavation (Figure 7). These comprised a 2-m long dark-fired clay threshold in the eastern end of the building, near massive daub fragments probably representing a monumental super-structure of the East entrance (Figure 12); a 10-m long fired clay 'podium', 30 cm high, built along the inside edge of the South wall; seven fired clay Raised Areas of varying sizes built up with two to four layers of fired clay, some decorated with incised motifs or a red painted wash and used to display special items during mega-structure ceremonial (Figure 13); and a large fired clay 'bin', which enjoyed a long and complex biography but which did not contain stored grain (Figure 14).

The living surface inside the mega-structure also raises complex issues of interpretation. The most convincing areas of fired clay 'paving' comprise the seven Raised Areas. Much of the daub that covered the living surface of the mega-structure was too irregular to be considered to form a floor. It is therefore possible that, just as we can identify variation in the form of different parts of the mega-structure, so it may be assumed that different kinds of floor covering were used for the different parts of the great building, including stamped earth surfaces for much of the central area.

The finds associated with the final phase of use of the mega-structure may be divided into three main categories: special deposits, deposits of large, potentially re-fitting sherds, and sherd scatters. The former is far rarer than the latter; in fact, before further analysis of the finds, we can be sure of only one major special deposit—a concentration of twenty-one miniature vessels, with a number of larger pots, in an area of *c*. 3 × 3 m just to the West of the western partition of the East end (Figure 15). A moderate number of sherds—in the hundreds rather than the thousands—were deposited in living floor deposits, sometimes forming clusters of re-fitting sherds and sometimes as 'orphan sherds'.[5] There are also several cases of sherds re-fitting from many metres apart.

Burnt area: Phase 3—the destruction of the mega-structure (Figures 16 and 17): there is a fundamental assumption that Trypillia houses have been burnt down deliberately at the end of their lives (Burdo, 2003; Kruts, 2003; Burdo *et al.*, 2013; Chapman, 2015). However, as we have seen already at the mega structure, the distribution of fired clay daub across the building is by no means continuous nor massive, revealing patches of dense, often vitrified daub, zones of medium density daub with little or no vitrification, and areas of low-density daub with no traces of vitrification. There seems little doubt, even at this preliminary stage of investigations, that there were major variations in the temperature at which different parts of the mega-structure burned down. This may have been a by-product of the

---

[4] The interior features are fully described in Chapman *et al.* (2014b).

[5] An 'orphan sherd' is Schiffer's (1976) term for sherds that did not re-fit to any other sherd on site.

Figure 12. Fired clay threshold, from East (photo: M. Videiko).

conditions of the fire or perhaps the different burning strategies designed to burn different areas in different ways.

Stratigraphic evidence from more than ten contexts showed the covering of the Phase 2 living surface of the mega-structure with a thin layer of dark soil prior to the first daub destruction deposits. This thin soil layer was found above the podium, two Raised Areas and the fired clay bin. It seems probable that this soil was derived from the local Chernozem and blew into the mega-structure over a period of time whose duration is currently difficult to assess. The suggestion is that a mega-structure that was relatively open may have been abandoned for a period of time before it was burned down.

The digitization of all destruction daub led to the insight that there were two stratigraphic stages of destruction daub—here termed Phases 3A (Figure 16) and 3B (Figure 17). These data show that different parts of the eastern block, the North wall, the western block, and the southern area (Figure 16) fell earlier than other parts of the building (Figure 17). However, these two stages of collapse may well have happened during the same destruction event, as indeed happened during the recent house-burning experiment at Nebelivka (Johnston *et al.*, in prep.).

Figure 13. The largest of the Raised Areas, from South East (photo: J. Chapman).

Figure 14. Fired clay bin, from South-West (photo: M. Videiko).

In summary, there were three final stages in the biography of the mega-structure: (1) the temporary or permanent cessation of social practices inside the building; (2) a period of as yet unknown duration allowing the build-up of thin levels of Chernozem-derived soil layers within the mega-structure; perhaps the mega-structure was not used in this period; and (3) two stages of the collapse of the building to produce the ploshchadka.

Burnt area: Phase 4—after the destruction of the mega-structure (Figure 18): the main characteristic of the period after the burning of the mega-structure was a period of soil formation, indicating an absence of cultural activity above where the mega-structure once stood. One can suppose that this period of soil formation was, at the same time, a period of little local deposition of artefacts or ecofacts. The ploughing of the soil above the mega-site in general, and the mega-structure in particular, was so deep as to leave traces of furrows in the top of the ploshchadka. It is this modern ploughing that has removed a large quantity of Trypillia pottery from its original location and created a large and varied plough-zone ceramic assemblage of at least 1500 sherds with Total Station recording. The best guess that we can make for the source of this plough-zone assemblage is supposedly near the top of the ploshchadka—a notion that would lend support to Burdo *et al.* (2013) view that there was much deposition on the burnt remains of Trypillia houses, viz., on the top of the ploshchadka. The alternative is that much pottery fell from shelves on walls in the mega-structure onto the growing mass of burnt daub during the course of the destruction by fire.

In summary, the Durham view is that it seems probable that some Trypillia pottery (Figure 18: red dots) was placed on, or fell onto, the top of the ploshchadka after the destruction of the building by fire. Over the ensuing millennia, but most probably in the modern period with the increasing depth of ploughing, the sherds placed on or near the top of the ploshchadka were transformed into a plough-zone assemblage, with the sherds distributed throughout the A horizon between 0.20 and 0.50 m in depth.

Interpretation of the mega-structure: the architectural remains of the Nebelivka mega-structure, together with its associated artefact assemblage, pose an intriguing problem of interpretation. Before our excavation, the teams shared an expectation of a large public building with a range of special finds, indicating some kind of administrative or ritual central place serving, at the very least, a cluster of houses in the South–East part of the mega-site. The size of the structure is not in doubt and the excavated remains provided a close match to the 2009 geophysical plan. However, there was only one part of the mega-structure with anything resembling monumental

Figure 15. Miniature vessel with graphite decoration: rim diameter 4 cm (photo: modified from M. Videiko).

Figure 16. Destruction daub, Phase 3A (source: B. Gaydarska and M. Nebbia).

architectural features—the East threshold with possible monumental wall features. The architectural emphasis on the eastern end of the mega-structure is heightened by the difference in sloping level between the East threshold and the surface of the unburnt area of at least 25–30 cm. This means that anyone approaching the mega-structure from the East side would have been confronted by a 2 m±high wall, with a possibly monumental entrance at the top of a slope. They would then have entered a loosely integrated structure which was partly roofed, partly open and with markedly different kinds of local 'spaces'—large open areas, small open areas, larger 'rooms', smaller 'rooms', and 'box rooms'.

The overall impression of the finds from the mega-structure is that there are few finds that differ greatly from the 'typical' Trypillia house assemblage. The most obvious special find is the group of twenty-one miniature vessels near the West partition of the East end. Some of them had burnished surfaces decorated with either a graphite wash or with painted graphite motifs—a feature unique not only at Nebelivka but for the whole of the Trypillia group. There was also the discovery of a tiny gold hair-ornament from one of the smaller 'rooms' in the East end (Figure 19)—one of the very few gold ornaments from the entire Trypillia-Cucuteni distribution. But the overwhelming mass of finds was ceramic, with a high proportion of fine wares. The total of twelve figurines is by no means impressive for such a large structure and the lithic assemblage of chipped, ground, and polished stone tools is small in comparison with other Trypillia

Figure 17. Destruction daub, Phase 3B (source: B. Gaydarska and M. Nebbia).

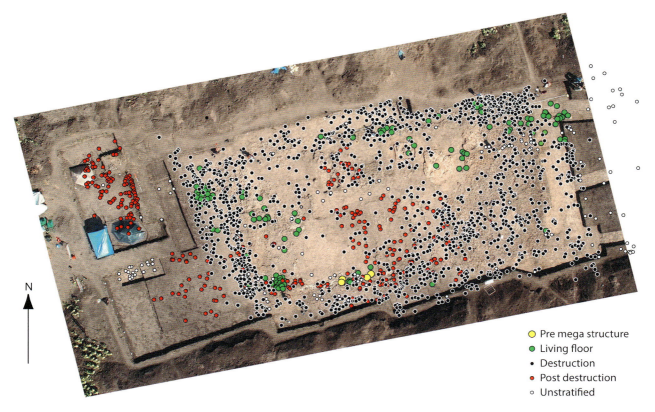

Figure 18. Pottery distribution, Phases 2–4 (source: E. Caswell).

house lithic assemblages. The group of over twenty small fired clay cones is perhaps a sign of an administrative practice (Videiko, 1987: 32–33), but may also be interpreted as gaming pieces (Figure 20). In general, there is little to make the mega-structure objects stand out from the typical artefact assemblage from a Trypillia house.

Several principal features (e.g. podium, cruciform Raised Areas) of the mega-structure are also similar to the features well known from Trypillia houses—but the Nebelivka examples are much larger (the podium, the Raised Areas) and more numerous (the Raised Areas). Preliminary research suggests that the fired clay bin, the largest Raised Area, and podium are the largest examples of their type so far known in the Trypillia culture. It would appear that the basic elements of the Trypillia house have been borrowed and adapted to fit the great size of what remains a public building but one without the depositional characteristics of a ritual or administrative centre. The layout of the rooms and internal features in both interpretations of the mega-structure does not fit any of the 'typical' domestic house layouts as defined by Chernovol (2012: figure 8.8). The mega-structure would have been a monumental building, visible from several km on the South part of the micro-region.

In short, the Nebelivka mega-structure is, in a sense, much more interesting than a ritual centre with all the trappings of a Late Neolithic temple (cf. Parța: Lazarovici *et al.*, 2001); it is a massive building with large versions of domestic features—'mega-features'—but with few objects differentiating the building from 'typical' Trypillia houses. Those expecting the architectural and artefactual reflections of a hierarchical society with elites ruling over thousands of inhabitants in a Trypillia mega-site will be disappointed. The resultant interpretation of the Nebelivka mega-structure requires a much more subtle model of site depositional practices than we have so far managed to create. Currently, there are more negatives than positives—relatively little storage capacity in fixed features or ceramics, with only five large storage-jars ('pithoi'); very restricted production of lithics or stone axes; no

Figure 19. Gold hair-ornament, mega-structure (photo: M. Videiko).

Figure 20. Fired clay cones, mega-structure (photo: M. Videiko).

production of copper or gold objects; no obvious cooking facilities—in particular, the striking absence of ovens or hearths, with the possible exceptions of a circular feature outside the West wall and the occasional use of the Raised Areas as hearths; rare special deposition with the exception of the miniature pots and little overt evidence for ritual practices. We are left with a building of great size, with a strong element of internal spatial differentiation, but with very few special artefacts. There is still little doubt that this is a public building, where meetings, and even ceremonies, could have taken place. The most obvious place for large meetings would have been the open central area, with its access to four major internal features—the podium, the fired clay bin, and the two largest Raised Areas. In addition, there may have been access to a set of small drinking-cups at the East end of the central area. But if those who attended the meetings brought their favourite objects with them, they seemed to have taken many of them away at the end of the ceremonies. The strong impression at the end of the excavation was of a mega-structure which had imitated the fittings and features of a domestic house on a large scale, without differentiating the mega-structure in an artefactual sense. We can therefore conclude that Trypillia mega-structures did indeed materialize spatial differentiation without the additional elaboration of artefactual differentiation.

OTHER ASSEMBLY HOUSES ON THE MEGA-SITES

In the same two mega-sites with perimeter boundaries—Nebelivka and Maidanetske—a similar pattern of spatial division has been recognized based on four spatial levels—the house, the Neighbourhood, the Quarter, and the entire site (Chapman *et al.*, 2014, 2014a; Ohlrau, 2014).

One of the key structuring elements of the Nebelivka plan is the series of larger-than-usual buildings provisionally termed 'assembly houses', on the assumption that these buildings were public places for meetings (Figure 1). Assembly houses were located at a variety of spacings around the outer and inner house circuits. They occurred in varying combinations: six isolates, five pairs, two trios, and one area with no assembly houses at all. Almost all of the assembly houses were rectangular, whereas one was apsidal and one was oval. Size was variable, with floor size ranging from 120 to 1320 m^2. Another variable was the extent of burning: one assembly house was burnt completely, two were not burnt at all, whereas the majority had only walls burnt. We consider the location of assembly houses to be of critical importance for the spatial division of the outer and inner house circuits and inner radial streets into the second level of spatial order—the 'Quarters'.[6] A critical question concerns the establishment of boundaries between the Nebelivka Quarters. Currently, eight criteria have been used to partition the mega-site into Quarters: (1) 'Natural' features, such as palaeo-channels (BUT there are only two palaeo-channels); (2) the border half-way between Assembly Houses (BUT this ignores local topographies); (3) the boundary between (pairs of) Assembly Houses (BUT sometimes there are three Assembly Houses or only one); (4) any large gaps between Neighbourhoods (BUT there is often a continuous spread of houses (e.g. E–F, F–G); (5) kinks in circuits (BUT these are absent in many parts of the circuit(s)); (6) major variations in the width of the middle (inter-circuit) space; (7) gaps in the ditch (BUT some one-third of the outer circuit has no surviving ditch); and (8) 'Obvious' entrances and passageways (BUT these gaps are not always obvious!).

The judicious combination of as many of the multiple criteria as possible has led to a preliminary partition of the Nebelivka mega-site into fourteen

---
[6]The term 'Quarter' is used in the sense of this term in studies of Near Eastern urbanism (Wilkinson *et al.*, 2013).

Quarters (Figure 1). It is possible that we shall re-define the Quarters at a later date, with the benefit of a wider range of information. It has been assumed that the location of single, paired, or groups of Assembly Houses was related to the structuring of domestic houses within the Quarters. It follows, then, that the distance separating Assembly Houses in adjacent Quarters would signify locational regularities (or otherwise) in the overall planning of the Quarters. The plot of these inter-Assembly House spacings (Figure 21) indicates great variability—ranging from 100 m (A.R. 2 in Quarter G to A.R. 2 in Quarter H) up to over 800 m (from the sole A.R. in Quarter M to A.R. 1 in Quarter B). This measure of the regularity of planning Quarters reveals a localized, bottom-up decision-making process rather than an overall 'centralized planning' that may have resulted in much more regular inter-Assembly Room spacing. A basic analysis of some of the locational and dimensional 'regularities' found at Nebelivka shows how Quarters developed in such markedly different ways that no single Quarter resembled any other Quarter in size or content. It is improbable that different partitioning of the mega-site would result in a different conclusion from this: namely, that the mega-site developed from the bottom-up within the overall constraints of the basic planning principles. It is intriguing that such variability could have been produced within identical planning principles.

Turning to the later, Phase CI mega-sites, the basic Nebelivka spatial structure was re-created a century or two later at Maidanetske, with an estimated total of fifteen Assembly Houses and a maximum mean ratio of almost 200 houses per Quarter (Ohlrau, 2014). A similar number of Assembly Houses is estimated for Dobrovody (Rassmann *et al.*, 2014: 126). It is even more intriguing, therefore, that only one possible Assembly House has been recognized at Taljanky— after all, the largest known mega-site in the Trypillia world. In view of the widespread geophysical coverage at Taljanky (195 ha), it is inconceivable that more Assembly Houses were present than have been recognized; we have to take the virtual absence of Assembly Houses at Taljanky as a genuine absence— and a phenomenon to be explained (NB the discussion of large houses and Assembly Houses at Taljanky in Rassmann *et al.*, 2016, 34 and Figs. 9b, 9c and 10b; see also Chapman and Gaydarska, 2016). The missing perimeter ditch and the absent Assembly Houses at Taljanky seem to us to be two sides of the same coin— an alternative social structure in which different ways of integrating a large population were used in contrast to those at Nebelivka and Maidanetske.

Conclusions

The presence of a perimeter boundary at two mega-sites—Nebelivka and Maidanetske—and their absence from the other two—Taljanky and Dobrovody— suggests major differences in social practices on these sites and the means that they used to integrate sub-groups with(out) communal building projects. The same is true for the absence from Taljanky of Assembly Houses, when these large structures were of such obvious social significance for the mega-sites of Nebelivka, Maidanetske, and Dobrovody.

The results of the excavation of the Nebelivka mega-structure have interesting implications for our understanding of the question of Trypillia urbanism. Rather than the creation of a completely new form of public buildings, with special functions materialized in dramatic, often monumental ways (e.g. the monumental temple complexes in the Late Chalcolithic and Early Bronze Age of southwest Asia (Matthews, 2009; Gates, 2011), Trypillian dwellers were content to reproduce their family houses *en gros* at certain strategic points of the settlement, with deposition on the same level as in family houses. It is interesting that three mega-structures were built in the same southern area of Nebelivka. But the mega-structure was by no means the same as a 'normal house', especially in its paucity of food storage, production, heating, and cooking facilities. This is not to say that all mega-

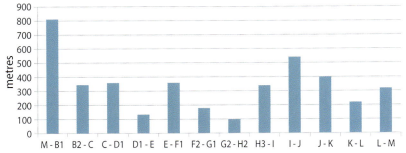

Figure 21. Spacings between Assembly Houses, Nebelivka (source: *J. Chapman*).

structures, whether at Nebelivka or at other mega-sites, will produce identical excavated results. Yet the first excavation of such a mega-structure has provided an intriguing combination of expanded scale and reduced object deposition. Further post-excavation studies will doubtless enable us to add more texture and colour to this provocative initial sketch, which contributes another layer of interpretation to the debate on Trypillia 'urbanism'.

ACKNOWLEDGEMENTS

This chapter could not have been written without the Kyiv–Durham research team of the AHRC-funded project 'Early urbanism in Europe? The case of the Ukrainian Trypillia mega-sites' (Grant No. AH/I025867/1). We thank the National Geographic Society for their much appreciated financial support for the mega-structure excavation (Grant No. 2012/211). We also thank Durham University, and especially the successive Chairs of Archaeology, Profs Chris Scarre and Chris Gerrard, for their support of the project. Our thanks are also due to the many villagers who made fieldwork in Nebelivka so enjoyable, Mayor Bobko and his son, the Director of the Nebelivka school, Larisa and Igor, Sergei the driver, Alina the best excavator in the village, Roma, and many more, as well as all of the students from Durham and other universities who worked so hard and long before evening drinks began.

REFERENCES

Andersen, N.H. 1997. *The Sarup Enclosures. The Funnel Beaker Culture of the Sarup site including two causewayed camps compared to the contemporary settlement in the area and other European enclosures.* Aarhus: *Sarup I*, Arhus University Press.

Becker, H. ed. 1996. *Archäologische Prospektion. Luftbild-Archäologie und Geophysik. Arbeitshefte des Bayerischen Landesamtes für Denkmalpflege.* München.

Braasch, O. 1995. 50 Jahre Verloren. In: O. Braasch, ed. Luftbildarchäin Ost- und Mitteleuropa. *Forschungen zur Archäologie im Land Brandenburg*, 3: pp. 109–22.

Braasch, O. 1996. Zur archäologischen Flugprospektion. *Archäologisches Nachrichtenblatt*, 1/1: 16–24.

Burdo, N. 2003. Sakralnyj aspekt arhitektury tripolskih protogorodov. In: O. G. Korvin-Piotrovskiy, V.O. Kruts & S.M. Ryzhov, ed. *Tripilski poselenya-giganti. Materiali mizhnarodnoi konferentsii.* Kiev: Korvin-press, pp. 18–21. Бурдо, Н. 2003. Сакральный аспект архитектуры трипольских протогородов. У зб.: О.Г. Корвін-Піотровський, В.О. Круц і С.М. Рижов, ред. *Трипільські поселення-гіганти. Матеріали міжнародної конференції.* Київ: Корвін-прес, с. 18–21.

Burdo, N., Videiko, M., Chapman, J. & Gaydarska, B. 2013. Houses in the Archaeology of the Tripillia-Cucuteni Groups. In: D. Hofmann & J. Smyth, eds. *Tracking the Neolithic house in Europe. Sedentism, architecture and practice.* New York: Springer, pp. 95–115.

Chapman, J. 2015. Burn or Bury? Mortuary Alternatives in the Neolithic and Chalcolithic of Central and Eastern Europe. In: A. Diachenko, F. Menotti, S. Ryzhov, K. Bunyatyan & S. Kadrow, eds. *The Cucuteni-Trypillia Cultural Complex and its Neighbours. Essays in Memory of Vlodomyr Kruts.* Lviv: Astrolyabia, pp. 259–78.

Chapman, J. & Gaydarska, B. 2016. Low-density Agrarian Cities: A Principle of the Past and the Present. In: J. Müller, K. Rassmann & M. Videiko, eds. *Trypillia Mega-Sites and European Prehistory: 4100–3400 BCE.* London and New York: Routledge, pp. 289–301.

Chapman, J. & Gaydarska, B. in press. Low-Density Urbanism: The Case of the Trypillia Group of Ukraine. In: M. Fernández-Götz & D. Krausse, eds. *Individualization, Urbanization and Social Differentiation: Eurasia at the Dawn of History.* Edinburgh: Edinburgh University Press.

Chapman, J. & Videiko, M. 2011. The Tripillia Culture Mega-Site Near Nebelivka: Summer 2009 Season. *Praehistorica (Prague)*, XXIX: 79–94.

Chapman, J., Videiko, M., Gaydarska, B., Burdo, N., Hale, D., Villis, R., Swann, N., Thomas, N., Edwards, P., Blair, A., Hayes, A., Nebbia, M. & Rud, V. 2014. The Planning of the Earliest European Proto-Towns: A New Geophysical Plan of the Trypillia Mega-Site of Nebelivka, Kirovograd Domain, Ukraine. *Antiquity Gallery*, 88 online gallery, http://antiquity.ac.uk.ezphost.dur.ac.uk/projgall/chapman339/.

Chapman, J., Videiko, M. Yu., Hale, D., Gaydarska, B., Burdo, N., Rassmann, K., Mischka, C., Müller, J., Korvin-Piotrovskiy, A. & Kruts, V. 2014a. The Second Phase of the Trypillia Mega-Site Methodological Revolution - A New Research Agenda. *European Journal of Archaeology*, 17/3: 369–406.

Chapman, J., Videiko, M. Y., Gaydarska, B., Burdo, N. & Hale, D. 2014b. An Answer to Roland Fletcher's Conundrum? Preliminary Report on the Excavation of a Trypillia Mega-Structure at Nebelivka, Ukraine. *Journal of Neolithic Archaeology*, 16: 135–57.

Chernovol, D. 2012. Houses of the Tomashevskaya Local Group. In: F. Menotti & A. G. Korvin-Piotrovskiy, eds. *The Tripolye Culture Giant-Settlements in Ukraine. Formation, Development and Decline.* Oxford: Oxbow Books, pp. 182–209.

Fletcher, R. 1995. *The Limits to Settlement Growth.* Cambridge: Cambridge University Press.

Fröhlich, S. ed. 1997. *Luftbildarchäologie in Sachsen-Anhalt.* Halle (Saale): Landesamt für archäologische Denkmalpflege.

Gates, C. 2011. *Ancient Cities: The Archaeology of Urban Life in the Ancient Near East, Egypt, Greece and Rome.* London: Routledge.

Goyda, M. 2006. Large Prehistoric Enclosures in Bohemia: The Evidence from the Air. In: A. Harding, S. Sievers & N. Venclová, eds. *Enclosing the Past: Inside and Outside in Prehistory.* Sheffield Archaeological Monographs, 15. Sheffield: J. R. Collis Publications, pp. 5–19.

Hale, D., Chapman, J., Swann, N., Videiko, M. & Villis, R. 2010. Early Urbanism in Europe? Geophysical Survey at Nebelivka, Ukraine. In: *Recent Work in Archaeological Geophysics.* The Geological Society. 15th

December 2010. Abstracts. London: Geological Society, pp. 35–36.

Harding, A., Sievers, S. & Venclová, N. eds. 2006. *Enclosing the Past: Inside and Outside in Prehistory*. Sheffield Archaeological Monographs 15. Sheffield: J. R. Collis Publications.

Johnston, S., Litkevych, V., Gaydarska, B., Voke, P., Nebbia, M. & Chapman, J. in prep. The Nebelivka Experimental House-Construction and House-Burning. In: Spasić, M., ed. *Housing in archaeological perspective*. Beograd: Muzej Grada Beograda.

Kruts, V. 2003. Tripolskie ploshchadki - rezultat ritualnogo sozhzheniya domov. In: O. G. Korvin-Piotrovskiy, V.O. Kruts & S.M. Ryzhov, ed. *Trypilski poselenya-giganty. Materialy mizhnarodnoi konferentsii*. Kiev: Korvin-pres, pp. 18–21. Круц, В.А. 2003. Трипольские площадки – результат ритуального сожжения домов. У зб.: О.Г. Корвін-Піотровський, В.О. Круц і С.М. Рижов, ред. *Трипільські поселення-гіганти. Матеріали міжнародної конференції*. Київ: Корвін-прес, с. 18–21.

Lazarovici, Gh., Draşovean, F. & Maxim, Z. 2001. *Parţa*. 2 vol. Timişoara: Waldpress.

Matthews, R. 2009. Peoples and Complex Societies of Ancient Southwest Asia. In: C. Scarre, ed. *The Human Past*. 2nd. ed. London: Thames & Hudson, pp. 432–71.

Mercer, R. J. 2006. The First Known Enclosures in Southern Britain: Their Nature, Function and Role, in Space and Time. In: A. Harding, S. Sievers & N. Venclová, eds. *Enclosing the Past: Inside and Outside in Prehistory*. Sheffield Archaeological Monographs 15. Sheffield: J. R. Collis Publications, pp. 69–75.

Mischka, C. 2010. Beispiele für Ähnlichkeit und Diversität neolithischer und kupferzeitlicher regionaler Siedlungsmuster in Rumänien anhand von geomagnetischen Prospektionen. In: S. Hansen, ed. *Leben auf dem Tell als soziale Praxis*. Bonn: Habelt, pp. 71–84.

Mischka, C. 2012. Late Neolithic Multiphased Settlements in Central and Southern Transylvania: A Geophysical Survey and Test Excavation. In: R. Hofmann, F-K. Moetz & J. Müller, eds. *Tells: Social and Environmental Space*. Bonn: Habelt, pp. 153–66.

Müller, J., Hofmann, R., Kirleis, W., Dreibrodt, S., Ohlrau, R., Brandtstätter, L., Dal Corso, M., Out, V., Rassmann, K. & Videko, M. in print. *Maidanetske 2013. New Excavations at a Trypillia Mega-site, Studien zur Archäologie in Ostmitteleuropa*. Bonn: Habelt.

Neustupný, E. 2006. Enclosures and Fortifications in Central Europe. In: A. Harding, S. Sievers & N. Venclová, eds. *Enclosing the Past: Inside and Outside in Prehistory*. Sheffield Archaeological Monographs 15. Sheffield: J. R. Collis Publications, pp. 1–4.

Ohlrau, R. 2014. Tripolje Großsiedlungen. Geomagnetische Prospektion und architektursoziologische Perspektiven. Unpub. MA Thesis. CAU Kiel.

Popa, A., Musteaţă, S., Rassmann, K., Bicbaev, V., Munteanu, O., Postică, G. & Sîrbu, G. 2010. Rezultate preliminare privind sondajele geofizice din anul 2009 şi perspectivele folosirii magnetometriei în Republica Moldova. In: S. Musteaţă, A. Popa & J-P. Abraham, eds. *Arheologia intre ştiinţă, politică şi economia de piată*. Chişinău: Pontos, pp. 145–57.

Rassmann, K., Ohlrau, R., Hofmann, R., Mischka, C., Burdo, N., Videjko, M. Yu. & Müller, J. 2014. High Precision Tripolye Settlement Plans, Demographic Estimates and Settlement Organization. *Journal of Neolithic Archaeology*, 16: 96–134.

Rassmann, K., Korvin-Piotrovskiy, A., Videiko, M. & Müller, J. 2016. The New Challenge for Site Plans and Geophysics: Revealing the Settlement Structure of Giant Settlements by Means of Geomagnetic Survey. In: J. Müller, K. Rassmann & M. Videiko, eds. *Trypillia Mega-Sites and European Prehistory: 4100–3400 BCE*. London and New York: Routledge, pp. 29–54.

Schiffer, M. B. 1976. *Behavioral Archaeology*. New York: Academic Press.

Smith, I. F. 1965. *Windmill Hill and Avebury: excavations by Alexander Keiller 1925–1939*. Oxford: Clarendon Press.

Videiko, M. Y. 1987. Glinyanye znaki-simvoly tripolskoi kultury. In: *Aktualnye problemy istoriko-arheologicheskih issledovanij. Tezisy dokladov VI respublikanskoj konferentsii molodyh arheologov*. Kiev: Naukova dumka, pp. 32–33. Видейко, М.Ю. 1987. Глиняные знаки-символы трипольской культуры. В сб.: *Актуальные проблемы историко-археологических исследований. Тезисы докладов VI республиканской конференции молодых археологов*. Киев: Наукова думка, с. 32–33.

Videiko, M.Y. 2013. *Kompleksnoe izuchenie krupnyh poselenij tripolskoj kultury V-IV tys. do n.e.*. Saarbrücken: Lambert Academic Publishing. Видейко, М.Ю. *Комплексное изучение крупных поселений трипольской культуры V-IV тыс. до н.э.* Saarbrücken: Lambert Academic Publishing.

Videiko, M. & Rassmann, K. 2016. Research on Different Scales: 120 Years Trypillian Large Sites Research. In: J. Müller, K. Rassmann & M. Videiko, eds. *Trypillia Mega-Sites and European Prehistory: 4100–3400 BCE*. London and New York: Routledge, pp. 17–28.

Whittle, A. W. R., Pollard, J. & Grigson, C. 1999. *The Harmony of Symbols: the Windmill Hill Causewayed Enclosure*. Cardiff Studies in Archaeology. Oxford: Oxbow Books.

Wilkinson, T. J., Gibson, McG. & Widell, M. eds. 2013. *Models of Mesopotamian Landscapes: How Small-Scale Processes Contributed to the Growth of Early Civilizations*. International Series, 2522. Oxford: Archaeopress.

CHAPTER 8

Chronology and Demography: How Many People Lived in a Mega-Site?

JOHANNES MÜLLER, ROBERT HOFMANN, LENNART BRANDTSTÄTTER, RENÉ OHLRAU
AND MYKHAILO VIDEIKO

INTRODUCTION

Since the discovery of the huge dimensions of Trypillia BII/CI mega-sites, estimations about their population size have mainly resulted magnitudes which are as extraordinary for European prehistory as the dimensions of the sites themselves. A variety of population calculations is known, usually (e.g. for Taljanky and Maidanetske) focusing on around 7500–25,000 inhabitants per site (Shmaglij, 1982; Shmaglij & Videiko, 1987; Kruts, 1989; Ohlrau, 2015). A basic assumption for these population estimations is the contemporaneity of the majority of houses in each mega-site, which might be problematic.

Also, for the reconstruction of the overall population density in the Southern Buh and Dnipro Interfluve, the question of the contemporaneity, or alternatively a sequential appearance, of mega-sites is very important. In many views, the mega-sites Nebelivka–Dobrovody–Taljanky–Maidanetske are described as a chronological sequence of about 15,000 people, moving after about fifty years from one site to the next, at a distance of about 20 km (Kruts, 1989). In other views, a contemporary existence of some of the mega-sites is supposed (Müller et al., in print). In such an argumentation, no less than about 30,000 people were projected as living contemporarily in mega-sites of the Volodymyrivsko-Tomashivska group.

In consequence, for Trypillia mega-sites, the question of the contemporaneity of the detected houses is still most important for further analyses and interpretations: are we really dealing with up to c. 1500–2500 contemporary house-units at one site? If this is the case, we would be dealing with probably more than c. 15,000 inhabitants per site; that makes them comparable on a demographic scale with early Mesopotamian cities. Furthermore, it is important to develop not only estimations, but also archaeological arguments for whether neighbouring mega-sites also existed contemporarily or if the aforementioned model of a population shift from one mega-site to the next is valid (cf. Diachenko & Menotti, 2012). Both aspects, the demographic dimension of one site and the population density within the region, are important for further aspects of economic, political, and social organization and, not least, questions of the environmental developments, in particular the carrying capacity of the landscape.

Thus, the main goals of this inquiry are twofold–regarding precise chronology and demography: How many houses existed contemporarily in a mega-site? How many mega-sites existed contemporarily? As a result, we might be able to answer the question: How many people lived in a mega-site? How many people lived in the Uman core area of the mega-sites?

Of basic importance for our approach is the interpretation of new ^{14}C-dates from Maidanetske; the first time that scientific dating has provided information about the chronology of mega-site house rings. Furthermore, consideration of typo-chronologies, as fundamental for the question of which sites existed contemporarily, might enable the formulation of probability models of population densities.

METHODS

Until recently, the arguments for different views of Trypillia demography were manifold, but still restricted because of the lack of reliable scientific dating. In principle, different interpretations of the same archaeological arguments are still possible:

1. The classical layout of a mega-site – a ground plan with concentric house rings around an empty central place and the very few stratigraphic overlaps of features – were used as an argument for the contemporaneity of the houses. Nevertheless, a succession of concentric house rings, for example, from an earlier inner ring to a later outer ring, would also result in such sophisticated settlement plans, but reduce the calculated number of inhabitants, for example, in Maidanetske with its nine house rings, by nearly eighty per cent.

© European Association of Archaeologists 2016

2. The regular burning of houses with the regular rectangular outline of the *ploschchadki* formed an argument for a consciously intended destruction of a whole settlement at the end of its duration. While this would imply the contemporaneity of most of the detected houses in mega-sites, alternative interpretations are also possible: for example, the burning of houses in one house ring after the other that would imply only a contemporaneity of the houses of one house ring (Zbenovich, 1990).
3. The intense studies of Trypillia ceramic shapes and ornamentation, especially BII/C ceramic ornamentation, proved statistically relevant typological clusters of features that have similar decoration and shapes (Ryzhov, 1999). These studies confirmed the typological division of Trypillia into the known main phases in their regional settings (cf. Diachenko & Menotti, 2015). Additionally, a typological differentiation of the Volodymyrivsko-Tomashivska and Kosenivska local group into several typological subgroups was undertaken. These typological sequences were interpreted as chronological sequences. Since with exceptions (Ryzhov, 1990; Shmaglij & Videiko, 1990) only one sub-phase was detected at each mega-site, the typological development was used as an argument for the contemporaneity of the features of each mega-site. Furthermore, the sequential sub-phases with each sub-phase of, for example CI, was used as an argument for the sequential appearance of mega-sites one after the other (cf. Kruts *et al.*, 2001; Diachenko, 2012). On the contrary, the lack of ^{14}C-dates and vertical stratigraphy made it clear that the different typological groups do not necessarily have to represent chronological phases. Different design systems also could reflect, for example, different contemporary social groups that express their differences and similarities in the medium of ceramic ornamentation among other things.
4. The methodological haziness of ^{14}C-dating in respect to the identification of short sequences, such as a two- to three-generation biography of mega-sites (*c.* fifty years by Kruts *et al.*, 2001; *c.* seventy to eighty years by Diachenko, 2012: figure 5.5), was used to underestimate the overlap of ^{14}C-dates from different sites (cf. Diachenko & Menotti, 2015). The reverse of this argument was taken by other scholars to describe the contemporaneity of mega-sites.

In consequence, a research strategy was developed, which included the following steps of analysis and interpretation:

1. In Maidanetske, the excavation strategy involved test-pits for each house ring, to gain radiometric dating samples (cf. Müller & Videiko, 2016). Context analyses of the samples and the evaluation of the sample material were involved in the interpretation of the data. The Bayesian approach was applied where possible.
2. The results were used to reconstruct a model of the contemporaneity of houses in Maidanetske. Using archaeological and ethnographic arguments in the reconstruction of the number of house inhabitants, a model of the demographic dimension of Maidanetske was developed.
3. Existing typological analyses of BII/CI ceramic inventories were used for correspondence analyses (CA) to estimate the statistical trajectories of stylistic differences. Through association with the already known and new ^{14}C-data, the CA-results were translated into a chronological pattern.
4. In doing so, a model on population dynamics within the Uman region was developed.

Dating a Mega-Site

In Maidanetske, during the 2013 campaign, both the trenches on house 44 and on two pits, as well additional small test trenches, which focus on geomagnetic features of houses in the concentric house rings 1–9, helped in dating the concentric house rings (Figure 1). These test trenches were carried out in eight cases, so that–together with the house and pit in trench 51/52–all nine house rings of the southwestern part of Maidanetske would yield information. Owing to the scarcity of datable material (due to the small amount of charcoal and bones in the house layers that are very near to the recent surface), only seven of the nine rings produced samples that could be used for radiometric dating. The Poznań laboratory succeeded in dating thirty-five samples (List 1; cp. also List 2). In spite of this, the spatial distribution of the dated houses allows judgement about the probability that the features were contemporary.

The context analyses of the samples mainly involved analyses of the stratigraphic location of the samples. An example of such a stratigraphy could be seen in house 44 (Müller *et al.*, 2014; Müller & Videiko, 2016).

The *ploschchadka* of house 44 was covered by a top layer of black soil with a very high concentration of humus, followed by a more greyish-brown sediment with less humus (Figure 2). Below these layers follows the daub package from the burnt house with a thickness of about 0.2–0.3 m. In the southwestern part of the house especially, a differentiation of the daub package into two layers was possible: a *c.* 10 cm thick top layer with small pieces of daub (nearly no organic intrusions), and a surface with smoothed horizontal

Figure 1. Maidanetske, SSW part of the settlement. The nine house rings, the excavation trenches and the numbers of the houses that were test-trenched or fully excavated (house 44). Pits 50, 52, and 60 are located in trenches with the same numbers. ^{14}C-data are available from nearly all features (see text).

daub pieces beneath the floor. The burnt floor layer consists of daub from a mineral-tempered pavement, with negative imprints of timber stakes at its bottom. The ground floor itself lies on top of a loess soil with a conserved fA_1 horizon. The upper edge of the loess soil beneath the floor level is characterized by different artefacts (pots, querns) that were placed there. In the areas outside of the ground floor layer the loess soil grew, probably as a result of domestic activities. This greyish loess sediment was partly covered by the top daub layer. Beneath the conserved loess soil and the anthropogenically influenced loess soil, the sediment of an fBw-horizon is visible that was hardly influenced by bioturbation. In all other trenches, the house stratigraphies were, in principle, similar to the one described for house 44.

The overall pattern of the settlement layout is the concentric arrangement of nine house rings, for each of which samples for dating were desired; this was possible for all except rings 3 and 5.

Ring 1 (house 44)

Besides one ^{14}C-date from a disturbance on top of the daub layer that represents a *terminus ante quem* (*c.* 750–450 cal BC), two ^{14}C-dates are relevant for dating the house. Poz-60162 (4965 ± 35 bp, bone, *Sus*, 3782–3702 cal BC) belongs to the daub layer, Poz-60161 (5015 ± 35 bp, bone, *Sus*, 3929–3715 cal BC) to the ground floor that indicates the usage of the house (List 1). The combination of the radiometric results, and of the vertical stratigraphy between both layers (Figure 2), makes usage of the house around *c.* 3700 BCE plausible, as also indicated by the sequential calibration of the two dates (Figure 3).

Four ^{14}C-dates belong to the lower part of the pit 52 that is associated with house 44 (List 1; cp. Müller & Videiko, 2016). Two of them represent *termini post quem* (possible old wood effect–60190 and 60347 *Quercus*), the two others *termini ad quem* (Poz-60292 4920 ± 40 bp (bos) from spit 1e (3713–3651 cal BC), and Poz-60296 4955 ± 35 bp from spit 1f (bone of a large mammal): 3775–3695 cal BC). Thus, the depositional processes probably took place in the 38th century BCE (Figure 3). Accordingly, there is a high probability that pit 52 existed contemporarily with house 44.

Ring 2 (house 46)

A similar stratigraphy was observed in trench 72, where the test-trench revealed the remains of the geomagnetic feature house 46 (*c.* 12 × 5 m). The ^{14}C-date Poz-60298 (4290 ± 40 bp, medium mammal, 2928–2879 cal BC) came from a layer on top of the house and represents a *terminus ante quem* (List 2).

List 1. Maidanetske ^{14}C-dates.

Sample name	Laboratory-ID	^{14}C age	Deviation	N (%)	C (%)	col (%)	find-ID	feature	level	find x	find y	trench	Material	Taxon	Description	Calibrated (68.2%)	Calibrated (95.4%)
Mai-50033 (feature 50004)	Poz-60157	4810	35	2.0	4.5	1.0	50033	50004	2	B	2	50	Bone	Bos		3645 BC (17.4%) 3630 BC; 3580 BC (50.8%) 3534 BC	3656 BC (26.4%) 3618 BC; 3611 BC (69.0%) 3521 BC
Mai-50038 (feature 50004)	Poz-60186	5050	35				50038	50004	2	A	1	50	Charcoal	Quercus		3942 BC (51.8%) 3857 BC; 3842 BC (1.5%) 3839 BC; 3820 BC (15.0%) 3794 BC	3957 BC (95.4%) 3766 BC
Mai-50073 (feature 50009)	Poz-60187	4980	35				50073	50009	3	A	2	50	Charcoal	Quercus		3790 BC (68.2%) 3707 BC	3930 BC (10.8%) 3877 BC; 3805 BC (84.6%) 3661 BC
Mai-50130 (feature 50008)	Poz-60158	5020	35	2.0	4.9	1.8	50130	50008	2	C	2	50	Bone	Ovis		3936 BC (33.9%) 3873 BC; 3810 BC (26.9%) 3761 BC; 3741 BC (3.3%) 3731 BC; 3725 BC (4.1%) 3715 BC	3943 BC (42.8%) 3855 BC; 3846 BC (3.1%) 3831 BC; 3824 BC (49.5%) 3710 BC
Mai-50140-1 (feature 50012)	Poz-60188	5005	30				50140	50012	4	A	3	50	Charcoal	Fraxinus		3905 BC (12.3%) 3880 BC; 3801 BC (55.9%) 3712 BC	3940 BC (28.6%) 3860 BC; 3814 BC (66.8%) 3704 BC
Mai-50140-2 (feature 50012)	Poz-60189	5125	35				50140	50012	5	A	4	51	Charcoal	Corylus		3975 BC (36.2%) 3938 BC; 3860 BC (32.0%) 3813 BC	3991 BC (50.7%) 3895 BC; 3881 BC (44.7%) 3800 BC

Continued

List 1. Continued

Sample name	Laboratory-ID	^{14}C age	Deviation	N (%)	C (%)	col (%)	find-ID	feature	level	find x	find y	trench	Material	Taxon	Description	Calibrated (68.2%)	Calibrated (95.4%)
Mai-50197 (feature 50012)	Poz-60159	5020	30	0.8	2.4	0.1	50197	50012	4	A	3	50	Bone	Bos		3933 BC (38.5%) 3875 BC; 3807 BC (29.7%) 3766 BC	3943 BC (44.5%) 3856 BC; 3843 BC (1.3%) 3835 BC; 3822 BC (49.6%) 3710 BC
Mai-51464 (feature 51007)	Poz-60160	2450	30	2.4	5.4	2.3	51464	51007	4	H	19	51	Bone	Bos		746 BC (24.6%) 686 BC; 666 BC (8.6%) 643 BC; 554 BC (28.8%) 475 BC; 463 BC (2.1%) 455 BC; 445 BC (4.1%) 431 BC	754 BC (26.7%) 681 BC; 670 BC (15.5%) 609 BC; 595 BC (53.2%) 411 BC
Mai-51498 (feature 51007)	Poz-60161	4965	35	2.6	4.3	1.3	51498	51007	4	L	20	51	Bone	Sus		3782 BC (68.2%) 3702 BC	3905 BC (3.4%) 3880 BC; 3801 BC (92.0%) 3655 BC
Mai-51606 (feature 51018)	Poz-60162	5015	35	2.2	5.8	3.0	51606	51018	4b	M	11	51	Bone	Sus		3929 BC (28.8%) 3877 BC; 3805 BC (27.9%) 3761 BC; 3742 BC (11.6%) 3715 BC	3943 BC (38.9%) 3855 BC; 3846 BC (2.5%) 3831 BC; 3824 BC (54.0%) 3707 BC
Mai-52029 (feature 52001)	Poz-60190	5165	35				52029	52001	1e	F	29	52	Charcoal	Quercus		4036 BC (12.1%) 4022 BC; 3995 BC (56.1%) 3954 BC	4045 BC (89.2%) 3940 BC; 3857 BC (6.2%) 3817 BC
Mai-52039 (feature 52001)	Poz-60295	4920	40	0.5	1.9	0.1	52039	52001	1e	F	29	52	Bone	Bos		3713 BC (68.2%) 3651 BC	3779 BC (95.4%) 3642 BC
Mai-52042 (feature 52001)	Poz-60347	5125	35				52042	52001	1f	F	30	52	Charcoal	Quercus		3975 BC (36.2%) 3938 BC; 3860 BC (32.0%) 3813 BC	3991 BC (50.7%) 3895 BC; 3881 BC (44.7%) 3800 BC

Continued

List 1. Continued

Sample name	Laboratory-ID	^{14}C age	Deviation	N (%)	C (%)	col (%)	find-ID	feature	level	find x	find y	trench	Material	Taxon	Description	Calibrated (68.2%)	Calibrated (95.4%)
Mai-52048 (feature 52001)	Poz-60296	4955	35	0.6	2.2	0.3	52048	52001	1f	H	31	52	Bone	Large mammal		3775 BC (68.2%) 3695 BC	3798 BC (95.4%) 3652 BC
Mai-60113 (feature 60002)	Poz-60348	5020	35	1.7	3.0	2.3	60113	60002	5	B	22	60	Bone	Large mammal		3936 BC (33.9%) 3873 BC; 3810 BC (26.9%) 3761 BC; 3741 BC (3.3%) 3731 BC; 3725 BC (4.1%) 3715 BC	3943 BC (42.8%) 3855 BC; 3846 BC (3.1%) 3831 BC; 3824 BC (49.5%) 3710 BC
Mai-60132 (feature 60006)	Poz-60191	4970	30			1.4	60132	60006	5	B	2	60	Charcoal	Quercus		3777 BC (68.2%) 3707 BC	3893 BC (1.6%) 3884 BC; 3799 BC (93.8%) 3661 BC
Mai-60145 (feature 60009)	Poz-60192	5060	35				60145	60009	6	D	2	60	Charcoal	Fraxinus		3942 BC (30.5%) 3895 BC; 3882 BC (17.4%) 3855 BC; 3845 BC (6.2%) 3834 BC; 3822 BC (14.1%) 3800 BC	3958 BC (95.4%) 3780 BC
Mai-60167 (feature 60009)	Poz-60349	4980	35	1.1	3.4		60167	60009	7	D	1	60	Bone	Bos		3790 BC (68.2%) 3707 BC	3930 BC (10.8%) 3877 BC; 3805 BC (84.6%) 3661 BC
Mai-60189 (feature 60009)	Poz-60350	5065	35	2.5	6.0	6.2	60189	60009	8	D-E	1-2	60	Bone	Bos		3944 BC (21.7%) 3907 BC; 3880 BC (46.5%) 3801 BC	3959 BC (95.4%) 3785 BC
Mai-70001 (Grotovine 1)	Poz-60196	6390	70		0.5							70	Soil organic matter		K7 dark brownish with loess	5466 BC (31.0%) 5404 BC; 5386 BC (37.2%) 5318 BC	5481 BC (95.4%) 5225 BC

Continued

Müller et al. — Chronology and Demography: How Many People Lived in a Mega-Site? 139

List 1. Continued

Sample name	Laboratory-ID	^{14}C age	Deviation	N (%)	C (%)	col (%)	find-ID	feature	level	find x	find y	trench	Material	Taxon	Description	Calibrated (68.2%)	Calibrated (95.4%)
Mai-70002 (Grotovine 2)	Poz-60197	4210	30									70	Soil organic matter		K5 dark brown	2890 BC (26.4%) 2864 BC; 2806 BC (39.7%) 2760 BC; 2717 BC (2.1%) 2713 BC	2900 BC (33.3%) 2848 BC; 2814 BC; (47.7%) 2737 BC; 2731 BC (14.5%) 2679 BC
Mai-70003 (Grotovine 3)	Poz-60198	4775	35									70	Soil organic matter		K8 dark brown	3636 BC (7.6%) 3626 BC; 3597 BC (60.6%) 3526 BC	3644 BC (91.9%) 3515 BC; 3411 BC (0.8%) 3405 BC; 3399 BC (2.7%) 3384 BC
Mai-72029 (feature 720005)	Poz-60298	4290	40	1.3	4.2	0.8	72029	720005	4		2	72	Bone	Medium Mammal		2928 BC (68.2%) 2879 BC	3022 BC (93.7%) 2871 BC; 2801 BC (1.7%) 2779 BC
Mai-73008 (feature 730005)	Poz-60351	4710	35	0.7	3.2	1.2	73008	730005	3		2	73	Bone	Ovis/Capra		3627 BC (16.3%) 3596 BC; 3527 BC (16.3%) 3498 BC; 3436 BC (35.6%) 3378 BC	3632 BC (26.5%) 3561 BC; 3537 BC (20.9%) 3492 BC; 3469 BC (48.0%) 3373 BC
Mai-73041 (feature 73005)	Poz-60199	4895	35	2.4	9.0	3.4	73041	73005	3		2	73	Bone	Medium mammel		3697 BC (68.2%) 3649 BC	3762 BC (6.3%) 3725 BC; 3715 BC (89.1%) 3637 BC
Mai-74001 (feature 740002)				0.2	2.4		74001	740002	2		2	74	Bone		not suitable		
Mai-74003 (feature 74004)							74003	74004	3		4	74	Bone		not suitable		

Continued

List 1. Continued

Sample name	Laboratory-ID	^{14}C age	Deviation	N (%)	C (%)	col (%)	find-ID	feature	level	find x	find y	trench	Material	Taxon	Description	Calibrated (68.2%)	Calibrated (95.4%)
Mai-75013 (feature 75002)	Poz-60352	4820	30	0.7	2.7	3.2	75013	75002	2		1-3	75	Bone	Bos		3650 BC (28.4%) 3631 BC; 3577 BC (2.4%) 3574 BC; 3564 BC (37.4%) 3536 BC	3656 BC (34.8%) 3626 BC; 3598 BC (60.6%) 3526 BC
Mai-77012 (feature 77003)	Poz-60194	4970	35	1.9	5.7	3.4	77012	77003	3	Q	5	77	Bone	Ovis/Capra		3783 BC (68.2%) 3705 BC	3909 BC (5.1%) 3879 BC; 3802 BC (90.3%) 3657 BC
Mai-79001 (feature 79003)	Poz-60195	4940	30	1.9	3.7	2.3	79001	79003	3		1	79	Bone	Sus		3761 BC (15.6%) 3741 BC; 3731 BC (3.4%) 3726 BC; 3715 BC (49.2%) 3661 BC	3777 BC (95.4%) 3654 BC
Mai-79005a (feature 79002)	Poz-60200	4875	35	1.1	6.7		79005	79002	2		1	79	Bone	Sheep/goat		3695 BC (21.7%) 3678 BC; 3670 BC (46.5%) 3640 BC	3748 BC (0.3%) 3745 BC; 3713 BC (92.2%) 3632 BC; 3557 BC (2.9%) 3538 BC
Mai-79005b (feature 79002)	Poz-60201	4450	30	2.5	10.1		79005	79002	2		1	79	Bone	Medium mammal		3320 BC (16.3%) 3272 BC; 3266 BC (14.5%) 3236 BC; 3170 BC (1.8%) 3164 BC; 3114 BC (14.5%) 3080 BC; 3070 BC (21.1%) 3025 BC	3336 BC (41.7%) 3210 BC; 3193 BC (7.9%) 3151 BC; 3139 BC (45.3%) 3011 BC; 2977 BC (0.4%) 2971 BC; 2948 BC (0.2%) 2945 BC
complex Zh, 1973	Bln-2087	4890	60										Charcoal			3761 BC (7.5%) 3741 BC; 3731 BC (1.9%) 3726 BC; 3715 BC (58.8%) 3636 BC	3893 BC (0.6%) 3883 BC; 3799 BC (84.7%) 3626 BC; 3597 BC (10.0%) 3526 BC

List 1. Continued

Sample name	find character	Number	Weight (g)	Remarks
Mai-50033 (feature 50004)	Bulk find	1	24	¹⁴C
Mai-50038 (feature 50004)	Sample	1	1	¹⁴C
Mai-50073 (feature 50009)	Sample	1	14	¹⁴C
Mai-50130 (feature 50008)	Bulk find	2	48	¹⁴C
Mai-50140-1 (feature 50012)	Sample	2	23.5	¹⁴C
Mai-50140-2 (feature 50012)	Sample	2	23.5	¹⁴C
Mai-50197 (feature 50012)	Single find	1	103	¹⁴C
Mai-51464 (feature 51007)	Single find	1	122	¹⁴C
Mai-51498 (feature 51007)	Single find	3	37	¹⁴C (part)
Mai-51606 (feature 51018)	Single find	1	17	¹⁴C
Mai-52029 (feature 52001)	Sample	2	9	¹⁴C
Mai-52039 (feature 52001)	Single find	1	97	¹⁴C
Mai-52042 (feature 52001)	Bulk find			¹⁴C
Mai-52048 (feature 52001)	Bulk find	2	58	¹⁴C
Mai-60113 (feature 60002)	Bulk find	4	35	¹⁴C (selection)
Mai-60132 (feature 60006)	Sample	1	2	¹⁴C
Mai-60145 (feature 60009)	Sample	1	3	¹⁴C
Mai-60167 (feature 60009)	Single find	11	330	¹⁴C (selection)
Mai-60189 (feature 60009)	Bulk find	18	440	¹⁴C (selection)
Mai-72029 (feature 720005)	Sample	1	1	¹⁴C
Mai-73008 (feature 730005)	Single find	7	13	¹⁴C
Mai-74001 (feature 740003)	Single find	1	14	¹⁴C
Mai-75013 (feature 75002)	Bulk find	1	37	¹⁴C
Mai-77012 (feature 77003)	Single find	2	4	¹⁴C
Mai-79001 (feature 79003)	Sample	1	7	¹⁴C

Sample name	Taxon	Element	Side	Epiphyseal Fusion	Fragmentopm	Meas (Bd)	Meas (Bp)	Meas (Glpe)	Dvl	Dvm	Meas (Head)	Modification
Mai-50033 (feature 50004)	Bos	OccipitalCondyle										
Mai-50038 (feature 50004)	Quercus											
Mai-50073 (feature 50009)	Quercus											
Mai-50130 (feature 50008)	Ovis	Femur	Right	FuPx	Px+		54.2				22.6	
Mai-50140-1 (feature 50012)	Fraxinus											
Mai-50140-2 (feature 50012)	Corylus											

142 *Trypillia-Mega-Sites and European Prehistory*

List 1. *Continued*

Sample name	Taxon	Element	Side	Epiphyseal Fusion	Fragmatopm	Meas (Bd)	Meas (Bp)	Meas (Glpe)	Dvl Dvm Meas (Head)	Modification
Mai-50197 (feature 50012)	Bos	Metacarpal	Right		Px+		58.7			Impact fracture, proximal side
Mai-51464 (feature 51007)	Bos	Metacarpal	Left	FuDs	6-	55.1			29.3 30.3	Impact fracture, lateral side
Mai-51498 (feature 51007)	Sus	Mandible								
Mai-51606 (feature 51018)	Sus	Radius	Right	FuPx	Px++		25.4			
Mai-52029 (feature 52001)	Quercus				6					
Mai-52039 (feature 52001)	Bos	Calcaneum	Right	FuPx	6					
Mai-52042 (feature 52001)	Quercus									
Mai-52048 (feature 52001)	Largemammal	Femur/Humerus			Frag					Impactfracture
Mai-60113 (feature 60002)	Largemammal	Tibia			Frag					
Mai-60132 (feature 60006)	Quercus									
Mai-60145 (feature 60009)	Fraxinus									
Mai-60167 (feature 60009)	Bos	Calcaneum	Right	FuPx	6			141.2		
Mai-60189 (feature 60009)	Bos	Patella	right		6					
Mai-72029 (feature 720005)	Medium Mammal	Long bonefragment								
Mai-73008 (feature 730005)	Ovis/Capra	Lumbarvertebra			6					
Mai-74001 (feature 740003)										
Mai-75013 (feature 75002)	Bos	Ph1		FuPx	6					
Mai-77012 (feature 77003)	Ovis/Capra	Mandible	ascending ramus							
Mai-79001 (feature 79003)	Sus	Tibia		UnDs	Px++	31.1	35.9	70.7		

List 2. *Cucuteni-Trypillia* ^{14}C-dates

LABNR	C14AGE	C14STD	Material	Species	Country	Site	Period	Culture	Phase	Locus
Ki-8086	5520	60	nd	nd	Ukraine	Bilshivtsy	3	C-T	T B1-B2	nd
Hd-19528	4499	24	Bone	Human	Romania	Grumezoaia	5	C-T	H	Inhumation burial
Ki-9623	4840	90	Bone	nd	Ukraine	Grygorivka	3	C-T	T B2	nd
Ki-9749	4830	90	Bone	nd	Ukraine	Grygorivka	3	C-T	T B2	nd
Ki-9622	4800	90	Charcoal	nd	Ukraine	Grygorivka	3	C-T	T B2	nd
Ki-9624	4740	90	Bone	nd	Ukraine	Grygorivka	3	C-T	T B2	nd
Hd-18678	5127	47	Charcoal	nd	Romania	Hancauti I	4	C-T	C B2	1986, H5, Pit 5, -1.30 m
Hd-19426	5106	49	Charcoal	nd	Romania	Hancauti I	4	C-T	C B2	1985, inferour level, -0.90-1.16 m
Hd-17930	4938	42	Charcoal	nd	Romania	Hancauti I	4	C-T	C B2	1986, H5, Pit 4, -1.23-1.50 m
Hd-18936	4884	54	Charcoal	nd	Romania	Hancauti I	4	C-T	C B2	S IV, H6, Pit 8, -1.45-1.58 m
Hd-17959	4621	95	Charcoal	nd	Romania	Hancauti I	5	C-T	H	1986, Surface IV, complex of firing pots no.1, from the oven mouth
Ki-9616	4650	90	Bone	nd	Ukraine	Grygorivka-Ignatenkova Gora	4	C-T	T C1	nd
Ki-11468	4630	90	Nd	nd	Ukraine	Grygorivka-Ignatenkova Gora	4	C-T	T C1	Pit 16
Ki-9614	4590	80	Bone	nd	Ukraine	Grygorivka-Ignatenkova Gora	4	C-T	T C1	nd
Ki-9615	4570	80	Bone	nd	Ukraine	Grygorivka-Ignatenkova Gora	4	C-T	T C1	nd
Ki-9617	4530	80	Bone	nd	Ukraine	Grygorivka-Ignatenkova Gora	4	C-T	T C1	nd
Ki-11469	4520	90	nd	nd	Ukraine	Grygorivka-Ignatenkova Gora	4	C-T	T C1	Pit 6, zr.3
Ki-9613	4520	80	Bone	nd	Ukraine	Grygorivka-Ignatenkova Gora	4	C-T	T C1	nd
Ki-10857	4515	90	nd	nd	Ukraine	Grygorivka-Ignatenkova Gora	4	C-T	T C1	R1,3, zr.2, -0.56 m
Ki-9618	4500	80	Bone	nd	Ukraine	Grygorivka-Ignatenkova Gora	4	C-T	T C1	nd
Ki-10856	4490	80	nd	nd	Ukraine	Grygorivka-Ignatenkova Gora	4	C-T	T C1	R1,3, zr.2, -0.56 m

Continued

List 2. Continued

LABNR	C14AGE	C14STD	Material	Species	Country	Site	Period	Culture	Phase	Locus
Ki-11467	4430	90	nd	nd	Ukraine	Grygorivka-Ignatenkova Gora	4	C-T	T C1	Pit 16, zr.1
Ki-9741	4490	90	nd	nd	Ukraine	Khomyne	4	C-T	T C1	nd
Ki-9740	4470	80	nd	nd	Ukraine	Khomyne	4	C-T	T C1	nd
Ki-9742	4390	90	nd	nd	Ukraine	Khomyne	4	C-T	T C1	nd
Ki-11455	4760	90	nd	nd	Ukraine	Ripnica 6	4	C-T	T C1	S2, Pit 1
Ki-11457	4670	90	nd	nd	Ukraine	Ripnica 6	4	C-T	T C1	S2, Pit 1
Ki-9745	4665	80	nd	nd	Ukraine	Ripnica 6	4	C-T	T C1	S2, Pit 1
Ki-9746	4620	90	nd	nd	Ukraine	Ripnica 6	4	C-T	T C1	S2, Pit 1
Ki-9743	4605	80	nd	nd	Ukraine	Ripnica 6	4	C-T	T C1	Nd
Ki-9744	4590	80	nd	nd	Ukraine	Ripnica 6	4	C-T	T C1	nd
Ki-11456	4580	90	nd	nd	Ukraine	Ripnica 6	4	C-T	T C1	S2, Pit 1
Ki-9747	4570	80	nd	nd	Ukraine	Ripnica 6	4	C-T	T C1	S2, Pit 1
Hd-19373	5163	36	charcoal	nd	Romania	Sofia 8	4	C-T	C B1/B2	Soundig II, Pit 1, -0.80-0.90m, beam of a platform
Hd-18826	4701	42	Bone	nd	Romania	Sarata Monteoru	4	C-T	C B2	1952, Surface R, -1-1.45 m
Hd-19419	4481	33	Bone	nd	Romania	Sarata Monteoru	4	C-T	C B2	1952, Surface T, -1.45 m
Hd-19573	4440	25	Bone	nd	Romania	Sarata Monteoru	4	C-T	C B2	1952, Surface R, Pit 1, -2 m
Gd-5858	5940	60	Charcoal	nd	Romania	Malnas-Bai	2	Cucuteni	C A2/A3	Sector D, level I/II, under the platform of H2
Gd-5861	5880	80	Charcoal	nd	Romania	Malnas-Bai	2	Cucuteni	C A2/A3	Level I/II, under the platform of H2
Hd-14118	5663	42	charcoal	nd	Romania	Malnas-Bai	2	Cucuteni	C A2/A3	Sector C, level I-II, under the platform of H2, m.10-11
Hd-14109	5497	100	Charcoal	nd	Romania	Malnas-Bai	2	Cucuteni	C A2/A3	Sector C, level II, posthole of H2, m.10-11
Gd-5860	5490	80	Charcoal	nd	Romania	Malnas-Bai	2	Cucuteni	C A2/A3	Sector B, level I/II, under the platform of H2
Gd-4682	5420	150	Charcoal	nd	Romania	Malnas-Bai	2	Cucuteni	C A2/A3	Sector B, Cas.1, level I

Continued

List 2. Continued

LABNR	C14AGE	C14STD	Material	Species	Country	Site	Period	Culture	Phase	Locus
Hd-15082	5407	20	Bone	nd	Romania	Malnas-Bai	2	Cucuteni	C A2/A3	SII, level II, fireplace 8
Hd-15278	5349	40	Bone	nd	Romania	Malnas-Bai	2	Cucuteni	C A2/A3	SI, Sector C, level I
Gd-4690	4950	100	Charcoal	nd	Romania	Malnas-Bai	2	Cucuteni	C A2/A3	Sector B, under the platform of H2, Level I
Bln-2803	5880	150	Grain	Wheat	Romania	Poduri-Dealul Ghindaru	1	Precucuteni	PC 3	nd
Bln-2804	5820	50	Charcoal	nd	Romania	Poduri-Dealul Ghindaru	1	Precucuteni	PC 2	nd
Bln-2782	5780	50	charcoal	nd	Romania	Poduri-Dealul Ghindaru	1	Precucuteni	PC 3	nd
Bln-2783	5690	50	charcoal	nd	Romania	Poduri-Dealul Ghindaru	2	Cucuteni	C A1	nd
Bln-2784	5680	60	Charcoal	nd	Romania	Poduri-Dealul Ghindaru	2	Cucuteni	C A1	nd
Hd-15401	5575	35	Charcoal	nd	Romania	Poduri-Dealul Ghindaru	2	Cucuteni	C A2	J4, H66,-1.85 m
Hd-15324	5529	29	Charcoal	nd	Romania	Poduri-Dealul Ghindaru	2	Cucuteni	C A2	I2, H66,-1.85 m
Bln-2824	5500	60	Charcoal	nd	Romania	Poduri-Dealul Ghindaru	2	Cucuteni	C A2	H2B
Lv-2153	5470	90	Bone	Human	Romania	Poduri-Dealul Ghindaru	2	Cucuteni	C A2	human skull, F1,-1.55 m
Bln-2802	5420	150	Charcoal	nd	Romania	Poduri-Dealul Ghindaru	2	Cucuteni	C A2	H2A
Bln-2805	5400	70	Charcoal	nd	Romania	Poduri-Dealul Ghindaru	2	Cucuteni	C A2	H2B
Hd-15039	5385	37	Grain	nd	Romania	Poduri-Dealul Ghindaru	2	Cucuteni	C A2	nd
Bln-2766	5350	80	Grain	Wheat	Romania	Poduri-Dealul Ghindaru	2	Cucuteni	C A2	H15
Ki-11462	4540	90	nd	nd	Ukraine	Usatovo	5	C-T	T C2	room 5 (?)
Ki-11459	4520	90	nd	nd	Ukraine	Usatovo	5	C-T	T C2	room 2 (?)
Ki-11460	4410	90	nd	nd	Ukraine	Usatovo	5	C-T	T C2	room 3 (?)
Ki-11461	4350	100	nd	nd	Ukraine	Usatovo	5	C-T	T C2	room 4 (?)
UCLA-1642A	4330	60	nd	nd	Ukraine	Usatovo	5	C-T	T C2	nd
Ki-11458	4270	100	nd	nd	Ukraine	Usatovo	5	C-T	T C2	Room 2 (?)
Bln-795	5345	100	Grain	Wheat	Romania	Leca-Ungureni	2	C-T	C A3	nd
Bln-1751	5635	50	Charcoal	nd	Romania	Margineni-Cetatuia	2	C-T	C A2	nd
Bln-1536	5625	50	Charcoal	nd	Romania	Margineni-Cetatuia	2	C-T	C A2	nd
Bln-1534	5610	55	Grain	Wheat	Romania	Margineni-Cetatuia	2	C-T	C A2	nd
Bln-1535	5485	60	Grain	Wheat	Romania	Margineni-Cetatuia	2	C-T	C A2	nd
Ki-369	5580	50	Bone	nd	Romania	Cainara	2	C-T	T B1	nd
Ki-870	4670	100	Charcoal	nd	Ukraine	Mayaki	5	Tripolye	T C2	nd
Ki-9751	4600	90	nd	nd	Ukraine	Mayaki	5	Tripolye	T C2	nd
Ki-282	4580	120	nd	nd	Ukraine	Mayaki	5	Tripolye	T C2	nd
Ki-11464	4530	90	nd	nd	Ukraine	Mayaki	5	Tripolye	T C2	nd

Continued

List 2. Continued

LABNR	C14AGE	C14STD	Material	Species	Country	Site	Period	Culture	Phase	Locus
Ki-9752	4490	90	nd	nd	Ukraine	Mayaki	5	Tripolye	T C2	9,1.36–1.61n, no.8370
Ki-281	4475	130	Charcoal	nd	Ukraine	Mayaki	5	Tripolye	T C2	nd
KiGN-281	4475	130	nd	nd	Ukraine	Mayaki	5	Tripolye	T C2	nd
Ki-11465	4460	90	nd	nd	Ukraine	Mayaki	5	Tripolye	T C2	nd
Bln-629	4400	100	Charcoal	Ulmus	Ukraine	Mayaki	5	Tripolye	T C2	Defensive ditch
UCLA-1642B	4376	60	nd	nd	Ukraine	Mayaki	5	Tripolye	T C2	nd
UCLA-1642G	4375	60	nd	nd	Ukraine	Mayaki	5	Tripolye	T C2	nd
Ki-11463	4370	100	nd	nd	Ukraine	Mayaki	5	Tripolye	T C2	nd
Ki-11466	4360	90	nd	nd	Ukraine	Mayaki	5	Tripolye	T C2	Defensive ditch
Le-645	4340	60	Charcoal	nd	Ukraine	Mayaki	5	Tripolye	T C2	nd
Ki-9753	4180	90	nd	nd	Ukraine	Mayaki	5	Tripolye	T C2	nd
Gd-6387	6320	110	Bone	nd	Romania	Scanteia	2	Cucuteni	C A3	1989, Cassette 3,3, H4,–0.60–0.70 m
Gd-4685	5750	110	Bone	nd	Romania	Scanteia	2	Cucuteni	C A3	1989, Section VI,13,–0.62 m
Hd-14701	5388	18	Bone	Human	Romania	Scanteia	2	Cucuteni	C A3	S VIII, Cassette 1, Grave 1,–0.82 m, child
Hd-14792	5370	26	Bone	Human	Romania	Scanteia	2	Cucuteni	C A3	S VIII, Cassette1, Grave 1,–0.87 m, woman
Hd-16700	5345	51	Bone	nd	Romania	Scanteia	2	Cucuteni	C A3	1992, Section VIII,13, Pit 62,–2.25 m
Gd-6388	5330	110	Bone	nd	Romania	Scanteia	2	Cucuteni	C A3	1989, Section VI,14,–0.55 m
Hd-19572	5280	27	Bone	nd	Romania	Scanteia	2	Cucuteni	C A3	S IX, m.37, Pit 7,–1.20 m
Hd-16701	5205	63	Bone	nd	Romania	Scanteia	2	Cucuteni	C A3	1992, Sectiopn VIII, Cassette 1, 16B-17C,–0.73m under the platform of H8
GrN-5088	4615	35	nd	nd	Moldova	Gorodnytsya-Gorodyshche	5	C-T	T C2	nd
GrN-1985	5340	80	nd	nd	Romania	Habasesti-Holm	2	C-T	C A3	nd
GrN-4424	5530	85	Charcoal	nd	Romania	Tarpesti	1	C-T	PC 3	nd
GrN-1982	4950	60	Grain	Wheat	Romania	Valea Lupului	4	C-T	C B2	nd
Lv-2152	5830	100	Bone	nd	Romania	Targu Frumos	1	C-T	PC 3	pit
Hd-15075	5065	19	Bone	nd	Romania	Cucuteni-Cetatuia	4	C-T	C B2	1961, LIV, CI

Continued

List 2. Continued

LABNR	C14AGE	C14STD	Material	Species	Country	Site	Period	Culture	Phase	Locus
Hd-14817	5423	26	Bone	nd	Romania	Preutesti-Halta	2	C-T	C A3	1978, S1, Pit1,-1.60 m
Le-1054	4600	60	Charcoal	nd	Moldova	Danku 2	5	C-T	H	nd
Hd-14710	5162	37	Bone	nd	Romania	Mihoveni-Cahla Morii	4	C-T	C B1b	1981, S5, Pit 5
Hd-14791	4890	29	Bone	nd	Romania	Mihoveni-Cahla Morii	4	C-T	C B2	1981, S5, m.80-81, H8
Bln-590	5565	100	Charcoal	Fraxinus	Moldova	Novye Ruseshti 1	2	C-T	T B1	nd
UCLA-1642F	4904	300	nd	nd	Ukraine	Novo-Rozanovka	4	C-T	T C1	nd
Le-1392	5990	60	wool	nd	Romania	Iablona 1	3	C-T	C A-B1	nd
Le-4538	5250	75	nd	nd	Romania	Iablona 1	3	C-T	C A-B1	nd
Le-1393	4170	40	Wool	nd	Romania	Iablona 1	3	C-T	C A-B1	nd
Bln-2431	5165	50	Charcoal	nd	Ukraine	Tsipleshty 1	3	C-T	T B2	nd
Bln-2426	5700	55	Charcoal	nd	Romania	Rogozhany 1	1	C-T	PC 3	nd
Bln-2480	4990	60	charcoal	nd	Moldavia	Varvarovka 15	4	C-T	T C1	nd
Ki-601	4370	180	nd	nd	Moldova	Varvarovka 8	4	C-T	T C1	nd
Bln-2447	5595	80	bone	nd	Moldova	Putineshti 3	2	C-T	T B1	nd
Lv-2156	5520	70	Charcoal	nd	Moldova	Putineshti 3	2	C-T	C A4	H3, Cassette 3,-1.70-1.80 m
Hd-19441	5379	32	Charcoal	nd	Moldova	Putineshti 3	2	C-T	C A4	Pit House 4,-2 m
Ki-613	5060	120	Bone	nd	Moldova	Putineshti 3	2	C-T	C A4	nd
Ki-609	4215	110	nd	nd	Moldova	Putineshti 3	2	Cucuteni	C A4	nd
IGAN-712	5730	50	Charcoal	nd	Moldova	Drutsy 1	2	Tripolye	T B1	nd
Ki-11491	5930	80	Bone	nd	Ukraine	Aleksandrovka	1	Early Tripolye	T A	nd
Bln-2428	5390	60	nd	nd	Ukraine	Cuconestii Vechi	2	C-T	C A3	nd
Bln-1060	5355	100	Charcoal	nd	Romania	Draguseni-Ostrov	2	C-T	C A3	nd
Bln-1195	5430	100	Charcoal	nd	Romania	Draguseni-Ostrov	2	C-T	C A4	nd
Hd-14761	5246	24	bone	nd	Romania	Draguseni-Ostrov	3	C-T	C A-B1	1963, e-f, -1.10 m
Bln-1194	5205	100	Charcoal	nd	Romania	Draguseni-Ostrov	2	C-T	C A4	nd
Hd-14544	5188	18	Bone	nd	Romania	Draguseni-Ostrov	3	C-T	C A-B1	1961, 6-10
Hd-14831	4996	26	Bone	nd	Romania	Draguseni-Ostrov	3	C-T	C A-B1	1961, complex V,-0.20 m
BM-495	4940	105	nd	nd	Moldova	Soroki-Ozero	4	C-T	T C1	nd
BM-494	4792	105	nd	nd	Moldova	Soroki-Ozero	4	C-T	T C1	nd

Continued

List 2. Continued

LABNR	C14AGE	C14STD	Material	Species	Country	Site	Period	Culture	Phase	Locus
Bln-3191	5700	70	Charcoal	nd	Ukraine	Timkovo	1	Precucuteni	PC 3	nd
Bln-2430	5020	60	nd	nd	Moldova	Brinzeni 4	2	C-T	T B1	nd
Bln-2429	5360	65	Charcoal	nd	Moldova	Brinzeni 8	3	C-T	T B2	nd
Ki-7203	5760	55	nd	nd	Ukraine	Berezovskaya GES	2	C-T	T B1	nd
Ki-7204	5710	60	nd	nd	Ukraine	Berezovskaya GES	2	C-T	T B1	nd
Ki-6683	5860	45	nd	nd	Ukraine	Grenovka	1	C-T	T A	nd
Ki-6682	5800	50	nd	nd	Ukraine	Grenovka	1	C-T	T A	nd
Ki-6656	6200	55	nd	nd	Ukraine	Babshin	1	C-T	T A	nd
Ki-6745	4530	50	Bone	nd	Ukraine	Zhvanets'-Shchovb	5	C-T	T C1-2	Pit House 1
Ki-6743	4480	40	Bone	nd	Ukraine	Zhvanets'-Shchovb	5	C-T	T C1-2	House 2
Ki-6754	4380	60	charcoal	nd	Ukraine	Zhvanets'-Shchovb	5	C-T	T C1-2	nd
Ki-6744	4355	60	Bone	nd	Ukraine	Zhvanets'-Shchovb	5	C-T	T C1-2	Pit House 6
Ki-6753	4290	55	Charcoal	nd	Ukraine	Zhvanets'-Shchovb	5	C-T	T C1-2	Embankment
Ki-6751	3960	50	Bone	Human	Ukraine	Tsviklovtsy	5	C-T	T C2	nd
Ki-11475	6520	90	Pottery	nd	Ukraine	Bernashovka 1	1	C-T	PC 3	nd
Ki-6681	6510	55	nd	nd	Ukraine	Bernashovka 1	1	C-T	PC 3	nd
Ki-11472	6445	90	Pottery	nd	Ukraine	Bernashovka 1	1	C-T	PC 3	nd
Ki-6670	6440	60	nd	nd	Ukraine	Bernashovka 1	1	C-T	PC 3	nd
Ki-6677	6180	60	nd	nd	Ukraine	Voronovitsy	1	C-T	T A	nd
GrN-5134	5440	70	Charcoal	nd	Ukraine	Polivanov Yar 3	2	C-T	T B1	nd
Ki-6675	6270	55	nd	nd	Ukraine	Korman'	1	C-T	T A	nd
Ki-6225	6225	60	nd	nd	Ukraine	Korman'	1	C-T	T A	nd
Ki-6676	6225	60	nd	nd	Ukraine	Korman'	1	C-T	T A	nd
Ki-7202	5805	65	nd	nd	Ukraine	Sabatinovka 1	1	C-T	T A	nd
Ki-6737	6100	55	nd	nd	Ukraine	Sabatinovka 2	1	C-T	T A	nd
Ki-6680	6075	60	nd	nd	Ukraine	Sabatinovka 2	1	C-T	T A	nd
Ki-11447	5620	100	nd	nd	Ukraine	Nezvisko 2	2	C-T	T B1	11/4-11, pottery
Ki-11448	5620	100	nd	nd	Ukraine	Nezvisko 2	2	C-T	T B1	10/D22, pottery
Ki-11446	5605	60	nd	nd	Ukraine	Nezvisko 2	2	C-T	T B1	Sl/3a/pottery
Ki-11449	5560	100	nd	nd	Ukraine	Nezvisko 2	2	C-T	T B1	Pottery
Bln-2087	4890	60	Charcoal	nd	Ukraine	Maidanetskoe	4	C-T	T C1	Same sample as Ki-1212

Continued

List 2. Continued

LABNR	C14AGE	C14STD	Material	Species	Country	Site	Period	Culture	Phase	Locus
Ki-1212	4600	80	Charcoal	nd	Ukraine	Maidanetskoe	4	C-T	T C1	nd
OxA-19840	5048	44	Charcoal	Fraxinus	Ukraine	Tal'yanki	4	W. Tripolye	T C1	House 41
OxA-22348	5032	31	Charcoal	Quercus	Ukraine	Tal'yanki	4	W. Tripolye	T C1	House 42
Ki-16026	4990	80	Bone	nd	Ukraine	Tal'yanki	4	W. Tripolye	T C1	House 40
OxA-22515	4976	29	Charcoal	Fraxinus	Ukraine	Tal'yanki	4	W. Tripolye	T C1	House 43
Ki-16025	4970	50	Bone	nd	Ukraine	Tal'yanki	4	W. Tripolye	T C1	House 41
Bln-4598	4936	40	nd	nd	Ukraine	Tal'yanki	4	W. Tripolye	T C1	nd
Ki-15993	4910	70	Bone	nd	Ukraine	Tal'yanki	4	W. Tripolye	T C1	House 41
Ki-6867	4810	55	Bone	nd	Ukraine	Tal'yanki	4	W. Tripolye	T C1	House 13/14
Ki-6868	4780	60	Bone	nd	Ukraine	Tal'yanki	4	W. Tripolye	T C1	House 13/14
Ki-6865	4755	50	Bone	nd	Ukraine	Tal'yanki	4	W. Tripolye	T C1	House 13/14
Ki-6866	4720	60	Bone	nd	Ukraine	Tal'yanki	4	W. Tripolye	T C1	House 13/14
Ki-15994	4550	70	Bone	nd	Ukraine	Tal'yanki	4	W. Tripolye	T C1	House 40
Ki-6671	6330	65	nd	nd	Ukraine	Okopi	1	Early Tripolye	T A	nd
Ki-6165	6165	55	nd	nd	Ukraine	Grebenyukov Yar	1	Early Tripolye	T A	nd
Ki-6673	6120	50	nd	nd	Ukraine	Grebenyukov Yar	1	Early Tripolye	T A	nd
Ki-6672	6040	65	nd	nd	Ukraine	Grebenyukov Yar	1	Early Tripolye	T A	nd
Ki-6684	5905	60	nd	nd	Ukraine	Luka Vrublevetskaya	1	Early Tripolye	T A	nd
Ki-6685	5845	50	nd	nd	Ukraine	Luka Vrublevetskaya	1	Early Tripolye	T A	nd
Bln-2137	5180	65	nd	nd	Ukraine	Veseliy Kut	3	E. Tripolye	T B1-B2	nd
Ki-903	5100	100	Charcoal	nd	Ukraine	Veseliy Kut	3	E. Tripolye	T B1-B2	nd
Ki-11450	4300	90	nd	nd	Ukraine	Ol'khovets 1	5	W. Tripolye	T C1-2	1993, Pit 1
Ki-11454	4280	90	nd	nd	Ukraine	Ol'khovets 1	5	W. Tripolye	T C1-2	1993, Pit 1
Ki-11452	4250	90	nd	nd	Ukraine	Ol'khovets 1	5	W. Tripolye	T C1-2	1993, Pit 1
Ki-10859	4240	90	nd	nd	Ukraine	Ol'khovets 1	5	W. Tripolye	T C1-2	1993, H1
Ki-6925	4225	55	Bone	nd	Ukraine	Ol'khovets 1	5	W. Tripolye	T C1-2	Pit 1
Ki-6924	4205	50	Bone	nd	Ukraine	Ol'khovets 1	5	W. Tripolye	T C1-2	Pit 1
Ki-10858	4190	90	nd	nd	Ukraine	Ol'khovets 1	5	W. Tripolye	T C1-2	1993, H1
Ki-9754	4190	80	nd	nd	Ukraine	Ol'khovets 1	5	W. Tripolye	T C1-2	1993, H1

Continued

List 2. Continued

LABNR	C14AGE	C14STD	Material	Species	Country	Site	Period	Culture	Phase	Locus
Ki-11451	4170	90	nd	nd	Ukraine	Ol'khovets 1	5	W. Tripolye	T C1-2	Pit 1
Ki-6922	4170	55	bone	nd	Ukraine	Ol'khovets 1	5	W. Tripolye	T C1-2	Pit 1
Ki-6923	4165	60	bone	nd	Ukraine	Ol'khovets 1	5	W. Tripolye	T C1-2	Pit 1
Ki-11453	4130	90	nd	nd	Ukraine	Ol'khovets 1	5	W. Tripolye	T C1-2	Pit 1
Ki-9625	4110	80	nd	nd	Ukraine	Ol'khovets 1	5	W. Tripolye	T C1-2	1993, H1, room 1
Le-1060	5100	50	Charcoal	nd	Ukraine	Klishchev	3	C-T	T B1-B2	nd
Ki-11488	4720	60	nd	nd	Ukraine	Zelena Dibrova	4	C-T	T C1	nd
Ki-882	5310	160	nd	nd	Ukraine	Krasnostavka	2	C-T	T B1	nd
Ki-11490	4780	70	nd	nd	Ukraine	Khutir Nezamoznyk	4	W. Tripolye	T C1	nd
Ki-11489	4910	70	nd	nd	Ukraine	Ol'shana	4	W. Tripolye	T C1	nd
Hd-14785	4495	18	Bone	nd	Moldova	Horodistea	5	Late Tripolye/Horodistea-Foltesti	H 1	S.L.,-1.50-1.70 m
Hd-15024	4377	21	Bone	nd	Moldova	Horodistea	5	Late Tripolye/Horodistea-Foltesti	H 2	1969, S.L., H1
Hd-14898	4235	30	Bone	nd	Moldova	Horodistea	5	Late Tripolye/Horodistea-Foltesti	H 2	S.L., H1
Ki-874	5770	120	nd	nd	Ukraine	Miropole	3	C-T	T B2	nd
Ki-1204	4700	90	Charcoal	nd	Ukraine	Shkarovka	2	C-T	T B1-B2	Platform 1
Ki-520	5015	105	nd	nd	Ukraine	Shkarovka	3	C-T	T B1-B2	nd
Bln-2088	4940	95	nd	nd	Ukraine	Shkarovka	3	C-T	T B1-B2	nd
Ki-2088	4940	95	nd	nd	Ukraine	Shkarovka	3	C-T	T B1-B2	nd
Ki-875	4840	95	nd	nd	Ukraine	Shkarovka	3	C-T	T B1-B2	nd
Ki-879	4710	130	nd	nd	Ukraine	Shkarovka	3	C-T	T B1-B2	nd
Ki-877	4690	80	nd	nd	Ukraine	Shkarovka	3	C-T	T B1-B2	nd
Ki-881	4620	100	nd	nd	Ukraine	Shkarovka	3	C-T	T B1-B2	nd
Ki-201	4320	170	nd	nd	Ukraine	Shkarovka	3	C-T	T B1-B2	nd

Continued

List 2. Continued

LABNR	C14AGE	C14STD	Material	Species	Country	Site	Period	Culture	Phase	Locus
Ki-6747	4210	45	bone	nd	Ukraine	Sandraky	5	C-T	T C2	3-7, cavity
Ki-6746	4175	50	Bone	nd	Ukraine	Sandraky	5	C-T	T C2	Bones on fireplace, 3-7
Ki-11486	4850	70	nd	nd	Ukraine	Pekari 2	4	C-T	T C1	nd
Ki-11487	4805	70	nd	nd	Ukraine	Pekari 2	4	C-T	T C1	nd
Ki-7207	5140	60	Bone	nd	Ukraine	Grebeni	3	C-T	T B2	nd
Ki-7205	5120	65	Bone	nd	Ukraine	Grebeni	3	C-T	T B2	nd
Ki-7208	5100	90	Bone	nd	Ukraine	Grebeni	3	C-T	T B2	nd
Ki-7206	5080	70	Bone	nd	Ukraine	Grebeni	3	C-T	T B2	nd
Ki-6750	4430	45	Bone	nd	Ukraine	Troyaniv	5	C-T	T C2	SIII, LV-b-7. House 25
Ki-6749	4410	50	Bone	nd	Ukraine	Troyaniv	5	C-T	T C2	House, XIII-19
Ki-6748	4360	55	Bone	nd	Ukraine	Troyaniv	5	C-T	T C2	House 28, LXXII-2, S18
Ki-5012	4320	70	Burnt bone	Human	Ukraine	Sofievka	5	E. Tripolye	T C2	Cemetery, Grave 1
Ki-5029	4300	45	Bone	nd	Ukraine	Sofievka	5	E. Tripolye	T C2	Cemetery
Ki-5013	4270	90	nd	nd	Ukraine	Sofievka	5	E. Tripolye	T C2	cemetery, Grave 11
Bln-631	4870	100	Charcoal	Fraxinus	Ukraine	Chapaevka	4	E. Tripolye	T C1	nd
Ki-880	4810	140	Charcoal	nd	Ukraine	Chapaevka	4	E. Tripolye	T C1	nd
Ki-5038	4280	110	Bone	Human	Ukraine	Chervony khutor	5	E. Tripolye	T C1-2	Cemetery, Grave 2
Ki-5039	4160	90	Bone	Human	Ukraine	Chervony khutor	5	E. Tripolye	T C1-2	Cemetery, Grave 98
Ki-5016	4140	110	Nd	nd	Ukraine	Chervony khutor	5	E. Tripolye	T C1-2	cemetery, Grave 6
UCLA-1671B	4890	60	nd	nd	Ukraine	Evminka 1	4	E. Tripolye	T C1	nd
UCLA-1466B	4790	100	nd	nd	Ukraine	Evminka 1	4	E. Tripolye	T C1	nd
Ki-5015	4290	90	nd	nd	Ukraine	Zavalovka	5	E. Tripolye	T C2	Cemetery, Grave 6
Ki-5014	4230	80	Bone	Human	Ukraine	Zavalovka	5	E. Tripolye	T C2	Cemetery, Grave 10
GrN-5099	4615	35	nd	nd	Ukraine	Gorods'k	5	Late Tripolye	T C2	nd
Ki-6752	4495	45	shell	nd	Ukraine	Gorods'k	5	Late Tripolye	T C2	nd
Ki-11862	4520	70	Bone	nd	Ukraine	Sharyn	5	W. Tripolye	T C1-2	Uman district, Cherkasy region, Yatran river, 2003, site 4, dug-out 3

Continued

152 Trypillia-Mega-Sites and European Prehistory

List 2. Continued

LABNR	C14AGE	C14STD	Material	Species	Country	Site	Period	Culture	Phase	Locus
Ki-12050	4575	60	Burnt bone	nd	Ukraine	Sharyn	5	W. Tripolye	T C1-2	Uman district, Cherkasy region, Yatran river, 2003, site 5, dwelling 2
Ki-11866	4530	80	Clay	nd	Ukraine	Sharyn	5	W. Tripolye	T C1-2	Uman district, Cherkasy region, Yatran river, 2003, site 5, dwelling 2
Ki-11867	4590	80	Clay	nd	Ukraine	Sharyn	5	W. Tripolye	T C1-2	Uman District, Cherkasy region, Yatran river, 2003, site 5, dwelling 2
Ki-11868	4520	80	Clay	nd	Ukraine	Sharyn	5	W. Tripolye	T C1-2	Uman district, Cherkasy region, Yatran river, 2003, site 5, dwelling 2
Ki-11869	4670	80	Clay	nd	Ukraine	Sharyn	5	W. Tripolye	T C1-2	Uman district, Cherkasy region, Yatran river, 2003, site 5, dwelling 2
Ki-9740	4470	80	Bone	nd	Ukraine	Rzhyschev-Ripnitsa	4	C-T	T C1	nd
Ki-9741	4490	90	Bone	nd	Ukraine	Rzhyschev-Ripnitsa	4	C-T	T C1	nd
Ki-9742	4390	90	Bone	nd	Ukraine	Rzhyschev-Ripnitsa	4	C-T	T C1	nd
Ki-9743	4605	80	bone	nd	Ukraine	Rzhyschev-Ripnitsa	4	C-T	T C1	nd
Ki-9744	4590	80	Bone	nd	Ukraine	Rzhyschev-Ripnitsa	4	C-T	T C1	nd
Ki-9745	4565	80	Bone	nd	Ukraine	Rzhyschev-Ripnitsa	4	C-T	T C1	nd
Ki-9746	4620	90	Bone	nd	Ukraine	Rzhyschev-Ripnitsa	4	C-T	T C1	nd
Ki-9747	4570	80	Bone	nd	Ukraine	Rzhyschev-Ripnitsa	4	C-T	T C1	nd

List 2. Continued

Labnr	Latitude	Longitude	Reference	Notice	Context	Duration	Quality	Incongr	Region	Megaregion	Database	Id
Ki-8086			Lazarovici (2010)	–	–	–	–	–	–	–	–	–
Hd-19528			Lazarovici (2010)	–	–	–	–	–	–	–	–	–
Ki-9623			Lazarovici (2010)	–	–	–	–	–	–	–	–	–
Ki-9749			Lazarovici (2010)	–	–	–	–	–	–	–	–	–
Ki-9622			Lazarovici (2010)	–	–	–	–	–	–	–	–	–
Ki-9624			Lazarovici (2010)	–	–	–	–	–	–	–	–	–
Hd-18678			Lazarovici (2010)	–	–	–	–	–	–	–	–	–
Hd-19426			Lazarovici (2010)	–	–	–	–	–	–	–	–	–
Hd-17930			Lazarovici (2010)	–	–	–	–	–	–	–	–	–
Hd-18936			Lazarovici (2010)	–	–	–	–	–	–	–	–	–
Hd-17959			Lazarovici (2010)	–	–	–	–	–	–	–	–	–
Ki-9616			Lazarovici (2010)	–	–	–	–	–	–	–	–	–
Ki-11468			Lazarovici (2010)	–	–	–	–	–	–	–	–	–
Ki-9614			Lazarovici (2010)	–	–	–	–	–	–	–	–	–
Ki-9615			Lazarovici (2010)	–	–	–	–	–	–	–	–	–
Ki-9617			Lazarovici (2010)	–	–	–	–	–	–	–	–	–
Ki-11469			Lazarovici (2010)	–	–	–	–	–	–	–	–	–
Ki-9613			Lazarovici (2010)	–	–	–	–	–	–	–	–	–
Ki-10857			Lazarovici (2010)	–	–	–	–	–	–	–	–	–
Ki-9618			Lazarovici (2010)	–	–	–	–	–	–	–	–	–
Ki-10856			Lazarovici (2010)	–	–	–	–	–	–	–	–	–
Ki-11467			Lazarovici (2010)	–	–	–	–	–	–	–	–	–
Ki-9741			Lazarovici (2010)	–	–	–	–	–	–	–	–	–
Ki-9740			Lazarovici (2010)	–	–	–	–	–	–	–	–	–
Ki-9742			Lazarovici (2010)	–	–	–	–	–	–	–	–	–
Ki-11455			Lazarovici (2010)	–	–	–	–	–	–	–	–	–
Ki-11457			Lazarovici (2010)	–	–	–	–	–	–	–	–	–
Ki-9745			Lazarovici (2010)	–	–	–	–	–	–	–	–	–
Ki-9746			Lazarovici (2010)	–	–	–	–	–	–	–	–	–
Ki-9743			Lazarovici (2010)	–	–	–	–	–	–	–	–	–
Ki-9744			Lazarovici (2010)	–	–	–	–	–	–	–	–	–
Ki-11456			Lazarovici (2010)	–	–	–	–	–	–	–	–	–
Ki-9747			Lazarovici (2010)	–	–	–	–	–	–	–	–	–
Hd-19373			Lazarovici (2010)	–	–	–	–	–	–	–	–	–
Hd-18826	45.15	26.63	Lazarovici (2010)	–	–	–	–	–	–	–	–	–

Continued

List 2. Continued

Labnr	Latitude	Longitude	Reference	Notice	Context	Duration	Quality	Incongr	Region	Megaregion	Database	Id
Hd-19419	45.15	26.63	Lazarovici (2010)	–	–	–	–	–	–	–	–	–
Hd-19573	45.15	26.63	Lazarovici (2010)	–	–	–	–	–	–	–	–	–
Gd-5858	46.03	25.82	Lazarovici (2010)	–	–	–	–	–	–	–	–	–
Gd-5861	46.03	25.82	Lazarovici (2010)	–	–	–	–	–	–	–	–	–
Hd-14118	46.03	25.82	Laszlo (1997)	–	–	–	–	–	–	–	–	–
Hd-14109	46.03	25.82	Laszlo (1997)	–	–	–	–	–	–	–	–	–
Gd-5860	46.03	25.82	Lazarovici (2010)	–	–	–	–	–	–	–	–	–
Gd-4682	46.03	25.82	Lazarovici (2010)	–	–	–	–	–	–	–	–	–
Hd-15082	46.03	25.82	Laszlo (1997)	–	–	–	–	–	–	–	–	–
Hd-15278	46.03	25.82	Laszlo (1997)	–	–	–	–	–	–	–	–	–
Gd-4690	46.03	25.82	Lazarovici (2010)	–	–	–	–	–	–	–	–	–
Bln-2803	46.49	26.53	Mantu (2000)	–	–	–	–	–	–	–	–	–
Bln-2804	46.49	26.53	Mantu (2000)	–	–	–	–	–	–	–	–	–
Bln-2782	46.49	26.53	Mantu (2000)	–	–	–	–	–	–	–	–	–
Bln-2783	46.49	26.53	Laszlo (1997)	–	–	–	–	–	–	–	–	–
Bln-2784	46.49	26.53	Laszlo (1997)	–	–	–	–	–	–	–	–	–
Hd-15401	46.49	26.53	Laszlo (1997)	–	–	–	–	–	–	–	–	–
Hd-15324	46.49	26.53	Laszlo (1997)	–	–	–	–	–	–	–	–	–
Bln-2824	46.49	26.53	Laszlo (1997)	–	–	–	–	–	–	–	–	–
Lv-2153	46.49	26.53	Mantu (1998)	–	–	–	–	–	–	–	–	–
Bln-2802	46.49	26.53	Laszlo (1997)	–	–	–	–	–	–	–	–	–
Bln-2805	46.49	26.53	Laszlo (1997)	–	–	–	–	–	–	–	–	–
Hd-15039	46.49	26.53	Laszlo (1997)	–	–	–	–	–	–	–	–	–
Bln-2766	46.49	26.53	Laszlo (1997)	–	–	–	–	–	–	–	–	–
Ki-11462	46.54	30.66	Lazarovici (2010)	–	–	–	–	–	–	–	–	–
Ki-11459	46.54	30.66	Lazarovici (2010)	–	–	–	–	–	–	–	–	–
Ki-11460	46.54	30.66	Lazarovici (2010)	–	–	–	–	–	–	–	–	–
Ki-11461	46.54	30.66	Lazarovici (2010)	–	–	–	–	–	–	–	–	–
UCLA-1642A	46.54	30.66	Telegin et al. (2003)	–	–	–	–	–	–	–	–	–
Ki-11458	46.54	30.66	Lazarovici (2010)	–	–	–	–	–	–	–	–	–
Bln-795	46.55	27.13	Laszlo (1997)	–	–	–	–	–	–	–	–	–
Bln-1751	46.58	26.86	Laszlo (1997)	–	–	–	–	–	–	–	–	–
Bln-1536	46.58	26.86	Laszlo (1997)	–	–	–	–	–	–	–	–	–
Bln-1534	46.58	26.86	Laszlo (1997)	–	–	–	–	–	–	–	–	–
Bln-1535	46.58	26.86	Laszlo (1997)	–	–	–	–	–	–	–	–	–

Continued

List 2. Continued

Labnr	Latitude	Longitude	Reference	Notice	Context	Duration	Quality	Incongr	Region	Megaregion	Database	Id
Ki-369	46.68	29.05	Ivanova (2008)	–	–	–	–	–	–	–	–	–
Ki-870	46.70	30.94	Telegin et al. (2003)	–	–	–	–	–	–	–	–	–
Ki-9751	46.70	30.94	Lazarovici (2010) + pers. comm.	–	–	–	–	–	–	–	–	–
Ki-282	46.70	30.94	Lazarovici; Patokova et al. (1989)	–	–	–	–	–	–	–	–	–
Ki-11464	46.70	30.94	Lazarovici (2010) + pers. comm.	–	–	–	–	–	–	–	–	–
Ki-9752	46.70	30.94	Lazarovici (2010) + pers. comm.	–	–	–	–	–	–	–	–	–
Ki-281	46.70	30.94	Lazarovici (2010) + pers. comm.	–	–	–	–	–	–	–	–	–
KiGN-281	46.70	30.94	Patokova et al. (1989); Telegin (2003)	–	–	–	–	–	–	–	–	–
Ki-11465	46.70	30.94	Lazarovici (2010) + pers. comm.	–	–	–	–	–	–	–	–	–
Bln-629	46.70	30.94	Quitta and Kohl (1969); Telegin (2003)	–	–	–	–	–	–	–	–	–
UCLA-1642B	46.70	30.94	Telegin et al. (2003)	–	–	–	–	–	–	–	–	–
UCLA-1642G	46.70	30.94	Telegin et al. (2003)	–	–	–	–	–	–	–	–	–
Ki-11463	46.70	30.94	Lazarovici (2010) + pers. comm.	–	–	–	–	–	–	–	–	–
Ki-11466	46.70	30.94	Lazarovici (2010) + pers. comm.	–	–	–	–	–	–	–	–	–
Le-645	46.70	30.94	Sementsov et al. (1969); Lazarovici	–	–	–	–	–	–	–	–	–
Ki-9753	46.70	30.94	Lazarovici (2010) + pers. comm.	–	–	–	–	–	–	–	–	–
Gd-6387	46.91	27.59	Lazarovici (2010) + pers. comm.	–	–	–	–	–	–	–	–	–
Gd-4685	46.91	27.59	Lazarovici (2010) + pers. comm.	–	–	–	–	–	–	–	–	–
Hd-14701	46.91	27.59	Ivanova (2008)	–	–	–	–	–	–	–	–	–
Hd-14792	46.91	27.59	Ivanova (2008)	–	–	–	–	–	–	–	–	–
Hd-16700	46.91	27.59	Lazarovici (2010) + pers. comm.	–	–	–	–	–	–	–	–	–
Gd-6388	46.91	27.59	Lazarovici (2010) + pers. comm.	–	–	–	–	–	–	–	–	–
Hd-19572	46.91	27.59	Lazarovici (2010) + pers. comm.	–	–	–	–	–	–	–	–	–

Continued

List 2. Continued

Labnr	Latitude	Longitude	Reference	Notice	Context	Duration	Quality	Incongr	Region	Megaregion	Database	Id
Hd-16701	46.91	27.59	Lazarovici (2010) + pers. comm.	–	–	–	–	–	–	–	–	–
GrN-5088	46.95	29.76	Telegin et al. (2003)	–	–	–	–	–	–	–	–	–
GrN-1985	47.15	26.96	Laszlo (1997)	–	–	–	–	–	–	–	–	–
GrN-4424	47.17	26.45	Mantu (2000)	–	–	–	–	–	–	–	–	–
GrN-1982	47.18	27.50	Laszlo (1997)	–	–	–	–	–	–	–	–	–
Lv-2152	47.21	27.01	Mantu (2000)	–	–	–	–	–	–	–	–	–
Hd-15075	47.30	26.92	Laszlo (1997)	–	–	–	–	–	–	–	–	–
Hd-14817	47.46	26.42	Laszlo (1997)	–	–	–	–	–	–	–	–	–
Le-1054	47.66	27.96	Dergachev (1980); Telegin (2003)	–	–	–	–	–	–	–	–	–
Hd-14710	47.68	26.17	Laszlo (1997)	–	–	–	–	–	–	–	–	–
Hd-14791	47.68	26.17	Laszlo (1997)	–	–	–	–	–	–	–	–	–
Bln-590	47.69	28.53	Quitta and Kohl (1969);Kohl (1970); Telegin(2003)	–	–	–	–	–	–	–	–	–
UCLA-1642F	47.79	32.38	Telegin et al. (2003)	–	–	–	–	–	–	–	–	–
Le-1392	47.80	27.62	Lazarovici (2010)	–	–	–	–	–	–	–	–	–
Le-4538	47.80	27.62	Lazarovici (2010)	–	–	–	–	–	–	–	–	–
Le-1393	47.80	27.62	Lazarovici (2010)	–	–	–	–	–	–	–	–	–
Bln-2431	47.83	28.14	Mantu (1998); Telegin et al. (2003);Rassamakin (2004)	–	–	–	–	–	–	–	–	–
Bln-2426	47.83	28.42	Mantu (2000)	–	–	–	–	–	–	–	–	–
Bln-2480	47.84	28.82	Telegin et al. (2003)	–	–	–	–	–	–	–	–	–
Ki-601	47.84	28.82	Telegin et al. (2003)	–	–	–	–	–	–	–	–	–
Bln-2447	47.97	28.02	Lazarovici (2010)	–	–	–	–	–	–	–	–	–
Lv-2156	47.97	28.02	Lazarovici (2010)	–	–	–	–	–	–	–	–	–
Hd-19441	47.97	28.02	Lazarovici (2010)	–	–	–	–	–	–	–	–	–
Ki-613	47.97	28.02	Telegin et al. (2003)	–	–	–	–	–	–	–	–	–
Ki-609	47.97	28.02	Boyadziev (1998)	–	–	–	–	–	–	–	–	–
IGAN-712	47.97	27.29	Kremenetski (1991); Zbenovich (1996)	–	–	–	–	–	–	–	–	–
Ki-11491	47.99	29.23	Lazarovici (2010); Palaguta (2007)	–	–	–	–	–	–	–	–	–
Bln-2428	48.00	27.18	Telegin et al. (2003)	–	–	–	–	–	–	–	–	–
Bln-1060	48.01	26.81	Laszlo (1997)	–	–	–	–	–	–	–	–	–
Bln-1195	48.01	26.81	Laszlo (1997)	–	–	–	–	–	–	–	–	–
Hd-14761	48.01	26.81	Laszlo (1997)	–	–	–	–	–	–	–	–	–

Continued

List 2. *Continued*

Labnr	Latitude	Longitude	Reference	Notice	Context	Duration	Quality	Incongr	Region	Megaregion	Database	Id
Bln-1194	48.01	26.81	Laszlo (1997)	–	–	–	–	–	–	–	–	–
Hd-14544	48.01	26.81	Laszlo (1997)	–	–	–	–	–	–	–	–	–
Hd-14831	48.01	26.81	Laszlo (1997)	–	–	–	–	–	–	–	–	–
BM-495	48.01	28.64	Telegin et al. (2003)	–	–	–	–	–	–	–	–	–
BM-494	48.01	28.64	Telegin et al. (2003)	–	–	–	–	–	–	–	–	–
Bln-3191	48.11	29.30	Patokova et al. (1989); Telegin (2003)	–	–	–	–	–	–	–	–	–
Bln-2430	48.29	27.49	Telegin et al. (2003)	–	–	–	–	–	–	–	–	–
Bln-2429	48.29	27.49	Lazarovici (2010); Telegin (2003)	–	–	–	–	–	–	–	–	–
Ki-7203	48.34	29.82	Lazarovici (2010)	–	–	–	–	–	–	–	–	–
Ki-7204	48.34	29.82	Lazarovici (2010)	–	–	–	–	–	–	–	–	–
Ki-6683	48.45	30.26	Telegin et al. (2003)	–	–	–	–	–	–	–	–	–
Ki-6682	48.45	30.26	Telegin et al. (2003)	–	–	–	–	–	–	–	–	–
Ki-6656	48.47	26.56	Telegin et al. (2003)	–	–	–	–	–	–	–	–	–
Ki-6745	48.55	26.49	Lazarovici (2010); Rassamakin (2004)	–	–	–	–	–	–	–	–	–
Ki-6743	48.55	26.49	Lazarovici (2010); Rassamakin (2004)	–	–	–	–	–	–	–	–	–
Ki-6754	48.55	26.49	Lazarovici (2010)	–	–	–	–	–	–	–	–	–
Ki-6744	48.55	26.49	Lazarovici (2010); Rassamakin (2004)	–	–	–	–	–	–	–	–	–
Ki-6753	48.55	26.49	Lazarovici (2010); Rassamakin (2004)	–	–	–	–	–	–	–	–	–
Ki-6751	48.58	26.63	Lazarovici (2010)	–	–	–	–	–	–	–	–	–
Ki-11475	48.58	27.48	Lazarovici (2010)	–	–	–	–	–	–	–	–	–
Ki-6681	48.58	27.48	Telegin et al. (2003)	–	–	–	–	–	–	–	–	–
Ki-11472	48.58	27.48	Lazarovici (2010)	–	–	–	–	–	–	–	–	–
Ki-6670	48.58	27.48	Lazarovici (2010)	–	–	–	–	–	–	–	–	–
Ki-6677	48.67	26.87	Telegin (2003); Lazarovici	–	–	–	–	–	–	–	–	–
GrN-5134	48.67	27.67	Telegin (2003)	–	–	–	–	–	–	–	–	–
Ki-6675	48.70	27.30	Lazarovici (2010)	–	–	–	–	–	–	–	–	–
Ki-6225	48.70	27.30	Telegin et al. (2003)	–	–	–	–	–	–	–	–	–
Ki-6676	48.70	27.30	Lazarovici (2010)	–	–	–	–	–	–	–	–	–
Ki-7202	48.74	29.88	Lazarovici (2010)	–	–	–	–	–	–	–	–	–
Ki-6737	48.74	29.88	Lazarovici (2010)	–	–	–	–	–	–	–	–	–
Ki-6680	48.74	29.88	Lazarovici (2010)	–	–	–	–	–	–	–	–	–

Continued

List 2. *Continued*

Labnr	Latitude	Longitude	Reference	Notice	Context	Duration	Quality	Incongr	Region	Megaregion	Database	Id
Ki-11447	48.78	25.27	Lazarovici (2010)	–	–	–	–	–	–	–	–	–
Ki-11448	48.78	25.27	Lazarovici (2010)	–	–	–	–	–	–	–	–	–
Ki-11446	48.78	25.27	Lazarovici (2010)	–	–	–	–	–	–	–	–	–
Ki-11449	48.78	25.27	Lazarovici (2010)	–	–	–	–	–	–	–	–	–
Bln-2087	48.80	30.69	Telegin et al. (2003)	–	–	–	–	–	–	–	–	–
Ki-1212	48.80	30.69	Telegin et al. (2003)	–	–	–	–	–	–	–	–	–
OxA-19840	48.80	30.53	Rassamakin & Menotti (2011)	–	–	–	–	–	–	–	–	–
OxA-22348	48.80	30.53	Rassamakin & Menotti (2011)	–	–	–	–	–	–	–	–	–
Ki-16026	48.80	30.53	Rassamakin & Menotti (2011)	–	–	–	–	–	–	–	–	–
OxA-22515	48.80	30.53	Rassamakin & Menotti (2011)	–	–	–	–	–	–	–	–	–
Ki-16025	48.80	30.53	Rassamakin & Menotti (2011)	–	–	–	–	–	–	–	–	–
Bln-4598	48.80	30.53	Kruts (2008)	–	–	–	–	–	–	–	–	–
Ki-15993	48.80	30.53	Rassamakin & Menotti (2011)	–	–	–	–	–	–	–	–	–
Ki-6867	48.80	30.53	Lazarovici (2010)	–	–	–	–	–	–	–	–	–
Ki-6868	48.80	30.53	Lazarovici (2010)	–	–	–	–	–	–	–	–	–
Ki-6865	48.80	30.53	Lazarovici (2010)	–	–	–	–	–	–	–	–	–
Ki-6866	48.80	30.53	Lazarovici (2010)	–	–	–	–	–	–	–	–	–
Ki-15994	48.80	30.53	Rassamakin & Menotti (2011)	–	–	–	–	–	–	–	–	–
Ki-6671	48.86	26.92	Telegin et al. (2003)	–	–	–	–	–	–	–	–	–
Ki-6165	48.87	30.82	Telegin et al. (2003)	–	–	–	–	–	–	–	–	–
Ki-6673	48.87	30.82	Telegin et al. (2003)	–	–	–	–	–	–	–	–	–
Ki-6672	48.87	30.82	Telegin et al. (2003)	–	–	–	–	–	–	–	–	–
Ki-6684	48.96	26.72	Telegin et al. (2003)	–	–	–	–	–	–	–	–	–
Ki-6685	48.96	26.72	Telegin et al. (2003)	–	–	–	–	–	–	–	–	–
Bln-2137	48.97	30.64	Kruts (2008)	–	–	–	–	–	–	–	–	–
Ki-903	48.97	30.64	Lazarovici (2010)	–	–	–	–	–	–	–	–	–
Ki-11450	49.04	30.85	Lazarovici (2010)	–	–	–	–	–	–	–	–	–
Ki-11454	49.04	30.85	Lazarovici (2010)	–	–	–	–	–	–	–	–	–
Ki-11452	49.04	30.85	Lazarovici (2010)	–	–	–	–	–	–	–	–	–
Ki-10859	49.04	30.85	Lazarovici (2010)	–	–	–	–	–	–	–	–	–

Continued

List 2. Continued

Labnr	Latitude	Longitude	Reference	Notice	Context	Duration	Quality	Incongr	Region	Megaregion	Database	Id
Ki-6925	49.04	30.85	Lazarovici (2010)	–	–	–	–	–	–	–	–	–
Ki-6924	49.04	30.85	Lazarovici (2010)	–	–	–	–	–	–	–	–	–
Ki-10858	49.04	30.85	Lazarovici (2010)	–	–	–	–	–	–	–	–	–
Ki-9754	49.04	30.85	Lazarovici (2010)	–	–	–	–	–	–	–	–	–
Ki-11451	49.04	30.85	Lazarovici (2010)	–	–	–	–	–	–	–	–	–
Ki-6922	49.04	30.85	Lazarovici (2010)	–	–	–	–	–	–	–	–	–
Ki-6923	49.04	30.85	Lazarovici (2010)	–	–	–	–	–	–	–	–	–
Ki-11453	49.04	30.85	Lazarovici (2010)	–	–	–	–	–	–	–	–	–
Ki-9625	49.04	30.85	Lazarovici (2010)	–	–	–	–	–	–	–	–	–
Le-1060	49.11	28.80	Zaets and Ryzhov (1993); Ivanova (2008)	–	–	–	–	–	–	–	–	–
Ki-11488	49.13	31.21	Lazarovici (2010)	–	–	–	–	–	–	–	–	–
Ki-882	49.18	30.79	Telegin et al. (2003)	–	–	–	–	–	–	–	–	–
Ki-11490	49.19	31.24	Lazarovici (2010)	–	–	–	–	–	–	–	–	–
Ki-11489	49.22	31.22	Lazarovici (2010)	–	–	–	–	–	–	–	–	–
Hd-14785	49.29	31.46	Laszlo (1997)	–	–	–	–	–	–	–	–	–
Hd-15024	49.29	31.46	Laszlo (1997)	–	–	–	–	–	–	–	–	–
Hd-14898	49.29	31.46	Laszlo (1997)	–	–	–	–	–	–	–	–	–
Ki-874	49.38	31.32	Lazarovici (2010)	–	–	–	–	–	–	–	–	–
Ki-1204	49.48	30.54	Telegin et al. (2003)	–	–	–	–	–	–	–	–	–
Ki-520	49.48	30.54	Telegin et al. (2003)	–	–	–	–	–	–	–	–	–
Bln-2088	49.48	30.54	Kruts (2008)	–	–	–	–	–	–	–	–	–
Ki-2088	49.48	30.54	Telegin et al. (2003)	–	–	–	–	–	–	–	–	–
Ki-875	49.48	30.54	Telegin et al. (2003)	–	–	–	–	–	–	–	–	–
Ki-879	49.48	30.54	Telegin et al. (2003)	–	–	–	–	–	–	–	–	–
Ki-877	49.48	30.54	Telegin et al. (2003)	–	–	–	–	–	–	–	–	–
Ki-881	49.48	30.54	Telegin et al. (2003)	–	–	–	–	–	–	–	–	–
Ki-201	49.48	30.54	Lazarovici (2010)	–	–	–	–	–	–	–	–	–
Ki-6747	49.55	27.95	Lazarovici (2010)	–	–	–	–	–	–	–	–	–
Ki-6746	49.55	27.95	Lazarovici (2010)	–	–	–	–	–	–	–	–	–
Ki-11486	49.70	31.55	Lazarovici (2010)	–	–	–	–	–	–	–	–	–
Ki-11487	49.70	31.55	Lazarovici (2010)	–	–	–	–	–	–	–	–	–
Ki-7207	50.02	30.97	Lazarovici (2010)	–	–	–	–	–	–	–	–	–
Ki-7205	50.02	30.97	Lazarovici (2010)	–	–	–	–	–	–	–	–	–
Ki-7208	50.02	30.97	Lazarovici (2010)	–	–	–	–	–	–	–	–	–

Continued

List 2. Continued

Labnr	Latitude	Longitude	Reference	Notice	Context	Duration	Quality	Incongr	Region	Megaregion	Database	Id
Ki-7206	50.02	30.97	Lazarovici (2010)	–	–	–	–	–	–	–	–	–
Ki-6750	50.11	28.52	Lazarovici (2010)	–	–	–	–	–	–	–	–	–
Ki-6749	50.11	28.52	Lazarovici (2010)	–	–	–	–	–	–	–	–	–
Ki-6748	50.11	28.52	Lazarovici (2010)	–	–	–	–	–	–	–	–	–
Ki-5012	50.22	31.51	Lazarovici (2010)	–	–	–	–	–	–	–	–	–
Ki-5029	50.22	31.51	Telegin et al. (2003)	–	–	–	–	–	–	–	–	–
Ki-5013	50.22	31.51	Lazarovici (2010)	–	–	–	–	–	–	–	–	–
Bln-631	50.30	31.19	Quitta and Kohl (1969); Telegin et al. (2003)	–	–	–	–	–	–	–	–	–
Ki-880	50.30	31.19	Telegin et al. (2003)	–	–	–	–	–	–	–	–	–
Ki-5038	50.30	31.19	Telegin et al. (2003)	–	–	–	–	–	–	–	–	–
Ki-5039	50.30	31.19	Telegin et al. (2003)	–	–	–	–	–	–	–	–	–
Ki-5016	50.30	31.19	Telegin et al. (2003)	–	–	–	–	–	–	–	–	–
UCLA-1671B	50.84	30.83	Telegin et al. (2003)	–	–	–	–	–	–	–	–	–
UCLA-1466B	50.84	30.83	Telegin et al. (2003)	–	–	–	–	–	–	–	–	–
Ki-5015	50.85	30.58	Lazarovici (2010)	–	–	–	–	–	–	–	–	–
Ki-5014	50.85	30.58	Lazarovici (2010)	–	–	–	–	–	–	–	–	–
GrN-5099	50.90	29.59	Telegin et al. (2003)	–	–	–	–	–	–	–	–	–
Ki-6752	50.90	29.59	Lazarovici (2010)	–	–	–	–	–	–	–	–	–
Ki-11862			Rassamakin (2012)	–	–	–	–	–	–	–	–	–
Ki-12050			Rassamakin (2012)	–	–	–	–	–	–	–	–	–
Ki-11866			Rassamakin (2012)	–	–	–	–	–	–	–	–	–
Ki-11867			Rassamakin (2012)	–	–	–	–	–	–	–	–	–
Ki-11868			Rassamakin (2012)	–	–	–	–	–	–	–	–	–
Ki-11869			Rassamakin (2012)	–	–	–	–	–	–	–	–	–
Ki-9740			Rassamakin (2012)	–	–	–	–	–	–	–	–	–
Ki-9741			Rassamakin (2012)	–	–	–	–	–	–	–	–	–
Ki-9742			Rassamakin (2012)	–	–	–	–	–	–	–	–	–
Ki-9743			Rassamakin (2012)	–	–	–	–	–	–	–	–	–
Ki-9744			Rassamakin (2012)	–	–	–	–	–	–	–	–	–
Ki-9745			Rassamakin (2012)	–	–	–	–	–	–	–	–	–
Ki-9746			Rassamakin (2012)	–	–	–	–	–	–	–	–	–
Ki-9747			Rassamakin (2012)	–	–	–	–	–	–	–	–	–

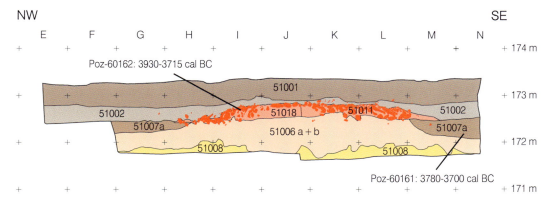

Figure 2. The short profile of house 44. The layers are described in the text, the location of the ^{14}C-samples that date termini ad quem are marked (graphics: R. Hofmann, UFG Kiel).

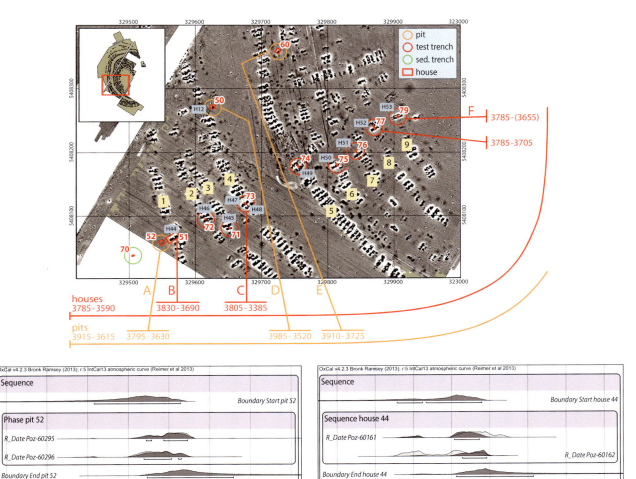

Figure 3. Modelling of ^{14}C-dates from Maidanetske. The sequential calibration of 6 groups of dates, which are related to different houses and pits, indicates the most probable chronological timeframe for the features. While for house 44, pit 50, and pit 60 the stratigraphic order of the samples could be integrated in the calculation, in all other cases phases were indicated by ^{14}C-dates of non-stratigraphic order. The median of each boundary calculation was used to display the most probable range for the dates in relation to their spatial order (cf. Müller et al., 2014; Bronk Ramsey, 2009; Reimer et al., 2013); Graphic: Karin Winter, UFG Kiel.

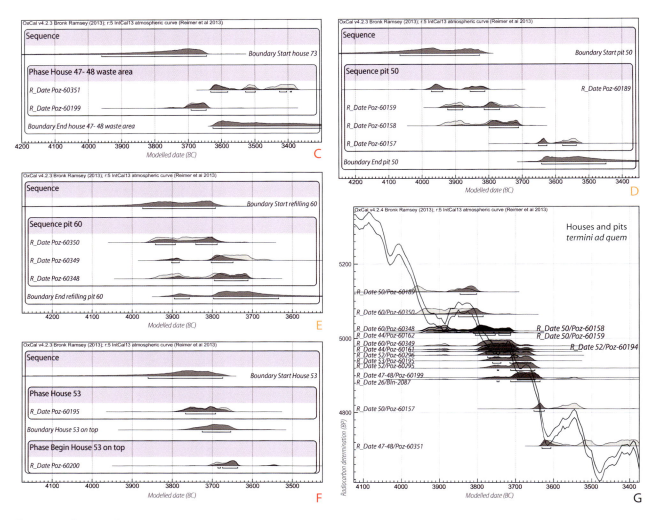

Figure 3. Continued.

Ring 4 (houses 47 and 48; pit 50)

In trench 73, a very similar stratigraphy provided information about the depositional processes of not only one, but also two houses, which are visible as the geomagnetic features 47 (15 m × 5 m) and 48 (15 m × 5 m). The small test-trench included the mere *c.* 0.5 m free space in between the two houses (Müller *et al.*, in print). From the layer of domestic use between the houses, two samples represent *termini ad quem* of house use (of both houses?), which dates to the 37th century BCE, probably to the first half of this century: Poz-60351 with a longer span (4710 ± 35 bp (*Ovis/Capra*) 3672–3378 cal BC) and Poz-60199 with a shorter span (4895 ± 35 bp (medium mammal) 3697–3649 cal BC) (Figure 3).

Pit 50 of trench 50 is associated with house 12, which also belongs to ring 4. From seven samples, in three cases, the sample material is from long-lived species (*Quercus* or *Fraxinus*). They should be handled as *termini post quem*. Of the remaining samples, Poz-60189 (5065 ± 35 bp, bone, *Bos*, 3944–3801 cal BC) is relevant for the deepest infilling, Poz-60159 (5020 ± 30 bp, bone, *Bos*, 3933–3766 cal BC) for a following infilling, Poz-60158 (5020 ± 35 bp, bone, *Ovis*, 3936–3725 cal BC) for a middle fill, and Poz-60157 (4810 ± 35 bp, *Bos*, 3645–3534 cal BC) for the youngest infilling of the pit. While the first three samples mentioned are clearly *termini ad quem*, the last also could be a *terminus ante quem* for latest infillings. In principle, there is a high probability that the first infilling took place in the 39th century BCE, the second in the 38th century BCE, and the third in the 37th century BCE (Figure 3).

An older date that was gained from excavation unit Zh (1973 excavation) probably also belongs to ring 4. This feature, house 26, lies in the southwest of the settlement. No context is known for the date Bln-2087 (4890 ± 60 bp; charcoal, 3761–3636 cal BP), but the date within the 37th and 36th centuries BCE fits with the general pattern of the radiometric dates (List 2).

Ring 5 (pit 60)

The pit was filled with an immense mass of daub and belonged probably to ring 5, or perhaps to ring 6 (cf. Müller & Videiko, 2016; Müller et al., in print). The five radiometric dates are distributed across each phase of the pit. While two dates represent *termini post quem* because of the longevity of their sample material (*quercus*, *fraxinus*), three could be termed as *termini ad quem*: Poz-60350 (5065 ± 35 bp, bone, *Bos*, 3944–3801 BC) for the oldest phase, Poz-60349 (4980 ± 35 bp, bone, *Bos*, 3790–3707 BC) for the middle phase, and Poz-60348 (5020 ± 35 bp, bone, large mammal, 3936–3715 cal BC) for the youngest phase. If we take into consideration the life span of the samples, the oldest phase 1 dates to the end of the 39th century BCE, the second phase to the turn of the 39th/38th centuries BCE, and the last phase to the 38th century BCE (Figure 3).

Ring 6 (house 50)

The burnt remains of house 50 (geomagnetic feature 13 m × 4 m) and the associated layers on the eastern side of the house were excavated in the 1 × 2 m test-pit. From the greyish layer on top of the daub beside the house, a sample represents a *terminus ante quem*. Nevertheless, the date from the second half of the 37th century/the first half of the 36th century BCE (Poz-60352: 4820 ± 30 bp, bone, *Bos*, 3650–3536 BC) is in line with other dates from the site.

Ring 8 (house 52)

In trench 77 (ring 8), parts of house 52 and the northern area beside house 52 could be included in a test trench (Figure 1). Within the stratigraphy, a sample from the daub layer represents a *terminus ad quem* for the use of the house that obviously dates to the 38th century BCE: Poz-60194, 4970 ± 35 bp, bone, *Ovis/Capra*, 3783–3705 cal BC.

Ring 9 (house 53)

In trench 79, house 53 with strongly burnt walls was identified in the test trench (Figure 1). Both layers, directly on top of the feature and the greyish layer that could be associated with the use-period of the house, yielded samples for radiometric dating. While the samples, Poz-60200 (4875 ± 35 bp, bone, *Ovis/Capra*, 3695–3640 BC) and Poz-60201 (4450 ± 30 bp, bone, medium mammal, 3320–3025 BC), represent *termini ante quem* in the 37th century BCE, Poz-60195 (4940 ± 35 bp, bone, *Sus*) represents a *terminus ad quem* (associated with the daub layer): 3761–3661 cal BCE. Linked with its stratigraphic position beneath the t.a.q.-samples, a date in the second half of the 38th century is most probable for house 53.

In conclusion, the series of thirty-five radiocarbon dates from Maidanetske, and the critical evaluation of their context, provides information about the chronological relevance of different features. For the first time, it was possible to gain dates from nearly all of the different rings of a Trypillia settlement as well as from pits. The context analyses of the radiometric dates showed that only fourteen dates are *termini ad quem*, which are associated with the use of the houses or the pits. The time interval of these fourteen dates could be reduced by using other *termini ante* and *post quem*, which were in a stratigraphic relation with *termini ad quem*. Of the fourteen dates from use-periods, seven are from houses and seven from pits. In general, the results are twofold:

1. The radiocarbon dates display statistically identical dates for all houses that were dated. As they are associated with burnt houses (no unburnt house was sampled), the dates support the model of a contemporary existence of these houses and their probably deliberate destruction around 3785/3590 BCE (Figure 3).

Furthermore, the dated pits also result in a similar timespan (*c.* 3915/3615 BCE). In consequence, burnt material from the houses and the upper fill of the pits represent the latest settlement event: the time at which (most of) the site burnt down. The vicinity and the full burning of whole houses, resulting in nearly rectangular remains of daub, was obviously a deliberate act. In consequence, the 2297 burnt houses which are known from the geophysical survey (cf. Rassmann et al., 2016; Müller & Videiko, 2016) date to the aforementioned timespan. Perhaps, we also could add the 671 partly eroded or unburnt houses, or maybe they belonged to a different stage in the development of the settlement (Ohlrau, 2015).

1. In contrast to most of the houses, whose remains represent the latest stage of the development, pits contain different stages of infilling that represent longer histories of the place. Evidence from pits 50 and 60 confirms that the earliest activities already took place *c.* 3940/3790 BCE. As pits are associated with single houses, this seems to confirm a dismantling of house structures from time to time so that primarily only the latest built structure remained in the Neighbourhood of the pits (cf. contribution Müller & Videiko, 2016).

The latest stage of infilling in both pits is dated to the 38th to 37th century BCE. In consequence, around 3700 cal BCE most of the settlement existed contemporarily. Both pits and houses were in use. The typo-chronological estimation of the excavated assemblages places Maidanetske in a final stage of the C1 phase 3 of the Tomashivska group (Müller et al., in print).

To sum up: the ^{14}C-dates from Maidanetske make a model in which at least the burnt houses could be in contemporary use much more probable. Thus, both the symmetrical ground plan of the site, and the burning of the houses, could be taken as further arguments which underline the contemporaneity of the structures.

Estimation of Maidanetske Population Size

The results of the dating of the settlement structures enable us, for the first time, to calculate the population size of Maidanetske based on a solid chronological assumption. While preliminary population estimations were based either on a general assumption that the contemporary existence of structures was visible from the symmetrical ground plan, or on calculations of the carrying capacity, the radiometric dates make the contemporaneous existence of a huge number of the detected houses more reliable. The reflection of house classes in the geomagnetic plan, as were detected in former and recent excavations, displays different types, but in general a standardization is obvious (cf. Kruts, 1989; Chernovol, 2012: 200). If we build a model of population size on this baseline, at least 2297 houses were in use more or less contemporarily, or perhaps even 2968 (including the unburnt houses).

All excavated houses from Maidanetske displayed very similar internal installations, including one fireplace each (cf. Shmaglij & Videiko, 2003; Müller & Videiko, 2016). The artefacts and macro-remains also characterize subsistence activities, which are bound to a 'living' household (cf. Kirleis & Dal Corso, 2016). Furthermore, the colluvial sediments that were formed during the time of occupation indicate significant human activities (cf. Kirleis & Dreibrodt, 2016). In consequence, there is no doubt that each house was occupied by residential groups, probably families.

The average Maidanetske house size of 77 m^2 enables us to calculate the inhabitants against the background of known space requirements for persons in sedentary societies (Ohlrau, 2015). There have been several attempts to calculate the correlation between house sizes and the size of the group of inhabitants living in a house. Classical intercultural studies by Naroll, Casselberry, and Brown result in the need for 6–10 m^2 for one person (Naroll, 1962; Casselberry, 1974; Brown, 1987), modified by Porčic with an index of mobility to an average of 6.97 m^2 (Porčic, 2012). If the deviations from the general median are taken into account, the synthesis of these ethnographical observations confirms that a person needs 5–15 m^2 in a house, averaging, for example, the 6.97 m^2 from Porčic.

The estimated population of Maidanetske adds up, under conservative estimations, to about 12,000 inhabitants, with an improbable maximum of about 46,000 inhabitants and a probable average of 29,000 inhabitants (Table 1), if we reconstruct the contemporary use of houses around c. 3700 BCE, as suggested by the radiometric dating. If we take into account the possibility that only half of the houses were contemporary in use, still about 14,500 ± 8,500 inhabitants are expected to have lived contemporarily in Maidanetske.

As no general differences between the mega-sites have been observed, an application of the Maidanetske demographic calculation model to other mega-sites is possible. Using the estimations of Porčic: for Dobrovody 14,100–16,200, for Taljanky 15,600–21,000, and for Maidanetske 22,300–23,800 inhabitants were calculated, if only the burnt structures were taken into consideration (Ohlrau, 2015). For Taljanky Kruts about 14,175 inhabitants had been already calculated (Kruts, 1989).

Typology, Chronology, and Spatial Developments in the Southern Buh and Dnipro Interfluve

As already emphasized, the validity of a precise regional chronological system for the Volodymyrivsko-Tomashivska and Kosenivska group (Trypillia BII/C)

Table 1. Population estimations for Maidanetske based on estimated maximal and minimal areas per person and estimated maximal and minimal numbers of contemporary houses (2297 houses: burnt houses; 2968: burnt and unburnt houses; 2633 houses: average between bot values).

Area/person	Houses 2297 (minimum house number)	Houses 2633 (mean house number)	Houses 2968 (maximum house number)	
	176,869 m^2	202,741 m^2	228,536 m^2	77 m^2 per house
5	35,373.8	40,548.2	**45,707.2**	
6,97	25,375.75	**29,087.66**	32,788.2	
15	**11,791.22**	13,516.33	15,235.7	

If only every second house was used contemporary, about 14.500 inhabitants lived in Maidanetske around 3700 BCE.

is of major importance for the reconstruction of the demographic processes and mobilities within the Southern Buh and Dnipro Interfluve, and to answer the question of whether mega-sites existed contemporarily, and if so, which ones.

Since the ground-breaking spatial and chronological analyses of Passek in the 1930s and 1940s (Passek, 1949), the division into a western and an eastern Trypillia spatial and stylistic tradition became clear (compare, for example, Ryzhov, 2012: 84). On the one hand, the general periodization and phasing of Trypillia is accepted by Moldovian and Ukrainian archaeology in general, on the other hand, regional and local patterns create typo-chronologies for regional and local groups that are sorely discussed (Wechler, 1994; Kruts, 2012: 73; Menotti, 2012: 2f. figure 2; Ryzhov, 2012: 80 ff.; Kadrow, 2013; Diachenko & Menotti, 2015).

Figure 4 compiles the relevant Trypillia periods, phases, and local group development with sub-phases and associated sites for the area under interest. In principle, periods identify general Trypillia developments that are seen in the whole distribution area; phases, the traditional division into general phases; local groups represent the typologically similar groups, which differ from area to area; sub-phases and stages, the division into local chronological units; further and associated sites, the key sites, which are related by Ukrainian research to the typological groups. For Maidanetske, whose assemblages are associated with Trypillia C1 and the Uman area the Volodymyrivsko-Tomashivska and Kosenivska local group is the especially relevant 'typological container', typological belonging to western Trypillia. While the general chronological development of Trypillia periods and phases is supported by some scientific dating, the typological division into sub-phases within the Volodymyrivsko-Tomashivska and Kosenivska local group is under discussion (Diachenko, 2012; Diachenko & Menotti, 2012). In particular, the typological differences during

BCE	Trypillia period	Trypillia phase	Trypillia local group	Subphase of local group		Associated sites	Ass 14C	Biggest site (estimation of inhabitants)
3350–3600	late	CII	Kosenivska (K)	K2/K3 (CII/1)		Vilkhovets 1 Kosherzhyntsi-Shulgivka		2500
				K1 (CII/1)		Apolianka Kosenivka		200
3600–3850		CI	Tomashivska (T)	T4		Tomashivka Rakhny Sobovi		
				T3	Stage 2	*Maidanetske*	3670–3800	15.000
					Stage 1	*Taljanky*	3730–3850	12.000
				T2		*Dobrovody* Yatranivka 1		10.000
				T1		Sushkivka		
3750–4100	middle	BII	Nebelivska (N)	N2	Stage 2			
					Stage 1	Glybochok Yampil Khrystynivka 1		4.500
				N1		*Nebelivka* Kryvi Kolina	3800–3970	9.000
			Volodymyrivska (V)	V late		Volodymyrivka Peregonivka		
				V early		Fedorivka		6.700
4100–4200		BI/BII						
4200–4600	early	BI						
4600–4800		A						

Figure 4. The chronology of Trypillia. Besides the main periodization and phasing, the Trypillia regional groups display characteristic inventories with sub-phases. The main mega-sites are indicated in italics *(after Diachenko, 2012; Kadrow, 2013; Kruts, 2012; Menotti, 2012; Ryzhov, 2012; Wechler, 1994). The radiometric data describe the chronological value also of CI-sub-phases.*

B2 and C1 might reflect partly non-chronological aspects of the Trypillia-settlements (cf. Videiko, 2003; Rassamakin & Menotti, 2011).

In principle, the typo-chronological model of Ryzhov (2012: 91 ff.) is generally used for the description of the Late Trypillia development in the Southern Buh and Dnipro Interfluve. Thus, the early B2 Volodymyrivska group is associated with one-colour, two-colours, incisions; incisions and colour pottery, while the late B2 Nebelivska local group displays painted pottery that shows links to the West. Beside the mega-sites, Nebelivka and Glybochek (<200 ha) settlements of only a few hectares are also known. In the established typo-chronology, the succeeding C1 Tomashivska local group is divided into four phases, defined by different quantities in the distribution of ceramic shapes and ornamentation, for which the 'Tomashivska-type' painting with, for example, the display of animals in the "ribbon" manner and the large number of 'tree of the world' drawings' is typical (Ryzhov, 2012: 101) (Phase 1: besides Nebelivka local group elements, the introduction of table crockery, for example, with comet-shaped and simplified line patterns. Phase 2: the sharp-ribbed nature of table crockery types is prominent, as is the standardization of Tangentenkreisband. Phase 3: the presence of sharp ribbing and high shoulders is prominent. Phase 4: sharp profiles). The prominent mega-sites are associated with C1 phase 2 (Dobrovody), Phase 3 (Stage 1: Taljanky; Stage 2 Maidanetske; cp. Diachenko & Menotti, 2012), while the size of sites is generally decreasing with C1 Phase 4 (Tomashivska) and the C2 Kosenivska local group.

Using the typological categories of ceramic shapes and ornamentation, which Ryzhov developed and described (Ryzhov, 1999, 2012), we conducted a CA to identify the statistical gradient of the probable typological similarity sequence. In principle, the first two eigenvectors of the CA verify the typological sequence as developed by Ryzhov (Figure 5). A continuum of a parabola-shaped 'cloud' of types and phase-markers identifies a steady and unbroken typological sequence for BII and CI inventories. Clusters of sets with typological similarities could be labelled, which in most cases are congruent with the typological sequences which were developed by Ryzhov. The CA sequence starts with the BII inventories of the Volodymyrivska local group (V), followed by Nebelivska group

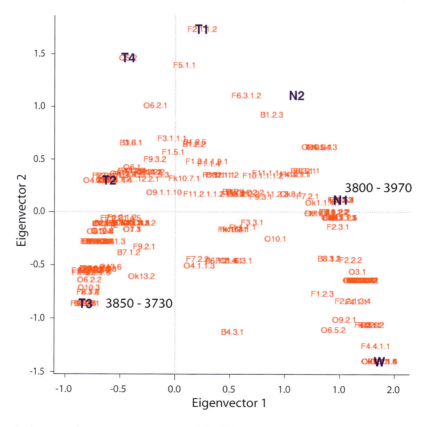

Figure 5. CA of ceramic shapes and ornamentation types of the Volodymyrivska-Nebelivska-Tomahivska local group sub-phases that were developed by Ryzhov (1999). The typological sequence displays a continuum with a normal distribution of the types that were analysed. The absolute chronological duration of Nebelivka, Taljanky, and Maidanetske, which is based on the available ^{14}C-data, confirms the chronological relevance of the sub-phases, but also indicates the contemporaneity of styles (graphics: L. Brandtstätter/J. Müller, UFG Kiel).

inventories of different typological stages (N1 and N2). For the CI Tomashivska local group, four different clusters of typological similarity groups (usually labelled as stages or sub-phases) were developed, of which at least three are in the 'right' sequence: First, eigenvector values for T1, T2, and T3 are in a steady reduction of the values. Only the CI/T4 phase has, judged on a statistical basis, more typological similarities with T1 and T2 than with T3. In principle, we would exclude T4 to be the latest stage in a typological sequence. Nevertheless, in general, the sequence supports the typological classification and sequencing of Ryzhov. The exception of CI/T4 might be due to the fact that mainly smaller and medium-sized sites are identified within this typological cluster, which are partly typologically linked with the other sites from T1 to T3 and only partly later.

Does the detailed typological sequence of the 12 phases, sub-phases, and stages (Figure 4) represent a chronological development or are we also confronted with typological differences that are due to other factors? Within the CA, we reduced the precise typological division to nine sub-phases, for which we could ask a similar question. Owing to the lack of vertical stratigraphies for the CI subgroups, a reliance on ^{14}C-data is a given.

Including Kyiv-data, at the moment there are about 282 radiometric dates published for Cucuteni-Trypillia (Lists 1 and 2). Excluding Kyiv-data, as they are extremely variable and not in line with other labs, only 43 dates remain for Ukrainian sites. In the regional sequence of radiometric dates, only information and data from Taljanky (Trypillia CI/T3 Stage 1) and Maidanetske (Trypillia CI/ T3 Stage 2) are published, and information on data from Nebelivka (Trypillia BII/N 1) is available (Chapman, 2015).

The information on the duration of the sites, which was reconstructed from radiometric dates, implies the chronological meaning of the typological sequence that we are discussing. Using the formalized statistical approach for ^{14}C-dates, Nebelivka existed from 3970 to 3800 BCE (Chapman, 2015); Taljanky from 3860 to 3730 BCE (Rassamakin & Menotti, 2011); and Maidanetske from 3800 to 3670 BCE (Figure 6).

As these radiometric data are the result of careful context analyses, they are very useful in the interpretation of the CA:

1. On the one hand, the chronological tendency of the CA is proven. On the other hand, the chronological overlap, for example, of the Nebelivka and Taljanky dates, which spans over six typological

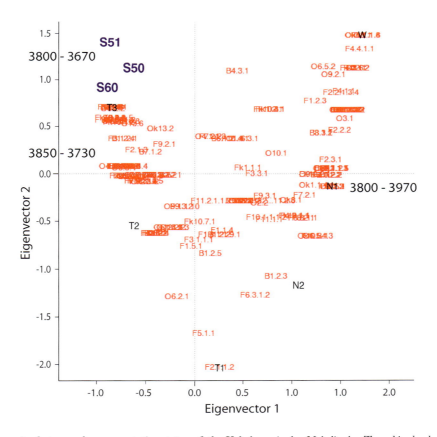

Figure 6. CA of ceramic shapes and ornamentation types of the Volodymyrivska-Nebelivska-Tomahivska local group sub-phases (BII/CI T 1–3) that were developed by Ryzhov (1999). In addition, inventories of the 2013 Maidanetske excavation are added. The ^{14}C-dates indicate chronological tendencies (graphics: L. Brandtstätter/J. Müller, UFG Kiel).

sub-phases and stages, clearly demonstrates the long duration of many of the ornamentation types and ceramic shapes. In consequence, only the main focus of their distribution in time is marked by the position of phases and sub-phases within the CA and in the chronological draft (Figures 4 and 5). This is in line with the observation of a continual increase and decrease of the different types.

2. The overlap, especially of the data from Maidanetske and Taljanky, suggests that, for these two mega-sites, besides a weak chronological tendency both existed more or less contemporarily (as also noted by Ryzhov, 1999; Shmaglij & Videiko, 2003; Diachenko, 2012).

In a further CA, the new inventories from the 2013 Maidanetske excavation were integrated (Figure 6). They mark the final stage of the development very clearly. Even the association of these units with their *termini ad quem* indicate chronological tendencies of the final stage of the Maidanetske development and the pit inventories.

Interpretation: Contemporary Mega-Sites

Consequently, in the development of ceramic ornamentation and ceramic shapes we could identify types, which are older and younger in tendency. The differentiation between sub-phases and stages is, for the majority, a question of different quantities in the distribution of ornament and shape types, as Ryzhov already remarked (Ryzhov, 2012). While in this sense, besides the similarities in the inventories, a 'progressive' development could be seen in a sequence from Nebelivka–Sushkovka–Dobrovody–Taljanky–Maidanetske; the contemporary existence of two to three mega-sites at a time is also most probable. Nebelivka lasted until Taljanky was already built up; Taljanky and Maidanetske are more or less contemporary.

As the population calculations indicate, an enlargement of the population in the mega-sites themselves from Dobrovody to Taljanky to Maidanetske took place; obviously a population flow between these sites existed throughout their occupation. In principle, there seems to be a tendency that the bigger the site, the more attractive it is. As the development is quite flexible, the temporal limits for the spatial detection of land-use patterns are artificial (cf. Ohlrau et al., 2016). Nevertheless, population values are quite high. For example, around 3750 BCE we have to deal with about 3500 houses minimum, thus a minimum of 17,500 inhabitants in an area of about 100 km^2 at the Taljanka River.

References

Boyadziev, J. 1998. Radiocarbon dating from southeastern Europe. In: M. Stefanovich, H. Todorova & H. Hauptmann, eds., *James Hawey Gaul. In Memoriam*. Sofia, The James Harvey Gaul Foundation, pp. 349–70.

Bronk Ramsey, C. 2009. Bayesian Analysis of Radiocarbon Dates. *Radiocarbon*, 51(1):337–360.

Brown, B.M. 1987. Population Estimation from Floor Area. A Restudy of 'Naroll's Constant'. *Cross-Cultural Research*, 21:1–49.

Casselberry, S.E. 1974. Further Refinement of Formulae for Determining Population from Floor Area. *World Archaeology*, 6:117–124.

Chapman, J. 2015. *About Time. Panel Nebelivka Exhibition*. Durham: Institute of Archaeology.

Chernovol, D. 2012. Houses of the Tomashovskaya Local Group. In: F. Menotti & A. Korvin-Piotrovskiy, eds., *The Tripolye Culture Giant-Settlements in Ukraine*. Oxford: Oxbow Books, pp. 182–209.

Dergachev, V. 1980. *Pamayatniki Pozdnego Tripol'ya*, Kishinev: Shtiintsa. Дергачев, В.А. 1980. Памятники позднего Триполья. Кишинев: Штиинца.

Diachenko, A. 2012. Settlement System of West Tripolye Culture in the Southern Bug and Dnieper Interfluve. Formation Problems. In: F. Menotti & A. Korvin-Piotrovskiy, eds. *The Tripolye Culture Giant-Settlements in Ukraine*. Oxford: Oxbow Books, pp. 116–38.

Diachenko, A. & Menotti, F. 2012. The Gravity Model: Monitoring the Formation and Development of the Tripolye Culture Giant-Settlements in Ukraine. *Journal of Archaeological Science*, 39:2810–17.

Diachenko, A. & Menotti, F. 2015. Cucuteni-Tripolye Contact Network. Cultural Transmission and Chronology. In: A. Diachenko, F. Menotti, S. N. Ryzhov, K. Bunytatyan & S. Kadrow, eds. *The Cucuteni-Trypillia Cultural Complex and its Neighbours. Essays in Memory of Volodymyr Kruts*. Astrolabe: Lviv, pp. 131–52.

Ivanova, M. 2008. *Befestigte Siedlungen auf dem Balkan, in der Ägäis und in Westanatolien, ca. 5000 - 2000 v.Chr.* Münster: Waxmann.

Kadrow, S. 2013. Werteba Site in Bilcze Zlote: Recent Research and Analyses. In: S. Kadrow, ed. *Bilce Zlote. Materials from the Werteba and the Ogród sites*. Kraków: Muzeum Aechaeologiczne Krakow, pp. 13–21.

Kirleis, W. & Dal Corso, M. 2016. Trypillian Subsistence Economy: Animal and Plant Expoitation. In: J. Müller, K. Rassmann & M. Videiko, eds. *Trypillia Mega-Sites and European Prehistory: 4100–3400 BCE*. London and New York: Routledge, pp. 195–205.

Kirleis, W. & Dreibrodt, S. 2016. The Natural Background: Forest, Forest Steppe or Steppe Environment. In: J. Müller, K. Rassmann & M. Videiko, eds. *Trypillia Mega-Sites and European Prehistory: 4100–3400 BCE*. London and New York: Routledge, pp. 171–180.

Krementski, K.V. 1991. *Paleoekogiya drevneishih zemledelcev i skotovodon Russkoi ravniny*. Moscow: Institute of Geography. Кременецкий, К.В. 1991. Палеоэкология древнейших земледельцев и скотоводов Русской равнины. Москва: Институт географии АН СССР.

Kruts, V. 2012. Giant-Settlements of Tripolye Culture. In: F. Menotti & A. Korvin-Piotrovskiy, eds. *The Tripolye*

Culture Giant-Settlements in Ukraine. Oxford: Oxbow Books, pp. 70–78.

Kruts, V.A. 1989. K istorii naseleniya tripolskoj kultury v mezhdurechje Yuzhnogo Buga i Dnepra. In: S. S. Berezanskaya, ed. *Pervobytnaya arkheologiya: Materialy i issledovaniya*. Kiev: Naukova Dumka, pp. 117–32. Круц, В.А. 1989. К истории населения трипольской культуры в междуречье Южного Буга и Днепра. В сб.: С.С. Березанская, ред. *Первобытная археология: материалы и исследования*. Киев: Наукова думка, с. 117–132.

Kruts, V.A., Korvin-Piotrovskiy, A.G. & Rizhov, S.N. 2001. *Talianki – Settlement-Giant of the Tripolian Culture. Investigations in 2001*. Kiev: Institute of archaeology of NASU.

Kruts, V.A., Korvin-Piotrovskiy, A.G., Ryzhov, S.N. & Chernovol, D. 2008. The 2005-2006 research in Talianki. In: A. Korvin-Piotrovskiy & A. Menotti, eds. *Tripolye Culture Culture in Ukraine: The Giant Settlement of Talianki*. Kiew: Academy of Science Ukraine, pp. 82–108.

László, A. 1997. *Datarea prin radiocarbon in arheologie*. Biblioteca Muzeului Național 2. Bucarest: Museum.

Lazarovici, C.-M. 2010. New data regarding the chronology of the Precucuteni, Cucuteni and Horodiştea-Erbiceni cultures. In P. Kalábková, B. Kovár, P. Pavúk & J. Suteková, eds. *PANTA REI. Studies in chronology and cultural development of the SE and Central Europe in Earlier Prehistory presented to Juraj Pavúk on the occasion of his 75. birthday*. Bratislava: Publishing house Comenius University in Bratislava and Archaeological center, Olomouc, pp. 91–114.

Mantu, C.-M. 1998. *Cultura Cucuteni : evolutie, cronologie, legaturi*. Piatra Neamt: Muzeul de Istorie Piatra Neamt.

Mantu, C.-M. 2000. Cucuteni-Tripolye cultural complex: relations and synchronisms with other contemporaneous cultures from the Black Sea area. *Studia Antiqua et Archaeologica*, 7: 267–284.

Menotti, F. 2012. Introduction. In: F. Menotti & A. Korvin-Piotrovskiy, eds. *The Tripolye Culture Giant-Settlements in Ukraine*. Oxford: Oxbow Books, pp. 1–5.

Müller, J., Hofmann, R., Rassmann, K., Mischka, C., Videyko, M. & Burdo, N.B. 2014. Maydanetskoe: Investigations, *Based on Updated Plan Stratum Plus*, 2:285–302. Мюллер, Й., Р. Хофманн, К. Рассман, К. Мишка, М.Ю. Видейко и Н.Б. Бурдо. 2014. Майданецкое: исследования по обновленному плану поселения. Stratum Plus 2: 285–302.

Müller, J., Hofmann, R., Kirleis, W., Ohlrau, R., Brandtstätter, L., Dal Corso, M., Out, V., Rassmann, K. & Videko, M., in print. *Maidanetske 2013. New excavations at a Trypillia megasite*. Studien zur Archäologie in Ostmitteleuropa. Bonn: Habelt.

Müller, J. & Videiko, M. 2016. Maidanetske: New Facts of a Mega-Site. In: J. Müller, K. Rassmann & M. Videiko, eds. *Trypillia Mega-Sites and European Prehistory: 4100–3400 BCE*. London and New York: Routledge, pp. 71–94.

Naroll, R. 1962. Floor Area and Settlement Population. *American Antiquity*, 27:587–589.

Ohlrau, R. 2015. Trypillian mega-sites – Geomagnetische Prospektion und architektursoziologische Perspektiven. *Journal of Neolithic Archaeology*, 17: 17–99 [doi:http://dx.doi.org/10.12766/jna.v17i0.116].

Ohlrau, R., Dal Corso, M., Kirleis, W. & Müller, J. 2016. Living on the Edge? Carrying Capacities of Trypillian Settlements in the Buh-Dnipro Interfluve. In: J. Müller, K. Rassmann & M. Videiko, eds. *Trypillia Mega-Sites and European Prehistory: 4100–3400 BCE*. London and New York: Routledge, pp. 207–220.

Palaguta, I. 2007. Tripolye Culture during the Beginning of the Middle Period (BI). *Brit. Arch. Rep. Int. Ser. 1666*. Oxford: Oxbow.

Patokova, E.F., Petrenko, V.G., Burdo, N.B. & Polishchuk, L. Yu. 1989. *Monuments of the Tripolye Culture in the North- Western Black Sea Area*. Kiev: Naukova Dumka. Патокова, Э.Ф., В.Г. Петренко, Н.Б. Бурдо и Л.Ю. Полищук. 1989. Памятники трипольской культуры Северо-Западного Причерноморья. Киев: Наукова думка.

Passek, T. S. 1949. Periodizatsiya tripolskih poselenij III-II tys. do n.e. Matrialy i issledovaniya po archeologii SSSR 10. Пассек, Т.С. 1949. Периодизация трипольских поселений III-II тыс. до н.э. Материалы и исследования по археологии СССР 10.

Porčic, M. 2012. Effects of Residential Mobility on the Ratio of Average House Floor Area to Average Household Size. Implications for Demographic Reconstructions in Archaeology. *Cross Cultural Research*, 46(1):72–86.

Quitta, H. & Kohl, G. 1969. Neue Radiocarbondaten zum Neolithikum und zur frühen Bronzezeit Südosteuropas und der Sowjetunion. *Zeitschrift für Archäologie* 3: 223–255.

Rassamakin, Y. 2004. *Die nordpontische Steppe in der Kupferzeit: Gräber aus der Mitte des 5. Jts. bis Ende des 4. Jt. v. Chr.* Mainz: Zabern.

Rassamakin, Y. 2012. Absolute chronology of Ukrainian Tripolian settlements. In: F.F. Menotti & A. Korvin-Piotrovskiy, eds., *The Tripolye Culture Giant-Settlements in Ukraine*. Oxbow Books, Oxford, pp. 19–69.

Rassamakin, Y. & Menotti, F. 2011. Chronological Development of the Tripolye Culture Giant-Settlement of Talianki (Ukraine). ^{14}C Dating vs. Pottery Typology. *Radiocarbon*, 53(4):645–57.

Rassmann, K., Korvin-Piotrovskiy, A., Videiko, M. & Müller, J. 2016. The New Challenge for Site Plans and Geophysics: Revealing the Settlement Structure of Giant Settlements by Means of Geomagnetic Survey. In: J. Müller, K. Rassmann & M. Videiko, eds. *Trypillia Mega-Sites and European Prehistory: 4100–3400 BCE*. London and New York: Routledge, pp. 29–54.

Reimer, P. J., Bard, E., Bayliss, A., Beck, J.W., Blackwell, P.G., Bronk Ramsey, C., Grootes, P.M., Guilderson, T.P., Haflidason, H., Hajdas, I., Hatt, C., Heaton, T. J., Hoffmann, D.L., Hogg, A.G., Hughen, K.A., Kaiser, K.F., Kromer, B., Manning, S.W., Niu, M., Reimer, R.W., Richards, D.A., Scott, E.M., Southon, J.R., Staff, R.A., Turney, C.S.M. & van der Plicht, J. 2013. IntCal13 and Marine13 Radiocarbon Age Calibration Curves 0–50,000 Years cal BP. *Radiocarbon*, 55(4):1869–87.

Ryzhov, S. N. 1990. Mikrochronologija tripoloskogo poseleniya u s. Taljanki. In: V. G. Zbenovich, ed. *Rannezemledelcheskie poseleniya-giganty tripolskoj kultury na Ukraine. Tezisy dokladov pervogo polevogo seminara*. Taljanki: Institute of Archaeology of the AS of the USSR, pp. 83–90. Рыжов, С.Н. Микрохронология трипольского поселения у с. Тальянки. В сб.: В.Г. Збенович, ред. *Раннеземледельческие поселения-гиганты трипольской культуры на Украине.*

Тезисы докладов первого полевого семинара. Тальянки: ИА АН УССР, с. 83–90.

Ryzhov, S.N. 1999. Keramika poselen trypilskoi kultury Bugo-Dniprovskogo mezhyrichcha yak istorychne dzerelo. *unpublished PhD Thesis*. Kyiv: Institute of Archaeology of the NASU. Рижов, С.М. 1999. Кераміка поселень трипільської культури Буго-Дніпровського межиріччя як історичне джерело (рукопис дисертації канд. істор. наук). Київ: Інститут археології НАНУ.

Ryzhov, S.N. 2012. Relative Chronology of the Giant-Settlement Period BII-CI. In: F. Menotti & A. Korvin-Piotrovskiy, eds. *The Tripolye Culture Giant-Settlements in Ukraine*. Oxford: Oxbow Books, pp. 139–68.

Sementsov, A., Romanova, E. & Dolukhanov, P. 1969. Radiouglerodnye daty laboratorii LOIA (Leningrad Branch of Institute of Archaeology) laboratory, *Soviet Archaeology* 1: 251–261. Семенцов, А., Е. Романова и П. Долуханов. 1969. Радиоуглеродные даты лаборатории ЛОИА (Ленинградского отделения Института Археологии). Советская археология 1: 251–261.

Shmaglij, N. 1982. Große Trypillia Siedlungen zwischen den Flüssen Dnjepr 134 und Südlichen Bug. *Supplementum Pulpudeva*, 3.

Shmaglij, N. & Videiko, M. 1987. Späte Trypillia Siedlungen in der Nähe des Dorfes Maidanetske in Tscherkassy. *Archäologie*, 60:58.

Shmaglij, N.M. & Videiko, M.Yu. 1990. Mikrochronologija poselenija Maidanetskoe. In: V. G. Zbenovich, ed. *Rannezemleelcheskie poseleniya-giganty tripolskoj kultury na Ukraine. Tezisy dokladov pervogo polevogo seminara*. Taljanki: Institute of Archaeology of the AS of the USSR, pp. 91–94. Шмаглий, Н.М. и Видейко, М.Ю. 1990. Микрохронология поселения майданецкое. В сб.: В. Г. Збенович, ред. *Раннеземледельческие поселения-гиганты трипольской культуры на Украине. Тезисы докладов первого полевого семинара.* Тальянки: ИА АН УССР, с. 91–94.

Shmaglij, N.M. & Videiko, M.Yu. 2003. Maidanetskoe – tripolskij protogorod. *Stratum Plus*, 2:44–140. Шмаглий, Н.М. и Видейко, М.Ю. 2003. Майданецкое – трипольский протогород. *Stratum Plus*, 2:44–140.

Telegin, D.Y., Lillie, M., Potekhina, I.D. & Kovaliukh, M. M. 2003. Settlement and Economy in Neolithic Ukraine: a New Chronology. *Antiquity* 77: 456–471.

Videiko, M. Y. 2003. Radiocarbon chronology of settlements of BII and CI stages of the Tripolye culture at the Middle Dnieper, Balitic-Pontic Studies. In: S. N. Bratchenko, ed. *The Foundations of Radiocarbon Chronology of Cultures Between the Vistula and Dnieper: 4000–1000 BC*. Poznań: Adam Mickiewicz University, pp. 7–21.

Wechler, K.-P. 1994. Zur Chronologie der Tripolje-Cucuteni-Kultur aufgrund von ^{14}C–Datierungen. *Zeitschrift für Archäologie*, 28:7–21.

Zaets, I. & Ryzhov, S. 1992. *Tripolskoe poselenie Klishchev na Yuzhnom Buge*. Kiev, MSNIP 'Tellus'. Заец, И. и С. Рыжов. 1992. Трипольское поселение Клищев на Южном Буге. Киев: МСНИП "Tellus".

Zbenovich, V.G. 1990. K probleme krypnyh tripolskih poselenij. In: V. G. Zbenovich, ed. *Rannezemledelcheskie poseleniya-giganty tripolskoj kultury na Ukraine. Tezisy dokladov pervogo polevogo seminara*. Taljanki: Institute of Archaeology of the AS of the USSR, pp. 10–12. Збенович, В.Г. 1990. К пробелеме крупных трипольских поселений. В сб.: В.Г. Збенович, ред. *Раннеземледельческие поселения-гиганты трипольской культуры на Украине. Тезисы докладов первого полевого семинара.* Тальянки: ИА АН УССР, с. 10–12.

CHAPTER 9

The Natural Background: Forest, Forest Steppe, or Steppe Environment

WIEBKE KIRLEIS AND STEFAN DREIBRODT

To reconstruct past human–environment interactions, it is important to gain an understanding of the creation of the modern environment. Crucial for the mega-site phenomenon that occurs in Central Ukraine in the 4th millennium BCE is the human impact of the Trypillia settlers on the former vegetation cover. A discussion of the Trypillia environment is provided, which considers the potential natural vegetation in the western Pontic area, as well as the recent biotic, climatic, and pedological conditions, and integrates these with palaeo-ecological and palaeopedological data.

The recent landscape in the Central Ukraine is characterized by small villages surrounded by arable fields, intersected by narrow river valleys. Large fields are ploughed and sown by Kolhosp (former collective farms), while small plots and gardens are arranged around the ribbon-built villages. The landscape appears as a cultural steppe with sunflower and soybean as main cultivars beside cereals. Lines of trees and shrubs accompany tracks and streets between the fields. Only small patches are covered with tree plantations. These tree plantations, exhibiting natural regeneration of oak and acer, indicate the potential of the natural settings for tree growth in the area. Consequently, the question occurs: since when is open steppe the dominant man-made plant cover in the region, and at what time did the degradation of the potential natural vegetation start?

THE NATURAL VEGETATION

The western Pontic plant region is characterized by a semi-arid forest steppe climate with a dry (but not drought) period. It is classified as a humid continental climate (Dfb-zone of the Köppen classification, Köppen & Geiger, 1939) with wet winters and warm summers. At Uman, the mean annual temperature is 7.1 °C and the mean sum of annual precipitation is 616 mm (http://de.climate-data.org/). As potential natural vegetation, oak-hornbeam forest, characteristic of the mesophytic deciduous broadleaved forest, finds its optimal growing conditions in Eastern–Central Europe. Its main components are common and sessile oak (*Quercus robur* and *Q. petraea*), hornbeam (*Carpinus betulus*), and lime (*Tilia cordata*). The geographic distribution of oak-hornbeam forest spreads from Central Europe to Belarus, Ukraine, and Romania. The potential habitat of the oak-hornbeam forest today is heavily transformed by human activity; it is among the most altered landscapes of Central Europe (Matuszkiewicz, 2004: 261). Towards the southeast, in the western Pontic plant region (Figure 1), the formation of mesophytic deciduous broadleaved forest reaches its distribution limit. Here, the subcontinental forest and forest steppe environment still comprises oak-hornbeam and oak woodlands (Walter & Breckle, 1986: 146ff.). The forest steppe ecotone connects the mesophilic deciduous forest in the North and the West, and true bunch grass steppe in the South and the East. In the mosaic-like forest steppe, the woodland patches alternate with patches of dryland scrub vegetation and of meadow or grassland steppe. The forest steppe, as a mosaic-like vegetation type, is characterized by forest-sustaining, forest-tolerant, and forest-hostile patches. In natural conditions, the forest steppe of Eastern Europe would consist of patches of deciduous forests dominated by common oak (*Quercus robur*), accompanied in the first and second canopy layer by maple (*Acer*), common ash (*Fraxinus*), hornbeam (*Carpinus*), and in particular lime (*Tilia cordata*), which is a very frost- and drought-resistant lime species. The patches of old-growth woodlands preferentially occur on drained soils, elevated areas, and northern slopes, as well as on river valleys and gorge slopes. Riverine woodlands accompany the river valley floor on the adjacent narrow alluvial deposits. In contrast, the plain loess areas and southwards facing slopes are predominantly characterized by steppe meadow vegetation (Doniță et al., 2004). Once established, the felted root system from the steppe grasses hinders tree growth. Although young tree shoots may develop, they are outcompeted in the long run due to insufficient water availability. The limiting factor for the development of old-growth

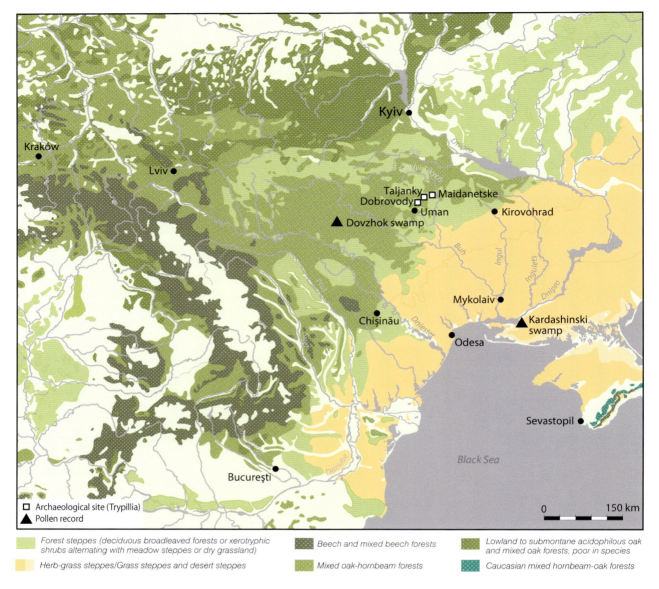

Figure 1. Natural vegetation: the distribution of forest, forest steppe, and true bunch grass steppe in the western Pontic plant region (after Bundesamt für Naturschutz, 2004).

deciduous woodlands in a forest steppe environment is the soil water balance in the summer months, because the woodlands have a higher water consumption than grasslands and young trees.

Vegetation Dynamics in Trypillia Times (4th millennium BCE)

As natural archives suitable for pollen studies, like lake sediments or peatbogs, are rare, the potential for landscape reconstruction by means of pollen analysis is limited in the western Pontic region. Investigations from a well-dated record from Dovzhok swamp are published by Kremenetski (1995). The Dovzhok swamp is situated in a typical natural vegetation habitat of mixed oak-hornbeam forest (Figure 1). In the pollen-record, the late Atlantic landscape is dominated by a mixed oak forest with oak, lime, elm (*Ulmus*), and hazel (*Corylus*). Hornbeam (*Carpinus*) is a late arrival in the region. It is present in the late Subboreal, but first dominates the broadleaved forests together with common oak at the onset of the Subatlantic period. The time between 4500 and 2900 BCE shows a very slow peat growth, indicative of a dry period, but relatively poor in temporal resolution. Nevertheless, this time is characterized by a regression of the deciduous trees and an increase in pine and non-arboreal pollen, indicating some severe changes in woodland composition. Steppe-indicating plants like Poaceae and Chenopodiaceae do not increase before medieval times at this western location. This is in opposition to a diagram from the Kardashinski swamp

(Figure 1) in the South (Kremenetski, 1995). Here, deciduous trees have much lower values in the late Atlantic and early Subboreal and pine dominates the arboreal spectrum, while high values of *Artemisia* and non-arboreal pollen indicate an open landscape with steppe components.

On-site pollen analyses from vessel fills from the archaeological excavations at Taljanky (Figure 1), carried out by Lucia Wick, Basel, hint to the existence of woodland habitats along the rivers; consisting of hazel (*Corylus*), alder (*Alnus*), lime (*Tilia*), common ash (*Fraxinus excelsior*), deciduous oak (*Quercus*), and elm (*Ulmus*). The high percentages of the pioneer taxa hazel and alder point to woodland exploitation for timber and animal fodder. Overall, these analyses show that the environment of the Taljanky settlement mainly consisted of steppe vegetation with patches of woodland growing along the rivers. Further pasture indicators and spores of coprophilous fungi point to cattle breeding in the vicinity of the site (Kruts *et al.*, 2008: 55). Pollen records from pits and archaeological features taken in Maidanetske during the 2013 excavation reveal poor pollen preservation (Müller *et al.*, in print). Accordingly, the interpretation has to be handled with care. Pine was the most common tree taxon in all of the samples (Figure 2). Oak, lime, and hazel occurred with just single grains in some of the samples. Thus, there is an indication for the existence of trees in the surrounding of the settlement. High values of Liguliflorae (Cichorioideae) show a strong selective decomposition of pollen in the soil. A single sample shows high values of Chenopodiaceae, but again this can be interpreted as pollen selection.

Cereal pollen is recorded in just a single sample (S52–200 cm) while a sample from the surface of a grinding stone (S51–11) did not yield any cereal pollen. Thus, the local pollen record can prove the presence of some tree stands in the vicinity of the settlement, but no statement is possible regarding the density of tree coverage or openness of the landscape. Imprints of leaves in the clay of settlement structures, as well as macro- and micro-charcoal, prove the use of timber for house construction, and thus make a local occurrence probable.

The main component of the charcoal assemblage at Maidanetske is common ash (*Fraxinus excelsior*), followed by oak (*Quercus*), and elm (*Ulmus*) (Figure 3). They all belong to the deciduous broadleaved oak-dominated forest species, which are typical for the regional natural forest steppe. Charcoal of common ash was also identified on the neighbouring site of Taljanky (Kruts *et al.*, 2008: 55, 2009). At Maidanetske, willow (*Salix*) supplements the wood spectrum; it is indicative for a riverine woodland that most probably grew alongside the Taljanka River in the vicinity of the site. These indications show that woodland patches existed between the Trypillia mega-sites, and that riverine forests accompanied the small rivers in the 4th millennium BCE. However, there is no clue identifying the extent of the woodland patches (Müller *et al.*, in print).

Charred curled-up awn fragments, most possibly of feather grass (*Stipa*), regularly occur in the Maidanetske samples (Figure 4). They concentrate in the upper excavation layers; in particular in those covering the cultural layers. These fragments are tiny and thus

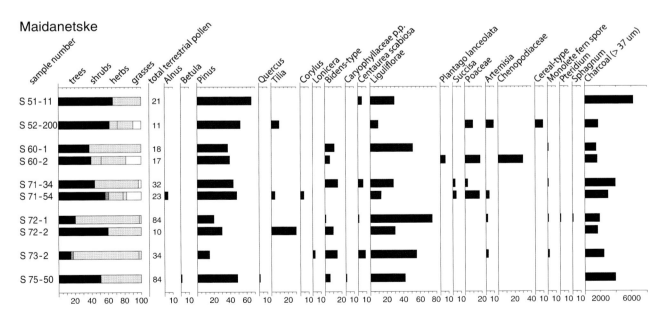

Figure 2. *On-site pollen spectra (Trenches 51, 52, 60, 71, 72, 73, and 75), excavation campaign Maidanetske 2013. Percentage values based on the terrestrial pollen sum (analyses: Carola Floors/Walter Dörfler, Kiel).*

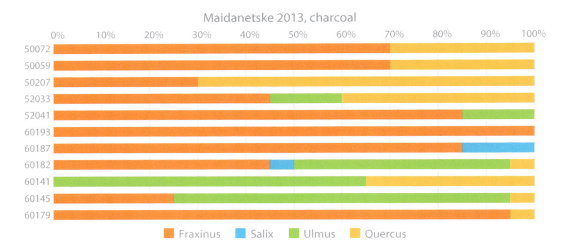

Figure 3. The charcoal assemblages from pit fills (Trenches 50, 52, and 60), excavation campaign Maidanetske 2013 (analysis: Vincent Robin, Kiel).

may have easily been dislocated into deeper layers, but this is unlikely to be the case. Feather grasses are characteristic for steppe environments. The eldest Central European feather grass finds stem from the Czech Republic and date to the Early Bronze Age (Bieniek & Pokorny, 2005). Feather grass awn fragments are light in weight and easily transported by wind. Thus, the awn fragments may well have been transported over long distances and give a regional signal for the expansion of grasslands. However, supported by the results from the pedological analyses, the Maidanetske finds in the upper occupation levels and above most probably hint to a local extension of steppe meadows in the phase shortly before and after abandonment of the mega-site. At this stage of investigation, this may be carefully interpreted as a sign of overexploitation of the semi-arid forest steppe environment (Müller *et al.*, in print).

The natural forest steppe is a mosaic-like vegetation type consisting of woodland patches alternating with meadow or grassland steppe, depending on topography, and soil conditions. It remains to be tested, whether the Trypillia mega-sites were preferentially situated on the former woodland patches, namely the drained soils, in elevated areas and on northern slopes, or if the preferred locations for establishing a megasite were the open meadow steppe patches in the natural forest steppe.

Palaeo-ecological and Palaeoclimatological Reconstructions

Different factors have influenced the Holocene vegetation development. According to Walter & Breckle (1997: 384), the border between woodland and true

Figure 4. (a) Cf. Stipa *(feathergrass), charred awn fragments, sample 51182_12; (b) Modern* Stipa ucrainica, *Botanical Garden, Halle University, Germany (photographs by Sara Jagiolla/Wiebke Kirleis, Kiel).*

steppe environment in the west Pontic region must have shifted in postglacial times. This is further attested through recent observation of krotovinas at Maidanetske, i.e. infilled burrows dug by the steppe animals, like the European ground squirrel, in the soils below the modern woodland vegetation. Compared with other European regions, the information about the Holocene environmental history of the Ukraine shows only a low temporal and spatial resolution. There are very few sedimentary archives with continuous environmental records like lakes or mires, resulting in a low spatial resolution of the existing information. A summary of palaeo-ecological and palaeoclimatological reconstructions shows the general trends at a supra-regional scale (Figure 5). Based on dated Holocene sediments (180 radiocarbon dates, eighty exposures) from the Russian part of the East European plain northeast of the Ukraine, pedo-lithogenic cycles, and the derived climatic conditions have been reconstructed (Sycheva, 2006). In Sycheva's model, Holocene soil formation is solely influenced by climate and occurred when there is no or few excess of precipitation compared with evapo(transpi)ration. Consequently, warmer and drier phases are characterized by soil formation (labelled as S1–S4), while erosion occurred during colder and wetter periods (Figure 5a). Some weak points in this model have to be mentioned. From other regions, it is clear that not only climate but also human activity affect Holocene geomorphologic processes (e.g. Dreibrodt *et al.*, 2010; James, 2014). Sycheva (2006) assumes that climate variability triggers processes synchronously at largely different geomorphic scales (like slopes and alluvial deposits) but this is probably more complex. Further, her assumption that more precipitation leads to increased erosion, disregards effects of the vegetation. A higher density of plant cover would rather reduce erosion during wetter periods. Figure 5b, representing

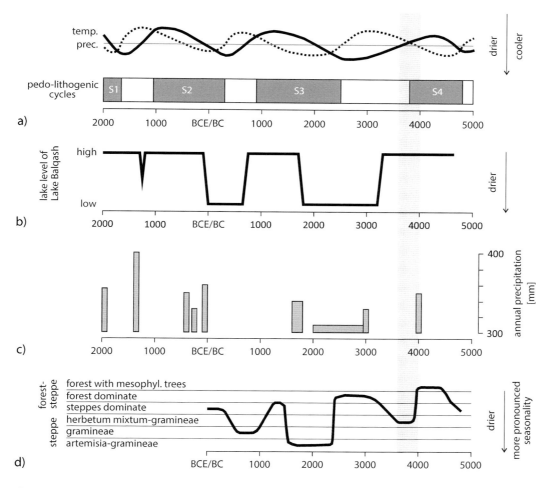

Figure 5. Summary of palaeo-ecological and palaeoclimatological reconstructions for the wider region. (a) Pedo-lithogenic cycles reconstructed by Sycheva (2006). S1–S4 represent regional phases of slope stability and soil formation, interrupted by erosive phases. Temperature and precipitation estimates are reconstructed from the record of soils and sediments. (b) Reconstruction of Lake Balquash lake level from Kremenetski (1997) (radiocarbon ages recalibrated). (c) Reconstruction of paleo-precipitation based on the magnetic properties of soils buried by burial mounds from Demkin et al. (2004). (d) Holocene palaeoclimatic summary of pollen diagrams given by Gerasimenko (1997) (radiocarbon ages recalibrated).

the lake level changes of Lake Balkhash, Eastern Kazakhstan, was taken and calibrated from Kremenetski (1997). It illustrates that the climate (relative humidity) of Central Asia was clearly connected to Eastern European climate change, but it is of limited value for the Central Ukraine since it is situated more than 1000 km to the East of Uman. The palaeohumidity reconstruction (Figure 5c) is based on the magnetic properties of more than 300 Holocene soils buried under burial mounds in the region from the Southern Lower Volga to the Ergeni uplands in southwestern Russia (Demkin et al., 2004). It illustrates a general problem of reconstructions that rely on the analysis of buried soils; since the number, age, and spatial distribution of burial mounds are limited, the same is true for the soils buried below. It is impossible under such conditions to reconstruct the soil history of a region in a continuous manner. To fill such gaps, it might be of interest to consider soils buried below slope deposits, since they occur ubiquitously in Holocene landscapes impacted by land use. A summary of Southern Ukrainian pollen records from Gerasimenko (1997) is further provided. It indicates a shift from forest-dominated vegetation towards a more open steppe environment in the first half of the 4th millennium BCE (Figure 5d). Bearing in mind the low resolution of the given palaeoclimate data sets, a look at the investigation interval is meaningful (grey column in Figure 5c). In the records of Sycheva (2006) and Gerasimenko (1997), a certain change in environmental conditions during Trypillia times appears. Yet, the character of change reconstructed by the authors differs. Sycheva (2006) points out a step from drier to wetter conditions, while Gerasimenko (1997) found indications for the opposite. This discrepancy might be explained by the different regions studied by the authors. The sites studied by Sycheva (2006) are situated north-eastwards of the ones studied by Gerasimenko (1997). It should be mentioned that a short dry spell at c. 3900 cal BCE has been reported for the North Atlantic region (Bond et al., 1997). The record of Lake Balkhash (Figure 5b) and the buried soils in the Volga region (Figure 5c) does not show any variability during Trypillia times.

SOIL DEVELOPMENT

The investigation of soils and buried soils is a method, which is widely used in Eastern Europe for palaeoenvironmental reconstructions, supplementary to palynology, and analysis of botanical macro-remains (e.g. Gerasimenko, 1997; Kremenetski, 1997; Demkina et al., 2003; Demkin et al., 2004; Sycheva, 2006; Mitusov et al., 2009). This is based on the observation that different formations of vegetation and types of land use lead to different soil types and properties; in the case of Trypillia sites namely forest soils, steppe soils, and as result of soil erosion, colluvial soils. The pedogenetic alteration of a given material starts at the surface. Thus, soils on stable surfaces exposed to these processes over a long time can reflect a multitude of varying conditions (multi-genetic soils), most often strongly influenced by the youngest intensive soil formation phase. Pedo-archives suited for reconstruction of the local environmental history are usually situated at and beneath slopes or below artificial layers like burial mounds. Here, surfaces and thus soils of decreasing age can be found buried and preserved under the subsequently deposited slope sediments (Butler, 1959) or the archaeosediments (e.g. Demkin et al., 2004).

New data from soil sciences offer a detailed view on the environmental dynamics in the 4th millennium BCE related to the archaeological site of Maidanetske in Central Ukraine. The mega-site is situated on the Chernozems high plateau, positioned at the confluence of a small watercourse with the Taljanky River, 170–190 m a.s.l., which drains into the Girskyj Tikych River to the East.

A preliminary hypothesis on the Holocene soil history at Maidanetske (Müller et al., in print) is based on investigations of a catenary transect formed by a small exposure at a slope adjacent to the excavation of the mega-site, supplementary auger cores, and observations of soil profiles within archaeological excavations. As a result of the deposition of colluvial layers, a typical forest soil (Cambisol) was buried and preserved. The start of Holocene soil erosion at the investigated slope accompanies or alternates with the onset of a steppe soil formation (Chernozem): the formation of the Chernozem before or after the burial of the basal Cambisol is indicated by the obvious enrichment of a large amount of soil organic matter in crumb peds of the upper layers, numerous filled krotovinas that penetrate the lower soil horizons to a maximum depth of almost 2 m, and secondary carbonates in the uppermost metre (Figure 6). These results are further reflected in the geochemical analyses on the elemental composition of sediment layers and soil horizons (Müller et al., in print).

The deposition of the loess was dated to the Weichselian Pleni-Glacial (c. 27 ka) and the Weichselian Late Glacial (c. 11 ka) via optically stimulated luminescence (Figure 6). This is very similar to reported ages of aeolian deposits from Central Europe (e.g. Hilgers et al., 2001). A change in colour, density, magnetic susceptibility, grain size distribution, and elemental contents observed in the field, supported by laboratory data, testify a pedogenic alteration of the upper 1.3 m of the loess after its deposition; indicating

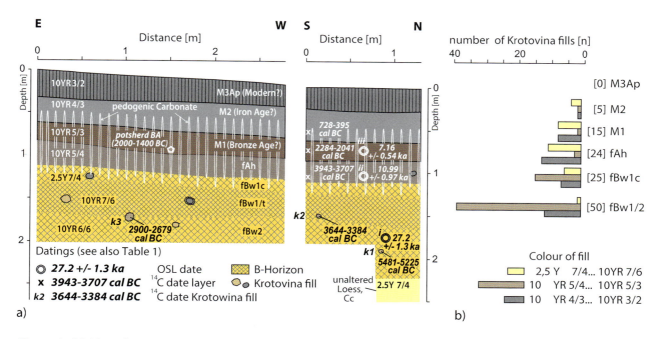

Figure 6. Maidanetske; stratigraphy of Trench 70. (a) Scaled drawing with age data. fBw: buried cambic horizon, fAh: buried humus surface horizon, M1-3: colluvial layers (M: lat. migrare). (b) Number and colour of krotovina fills from different horizons and layers.

the formation of a typical immature Holocene forest soil (Cambisol) with slightly increased clay content and enrichment of pedogenic iron content. The presence of the Cambisol indicates a phase of woodland development at the site. It pre-dates the occupation phase as the pits of the Trypillia settlement were dug into the Cambisol horizon. The buried Bw horizon of the Cambisol was found to be present across the whole excavated area (at the slope as well as on the plateau). Although information on the canopy density and the tree composition of this woodland patch is sparse, it can be concluded from the pedological and geomorphological data that the landscape of Maidanetske was probably completely forested during the early Holocene before the Trypillia occupation. A co-evolution of a steppe soil with the occupation of the Maidanetske settlement is indicated by the radiocarbon ages of the soil organic matter of respective soil horizons (thick fAh) and krotovina fills (k1, k2, and k3). The surface A-horizon of the soil grew in thickness and intensive bioturbation by dwelling animals (probably ground squirrel) began. The apparent age of the soil organic matter filling the deepest dated krotovina fill (k1) is about 1500 years older than the houses of the settlement and the buried remnant of the surface horizon. This shift to apparently older ages makes sense, since the radiocarbon age of the organic matter of buried soils reflects the stage of equilibrium of the input of young organic matter and decomposition reached at the time of burial; called the 'apparent mean residence time' of organic matter (e.g.

Paul *et al.*, 1964; Campbell *et al.*,1967). Similar equilibrium ages of buried soils of 950–1550 years were found by Alexandrovskiy & Chichagova (1998) in buried soils from the Russian part of Eastern European steppe, or 550–2000 years at sites in Germany (Dreibrodt *et al.*, 2009, 2013). Therefore, the radiocarbon age of k1 might reflect the onset of intensive bioturbation associated with the start of settlement activity at the investigated Trypillia site. The presence of a wooded landscape before and at the onset of the Trypillia occupation phase at Maidanetske would explain both the buried forest soil (Cambisol) and the large number of concurrent houses consuming an immense amount of wood for construction, fuel, and tools.

The large number of krotovina fills that exhibit the same colour as the Trypillia surface horizon (fAh) further supports the idea of coincidence in the onset of Chernozem formation and the Trypillia settlement. More importantly, the location of the excavated houses explicitly excludes a greater age for the Chernozem compared with the Trypillia settlement, since the Chernozem was clearly situated above the house remains and only thin A-horizons correspond to the level of the Trypillia surface. Since there are hardly any pronounced climatic indications to explain the shift in soil formation processes (Figure 5), local clearance by the settlers and subsequent land use might explain the change of edaphic conditions.

To summarize, the geomorphologic and paleopedologic results indicate a wooded landscape before and at the onset of the occupation of the Trypillia settlement, and subsequent landscape openness. Considering the palaeoclimatic data from the region, the formation of the Chernozem at Maidanetske reflects the environmental conditions of an agricultural steppe rather than a climatic one.

Conclusions about the Trypillia Environmental History in Central Ukraine

The Ukrainian vegetation history in the timespan of 4500–2900 BCE displays a mode of change. In the West, a change in the woodland cover, namely a regression of deciduous trees, an increase in pine, and increasing openness are observed. In the Southern Ukraine, a pine-dominated forest steppe with a high degree of openness and steppe components was present. On-site plant remains from Central Ukrainian mega-sites (Maidanetske and Taljanky) hint to an environment that was dominated by steppe vegetation with the existence of some trees in the immediate vicinity of the settlements, and to the presence of riverine woodland along the small rivers. For both mega-sites, estimates of the degree of woodland cover are not possible on the basis of palaeo-botanical data alone. With the addition of paleo-pedological information, indicating a coincidence of the alteration of the forest Cambisol to steppe Chernozem during the settlement occupation, the picture becomes more complete. The local development of an open steppe environment was most probably triggered by woodland clearance and subsequent land-use activities by the settlers. The scenario of a land-use-induced steppe formation (agricultural steppe) is further corroborated by the macrobotanical data, shown by the charred remains of the steppe indicator feather grass, which date to the latest to post-settlement phase.

The new palaeo-ecological data clearly show the human impact on the landscape in the 4th millennium BCE. Human activity linked to the Trypillian mega-sites, in particular overexploitation, seems to have been the main trigger towards a severe increase in the meadow or grassland steppe formations. In the long run, the modern cultural steppe in Central Ukraine is related to the early man-made establishment of grassland steppe on soils that would carry the patchy tree cover of a forest steppe or even of an oak-hornbeam forest as potential natural vegetation.

References

Alexandrovskiy, A.L. & Chichagova, O.A. 1998. Radiocarbon Age of Holocene Palaeosols of the East European Forest-Steppe Zone. *Catena*, 34:197–207.

Bieniek, A. & Pokorny, P. 2005. A new Find of Macrofossils of Feather Grass (*Stipa*) in an Early Bronze Age Storage Pit at Vlineves, Czech Republic: Local Implications and Possible Interpretation in a Central European Context. *Vegetation History and Archaeobotany*, 14:295–302.

Bond, G., Showers, W., Cheseby, M., Lotti, R., Almasi, P., Demenocal, P., Priore, P., Cullen, H., Hajdas, I. & Bonani, G. 1997. A Pervasive Millennial-Scale Cycle in North Atlantic Holocene and Glacial Climates. *Science*, 278:1257–66.

Bundesamt für Naturschutz (BfN)/Federal Agency for Nature Conservation. 2004. *Karte der natürlichen Vegetation Europas/Map of the Natural Vegetation of Europe, Maßstab/Scale 1: 2,500,000. Erläuterungstext, Legende, Karten / Explanatory Text, Legend, Maps.* Münster: Landwirtschaftsverlag. Interactive CD-rom/ Interactive CD-rom. http://www.floraweb.de/vegetation/dnld_eurovegmap.html; [accessed 24 May 2015].

Butler, B.E. 1959. *Periodic phenomena in landscapes as a basis for soil studies.* CSIRO, Soil Publ. 14, Canberra: CSIRO.

Campbell, C.A., Paul, E.A. & Rennie, D.A. 1967. Factors Affecting the Accuracy of the Carbon-Dating Method of Soil Humus Studies. *Soil Science*, 104:81–85.

Demkina, T.S., Borisov, A.V. & Demkin, V.A. 2003. Paleosol and Paleoenvironment in the Northern Ergeny Upland in the Latest Neolithic and Bronze Ages 4–2 ka. B.C. *Eurasian Soil Science*, 36:586–98.

Demkin, V.A., Eltsov, M.V., Alekseev, A.O., Demkina, T.S., Alekseeva, T.V. & Borisov, A.V. 2004. Soil Development in the Lower Volga area During the Historical Period. *Eurasian Soil Science*, 37:1324–33.

Doniță, N. & Karamyševa, Z.V. with contributions by Attila Borhidi and Udo Bohn. 2004. L Forest Steppes (Meadow Steppes Alternating with Nemoral Deciduous Forests) and Dry Grasslands Alternating with Dry Scrub. In: Bundesamt für Naturschutz (BfN) (Hrsg.) U. Bohn, R. Neuhäusl & G. unter Mitarbeit von Gollub et al. (2000/2003): Karte der natürlichen Vegetation Europas/Map of the Natural Vegetation of Europe. Maßstab/Scale 1:2.500.000. Teil 1: Erläuterungstext mit CD-ROM; Teil 2: Legende; Teil 3: Karten. Münster: Landwirtschaftsverlag, pp. 375–89.

Dreibrodt, S., Nelle, O., Lütjens, I., Mitusov, A., Clausen, I. & Bork, H-R. 2009. Investigations on Buried Soils and Colluvial Layers Around Bronze Age Burial Mounds at Bornhöved (Northern Germany): An Approach to Test the Hypothesis of 'Landscape Openness' by the Incidence of Colluviation. *The Holocene*, 19(3):487–97.

Dreibrodt, S., Lubos, C., Terhorst, B., Damm, B. & Bork, H-R. 2010. Historical Soil Erosion by Water in Germany: Scales and Archives, Chronology, Research Perspectives. *Quaternary International*, 222:80–95.

Dreibrodt, S., Jarecki, H., Lubos, C., Khamnueva, V.S., Klamm, M. & Bork, H.-R. 2013. Holocene Soil Formation and Erosion at a Slope Beneath the Neolithic Earthwork Salzmünde (Saxony-Anhalt, Germany). *Catena*, 107:1–14.

Gerasimenko, N. 1997. Environmental and Climatic Changes between 3 and 5 ka BP in Southeastern Ukraine. In: H. N. Dalfes, G. Kukla & H. Weiss eds. *Third Millennium BC Climate Collapse and Old World Change.* Berlin: Springer, pp. 371–99.

Hilgers, A., Gehrt, E., Janotta, A. & Radtke, U. 2001. A contribution to the Dating of the Northern Boundary of the Weichselian Loess Belt in Northern Germany by Luminescence Dating and Pedological Analysis. *Quaternary International*, 76/77:191–200.

http://de.climate-data.org/ [accessed 22 September 2015].

James, L.A. 2014. Legacy Sediment: Definitions and Processes of Episodically Produced Anthropogenic Sediment. *Anthropocene*, 2:16–26.

Köppen, W. & Geiger, R. 1939. *Handbuch der Klimatologie Bd. 3: Regionale Klimakunde: Europa und Nordasien, Teil N: Klimakunde von Rußland in Europa und Asien, Hälfte 2: Klimakunde von Rußland: Tabellen*. Berlin: Bornträger.

Kremenetski, C.V. 1995. Holocene Vegetation and Climate History of Southwestern Ukraine. *Review of Palaeobotany and Palynology*, 85:289–301.

Kremenetski, C.V. 1997. The Late Holocene Environmental and Climate Shift in Russia and Surroundings Lands. In: H. N. Dalfes, G. Kukla & H. Weiss eds. *Third Millennium BC Climate Collapse and Old World Change*. Berlin: Springer, pp. 351–70.

Kruts, V.A., Korvin-Piotrovskiy, A.G., Menotti, F., Ryzhov, S.N., Chernovol, D.K. & Chabanyuk, V.V. 2008. *The Trypillia Culture giant-settlement of Talianki. The 2008 Investigations*. Kiev: Institute of Archaeology of the National Academy of Sciences of Ukraine.

Kruts, V.A., Korvin-Piotrovskiy, A.G., Menotti, F., Ryzhov, S.N., Chernovol, D.K., Tolochko, D.V. & Chabanyuk, V.V. 2009. *The Trypillia Culture Giant-Settlement of Talianki. The 2009 Investigations*. Kiev: Institute of Archaeology of the National Academy of Sciences of Ukraine.

Matuszkiewicz, W. 2004. F.3 Mixed Oak-Hornbeam Forests (*Carpinus betulus, Quercus robur, Q. petraea, Tilia cordata*). In: Bundesamt für Naturschutz (BfN) / Federal Agency for Nature Conservation (2004) Karte der natürlichen Vegetation Europas / Map of the Natural Vegetation of Europe, Maßstab / Scale 1: 2,500,000. *Erläuterungstext, Legende, Karten / Explanatory Text, Legend, Maps*. Münster: Landwirtschaftsverlag, pp. 257–68.

Mitusov, A., Mitusova, O.E., Pusovoytov, K., Lubos, C. C.-M., Dreibrodt, S. & Bork, H.-R. 2009. Palaeoclimatic indicators in soils buried under archaeological monuments in the Eurasian steppe: a review. *The Holocene*, 19,8, 1153–1160.

Müller, J., Hofmann, R., Kirleis, W., Ohlrau, R., Brandtstätter, L., Dal Corso, M., Out, V., Rassmann, K. & Videiko, M., in print. Maidanetske 2013. New Excavations at a Trypillia megasite. Studien zur Archäologie in Ostmitteleuropa. Bonn: Habelt.

Paul, E.A., Campbell, C.A., Rennie, D.A. & McCallum, K.J. 1964. Investigations on the Dynamics of Soil Humus Utilizing Carbon Dating Techniques. *Eighth International Congress of Soil Science*, 3:201–08.

Sycheva, S.A. 2006. Long-term pedolithogenic rhythms in the Holocene. *Quaternary International*, 152–153: 181–91.

Walter, H. & Breckle, S.-W. 1986. *Ökologie der Erde, Geo-Biosphäre. Band 3: Spezielle Ökologie der gemäßigten und arktischen Zonen Euro-Nordasiens. Zonobiom VI-IX*. Stuttgart: Fischer Verlag.

Walter, H. & Breckle, S.-W. 1997. *Vegetation und Klimazonen*. 7th ed. Stuttgart: Ulmer.

CHAPTER 10

Demography Reloaded

ALEKSANDR DIACHENKO

INTRODUCTION

Were prehistoric settlements built by amorphous peoples of some 'archaeological culture' or particular population groups of a certain size, growth rate, and density of distribution in a given area? Population estimates and demographic development are considered by 'social demographers' as a reflection of socio-political organization and economic development, rather than simply valued properties of inhabitants of some site or region. Recent studies in archaeological demography, which are based upon the concept of punctuated equilibrium, went far from equating certain numbers of people with types of settlement form or socio-political organization. However, even taking into account much more complex structural relations between social organization, economy and population, demographic development could tell us a lot about the societies of remote past.

Cucuteni–Trypillia demography is not a new topic. In the 1930s, estimations were made by Soviet archaeologists and, dozens of years later, Romanian scholars (for the most recent overviews see Preoteasa, 2009; Diachenko, 2013; Videiko, 2013). Passek (1940: 31–32, 1949) simply introduced ethnographic evidence to the Trypillia settlements, following Struve's scheme, i.e. oversimplified Soviet Marxism. Further estimations resulted in notable trends. Calculating the population values and catchment areas for the sites in the Middle Dnipro region, Bibikov (1965) faced a typical Malthusian catastrophe. The productivity of the catchment areas in his estimations appeared to be too low to support a sustainable life at these settlements. Bibikov concluded that the 'Trypillians' harvested twice per year and, ironically, since that time the shadow of Malthus instead of a 'ghost of communism' followed one of two directions in studies of the Cucuteni–Trypillia demography in the Soviet bloc and the so-called post-socialist states. This is especially evident in the case of the mega-sites that were discovered in the late 1960s. A possible discrepancy between population estimates and the economic potential of the 'Trypillians' or, at least, significant population pressure on the local environment, was recognized both in the East and the West (e.g. Kruts, 1989, 2012; Fletcher, 1995; Nikolova, 2002; Gaydarska, 2003; Nikolova & Pashkevich, 2003; cf. Videiko, 2013; Ohlrau et al., 2015).

The second direction in related studies was initiated by Shmaglij. Generally speaking, his work on population estimates for Maidanetske, reaching 10,000–15,000, then 20,000–24,000, and finally 6000–9000 people (Shmaglij et al., 1975; Shmaglij, 1980; Shmaglij & Videiko, 1990a), corresponded to the concept implemented into Soviet Marxism of linear socio-economic and demographic development worldwide, that 'spread' the Near Eastern model to other territories. Followers of Shmaglij postulated the rejection of Marxism (Burdo, 2004). Meanwhile, their studies, which included estimations of the monumentality of the clay-and-wood houses in man-hours and assumptions regarding the ruling elites focused on obtaining surpluses, seem to be heavily influenced by Marx's (1909) labour theory of value (e.g. Videiko, 2002, 2006).

New concepts for the development of prehistoric populations and high precision settlement plans that were recently obtained by international research teams in Ukraine, Moldova, and Romania enable reworking of the Cucuteni–Trypillia demography. Surely, it is also important to briefly discuss the previous ideas prior to this reworking. This study focuses on the Western Trypillia culture (WTC) settlements in the Southern Buh and Dnipro interfluve, a region well-known for the largest Chalcolithic sites in Europe. The estimations traditionally include several spatial tiers. Placing the obtained values against a time-scale, I aim to reconstruct the dynamic demographic processes in this region and the surrounding areas. Finally, some issues of the structural relations between economic development, socio-political organization, and population are considered.

ESTIMATIONS

High-precision demographic reconstructions are possible with a representative sample of excavated settlements and synchronous cemeteries. However, this is not the case for the WTC in the Southern Bug and Dnieper interfluve. Trypillia graves were not found in this region. A lack of sex–age profiles makes the precise estimation of population values impossible (e.g. Hassan, 1981; Bocquet-Appel, 2002; Chamberlain, 2006). Meanwhile, the highly clustered spatial distribution of the 'Trypillians' enables approximations for four spatial tiers, represented by house, settlement, micro-regional, and regional groups. Let us consider the corresponding values.

House

The WTC house in the Sothern Buh and Dnipro interfluve is usually associated with one nuclear family (Kruts, 1989, 1993 and earlier conference papers). This conclusion is based upon regularities in the interior of houses that mostly included one living-room. Each building contained one oven (Chernovol, 2012). The 9.8 per cent of dwellings in Maidanetske that were inhabited by two families were among the few exceptions (Videiko, 1992: 61). However, the interpretation of the internal structure of houses was not confirmed by further studies (Chernovol, 2012; Videiko, 2013). Most of the previous estimates for the WTC populations in the area are based upon the amount of floor area required for one person and analogies taken from other archaeological studies or ethnographic evidence (for the recent overviews see Preoteasa, 2009; Diachenko, 2013; Videiko, 2013). I follow the approach that considers dynamics of the family development; the growth and decline of families over time is obvious, therefore, the related simulations lead to more precise approximations (Porčić, 2010, 2011).

Let us assume two families exchanging marriage partners with each other. Sex–age profiles of these families directly correspond to the demographic structure of people buried in the Vykhvatyntsi cemetery (Trypillia CII, Dniester region). Despite of the high percentage of children–people under the age of 14 reached sixty-three per cent of the total number of buried at the cemetery (Kyslyi, 2005)–this site is the only known Cucuteni–Trypillia cemetery that provides representative sex–age profile for the particular population group (Velikanova, 1975; Potekhina, 1999). Women who died between the ages of twenty-five and thirty years represented forty-four per cent of the total number of buried women, while buried women between the ages of forty and sixty years are distributed as follows: forty years–twenty per cent, forty-five to fifty years–forty per cent, and fifty-five to sixty–forty per cent (Velikanova, 1975: 12–14, table 2). Calculations are presented in Table 1. Since we deal with numerous assumptions, the obtained values are rounded to integers or an average family of four to five persons. The annual growth rate of population in this case equals 0.3 per cent.

It should be noted that the obtained values approximately equal to the average family size in hunter–gatherers groups worldwide, except Australia (Hamilton et al., 2007: table 2). The annual population growth rate corresponds to the values for Europe that are associated with the spread of agriculture (Gignoux et al., 2011; Müller, 2013, 2015).

Settlement

Simulation of family development also enables calculation of the approximate number of abandoned houses, which according to the model results reaches up to twenty-five per cent. Of course, the proportion of abandoned dwellings could vary at different settlements depending upon the sex–age structure of a particular population group. The value of 78.4 per cent synchronous dwellings that balances well with the figure of twenty-five per cent for abandoned houses was also derived from the scheme of Maidanetske development from Shmaglij & Videiko (2003) and applied to population estimates (Diachenko, 2012; Diachenko & Menotti, 2012). These values are confirmed by the earlier houses in Taljanky and Maidanetske identified in stratigraphy and as the result of the typo-chronological analysis of ceramics (Ryzhov, 1990; Shmaglij & Videiko, 1990b). However, according to our simulations, only half of the abandoned houses include ceramic complexes that are different from the overall pottery at the site. The approximate number of abandoned dwellings in the small settlements reaches 12.5 per cent with just one exception.

Table 1. Estimation of the average family size based upon sex–age structure of people buried in Vykhvatyntsi cemetery

Nuclear families (assumptions and estimations)	Nuclear family 1 (model results)				Nuclear family 2 (model results)			
Number of children	3		4		6		8	
Mean size of a family (persons per house)	3.1	4	4.7	4.5	3.1	5.7	5.6	5.3
Portion of families (%)	60		40		60		40	
Intermediate results based on the sex–age structure in Vykhvatintsy (persons per house)	3.7–4.3 (71% of families)				4–5.7 (29% of families)			
Average size of family (persons per house)	3.9–4.7 (100% of families)							

Application of the gravity model to the WTC sites in the Southern Buh and Dniepro interfluve identified the newly developed villages that were branches of the settlements of medium and large size, for instance, Talne 2 and 3 that are seen as 'satellites' of Maidanetske (Diachenko & Menotti, 2012). Most probably, the formation of these 'satellites' was caused by economic purposes, i.e. the increase of the catchment area of the centre (Shmaglij & Videiko, 2003). Therefore, these villages could have been founded by the younger generations. As a result, the dwellings within these sites could be considered as synchronous.

The high precision settlement plans that were recently obtained as the result of geomagnetic surveys in many ways rebooted the general understanding of the internal structure of WTC mega-sites (Chapman et al., 2014; Kruts et al., 2011, 2013; Müller et al., 2014; Rassmann et al., 2014). This is also the case for population estimates.

First of all, some sites appeared to be much smaller than suggested previously. Due to the geophysical surveys, the settlement of Apolianka, assumed to be 106–120 ha and include c. 400 dwellings (Diachenko, 2010; Videiko, 2013), was revealed to be limited in size to 30 ha and just thirty houses (Rassmann et al., 2014). The size of Dobrovody 'decreased' from 210–250 to 150 ha, but the number of buildings 'increased' from c. 1380 to c. 1800 (cf. Diachenko, 2010; Videiko, 2013; Rassmann et al., 2014).

The so-called unburnt and/or eroded dwellings were recognized at all surveyed mega-sites. The relative frequency of these features varies from 14.2 or 15.9 per cent in Taljanky to 33.2 per cent in Nebelivka (Chapman personal comment on 05 December 2014; Rassmann et al., 2014: 110). At first glance, this corresponds to the approximate number of abandoned houses that we obtained as a result of simulating the average family. However, one of these complexes, excavated in Nebelivka, did not contain any evidence; supporting the interpretation of the so-called unburnt dwellings as houses. Details of the 'platform' that is interpreted as the remains of a floor from the second storey and elements of interior were not found (Vitaliy Rud presentation given at the Department of the Eneolithic and Bronze Age archaeology, IA NASU on 10 March 2015). At the same time, storage facilities are known for Trypillia settlements outside the Southern Buh and Dnipro interfluve; for instance, the two-storey (!) construction at the WTC settlement of Bernashivka 2 in the Middle Dniester region that had dimensions of 5.5–7.5 m and contained seven large unburnt clay container vessels standing in the dwelling (Chernovol, 2013). Kruts (1989) estimated every fourth construction in Taljanky to be storage in the 1980s to early 2000s, but later abandoned this assumption. Shmaglij and Videiko followed the Kruts' ratio of storage facilities to houses, calculating the population values for Maidanetske (Shmaglij & Videiko, 2003: 126). However, no evident storage was found in Maidanetske, denying us the corresponding ratio for this site as well (Videiko, 2013).

Interpretation of the so-called unburnt and/or eroded dwellings, in fact geophysical anomalies of lower strength, raises numerous questions. Why is the difference in the relative frequencies of these anomalies at different sites so significant (Table 2)? What is the ratio of unburnt to eroded buildings? Is the number of lower strength anomalies dependent upon the state of dwelling preservation? Could a proportion of the so-called unburnt structures be interpreted as storage structures? Is this really the case for abandoned houses? Or maybe these structures were simply burnt in a lower temperature fire, and their amount does not reflect any chronological difference. Due to the lack of evidence to answer all these questions, estimations of three possible population values for each settlement were obtained.

Comparison of the new and old geomagnetic plan of Maidanetske also resulted in the identification of a higher number of burnt houses and so-called unburnt and/or eroded dwellings than previously estimated. The extrapolation coefficients for Maidanetske are 1.85 and 4.02, respectively (Rassmann et al., 2014: 120, table 1). Could these coefficients be applied to other WTC sites in the Southern Buh and Dnipro interfluve? At least three related issues have to be considered to answer this question. These are: (1) the number of comparisons, (2) the development of methodology and equipment, and (3) different methodologies that could also be impacted by subjective factors.

The results of new and old surveys could only be compared for the settlements Taljanky and Maidanetske. According to the number of dwellings represented by old and new plans of Taljanky (Kruts et al., 2013), the extrapolation coefficient for burnt houses at this site is equal to c. 1.25. The difference in extrapolation coefficients for Taljanky and

Table 2. Number of burnt and the so-called 'unburnt and/or eroded dwellings' at the recently prospected settlements (after Chapman et al., 2014; Rassmann et al., 2014)

Settlement	Portion of dwellings (%)	
	Burnt	Unburnt and/or eroded
Apolianka	73.3	26.7
Dobrovody	83.3	16.7
Maidanetske	77.4	22.6
Nebelivka	66.8	33.2
Taljanky	84.1	15.9

Maidanetske, as well as the difference in the ratio of the surveyed areas and total area of sites represented in Table 2, may be explained by the development of geophysical equipment and methodology. Maidanetske was one of the first Trypillia settlements surveyed. The work at this site was conducted in 1971–1974 using 'M-23' and 'M-27' magnetometers, while the site of Taljanky was surveyed in 1983–1986 with the 'ММП-203' magnetometer (Videiko, 2013: 40–46).

Plans of the settlements Glybochok, Fedorivka, Vilkhovets 1, Yampil, and Yatranivka were also produced with a 'ММП-203' magnetometer. However, the methodologies for the interpretation of the anomalies were different (cf. Dudkin, 2007; Koshelev, 2005a, 2005b). Koschelev's work resulted in much higher values for the density of dwellings than estimated by the Frankfurt-Kiel team who applied the 16-channel SENSYS MAGNETO®-MX ARCH magnetometer (cf. Koshelev, 2005b; Müller et al., 2014; Rassmann et al., 2014). At the same time, pits are not represented in Koschelev's plans. Assuming the possibility of Koschelev interpreting these features as part of the 'houses', and c. 1 pit per 1 house similar to other settlements (Chapman, et al., 2014; Rassmann et al., 2014), one may find a correspondence between the estimates of Koschelev and Dudkin, as well as the results that are based upon Dudkin's plans (Dudkin, 2007). These values are considered in our calculations. The extrapolation coefficient, valued at c. 1.25, is based upon comparison of the new and old estimates for the southern part of Taljanky (Kruts et al., 2011).

Population estimates for the sites are given in Table 3. The values were calculated according to three possible scenarios: the first scenario considers the lower strength anomalies as non-residential dwellings, with 78.4 per cent synchronous houses that are represented by burnt structures (Table 3A). According to

Table 3. Population estimates for the settlements

Settlement	Number of dwellings			Number of people per house	Number of people per settlement
	Burnt dwellings	Unburnt dwellings	Synchronous houses		
A. Scenario 1					
Apolianka	22	8	17	4–5	68–85
Dobrovody	1500	300	1176	4–5	4704–5880
Maidanetske	2297	671	1801	4–5	7204–9005
Nebelivka	907	450	711	4–5	2844–3555
Taljanky	1750	330	1372	4–5	5488–6860
B. Scenario 2					
Apolianka	22	8	22	4–5	88–110
Dobrovody	1500	300	1500	4–5	6000–7500
Maidanetske	2297	671	2297	4–5	9188–11,485
Nebelivka	907	450	907	4–5	3628–4535
Taljanky	1750	330	1750	4–5	7000–8750

Settlement	Number of dwellings (initial data)	Extrapolation coefficient	Number of dwellings (estimations)	Number of synchronous houses	Number of people per house	Number of people per settlement
C. Scenario 3						
Apolianka*	30	1	30	24	4–5	96–120
Dobrovody*	1800	1	1800	1411	4–5	5644–7055
Fedorivka**	1362	1.25	1703	1335	4–5	5340–6675
Glybochok**	924	1.25	1155	906	4–5	3624–4530
Maidanetske*	2968	1	2968	2327	4–5	9308–11,635
Nebelivka***	1357	1	1357	1064	4–5	4256–5320
Taljanky**	2080	1	2080	1631	4–5	6524–8155
Vilkhovets 1****	518	1.25	648	508	4–5	2032–2540
Yampil*	378	1.25	473	371	4–5	1484–1855
Yatranivka 1**	660	1.25	825	647	4–5	2588–3235

Sources:
*Rassmann et al. (2014).
**Dudkin (2007), Diachenko and Menotti (2012).
***Chapman, personal comment on 05 December 2014.
****Diachenko (2010).

the second scenario, the number of burnt buildings is equal to the number of synchronous houses, while the so-called unburnt and/or eroded houses are assumed to be abandoned during the life of a settlement (Table 3B). The third scenario interprets the lower strength anomalies as the houses that, for some reason, were burnt in a lower temperature fire. Therefore, the total number of dwellings is equal to the sum of burnt and unburnt buildings; 78.4 per cent of which are suggested to be synchronous. One should note that the number of dwellings in Fedorivka, Glybochok, Vilkhovets 1, Yampil, and Yatranivka was obtained by multiplication of the earlier estimations by an extrapolation coefficient of 1.25. The number of buildings at other sites were multiplied by 1 or remained the same (Table 3B). It should be noted that the obtained results are nearly proportional to the average value of 185 houses in the 'quarters' of Maidanetske that could suggest similar principles in organizational structure (Ohlrau, 2014: 85, table 10). Since the relative frequency of the lower strength anomalies varies from site to site, it is only possible to obtain the results for scenarios 1 and 2 for those settlements that were surveyed recently.

Scenarios 2 and 3, as could have been expected, resulted in similar population values, because of the nearly equal relative number of lower strength anomalies at some sites. Maidanetske had the highest number of inhabitants according to all three scenarios. Estimates for Dobrovody, Fedorivka, and Taljanky, as well as Glybochok and Nebelivka seem to reflect stabilization points in population growth, probably reflecting a balance between reproductive activity and successive subsistence (Shennan, 2009). Values for the small village of Apolianka vary from 68 to 120 people depending on the particular scenario.

The results obtained enable calculations for the higher spatial tiers. Let us estimate the values for the micro-regions and the entire region.

Micro-regions and regions are represented respectively, by settlement clusters and two spatial variants (SV) of the Volodymyrivsko-Tomashivska line sites in the Southern Buh and Dnipro interfluve. Each SV included one or more settlement clusters.

The work on micro-regional and regional population estimates requires a chronological framework of course. Experts in Cucuteni-Trypillia studies have the ambitious goal of proving that the duration of a single phase or stage of development corresponding to the lifespan of an ordinary settlement was *c.* fifty years (Markevich, 1981; Kruts, 1989). This threshold exceeds the accuracy of radiocarbon dating, including the possibilities of Bayesian modelling. Meanwhile, typo-chronologies that are based on this assumption, partly supported by stratigraphic evidence and radiocarbon dates, endorse the aforementioned interval as a quite precise approximation. The logic of these schemes also suggests that the duration of the mega-sites was *c.* eighty years, and *c.* twenty-five to thirty years for the villages that branched off the medium and large settlements (Diachenko, 2012).

The relative chronology of the WTC sites in the Southern Buh and Dnipro interfluve is based upon the typo-chronology proposed by Ryzhov (1993, 1999, 2000, 2007, 2011, 2012) and improved by the application of the gravity model to these settlements (Diachenko & Menotti, 2012). The Volodymyrivsko-Tomashivska line of development includes the Volodymyrivska, Nebelivska, and Tomashivska groups, with subsequent sub-division into phases and stages. After a chronological gap of *c.* fifty years, this region was populated by the peoples of the Kosenivska group as the result of a migration wave from the Dniester region (Kruts, 1989; Ryzhov, 1999; Diachenko, 2012). The late sites of the Volodymyrivska group and the early sites of the Nebelivska group, as well as the late settlements of the Nebelivska group and the early settlements of the Tomashivska group, were chronologically overlapped. Thus, the sites of the Volodymyrivsko-Tomashivska line were combined into ten analytical periods (Diachenko & Menotti, 2012). Settlements of the Kosenivska group were divided into three phases, with possible further sub-division of the third phase of this group, also known as sites of the Kocherzhyntsi-Shulgivka type (Ryzhov, 2002). The settlements that are considered in this study correspond to six of ten analytical periods of the Volodymyrivsko-Tomashivska line and two of three phases of the Kosenivska group (Table 4).

Estimates for the four settlement clusters are given in Table 5. The WTC population in the Southern Buh and Dnipro interfluve probably reached its peak in the third phase of the Tomashivska group. One of the considered settlement clusters is represented by a

Table 4. Relative chronology of sites considered in this study

	Vladimirovsko-Tomashovskaya line										Kosenovskaya group		
Analytical period	1	2	3	4	5	6	7	8	9	10	1	2	3
Settlements	Fedorivka			Nebelivka, Yampil	Glybochok		Dobrovody, Yatranivka 1	Taljanky	Maidanetske		Apolianka	Vilkhovets 1	

Table 5. Population estimates for the settlement clusters

Centre	Other settlements in cluster	Population estimates according to scenario 3
Fedorivka	Not known	5340–6675
Nebelivka	Kryvi Kolina, Leshchivka, Pishchana	7272–9090
Dobrovody	Yatranivka 1	8232–10,290
Maidanetske	Moshuriv 1, Romanivka, Talne 2 and 3	12,120–15,150

single site, namely Fedorivka. Synchronous settlements in the micro-region are not known (Table 5). One should note that calculations corresponding to scenario 3 were only possible in estimating the regional and micro-regional population values. The estimates for the settlement cluster with a centre in Dobrovody are based upon the data obtained as the result of geophysical surveys. The number of dwellings and corresponding population estimates for several sites in other clusters were obtained based upon the same coefficients as applied to Fedorivka, Glybochok, etc.

Population size for the regional tier also allows the estimation of the WTC population density in the Southern Buh and Dnipro interfluve. Corresponding values for clusters of sites are quite speculative, because of the set of issues related to the measurement of catchment areas. The territory of the WTC in the region is measured at *c.* 8000 km^2 (Kruts, 1989). Thus, considering scenario 3 and the possibility of discovering sites belonging to analytical period 3 in the area of SV-2, the population density in the region is estimated as somewhat exceeding 1.5–1.9 persons per 1 km^2.

The peoples of the Kosenivska group are characterized by a lower population density. Taking into account the estimates for the number of dwellings in Zavadivka, Vilkhovets 1, and Vilshana Slobidka that represent three settlement clusters, the total population size at the peak of the Kosenivska group population growth reached 3152–3940 persons. Therefore, assuming some unknown sites from the second phase of development of this group, we estimate the population density in the region as somewhat exceeding 0.4–0.5 persons per square kilometre.

The changes in population values may be considered as proxies for the reconstruction of demographic processes. Let us focus on the dynamics of demographic development more precisely.

DEMOGRAPHIC PROCESSES

Figure 1 represents the changes in population size of the mega-sites and clusters of settlements that belonged to SV-1 of the Volodymyrivsko-Tomashivska line, where these mega-sites are supposed to be the centres. Besides the different relation of values obtained for analytical period 3, i.e. decrease/increase, and a significant decrease in population in analytical period 8, trends for the mega-sites and settlement clusters are quite similar. However, some notable dynamics are not represented in these charts due to the lack of settlements that belong to analytical periods 2, 3, and 6.

First, settlements of analytical periods 2 and 3 decreased in size and probably in number of dwellings compared to analytical period 1. The settlement of Fedorivka was founded by immigrants from the West, who later abandoned this mega-site and formed new settlements in both area SV-1 and SV-2 of the Volodymyrivsko-Tomashivska line (Diachenko & Menotti, 2012). Therefore, instead of a decrease or

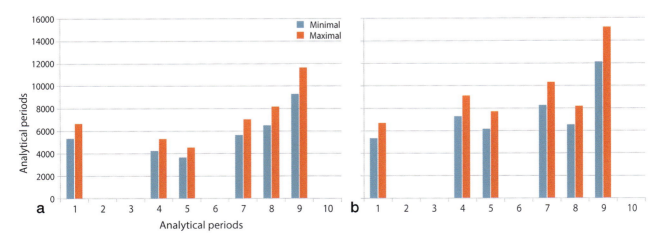

Figure 1. Population estimates for SV-1 of the Volodymyrivsko-Tomashivska line of the WTC. (a) All sites; (b) largest settlements.

slight growth of the population from analytical period 1 to analytical period 4, as represented in Figure 1, the transition between analytical periods 3 and 4 was characterized by abnormally high population growth.

Second, an increase in the number of people from analytical period 5 to analytical period 7 corresponds to the annual growth rate of *c*. 0.30 per cent for the settlement clusters and *c*. 0.45 per cent for the mega-sites. However, a part of the SV-1 population probably migrated to the SV-2 settlements during analytical periods 5 and 6 (Diachenko, 2012). Therefore, abnormally high population growth in SV-1 settlements during analytical period 6 and/or 7 is also obvious.

In both cases, the abnormally high population growth was accompanied by significant changes in pottery styles (Ryzhov, 1993, 1999, 2000, 2007, 2012). This allows the assumption of two migration waves into the Southern Buh and Dnipro interfluve that followed the earlier migration that resulted in the formation of Fedorivka.

Besides previously identified emigration of the SV-1 population to the settlements of SV-2 in analytical periods 2, 5, and 6, population movement in the opposite direction is assumed, according to the data from new high-precision settlement plans. Abnormally high population growth in analytical period 9 corresponds temporally with the decline of SV-2 settlements in their number of inhabitants (Diachenko, 2012). The highest number of houses in Maidanetske, comparing to other Trypillia mega-sites, could be caused by migration from the East to the West. Moreover, synchronous settlements of the Chechelnytska group also declined in population in this time (Tarapata forthcoming). This corresponds to the high number of imitations of Chechelnytska pottery in the ceramic complexes of Maidanetske (Shmaglij & Videiko, 2003). Hence, the formation of the most populated Cucuteni–Trypillia mega-site could have been caused by two migrations waves coinciding in time. These migrations were directed both from the East to the West and from the west to the east.

A population decline in analytical period 10 is usually explained by the emigration to the west, where 'imports' of Tomashivska pottery are known as far away as Romania (Ryzhov, 2000). It cannot be excluded that this 'great movement' of the Tomashivska group population started earlier, during analytical period 8 (Table 2b: analytical period 8). On the other hand, the decline in population size for analytical period 8 could be also explained in different way; we did not include the settlement of Kocherzhyntsi-Pankivka, belonging to the other settlement cluster, in the calculations. Its population size is estimated to 1392–1740 persons.

As mentioned above, the Southern Buh and Dnipro interfluve was populated by WTC populations again after a short chronological hiatus. The new migration wave resulted in the formation of the Kosenivska group settlements. The data derived from new geophysical plans solve the issue of earlier estimations, which showed a significant decrease in the number of people between phases 1 and 2 of this group (Diachenko, 2012). Since the settlement of Kosenivka, which belongs to the first phase, was prospected by Golub, it is not possible to calculate the extrapolation coefficient and, consequently, the population values. However, new evidence for the site of Apolianka seems to change the mentioned trend to a slight increase in number of people.

Even considering the issues with estimating population values for the sites that belong to analytical periods 3 and 6, it is obvious that the general trend corresponds to the old idea of Ravenshtein (1885); supposing the 'gravitation' of migration flows to the largest settlements. This was also the case for long-distance migrations into the Southern Buh and Dnipro interfluve. Population movement from one micro-region to the other, located nearby, resulted in a more intensive increase in the population size of mega-sites, than the growth of inhabitants in other settlements in the corresponding settlement clusters. Comparison of the population values for Maidanetske and other settlements in its cluster with the number of people in Taljanky, as well as the population values for Nebelivka and other sites in its cluster, resulted in the same conclusion.

The territory of modern Ukraine is usually seen as densely populated in the Chalcolithic. In this respect, long-distance migrations are considered as impossible. However, our estimations have shown relatively low values for one of the most intensively populated areas within the territory of the Cucuteni–Trypillia cultural complex (Kruts, 1993; Harper, 2013) that correspond to, or even exceed, the global values and trends for the regions that include non-settled or less settled areas, including south-eastern Europe (Müller, 2013, 2015: 204, 208, figures 17.1 and 17.5). It is notable that the peak of growth of the Volodymyrivsko-Tomashivska line populations corresponds temporally with the significant decline of population densities in south-eastern Europe (Müller, 2013, 2015: 208, figure 17.5). Considering these arguments, migrations into the Southern Buh and Dnipro interfluve were possible. They resolved the demographic issues, probably overpopulation, in other areas, including the Middle Dniester, Upper Dniester, and Middle Southern Buh region. Some waves of massive population movement correspond to indirect evidence for climate change and increase in number of the fortified settlements and weapons (Anthony, 2007; Dergachev, 2007; Ryzhov,

2007; Diachenko, 2012; Harper, 2013). However, what does the 'overpopulation' mean in case of the Neolithic Eastern Europe and, particularly, the Cucuteni–Trypillia cultural complex?

Besides the discussion of migratory behaviour, work with new data resulted in the identification of two stabilization points in population growth for the mega-sites and settlement clusters. The corresponding values are estimated as 3624–5320 and 5644–8155 persons for the mega-sites, and 6144–9090 and 6524–10290 persons for the settlement clusters, respectively (Figure 1). The increase in the number of people between the two stabilization points probably reflects a slight growth of carrying capacity. This could be influenced by changes in the climate that, according to some indirect evidence, became more humid in Trypillia CI (Gerasimenko, 2004; Anthony, 2007; Diachenko, 2012; Harper, 2013). It should be noted that these values do not exceed the number of people in Maidanetske and other settlements in its cluster, supporting the idea of stabilization in population growth below the carrying capacity (Milisauskas & Kruk, 1989; Strogatz, 1994: 18–24; Hastings, 1997: 90–92; Diachenko & Zubrow, 2015). In this respect, Maidanetske appears to be one of the earliest known cases of a significant non-equilibrium state between population values and economic development as well as socio-political organization. Identical non-equilibrium trends in the development of modern cities is known as 'false urbanization'. Finding theses similarities in the present and the past, we could question the structural relationship between different subsystems of the WTC societies.

Some Notes Regarding Economic Development, Socio-Political Organization and Population

First, let us consider the issue of the relationship between population density, number of people and local environment. A huge population pressure in the Southern Buh and Dnipro interfluve was not confirmed. This corresponds to the trends in other agrarian-occupied regions in the Near East and Europe before 3500 BCE. However, differences in population density might lead to population spread to previously uninhabited regions (Müller, 2015). This is especially evident for the Cucuteni–Trypillia cultural complex. To some extent, the values for population density underestimate the human impact on the environment in this case. Developed typo-chronologies, taken together with ethnographical analogies and radiocarbon dates, led to the conclusion that a single settlement existed over a period of about fifty years (Markevich, 1981; Kruts, 1989, 1993). Deforestation, and possibly degradation of soils, caused the necessity of re-settling to other places. Previously settled areas could not be reforested, because new-growth pioneer forest would take an entire settlement generation to become established, with maturity only reached in another seventy to eighty years (Kruts, 1989). Therefore, a few phases of development should be considered simultaneously to analyse the population pressure. Despite this underestimation, a high amount of 'no-man's land' was available in the Southern Buh and Dnipro interfluve. According to Saiko, the development of the Trypillia populations in this region was conditioned by almost unlimited possibilities for spatial expansion. Instead of intensification, the prevailing economic strategy when spatial expansion was not possible, the Trypillians were able to move their homes to new places (Masson, 1990; Saiko, 1990).

The availability of 'no-man's land' is confirmed by the dynamics of changes in the density of dwellings within the large settlements of the Volodymyrivsko-Tomashivska line (Table 6). The significant growth in size of the mega-sites is the result of migrations, which at the same time resulted in a significant decrease in the density of dwellings (e.g. in Nebelivka and Maidanetske; this is probably also true for Dobrovody, but geophysical surveys of the sites that belong to analytical period 6 are required to prove this assumption). Settlements of the Volodymyrivska and Nebelivska group, belonging to analytical periods that follow the time of the migrations, increased in density of dwellings but decreased in settlement size and the number of houses (Diachenko, 2012). These trends confirm that the demographic development in the Eastern European periphery and the Near East was clearly divergent (Müller, 2015).

Sites of the Tomashivska group that belong to analytical periods 7 and 8 reflect the stabilization in population growth, as noted above (Figure 1). The

Table 6. Density of dwellings at the largest settlements

Settlement	Size (ha)	Number of synchronous houses after scenario 3	Density of synchronous houses after scenario 3 (houses per 1 ha)
Fedorivka	122.7*	1411	11.5
Nebelivka	236.0**	1064	4.5
Glybochok	100.0*	906	9.1
Dobrovody	150.0***	1411	9.4
Taljanky	320.0***	1631	5.1
Maidanetske	200.0***	2327	11.6

Sources:
*Diachenko & Menotti (2012).
**Chapman, personal comment on 05 December 2014.
***Rassmann et al. (2014).

settlement of Maidanetske drops out of this general trend (Table 6). The values for the Tomashivska group settlements correspond to our conclusions regarding the slight increase of carrying capacity and the stabilization of population growth below it.

Meanwhile, population size itself cannot be ignored. A high number of people living in one place requires socio-political institutions to organize daily and seasonal activities, as well as general life (Renfrew, 1978; Masson, 1980; Johnson, 1982; Johnson & Earle, 2000). Ethnological evidence also suggests that the organization of migrations ordinarily results in an increase in social complexity (e.g. Earle, 1996; Latushko, 2003). However, the further development of chiefdoms could take different paths, including stagnation, decay into smaller socio-political units, or decrease in complexity (Semenov, 1993).

Conclusion and Discussion

Thus, current knowledge regarding the WTC settlements in the Southern Buh and Dnipro interfluve allows three possible scenarios for the estimation of population size. The difference in the obtained values is caused by three possible interpretations of the so-called 'unburnt and/or eroded dwellings' that were identified as a result of the recent geomagnetic surveys. At the same time, the lack of evidence for the sex–age structure of the populations has led to the constant value for the average family size, which is estimated at *c.* four to five persons. This value was obtained as the result of simulations basing upon the sex–age structure of the people buried in Vykhvatyntsi cemetery, Dniester region.

The relatively low values for the growth and density of population reflect the high amount of unoccupied land in the Southern Buh and Dnipro interfluve. On the one hand, this made migrations into this region possible, as well as population movement between micro-regions; labelled as locations for the sites of SV-1 and SV-2 of the Volodymyrivsko-Tomashivska line of the WTC. On the other hand, the availability of unoccupied land most likely decreased population pressure on the environment, hence slowing down economic intensification.

Stabilization points in population growth were also identified in this study. It is notable that population size in some of the largest settlements exceeds these stabilization points, confirming the hypothesis regarding the stabilization in growth below carrying capacity. This also raises an important issue for simulations in spatial archaeology. Many of the spatial models applied to archaeological settlement systems include population values as the variables inverse to distance between the sites. Moreover, in most of the applications, this mathematical logic is based upon the assumption of a certain correspondence between the population values for a given settlement and the number/volume of its functions (e.g. Christaller, 1966: 67). Considering 'false urbanization' in prehistory, for instance the case of the WTC in the Southern Buh and Dnipro interfluve, it might be a good idea to quantify the 'population size' in spatial simulations as the 'population' at the stabilization point instead of the application of values estimated in ordinary way.

References

Anthony, D.W. 2007. *The Horse, the Wheel and Language. How Bronze-Age Riders from Eurasian Steppe Shaped the Modern World.* Princeton: Princeton University Press.

Bibikov, S.N. 1965. Hoziajstvenno-ekonomicheskij kompleks razvitogo Tripolya. *Sovetskaya Archaeologiya*, 1:48–62. Бибиков, С.Н. Хозяйственно-экономический комплекс развитого Триполья. *Советская археология*, 1:48–62.

Bocquet-Appel, J.-P. 2002. Paleoanthropological Traces of a Neolithic Demographic Transition. *Current Anthropology*, 43(4):637–50.

Burdo, N.B. 2004. Sakralnyj svit Trypilskoi tsyvilizatsii. In: M.Yu. Videiko, ed. *Entsiklopediya trypilskoi tsyvilizatsii v 2 tomah, Tom 1.* Kyiv: Ukrpoligraphmedia, pp. 344–419. Бурдо, Н.Б. 2004. Сакральний світ Трипільської цивілізації. В кн.: М.Ю. Відейко, ред. *Енциклопедія трипільської цивілізації в 2х томах, Том 1.* Київ: Укрполіграфмедіа, с. 344–419.

Chamberlain, A.T. 2006. *Demography in Archaeology.* Cambridge: Cambridge University Press.

Chapman, J., Videiko, M., Hale, D., Gaydarska, B., Burdo, N., Rassmann, K., Mischka, C., Müller, J., Korvin-Piotrovskiy, A. & Kruts, V. 2014. The Second Phase of the Trypillia Mega-Site Methodological Revolution: A New Research Agenda. *European Journal of Archaeology*, 17(3):369–406.

Chernovol, D. 2012. Houses of the Tomashovskaya Local Group. In: F. Menotti & A.G. Korvin-Piotrovskiy, eds. *The Tripolye Culture Giant-Settlements in Ukraine. Formation, Development and Decline.* Oxford: Oxbow Books, pp. 182–209.

Chernovol, D. 2013. Postrojki petrenskoj localnoj gruppy. *Revista Archeologică*, IX(1):72–87. Черновол, Д.К. 2013. Постройки петренской локальной группы. *Revista Archeologică*, IX(1): 72–87.

Christaller, W. 1966. *Central Places in Southern Germany.* Englewood Cliffs, NJ: Prentice Hall.

Dergachev, V.A. 2007. *O skipetrah, o loshadiah i o voine. V zashchitu migratsioonoj kontseptsii M. Gimbutas.* Sankt-Peterburg: Nestor-Istoriya. Дергачев, В.А. 2007. *О скипетрах, о лошадях и о войне. В защиту миграционной концепции М. Гимбутас.* Санкт-Петербург: Нестор-История.

Diachenko, A. 2010. *Tripolskoe naselenie Bugo-Dneprovkogo mezhdurechya: prostranstvenno-vremennoj analiz.* Unpublished PhD Thesis. Kiev: Institute of

Archaeology of the NASU. Дяченко, А. 2010. *Трипольское население Буго-Днепровского междуречья: пространственно-временной анализ (рукопись дис. канд. истор. наук)*. Киев: Институт археологии НАНУ.

Diachenko, A. 2012. Settlement System of West Tripolye Culture in the Southern Bug and Dnieper Interfluve: Formation Problems. In: F. Menotti & A. G. Korvin-Piotrovskiy, eds. *The Tripolye Culture Giant-Settlements in Ukraine: Formation, Development and Decline*. Oxford: Oxbow Books, pp. 116–38.

Diachenko, A. 2013. Paleodemograficheskie rekonstruktsii Cucuteni-Tripolskogo naseleniya: sovremennoe sostoyanie, problemy i perspektivy. *Revista Archeologică*, IX (1):98–107. Дяченко, А.В. 2013. Палеодемографические реконструкции Кукутень-Трипольского населения: современное состояние, проблемы и перспективы. *Revista Archeologică*, IX(1): 98–107.

Diachenko, A. & Menotti, F. 2012. The Gravity Model: Monitoring the Formation and Development of the Tripolye Culture Giant-Settlements in Ukraine. *Journal of Archaeological Science*, 39(4):2810–17.

Diachenko, A. & Zubrow, E.B.W. 2015. Stabilization Points in Carrying Capacity: Population Growth and Migrations. *Journal of Neolithic Archaeology*, 17:1–15.

Dudkin, V.P. 2007. Magnitometrychni doslidzhennia poselen Trypilskoi tsyvilizatsii. In: M. Videiko & S. Kot, eds. *Trypilska kultura. Poshuky. Vidkryttia. Svitovyj kontekst (do 100-richchia z dnia narodzennia O. Olzhycha)*. Kyiv: Spadshchyna Ltd, pp. 57–70. Дудкін, В.П. 2007. Магнітометричні дослідження поселень Трипільської цивілізації. У зб.: М. Відейко та С. Кот, ред. *Трипільська культура. Пошуки. Відкриття. Світовий контекст* (до 100-річчя з дня народження О. Ольжича). Київ: Спадщина LTD, с. 57–70.

Earle, T.K. 1996. Specialization and the Production of Wealth: Hawaiian Chiefdoms and the Inka Empire. In: R.W. Preucel & I. Hodder, eds. *Contemporary Archaeology in Theory. A Reader*. Oxford: Blackwell Publishing, pp. 165–87.

Fletcher, R. 1995. *The Limits of Settlement Growth: A Theoretical Outline*. Cambridge: Cambridge University Press.

Gaydarska, B. 2003. Application of GIS in Settlement Archaeology: An Integrated Approach to Prehistoric Subsistence Strategies. In: O.G. Korvin-Piotrovskiy, V.O. Kruts & S.M. Ryzhov, eds. *The Tripolye Giant-Settlements. Materials of the International Conference*. Kiev: Institute of Archaeology of the NASU, pp. 212–5.

Gerasimenko, N.P. 2004. *Razvitie zonalnykh landshaftov chetvertichnogo perioda na Ukraine*. Unpublished Dr Hab. Thesis. Kiev: Institute of Geography of the NASU. Герасименко, Н.П. 2004. Развитие зональных ландшафтов четвертичного периода на Украине (рукопись дис. док. геогр. наук). Киев: Институт географии НАНУ.

Gignoux, C.R., Henn, B.M. & Mountain, J.L. 2011. Rapid, Global Demographic Expansions after the Origins of Agriculture. *Proceedings of the National Academy of Sciences of the USA*, 108(15):6044–9.

Hamilton, M.J., Milne, B.T., Walker, R.S., Burger, O. & Brown, J.H. 2007. The Complex Structure of Hunter-Gatherer Social Network. *Proceedings of the Royal Society B*, 274(1622):2195–202.

Harper, T.K. 2013. The Effect of Climate Variability on Population Dynamics of the Cucuteni-Tripolye Cultural Complex and the Rise of the Western Tripolye Giant-Settlements. *Chronika*, 3:28–46.

Hassan, F. 1981. *Demographic Archaeology*. New York: Academic Press.

Hastings, A. 1997. *Population Biology: Concepts and Models*. New York: Springer.

Johnson, G.A. 1982. Organizational Structure and Scalar Stress. In: C. Renfrew, M. Rowlands & B. A. Segraves-Whallon, eds. *Theory and Explanation in Archaeology. The Southampton Conference*. New York: Academic Press.

Johnson, A.W. & Earle, T.K. 2000. *The Evolution of Human Societies: From Foraging Group to Agrarian State*. Stanford, CA: Stanford University Press.

Koshelev, I.N. 2005a. *Magnitnaya razvedka archeologicheskih pamiatnikov*. Kiev: Biblioteka V.I. Vernadskogo. Кошелев, И.Н. 2005а. Магнитная разведка археологических памятников. Киев: Библиотека В. И. Вернадского.

Koshelev, I.N. 2005b. *Pamiatniki tripolskoj kultury po dannym magnitnoj razvedki*. Kiev: Biblioteka V.I. Vernadskogo. Кошелев, И.Н. 2005b. Памятники трипольской культуры по данным магнитной разведки. Киев: Библиотека В.И. Вернадского.

Kruts, V.A. 1989. K istorii naseleniya Tripolskoj kultury v mezhdurechye Uzhnogo Buga i Dnepra. In: S. S. Berezanskaya, ed. *Pervobytnaya archeologiya: Materialy i issledovaniya*. Kiev: Naukova Dumka, pp. 117–32. Круц, В.А. 1989. К истории населения трипольской культуры в междуречье Южного Буга и Днепра. В сб.: С.С. Березанская, ред. *Первобытная археология: материалы и исследования*. Киев: Наукова думка, с. 117–32.

Kruts, V.O. 1993. Pytannia demographii Trypilskoi kultury. *Archeologiya*, 3:30–6. Круц, В.О. 1993. Питання демографії Трипільської культури. *Археологія*, 3: 30–36.

Kruts, V.A. 2012. Giant-settlements of Tripolye culture. In: F. Menotti & A. Korvin-Piotrovskiy, eds. *The Tripolye Culture Giant-Settlements in Ukraine. Formation, Development and Decline*. Oxford: Oxbow Books, pp. 70–78.

Kruts, V.A., Korvin-Piotrovskiy, A.G., Rassmann, K. & Peters, D. 2011. Talianki: reloaded. Geomagnetic prospection three decades after V.P. Dudkin's work. In: A. G. Korvin-Piotrovkiy & F. Menotti, eds. *Talianki – Settlement-Giant of the Tripolian Culture. Investigations in 2011*. Kiev: Institute of Archaeology of the NASU, pp. 60–85.

Kruts, V.A., Korvin-Piotrovkiy, A.G., Mischka, C., Ohlrau, R., Windler, A. & Rassmann, K. 2013. Talianki-2012. The geomagnetic prospection. In: A. G. Korvin-Piotrovskiy & K. Rassmann, eds. *Talianki – Settlement-Giant of the Tripolian Culture. Investigations in 2012*. Kiev: Institute of Archaeology of the NASU, pp. 85–103.

Kyslyi, O. 2005. *Demographichnyj vymir istorii*. Kyiv: Aristej. Кислий, О. 2005. *Демографічний вимір історії*. Київ: Арістей

Latushko, Yu.V. 2003. Migratsionnye protsessy v Vostochnoj Polinezii i ikh vliyanie na formirovanie ierarkhicheskih struktur (Gavaiskaya model). In: A. P. Derevianko, ed. *Problemy archeologii i paleoekologii Severnoj, Vostochnoj i Centralnoj Azii*. Novosibirsk:

Izdatelstvo Instituta archeologii i etnografii SO RAN, pp. 442–5. Латушко, Ю.В. 2003. Миграционные процессы в Восточной Полинезии и их влияние на формирование иерархических структур (Гавайская модель). В сб.: А.П. Деревянко, ред. Проблемы археологии и палеоэкологии Северной, Восточной и Центральной Азии. Новосибирск: Издательство Института археологии и этнографии СО РАН, с. 442–5.

Markevich, V.I. 1981. *Pozdnetripolskie plemena Severnoi Moldavii*. Kishinev: Shtiintsa. Маркевич, В.И. 1981. *Позднетрипольские племена Северной Молдавии*. Кишинев: Штиинца.

Marx, K. 1909 [1867]. *Capital: A Critique of Political Economy*. Chicago: C.H. Kerr.

Masson, V.M. 1980. Dinamika razvitiya tripolskogo obshchestva v svete paleodemograficheskih otsenok. In: I.I. Artemenko, ed. *Pervobytnaya archeologiya: Poiski i nakhodki*. Kiev: Naukova Dumka, pp. 204–12. Массон, В.М. 1980. Динамика развития трипольского общества в свете палеодемографических оценок. В сб.: И.И. Артеменко, ред. *Первобытная археология: поиски и находки*. Киев: Наукова думка, с. 204–12.

Masson, V.M. 1990. Tripolskoe obshchestvo i ego sotsialno-ekonomicheskie charakteristiki. In: V.G. Zbenovich, ed. *Rannezemledelcheskie poseleniya-giganty tripolskoj kultury na Ukraine. Tezisy dokladov pervogo polevogo seminara*. Taljanki: Institute of Archaeology of the AN USSR, pp. 8–10. Массон, В.М. 1990. Трипольское общество и его социально-экономические характеристики. В сб.: В.Г. Збенович, ред. *Раннеземледельческие поселение-гиганты трипольской культуры на Украине. Тезисы докладов первого полевого семинара*. Тальянки: Институт археологии АН УССР.

Milisauskas, S. & Kruk, J. 1989. Neolithic Economy in Central Europe. *Journal of World Prehistory*, 3 (4):403–46.

Müller, J. 2013. Demographic Traces of Technological Innovation, Social Change and Mobility: From 1 to 8 Million Europeans (6000–2000 BCE). In: S. Kadrow & P. Włodarczak, eds. *Environment and Subsistence – Forty Years After Janusz Kruk's "Settlement Studies…"*. Bonn & Rzeszow: Rudolf Habelt GmbH & Mitel, pp. 493–506.

Müller, J. 2015. Eight Million Neolithic Europeans: Social Demography and Social Archaeology on the Scope of Change – From the Near East to Scandinavia. In: K. Kristiansen, L. Smedja & J. Turek, eds. *Paradigm Found. Festschrift on Occasion of Evzen Neustupny's 80th birthday*. Oxford: Oxbow Books, pp. 200–14.

Müller, J., Hofmann, R., Rassmann, K., Mischka, C., Videiko, M.Yu. & Burdo, N.B. 2014. Maidanetskoe: issledovaniya po obnovlennomu planu poseleniya. *Stratum Plus*, 2:285–302.

Nikolova, A.V. 2002. Zametki k paleoekonomicheskim rekonstruktsiyam rannikh form zemledeliya. In: S.D. Kryzhitskyi, ed. *Suchasni problemy archeologii*. Kyiv: Institute of Archaeology of the NASU, pp. 161–63. Николова, А.В. 2002. Заметки к палеоэкономическим реконструкциям ранних форм земледелия. В сб.: С.Д. Крыжицкий, ред. *Сучасні проблеми археології*. Київ: Інститут археології НАНУ, с. 161–3.

Nikolova, A.V. & Pashkevich, G.A. 2003. K voprosu ob urovne razvitiya zemledeliya Tripolskoj kultury. In: O.G. Korvin-Piotrovskiy, V.O. Kruts & S.M. Ryzhov, eds. *The Tripolye Giant-Settlements. Materials of the International Conference*. Kiev: Institute of Archaeology of the NASU, pp. 89–95. Николова, А.В. и Пашкевич, Г.А. 2003. К вопросу об уровне развития земледелия Трипольской культуры. In: O.G. Korvin-Piotrovskiy, V.O. Kruts and S.M. Ryzhov, eds. *The Tripolye Giant-Settlements. Materials of the International Conference*. Kiev: Institute of Archaeology of the NASU, pp. 89–95.

Ohlrau, R. 2014. Tripolje Großsiedlungen. Geomagnetische Prospektion und architektursoziologische Perspektiven. Unpublished MA Thesis. Kiel: CAU.

Ohlrau, R., Dal Corso, M., Kirleis, W. & Muller, M. 2015. Living on the edge? Carrying capacities of Trypillian settlements in the Buh-Dnipro interfluve. In: J. Muller, K. Rassmann & M. Videiko, eds. *Trypillia-Megasites and European Prehistory, 4100–3400 B.C.*

Passek, T.S. 1940. Trypilske poselennya Kolomyishchyna (rozkopky 1934–1938 rr.). In: M.I. Yachmenov, T.S. Passek & L.M. Slavin, eds. *Trypilska kultura. Tom 1*. Kiev: Drukarnia-litografiya AN URSR, pp. 9–41. Пассек, Т.С. 1940. Трипільське поселення Коломийщина (розкопки 1934–1938 рр.). У кн.: М.І. Ячменьов, Т.С. Пассек і Л.М. Славін, ред. *Трипільська культура. Том 1*. Київ: Друкарня-літографія АН УРСР, с. 9–41.

Passek, T.S. 1949. *Periodozatsiya tripolskikh poselenij (III – II tys. do n.e.). Materialy i issledovaniya po archeologii SSSR*, 10. Пассек, Т.С. 1949. *Периодизация трипольских поселений III – II тыс. до н.э. Материалы и исследования по археологии СССР*, 10.

Porčić, M. 2010. House Floor Area as a Correlate of Marital Residence Pattern: A Logistic Regression Approach. *Cross-Cultural Research*, 44(4):405–24.

Porčić, M. 2011. An Exercise in Archaeological Demography: Estimating the Population Size of Late Neolithic Settlements in the Central Balkans. *Documenta Praehistorica*, XXXVIII:323–32.

Potekhina, I.D. 1999. *Naselenie Ukrainy v epokhu neolita i rannego eneolita po antropologichesim dannym*. Kiev: Institute of Archaeology of the NASU. Потехина, И.Д. 1999. *Население Украины в эпоху неолита и раннего энеолита по антропологическим данным*. Киев: Институт археологии НАНУ.

Preoteasa, C. 2009. Considerations d'ordre demographique et social concernant le complexe culturel Precucuteni – Cucuteni – Tripolye. *Annales d'Université Valahia Targoviste, Section d'Archéologie et d'Histoire*, IX (2):105–18.

Rassmann, K., Ohlrau, R., Hofmann, R., Mischka, C., Burdo, N., Videiko, M. & Müller, J. 2014. High Precision Tripolye Settlement Plans, Demographic Estimations and Settlement Organization. *Journal of Neolithic Archaeology*, 16:63–95.

Ravenshtein, E.G. 1885. The Laws of Migration. *Journal of the Statistical Society of London*, 48(2):167–235.

Renfrew, C. 1978. Space, Time and Polity. In: J. Friedman & M. Rowlands, eds. *The Evolution of Social Systems*. London: Duckworth, pp. 89–112.

Ryzhov, S.N. 1990. Mikrohronologiya poseleniya u s. Talyanki. In: V.G. Zbenovich, ed. *Rannezemledelcheskie poseleniya-giganty tripolskoj kultury na Ukraine. Tezisy dokladov pervogo polevogo seminara*. Taljanki: Institute of Archaeology of the AN USSR, pp. 83–90. Рыжов,

С.Н. 1990. Микрохронология поселения у с. Тальянки. В сб.: Раннеземледельческие поселения-гиганты трипольской культуры на Украине. Тезисы докладов первого полевого семинара. Тальянки: Институт археологии АН УССР, с. 83–90.

Ryzhov, S.M. 1993. Nebelivska grupa pamjatok trypilskoi kultury. *Archeologiya*, 3:101–14. Небелівська група пам'яток трипільської культури. Археологія, 3:101–14.

Ryzhov, S.M. 1999. *Keramika poselen trypilskoi kultury Bugo-Dniprovskogo mezhyruzhzhia yak istorychne dzerelo*. Unpublished PhD Thesis. Kyiv: Institute of Archaeology of the NASU. Рижов, С.М. 1999. *Кераміка поселень трипільської культури Бугo-Дніпровського межиріччя як історичне джерело (рукопис дис. канд. істор. наук)*. Київ: Інститут археології НАНУ

Ryzhov, S.N. 2000. Raspisnaya keramika tomashovskoj localno-khronologicheskoj gruppy tripolskoj kultury. *Stratum Plus*, 2:459–73. Рыжов, С.Н. 2000. Расписная керамика томашовской локально-хронологической группы трипольской культуры. *Stratum Plus*, 2: 459–73

Ryzhov, S.N. 2002. Pozdnetripolskie pamyatniki Bugo-Dneprovskogo mezhdurechya. *Stratum Plus*, 2:187–95. Рыжов, С.Н. 2002. Позднетрипольские памятники Буго-Днепровского междуречья. *Stratum Plus*, 2:187–95.

Ryzhov, S.M. 2007. Suchasnyj stan vyvchennia kulturno-istorychnoi spilnosti Cucuteni–Trypillya. In: Yu.Ya. Rassamakin & S.M. Ryzhov, eds. *O. Olzhych. Archeologiya*. Kiev: Vydavnytstvo im. Oleny Teligy, pp. 437–77. Рижов, С.М. 2007. Сучасний стан вивчення культурно-історичної спільності Кукутень-Трипілля. У зб.: Ю.Я. Рассамакін і С.М. Рижов, ред. *О. Ольжич. Археологія*. Київ: Видавництво ім. Олени Теліги.

Ryzhov, S.N. 2011. Western-Tripolye Settlements of the Vladimirovskaya Local Group in the Southern Bug and Dnieper interfluve. In: A.G. Korvin-Piotrovskiy, ed. *Earliest farmers of South-Eastern Europe. Abstracts of International Scientific Conference*. Kiev-Taljanky: Institute of Archaeology of the NASU, pp. 78–79.

Ryzhov, S.N. 2012. Relative chronology of the giant-settlement period BII—CI. In: F. Menotti & A.G. Korvin-Piotrovskiy, eds. *The Tripolye Culture Giant-Settlements in Ukraine: Formation, Development and Decline*. Oxford: Oxbow Books, pp. 79–115.

Saiko, E.V. 1990. Stadialnaya differentsiatsiya istoricheski raznykh tipov rasseleniya: poselenie i gorod-derevnia. In: V.G. Zbenovich, ed. *Rannezemledelcheskie poseleniya-giganty tripolskoj kultury na Ukraine. Tezisy dokladov pervogo polevogo seminara*. Taljanki: Institute of Archaeology of the AN USSR, pp. 17–21. Сайко, Э.В. 1990. Стадиальная дифференциация исторически разных типов расселения: поселение и город-деревня. В сб.: В.Г. Збенович, ред. *Раннеземледельческие поселения-гиганты трипольской культуры на Украине. Тезисы докладов первого полевого семинара*. Тальянки: Институт археологии АН УССР.

Semenov, Yu.I. 1993. Perehod ot pervobytnogo obshchestva k klassovomu: puti i varianty razvitiya (chast 1). *Etnograficheskoe obozrenie*, 1:52–70. Семенов, Ю.И. 1993. Переход от первобытного общества к классовому: пути и варианты развития (часть 1). *Этнографическое обозрение*, 1: 52–70.

Shennan, S. 2009. Evolutionary Demography and the Population History of the European Early Neolithic. *Human Biology*, 81(2–3):339–55.

Shmaglij, N.M., Dudkin, V.P. & Zinkovskij, K.V. 1975. Nekotorye voprosy sotsialno-ekonomicheskoj rekonstruktsii krupnogo tripolskogo poseleniya (po materialam poselenij Umanshchiny). In: V.D. Baran, ed. *Noveishie otkrytiya sovetskikh archeologov. Chast 1*. Kiev: Akademiya Nauk SSSR, pp. 68–9. Шмаглий, Н.М., Дудкин, В.П. и Зиньковский, К.В. 1975. Некоторые вопросы социально-экономической реконструкции крупного трипольского поселения (по материалам поселений Уманщины). В сб.: В.Д. Баран, ред. *Новейшие открытия советских археологов. Часть 1*. Киев: Академия наук СССР.

Shmaglij, N.M. 1980. Krupnye tripolskie poseleniya v mezhdurechye Dnepra i Yuzhnogo Buga. In: I.I. Artemenko, ed. *Pervobytnaya archeologiya: Poiski i nakhodki*. Kiev: Naukova Dumka, pp. 198–203. Шмаглий, Н.М. 1980. Крупные трипольские поселения в междуречье Днепра и Южного Буга. В сб. И.И. Артеменко, ред. *Первобытная археология: поиски и находки*. Киев: Наукова думка, с. 198–203.

Shmaglij, N.M. & Videiko, M.Yu. 1990a. Krupnye tripolskie poseleniya i problema rannih form urbanizatsii. In: V.G. Zbenovich, ed. *Rannezemledelcheskie poseleniya-giganty tripolskoj kultury na Ukraine. Tezisy dokladov pervogo polevogo seminara*. Taljanki: Institute of Archaeology of the AN USSR, pp. 12–6. Шмаглий, Н.М. и Видейко, М.Ю. 1990a. Крупные трипольские поселения и проблема ранних форм урбанизации. В сб.: В.Г. Збенович, ред. *Раннеземледельческие поселения-гиганты трипольской культуры на Украине. Тезисы докладов первого полевого семинара*. Институт археологии АН УССР, с. 12–6.

Shmaglij, N.M. & Videiko, M.Yu. 1990b. Mikrochronologiya poseleniya Maidanetskoe. In: V.G. Zbenovich, ed. *Rannezemledelcheskie poseleniya-giganty tripolskoj kultury na Ukraine. Tezisy dokladov pervogo polevogo seminara*. Taljanki: Institute of Archaeology of the AN USSR, pp. 91–94. Шмаглий, Н.М. и Видейко, М.Ю. 1990b. Микрохронология поселения Майданецкое. В сб.: В.Г. Збенович, ред. *Раннеземледельческие поселения-гиганты трипольской культуры на Украине. Тезисы докладов первого полевого семинара*. Институт археологии АН УССР, с. 91–94.

Shmaglij, N.M. & Videiko, M.Yu. 2003. Maidanetskoe – tripolskij protogorod. *Stratum Plus*, 2:44–140. Шмаглий, Н.М. и Видейко, М.Ю. 2003. Майданецкое – трипольский протогород. *Stratum Plus*, 2: 44–140.

Strogatz, S.H. 1994. *Nonlinear Dynamics and Chaos with Applications to Physics, Biology, Chemistry, and Engineering*. Cambridge, MA: Perseus Publishing.

Tarapata D. 2015. Trends in Demographic Development as a Tool for Relative Dating (with Application to Settlements of the Chechelnitskaya Local Group). *Acta Archaeologia Conservativa*, 1.

Velikanova, M.S. 1975. *Paleoantropologiya Prutsko-Dnestrovskogo naseleniya*. Moskva: Nauka. Великанова, М.С. 1975. *Палеоантропология Прутско-Днестровского населения*. Москва: Наука.

Videiko, M.Yu. 1992. Ekonomika ta suspilnyj lad trypilskogo naselennia Seredniogo Pobuzhzhya. Unpublished PhD Thesis. Kyiv: Institute of Archaeology of the NASU. Відейко. М.Ю. 1992. *Економіка та суспільний лад трипільського населення Середнього Побужжя (рукопис дис. канд. істор. наук)*. Київ: Інститут археології НАНУ.

Videiko, M.Yu. 2002. *Trypilski protomista: Istoriya doslidzhen*. Kyiv: Institute of Archaeology of the NASU. Відейко, М.Ю. 2002. *Трипільські протоміста: історія досліджень*. Київ: Інститут археології НАНУ.

Videiko, M.Yu. 2006. Hliborobstvo trypilskykh plemen. In: G.O. Pashkevych & M.Yu. Videiko. *Rilnytsvo plemen trypilskoi kultury*. Kyiv: Institute of Archaeology of the NASU, pp. 81–122. Відейко, М.Ю. 2006. Хліборобство трипільських племен. У кн.: Г.О. Пашкевич і М.Ю. Відейко. *Рільництво племен трипільської культури*. Київ: Інститут археології НАНУ, с. 81–122.

Videiko, M. 2013. *Kompleksnoe izuchenie krupnykh poselenij Tripolskoj kultury V – IV tys do n.e.* Saarbrücken: Lambert Academic Publishing. Видейко, М.Ю., 2013. Комплексное изучение крупных поселений Трипольской культуры V – IV тыс. до н.э. Saarbrücken: Lambert Academic Publishing

CHAPTER 11

Trypillian Subsistence Economy: Animal and Plant Exploitation

WIEBKE KIRLEIS AND MARTA DAL CORSO

From geophysical and archaeological investigations, it is known that about 15,000 people were living together in the late Trypillia mega-sites in the 4th millennium BCE (Müller *et al.*, 2016; Kruts *et al.*, 2008; Kruts *et al.*, 2009). To function, such prehistoric population agglomerations need a reliable anchoring in subsistence economy and—most probably—a complex social organization. In any human society, the provision of an adequate food supply is a key component to avoid conflict and social upheaval. Facing the enormous dimensions of the population figures for late Trypillian mega-sites, exceptional for prehistoric times, the central question is how population maintenance was managed; if limitations of the natural resources finally furthered the decline of the mega-sites, and which measures were used to buffer potential scarcity in basic requirements. An attempt to develop a model for the carrying capacity of the environment, especially of the Trypillian phase C1, when the population is gathered in the huge agglomerations of the mega-sites, is given in Ohlrau *et al.* (2016).

The following overview of animal and plant exploitation from the early to late Trypillian phases provides some basic data to reconstruct Trypillian subsistence economy. From a diachronic perspective, it is important to bear in mind that three main Trypillia phases (A–C) are distinguished. Relevant for the reconstruction of subsistence economy is the fact that the settlement system changes over the course of time. An early phase is characterized by villages that covered an area of 0.5–6 ha and contained no more than fifteen dwellings. It is followed by settlements of 20–40 ha in size consisting of around two hundred dwellings (Zbenovich, 1996a, 1996b), and a late phase with the mega-site phenomenon, when areas up to 300 ha were settled by about 15,000 inhabitants (Müller *et al.*, 2016). The early settlements cluster on the lower river bench of the Dniester and at the Southern Buh. These early settlements are usually found near the edge of the first river terrace, 2–7 m above the water level, or on the slopes of terraces and gullies. Sites of the middle and late Trypillia periods occur further to the East, between the Southern Buh to the West and the Dnipro to the East. The mega-sites, especially, are mostly perched on promontories of steep river banks or on plateaux (Zbenovich, 1996a).

ANIMAL EXPLOITATION

The archaeozoological state of the art for the early Trypillia phase is compiled by Zbenovich (1996b: 51ff.). The data compilation is based on minimum numbers of individuals per species. A more general compilation can be found in Kruts *et al.* (2001: 79ff.). The latter provides percentage data per species and site, taking into consideration the three Trypillia phases A–C, including the sub-phases.

In the early Trypillia phase A, finds of wild species, most prominently red deer (*Cervus elaphus*), wild boar (*Sus scrofa ferus*), and roe deer (*Capreolus capreolus*), dominate compared with those from domestic animals at four of seven sites (Zbenovich, 1996b: 52). Red deer and wild boar are reliant on woodland habitats, while roe deer prefer the ecotone occurring at the intersection of woodland to open vegetation. Species indicative for open grassland environments, like the horse (*Equus caballus*), are present but rare, occurring more numerously in settlements of the eastern distribution of early Trypillia (Kruts, 2001: 80), an area closer to the natural grassland steppe environment and thus fitting the natural habitat of wild horses (Kirleis & Dreibrodt, 2016: Figure 1). The dominance of species related, under natural conditions, to woodland environments proves that the early Trypillia settlements were located in a woodland steppe that is composed of woodland patches interspersed with areas of grassland. The list of wild animals comprises twenty species, including beaver (*Castor fiber*) and European otter (*Lutra lutra*) from the riverine environment (Zbenovich, 1996b: 51 ff.). According to Kruts *et al.* (2001: 83, table 7), in the early Trypillia phase A on average fifty-four per cent of the species belong to domestic, and forty-six per cent to wild animals.

Among the early Trypillia domestic animals, cattle (*Bos taurus*) are most important, followed by pig (*Sus*

© European Association of Archaeologists 2016

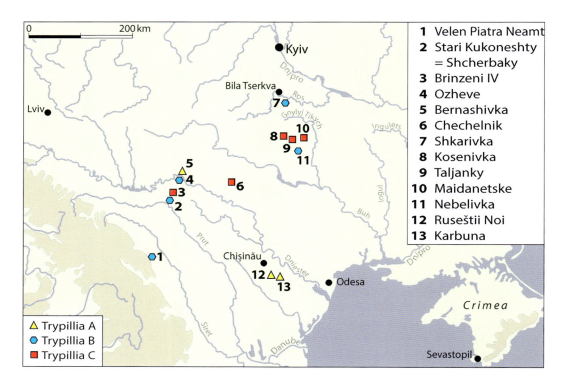

Figure 1. Map of Trypillia sites with charred botanical macro-remains differentiated according to phases A–C. Source: K. Winter, Kiel

domesticus) and sheep/goat (*Ovis aries* and *Capra hircus*). The only exception to this species composition is found at the site Luka Vrublivetska, a site with a special artefact composition. Here, pigs are the dominant species. Dogs (*Canis familiaris*) are regularly proven to have accompanied the early Trypillia settlers (Zbenovich, 1996b: 51 ff.).

Detailed and profound information is available for the two early Trypillian A settlements of Bernove-Luka and Bernashivka, where the hunted species represent about sixty-one per cent of the individuals. However, meat production of wild versus domestic animals has to be converted by the factor 2–2.5. Thus, in the early Trypillia A settlements, the main meat contribution to the diet was provided by animal husbandry. Fish and molluscs complemented the diet. Concentrations of shells from riverine molluscs (*Unio* sp.) are proven for both early Trypillia settlement clusters. The use of shells as ornamental discs for the decoration of textiles is shown by the finds of shell fragments with tiny drill holes (Zbenovich, 1996b: 51 ff.).

At the beginning of the middle Trypillia phase B, in sub-phase BI, the composition of the animal spectrum remains stable, with cattle and pig dominating, supplemented by the small livestock sheep and goat (Kruts *et al.*, 2001: 79ff.). Again, evidence for horses at the eastern edge of the Trypillian distribution area shows the relation of the farming communities to the steppe environment and the contact to the steppe inhabitants. Hunting of wild animals continued to be an important contribution to daily nutrition.

In the following sub-phase BII, animal husbandry gains importance. Among the domestic animals, diversity is observable in the preferences for either cattle, pig, or small livestock. Local preferences as well as environmental traits seem to influence the different proportions of cattle, pig, small livestock, and horse.

Development in the Trypillian stage CI is twofold. In general, a further increasing importance of animal husbandry is observed, while hunted game becomes less relevant. Cattle become established as the favourite domestic animal species. However, the Middle Dnipro region shows a divergent development. Here, the ratio of wild versus domestic species varies extremely from site to site. Nevertheless, on average, the Trypillia CI populations in the Middle Dnipro region also primarily depended on animal husbandry for meat consumption. However, in contrast to the general development, cattle seem to have been less important here, while pig or small livestock were preferred.

In the latest Trypillia C phase, sub-phase CII, husbandry is the main strategy of animal exploitation. Three regions are separated according to a divergent relevance of cattle. In the region of the Usatove-group in the northwest of the Black Sea, small livestock prevails, followed in relevance by cattle and horse. Pigs were hardly indicated. In contrast, in the Volyn region and in the Middle Dnipro region, the preference is for cattle. The only exception being the site Syrets in the Middle Dnipro region, where small livestock (sheep and goat) were the dominant species in the archaeozoological record.

From a diachronic perspective, the Trypillia animal exploitation shows a decreasing importance of hunting game. The animal husbandry strategy is characterized in general by a high degree of diversity. The main domestic animals are cattle, pig, and small livestock, supplemented by horse. The preferences among these species differ from region to region. They are influenced by the environmental conditions as well as by cultural traditions.

PLANT USE

Archaeobotanical studies on the plant economy of the Trypillian culture have been carried out since the 1930s. The compilation by Pashkevych & Videiko (2006) gives an overview of the main components of Trypillian plant use. Plant imprints in clay and ceramics were the focus of analyses, due to the high number of clay fragments regularly discovered as a main component of house remains and numerous ceramic fragments with organic tempering. Analysis of the imprints has, in general, provided the following plant identifications: the hulled wheats emmer (*Triticum turgidum* subsp. *dicoccon*) and einkorn (*Triticum monococcum*); free threshing barley (*Hordeum vulgare* var. *coeleste* synonym *Hordeum vulgare* var. *nudum*), the pulses pea (*Pisum sativum*), bitter vetch (*Vicia ervilia*), grass pea (*Lathyrus sativus*), and lentil (*Lens culinaris*); and hemp (*Cannabis* sp.). Imprints of naked wheat (*Triticum aestivum* s.l.) and spelt (*Triticum spelta*) are sparse, those of oat (*Avena* sp.) questionable, and imprints of broomcorn millet (*Panicum miliaceum*) relate to the late Trypillian phase C. From the lack of imprints of corn stalks in clay, Yanushevich (1975) infers that cereals were harvested by cutting the culm just below the ear—but this can also be explained by the details of crop processing, such as the separation of culms from chaff and grains at the threshing floor and the presence of only chaff, grains, and weeds at consumption sites. The gathering of wild fruits from the native woodland flora is proven by imprints of fruits, seeds, and stones of apple and pear (*Malus* sp. and *Pyrus* sp.); the stone fruits cherry and sloe (*Prunus avium*, *P. spinosa*); cornelian cherry (*Cornus mas*), hawthorn (*Crataegus* sp.), arrowwood (*Viburnum lantana*), dwarf elder (*Sambucus ebulus*), black nightshade (*Solanum nigrum*), hazel (*Corylus avellana*), and acorns (*Quercus* sp.). The genus *Vitis* is proven by imprints of large-sized grape seeds at the Moldovian Trypillia A/B-site Ruseștii Noi and the Moldovian Trypillia C-site Varvarivka 8. Wild grape (*Vitis sylvestris*) is native to the Ukraine and is considered to have been used in the past. The introduction of fruit plants with wild origins in Central and Eastern Asia and Transcaucasia is shown by imprints of remains from apricot, damson, and cherry plum (*Prunus armeniaca*, *P. insititia*, and *P. cerasifera*; Körber-Grohne, 1996: 181 and 211; Pashkevych & Videiko, 2006: 41; Yanushevich, 1975, 1978, 1980; Zohary et al., 2012; Gluza, 2013).

Quantification and estimates of the relevance of the different crops and gathered plants for the economy, solely based on the interpretation of plant imprints, are difficult. Moreover, plant imprints in pottery may well provide only a selection of the taxa exploited (McClatchie & Fuller, 2014). However, it remains an important source of information about plant exploitation for the investigated region and period, since evidence for charred plant remains is extremely rare. Most of the charred plant assemblages from Trypillian sites are chance finds from different archaeological contexts, including the content of at least five ceramic vessels. Systematic sampling for archaeobotanical analyses has recently started to be applied at the Trypillian sites Bernashivka, Ozheve, and Nebelivka (Pashkevich, 2014). The sites with charred plant assemblages (Table 1/Figure 1) are assigned to the three phases (A–C) of the Trypillian Culture (Pashkevych & Videiko, 2006: pp. 45). From phase A, there is a mass find of three-hundred charred seeds of bitter vetch discovered at the Moldovian site Karbuna (Yanushevich, 1980). At the Ukrainian Trypillia A2 site Bernashivka, a single soil sample from pit 2 contained an even mixture of einkorn and emmer grains with some free-threshing barley and spelt, plus a stone of cornelian cherry (Pashkevich, 2011). Numerous charred finds of remains from stone fruits (*Prunus* sp.), including finds of apricot at the Moldovian site Ruseștii Noi, provide insight into the use of fruits.

For phase B, the Trypillia A/AB site Shkarivka shows some evidence of hulled barley and emmer grains with traces from a crop parasite; the weevil (most possible from *Sitophilus granarius*). At the Trypillia B1 site Ozheve, flotation of soil samples brought evidence for hulled wheats, free-threshing and hulled barley, and lots of fragmented cereal grains (Pashkevich, 2014). A special find from the Ozheve site is a ceramic vessel that contained a concentration of gromwell (*Lithospermum* sp.; pers. comm. Dmytro Chernovol, Kiev, and Helmut Kroll, Kiel). Archaeobotanical comparison allows for interpretation of the shiny white seeds as being a hoard of beads that possibly were used for the decoration of wooden vessels or on textile (Jiang et al., 2007). About 3 l of charred emmer grains, mixed with some einkorn and free-threshing barley, and including some unspecified weed seeds, was found at the northern Moldovian Trypillia B site Shcherbaky (synonymous with Stari Kukoneshty; Kuzminova, 1991). In addition, a ceramic vessel from Shcherbaky contained grains of the foxtail

198 *Trypillia–Mega-Sites and European Prehistory*

Table 1. *(Belongs to Figure 1) Compilation of charred and mineralized botanical remains from Trypillian sites. n=single finds, nnn=numerous finds*

Phases according to Pashkevych/Videiko 2006, 45ff.	Phase A				Phase B					Phase C				
Country	Moldavia	Ukraine	Moldavia	Ukraine	Ukraine	Ukraine	Moldavia	Romania	Ukraine	Ukraine	Ukraine	Ukraine	Moldavia	Ukraine
Archaeological period	Trip A	Trip A2	Trip A/B	Trip A/AB	Trip B1	Trip B2	Trip B2	Cucuteni A	Trip C1	Trip C1	Trip C1	Trip C2	Trip C	Trip C
Sample type	Mass find	Soil sample, pit 2	No information	No information	Soil sample and vessel filling	Soil samples	? and vessel filling	No information	Vessel filling	Soil samples	Soil samples	Vessel filling	ritual place	Vessel filling
	Karbuna, Yanushevich (1980)	Bernashivka, Pashkevich (2011)	Rusești Noi, Kuzminova (1991)	Shkarivka, Pashkevych & Videiko (2006, 49)	Ozheve, Pashkevych (2014)/pers. communication with Dimitri Chernovol/Helmut Kroll, Kiel	Nebelivka, Pashkevich (2014)	Shcherbaky, Pashkevych & Videiko (2006, 49/50=Stari Kukoneshty, Kuzminova (1991)	Velen Piatra Neamt, Pashkevych & Videiko (2006, 47)	Maidanetske, Pashkevych & Videiko (2006, 51)	Maidanetske 2013, Kirleis et al. in prep.	Taljanky, Kruts et al. (2008, 2009)	Kosenivka, Pashkevych & Videiko (2006, 51/52)	Brinzeni IV, Kuzminova (1991)	Chechelnyk, Pashkevych & Videiko (2006)
Cereal grains		209		26	n	72	nnn		267	47		218	275	>500
Triticum dicoccum		90		4		33	nnn		264	9		139	15	>500
Triticum monococcum		81				17	n			5		77		n
Triticum cf. spelta		2				6							7	
Triticum, hulled					n									
Triticum aestivo-compactum													3	
Triticum aestivum s.l.						1						1		n
Hordeum vulgare var. vulgare				22	n	4			3	2			1	
Hordeum vulgare var. nudum		36			n	11	n						249	
Hordeum vulgare										6				
Cerealia indet.										23				
Setaria glauca					nnn									
Panicum miliaceum							nnn			2		1		
Threshing remains									10	49				
Triticum dicoccum, glume bases									8	37				
Triticum monococcum, glume bases									2	7				
Triticum, glume bases											n			
Hordeum vulgare, rhachis fragments										5				
Pulses	300					8		3000	777	30			1	
Pisum sativum						4		3000	777	29			1	
Lens culinaris						1				1				
Vicia ervilia	300					3								

Taxon	300	210	nnn	26	nnn	80	nnn	3000	1054	nnn	218	276	nnn
Leguminosae sativae indet.									5				
Fruit remains		**1**	**nnn**						**4**	**nnn**			
Prunus armeniaca			n										
Prunus sp.			nnn										
Cornus mas		1											
Corylus avellana									4				n
Lithospermum (dry preservation)			nnn										
Herbs							**22**		**6084**				
Chenopodium album									2811				
Chenopodium sp.									1148				
Chenopodiaceae p.p.									2088				
Galium aparine									17				
Bromus secalinus-Typ									2				
Bromus sp.									3				
Echinochloa crus-galli									4				
Setaria viridis									3				
Anagallis sp.									1				
Hyoscyamus niger									1				
Solanum (nigrum)									1				n
Polygonum aviculare									1				
Polygonum sp.									1				
Lamiaceae									1				
Poaceae p.p.									1				
Rosaceae									1				
cf. Stipa (curled awn fragments)									175				
weeds, p.p.							22						
Indeterminate									28				n
sum	**300**	**210**	**nnn**	**26**	**nnn**	**80**	**nnn**	**3000**	**1054**	**nnn**	**218**	**276**	**nnn**

species *Setaria glauca* (Pashkevych & Videiko, 2006: 49–50). More detailed information is available for the Trypillia BII site Nebelivka, close to Maidanetske (Pashkevich, 2014). Systematic sampling revealed the following species, listed here in their order of frequency: emmer, einkorn, free-threshing barley, spelt, hulled barley, free-threshing bread wheat/club wheat, three seeds of bitter vetch, four peas, and one lentil. Concerning their importance, it must be noted that pulses are systematically underrepresented in the archaeobotanical record for the Trypillia B sites. However, the contemporaneous Romanian Cucuteni A site Velen Piatra Neamt provided about 3000 charred peas (Pashkevych & Videiko, 2006: 47).

Dating to phase C, a ceramic vessel from Maidanetske was filled with 40 ml of charred remains; a mixture of emmer grains and peas, with minor additions of hulled barley grains and a few einkorn and emmer threshing remains. The peas show traces from weevils (most probably *Sitophilus granaria*) (Pashkevych & Videiko, 2006: 51). The charred assemblage from a ritual place at the Moldovian site Brinzeni IV consists of free-threshing barley grains mixed with some emmer, spelt, free-threshing wheat (*Triticum aestivo-compactum*), and one pea (Kuzminova, 1991). The fill of a ceramic vessel from the Ukrainian site Kosenivka consisted of a mixture of emmer and einkorn grains. Further, there is evidence for broomcorn millet. Recently, a team from Basel University analysed soil samples and fills of ceramic vessels from Taljanky (Kruts et al., 2008: 53 ff.; Kruts et al., 2009: 50 ff.). Charred botanical macro-remains were sparse. Charcoal from ash (*Fraxinus* sp.) and oak (*Quercus* sp.) was accompanied by fragments of hazelnut shells, some threshing remains of hulled wheat and charred seeds of nightshade (*Solanum* sp.). Pollen analyses on the fills of eight pots resulted in evidence for steppe environment, riverine forest, and an indication of wheat and buckwheat (*Fagpopyrum esculentum*) as crop plants. However, there is no evidence from botanical macro remains for the growing of buckwheat available for the Trypillian culture. Another ceramic vessel with charred material originates from the site Chechelnyk. It contained more than 500 emmer grains with some admixture of einkorn, free-threshing wheat, and barley grains. To sum up, Trypillian arable farming was based, in general, on the cultivation of the hulled wheats emmer and einkorn and free-threshing barley. Bitter vetch accompanies the cereals from the Trypillia A period onwards and was possibly replaced by pea in the later phases. In particular for the Moldovian sites of the late stage of Trypillia (mid to late 3rd millennium BCE), broomcorn millet is considered as a domestic plant because of evidence for an increasing number of clay imprints of this species (Kuzminova, 1991). Crop growing was supplemented by gathering of fruits in the nearby woodlands and possibly the cultivation of fruit trees in the vicinity of at least some of the settlements, e.g. at the Moldovian site Ruseștii Noi.

NEW ARCHAEOBOTANICAL DATA, NEW ARCHAEOBOTANICAL PROXY

New data for the Trypillia C1 site Maidanetske are available since systematic sampling for archaeobotanical investigations was applied at the joint excavation of the Academy of Sciences in Kyiv and Kiel University in 2013 (Müller et al., in print). A total of 137 macro-remain samples corresponding to 1370 l of sediment from three different archaeological contexts (inner house, area outside of the house, pit) were floated through meshes with a width of 300 μm. Therefore, next to crop fruits, threshing remains and small weed seeds and fruits were also part of the analysed subfossil assemblages. In addition, a targeted test study on the phytolith assemblage was carried out. This preliminary analysis focused on the anthropogenic contexts that were expected to yield phytoliths and provide information about plant exploitation, i.e. an ash layer from the pit and two of the many daub fragments that show plant impressions (Müller et al., in print).

Altogether, about 6400 charred and mineralized plant remains were found at the Maidanetske site (Table 1). Among these were six crop species. There is evidence for four cereals, listed here in order of importance based on the number of charred grains: emmer, einkorn, barley, and broomcorn millet. The finds of threshing remains follow the same species ordering in sheer numbers; however, as numbers of finds in both categories are low, this does not necessarily relate to the relevance of the species as food plants. For the hulled wheat species emmer and einkorn, there is evidence for glume bases, while only rachis fragments were identified from barley, which can be explained by the fact that this is a free-threshing species. However, no threshing remains from millet were present. It is not yet clear whether the millets were already cultivated in this period or if they represent weed species. Next to the cereals, pea and lentil present two pulses species that supplemented the cereal spectrum at Maidanetske. In general, the Maidanetske finds are in accordance with the expected crop spectrum for the Trypillian culture (Kruts et al., 2001; Pashkevych & Videiko, 2006; Kruts et al., 2008; Pashkevich, 2014), although–in contrast to other sites–there is no hint of bitter vetch. The only gathered plants in the archaeological plant assemblage from Maidanetske are hazelnut and possibly black henbane (*Hyoscyamus niger*). Next to the domestic plants, five weed species were identified which indicate nutrient-rich soils: cleavers (*Galium aparine*), caryopses of brome (*Bromus secalinus*-type), common knotweed (*Polygonum aviculare*), black nightshade (*Solanum nigrum*), and most numerous, fat hen (*Chenopodium album*). The height of these weed species further suggests that the cereals at Maidanetske were harvested at ear-level. There is additional weed evidence for the two Panicoideae species green foxtail (*Setaria viridis*) and cockspur (*Echinochloa crus-galli*).

For the first time, phytolith analyses have been applied to sediment samples from a Trypillian site at Maidanetske (Figure 3). Phytoliths are microfossils formed in plant tissue consisting of silica that persists after the decay of the plant. This additional archaeobotanical proxy widens the view on past subsistence strategies. It is particularly valuable where proxies depend on high soil humidity for proper preservation fail, e.g. pollen. Grasses (including cereals) usually contain a high amount of phytoliths. This combined with the fact that different phytolith morphotypes occur in specific parts of the plant (inflorescence, leaves/culms) makes them an excellent tool to trace activities related to crop processing, the use of by-products, and food preparation.

The preliminary study of phytoliths at Maidanetske shows the high suitability for this kind of analysis for application to Trypillian contexts. The microfossils from a daub layer in the house and an ash layer of a pit fill present a good state of preservation, which allows for counting at least 400 phytoliths from identifiable morphotypes per sample. As it is usually the case, dicotyledons are highly under-represented, while phytoliths from monocotyledons dominate the assemblages. Within the monocotyledons, several types of grass short cell phytoliths (GSCP) have been identified that are diagnostic of different subfamilies of the grass family (Poaceae). The subfamily of the Pooideae that comprises the C3 grasses, represented by rondel and trapeziform GSCPs (2a and b), is widely attested in all samples. Thus, C3 grasses, which include the cereals of the 'Neolithic package', were common components of the plants used on-site and possibly of the local vegetation. Indeed, dendritic long cells typical of wheat and barley chaff have been attested, which is also confirmed by the macrobotanical evidence. In addition, bilobates (Figure 2c) and polylobates, which are indicative for C4 Panicoideae grasses like the millets, are present in the archaeological samples in very small quantities. They are slightly more abundant in the topsoil. This presence of Panicoideae corresponds with the macrobotanical record, which contains both wild and domestic millets (Table 1). Finally, the ash layer in the pit contained saddles, which are grass short cells that are usually related to the C4 Chloridoideae grass subfamily.

The conjoined aggregate of cells forming so-called silica skeletons (Figure 4) are particularly suitable for obtaining information about the presence and use of plant parts. The silica skeletons seem to be safely related to plant use by people because they are concentrated in the archaeological contexts and absent in the topsoil at Maidanetske. Dendritic long cells (Figure 2d) are usually attributed to domestic C3 grass inflorescences, i.e. to chaff of *Hordeum* sp. or *Triticum* sp. (cf. e.g. Albert *et al.*, 2008; Ball *et al.*, 2009), while echinate long cells may also be interpreted as grass inflorescences, but could, however, also represent wild grasses that might be related to weeds. The presence of cereal chaff in the daub indicates the intentional use of crop-processing remains as temper, as is supported by the observation of plant impressions in many more daub fragments. The presence of dendritic and echinate long cells from grass inflorescences in the pit might derive from the waste after on-site crop processing activities, e.g. dehusking. Apart from silica

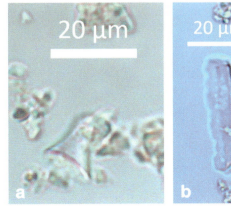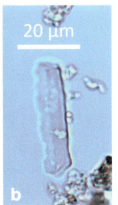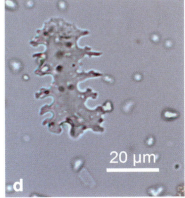

Figure 2. The main phytolith morphotypes in the assemblages from Maidanetske 2013 give indications of Pooideae ((a) rondel, (b) trapeziform), Panicoideae ((c) bilobate), and pooid cereal chaff ((d) dendritic long cell) (photos M. Dal Corso, Kiel).

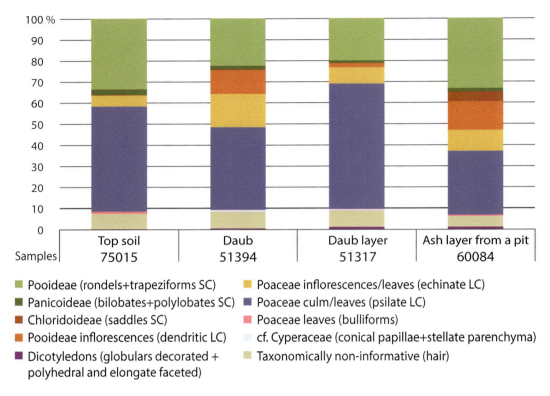

Figure 3. The phytolith single cells assemblage from the 2013 excavation campaign in Maidanetske according to archaeological context. SC = short cells, LC = long cells.

skeletons providing information about the use of grass inflorescences, there is also evidence of silica skeletons characterized by psilate long cells, pointing to the presence of culms and leaves (Figure 4). Such cells are also ubiquitously found in the assemblage of single phytolith cells (Figure 3). These skeletons most

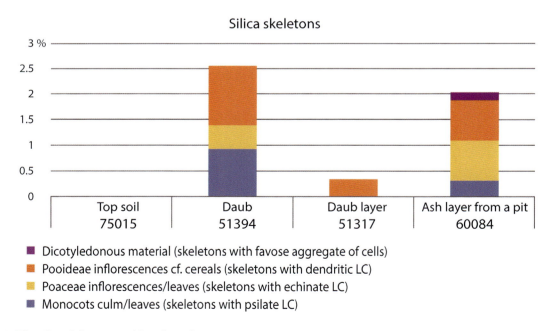

Figure 4. The silica skeleton assemblage from the 2013 excavation campaign in Maidanetske according to archaeological context in % on the sum of phytoliths and skeletons (calc. after Jenkins et al. 2011). LC = long cells.

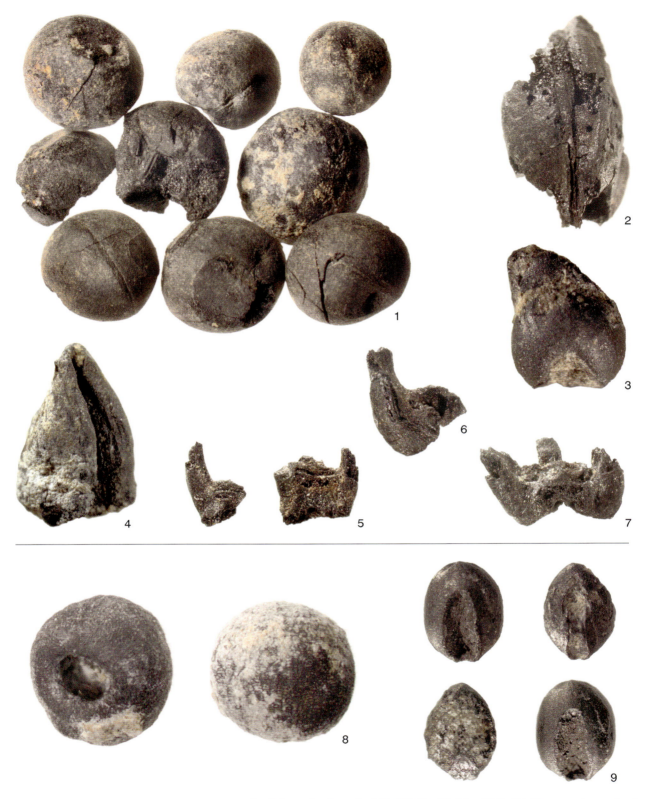

Plate Charred macro-remains from Maidanetske (Photos by Sara Jagiolla/Wiebke Kirleis, Kiel) (1) Pisum sativum *(pea), sample 51647, house context.* (2) Hordeum vulgare *(barley), sample 600191, refuse pit.* (3) Panicum miliaceum *(broomcorn millet), sample 51182, house context.* (4) Triticum monococcum *(einkorn), sample 60079, refuse pit.* (5) Triticum monococcum *(einkorn), glume bases, sample 60165, refuse pit.* (6) Triticum monococcum/dicoccon *(einkorn/emmer), glume base, sample 60165, refuse pit.* (7) Triticum dicoccon *(emmer), glume bases, sample 60165, refuse pit.* (8) Galium aparine *(cleavers), sample 60145, refuse pit.* (9) Setaria viridis *(green foxtail), sample 51182, house context. Scale: (1) 10:1; (2)–(9) 20:1.*

probably represent grass culms, because typical phytoliths from grass leaves such as bulliform cells are very rare and stomata are completely absent.

The preliminary phytolith studies at the Chalcolithic Maidanetske mega-site allow the reconstruction of activities related to crop processing and the use of cereal by-products that are not represented by the macro-remains assemblage (e.g. grass culms/leaves). Both give further information about social and technological aspects (cf. Harvey & Fuller, 2005; Fuller et al., 2014). Dehusking of spelt wheat was carried out within the settlement and was part of daily food preparation. In the chain of reasoning, the hulled wheat species were most probably stored in the spikelets. The waste of dehusking was partly deposited in the pit next to the house. Another proportion of the by-products was used as temper for daub production. At the moment, it remains an open question whether, and to what extent, crop by-products were also used as animal fodder.

In Maidanetske, the new results from archaeobotany mainly contribute to explaining the mode of the subsistence economy of a single house, the resource management of building activities, and waste management. The combination of macro-remains and phytoliths allows the reconstruction of the crop assemblage of Maidanetske. It can be concluded that the plant-based part of the diet was based on pea and the hulled wheat species emmer and einkorn, with the addition of barley. Broomcorn millet is present in the latest stages of the settlement. The daily diet was supplemented by gathered hazelnuts. An addition to the current state of the art is the documentation of the weed spectrum. The ecological indications from weeds, in agreement with the results from pedology (Kirleis & Dreibrodt, 2016; Müller et al., in print), hint to crop growing on rich loamy soils that were highly suitable for arable farming. Further, the weeds give insight into Trypillian agrarian technics, since the growing height of the proven species indicates cereal harvesting at ear-level. The phytoliths provide additional detailed insight into dehusking and by-product management, i.e. its deposition as waste in a pit and its use as daub temper.

Conclusions on Trypillian Subsistence Economy

In general, the Trypillian subsistence strategy is characterized by a high degree of diversity, determined by the environment, way of life, and economic traditions of the population of each particular region (Zbenovich, 1996a). As far as the use of the natural biotic resources is concerned, only slight changes occur in the subsistence strategy over time. This is surprising, as the settlement dimensions differ greatly from sites with up to 15 dwellings in the early Trypillian phase A towards the late Trypillian phase C1 mega-sites with 15,000 inhabitants. Throughout all three Trypillian phases, the early farmers' animal husbandry of mainly cattle, pig, and small livestock was supplemented by hunting of game. The importance of animal husbandry increases in the Trypillian phase C and the use of wild animals declines. The plant economy is generally built upon a wide range of cereals (emmer, einkorn, free-threshing and hulled barley, bread wheat, spelt, broomcorn millet) and pulses (bitter vetch, pea, lentil), supplemented by gathered and possibly cultivated fruits. Diachronic developments concern bitter vetch and broomcorn millet. While the bitter vetch is prominent in the early Trypillian phase A, it may have been replaced by pea in phase C at the latest. For the broomcorn millet, it remains to be proven in which stage of the Trypillian phase C it was grown. The late occurrence of broomcorn millet may relate to the very latest Trypillian stages and coincide with the decline of the mega-sites.

References

Albert, R.M., Shahack-Gross, R., Cabanes, D., Gilboa, A., Lev-Yadun, S., Portillo, M., Sharon, I., Boaretto, E. & Weiner, S. 2008. Phytolith-rich Layers from the Late Bronze and Iron Ages at Tel Dor (Israel): Mode of Formation and Archaeological Significance. *Journal of Archaeological Science*, 35(1):57–75.

Ball, T.B., Ehlers, R. & Standing, M.D. 2009. Review of Typologic and Morphometric Analysis of Phytoliths Produced by Wheat and Barley. *Breeding Sciences*, 59:505–12.

Fuller, D.Q., Stevens, C. & McClatchie, M. 2014. Routine Activities, Tertiary Refuse, and Labor Organization: Social Inferences from Everyday Archaeobotany. In: M. Madella, C. Lancelotti & M. Savard, eds. *Ancient Plants and People: Contemporary Trends in Archaeobotany*. Tucson: University of Arizona Press, pp. 174–217.

Gluza, I. 2013. Plant Impressions on the Ceramics. In: S. Kadrow, ed. *Bilcze Zlote: Materials of the Tripolye Culture from the Werteba and the Ogród sites. TOM V*. Krakow: Biblioteka Muzeum Archeologicznego w Krakowie, pp. 87–99.

Harvey, E.L. & Fuller, D. Q. 2005. Investigating Crop Processing Using Phytoliths Analysis: The Example of Rice and Millets. *Journal of Archaeological Sciences*, 32(5):739–52.

Jenkins, E., Baker, A. & Elliott, S. 2011. Past plant use in Jordan as revealed by archaeological and ethnoarchaeological phytolith signatures. In: E. Black & S. Mithen, eds. *Water, life and civilisation: climate, environment and society in the Jordan Valley*. Cambridge UP, UK, Cambridge, pp. 381–400.

Jiang, H.-E., Li, X., Liu, C.-J., Wang, Y.-F. & Li, C.-S. 2007. Fruits of Lithospermum Officinale L. (Boraginaceae) Used as an Early Plant Decoration (2500 years BP) in Xinjiang, China. *Journal of Archaeological Sciences*, 34(2):167–70.

Kirleis, W. & Dreibrodt, S. 2016. The Natural Background: Forest, Forest Steppe, or Steppe Environment. In: J. Müller, K. Rassmann & M. Videiko, eds. *Trypillia Mega-Sites and European Prehistory: 4100–3400 BCE*. London and New York: Routledge, pp. 171–180.

Körber-Grohne, U. 1996. *Pflaumen, Kirschpflaumen, Schlehen. Heutige Pflanzen und ihre Geschichte seit der Frühzeit*. Stuttgart: Theiss.

Kruts, V. A., Korvin-Piotrovskiy, A. G. & Ryzhov, S. N. 2001. *Talianki – Giant-Settlement of the Tripolian Culture. Investigations in 2001*. Kiev: Institute of Archaeology of the NASU.

Kruts, V.A., Korvin-Piotrovskiy, A.G., Menotti, F., Ryzhov, S.N., Chernovol, D.K. & Chabanyuk, V.V. 2008. *The Trypillia Culture Giant Settlement of Talianki. Investigations in 2008*. Kiev: Institute of Archaeology of the National Academy of Sciences of Ukraine.

Kruts, V.A., Korvin-Piotrovskiy, A.G., Menotti, F., Ryzhov, S.N., Tolochko, D.V. & Chabanyuk, V.V. 2009. *The Trypillia Culture Giant Settlement of Talianki. Investigations 2009*. Kiev: Institute of Archaeology of the National Academy of Sciences of Ukraine.

Kuzminova, N. N. 1991. Crops and Weeds in the Tripolye Culture Sites in Moldavia. In: E. Hajnalová, ed. *Palaeoethnobotany and Archaeology. International Workgroup for Palaeoethnobotany, 8th symposium, Nitra-Nové Vozokany 1989. Acta Interdisciplinaria Archaeologica Tomus VII*. Nitra: Archaeological Institute of the Slovak Academy of Sciences, pp. 199–201.

McClatchie, M. & Fuller, D. 2013. Leaving a Lasting Impression: Arable Economies and Cereal Impressions in Africa and Europe. In: C.J. Stevens, S. Nixon, M. A. Murray & D.Q. Fuller (Eds.), *Archaeology of African Plant Use*. Walnut Creek: Left Coast Press, pp. 259–266.

Müller, J., Hofmann, R., Brandtstätter, L., Ohlrau, R. & Videiko, M. 2016. Chronology and Demography: How Many People Lived in a Mega-Site? In: J. Müller, K. Rassmann & M. Videiko, eds. *Trypillia Mega-Sites and European Prehistory: 4100–3400 BCE*. London and New York: Routledge, pp. 133–169.

Müller, J., Hofmann, R., Kirleis, W., Ohlrau, R., Brandtstätter, L., Dal Corso, M., Out, V., Rassmann, K. & Videiko, M., in print. *Maidanetske 2013. New excavations at a Trypillia megasite. Studien zur Archäologie in Ostmitteleuropa*. Bonn: Habelt.

Ohlrau, R., Dal Corso, M., Kirleis, W. & Müller, J. 2016. Living on the Edge? Carrying Capacities of Trypillian Settlements in the Buh-Dnipro Interfluve. In: J. Müller, K. Rassmann & M. Videiko, eds. *Trypillia Mega-Sites and European Prehistory: 4100–3400 BCE*. London and New York: Routledge, pp. 207–220.

Pashkevich, G. 2011. Value Bernashivka-1 for Palaeoethnobotanical Characteristics of Early Tripolje. In: A. G. Korvin-Piotrovskiy, ed. *Earliest farmers of South-Eastern Europe. Abstracts of International Scientific Conference*. Kiev-Taljanky: Institute of Archaeology of the NASU, pp. 67–68.

Pashkevich, G. 2014. Data of the Trypillian Agriculture: New Palaeobotanical Evidence. In: G. Dumitroaia, C. Preoteasa & C.-D. Nicola, eds. *Cucuteni Culture within the European Neo-Eneolithic Context. International Colloquium, Cucuteni 130, Abstracts*. Piatra-Neamt, 15–17 octombrie 2014. Piatra-Neamţ: 'Constantin Matasă', pp. 24–27.

Pashkevych, G. O. & Videiko, M. Yu. 2006. *Rilnytsvo plemen trypilskoi kultury*. Kyiv: Institute of Archaeology of the NASU. Пашкевич, Г.О. і Відейко, М.Ю. 2006. *Рільництво племен трипільської культури*. Київ: Інститут археології НАНУ.

Yanushevich, Z. V. 1975. Fossil Remains of Cultivated Plants in the South-West of the Soviet Union. *Folia Quaternaria*, 46:23–30.

Yanushevich, Z. V. 1978. Prehistoric Food Plants in the south-west of the Soviet-Union. Berichte der Deutschen Botanischen Gesellschaft, 91(1), Special Issue: In: K.-E. Behre, H. Lorenzen & U. Willerding, eds. *Beiträge zur Paläo-Ethnobotanik von Europa*. Stuttgart: G. Fischer, pp. 59–66.

Yanushevich, Z. V. 1980. *Zemledelie v rannem Tripolje (po dannym palaeobotaniki)*. In: I. I. Artemenko, ed. *Pervobytnaya archeologiya:– poiski i nakhodki*, Kiev: Naukova Dumka, pp. 225–34. Янушевич, З.В. 1980. Земледелие в раннем Триполье (по данным палеобо таники). В сб.: И.И. Артеменко, ред. *Первобытная археология: поиски и находки*. Киев: Наукова думка, с. 225–34.

Zbenovich, V. G. 1996a. The Tripolye Culture: Centenary of Research. *Journal of World Prehistory*, 10(2): 199–241.

Zbenovich, V. G. 1996b. *Siedlungen der frühen Tripolje-Kultur zwischen Dnestr und Südlichem Bug. Archäologie in Eurasien 1*, Espelkamp: Marie Leidorf.

Zohary, D., Hopf, M. & Weiss, E. 2012. *Domestication of Plants in the Old World*, 4 ed., Oxford University Press, Oxford.

CHAPTER 12

Living on the Edge? Carrying Capacities of Trypillian Settlements in the Buh-Dnipro Interfluve

René Ohlrau, Marta Dal Corso, Wiebke Kirleis and Johannes Müller

One of the striking questions concerning the Trypillian mega-sites is about sustainability. How could these settlements emerge from an economic point of view? What led to their decline? Was persistence even possible? For now, the settlement pattern seems to show a fast development of partially contemporary sites with a short runtime leading to possible migrations between them (Diachenko & Menotti, 2012; Diachenko & Zubrow, 2015). Explanations for this pattern are diverse. Besides emerging out of internal or external conflict (Kruts, 1989; Zbenovich, 1990; Videiko, 1998), the short duration of settlements is explained by depletion of resources. This hypothesis of environmental stress includes soil degradation, deforestation, and epidemics (Kruts, 2008a: 44). To address this scenario, a detailed picture of the palaeo-environment in the direct vicinity of the mega-sites has yet to be drawn, but advances in this field of research have already been illustrated (see Kirleis & Dreibrodt, 2016).

The reconstruction of Trypillian subsistence economy has been of concern since the influential work of Bibikov (1965), Gaydarska (2003), Harper (2012), Kruts (1989), (1993), Kruts *et al.* (2001), Nikolova & Pashkevich (2003), Pashkevich & Videiko (2006), and Preoteasa (2015). Despite diverse empirical variables and analogies, drawing conclusions about a complex economic and ecological system proves to be very challenging. A simple model is presented here, based on new empirical data and robust assumptions. A first aim of this model is to depict and quantify the catchment areas of Trypillian sites in the Buh-Dnipro interfluve, according to their size. A second aim consists in finding crucial limiting factors for the development of mega-sites that emerged after (1) the contemplation of demanded resources at each individual site, and (2) the comparison of landscape use in different chronological phases. Before discussion of the preliminary outcome of such a model, in the following paragraphs the variables adopted are illustrated according to the literature and new archaeological data. The latter come from the recent multi-disciplinary investigations carried out at the mega-sites of Maidanetske and Taljanky, which therefore constitute the core of the present model.

Population Size

For modelling carrying capacity, first of all demographic data are needed, which derive here from the calculation of the total number of contemporary households per settlement. By combining data from recent high-resolution surveys and existing geophysical plans of Maidanetske and Taljanky by Dudkin (1978), the total number of buildings per site has been estimated (Ohlrau, 2015; Rassmann *et al.*, 2014). Taljanky consisted of 2200 buildings and Maidanetske had about 3000 structures, which is roughly twice the amount previously estimated (Dudkin, 1978). At both sites, the new geomagnetic survey also revealed unburnt or eroded buildings, which are included in the aforementioned estimation. A recent programme of radiocarbon dating concerning burnt houses at Maidanetske suggests that they were contemporary (Müller *et al.*, 2016). Nevertheless, considering that the fine-tuning of internal phasing is still in progress, for now not all of the detected archaeological features are expected to be contemporary. For instance, a distinction between burnt and unburnt buildings seems to occur. On the basis of this distinction, the percentage of burnt to unburnt buildings in Maidanetske (seventy-eight per cent) and Taljanky (eighty-three per cent) was used to detect contemporaneity. Interestingly, this fits former calculations of contemporary structures based on a typological chronology (Videiko, 1996). For further calculations, we can assume 2300 contemporary buildings (based on 3000 known buildings) and 1830 (based on 2200) at Maidanetske and at Taljanky, respectively.

Different methods for population estimation were tested on this high quality dataset. Estimates of average people per household, resulting in 4.5–7 people (Kolb, 1985); built space, with a demand of 7 m² per person (Porčic, 2012); as well as roofed living space (LeBlanc, 1971), derived as one-third of the floor area in Trypillian houses, based on Chernovol's house typology (Chernovol, 2012), suggests a population of, on average, over 11,100 people per settlement at each of these two mega-sites (Table 1). For other settlements of the study area, such data were obtained from calibrated settlement size and an approximated number of buildings per hectare (Diachenko & Menotti, 2012). Additionally, in such cases contemporary structures are calculated as seventy-eight per cent of the total structures. Following the aforementioned parameters, an average of five people per building is used to transfer the population estimation to the whole area.

Woodland Cover According to Timber Demand

A reconstruction of the landscape is crucial for economic modelling and for defining the carrying capacities of Trypillian sites, especially in relation to the availability of wood for construction. It is assumed that Trypillian settlers arrived in a natural forest steppe environment; a transitional zone with mixed grasslands and patches of temperate broadleaf forest. This scenario is supported by current palaeoecological research at Maidanetske that provides a more detailed view (Müller et al., in print; Kirleis & Dreibrodt, 2016). Despite bad preservation, on-site pollen archives prove the presence of deciduous oak, lime, and hazel. Unfortunately, high resolution and long-term archives are yet to be found, and quantifications of woodland cover are still pending. Preliminary on-site charcoal analyses also point to a mixed oak-dominated forest with ash, deciduous oak, and elm, and to the use of riparian trees, such as willow, from the riverine environment. The pedological analyses hint at local forest cover before the first settlement activities at Maidanetske, due to the presence of a Cambisol that forms in forested areas. Instead, it seems that the development of highly fertile Chernozem soils, typical of steppe environment, coincided with the foundation of the site. These results have some interesting implications for further modelling.

In order to understand the amount of timber needed for the construction of a single house, former studies assumed a surface equal to fifty per cent of the settlement perimeter to be covered by woodland (Bondar, 1981: 116; Kruts et al., 2001: 77), while 300 m³ of timber are considered available per hectare (Kruts et al., 2001: 77). Based on archaeological experiments, 20 m³ of timber was necessary to construct a typical Trypillian house and to produce wooden imprints on daub similar to those found in the archaeological record (Korvin-Piotrovskiy et al., 2012: 219). Thus, 1 ha of woodland could provide timber for fifteen houses. Similar data have also been adopted for the contemporaneous Cucuteni sites in Moldova, where timber demand for a house is considered even lower (8–17 m³, according to the size of the house; Preoteasa, 2015: 119).

The area of woodland needed to build a settlement does not, in most cases, exceed the size of the settlements and corresponds on average to sixty-seven per cent of the settlement area (Table 5). Maidanetske again offers an example for maximal demand: here, according to the new number of houses, the area of woodland needed equals that of the final extension of the site.

Based on the pollen and charcoal data available until now, these estimations of woodland loss due to construction activity are expected to refer mainly to the mixed broadleaf forest. This forest offers qualitatively good wood for dwelling constructions, and consequently human selection, generally observed at prehistoric sites, can be expected. This woodland type has a canopy regeneration rate of c. thirty years, based on studies of modern analogues in Europe (Walker et al., 2000; Harmer et al., 2001). For this reason, in this model the previously used land surface, inclusive of that derived after woodland clearance, is taken into account. Although information on wood selection for specific structures is still missing, the use of the wood resources from the riparian zones, at the moment underestimated, should be considered in the future as well. According to the geomorphology of the region, the Buh-Dnipro interfluve is indeed an area where hygrophilous forest stands could have been largely available and appealing, even if not favoured in term of resources (Harper, 2012: 57).

Table 1. Estimated total and contemporary population sizes of Maidanetske and Taljanky

	Maidanetske		Taljanky	
	Total	Contemporary	Total	Contemporary
Minimum	8750	6600	6200	5100
Mean	14,750	11,150	13,800	11,450
Maximum	31,700	23,800	25,300	21,000

Table 2. *Calculation of crops demand, assuming them to cover the seventy-seven per cent of kilocalories in the diet (cp. Ebersbach 2002, 129).*

	Variable(s)	Source		Calculation
Emmer	Yield 1000 kg/ha/year	Gregg (1988, 58); Kruk & Milisauskas (1999, 294); Harper (2012, 38)		
	Correction (Wheat/Emmer) 65%	Habeck & Longin (2014)	1000×0.65	=650 kg/ha
	Processing—10%	Clark & Haswell (1967, 67)	650×0.9	=585 kg/ha
	Loss/Seed stock −25%	Harper (2012, 40)	585×0.75	=43,875 kg/ha
	Demand/yield		106.7/438.75	=0.24 ha/capita/year
Field pea	Yield 1400 kg/ha/year			
	Loss/Seed stock −25%	Harper (2012, 40)	1400×0.75	=1050 kg/ha/year
	Demand/yield		60.3/1050	=0.06 ha/capita/year

ARABLE LAND

Most studies on the carrying capacities of Trypillian sites are based on arable land, which is established using calculations often based on the assumption that the complete demand for kilocalories, protein, and nutrients was met by cereals (Bibikov, 1965; Kruts, 1989; Gaydarska, 2003). Since this is a rather unrealistic assumption for ancient diet, because it does not consider other sources of nutrients (e.g. meat, wild fruits), the crop yield per person was overestimated. In this study, further corrections to these models that consider meat consumption have been taken into account (Harper, 2012). To come to robust conclusions, a calculation of diet compositions and crop yields is needed to estimating the pro capita demand for arable land.

Regarding diet, for calibration of older models we can use the established amount of 210 kg of cereals to fit the kilocalorie demand per person per year (Clark & Haswell, 1967), as well as the thirteen per cent lower energy yield of legumes to cereals (Harper, 2012: 38), and reduce them according to diet composition. To do so, we have to consider ethnographic studies as well as empirical data from Trypillian sites, as illustrated by Kirleis & Dal Corso, 2016. The influential study by Ebersbach (2002) about Neolithic agropastoral economies shows that in traditional societies, crops are only part of the overall diet. In a sample of thirty societies, the mean percentage of crops, including cereals and legumes, lies around seventy-seven per cent with missing kilocalories mainly coming from meat resources (Ebersbach, 2002: 129).

Besides the assumed percentage of crops, we have empirical data on the ratio between cereals and legumes, which is roughly 2:1 for Trypillia C settlements according to Harper (2012). Following these calculations, we assume a calibrated demand of 106.7 kg/year emmer and 60.3 kg/year field pea per capita (Table 2) and at least 0.3 ha of arable land per capita (Table 3).

PASTURES

According to zooarchaeological records available until now, animal husbandry and especially cattle played a major role in the Trypillian subsistence economy. This is visible also in the prominent applications of bucrania on various vessels, sledge models, and zoomorphic figurines.

To calculate an estimation of cattle pro capita or household, there are different assumptions for agrarian Neolithic societies. The most advanced land-use models that include cattle were developed for the Linear Pottery Culture (*Linearbandkeramik*/LBK) in Central Europe; calculating one or two animals per capita based on ethnographic analogy (Ebersbach & Schade, 2005: 265). Archaeological evidence for Trypillian sites shows a slightly different picture; about one cow per household (Kruts *et al.*, 2001: 80). For the present model, the data from several excavated Trypillian households of stage CI are used (Table 4).

Table 3. *Comparison of estimations regarding demanded hectare of arable land per capita per year*

ha/capita/year	Source
0.3–0.6	Bibikov (1965)
0.30	Kruts (1989)
1.77	Kruts (1993)
1.05	Gaydarska (2003)
0.53–0.58	Nikolova & Pashkevich (2003)
0.6–1.5	Pashkevich & Videiko (2006)
0.28	Harper (2012)
0.30	This model

Table 4. *Herd composition per household used in this model, after Kruts et al. (2001, 85)*

Animals	Trypillia BII	Trypillia CI
Cattle	1	1
Small livestock	1	0.4
Pig	0.7	0.8
Horse	0.4	0.2

Besides the amount of livestock, the land needed to provide fodder for the animals has to be estimated. For this, we rely on the LBK model and take into account 10 ha per large livestock animal and 5 ha for small ones (Ebersbach & Schade, 2005). This high estimation is due to the uncertainty about herd management and fodder type during Trypillian times. According to the LBK model, multiple sources of fodder should be considered, including broadleaf fodder from woodland pasture and grazing from grasslands in forest openings. If woodland pasture was used, as suggested for LBK sites (Ebersbach & Schade, 2005), the fact that it presents a low edible biomass compared to modern pastures should be taken into account. However, in the forest steppe environment, the situation was probably inverse with respect to the close broadleaf forests of Neolithic central Europe, and openings with grasslands and shrubs, together with forest patches, should be considered as part of the natural environment surrounding Trypillian sites. According to the LBK model (Ebersbach & Schade, 2005), crop processing by-products such as straw and chaff (i.e. produced in the crop fields) could also be fed to animals, if and when these were kept close to the site. On the other hand, such cereal by-products in Trypillian sites were probably used for other purposes as well (e.g. as temper), and they would not have lasted for the whole year. Due to these reasons and to the fact that we do not know yet the extent of openness of the forest steppe environment, the demanded hectare per animal here is much higher than in present times. Despite the mixture of practices and vegetation types expected, the land devoted to fodder provision has, for simplicity, been labelled 'pasture' in the model.

Modelling Per Chronological Phases

By modelling the different variables of agro-pastoral land use and woodland consumption, it is possible to see whether one of these factors had a limiting effect on settlement development. An overview of the data obtained by applying such variables in the present model is given in Table 5. The distribution map of the sites quoted in Table 6 is provided in Figure 1.

To compare land use areas, the evaluated variables above were tested after the subdivision of the sites into three phases, from BI/BII to CI, following the relative chronology established by Ryzhov (1999), and after the estimated duration of fifty years for the peak of contemporary households (see Diachenko & Menotti, 2012: table 1). A new refinement of these chronological phases is presented in this volume (Müller et al., 2016) and this has been used here to follow the evolution of land use in the maps in Figures 2–4. The first Figure 2 shows the results of the model for sites of the Trypillian phase BII (Volodymyrivska Group V1 and Nebelivska group N1) that lasted from c. 4000 to 3900 cal BCE. The second map (Figure 3) presents the period of occupation at the transition between the Trypillian phases BII and CI (Nebelivska group N2 and Tomashivska group T2), dating between c. 3900 and 3750 cal BCE. The last Figure 4 shows the sites of the Trypillian phase CI (Tomashivska group T3 and T4) active c. 3750–3600 cal BCE. Each map represents a time period of occupation of c. 100–150 years. In addition, in each map the previous occupation is also shown under the label 'former land use' corresponding to the areas of influence (i.e. settlement, arable land, and woodland used) of settlements from the previous phase. In Figure 5, a diachronic perspective is given that allows visualization of all the aforementioned occupation phases.

Discussion

At this stage of research, topography is not yet integrated in this preliminary model. Nevertheless, it is clearly visible that arable land was not a limitation, even for maximal probable population estimations of the biggest sites. Indeed, chronological phasing shows that most of the site locations avoid intersections of land use with areas of former land use (Figure 5). This implies that newly founded settlements exploited new areas. This suggests that land and timber used by Trypillian B sites (Figure 2) affected resources locally but not overall in the region and, for instance, enough woodland for timber and arable land for cultivation were available for newly founded settlements. Only with the establishment of the Trypillian C sites does a permanent transformation from forest-steppe to steppe seem to occur; for instance, as shown by the investigations at Maidanetske, where the village was settled on a previously forested area. Moreover, it should be remembered that the ecotone of the forest steppe environment can be considered transitional and thus more exposed to changes in openness.

In contrast to arable land and the required woodland, the surface estimated for fodder production ('pasture' on the maps) often intersects between sites catchments. This may imply that neighbouring sites were coping with their vicinity through joint use of woodlands pastures and of grasslands. Otherwise some kinds of seasonal and long-distance herding practices could be assumed, which kept the cattle away from the direct vicinity of the settlement, allowing two very close sites to distribute their livestock across a wider

Table 5. *Required land for the subsistence economy of Trypillian settlements in the Southern Buh-Dnipro interfluve by variables discussed in the text (for reference cp. list 1)*

Settlement	No. used in Figure 1 Diachenko & Menotti (2012)	Sub-phase	Size (ha)	Total houses	Contemporary houses	Woodland/ construction (ha)	Pasture (ha)	Arable land (min. ha)	Arable land (mean ha)	Arable land (max ha)
Popudnia	1	t1	11.8	119	119	8	1428	107.1	178.5	428.4
Khrystynivka 1	2	n2	72.3	770	604	51	6160.8	543.6	906	2174.4
Tomashivka	3	t4	117.4	1191	935	79	9537	841.5	1402.5	3366
Cherpovody 2	4	t4	0.8	8	8	1	81.6	7.2	12	28.8
Gorodnytsia	5	t4	19.6	198	198	13	2019.6	178.2	297	712.8
Kocherzhyntsi-Pankivka	6	t3	27.5	278	278	19	2835.6	250.2	417	1000.8
Dobrovody	7	t2	210.9	1384	1084	92	11,056.8	975.6	1626	3902.4
Sushkivka	8	t1	76.9	819	642	55	6548.4	577.8	963	2311.2
Korzhova Slobidka	9	n2	12.6	127	127	8	1295.4	114.3	190.5	457.2
Yatranivka 1	10	t2	60	660	517	44	5273.4	465.3	775.5	1861.2
Peregoiovka	11	v3	50	533	418	36	4263.6	376.2	627	1504.8
Romanivka	12	t3	57.7	615	482	41	4916.4	433.8	723	1735.2
Moshuriv 1	13	t3	7.1	50	50	3	510	45	75	180
Taljanky	14	t3	320	2200	1826	147	18,625.2	1643.4	2739	6573.6
Maidanetske	15	t3	200	3000	2300	200	23,460	2070	3450	8280
Ostrovets	16	n2	7.1	72	72	5	734.4	64.8	108	259.2
Nebelivka	17	n1	235.5	1370	1070	91	10,914	963	1605	3852
Volodymyrivka	18	v2	50.2	533	418	36	4263.6	376.2	627	1504.8
Polonyste	19	v3	16.6	72	72	5	734.4	64.8	108	259.2
Tsyurupy	20	n2	9.4	95	95	6	969	85.5	142.5	342
Leshchivka	21	n1	11.8	119	119	8	1213.8	107.1	178.5	428.4
Fedorivka	22	v1	122.7	1362	1068	91	10,893.6	961.2	1602	3844.8
Stara Buda	23	t1	1.2	12	12	1	122.4	10.8	18	43.2
Nemorozh	24	n2	35.3	376	295	25	3009	265.5	442.5	1062
Gordashivka 1	25	v3	7.1	168	168	11	1713.6	151.2	252	604.8
Talne 1	26	t1	7.9	80	80	5	816	72	120	288
Talne 3	27	t3	3.1	31	31	2	316.2	27.9	46.5	111.6
Talne 2	28	t3	4.9	49	49	3	499.8	44.1	73.5	176.4
Rozsohuvatka	29	n2	55	586	459	39	4681.8	413.1	688.5	1652.4
Bondarka 2	30	t4	12.6	127	127	8	1295.4	114.3	190.5	457.2
Glybochok	31	n2	100	924	724	62	7384.8	651.6	1086	2606.4
Kolodyste 1	32	n2	7.9	80	80	5	816	72	120	288
Kolodyste 2	33	n2	12.6	127	127	8	1295.4	114.3	190.5	457.2
Kryvi Kolina	34	n1	38.2	407	319	27	3253.8	287.1	478.5	1148.4
Pishchana	35	n1	16.3	165	165	11	1683	148.5	247.5	594
Yampil	36	n2	36.7	378	296	25	3019.2	266.4	444	1065.6
Komarivka	37	n2	7.1	72	72	5	734.4	64.8	108	259.2
Peremozhyntsi	38	n2	37.7	402	315	27	3213	283.5	472.5	1134
Kvitky 2	39	n2	14.1	142	142	9	1448.4	127.8	213	511.2
Valiava	40	n1	80	852	668	57	6813.6	601.2	1002	2404.8
Nezamozhnyk	41	n1	15.7	159	159	11	1621.8	143.1	238.5	572.4
Vilshana 1	42	n2	39.3	419	328	28	3345.6	295.2	492	1180.8
Khlystunivka	43	n2	3.9	39	39	3	397.8	35.1	58.5	140.4
Buda Orlovetska	44	n2	23.6	238	187	16	1907.4	168.3	280.5	673.2
Ksaverove	45	n2	23.6	238	238	16	2427.6	214.2	357	856.8
Zelena Dibrova	46	t1	9.6	97	97	6	989.4	87.3	145.5	349.2
Novo-Ukrainka	47	t2	23.6	238	238	16	2427.6	214.2	357	856.8
Chychykozivka	48	t2	254.3	1668	1308	111	13,341.6	1177.2	1962	4708.8
Vasylkiv	49	t3	113	1147	889	76	9067.8	800.1	1333.5	3200.4
Lebedyn	50	t4	3.1	31	31	2	316.2	27.9	46.5	111.6

Continued

Table 5. Continued

Settlement	No. used in Figure 1 Diachenko & Menotti (2012)	Sub-phase	Size (ha)	Total houses	Contemporary houses	Woodland/ construction (ha)	Pasture (ha)	Arable land (min. ha)	Arable land (mean ha)	Arable land (max ha)
Andriivka	51	v2	35.3	254	199	17	2029.8	179.1	298.5	716.4
Likareve	52	n1	43.2	460	361	31	3682.2	324.9	541.5	1299.6

V1–3 Volodymyrivska Group; N1–2 Nebelivska group; T1–4 Tomashivska group.

area. Another possibility relates to a more intense use of spaces and resources, including cereal by-products and probably riparian environments, as suggested also by Harper (2012: 57), which could allow reduction of the area calculated for pastures and their overlapping. Regarding herd management, ethnographic comparison with the Bantu village of Mukobela (Upjohn Light & Upjohn Light, 1938) could provide interesting hints. This village had a population of about 2000 inhabitants in about 1000 buildings. In the village, which is circular in shape, people used the inner space to keep their cattle (5000 individuals!) and had additional kraals for each household. The entrance of the village was chosen according to the wind direction, so that when the cattle moved into the central space the village was not covered in dust.

Future perspectives

The model here presented constitutes a starting point for the estimation of Trypillian carrying capacity, which could benefit from future improvements. In particular, an integration of the geomorphology and hydrology of the study area would be relevant in terms of resource availability. From the ecological point of view, the forest steppe ecotone would have consisted of gallery forests along the rivers and patches of deciduous woodland on elevated areas and shaded slopes. In contrast, plain loess areas and south-facing slopes would have been predominantly characterized by steppe meadow vegetation. Such information on topography and vegetation cover, sustained by further pedological, archaeobotanical, and zooarchaeological data, could

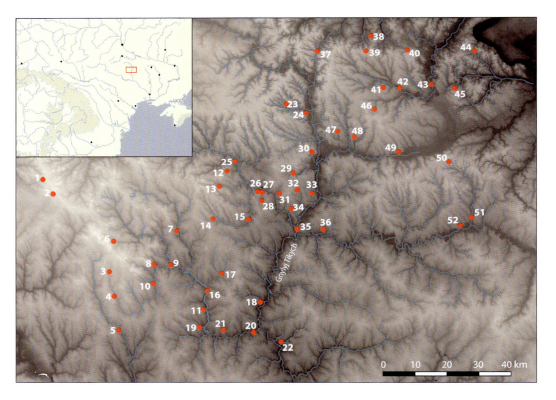

Figure 1. *Distribution map of Trypillian sites in the Buh-Dnipro interfluve considered in this model. The names of the settlements are provided in Table 5.*

List 1. *Uman region resource demands (for reference)*

Settlement	Nr. Diachenko/ Menotti 2012	Stage	Size (ha)	Total (h)	Contemporary (h)	Total (p) min	Total (p) mean	Total (p) max	Contemporary (p) min	Contemporary (p) mean	Contemporary (p) max	Construction timber (m³)	Deforestation/ construction (ha)	Cattle/ h	Small livestock/ h
Popudnia	1	t1	11.8	119	119	357	595	1428	357	595	1428	2380	7.9	119	47.6
Khristinovka 1	2	n2	72.3	770	604	2310	3850	9240	1812	3020	7248	15,400	51.3	604	241.6
Tomashovka	3	t4	117.4	1191	935	3573	5955	14,292	2805	4675	11,220	23,820	79.4	935	374
Cherpovody 2	4	t4	0.8	8	8	24	40	96	24	40	96	160	0.5	8	3.2
Gorodnitsa	5	t4	19.6	198	198	594	990	2376	594	990	2376	3960	13.2	198	79.2
Kocherzhintsy-Pankovka	6	t3	27.5	278	278	834	1390	3336	834	1390	3336	5560	18.5	278	111.2
Dobrovody	7	t2	210.9	1384	1084	4152	6920	16,608	3252	5420	13,008	27,680	92.3	1084	433.6
Sushkovka	8	t1	76.9	819	642	2457	4095	9828	1926	3210	7704	16,380	54.6	642	256.8
Korzhova Slobodka	9	n2	12.6	127	127	381	635	1524	381	635	1524	2540	8.5	127	50.8
Yatranovka 1	10	t2	60	660	517	1980	3300	7920	1551	2585	6204	13,200	44.0	517	206.8
Peregonovka	11	v3	50	533	418	1599	2665	6396	1254	2090	5016	10,660	35.5	418	167.2
Romanovka	12	t3	57.7	615	482	1845	3075	7380	1446	2410	5784	12,300	41.0	482	192.8
Moshurov 1	13	t3	7.1	50	50	150	250	600	150	250	600	1000	3.3	50	20
Talianki	14	t3	320	2200	1826	6600	11,000	26,400	5478	9130	21,912	44,000	146.7	1826	730.4
Maidanetske	15	t3	200	3000	2300	9000	15,000	36,000	6900	11,500	27,600	60,000	200.0	2300	920
Ostrovets	16	n2	7.1	72	72	216	360	864	216	360	864	1440	4.8	72	28.8
Nebelivka	17	n1	235.5	1370	1070	4110	6850	16,440	3210	5350	12,840	27,400	91.3	1070	428
Vladimirovka	18	v2	50.2	533	418	1599	2665	6396	1254	2090	5016	10,660	35.5	418	167.2
Polonistoe	19	v3	16.6	72	72	216	360	864	216	360	864	1440	4.8	72	28.8
Tsyurupy	20	n2	9.4	95	95	285	475	1140	285	475	1140	1900	6.3	95	38
Leshchevka	21	n1	11.8	119	119	357	595	1428	357	595	1428	2380	7.9	119	47.6
Fedorovka	22	v1	122.7	1362	1068	4086	6810	16,344	3204	5340	12,816	27,240	90.8	1068	427.2
Staraya Buda	23	t1	1.2	12	12	36	60	144	36	60	144	240	0.8	12	4.8
Nemorozh	24	n2	35.3	376	295	1128	1880	4512	885	1475	3540	7520	25.1	295	118
Gordashevka 1	25	v3	7.1	168	168	504	840	2016	504	840	2016	3360	11.2	168	67.2
Talnoe 1	26	t1	7.9	80	80	240	400	960	240	400	960	1600	5.3	80	32
Talnoe 3	27	t3	3.1	31	31	93	155	372	93	155	372	620	2.1	31	12.4
Talnoe 2	28	t3	4.9	49	49	147	245	588	147	245	588	980	3.3	49	19.6
Rassohovatka	29	n2	55	586	459	1758	2930	7032	1377	2295	5508	11,720	39.1	459	183.6
Bondarka 2	30	t4	12.6	127	127	381	635	1524	381	635	1524	2540	8.5	127	50.8
Glubochek	31	n2	100	924	724	2772	4620	11,088	2172	3620	8688	18,480	61.6	724	289.6
Kolodistoe 1	32	n2	7.9	80	80	240	400	960	240	400	960	1600	5.3	80	32
Kolodistoe 2	33	n2	12.6	127	127	381	635	1524	381	635	1524	2540	8.5	127	50.8
Krivye Kolena	34	n1	38.2	407	319	1221	2035	4884	957	1595	3828	8140	27.1	319	127.6

Continued

List 1. Continued

Settlement	Nr. Diachenko/Menotti 2012	Stage	Size (ha)	Total (h)	Contemporary (h)	Total (p) min	Total (p) mean	Total (p) max	Contemporary (p) min	Contemporary (p) mean	Contemporary (p) max	Construction timber (m³)	Deforestation/construction (ha)	Cattle/h	Small livestock/h
Peschane	35	n1	16.3	165	165	495	825	1980	495	825	1980	3300	11.0	165	66
Yampol	36	n2	36.7	378	296	1134	1890	4536	888	1480	3552	7560	25.2	296	118.4
Komarovka	37	n2	7.1	72	72	216	360	864	216	360	864	1440	4.8	72	28.8
Peremozhintsy	38	n2	37.7	402	315	1206	2010	4824	945	1575	3780	8040	26.8	315	126
Kvitki 2	39	n2	14.1	142	142	426	710	1704	426	710	1704	2840	9.5	142	56.8
Valiava	40	n1	80	852	668	2556	4260	10,224	2004	3340	8016	17,040	56.8	668	267.2
Nevamozhnik	41	n1	15.7	159	159	477	795	1908	477	795	1908	3180	10.6	159	63.6
Olshana 1	42	n2	39.3	419	328	1257	2095	5028	984	1640	3936	8380	27.9	328	131.2
Khlystunovka	43	n2	3.9	39	39	117	195	468	117	195	468	780	2.6	39	15.6
Buda Orlovetskaya	44	n2	23.6	238	187	714	1190	2856	561	935	2244	4760	15.9	187	74.8
Ksaverovo	45	n2	23.6	238	238	714	1190	2856	714	1190	2856	4760	15.9	238	95.2
Zelenaya Dibrova	46	t1	9.6	97	97	291	485	1164	291	485	1164	1940	6.5	97	38.8
Novo-Ukrainka	47	t2	23.6	238	238	714	1190	2856	714	1190	2856	4760	15.9	238	95.2
Chichirkozovka	48	t2	254.3	1668	1308	5004	8340	20,016	3924	6540	15,696	33,360	111.2	1308	523.2
Vasilkov	49	t3	113	1147	889	3441	5735	13,764	2667	4445	10,668	22,940	76.5	889	355.6
Lebedin	50	t4	3.1	31	31	93	155	372	93	155	372	620	2.1	31	12.4
Andreevka	51	v2	35.3	254	199	762	1270	3048	597	995	2388	5080	16.9	199	79.6
Likareve	52	n1	43.2	460	361	1380	2300	5520	1083	1805	4332	9200	30.7	361	144.4

Settlement	pasture/ cattle (ha)	pasture/ small livestock (ha)	pasture ∑ (ha)	arable land min (ha)	arable land mean (ha)	arable land max (ha)	pastoral landuse (ha)	radius mean agrar landuse (m)	woodland consumption ∑ (ha)	radius deforestation (m)	radius settlement (m)	radius deforestation construction (m)	arable land min (ha)	arable land max (ha)	radius min agrar landuse (m)	radius min agrar landuse (m)
Popudnia	1190	238	1428	107.1	178.5	428.4	3273	948	732	1720	194	159	107.1	428.4	778	1362
Khristinovka 1	6040	120.8	6160.8	543.6	906	2174.4	7086	2178	3726	3923	480	404	543.6	2174.4	1795	3111
Tomashovka	9350	187	9537	841.5	1402.5	3366	8845	2724	5767	4896	611	503	841.5	3366	2248	3885
Cherpovody 2	80	1.6	81.6	7.2	12	28.8	806	246	49	446	50	41	7.2	28.8	202	353
Gorodnitsa	1980	39.6	2019.6	178.2	297	712.8	4007	1222	1218	2219	250	205	178.2	712.8	1003	1756
Kocherzhintsy-Pankovka	2780	55.6	2835.6	250.2	417	1000.8	4748	1448	1710	2629	296	243	250.2	1000.8	1188	2081
Dobrovody	10,840	216.8	11,056.8	975.6	1626	3902.4	9846	3094	6687	5433	819	542	975.6	3902.4	2582	4344
Sushkovka	6420	128.4	6548.4	577.8	963	2311.2	7306	2246	3960	4045	495	417	577.8	2311.2	1851	3207
Korzhova Slobodka	1270	25.4	1295.4	114.3	190.5	457.2	3210	979	781	1777	200	164	114.3	457.2	803	1407
Yatranovka 1	5170	103.4	5273.4	465.3	775.5	1861.2	6542	2008	3189	3623	437	374	465.3	1861.2	1654	2871
Peregonovka	4180	83.6	4263.6	376.2	627	1504.8	5895	1812	2578	3264	399	336	376.2	1504.8	1493	2588
Romanovka	4820	96.4	4916.4	433.8	723	1735.2	6330	1946	2973	3505	429	361	433.8	1735.2	1604	2779
Moshurov 1	500	10	510	45	75	180	2063	639	308	1140	150	103	45	180	529	907
Talianki	18,260	365.2	18,625.2	1643.4	2739	6573.6	12,671	3962	11,255	6995	1009	683	1643.4	6573.6	3296	5584
Maidanetske	23,000	460	23,460	2070	3450	8280	13,551	4112	14,192	7519	798	798	2070	8280	3365	5932
Ostrovets	720	14.4	734.4	64.8	108	259.2	2416	737	443	1338	150	124	64.8	259.2	604	1059
Nebelivka	10,700	214	10,914	963	1605	3852	9886	3126	6601	5449	866	539	963	3852	2617	4367
Vladimirovka	4180	83.6	4263.6	376.2	627	1504.8	5896	1812	2578	3265	400	336	376.2	1504.8	1494	2588
Polonistoe	720	14.4	734.4	64.8	108	259.2	2575	816	443	1417	230	124	64.8	259.2	684	1138
Tsyurupy	950	19	969	85.5	142.5	342	2776	846	584	1537	173	142	85.5	342	695	1216
Leshchevka	1190	23.8	1213.8	107.1	178.5	428.4	3107	948	732	1720	194	159	107.1	428.4	778	1362
Fedorovka	10,680	213.6	10,893.6	961.2	1602	3844.8	9397	2883	6588	5204	625	538	961.2	3844.8	2374	4123
Staraya Buda	120	2.4	122.4	10.8	18	43.2	987	301	74	546	62	50	10.8	43.2	247	433
Nemorozh	2950	59	3009	265.5	442.5	1062	4952	1522	1820	2742	335	282	265.5	1062	1255	2174
Gordashevka 1	1680	33.6	1713.6	151.2	252	604.8	3532	1046	1033	1964	150	189	151.2	604.8	844	1538
Talnoe 1	800	16	816	72	120	288	2547	777	492	1410	159	130	72	288	637	1116
Talnoe 3	310	6.2	316.2	27.9	46.5	111.6	1587	484	191	878	99	81	27.9	111.6	397	695
Talnoe 2	490	9.8	499.8	44.1	73.5	176.4	1995	609	301	1104	125	102	44.1	176.4	500	874
Rassohovatka	4590	91.8	4681.8	413.1	688.5	1652.4	6178	1899	2831	3420	418	353	413.1	1652.4	1565	2712
Bondarka 2	1270	25.4	1295.4	114.3	190.5	457.2	3210	979	781	1777	200	164	114.3	457.2	803	1407
Glubochek	7240	144.8	7384.8	651.6	1086	2606.4	7836	2423	4466	4335	564	443	651.6	2606.4	2004	3445
Kolodistoe 1	800	16	816	72	120	288	2547	777	492	1410	159	130	72	288	637	1116

Continued

List 1. Continued

Settlement	pasture/ cattle (ha)	pasture/ small livestock (ha)	pasture ∑ (ha)	arable land min (ha)	arable land mean (ha)	arable land max (ha)	pastoral landuse (ha)	radius mean agrar landuse (m)	woodland consumption ∑ (ha)	radius deforestation (m)	radius settlement (m)	radius deforestation construction (m)	arable land min (ha)	arable land max (ha)	radius min agrar landuse (m)	radius min agrar landuse (m)
Kolodistoe 2	1270	25.4	1295.4	114.3	190.5	457.2	3210	979	781	1777	200	164	114.3	457.2	803	1407
Krivye Kolena	3190	63.8	3253.8	287.1	478.5	1148.4	5150	1583	1968	2851	349	294	287.1	1148.4	1305	2261
Peschane	1650	33	1683	148.5	247.5	594	3658	1115	1015	2025	228	187	148.5	594	915	1603
Yampol	2960	59.2	3019.2	266.4	444	1065.6	4972	1531	1826	2753	342	283	266.4	1065.6	1263	2184
Komarovka	720	14.4	734.4	64.8	108	259.2	2416	737	443	1338	150	124	64.8	259.2	604	1059
Peremozhintsy	3150	63	3213	283.5	472.5	1134	5117	1573	1943	2833	346	292	283.5	1134	1296	2246
Kvitki 2	1420	28.4	1448.4	127.8	213	511.2	3394	1035	873	1879	212	174	127.8	511.2	850	1487
Valiava	6680	133.6	6813.6	601.2	1002	2404.8	7452	2291	4120	4126	505	425	601.2	2404.8	1888	3271
Nevamozhnik	1590	31.8	1621.8	143.1	238.5	572.4	3590	1095	978	1988	224	184	143.1	572.4	898	1573
Olshana 1	3280	65.6	3345.6	295.2	492	1180.8	5222	1605	2023	2891	354	298	295.2	1180.8	1323	2292
Khlystunovka	390	7.8	397.8	35.1	58.5	140.4	1780	543	240	985	111	91	35.1	140.4	446	780
Buda Orlovetskaya	1870	37.4	1907.4	168.3	280.5	673.2	3957	1219	1153	2190	274	225	168.3	673.2	1006	1738
Ksaverovo	2380	47.6	2427.6	214.2	357	856.8	4394	1340	1464	2433	274	225	214.2	856.8	1100	1926
Zelenaya Dibrova	970	19.4	989.4	87.3	145.5	349.2	2805	855	597	1553	175	143	87.3	349.2	702	1229
Novo-Ukrainka	2380	47.6	2427.6	214.2	357	856.8	4394	1340	1464	2433	274	225	214.2	856.8	1100	1926
Chichirkozovka	13,080	261.6	13,341.6	1177.2	1962	4708.8	10,815	3399	8068	5967	900	595	1177.2	4708.8	2835	4771
Vasilkov	8890	177.8	9067.8	800.1	1333.5	3200.4	8632	2660	5485	4778	600	493	800.1	3200.4	2196	3791
Lebedin	310	6.2	316.2	27.9	46.5	111.6	1587	484	191	878	99	81	27.9	111.6	397	695
Andreevka	1990	39.8	2029.8	179.1	298.5	716.4	4187	1310	1228	2312	335	232	179.1	716.4	1090	1845
Likareve	3610	72.2	3682.2	324.9	541.5	1299.6	5478	1684	2227	3033	371	312	324.9	1299.6	1388	2405

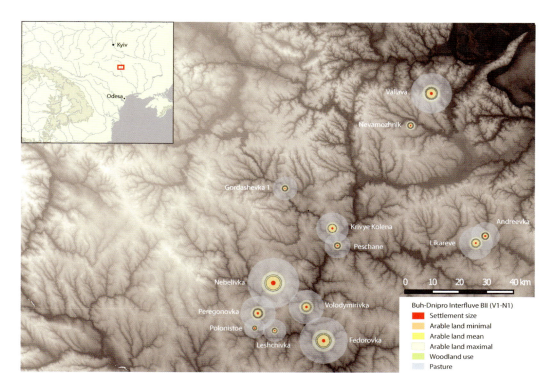

Figure 2. Modelled land-use for sites in the Southern Buh-Dnipro interfluve. Trypillia BII (Volodymyrivska 1–Nebelivska 1).

improve the understanding of landscape use and the extent of human impact. Other variables that need further investigation and refinement are, for example, the economic importance of riparian habitats for timber and fodder, and pastoral practices for the definition of pastures. For this purpose, the application of phosphate analysis could aid understanding of the function of the space in the middle of the sites, usually considered as

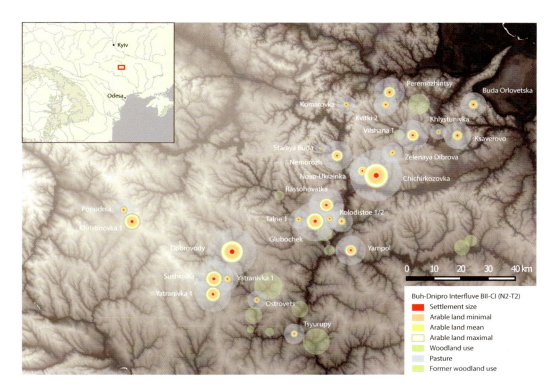

Figure 3. Modelled land-use for sites in the Southern Buh-Dnipro interfluve and remains of former land-use from previous stage. Trypillia BII-C1 (Nebelivska 2–Tomashivska 2).

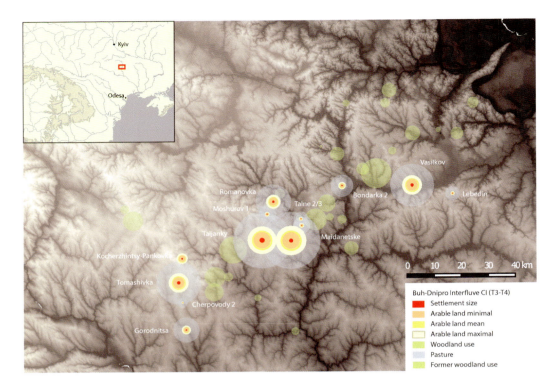

Figure 4. Modelled land-use for sites in the Southern Buh-Dnipro interfluve and remains of former land-use from previous stage. Trypillia CI (Tomashivska 2–4).

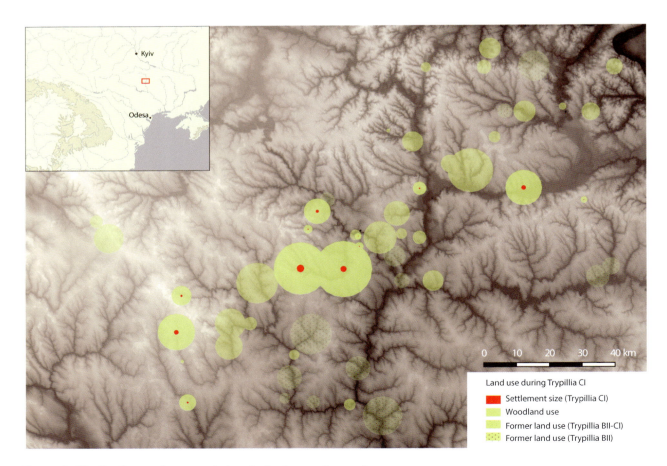

Figure 5. Woodland use and recovery during the final stage of mega-sites.

empty but where rural activities could have taken place; including animal penning areas, as attested ethnographically. Finally, analysis of wood imprints in daub are in progress, which could give information on the mean timber diameter in constructions and, consequently, on woodland management.

REFERENCES

Bibikov, S.N. 1965. Hozyajstvenno-ekonomicheskij kompleks razvitogo Tripolja. *Sovetskaya Arheologiya*, 1:48–62. Бибиков, С.Н. 1965. Хозяйственно-экономический комплекс развитого Триполья. *Советская археология*, 1:48–62.

Bondar, V.S. 1981. Dnestro-Dneprovskiy lesostepnoj okrug. In: S. A. Khensyruk, ed. *Kompleksnoe lesohoziajstvennoe rajonirovanie Ukrainy i Moldavii*. Kyiv: Naukova dumka, pp. 114–5. Бондарь, В.С. 1981. Днестро-днепровский лесостепной округ. В сб.: С. А. Хенсирук, ред. Комлексное лесохозяйственное районирование Украины и Молдавии. Киев: Наукова думка, с. 114–5.

Chernovol, D. 2012. Houses of the Tomashovskaya Local Group. In: F. Menotti & A. G. Korvin-Piotrovskiy, eds. *The Tripolje Culture. Giant-Settlements in Ukraine. Formation, Development and Decline*. Oxford: Oxbow Books, pp. 183–209.

Clark, C. & Haswell, M. 1967. *The Economics of Subsistence Agriculture*. London: Macmillan.

Diachenko, A. & Menotti, F. 2012. The Gravity Model: Monitoring the Formation and Development of the Tripolye Culture Giant-Settlements in Ukraine. *Journal of Archaeological Science*, 39:2810–7.

Diachenko, A. & Zubrow, E.B.W. 2015. Stabilization Points in Carrying Capacity: Population Growth and Migrations. *Journal of Neolithic Archaeology*, 17:1–15 [doi 10.12766/jna.2015.1].

Dudkin, V. P. 1978. Geofizicheskaya razvedka krupnyh tripolskih poselenij. In: V. F. Gening, ed. *Ispolzovanie metodov estestvennyh nauk v arheologii*. Kyiv: Naukova Dumka, pp. 35–45. Дудкин, В.П. 1978. Геофизическая разведка крупных трипольских поселений. В сб.: В.Ф. Генинг, ред. Использование методов естественных наук в археологии. Киев: Наукова думка, с. 35–45.

Ebersbach, R. 2002. *Von Bauern und Rindern. Eine Ökosystemanalyse zur Bedeutung der Rinderhaltung in bäuerlichen Gesellschaften als Grundlage zur Modellbildung im Neolithikum*. Basler Beiträge zur Ur- und Frühgeschichte 15. Basel: Schwabe.

Ebersbach, R. & Schade, C. 2005. Modelle zur Intensität der bandkeramischen Landnutzung am Beispiel der Altsiedellandschaft Mörlener Bucht/Wetterau. In: J. Lüning, Ch. Fridrich & A. Zimmermann, eds. *Bandkeramik in the 21st Century. Symposium in the Brauweiler abbey near Cologne, 16th - 19th of September 2002*. Internationale Archäologie - Arbeitsgemeinschaft, Symposium, Tagung, Kongress 7. Rahden/Westf: Leidorf, pp. 259–73.

Gaydarska, B. 2003. Application of GIS in Settlement Archaeology: An Integrated Approach to Prehistoric Subsistence Strategies. In: O. G. Korvin-Piotrovskij, V. O. Kruts & S. M. Ryzhov, eds. *Tripolian Settlements-Giants: The International Symposium Materials*. Kyiv: Korvin-Pres, pp. 212–6.

Gregg, S.A. 1988. *Foragers and Farmers: Population Interaction and Agricultural Expansion in Prehistoric Europe*. University of Chicago Press, Chicago.

Habeck, B. & Longin, F. 2014. Von Spezialisten für Spezialisten. Emmer erfolgreich in den Markt einführen? *BWagrar*, 17: 1–8.

Harmer, R., Peterken, G., Kerr, G. & Poulton, P. 2001. Vegetation Changes during 100 Years of Development of Two Secondary Woodlands on Abandoned Arable Land. *Biological Conservation*, 101(3):291–304.

Harper, T.K. 2012. Sustaining Tal'yanki: A Model Of Eneolithic Subsistence Economics At A Giant-Settlement Of The Western Tripol'ye Culture, *Unpublished Master's Thesis*. Buffalo, Ukraine.

Kirleis, W. & Dal Corso, M. 2016. Trypillian Subsistence Economy: Animal and Plant Exploitation. In: J. Müller, K. Rassmann & M. Videiko, eds. *Trypillia Mega-Sites and European Prehistory: 4100–3400 BCE*. London and New York: Routledge, pp. 195–205.

Kirleis, W. & Dreibrodt, S. 2016. The Natural Background: Forest, Forest Steppe or Steppe Environment. In: J. Müller, K. Rassmann & M. Videiko, eds. *Trypillia Mega-Sites and European Prehistory: 4100–3400 BCE*. London and New York: Routledge, pp. 171–180.

Kolb, C. 1985. Demographic Estimates in Archaeology: Contributions from Ethnoarchaeology on Mesoamerican Peasants. *Current Anthropology*, 26:581–99.

Korvin-Piotrovskiy, A.G., Chabanyuk, V. & Shatilo, L. 2012. Tripolian House Construction. Concepts and Experiments. In: F. Menotti & A. Korvin-Piotrovskiy, eds. *The Tripolye Culture Giant-Settlements in Ukraine: Formation, Development and Decline*. Oxford: Oxbow Books, pp. 210–29.

Kruk, J. & Milisauskas, S. 1999. Rozkwit i upadek społeczeństw rolniczych neolitu. *The Rise and Fall of Neolithic Societies (Abbreviated English Version)*. Kraków: Instytut Archeologii i Etnologii Polskiej Akademii Nauk.

Kruts, V.A. 1989. K istorii naseleniya tripolskoy kultury v mezhdurechje Yuzhnogo Buga i Dnepra. In: S. S. Berezanskaya, ed. *Pervobytnaya arkheologiya: Materialy i issledovaniya*, Kyiv: Naukova Dumka, pp. 117–32. Круц, В.А. 1989. К истории населения трипольской культуры в междуречье Южного Буга и Днепра. В сб.: С.С. Березанская, ред. *Первобытная археология: материалы и исследования*. Киев: Наукова думка, с. 117–32.

Kruts, V.O. 1993. Pytannia demographii Trypilskoi kultury. *Archeologiya*, 3:30–6. Круц, В.О. 1993. Питання демографії Трипільської культури. Археологія, 3: 30–36.

Kruts, V.A. 2008a. Giant-Settlements of the Tripolian Culture. In: A. G. Korvin-Piotrovskiy & F. Menotti, eds. *Tripolye Culture in Ukraine: the Giant-Settlement of Talianki*. Kiev: National Academy of Sciences of Ukraine, pp. 42–8.

Kruts, V.A., Korvin-Piotrovskiy, A.G. & Ryzhov, S. 2001. *Tripolskoe poselenie-gigant Taljanki. Issledovaniya 2001 goda*. Kyiv: Inst. Archeologii Nacional'noj Akad. Nauk Ukrainy

LeBlanc, S. 1971. An Addition to Naroll's Suggested Floor Area and Settlement Population Relationship. *American Antiquity*, 36:210–1.

Müller, J., Hofmann, R., Brandtstätter, L., Ohlrau, R. & Videiko, M. 2016. Chronology and Demography:

How Many People Lived in a Mega-Site? In: J. Müller, K. Rassmann & M. Videiko, eds. *Trypillia Mega-Sites and European Prehistory: 4100–3400 BCE*. London and New York: Routledge, pp. 133–169.

Müller, J., Hofmann, R., Kirleis, W., Ohlrau, R., Brandstetter, L., Dal Corso, M., Out, V., Rassmann, K. & Videko, M. in print. Maidanetske 2013. New excavations at a Trypillia megasite. *Studien zur Archäologie in Ostmitteleuropa*. Bonn: Habelt.

Nikolova, A.V. & Pashkevich, G.A. 2003. K voprosu ob urovne razvitiya zemledeliya Tripolskoj kultury. In: O. G. Korvin-Piotrovskij, V. O. Kruts & S. M. Ryzhov, eds. *Tripolian Settlements-Giants: The International Symposium Materials*. Kyiv: Korvin-Pres, pp. 89–95. Николова, А.В. и Пашкевич, Г.А. 2003. К вопросу об уровне развития земледелия Трипольской культуры. У зб.: Корвін-Піотровський, О.Г., Круц, В.О. і Рижов, С.М. Трипільські поселення-гіганти: матеріали міжнародної конференції. Київ: Корвін-прес, с. 89–95.

Ohlrau, R. 2015. Trypillia Großsiedlungen: Geomagnetische Prospektion und architektursoziologische Perspektiven (MA thesis, Kiel University), *Journal of Neolithic Archaeology 17*, 17–99.

Pashkevich, G.O. & Videiko, M.Y. 2006. *Rilnytsvo plemen Trypilskoi kultury*. Kyiv: Institute of Archaeology of the NASU. Пашкевич, Г.О. і Відейко, М.Ю. 2006. *Рільництво племен трипільської культури*. Київ: Інститут археології НАНУ.

Preoteasa, C. 2015. The habitat of the Cucuteni Culture wihin the Neamt Depression (Ozana – Topolita) in Moldavian Sub-Carpathians, Romania. In: A. Diachenko, F. Menotti, S. Ryzhov, K. Bunyatyan & S. Kadrow, eds. *The Cucuteni – Trypillia Cultural Complex and its Neighbours: Essays in Memory of Volodymyr Kruts*. Kiev/Rzeszow: Institute of Archaeology of the NAS of Ukraine and Institute of Archaeology, Rzeszow, pp. 111–28.

Porčič, M. 2012. Effects of Residential Mobility on the Ratio of Average House Floor Area to Average Household Size. Implications for Demographic Reconstructions in Archaeology. *Cross Cultural Research*, 46(1):72–86.

Rassmann, K., Ohlrau, R., Hofmann, R., Mischka, C., Burdo, N., Videiko, M.Y. & Müller, J. 2014. High Precision Tripolye Settlement Plans, Demographic Estimations and Settlement Organization. *Journal of Neolithic Archaeology*, 16:96–134. [doi 10.12766/jna.2014.3].

Ryzhov, S.M. 1999. Keramika poselen trypilskoi kultury Bugo-Dniprovskogo mezhyrichchia yak istorychne dzherelo *unpublished PhD thesis*. Kyiv: Institute of Archaeology of the NASU. Рижов, С.М. *Кераміка поселень трипільської культури Бугo-Дніпровського межиріччя як історичне джерело (рукопис дис. канд. істор. наук)*. Київ: Інститут археології НАНУ.

Upjohn Light, R. & Upjohn Light, M. 1938. Contrasts in African Farming. Aerial Views from the Cape to Cairo. *Geographical Review*, 28(4):529–55.

Videiko, M. 1996. Großsiedlungen der Tripol'e-Kultur in der Ukraine. *Eurasia Antiqua*, 1:45–80.

Videiko, M. 1998. Prychyny vynyknennia i rozvytku trypilskyh protomist. *Archeologiya*, 4:145–51. Відейко, М.Ю. Причини виникнення і розвитку трипільських протоміст. Археологія, 4:145–51.

Walker, K.J., Sparks, T.H. & Swetnam, R.D. 2000. The Colonisation of Tree and Shrub Species within a Self-Sown Woodland: the Monks Wood Wilderness. *Aspects of Applied Biology*, 58:337–44.

Zbenovich, V.G. 1990. K porbleme krupnyh tripolskih poselenij. In: V. G. Zbenovich, ed. *Rannezemledelcheskie poseleniya-giganty Tripolskoj kultury na Ukraine: Tezisy dokladov pervogo polevogo seminara*. Taljanki: Institute of Archaeology of the AS of the USSR, pp. 10–12. Збенович, В.Г. 1990. К проблеме крупных трипольских поселений. В сб.: В.Г. Збенович, ред. *Раннеземледельческие поселения-гиганты на Украине. Тезисы докладов первого полевого семинара*. Тальянки: Институт археологии АН СССР, с. 10–2.

CHAPTER 13

Pottery Kilns in Trypillian Settlements. Tracing the Division of Labour and the Social Organization of Copper Age Communities

ALEKSEY KORVIN-PIOTROVSKIY, ROBERT HOFMANN, KNUT RASSMANN, MYKHAILO YU. VIDEIKO AND LENNART BRANDTSTÄTTER

INTRODUCTION

The Trypillia culture, which is famous for its high-quality ceramic vessels, also provides evidence for complex pottery kilns, as revealed by excavations on Trypillian sites more than fifty years ago. These have been reviewed in recent decades by Ellis (1984), Petrasch (1986), and Willms (1999) and, most recently, a detailed analysis by Tsvek (2004) has been published (Figure 1). Until recently, the Trypillian pottery kilns which were known were more or less randomly found during settlement excavations. Within the area of the large Trypillian settlements, three specialized pottery workshops were found in the BI/II and BII settlements of the East Trypillia culture in Veselyj Kut and Myropillya, Trostyanchyk (Tsvek, 2004: 290). However, it should be emphasized that kilns have not been found on the largest settlements in the South Bug-Dnipro region to date. There was only one indication in the central part of Maidanetske: here, in 1985, a pit with an assemblage of vitrified pottery was excavated, which could represent production remains from a pottery workshop located within the Neighbourhood. The first direct evidence for ceramic production on very large settlements is the result of the recent large-scale geomagnetic survey of those sites. In the first campaign in 2011 at Taljanky and Maidanetske, a small number of characteristic magnetic anomalies were detected (Kruts et al., 2011: 65, 81: figure 12). Besides other different opinions, the interpretation of these objects as pottery kilns was the most favoured one which was later also published (Rassmann et al., 2014a: 109). In 2013, Vladimir Kruts and Aleksey. Korvin–Piotrovskiy excavated three of these anomalies in the northern area of the settlement of Taljanky. This fieldwork confirmed the assumption that all these anomalies were indeed pottery kilns characterized by a complex construction. Based on these results, similar anomalies in Taljanky, Maidanetske and in Nebelivka were excavated in 2014 (Videiko et al., 2015a).

The following paper will provide an overview of the current state of research and the new excavation results in Taljanky and Maidanetske. Furthermore, we will discuss the implications for the reconstruction of specialization and division of labour in Trypillian settlements.

POTTERY KILNS AND DIVISION OF LABOUR

From a technological point of view pottery kilns represent a technical solution to achieve certain qualities of the intended finished product. They allow higher and better controlled temperatures, better controlled firing atmospheres, and have a higher degree of efficiency with regard to the input of fuel compared to other pottery burning techniques (e.g. Rice, 1987; Ellis, 1984: 130–164). Pottery kilns are an indicator of intensified pottery production, a certain degree of division of labour, and craft specialization: special knowledge and experience would have been necessary to handle the process of firing properly. Furthermore, the maintenance of pottery kilns had to be managed, requiring labour and capital investment, and for their preservation and repair.

Based on archaeological evidence and the increasing quality of the finished products, several authors (e.g. Kaiser & Voytek, 1983; Ellis, 1984; Parzinger, 1992; Scharl & Suhrbier, 2005) argue that pottery production became more specialized in Southeastern and Eastern Europe possibly from the early Neolithic and certainly from the late Neolithic and Copper Age. Current research allows us to trace the process of how production capacities and firing temperatures were improving (e.g. Petrasch, 1986: 47–49; Dusek, 1984). In contrast, it is still difficult to answer the question of precisely how this specialization worked, as well as

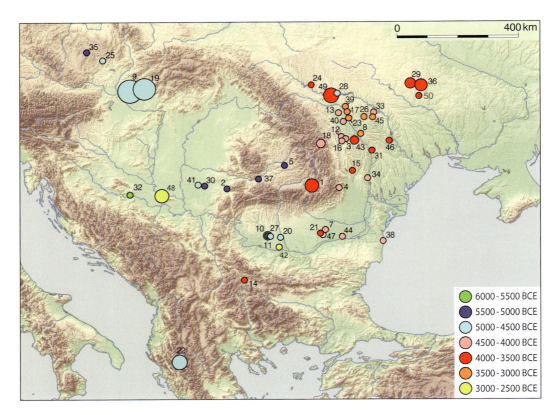

Figure 1. The distribution of kilns in Southeastern and Eastern Europe and their absolute dating in 500-year increments. The size of the points represents the number of kilns per site. The values are displayed in List 1.

how, and on which societal levels, pottery production was localized. To find answers to these questions, additional arguments have to be taken into consideration (e.g. Costin, 1991).

One crucial point is how the production was spatially organized: the distribution of production units between settlements shows whether, for example, only certain communities were specialized in pottery production or, alternatively, production units were distributed evenly. The number, size, and distribution of kilns within settlements can explain how many producer groups took part in the production process and how production units were composed. Are these organized as single kilns or as 'kiln batteries' as are proven in several contemporary sites (Hampe & Winter, 1965)? In the case of the Trypillian mega-sites, evidence of pottery kilns in the geomagnetic surveys on the one hand, and targeted excavation of pottery kilns on the other hand, provide excellent indicators for dealing with these questions in relation to, for example, the number of contemporary houses. Other important points are the scale of production and–connected to that–the estimated amount of time which the producers needed to spend on their craft. Starting, for example, from the estimated time which was necessary to produce vessels, from the amount and composition of production waste and also from the amount of pottery which was consumed in houses and disposed of in pits, extrapolations for whole settlements can potentially give us important clues regarding these questions.

In the following sections, we will evaluate at least some of the aspects mentioned above from the perspective of the new evidence from Taljanky and Maidanetske.

KILNS–SURVEY AND EXCAVATION

Survey

High resolution geomagnetic survey on giant settlements confirmed the large number of house anomalies already detected by Dudkin's surveys (Kruts *et al.*, 2001: 10). Besides the 1550 houses in Taljanky, nearly 1800 pits were revealed (Figure 2). Their size and magnetic characteristics vary widely. A small group of objects (seventy-four anomalies with a size of 3–10 m^2) shows high-magnetic flux density, in a range between 10 and 50 nT. These objects are surrounded by circular zones with low nT-values around zero. As exemplified by kiln C from Taljanky, kiln-anomalies with a diameter of 2.5 m were clearly larger than the kiln itself, which was *c.* 1.5 × 1.5 m (Figure 3). Here, the borders of the kiln construction

Korvin-Piotrovskiy et al. — Pottery Kilns in Trypillian Settlements   223

List 1. List of Southeast European and North Pontic Neolithic, and Chalcolithic kilns

Id	Site	Count	Latitude	Longitude	6000–5500	5500–5000	5000–4500	4500–4000	4000–3500	3500–3000	3000–2500	Used references
1	Ariuşd, Erösd, Priesterhügel	5	45,778	25,677					x			Comşa (1976: 358); Ellis (1984: 145f.); Willms (1999: 746)
2	Balta Sarata-Cîmpul lui Posta	1	45,583	22,083		x						Lazarovici/Lazarovici (2006: 190)
3	Bălţaţi	1	47,223	27,120				x				Ellis (1984: 150)
4	Tîrgu Bereşti	1	45,717	26,833				x				Ellis (1984: 150)
5	Bernadea	1	46,383	24,483		x						Comşa (1976: 355); Ellis (1984: 142)
6	Bodeşti-Frumuşica	1	47,026	26,425				x				Comşa (1976: 359); Ellis (1984: 147); Willms (1999: 742)
7	Cernica I-III-Mănăstirea Iezărul	1	44,424	26,270				x				Comşa (1976: 355)
8	Chirileni III	1	47,380	27,774						x		Sîrbu (2015: 172)
9	Cifer-Pác	15	48,305	17,520			x					Willms (1999: 746)
10	Circea-La Viaduct, 'Hanuri'	4	44,200	23,883	x							Comşa (1976: 355); Ellis (1984: 135); Willms (1999: 743)
11	Circea-La Viaduct, 'Hanuri'	5	44,200	23,883		x						Comşa (1976: 355); Ellis (1984: 135); Petrasch (1986: 44); Willms (1999: 743)
12	Cucuteni-Cetăţuia	1	47,288	26,930				x				Ellis (1984: 150)
13	Drăguşeni-Ostrov	1	48,019	26,806				x				Comşa (1976: 359); Ellis (1984: 150)
14	Gălibovtz; Gălibovtsi	1	42,812	23,007					x			Comşa (1976: 361); Ellis (1984: 142); Willms (1999: 741)
15	Glăvăneştii Vechi - Malul Jijiei	1	46,247	27,396					x			Comşa (1976: 359); Ellis (1984: 150); Petrasch (1986: 44); Willms (1999: 741)
16	Hăbăşeşti-Holm	1	47,156	26,958				x				Ellis (1984: 147–150); Willms (1999: 742)
17	Hancăuţi-I La Frasin	1	48,050	27,188						x		Sîrbu (2015: 172)
18	Hangu	2	47,078	26,042				x				Comşa (1976: 359); Ellis (1984: 147)
19	Horné Lefantovce	13	48,424	18,143			x					Willms (1999: 745)
20	Hotărani, Hotărani-La scoala	1	44,163	24,410			x					Ellis (1984: 139)
21	Jilava, Magura Jilavei	1	44,317	26,067					x			Comşa (1976: 355); Ellis (1984: 142)
22	Kamnik	6	40,183	20,650			x					Willms (1999: 746)
23	Kosteşty 9	1	47,858	27,260						x		Ellis (1984: 154); Petrasch (1986: 44); Willms (1999: 742)
24	Koszylowce Oboz	1	48,871	25,579					x			Ellis (1984: 152)
25	Kramolin	1	49,133	16,130			x					Petrasch (1986: 44); Willms (1999: 742)
26	Lazo XI - Tăurele	1	47,894	27,928						x		Sîrbu (2015: 172)
27	Leu - La Tei	1	44,183	24,000			x					Nica/Niţa (1979: 37–38); Petrasch (1986: 44); Willms (1999: 743)
28	Luka-Vrubleveckaja, Vrublevetskaia, Luka Vrublevet	1	48,617	26,750			x					Ellis (1984: 152); Willms (1999: 742)
29	Maidanetske	3	48,882	30,045					x			Videiko (2015b)

Continued

List 1. Continued

Id	Site	Count	Latitude	Longitude	6000–5500	5500–5000	5000–4500	4500–4000	4000–3500	3500–3000	3000–2500	Used references
30	Parța I (-Ost)	1	45,630	21,139		x						Comșa (1976: 355)
31	Sinești	1	46,861	28,251					x			Ellis (1984: 152)
32	Slavonski Brod-Galovo	2	45,159	18,053	x							Minichreiter (2007: 48, 59)
33	Stoicani	1	48,027	28,359				x				Ellis (1984: 142)
34	Suceveni(Galați)-Stoborani	1	46,011	28,042				x				Ellis (1984: 142)
35	Sváby	1	49,309	15,357		x						Willms (1999: 743)
36	Talianki	4	48,807	30,521					x			Kruts et al. (2014)
37	Tărtăria-Gura Luncii	1	45,933	23,400		x						Comșa (1976: 355); Petrasch (1986: 44); Willms (1999: 743); Lazarovici & Lazarovici (2011: 56)
38	Techirghiol	1	44,067	28,650				x				Comșa (1976: 355); Ellis (1984: 142)
39	Trinca-Izvorul lui Luca	1	48,210	27,115						x		Sîrbu (2015: 172)
40	Trusești, Tuguieta	1	47,750	27,017				x				Ellis (1984: 147)
41	Uivar-Gomilă	1	45,648	20,862			x					Scharl & Suhrbier (2005: 50 f.)
42	Vădastra-Măgura Fetelor	1	43,865	24,368							x	Comșa (1976: 355); Ellis (1984: 139)
43	Valea Lupului	2	47,180	27,499					x			Comșa (1976: 359); Ellis (1984: 150); Willms (1999: 742)
44	Vărăști A-Grădiștea Ulmilor	1	44,215	26,968				x				Comșa (1976: 355); Ellis (1984: 142)
45	Vărvăreuca	1	47,879	28,313						x		Sîrbu (2015: 172)
46	Varvarovka 8	1	47,150	29,017					x			Ellis (1984: 152)
47	Vidra-Măgura Jidovilor	1	44,264	26,166			x					Comșa (1976: 355); Ellis (1984: 142)
48	Vučedol-Vinograd	5	45,220	19,377							x	Willms (1999: 746)
49	Žvanec	6	48,550	26,483					x			Ellis (1984: 154); Petrasch (1986: 44); Willms (1999: 746)
50	Nebelivko	1	48,642	30,558					x			Videiko et al. (2015a)

Figure 2. Taljanky (Talne district). Overview of the geomagnetic survey.

correlate with the 20 nT line. This pattern is a well-known characteristic feature for kilns (cf. Jáuregui, 2010: 478, figure 5). It should be mentioned in this context that the detection of pottery kilns of the Roman Period by Martin J. Aitken in winter 1958 marked the earliest application of geomagnetic survey in archaeology (Aitken, 1959).

In 2013, the first three anomalies were excavated and proven indeed to be pottery kilns. The GIS-based comparison of the geomagnetic data and excavated pottery kiln exhibits a clear pattern which sharpens our understanding of the geomagnetic data. Based on this information, in 2014 further anomalies were classified as kilns and selected for excavation; one object in Taljanky and a further two in Maidanetske and Nebelivka.

Based on the new excavation data, the large-scale geomagnetic surveys on other Copper Age sites have revealed a large number of 'kiln-like anomalies'. In Taljanky this amounted to seventy-four kilns (1550 houses, 1:21), in Maidanetske to eighteen kilns (ca. 1850–2350 houses, ca. 1:130/100), and in Petreni (Moldova) to twenty-one kilns (c. 500 houses, 1:25). It is very likely that the classification of kilns has its uncertainties; some anomalies were maybe fireplaces and not pottery kilns. Nevertheless, the ratio between 'kiln-like anomalies' and house numbers delivers valuable information: it is quite similar in Taljanky and Petreni, but much lower in Maidanetske. The excavation in Taljanky revealed single-phase kilns, whereas the kiln in Maidanetske has three phases. It should be taken into consideration that maybe proper 'kiln places' were used over three generations on exactly the same place. The observations are too few to draw extensive conclusions, but at least they hint to the possibility that the true number of kilns in Maidanetske was higher, and presumably in a similar ratio to the houses as in Taljanky or Petreni.

Excavation

The excavation of pottery furnaces in Taljanky–Archaeological description

As already mentioned, the northern section of the settlement has, due to the high density of buildings, been an interesting area for research. Furthermore, besides numerous pits which were likely used for clay exploitation, the geomagnetic plan of its northwestern part shows several kiln-like roundish anomalies at the periphery of the settlement (Figures 4 and 5). Since the location of the objects was highly unusual, two small-sized anomalies near excavation site XX, where the dwellings 45–47 and three pits have been investigated (Kruts *et al.*, 2011, 2013), were selected for excavation, one to the northwest of it and one to the West. Moreover, to verify the attribution of these objects, we chose one more similar, small-sized anomaly. It was located 220 m to the West of the

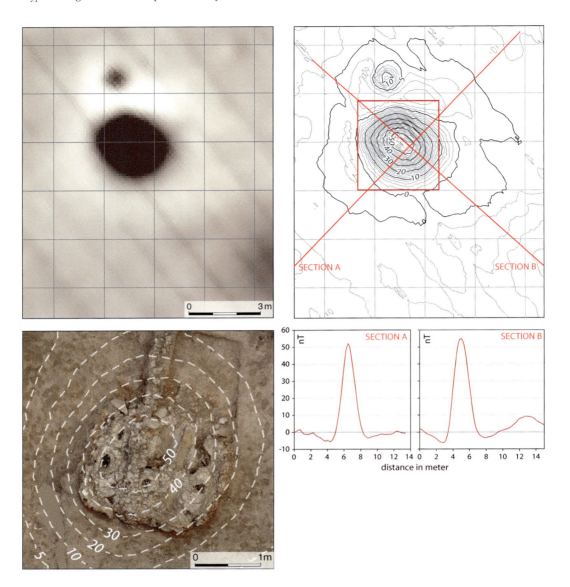

Figure 3. Taljanky (Talne district). Kiln C. Comparison of the excavated kiln and the geomagnetic data. Visible are the differences regarding the size of the geomagnetic anomaly and the real size of the kiln. The 20 nT line correlates with the size of the kiln.

anomalies mentioned above within the settlement's limits (Figure 4).

For each of the selected anomalies, trenches of the same size (6 × 4 m) were excavated. The excavations were carried out on a square grid of 2 × 2 m. The names of the squares are alpha-numeric. The letters from the West to the East are 'A', 'Б', and 'В' (cyrillic), the numbers north–south '1', '2', and '3'. Each of the excavations/features was given a name: Excavation 'A'/kiln 'A', 'B', 'C' (2013), and 'D' (2014) (Latin).

Excavation/kiln 'A'

At excavation 'A', an object was investigated which is interpreted as pottery furnace. The surface of the structure with an area of 2.5 × 2.0 m, at a depth from 0.4 to 0.55 m, was filled with fragments of pottery, often baked with vitrified coating, as well as pieces of slagging plastering (Figures 6–11). In addition, inside the fill there were also some unburnt animal remains that were apparently deposited after the feature had ceased to function. To the south of the object, on an area of 1.2 × 0.9 m and at the depth of 0.65–0.75 m, there was some slagging plastering, ceramic fragments, and some animal bones that determine the level of the ancient ground surface on which the debris was deposited.

After the debris was removed from the surface of the structure, it became possible to determine its shape and dimensions: it was a structure of rectangular shape (2.2 × 1.6 m) with rounded corners (Figures 12 and 13). The long axis of the feature was oriented north–

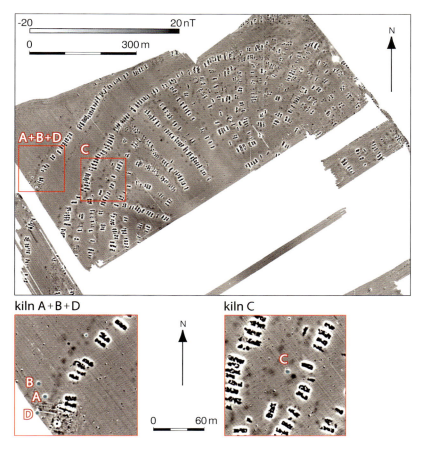

Figure 4. *Taljanky (Talne district). Overview on the northern part of the settlement with detailed plans of the excavation areas with pottery kilns A, B, and D in the first, and kiln C in the second.*

south with a slight deviation to northeast–southwest. The feature was framed with a wall on the West, North, and East sides with a height of about 20 cm and a width of about 15 cm, covered with several (at least four) layers of clay plaster 3–5 cm thick on a wooden frame. There were well-preserved holes from the upright poles, located at a distance of 15–20 cm apart, which had been part of the wall's wooden frame. The diameter of the posts ranged from 5 to 7 cm.

Between the walls, under the fill, the platform was found (hearth of the burning compartment). Its thickness was approximately 15 cm, and it included ceramic fragments. The edges of the platform rested on the walls, and the central part rested on two longitudinal supporting channel walls built of loam of about 40 cm wide at the bottom and 20–25 cm at the top and a height of 30 cm, oriented NNE–SSW.[1] Thus, the space beneath the hearth (platform) was divided into three channels, the walls and bottom of which were coated with clay and well-baked. Note that the bottom of the channels was at the depth of 0.85 cm, i.e. they had been deepened 10 cm in regard to the ancient surface. The height of the channels under the platform was about 30 cm, the width 40 cm. The southern part of the walls of the structure and the longitudinal retaining supports were lined with granite stones. In the platform, above each channel, there were round holes for blowing. There were three holes above each of the lateral channels and two above the one in the middle. The diameter of all the holes, except the two above the lateral channels under the northern wall, was about 15 cm; for the remaining two the diameter was about 10 cm. On the southern side of the object, at the bottom of the channels, there was an area made of fired clay of about 3 cm thick, the soil underneath which was burned.

This structure was undoubtedly a pottery furnace with the fuel loading area on the south side, and a three-channel combustion chamber. The platform above the firebox rested on two 'goats', with eight holes for blowing and a furnace dome, erected on a wooden frame, which had burned during use. The dome of the baking chamber did not survive. In the south-western and south-eastern parts of the hearth, above the platform, there were flat baked-clay blocks

---

[1] Below, these two-fold internal partitions, which divide the firebox into three channels, are referred to as 'goats' in translation of the term козел (Ukrainian) or козёл (Russian) which is used in the Ukrainian- and Russian-speaking literature about kilns as a *terminus technicus*. This term means he-goat and is used in the Ukrainian and Russian languages as the equivalent to the English term 'trestle'.

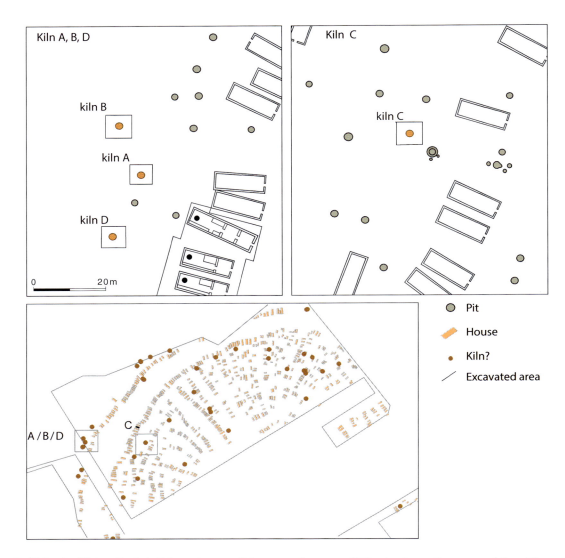

Figure 5. Taljanky (Talne district). Schematic map of the excavation area of kilns in the northern area of the settlement. Houses and pits are drawn in idealized form.

(up to 5 cm thick), probably representing part of the fallen inner coating of the walls or roof. All the design details of the furnace were badly burned, sometimes up to the point of vitrification, including the walls of the roof, the base of which was baked up to a depth of 15 cm.

While clearing the surface of the platform of the baking chamber, it was revealed that two blowholes on the eastern side were closed with halves (pieces) of conical-shaped bowls, and the mid blowhole on the western side with a large fragment of a bottom part of a biconical vessel. Also above the platform a flat, up to 3 cm thick, rounded (up to 18 cm in diameter)- -baked-circular disk was found. It can be assumed that these objects were used to regulate the temperature in the baking chamber. In addition, the entrance to the eastern channel was blocked with a large granite stone. Apparently, in case of necessity, any channel could be blocked in such a way, for the same purpose.

Excavation/kiln 'B'

Excavation 'B', with a second pottery furnace, was located 10 m north–north-west of excavation 'A' (Figures 4 and 5). It was of rectangular shape with rounded corners, measuring 1.9 × 1.75 m, and its long axis was oriented west-east (Figures 14–19). Unlike the pottery furnace in pit 'A', on the surface of this one there was no slagging clay baked with ceramics. The interior of the structure, at a depth of 0.4–0.6 m, was filled with fragments of pottery, and they were accumulated near the walls, out of which they seem to have fallen during the destruction of the dome. Here,

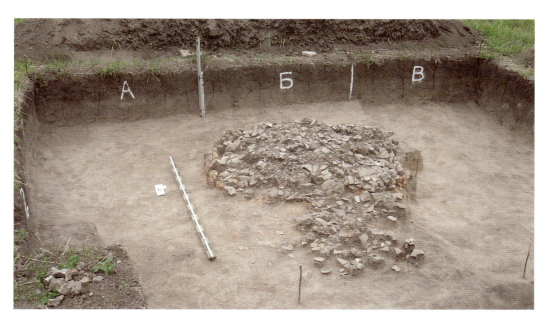

Figure 6. Taljanky (Talne district). Kiln A. View from the South.

there were also layered pieces of plaster, apparently from the collapsed walls and dome.

On the southern, western, and northern sides of the structure, its vertical walls were perfectly preserved; 15 cm thick and 25 cm high. The design of the walls and roof of furnace 'B' differs from the walls of kiln 'A'. In the middle of the area of the walls/dome of the furnace, a dense fill of ceramic fragments represented a separate layer. Here, ceramics serve as a constructive element to safeguard, upon firing, the rigidity of the arch of the firing chamber and increase its resistance to heat. It was because of this design of walls that we could not see any traces of the wooden uprights inside of them. In this furnace, the traces of wooden structures–uprights–could be seen on the inside walls on the platform (the hearth) of the firing chamber. Altogether, there were four carefully made holes of about 5 cm in diameter. Two of them were at the western wall of the furnace (respectively, in the northwest and southwest corners). The third and fourth ones were in the middle of the long northern and southern walls. We can assume that another pair of these holes had to be in the eastern part of the furnace, completing the northern and southern walls.

Figure 7. Taljanky (Talne district). Kiln A. View from the southeast.

Figure 8. Taljanky (Talne district). Kiln A. View from the East.

Most likely, these holes served as a place for setting poles that supported the frame of the dome of the firing chamber.

After removing fragments of ceramics and layered coating, the partially preserved platform (hearth) of the firing chamber was discovered; up to 15 cm thick, resting on two longitudinal west–east oriented 'goats'.

At the base of the platform along the central axis, granite slabs laid in a north–south direction were used as a transverse sub-structure of the hearth. The northern end of one of these measured 50 × 30 cm and was positioned partly on the northern wall and partly on the 'goat' in the central part of the northern channel. The other granite slab was about 0.5 m long and split

Figure 9. Taljanky (Talne district). Kiln A. View from the northeast.

Figure 10. Taljanky (Talne district). Kiln A. View from the North.

into five pieces; it was the continuation of the first one, and rested on both 'goats' of the central canal. Similar granite bridges were over the front and final parts of the northern canal. Similar stone structures were discovered near the eastern edge and the western end of the southern canal. Two more large granite stones supported the north-eastern and south-eastern corners of the structure, as if framing the furnace mouth. The hearth was probably designed as a stone grid with three stone lintels stacked on each of the canals, partly supported by the base of the oven walls and partly by the 'goats'. In this case, the daub part of

Figure 11. Taljanky (Talne district). Kiln A. View from the northwest.

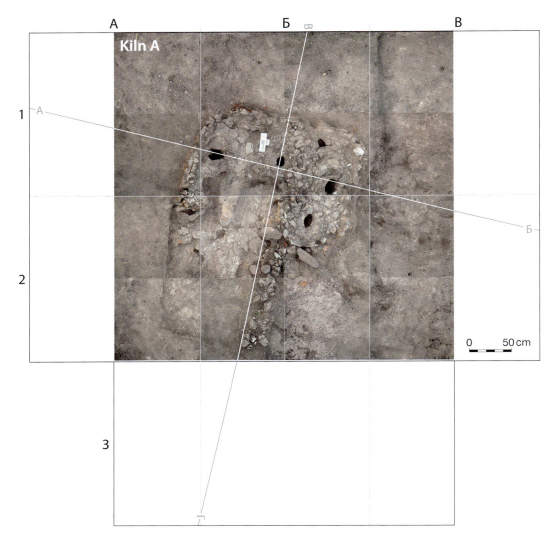

Figure 12. Taljanky (Talne district). Kiln A. After uncovering.

the platform (hearth) of the firing chamber was poorly preserved.

At the same time, blowholes are clearly visible in the part of the clay platform that survived. Altogether there are eight of them: three above the northern and southern canals, and two above the middle one. The diameter of all of them, except the two in the corners, is about 15 cm; the corner ones at the western wall measure about 10 cm. The surface of the platform of the hearth burning compartment, judging from the design of heat blow holes, had been carefully smoothed. There were fragments of two plane covers for heat blow holes for adjusting the temperature, similar to the ones from furnace 'A', found on the platform.

The height of the flue channels was about 30 cm, the width of the northern one about 40 cm and the other two about 30 cm. The width of the ground 'goats' measured about 20 cm. In the central part of the northern 'goat' the soil was replaced with granite slabs, and in the body of the southern 'goat' there were pieces of granite. The bottom and walls of the flue channels were covered with a layer of clay with the addition of sand. The eastern part of the flue channels smoothly lowered into the combustion area in front of the oven, as a layer of clay about 3 cm thick and burned. The flue channel area was about 20 cm deep and about 80 cm long.

Thus, this furnace, being two-tiered with a three-channelled vertical combustion chamber, is somewhat different from kiln 'A' in its design. The difference consists of the construction of walls and the existence of remains of the construction of the burning compartment, as well as in the use of stone in the hearth of the firing chamber and the 'goats'.

Excavation/kiln 'C'

In excavation 'C', at the depth of 0.45–0.55 cm and on an area of 3 × 4 m, there was a massive layer of Trypillia ceramics which covered the remains of kiln

Figure 13. Taljanky (Talne district). Kiln A. View from the West.

C (Figure 20). They were all scattered fragments of different origin. Judging from the fact that under the rubble there were the remains of a pottery furnace, most of these ceramics were probably part of the dome of the firing chamber. It can be assumed that the layer with these ceramic fragments provided toughness and heat resistance to the vault; the construction is similar to the vault of hearth 'B'.

Pottery furnace 'C' was similar to the ones described above in its design: with a three-channel vertical

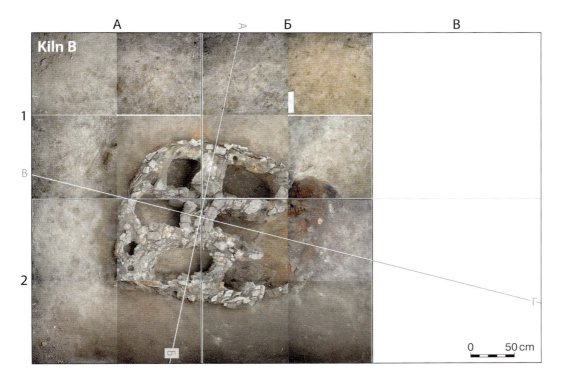

Figure 14. Taljanky (Talne district). Kiln B. View from the South.

Figure 15. Taljanky (Talne district). Kiln B. View from the East.

combustion chamber (Figures 21–25). The only difference is its shape: the kiln was not rectangular with rounded corners but formed like a horseshoe with a diameter of about 2 m. On the North, West, and South, the furnace was framed with well-burnt clay walls, preserved to a height of about 10 cm and representing the base of the firing chamber vault. Judging by the well-preserved part in the north-western section of the furnace, it was about 13 cm thick. Fragments of pottery were inserted in the clay walls as filler. The mouth of the kiln was located on the east side.

The combustion chamber consisted of three channels of 35 cm (southern), 25 cm (middle), and 30 cm (northern) width and up to 30 cm height. The channels were separated by two 'goats' of 25 cm (southern) and 30 cm (northern) width. The walls and the bottom of the channels were lined with clay without plant inclusions. The covering clay was badly burned, even scorified. The bottom of the northern channel was partially paved with large fragments of table and kitchen vessels, under which baked clay formed the bottom and walls of the channels, the same as in the other channels. A profile through the eastern end of the northern 'goat' and the edge of the furnace platform showed that the 'goat' consisted of separate pieces of coating and ceramic fragments, bonded and covered with clay on the outside, and was built on the smoothed (probably

Figure 16. Taljanky (Talne district). Kiln B. View from the East.

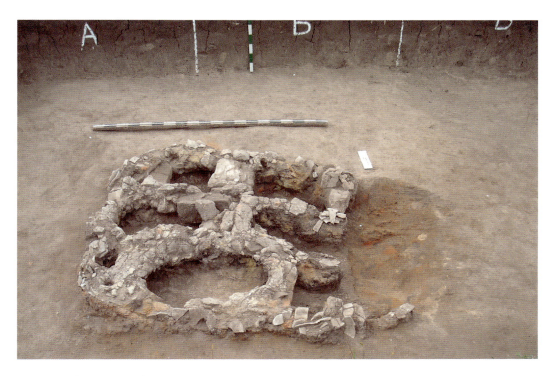

Figure 17. Taljanky (Talne district). Kiln B. View from the South.

watered) surface, which in this place, during the life of the hearth, was burned to a depth of 17–19 cm.

In the upper part of the northern channel, across it at the base of the firing chamber, there were seven broken stones of different sizes that were located in a line. It is possible that these stones were originally one oblong stone, one end of it leaning against the northern wall of the hearth, and the other one on the northern 'goat', as the basis of the hearth of the firing chamber. Such stones were used in the construction of

Figure 18. Taljanky (Talne district). Kiln B. View from the West.

Figure 19. Taljanky (Talne district). Kiln B, View from the North.

furnace 'B' (see above). Most likely, the construction of the hearth platform of the firing chamber was a combination of types, consisting of a stone grill and clay with inclusions of ceramics. As the hearth platform was badly fragmented it was not possible to restore the system of heat blow holes, except at the western side of the northern and central channels where their remains could be traced.

As already noted, the mouth of the furnace was on the east side. Here, the coating of the channels appeared to be a solid platform that was put on the surface as a layer of clay, without plant inclusions, of about 3 cm thick, protruding 0.6 m beyond the contour of the furnace. 40 cm to the northeast of the north-eastern edge of the furnace there was a large quantity of overheated burnt plaster, separate ceramic fragments, and two stones with diameters of 20 and 15 cm. It is possible that this cluster is part of the roof of the burning compartment that collapsed to the outside.

Excavation/kiln 'D'

Excavation 'D' was located 3 m southwest of the pit-quarry (Figures 4 and 5). There, remains of another pottery furnace were found. It was of rectangular shape with rounded corners, measuring 1.9 × 1.6 m; its long axis was oriented north–south (Figures 26–29). The interior of the structure was filled with fragments of pottery at a depth of 0.4–0.5 m. These had accumulated near the walls, out of which they seem to have fallen during the destruction of the roof. Here, there were also layered pieces of plastering, apparently stemming from the collapsed walls and roof.

On the southern, western, and northern sides of the structure its vertical walls were perfectly preserved, 10 cm thick and 20 cm high. A dense filling of ceramic fragments in the middle of the furnace represented a separate layer. Here, ceramics serve as a construction element to safeguard, upon firing, the rigidity of the arch of the firing chamber and increase its resistance to heat. In this wall design, we see no trace of the wooden uprights inside the walls. In this furnace the traces of wooden structures–uprights– could be seen on the inside walls on the platform (the hearth) of the firing chamber.

After removing fragments of ceramics and the layered coating, we discovered the partially preserved platform (hearth) of the firing chamber, up to 15 cm thick, that rested on two longitudinal west–east directed 'goats'. The construction of the channels and 'goats' of the stove is analogous to the construction of kiln 'B'.

In the part of the clay platform that survived, we can quite clearly see heat blow holes. Altogether there are nine of them: three above each channel. Their diameters vary within the limits of 10–15 cm. The surface of the platform of the hearth burning compartment, judging from the design of the blowing holes, had been carefully smoothed.

The height of the flue channels was about 25 cm and the width about 25–30 cm. The width of the ground/granite 'goats' measured about 25 cm. The

Figure 20. Taljanky (Talne district). Kiln C. Upper level with pottery remains.

bottom and walls of the flue channels were covered with a layer of clay with the addition of sand. The eastern part of the flue channels smoothly lowered into the combustion area in front of the oven, as a layer of clay about 3-cm thick and burned. In front of the kiln (on the east side) there was a pit (20 cm width and about 80 cm long) in which a fire for ceramics in the kiln was made.

The excavation of a pottery kiln from Maidanetske–Archaeological description

Since the identification of pottery kilns was successful in several cases based on the results of the geomagnetic survey in Taljanky (Rassmann *et al.*, 2014a), in August and September 2014 a similar magnetic anomaly was excavated in Maidanetske (Videiko *et al.*, 2015b). The feature was located in the North of the settlement within one of the innermost groups of houses close to the free space in the centre of the settlement (Figure 30). Here, it was situated in the free space between houses of different alignment and intensity as regards the geomagnetic survey; 25 m further to the east at least one further similar feature is visible. The divergent alignment and flux density of the houses is potentially because they are not contemporary. In the plan of the geomagnetic survey, the pottery kiln was visible as an almost round structure with a diameter of 3.2 m and a maximum geomagnetic flux density of 75 nT, close to the gable wall of a house which was only poorly visible.

Together with its surrounding space, the kiln was uncovered in an excavation area of 10 m by 11 m (trench 80). In the excavation area two pit features,

Figure 21. Taljanky (Talne district). Kiln C. View from the South.

which in the plan of the geomagnetic survey clearly display lower magnetic flux density, were completely and partly included, respectively. From these pits, a huge amount of pottery remains originated which show distinct traces of misfiring. A large proportion of this strongly fragmented material has a light to medium grey colour, shows deformations, and hard-fired up to the stage of almost complete vitrification. In many cases, pottery fragments were baked with almost completely scorified clay, likely remains of the kiln construction.

In the area of trench 80, the top ground surface was situated at a level of 174.4–174.8 m a.s.l. Under a layer of Chernozem, the first remains of the kiln came

Figure 22. Taljanky (Talne district). Kiln C. View from the West.

Figure 23. Taljanky (Talne district). Kiln C. View from the West.

to light at a level of 174.2 m as a rather strong disturbed structure, at first consisting of relatively small pieces of daub and pottery fragments; at deeper levels the remains were better preserved. Judging from sherd scatters beside the kiln, the ancient top ground surface existed at a level of about 174.1 m a.s.l. The remains of the kiln reached down to a level of 173.6 m a.s.l.; accordingly, it was dug into the ground up to 0.5 m.

Figure 24. Taljanky (Talne district). Kiln C. View from the East.

Figure 25. Taljanky (Talne district). Kiln C. Burned ground under the kiln.

The higher magnetic flux density of the kiln in the geomagnetic survey, compared to other cases (see above), could be caused by the fact that here three ovens were built on top of each other in the same place. Before we come to an interpretation of the remains uncovered, in the following section the construction phases are described, starting from the oldest and ending with the youngest (Figure 31).

Construction phase 1

The remains of the first pottery kiln in trench 80 were an almost round, NNW–SSE aligned building structure with a size of 1.9 × 1.7 m (Figures 31a and 32). The construction was partitioned into three parallel, 0.3–0.38 m wide, maximally 1.25 m long, and 0.2 m deep channels with almost vertical walls, which were separated by 0.15 m wide partition walls. In the NNW, these channels were semi-circularly closed, in the SSO they were open; however, their SSE end with the loading mouth of the kiln was not preserved.

Laterally, the pit–which was dug as one of the first construction steps of the pottery kiln–was lined with 0.1-m thick clay; at the bottom a 0.1 m thick clay floor was inserted, whose upper edge ran at a level of 173.75 m a.s.l. and there with approximately 0.35 m below the ancient ground level. In the south, in front of the mouth of the pottery kiln, a working pit could have existed which was, however, not registered during excavation.

Within the partition walls, numerous large vessel fragments–mainly of storage vessels and bowls–have been incorporated for stabilization (Figure 33). The

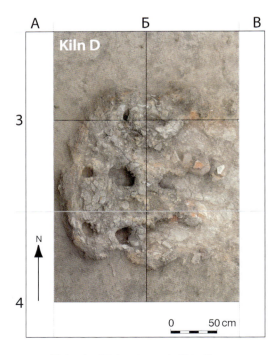

Figure 26. Taljanky (Talne district). Kiln D.

Figure 27. Taljanky (Talne district). Kiln D.

upper edge of the partition walls was rounded (Figure 34a) while on top of the outer wall flat beddings were partly preserved (Figure 34b), whose upper edge ran a few centimetres deeper than the upper edge of the partition walls. At the moment it is not clear if this bedding served as a support for the cover of the channels or as a foundation for the (not preserved) superstructure of the kiln. Additionally, in the NNW of the outer wall of the kiln a bedding, sloped towards the centre of the construction, was partly preserved which could alternatively be considered as the foundation for the superstructure (Figure 34c).

Construction phase 2

In the second construction phase of the pottery kiln, the three channels were filled up with clay and new channel walls were built above those of construction phase 1. Afterwards, a new clay floor was inserted about 0.15 m above the clay floor of the previous construction phase (Figures 31b and 35). From the newly

Figure 28. Taljanky (Talne district). Kiln D.

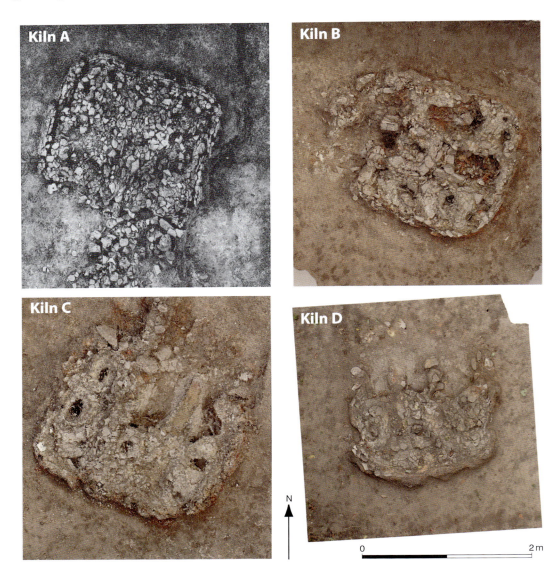

Figure 29. Taljanky (Talne district). Compilation of the ground plans of the four pottery kilns which were excavated in Talianki in 2013 and 2014.

built channel walls of the second construction phase, only few remains are preserved at the connection zone of the new floor to the wall plastering. Later, at the beginning of construction phase 3, the walls of construction phase 2 were almost completely removed.

Construction phase 3

In the third construction phase of the pottery kiln, the channel walls of construction phase 2 were removed and a completely new kiln was constructed. It was built directly upon the pre-existing structure (Figures 31c and 36). At its southern part this feature was substantially more strongly disturbed by post-depositional processes than the remains of the first construction phases. This pottery kiln shows the same characteristics as the previous ones: a round overall shape with a size of 2.05 × 1.95 m (due to the continuing use of the pre-existing oven structure), and three channels.

During the third construction phase of the pottery kiln, the combustion chamber (channels) was no longer situated significantly below the ground level but more or less level with the ground. The clay floor of the channels ran at the level of 173.95 m a.s.l. In contrast to the previous construction phases, in this phase the channels were aligned ENE–WSW, thus rotated 90° counter-clockwise. The rounded ends of the channels are located in the WSW; loading of the pottery kiln was carried out from ENE.

On the upper edge the channels had a width of 0.35 m, near the clay floor 0.2 m. Their height from the bottom up to the rounded upper edges of the partition walls amounts to 0.25 m. The channels were preserved only in their western part for an overall length of about 1 m. As in the case of the pottery kiln of the first construction phase, the mouth of the pottery kiln was destroyed.

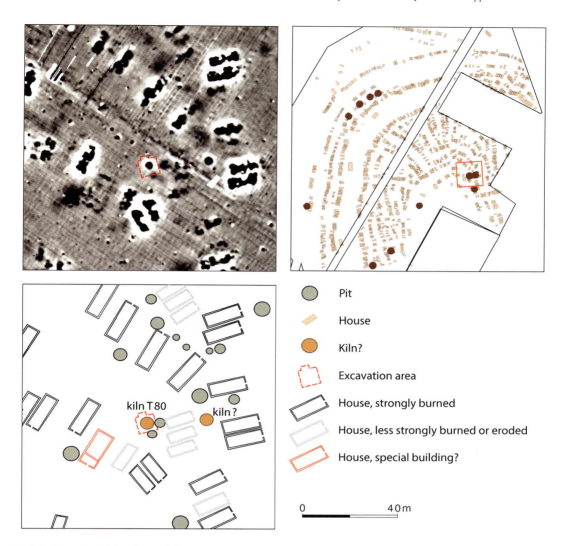

Figure 30. Maidanetske (Talne district). Schematic map of the excavation area of the kilns in trench 80. Houses are drawn in an idealized form. Some of the pits were used for the deposition of misfired pottery and other production remains, as the two pits close to pottery kiln T80 indicate.

The channel walls were not vertical but rather inclined. They show traces of intensive firing and partly a laminated structure which could be due to repeated repairing. For that, the builders of the pottery kiln used large pottery fragments which were vertically implemented into the walls. The surfaces of the channel walls and particularly their rounded endings show traces of intensive slagging, indicating that at these points the highest temperatures where reached.

On the northern outer edging of the kiln, a partly flat and partly internally inclined bedding is preserved, which had a width of 0.1–0.15 m (Figure 37). Since the level of this bedding clearly lies below the upper edge of the channel walls, with some probability it did not serve as support for the channel covering but rather as a foundation for the superstructure of the pottery kiln. From this superstructure only a few remains were found within and above the channels. On top and south of the remains of the pottery kiln, quite numerous large pottery fragments were scattered, which could represent parts of the superstructure.

Discussion of the Maidanetske kiln

From the typological point of view the pottery kilns which have been uncovered in Maidanetske can most likely be classified as freestanding updraft kilns, with a separated three-chambered firebox and a firing chamber above a round ground plan (cf. Rice, 1987: 158 f.; Ellis, 1984: 133). The basal area of the cylindrical firing chambers amounts to 2 m². From the kilns, only the fireboxes were partly preserved, while remains of the firing chambers are largely lost. During the first phase of the kiln, the firing box was situated slightly below ground level. In contrast, in the second and third stage of the kiln the loading of the kiln could be carried out at ground level.

At the current stage of evaluation, it is hard to estimate how the division of the firebox and the firing

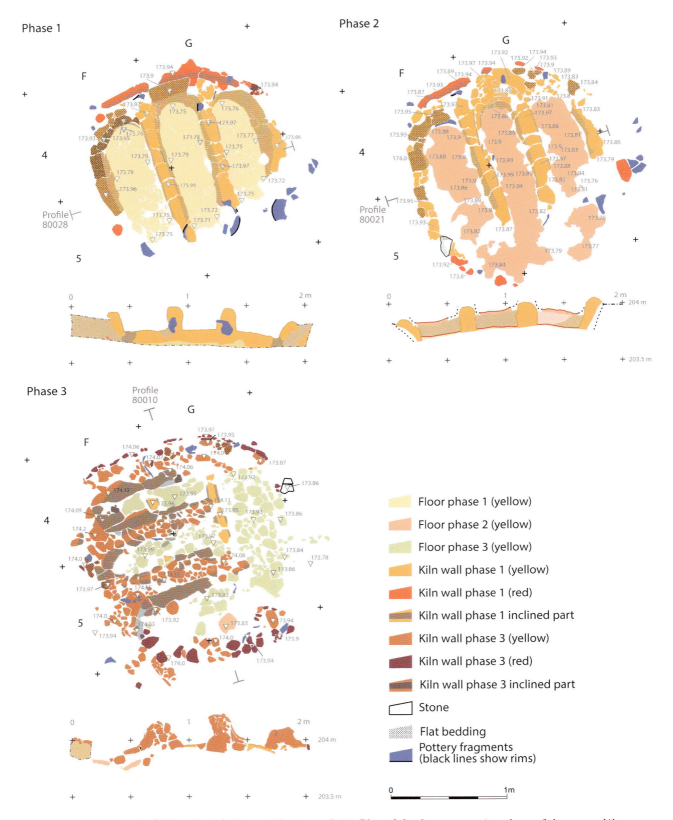

Figure 31. Maidanetske (Talne district). Pottery kiln in trench 80. Plan of the three construction phases of the pottery kiln.

chamber was constructed in the Maidanetske kilns. In other Neolithic and Chalcolithic kilns, different technical solutions have been observed for this problem: in several cases grates with holes (German: *Lochtenne*) are proven as, for example, in the cases of the Taljanky kilns A and D (see above). In other cases, vaults or

Figure 32. Maidanetske (Talne district). Pottery kiln in trench 80. Photogrammetric picture of construction phase 1 remains.

grates were constructed from clay cylinders (cf. Comşa, 1976: 359 f.). In Nebelivka,[2] in the surrounding of a kiln, numerous burnt clay slabs with angled outer edges were found which are interpreted as mobile coverings for the channels (Videiko *et al.*, 2015a: figure 7, 3). The diameter of these clay slabs measures about 40 cm (±2 cm) and would therefore also fit to the channels in Maidanetske. A few similar objects were also found in trench 80 of Maidanetske, in the surrounding of the pottery kiln.

Another question is how we have to interpret the divergent alignment of the kilns between construction phases 2 and 3: is it a result of better adaptation or optimization to the conditions in Maidanetske, for example, regarding the wind direction, etc., or could considerations regarding the engineering of the new constructed kiln have been the critical point for this modification?

However, using exactly the same place for the construction of three pottery kilns could indicate a long-lasting production within a larger social unit, visible in the clustering of houses in their surroundings. The recently uncovered pottery kiln, and at least one another, was situated in the proximity of a building which is visible in the geomagnetic survey only as linear wall structures (Figure 30). This characteristic appearance normally occurs only in cases of freestanding special buildings which are often clearly larger than normal houses and which are interpreted as communal buildings (cf. Müller *et al.*, 2016a). The spatial proximity of this building on the one hand and of pottery kilns on the other hand, could indicate that kilns were communal institutions. However, according to the currently available analysis of the geomagnetic survey, similar relations between kilns and seem not to be the rule.

The Number of Pottery Kilns and Houses–Proxies for Modelling Division of Labour

Geomagnetic surveys have delivered representative plans for the settlements of Petreni, Maidanetske, and Taljanky, with detailed information on houses and the respective location of kilns. To use these new data for investigating pottery production is a promising option. However, the accompanying uncertainties should not be overlooked (Figure 38). One goal of the new research in Maidanetske is focused on the establishment of an internal chronology of the settlement. A series of ^{14}C-dates enables us to detect general trends, but the number of dates is not yet large enough to establish a high-resolution chronology of the settlement (Müller *et al.*, in print). The geomagnetic data show around 1550 houses in Taljanky and 1980–2300 in Maidanetske (Rassmann, 2015a; Rassmann *et al.*, 2014b: 107–108, 116–118), but it remains unclear how many of these existed coevally; a key variable for

---
[2]For a description of this feature: Burdo and Videiko, 2016.

Figure 33. Maidanetske (Talne district). Pottery kiln in trench 80. Section 28 through the first construction phase of the kiln. Large vessel fragments are integrated into the internal partition of the kiln basement.

calculating consumption. There are some conventional models based on the typological investigations of the rich ceramic inventory of houses (Ryzhov, 1999). A second question concerns the life span of a kiln. There are ethnographical observations of the usage of kilns over a period of one generation (Hampe & Winter, 1965). For an evaluation of these points, further investigations are needed. The excavation in Taljanky revealed single phase kilns, whereas the kiln in Maidanetske has two or three phases. At the latter site the 'kiln places' were maybe used over two to three generations in exactly the same place, in contrast to Taljanky where the potter changed the place of their kilns, as we can see from kilns A, B, and D (Figure 7).

A third question concerns the consumption of, and demand for, ceramic vessels per household. The excavation of a large number of Trypillian houses shows a variation of 30–150 vessels in the inventory of a burnt house (Videiko, 2004). Despite these uncertainties, we would like to discuss the detected kilns in the context of recent experiments with kiln construction. On a

Figure 34. Maidanetske (Talne district). Pottery kiln in trench 80, northern part of construction phase 1 with rounded ends of the channels. (a) Partition wall, rounded on the upper edge; (b) flat bedding on top of the outer wall; (c) bedding at the outer wall, sloped towards the centre of the kiln.

Figure 35. Maidanetske (Talne district). Pottery kiln in trench 80. 3D-model of construction phase 2 remains.

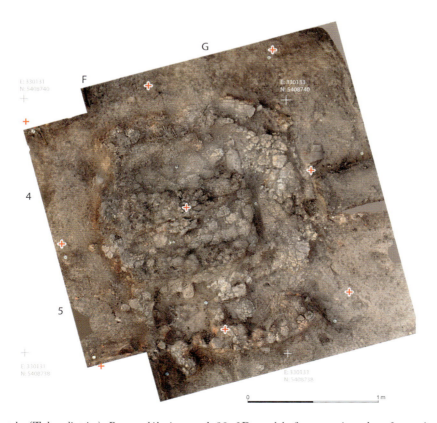

Figure 36. Maidanetske (Talne district). Pottery kiln in trench 80. 3D-model of construction phase 3 remains.

Figure 37. Maidanetske (Talne district). Pottery kiln in trench 80. Flat bedding at the outer side of construction phase 3.

settlement of the Roman Period in Haarhausen in Central Germany, kilns with a similar construction were excavated and later reconstructed for experimental studies (Dusek, 1984). Based on these data, a kiln can be used approximately once a week due to the time needed for firing up the kiln, for firing the ceramics, and for cooling down the kiln. The production volume consisted of 150 vessels of different sizes. Each firing consumes a volume of 1.5 m^3 of wood (Dusek, 1984: 13).

The ratio between kilns and houses at the settlements discussed varies from *c.* 1:20 in Petreni and Taljanky, to 1:100 in Maidanetske. To calculate the ceramic consumption of a Trypillian house M. Videiko's archaeological data from the Uruk excavation were used; here, the average consumption was

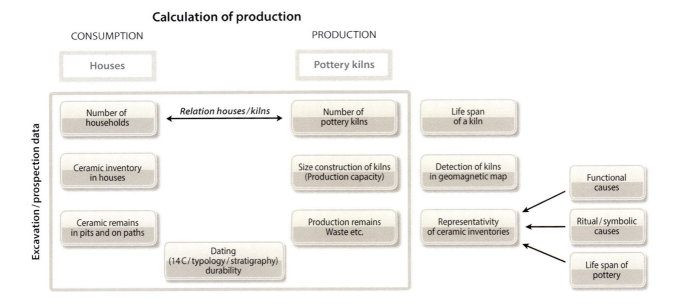

Figure 38. Overview of the calculation of the production and consumption of pottery, in respect to the archaeological data and specific uncertainties in the excavation record.

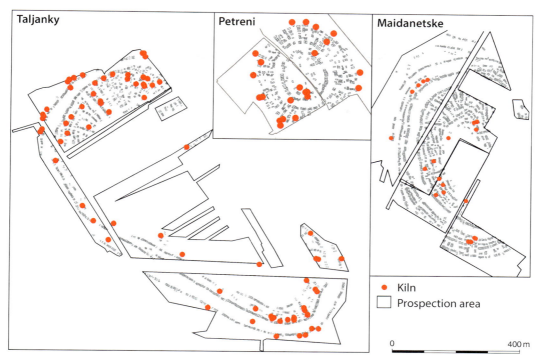

Figure 39. Schematic map of the location of kilns in the settlements of Maidanetske and Taljanky (both Talne district) and Petreni (district Drochia, Moldova). The identification of the pottery kilns is based on the geomagnetic data. Five such anomalies at Maidanetske and Taljanky were correctly proven to be kilns by excavation in 2013 and 2014.

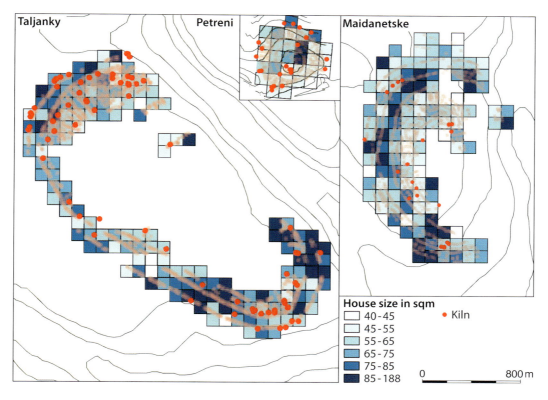

Figure 40. Schematic map of the location of kilns in the settlements of Maidanetske and Taljanky (both Talne district) and Petreni (district Drochia, Moldova) in relation to the size of houses. The house size is calculated based on the median in 100 × 100 m raster cells.

calculated at *c.* 80 vessels per year. The total number of workshops based on this case study was calculated as thirty at Maidanetske and up to forty-one in Taljanky (Videiko, 2004).[3] Based on the excavation data from Late Neolithic Okolište (Central Bosnia), Hofmann (forthcoming) calculated a much lower consumption of 1.5 vessels per household per year on average. Taking the Uruk calculation as an upper limit, the production rate of a kiln can yield a volume of 50 × 150 vessels per year, enough for around one-hundred houses. Despite these rough calculations, the observed kilns in Maidanetske could satisfy the need of all the 3000 houses. It seems more realistic to us that the number of contemporaneous houses was smaller, especially if we consider the new ^{14}C-dates (Müller *et al.*, 2016b). This will be discussed in a future publication.

The spatial distribution of the kilns in the settlements differs in their relation to the houses. In Maidanetske, the geomagnetic data of nearly sixty percent of the settlement revealed four or five groups of kilns, and three single kilns (Figure 39). The spatial pattern indicates a concentration of pottery production in larger social units. For the whole settlement, we estimate no more than eight to ten production groups. In Maidanetske, the identified kilns are not connected with areas of larger houses (Figure 40). The situation is different to Petreni and Taljanky, where the kilns are distributed more widely. Some of them are close to areas with larger buildings, but they are also close to medium-sized and smaller houses. A remarkable difference in relation to Taljanky and Petreni compared to Maidanetske is the divergent ratio of kilns to houses, and the resulting sparser distribution at the latter site. The question arises of whether this difference also indicates differences in specialization and the degree of the division of labour. To answer this, new data and a more detailed analysis are obviously needed.

Conclusions

Pottery kilns (furnaces, stoves) are widely known for the Cucuteni–Trypillia communities in Romania, Moldova, and Ukraine at all stages of their development. At present, they are most fully described in 'Pottery production of Trypillia cultural society' by Tsvek (2004), where the author has identified four types of furnaces: single-chamber, single-chamber 'tandoor' type, dual chamber with a horizontal connection of chambers, and double chamber with vertical chamber articulation (bunk).

At the same time, the previously investigated furnaces do not allow us to determine the volume of ceramic production, which, judging from the amount of ceramic finds obtained in the course of the archaeological excavation of residential complexes, was significant. The pottery furnaces investigated in 2013/2014 enable us to look into the problem of ceramic production in a different way.

First, all the investigated furnaces belong to a different, more advanced type. They can be defined as three-channel combustion chamber with dual vertical bunk ('goat'/'salamander'/'trestle') and a large burning compartment with adjustable temperature (Figure 41). Second, the size of the baking chambers raises the question of the possible production volumes for a single kiln. Third, the determination of the total number of furnaces in the settlement, according to the geomagnetic survey, offers the possibility to calculate the total amount of ceramic production in a given settlement. And finally, the spatial distribution of anomalies corresponding to pottery furnaces within the territory of the settlement, and within the context of the dwelling structural elements, allows us to investigate the social significance of ceramic production within the community.

The detection of kilns by geomagnetic survey, and the first excavations carried out by precisely targeting them, demonstrate the great potential of an integrative approach in combining survey data and excavation.

Our first analysis of the spatial distribution of kilns in the context of other settlement data illustrates a promising approach to investigating pottery production on different scales. The wide range of social, technical, typological, and economical aspects obviously needs

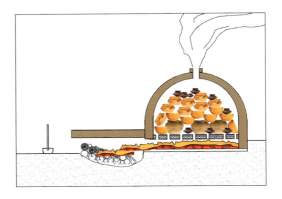

Figure 41. First attempt at a schematic reconstruction of the pottery kilns from Maidanetske and Taljanky: (a) firebox with three channels (here: longitudinal section); (b) grate (platform) or mobile covering of round clay slabs; (c) firing chamber; (d) fire or loading pit; (e) loading mouth. The tunnel-like loading mouth of the kiln which is displayed in the reconstruction is not proven in the archaeological record. The same is true for the shape of the fire chamber above the grate.

---

[3] The starting point of his extrapolation was a figure of around 2000 households in Maidanetske and 2700 in Talianki (Kruts *et al.*, 2001: 77).

representative excavation data, which is a realistic task for the forthcoming fieldwork.

Acknowledgements

We sincerely like to thank Steve Davis (Dublin), Nils Müller-Scheeßel (Frankfurt a. M.), Aleksandr Diachenko (Cherkasy), and Nicole Taylor (Kiel) for correcting the text, and Karl-Heinz Till (Rabenau) for discussing the wide field of ceramic production. We also thank Ingmar Franz (Kiel) for his help with producing 3D-models of kilns and Johannes Kalmbach (Frankfurt a. M.) for manifold kinds of support.

References

Aitken, M.J. 1959. Magnetic Prospection. I – The Water Newton Survey. *Archaeometry*, 1:24–9.

Burdo, N. & Videiko, M. 2015. Nebelivka: From Magnetic Prospection to New Features of Mega-Sites. In: J. Müller, K. Rassmann & M. Videiko, eds. *Trypillia-Mega-Sites and European Prehistory: 4100–3400 BCE*. London and New York: Routledge, pp. 95–116.

Comşa, E. 1976. Die Töpferöfen im Neolithikum Rumäniens. *Jahresschrift für mitteldeutsche Vorgeschichte*, 60:353–64.

Costin, C.L. 1991. Craft Specialization: Issues in Defining, Documenting, and Explaining the Organization of Production. *Archaeological Method and Theory*, 3:1–56.

Dusek, S. 1984. Die Produktion römischer Drehscheibenkeramik in Thüringen – Technologie, ökonomische und gesellschaftliche Konsequenzen. In: R. Feustel, ed. *Römerzeitliche Drehscheibenware im Barbaricum. Weimarer Monographien zur Ur- und Frühgeschichte 11*. Weimar: Druckerei Fortschritt Erfurt, pp. 5–18.

Ellis, L. 1984. *The Cucuteni-Tripolye Culture: A Study in Technology and the Origins of Complex Society. International Series I-217*. Oxford: BAR.

Hampe, R. & Winter, A. 1965. *Bei Töpfern und Zieglern in Süditalien, Sizilien und Griechenland*. Mainz: Verlag RGZM.

Hofmann, R. Forthcoming. Pottery Standardization and Specialization in the late Neolithic Okolište: A case study from Central Bosnia (5200–4700 BCE).

Jáuregui, C.N. 2010. Definición de contextos materiales en área lferas. In: S. Biegert, ed. *Congressus Vicisemus Sextus Rei Cretariae Romanae Favtorum Gadibus Habitus MMVIII. Rei Cretariae Romanae Favtorum 41*. Bonn: Dr. Rudolph Habelt Verlag, pp. 473–80.

Kaiser, T. & Voytek, B. 1983. Sedentism and Economic Change in the Balkan Neolithic. *Journal of Anthropological Archaeology*, 2:323–53.

Kruts, V.A., Korvin-Piotrovskij, A.G., Mischka, C., Ohlrau, R., Windler, A. & Rassmann, K. 2013. Taljanki 2012. The Geomagnetic Prospection. In: A. G. Korvin-Piotrovkiy & K. Rassmann, eds. *Talianki – Settlement-Giant of the Tripolian Culture. Investigations in 2012*. Kiev: Institute of Archaeology of the NASU, pp. 85–103.

Kruts, V.A., Korvin-Piotrovskiy, A., Peters, D. & Rassmann, K. 2011. Taljanki Reloaded: Geomagnetic Prospection Three Decades after V. P. Dudkins Work. In: A. G. Korvin-Piotrovskiy & F. Menotti, eds. *Settlement Giants of the Tripolian Culture. Investigations in 2011*. Kiev: Institute of Archaeology of the NASU, pp. 60–85.

Kruts, V., Korvin-Piotrovskiy, A.G., Chabanyuk, V. V. & Shatilo, L. A. 2013. Talianki: Settlement-Giant of the Tripolian Culture. Investigations in 2012. Kiev: Institute of Archaeology of the NASU, pp. 4–84.

Kruts, V., Korvin-Piotrovskiy, A.G. & Rassmann, K. 2014. New Discovery of the Kilns in the Tripolian Giant-Settlement Talianki. In: G. Dumitroaia, C. Preoteasa & N. Ciprian-Dorin, eds. *Cucuteni Culture within the European Neo-Eneolithic Context. Abstracts of the International Colloquium 'Cucuteni – 130' in Pietra Neamț from 15th–17th October 2014*. Piatra Neamț: Editura "Constantin Matasă", pp. 117–21.

Kruts, V.A., Korvin-Piotrovskiy, A.G. & Ryzhov, S.N. 2001. *Talianki – Settlement-Giant of the Tripolian Culture*. Kiev: Korvin-Press.

Lazarovici, C.-M. & Lazarovici, G. 2006. *Arhitectura Neoliticului şi Epocii Cuprului din România. I Neoliticul*. Bibliotheca Archaeologica Moldaviae. Trinitas Iaşi.

Lazarovici, G. & Lazarovici, C.-M. 2011. Architecture of the Settlement. In: G. Lazarovici, C.-M. Lazarovici & M. Merlini, eds. *Tărtăria and the Sacred Tablets*. Cluj-Napoca: Editura Mega, pp. 47–56.

Minichreiter, K. 2007. *Slavonski Brod Galovo. Deset godina arheoloških istraživanja (Ten Years of Archaeological Excavations) 1*. Zagreb: Monografije Instituta za arheologiju MIARH 1.

Müller, J., Hofmann, R. & Ohlrau, R. 2016a. From Domestic Households to Mega-Structures: Proto-Urbanism? In: J. Müller, K. Rassmann & M. Videiko, eds. *Trypillia Mega-Sites and European Prehistory: 4100–3400 BCE*. London and New York: Routledge, pp. 253–268.

Müller, J., Hofmann, R., Brandtstätter, L., Ohlrau, R. & Videiko, M. 2016b. Chronology and Demography: How Many People Lived in a Mega-Site? In: J. Müller, K. Rassmann & M. Videiko, eds. *Trypillia Mega-Sites and European Prehistory: 4100–3400 BCE*. London and New York: Routledge, pp. 133–169.

Müller, J., Hofmann, R., Kirleis, W., Ohlrau, R., Brandtstätter, L., Dal Corso, M., Out, W. & Videko, M., eds. In print. *Maidanetske 2013. New Excavations at a Trypillia megasite. Studien zur Archäologie in Ostmitteleuropa*. Bonn: Habelt.

Nica, M. & Niţa, T. 1979. Les etablissements neolithiques de Leu et Padea, de la zone d'interference des cultures Dudeşti et Vinča. *Dacia N. S.*, 23:31–64.

Parzinger, H. 1992. Zentrale Orte–Siedelverband und Kultgemeinschaft im karpatenländischen Neo- und Äneolithikum. *Balcanica*, 23:221–30.

Petrasch, J. 1986. Typologie und Funktion neolithischer Öfen in Mittel- und Südosteuropa. *Acta Praehist. et Arch. Berlin*, 18:33–83.

Rassmann, K., Ohlrau, R., Hofmann, R., Mischka, C., Burdo, N., Videjko, M.Y. & Müller, J. 2014a. High Precision Tripolye Settlement Plans, Demographic Estimations and Settlement Organization. *Journal of Neolithic Archaeology*, 16:63–95.

Rassmann, K., Videjko, M., Peters, D. & Gauss, R. 2014b. Großflächige geomagnetische Untersuchungen kupferzeitlicher Siedlung der Trypillia-Kultur. Aktuelle Prospektionen in Taljanky und Maydanetske (Ukraine) im Vergleich mit früheren Forschungen. In: W. Schier & F. Drasovean, eds. *The Neolithic and Eneolithic in Southeast Europe. New Approaches to Dating and Cultural Dynamics in the 6th to the 4th Millennium BC*. Rahden: Verlag Marie Leidorf, pp. 99–112.

Rice, P.M. 1987. *Pottery Analysis. A Sourcebook*. Chicago: University of Chicago Press.

Ryzhov, S.M. 1999. Keramika poselen trypilskoi kultury Bugo-Dniprovskogo mezhyrizhzhia yak istorychne dzerelo, *unpublished PhD Thesis*, Kyiv: Institute of Archaeology of the NASU. Рижов, С. М. 1999. Кераміка поселень трипільської культури Буго-Дніпровського межиріччя як історичне джерело (рукопис дис. канд. істор. наук). Київ: Інститут археології НАНУ.

Scharl, S. & Suhrbier, S. 2005. Ton, Steine, Knochen– Handwerk und Kunst der Vinča-Kultur. In: W. Schier, ed. *Katalog zur Sonderausstellung Masken–Menschen– Rituale. Alltag und Kult vor 7000 Jahren in der prähistorischen Siedlung von Uivar, Rumänien im Martin-von-Wagner-Museum der Universität Würzburg, 21. April – 10. Juli 2005*. Würzburg: Xpress, Würzburg, pp. 48–53.

Sîrbu, G.V. 2015. Late Eneolithic Pottery Kilns of the Prut-Dniester Interfluve (on the basis of materials from the Trinca-Izvorul lui Luca settlement). *Stratum Plus*, 2:171–80. Г. В. Сырбу 2015. Гончарные комплексы позднего энеолита Пруто-Днестровского межд уречья (по материалам поселения Тринка-Изворул луй Лука).

Tsvek, O.V. 2004. Goncharne vyrobnytstvo plemen trypilskoi kultury. In: M. Yu Videiko, ed. *Entsyklopediya trypilskoi tsyvilizatsii. Tom 1*. Kyiv: Ukrpoligrafmedia, pp. 273–99. Цвек, О. В. 2004. Гончарне виробництво племен Трипільської культури. В кн.: Відейко, М. Ю., ред. *Енциклопедія трипільської цивілізації, Том 1*. Київ: Укрполіграфмедіа: с. 273–99.

Videiko, M.Yu. 2004. Pro haracter ta obsiagy vyrobnytstva glynianogo posudu v trypilskyh protomistah. *Ukrainskyi keramologichnyj zhurnal*, 1:30–36. Відейко, М. Ю. 2004. Про характер та обсяги виробництва глиня ного посуду в трипільських протомістах. *Українсь кий керамологічний журнал* 1, Опішня: 30–6.

Videiko, M.Y., Chapman, J., Burdo, N.B., Gaydarska, B., Ţerna, S.V., Rud, V.S. & Kiosak, D.V. 2015a. Kompleksnye issledovaniya sooruzhenij, proizvodstvennyh kompleksov i ostatkov postroek na tripolskom poselenii u s. *Nebelevka. Stratum Plus*, 2:147–70. Видейко, М.Ю., Чэпмен, Дж., Бурдо, Н.Б., Гайдарска, Б., Церна, С., Рудь В. и Киосак, Д. 2015а. Комплексные исследования оборонительных сооружений, произв одственных комплексов и остатков построек на трипольском поселении у села Небелевка–Complex Investigations of Defensive Systems, Production Complexes and Remains of Constructions on the Tripolye Site near the Village of Nebelevka. *Stratum Plus*, 2:147–70.

Videiko, M.Yu., Müller, J., Burdo, N.B., Hofmann, R. & Cerna, S. 2015b. Doslidzhennya v tsentralnij chastyni Maidanetskogo. *Archeologiya*, 1:71–78. Відейко, М. Ю., Мюллер Й., Бурдо Н.Б., Хофманн Р. і Церна С. 2015. Дослідження у центральній частині Майданецького. *Археологія*, 1:71–78.

Willms, C. 1999. Neolithische Töpferöfen in Mittel- und Osteuropa. In: F.-R. Herrmann, ed. *Festschrift für Günter Smolla. Materialien zur Vor- und Frühgeschichte Hessens 8*. Wiesbaden: Landesamt für Denkmalpflege Hessen, pp. 739–49.

CHAPTER 14

From Domestic Households to Mega-Structures: Proto-Urbanism?

JOHANNES MÜLLER, ROBERT HOFMANN AND RENÉ OHLRAU

INTRODUCTION

During the last decades, the excavations of Trypillia structures at three mega-sites of the Uman region resulted in new information about question which have been intensely discussed during the last century; house architecture, household and house place organization, and the economic, political, and social constitution of household-units and mega-sites. With the new information available today, it is much easier to tackle many implications with respect to questions linked to notions of village life and, in the case of Trypillia C1 proto-urbanism.

For the political and social organization of a mega-site, both the level of the household organization, and the level of the interacting activities at the site-level are important. How is a typical Trypillian household in a mega-site organized, and which kind of architecture is used? Are house features as standardized as ascertained by the research? Are differences between domestic households within mega-sites still detectable? What is the relation between households and mega-structures? These questions are related to the main 'bigger' aspect of how it was possible for Chalcolithic communities to organize such population agglomerations.

In consequence, a model of the economic, political, and social organization of an idealized mega-structure, which integrates observations of material culture and architecture, is needed. From a methodological point of view, we would like to focus on the spatial distribution of material culture within the analysed structures.

Since new excavation techniques were applied, the recent excavations at Taljanky, Maidanetske, and Nebelivka, an evaluation of spatial relations, material culture, and structures at the household level has been made much easier than before (e.g. Müller *et al.*, in print). The applied documentation technique, which includes photogrammetry and the exact documentation of the spatial location of artefacts and samples, as well as the documentation of daub imprints and sherd-distributions from single pots, aids in the reconstruction of domestic features and the depositional processes within them (Müller *et al.*, in print).

Furthermore, with the new geomagnetic surveys we also gained some knowledge of the size and location of most unexcavated structures from Trypillian mega-sites (Rassmann *et al.*, 2014). Based on the combination of data from excavated features and non-excavated geophysical features, the application of theories and methods from present-day settlement planning aids in developing settlement models for Trypillia mega-sites. Built space and its configuration as a 'social medium' is a crucial element of this approach (Trebsche *et al.*, 2010). Thus, the main aim of the inquiries is to disentangle a social structure behind Trypillia socio-architectural principles.

From *ploschchadki* to household organization

In all geophysical plans of the mega-sites, the spatial link between the remains of burnt houses and pits is usually visible. Thus, the spatial definition of a 'house place' is possible in spite of the close proximity of houses in many cases. A house place usually consists of the house itself, represented first by the *ploschchadki* with the remains of walls, floors, and installations, second by an extraction pit (later with different functions), and third by an activity and waste zone in the direct vicinity. Within the two houses that were excavated by the Maidanetske team, an internal division into a first and second floor was visible, with household-installations and activities mainly on the second floor and storage purposes mainly on the first floor. To verify our model, the analyses of the spatial patterns within a house should be described.

The house, the pit, and the bench: reconstructing activities

In the 2013, Maidanetske campaign, excavation unit house place 44, was chosen for excavation; it was identified in the plan of the geomagnetic survey as

© European Association of Archaeologists 2016

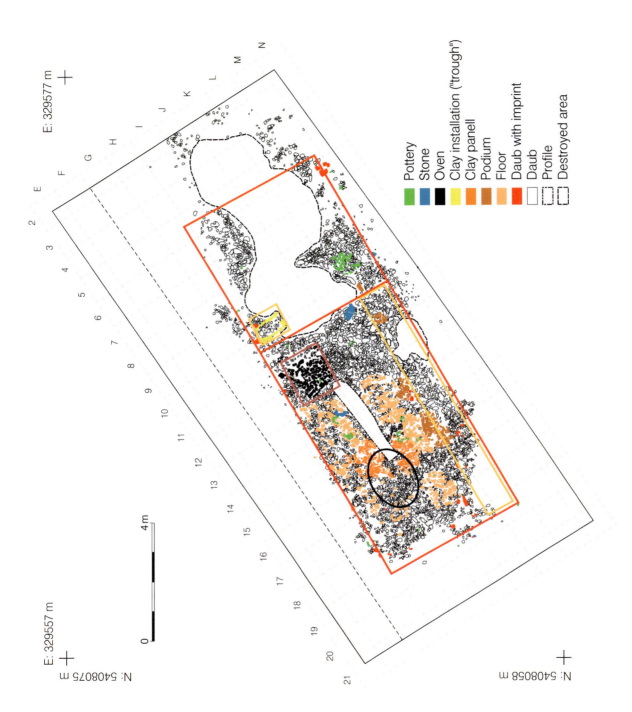

Figure 1. Maidanetske house 44 displays a typical ploschchadka with internal divisions into several features that are known from most domestic Trypillian C1 houses (cf. Chernovol, 2012). Source: R. Ohlrau/R. Hofmann/J. Müller/K. Winter, UFG Kiel.

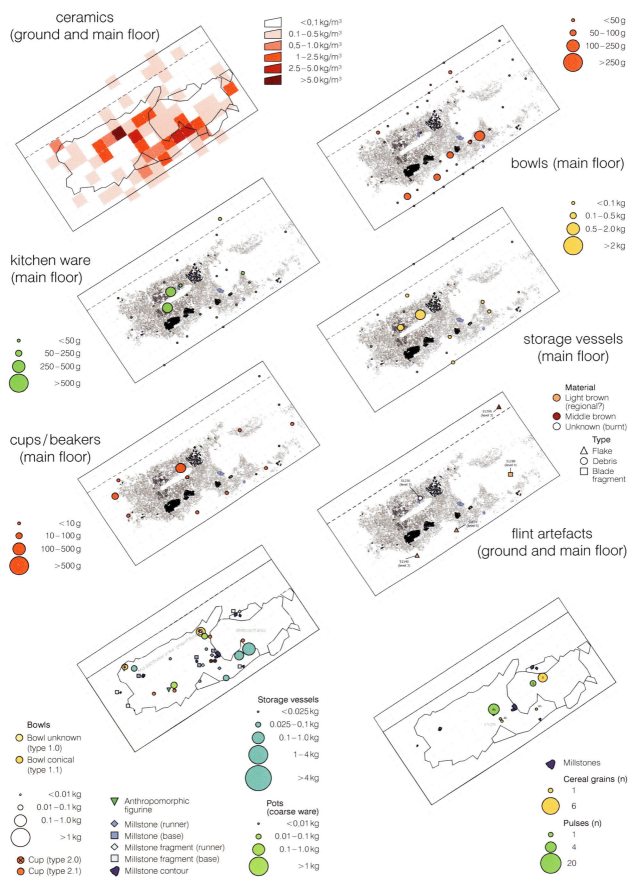

Figure 2. Artefact distributions on the ground floor, on the main floor, and in the vicinity of house 44 display different spatial patterns that aid in the reconstruction of activity areas within and around the house. Source: R. Hofmann/K. Winter, UFG Kiel.

being composed of a house and a pit that obviously belong together. The package of daub (*ploschchadka*) implies a maximal house size of 15.5 m × 5.0 m, but mapping the weight of daub pieces makes it plausible that the real size of the feature was originally 14.0 m × 5.0 m (Figure 1).

The *c.* 10 cm thick top layer with small pieces of daub (and nearly no organic intrusions) showed only a few wood imprints. Beneath this layer, the top of the floor surface, with smoothed horizontal daub pieces, became visible. The burnt floor layer consists of daub from a mineral-tempered pavement of 3–5 cm thickness and a 3–6.5 cm thick ground floor, with negative imprints of timber stakes at their base. Most of the further clay or other installations were constructed on top of the ground floor and beneath the upper daub layer. The ground floor itself lies on top of a loess soil with a conserved fA_1 horizon. The upper edge of the loess soil beneath the floor level is characterized by different artefacts (pots, querns) that were placed there. Beneath the conserved loess soil and the anthropogenically influenced loess soil, the sediment of an fBw-horizon is visible.

Accordingly, the burnt ground floor with the negative impressions of split boards (*Spaltholzbohlenabdrücke*) was a second floor on top of an empty space with areas for storage. When the house burnt down, the material from the top floor walls etcetera was also spread over parts of the occupation layer of the activity zone that is situated beside the house.

The house itself has a northeast–southwest orientation. Since the daub package displayed no perforations or irregularities at its edges, which usually occurs if daub falls into postholes, no posts are reconstructed for the walls (Figure 1). The greater thickness of the daub package along the central axis of the house and its decreasing thickness towards the borders imply that the daub which was situated on top represents parts of the burnt roof or an inserted ceiling, in which clay was obviously one component as a building material.

The top floor ('second floor') of the house was the main floor for living. This floor was constructed from horizontal split timber boards (*Spaltbohlen*) that were oriented axial to the house and formed the bottom of the ceiling, visible in negative imprints. A chuff-tempered clay screed was distributed on top of the timber boards, and again on top of a further mineral-tempered clay screed (together *c.* 15 cm thick), which was then smoothed. The width of the timber imprints varied between 1 and 15 cm, with a mean of about 6.75 cm. Thus, we could reconstruct a ceiling of *c.* 15 cm thick horizontal timber boards that were overlaid by about 10 cm of clay-like floor.

Different features existed upon this floor. In the much-destroyed eastern part of the house, a 'trough' was discovered; it was not free-standing, rather its southwest part was associated with the former partition wall that can also be reconstructed next to the northwest end of the podium. Thus, the top floor was divided into an entrance room (5 × 5 m) and the main 'residential' room (9 × 5 m), very similar to what is known for houses in Taljanky, for example.

In the residential room, four installations were placed directly on top of the floor (Figure 1):

1. On the southeastern longitudinal side, the remains of a clay construction with rounded long edges and a smoothed surface was detected, built of yellowish, crumbly clay (6.3 m × 1.4 m × 0.2 m); the base showed negative imprints along the axial orientation of the house. This demonstrates that the construction was built from both timber and clay. In other contexts, this type of installation is usually labelled a 'podium'/bench for displaying or storing items; the artefact distribution supports such an interpretation.
2. An oval areal of 2.15 × 1.5 m was covered with thin, small broken daub fragments (1 cm thick) in several layers. Its spatial position in the centre of the residential room makes it probable that we are dealing here with a kind of installation which is labelled as the 'altar' in other cases (Chernovol, 2012).
3. In the northern corner near the partition wall (quadrant H–I/11–12), massive burnt daub pieces formed a square construction (1.3 × 1.3 m): the remains of the 'fireplace'.
4. Negative impressions of a former vertical wooden pillar near the partition wall might be associated with the main room, as part of its entrance construction.

In the entrance room, a U-shaped, *c.* 0.6 m wide and 0.9 m long construction at the northeastern wall of the house, linked to the partition wall, consisted of a small rounded wall 10–15 m wide and at least 10 cm high, that was built from heavily chuff-tempered clay and constructed in different consecutive layers. Ukrainian Trypillia archaeologists usually identify such a construction as a trough (Chernovol, 2012). On the ground floor, no further installation was found but ceramics and querns imply the use of this area for storage purposes.

In consequence, house 44 displays a construction and installations which are similar to Trypillian houses that have long been known (cp. Chernovol, 2008; Chernovol, 2012). House 44 is a two-storeyed, rectangular house with two rooms on the top floor and an activity zone in the surrounding of the house, forming the house place. The distribution of artefacts within and around the house aids in the identification of household patterns of household production and consumption (Figure 2).

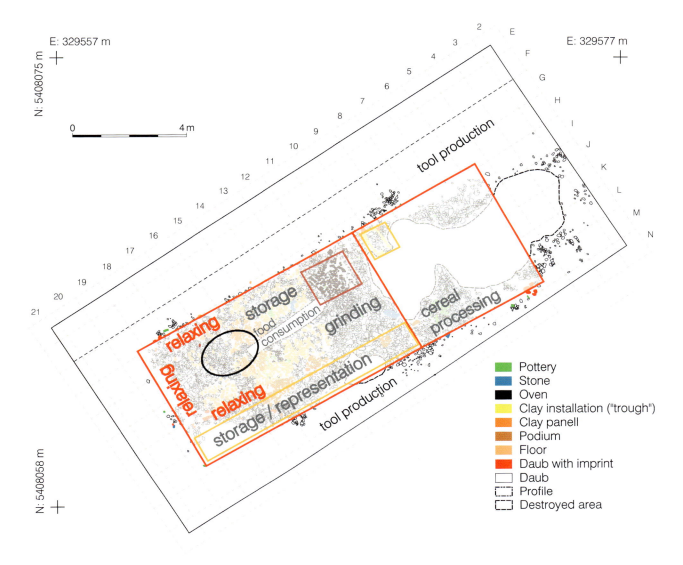

Figure 3. Maidanetske house 44 with reconstructed activity areas. Source: R. Hofmann/J. Müller/K. Winter, UFG Kiel.

The artefacts as proxies for activities

Approximately 1900 artefacts are associated with house 44. They are distributed across the layers of the ground floor, the first floor, and the surrounding activity zone of the house. Our interest is focused on the spatial differences in the distribution of different artefact categories between and within the three spatial units; to identify functional differences within the house and between internal and external activities. This issue is related to the taphonomy of artefact distribution that includes depositional processes before, during, and after the use of the house. Since no signs of later activities were observed within the house place, the moment of 'burning', and therefore the deliberate destruction of the house, is associated with the 'closing' of the inventory. The location of the artefacts on the ground and first floor of the house gives the impression of their having not been moved, and their association with the last household activities, or at least the final storage of tools on the ground floor. Hence, artefacts from the surrounding zone might also reflect 'secondary' waste that can be associated with earlier activities at the site, or just waste contemporary with the house occupation. Since radiometric dates, as well as typo-chronological considerations, point to a short house duration (less than one-hundred years? See Müller *et al.*, 2015; Müller *et al.*, in print; Brandtstätter, in print), all artefacts could be seen as one single 'house inventory'.

In principle, the house inventory displays a huge amount of pottery; at least fifty pots can be reconstructed (Müller *et al.*, in print). In contrast, the almost complete lack of flint tools is also known from other Trypillia C1/C2 sites, but is still surprising (e.g. Kruts *et al.*, 2001: 63–64). The quantity of millstones and other ground stone tools might be related to economic differences between the households (see below). The small number of bone tools and bones, as well as archaeozoological and archaeobotanical macro-remains, is probably due to preservation conditions (high temperature fire).

In general, artefacts were concentrated in the house, while their number in the surrounding area is quite small. Ceramics are distributed with a density of up to 5 kg/m³ in the central part of the house but less than 0.5 kg/m³ in the surrounding activity zone (Figure 2). Animal bones display the opposite distribution pattern but this might be due to the taphonomic influences of the house fire. This pattern might alternatively reflect the behaviour of keeping the internal house areas clear of consumption waste. On the whole, the spatial distribution of artefact categories clearly differs within the top floor, the ground floor, and also between both. Qualitative differences in artefact distributions are also recognizable between the house and the surrounding open space (Figure 2).

Striking distribution patterns have been observed for the first floor and the surrounding activity zone (Figure 2): Bowls are concentrated within the house (southeastern corner of the entrance room and northeastern area of the main room on the podium) and outside the house alongside the two longitudinal walls, mainly in front of the southeastern wall. Beakers and goblets are additionally distributed at the outer edge of the southeastern longitude, but also at the southwestern latitudinal wall. A concentration is visible between the fire place and the 'altar' of the main room. Tableware is concentrated in the main room between the 'altar' and the fire place as well as between the 'altar' and the podium. Storage vessels display a quite similar spatial distribution, with a concentration between the fire place and the 'altar', but in this case also including the direct vicinity of the 'altar'.

Two ceramic balls are distributed in the entrance room, two figurines possibly come from the northeastern and central part of the podium in the main room, one spindle whorl was found outside the house, in front of the southeastern longitude wall. Querns are distributed in the southwestern corner of the entrance room and in the main room between the fireplace and the 'altar'. The few flint artefacts are distributed outside the house except for one burnt object from near the fireplace. The few remains of cereal grains, pulses, and threshing remains are distributed all over the house.

We could use these distribution patterns to reconstruct the spatial order of production and consumption in the upper floor and the surroundings of house 44, as long as we take possible taphonomic processes into consideration. Most of the artefacts were found *in situ* (e.g. the pots still standing on their base). For example, the distribution of cups and storage vessels at and outside the southeastern wall of the house is obvious. They fell into this position during the collapse of the wall, probably hanging on the inner wall or placed on the podium beforehand.

The spatial division in the main room indicates production, distribution, and consumption activities, which we can associate with the artefact categories. Besides the location of vessels, figurines, and other items for storage or representation in the area and probably on the podium along the southeastern wall, the division of the remaining space is evident; an area of many activities to the East of the 'altar' and an area West of this without signs of activities (Figure 3–4). Thus, space for cereal processing, food consumption, but also for storage facilities, existed between the fireplace and the altar, while the southwestern part of the main room was probably used for relaxing (including

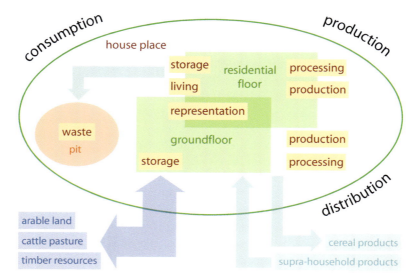

Figure 4. Scheme of the house place organisation. Source: J. Müller/K. Winter, UFG Kiel.

sleeping). Due to the recent disturbance, the reconstruction of activities in the entrance room is not possible; however, outside the house the production of flint tools and the deposition of some waste (animal bones) obviously took place.

On the ground floor, the artefact distribution was completely different (Figure 2). The spatial distributions of bowls, kitchen-ware, and storage vessels are the opposite of their spatial distribution pattern on the top floor. In addition, cups and goblets that were distributed on the top floor mainly at the borders of the house were distributed beneath the inner part of the ceiling on the ground floor. Querns, which show at least a similar distribution pattern to those on the top floor, are nevertheless distributed in a special way on the ground floor: they were found alone or in pairs at the four locations; at the last three locations, a base and a runner were deposited together. Besides these obvious distribution patterns, the lower part of a figurine and some botanical macro-remains should also be mentioned, of which twenty peas were found in the direct vicinity of a group of querns. Even if evidence is still weak and the artificial modern disturbance in the northeastern area of the house does not really allow for clear conclusions, the interpretation of the ground floor as storage facilities–both for items in storage vessels and for tools like querns–might be the most plausible interpretation of the artefact distribution.

An empty pit and the house vicinity

A pit was excavated 9 m southwest of the southwestern gable side of house 44 (diameter of 4.6 m; depth 1.5 m with a basal diameter of 1.5 m). The fill was a homogenous black-brown sediment without daub. At least 9.2 m^3 soil was extracted during the Chalcolithic; due to erosional processes, we can reckon with 10 m^2. In comparison with the other excavated pits and features, the artefact density of this pit was very low. The few finds, including animal bones and daub, were concentrated at the base and near the borders of the pit. The two pots are very much reduced to small pieces. If at all identifiable, they belong to a biconical vessel and a bowl. Accordingly, there is a high probability that pit 52 existed contemporarily with house 44. It possibly originated as an extraction pit for building purposes. In the vicinity of both the house and the pit mainly flint flakes and animal bones were found.

Consequences

Based on the distribution patterns of artefacts and macro-remains, the excavated features from house place 44, especially the reconstruction of the activities within house 44, underline a clearly organized spatial order for activities that relate to subsistence. Obviously, on the ground floor of the house different millstones were stored and probably removed only occasionally for processing. Different sizes of the querns imply their possible use for different plant species, as documented from ethnographic examples (e.g. Schön & Holter, 1988). While the dehusking and winnowing of cereals took place in the entrance room or outside the house, grinding took place in the residential room on the first floor near the fire place, and perhaps also in one corner of the entrance room. Consumption and storing can also be associated with the areas that are identified for that purpose by different vessel categories: mainly in the centre of the residential room on the second floor.

As both animal bones and the few hints for the use of secondary products (spindle whorls) are mainly distributed around the house, it is probable that processing and production activities related to animals took place in the activity zone of the house place. It is not clear where animals were kept and arable land was located. The most probable model would imply the keeping of stock near the houses by the household communities (Kruts et al., 2001: 79 ff.), but keeping them all in the central free space at Maidanetske could also be an option. Additionally, arable land is usually linked to the direct surroundings of the settlement, but that also could have been possible within the central area. The high percentage of storage vessels and the keeping of cattle by household 44, for example, indicate an economy that is based on longer planning and even the accumulation of subsistence goods.

Indications for differences between households (see below) would suggest that Maidanetske house 44 had a household economy that was engaged predominantly in primary subsistence, while other (larger) houses were mainly engaged in secondary subsistence activities or even ritual economies.

The excavation of house 44 left no doubt that the house was used for domestic purposes and the daily activities of a household community. The separation into a ground floor (mainly for storing equipment and special resources) and a second floor (for food processing and consumption, perhaps also house rituals) indicates a clear spatial pattern of activities. In the direct vicinity of the house, tool production also took place. The spatial patterning of the installations reflects patterns which are also visible in house models like the one from Sushkivka (Uman district, Cherkasy oblast), which was excavated in 1916 by V. Ye. Kozlovska (Ciuk, 2008: 180); especially the podium to the right side of the entrance in the main room, the fireplace to the left and the altar in the centre is quite similar to the model from Sushkivka. Both the ceramic types and the other tools reflect a special distribution that could be linked to daily activities. Related to this is the inventory of the pit 52; the waste management seems to be clear.

Domestic Houses: Differences in Size and Function?

While the difference between mega-structures and 'normal' houses has been underlined in different inquiries, differences between domestic houses were also described. A 'high level of standardization' was detected (Chernovol, 2012: 200). Besides the clear design of settlement planning, the similarity of different house categories implies a heavily structured society. Three categories of domestic houses were differentiated; first, the standard house with an oven, altar and podium; second, a type of house with a household annex attached to the short side of the house; and third, a group of houses which were 'over-equipped' (*Überausstattung*) especially in terms of ritual installations like altars, etc. Besides these differences, pointing to a certain degree of difference in household activities of the households that might be additional to their involvement in subsistence economy, differences in some of the tools for economic activities should also be estimated.

With respect to the quantities of millstones and loom-weights within the house places, different tendencies were observed e.g. for Taljanky houses (Figure 5). Despite dealing with a small amount of data, a tendency seems to be clear: the smaller a house, the more millstones are found there–the bigger a house, the fewer of these items were found. Since especially houses with smaller floor sizes yield the highest number of millstones, and the steepest decrease in their quantity is visible for houses bigger than 60 m², a qualitative 'cut-off point' is obviously reached. Houses between 60 and 75 m² present a very small number of millstones but could contain a huge number of loom weights, which are more or less absent in smaller houses. Houses that are larger than 75 m² do not primarily contain such objects as millstone or loom-weights.

These differences in two examples of processing, in one case related to primary products, in the other to secondary products, are of interest because until now the evidence for typological differences in the ceramic design of neighbouring households points to a further pattern of household links: in general, the closer houses stand together in the house-rings, the more identical their ornamentation systems are; the farther

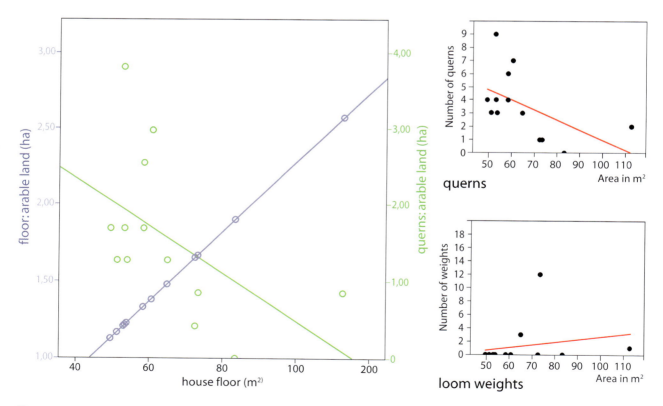

Figure 5. Differences in the reconstructed demand on arable land, using the floor size of houses in Taljanky for population estimations, and the reconstructed use of arable land using the number of millstones per house as a proxy for the amount of cereal processing (cf. Müller et al., in print). The number of millstones and loom-weights implies a division into three categories of houses: with many millstones, with millstones and loom-weights, and without both. Source: J. Müller/K. Winter, UFG Kiel.

apart they are, the more different their decoration is (Figure 6). Besides this general trend, interrelations between house groups are also visible. In spite of the fact that, until now, such spatial-typological analyses were only possible for a southeastern ring of the Maidanetske settlement (Tkachuk & Melnik, 2005), the pattern is independent of house size. Translated into the communication within the settlement, this indicates an open society in which peaceful relations with neighbours make an exchange of design systems, and perhaps also of other goods, possible. In principle, there seems to be no restriction in the communication of different house categories.

Beyond the house place level, houses are combined in small clusters at all mega-sites. To ensure a comparability between different mega-sites, a standardized methodology was developed for determinations of such house clusters (Ohlrau, 2015). Via reduction of plotted buildings to edges and network analysis (minimum spanning tree), it is possible to determine standard distances of buildings per settlement. Here, half of the first quartile of house distances (5.7 m) is

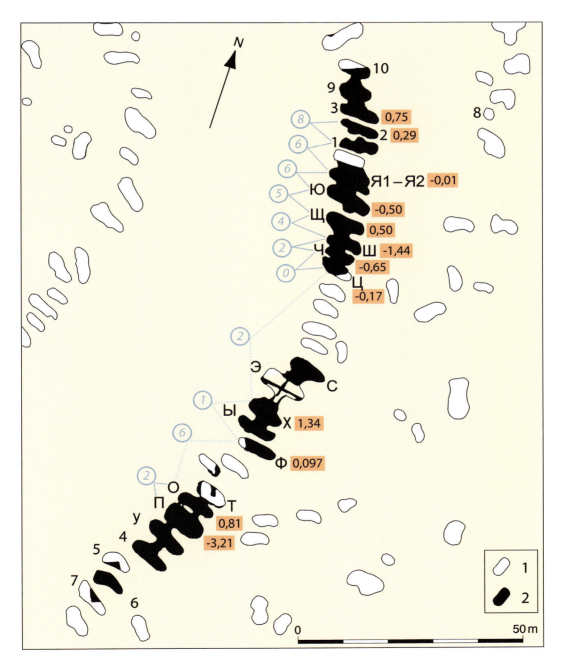

Figure 6. *The typological dissimilarities and similarities between houses in the southeastern house-ring of Maidanetske are expressed in the amount of shared ornamentation types and in the eigenvector value of the first eigenvector of a correspondence analyses on pottery decoration (Brandtstätter, in print; Tkachuk & Melnik, 2005). Source: K. Winter, UFG Kiel.*

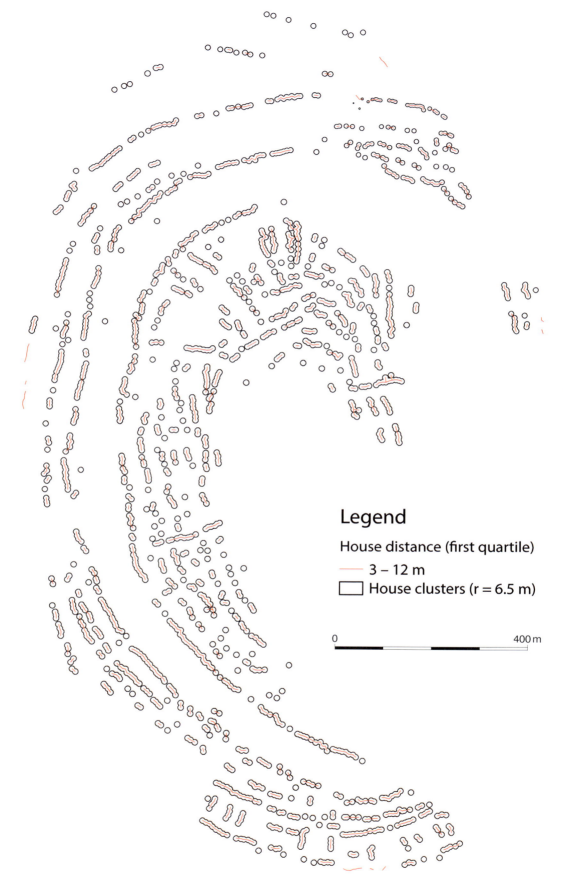

Figure 7. The reconstruction of house clusters by the average distance between neighbouring houses. Source: R. Ohlrau, UFG Kiel.

used to produce clusters by means of intersecting buffers (Figure 7). As a result, Maidanetske can be divided into 533 clusters with 2–41 (with a median of five) buildings per group (Table 1). Mainly neighbouring houses in the house-rings form groups which average five to six houses (Figure 7). While this pattern is not necessarily normative (in contrast to the single house layouts), the impression is of a link to a kind of organizational level that could not be more closely identified yet. In any case, the flow of typological similarities does not indicate any clear division between the house clusters in the southeastern part of the Maidanetske mega-site.

We can observe on the one hand differences between the contribution of different sized domestic houses to subsistence production and secondary products, and on the other hand the open relationships within at least one ring at Maidanetske, which displays the different attitudes of the political organization of the households. The role of the mega-structures remains in clear contrast to such a pattern for 'domestic houses'.

MEGA-STRUCTURES IN PUBLIC SPACE?

Until recently, only one mega-structure was excavated; in Nebelivka the Ukrainian–British team managed to uncover one whole mega-structure (Chapman *et al.*, 2014). Besides differences in the interpretation of the structure within the team (roofed/not roofed; temple/bakery), the difference to the previously described domestic houses is obvious: not only in respect to size and architecture, but also in respect to the artefact assemblage recovered. For example, golden objects are not known in any domestic Trypillian house until now, but occur in the Nebelivka mega-structure. While our knowledge about mega-structures remains very weak because of the lack of excavations, we cannot discuss their character in an adequate manner. Instead, a spatial analysis of mega-structures within the overall settlement plan should be our main point of departure, as their locations show clear differences to domestic house locations.

In Maidanetske, the design of the settlement depicts a clear pattern that combines the open house-rings, the main ring, radial open track ways, and the central area of the site. The distribution of mega-structures in the geomagnetic survey shows their special localization: we find them both in longitude orientation in the rings, especially the main ring of the site, and in 'blocking' radial tracks that lead into the centre of the site. Even if the geophysically detected size of the eight observed Maidanetske mega-structures varies, the contrast to other houses is visible.

A view-shed analysis of Maidanetske displays areas that are more visible than others (Figure 8). In this case, we would like to define 'public' areas as those which are most visible. Except for the central space, which is not taken into account here, the mega-structures of Maidanetske are placed in the most public areas of the mega-site. Therefore, a political meaning can be reconstructed for these foci, with general tasks of a supra-household political institution, even when their chronology is not yet clear. Differences, for example, in the numbers of pits associated with the mega-structures, might indicate individual differences which could be interpreted as reflecting the autonomy of possible quarters, which we might associate with mega-structures.

In general, mega-structures can be recognized at a regular distance from each other within the inner ring of Maidanetske. Despite this, it is challenging to group neighbouring houses as belonging to the nearest mega-structure. Even if it is difficult to identify clear boundaries between such house clusters (except perhaps those separated by radial track ways or small longitudinal depressions), a clustering of neighbouring domestic houses according to the shortest distances to a nearby mega-structure is plausible.

In principle, by applying the method of shortest distances to nearest features, in this case mega-structures, catchment areas can be calculated (Table 2). Except for two artificially oversized areas due to missing survey data, a regular distribution of features in 'districts' of about 9 ha is visible. Categorizing the different types of features in hierarchical order, there are on average 185 house places (D) in sixty-six clusters (C). The next category of larger-than-average buildings of 150–300 m² (B1) is accompanied in some cases by probable kilns (B2), forming a kind of economic unit. They are best recognized in the central western part of the site. Mega-structures were classified as organizing units (A). Taking into account the average size of the districts, the standard distance of mega-structures and the estimated overall size of built space at Maidanetske (175 ha), a total of nineteen to twenty districts seems plausible (Figure 9). In comparison to Nebelivka, this estimation seems to fit quite well.

Except for the mega-structures that are placed across the radial tracks, all mega-structures are found along the main public 'street' of the village. Obviously,

Table 1. Statistics for buildings in the clusters at Maidanetske (Ohlrau, 2015)

Statistic value	Maidanetske
n	533
Minimum	2
Maximum	41
Mean	7
Standard deviation	5.75
Median	5

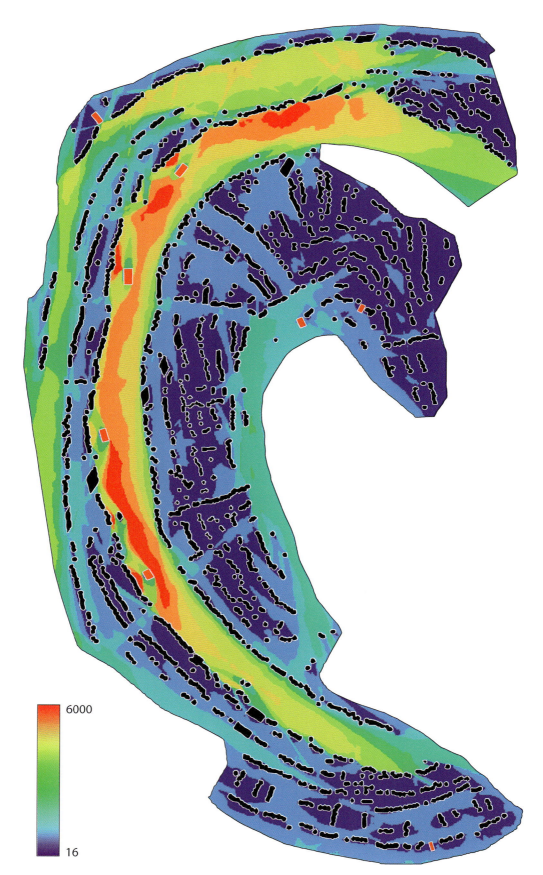

Figure 8. View-shed analysis of the Y-space at Maidanetske. The visibility increases from blue to red (number of cell connectivity). Mega-structures are mainly placed in the 'public' space or blocking radial accesses to the central space. Source: R. Ohlrau, K. Winter, UFG Kiel.

Table 2. Statistics on mega-structure areas in relation to house groups and kilns. The division into four spatial classes A–D represents one of the possible models for the organization of Maidanetske (Ohlrau, 2015)

	Mega-structures (A)	Houses (D)	Clusters (C)	Economic units (B1)	Kilns (B2)
n	8	1906	533	26	6
Minimum	5.9 ha	64	21	0	0
Maximum	25.9 ha	386	141	4	2
Mean	11.8 ha	212	75	1	0.7
Stand. dev	7.08 ha	94.39	66.51	1.22	0.86
Median	8.9 ha	185	66	1	0

the spatial structure links several parts of the house-rings at a different organization level, with mega-structures playing a central role. Again, a different meaning for spatial structuring with a completely different appearance is visible; not the Neighbourhood within the house-rings, but a political institution beyond Neighbourhood principles, associated with the mega-structures, implies a further political level of decision-making.

Craftsmanship and Specialization

Interestingly, a distribution pattern is observable for pottery kilns that is similar to that of the mega-structures, if our interpretation of the geophysical values is correct: kilns are distributed all over the settlement, but because of their small number they could easily be associated with the reconstructed house clusters around the mega-structures. In principle, the observation that pottery kilns are distributed in association with the quarters and do not cluster in one part of the settlement, might indicate an organization of specialization that is not bound to the household level but organized at the level of quarters. Future research regarding producion rates of these kilns and comparisons with household demands for pots will enlight the question if the demand of one quarter could be satisfied by one kiln (see Korvin-Piotrovskiy *et al.*, 2016). In consequence, besides production and processing of primary and secondary products (and tools, for example) in the households, a further class of production probably took place at the supra-household level of the quarters. The issue of kilns and specialized potters might be only the top of an as yet undiscovered bundle of supra-household production and managing processes.

Mega-Sites and Limits of Settlement Growth

To derive a social interpretation of the presented spatial model for Maidanetske, social network theory can be applied. In his influential article, Johnson (1982) describes a communication theory of decision performances and ideal group sizes. He predicted that with increasing group size the communications load increases exponentially, leading to rising social stress, conflict potential, and splitting of groups. This model of scalar stress would, in theory, allow infinite levels of human organization, by maintaining an ideal of 6 ± 2 decision makers per group. A maximal level of communications load was estimated at between fifteen and twenty individual per group (Johnson, 1982: 393).

Taking into account categories A–D (Table 2) for the idealized mega-site organizational model, it is possible to apply calculations of scalar stress. To do so, a hierarchy for these categories is assumed. Beginning at the lowest organizational level, the household (D); given a robust estimation of five individuals, ranging from three to twelve, an ideal decision group according to Johnsons model seems plausible. The category (C) of various house clusters also fits in the ideal grouping, with a ratio of 5:1, assuming one decision maker per household. The following organizational levels of economic units (B) to house clusters (ratio 15:1) and economic units to exceptional buildings (A) (ratio 3:1) depict a decreasing decision performance with increasing organizational levels, leading to Johnson's assumed limit of up to twenty exceptional buildings per mega-site (Figure 10).

If we accept this model, it has strong implications for the organizational limits Trypillian inhabitants were facing when building the mega-sites. It seems that, in the case of Maidanetske with its very high building density, we have a convincing example for a society living at the edge of their possibilities in respect to decision performance.

Mega-Site Organization and Proto-Urbanism

Both the clear site-wide planning of Maidanetske, for example, and the spatial distribution of mega-

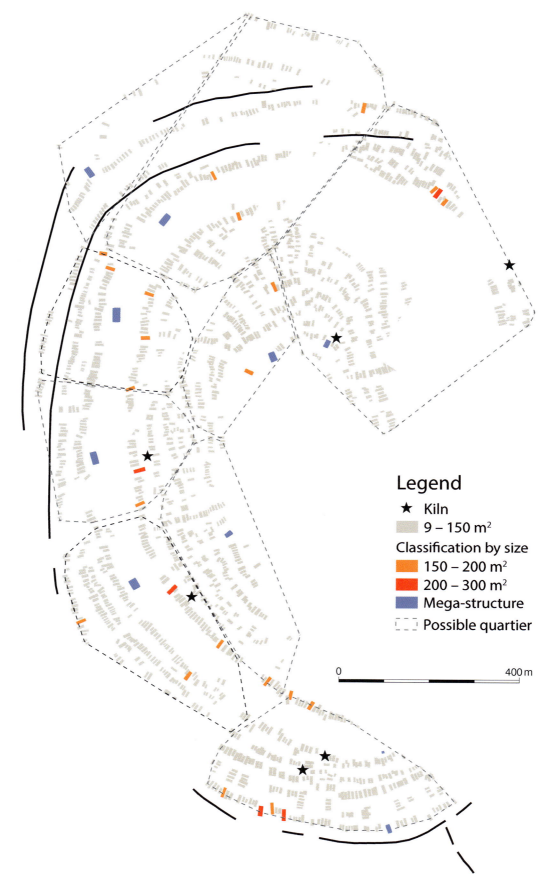

Figure 9. Reconstruction of quarters in Maidanetske by mapping nearest distances of houses to mega-structures. Clusters of kilns are also associated with these quarters. Source: R. Ohlrau, K. Winter, UFG Kiel.

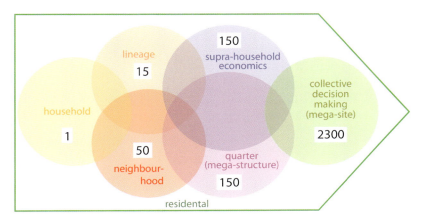

Figure 10. The model of decision-making processes in a mega-site. The numbers indicate estimated households per category. Source: *J. Müller/K. Winter, UFG Kiel.*

structures and kilns, indicate that we are dealing with constitutionalized political institutions at different spatial and demographic levels, which managed both the economic and social reproduction of the society. While domestic houses are already organized in a normative way, house clusters and quarters depict further levels of probable decision-making institutions within the settlement. Even if no potter quarters exist, the overall demand for fine wares is satisfied by a potter's full-time or part-time specialization, which is bound to the political organization of the quarters.

Since the artefact distributions in the houses indicate that most of the houses are engaged in agricultural subsistence activities, the pure population size cannot be compared with the European form of urbanism that is defined by a developed specialization of many craftspeople and traders within the towns and cities, and the contrast between urban centres and the countryside. Neither in Nebelivka nor in Taljanky or Maidanetske did a sufficient number of contemporary small sites in the 'countryside' exist (Müller *et al.*, in print).

Nevertheless, both the demographic size of the mega-sites and the normative organization are important arguments for talking about urbanism. As the settlements are not very stable, and existed for less than 150 years, the term proto-urbanism might be adequate.

Proto-urbanism

Another argument for a label proto-urbanism is the complicated system of rules and networks at different social levels, which we were able to reconstruct by bringing together the still mosaic-like state of evidence: (1) the household level, with open communication between neighbours and the whole settlement, linking together neighbouring households but not separating them from others (the peaceful neighbourhood principle); (2) the specialization between households at an economic level in respect to their integration in processing primary and secondary products; (3) household clusters of five houses on average, which link households spatially for reasons unknown until now (the residential house-ring principle [of generational contracts/lineages?]); (4) the economic and political linkage of households to quarters, represented by mega-structures as the focal point and by supra-household economic specializations (the mega-structure principle); (5) the overall settlement, which needs a political institution to direct the spatial planning of the whole site and perhaps combined economic activities (the mega-site principle). Consequently, an individual in a mega-site was bound in at least five identities, which operated at different spatial and non-spatial levels of the site.

Triggers of proto-urbanism and agglo-control

While most scholars link the appearance of mega-sites in a border region between forest steppe and steppe with the advantages that larger groups accumulate in respect to defence purposes, we would like to stress a different factor. With the increase in specialization, visible in the appearance of sophisticated kilns, the delivery and knowledge about special demands is much easier to satisfy if the consumers settle as close together as possible. While such an agglomeration is of advantage for craft specialization, with regard to subsistence economy distances to arable land and timber sources increases. In this respect, the first archaeological detection of new sledge models indicates changes in the transportation system that could overcome these disadvantages, especially in a forest steppe (with a canopy-like distribution of trees) or even a steppe. In conclusion, the creation of mega-sites at a time when the system of transportation was reducing the time required to reach farther land is not accidental, but was made possible by such a development. Furthermore, societal control of large human groups is much easier under such conditions: the described system of overlapping political institutions is a new form of an agglomerated organization and control system in agrarian societies ('agglo-control'). Such a new system also enabled the inhabitants of a mega-site to take decisions about the abandonment of a huge settlement–like they did.

REFERENCES

Brandtstätter, L. in print. Die Keramik aus Maidanetske im Tripolje-Zusammenhang. *Journal of Neolithic Archaeology*.

Chapman, J., Videiko, M., Gaydarska, B., Burdo, N. & Hale, D. 2014. Architectural Differentiation on a Trypillia Mega-Site: Preliminary Report on the Excavation of a Mega-Structure at Nebelivka, Ukraine. *Journal of Neolithic Archaeology*, 16:135–57.

Chernovol, D. 2008. Interior of the Tripolian House. In: A. Korvin-Piotrovskiy & F. Menotti, eds. *Tripolye Culture in Unkraine: The Giant Settlement of Talianki*. Kiew: Academy of Science Ukraine, pp. 177–91.

Chernovol, D. 2012. Houses of the Tomashovskaya Local Group. In: F. Menotti & A. Korvin-Piotrovskiy, eds. *The Tripolye Culture Giant-Settlements in Ukraine*. Oxford: Oxbow Books, pp. 182–209.

Ciuk, K. 2008. *Mysteries of Ancient Ukraine: The Remarkable Trypilian Culture, 5400–2700 BC*. Toronto: Royal Ontario Museum.

Johnson, G. 1982. Organizational Structure and Scalar Stress. In: C. Renfrew, M. Rowlands & B. A. Segraves, eds. *Theory and Explanation in Archaeology*. New York: Academic Press, pp. 389–421.

Korvin-Piotrovskiy, A. G., Hofmann, R., Rassmann, K., Videiko, M. Y. & Brandtstätter, L. 2016. Pottery Kilns in Trypillian settlements. Tracing the division of labour and the social organisation of Copper Age communities. In: J. Müller, K. Rassmann & M. Videiko, eds. *Trypillia Mega-Sites and European Prehistory: 4100–3400 BCE*. London and New York: Routledge, pp. 221–252.

Kruts, V.A., Korvin-Piotrovskiy, A.G. & Rizhov, S.N. 2001. *Talianki–Settlement-Giant of the Tripolian Culture. Investigations in 2001*. Kiew: Institute of archaeology of NASU.

Müller, J., Hofmann, R., Kirleis, W., Ohlrau, R., Brandtstätter, L., Dal Corso, M., Out, V., Rassmann, K. & Videko, M. in print. *Maidanetske 2013. New excavations at a Trypillia megasite. Studien zur Archäologie in Ostmitteleuropa*. Bonn: Habelt.

Ohlrau, R. 2015. Trypillian mega-sites: Geomagnetische Prospektion und architektursoziologische Perspektiven. *Journal of Neolithic Archaeology*, 17: 17–99 [doi: http://dx.doi.org/10.12766/jna.v17i0.116].

Rassmann, K., Ohlrau, R., Hofmann, R., Mischka, C., Burdo, N., Videjko, M.Y. & Müller, J. 2014. High Precision Tripolye Settlement Plans, Demographic Estimations and Settlement Organization. *Journal of Neolithic Archaeology*, 16:96–134.

Schön, W. & Holter, U. 1988, Zum Gebrauch von Mahl- und Schleifsteinen in der Ostsahara. *Archäologische Informationen* 11, 1988, 156–60.

Tkachuk, T. & Melnik, J. 2005. *Semiotycnyj analiz Trypilsko-Kukutenskich znakovych system (Malowanij Posud)*. Vinnytsia: Nova Knyha.

Trebsche, P., Müller-Scheeßel, N. & Reinhold, S. eds. 2010. *Der gebaute Raum. Bausteine einer Architektursoziologie vormoderner Gesellschaften. Tübinger Archäologische Taschenbücher 7*. Münster: Waxmann.

CHAPTER 15

Small is Beautiful: A Democratic Perspective?

ALEKSANDR DIACHENKO

INTRODUCTION

How many people could list five classic period small villages near Tikal? Meanwhile, huge sites and monumental structures–the objects of tourist attraction and endless pseudo-scientific narratives–are well known to almost everyone. For different reasons, many archaeologists also choose to work on the 'mega'; preferring examination of 'increase' and 'formation' over analysis of 'decline' and 'collapse'. The corresponding trend in studies of the Trypillia giant-settlements was noted by Anthony, who recognized a set of contradictions among suggested suppositions for the formation and decline of these mega-sites (Anthony, 2013: 1235; also see the recent overview of the ongoing debates in Chapman et al., 2014). Hence, the purpose of this chapter is the revisal of imbalance in the 'huge'–'small' and 'formation'–'collapse' studies. The chapter targets three related issues regarding the large Trypillia settlements between the Southern Buh and the Dnipro. These are as follows.

First, recent case studies showed that, despite the crises, socio-political changes, and alteration of landscapes, societies mostly did not collapse in an apocalyptical sense, because of human resilience and ecological vulnerability (McAnany & Yoffee, 2010: 5–6). Thus, what is the particular case for the Trypillia giant-settlements–collapse, decline, or transformation?

Second, the issue of the collapse/decline/transformation of the mega-sites could be scaled to different spatio-chronological tiers. Should it be discussed as a general phenomenon or a set of individual declines/collapses/transformations? Trypillia is no longer recognized as a unified socio-cultural group. Classifications that were developed for the territory between the Southern Buh and the Dnipro include sites of the Eastern Trypillia culture (ETC) and the Western Trypillia culture (WTC); both subdivided into lines of development, local groups, or variations and types of settlements (e.g. Tsvek, 2006; Ryzhov, 2007, 2012). Thus, was the collapse/decline/transformation of the mega-sites belonging to different Trypillia units also different?

Finally, suggested social complexity of Trypillia populations during the mega-sites period is, to some extent, based on the observed settlement hierarchy (Kruts, 1989, 2012a; Videiko, 2002b, 2013; Diachenko, 2012; cf. Ohlrau, 2014). Does it mean that collapse/decline/transformation of the large settlements led to some other forms of social organization and a democratic perspective must dominate the related reconstructions?

Surely, the spatio-temporal framework of this study should be discussed prior to considering the listed issues. Definitions of 'small' and 'large' settlements have to be given as well.

THE GENERAL SPATIO-TEMPORAL FRAMEWORK OF THIS STUDY

The significant size increase of Cucuteni–Trypillian sites started in Late Trypillia BI–Trypillia BI-II period and ended up in Trypillia CII/1 (Videiko, 2013: 98–106, figure 68, tables 1–4). The ETC settlement of Onopriivka is the largest known Trypillia BI site, while the WTC Vilkhovets 1 is the largest known Trypillia CII/1 site (Figures 1 and 2). It is noteworthy that both of these settlements are located in the Southern Buh and Dnipro interfluve; the eastern periphery of the Cucuteni–Trypillia cultural complex (CTCC).

Since most of radiocarbon dates that were obtained for the Trypillia BI-II sites are overlapped by the intervals of dates for the Trypillia BII settlements, accurate estimation of the absolute chronology of the Trypillia BI-II period remains an issue (Manzura, 2005; Rassamakin, 2012). It should not be forgotten that the modern typo-chronological schemes are caused by the scale and rate of the innovation flow in remote past. The mobility of people and the diffusion of ideas that spread innovations had different directions and intensities, mainly depending on the structure of settlement systems (Diachenko & Menotti, 2015). That is why the Trypillia BI-II sites at the periphery could be contemporaneous to the early Trypillia BII settlements in

© European Association of Archaeologists 2016

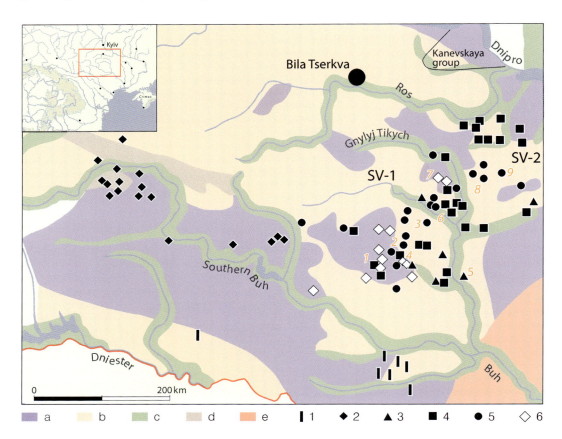

Figure 1. The WTC settlements between the Dniester and the Dnipro. Landscapes: (a) forest-steppe upland dissected landscapes; (b) loess upland terrace landscapes; (c) floodplain landscapes; (d) pine forest terraces; and (e) northern steppe upland and slope landscapes. Settlements: (1) Chechelnytska local group; (2) Serednobuzka local group; (3) Volodymyrivska local group; (4) Nebelivska local group; (5) Tomashivska local group; and (6) Kosenivska local group and Kocherzhyntsi-Shulgivka type. Settlements concerned in this study: (1) Tomashivka; (2) Dobrovody; (3) Maidanetske; (4) Nebelivka; (5) Fedorivka; (6) Glybochok; (7) Vilkhovets 1; (8) Chychyrkozivka; and (9) Vasylkiv.

core areas, while some of the late Trypillia BI sites located in margin regions may be synchronous with the Trypillia BI-II settlements in core areas, especially when taking into account the short approximate duration of 'Trypillia BI-II'. Moreover, the latter category has to be considered as a reflection of socio-cultural transformation rather than a chronological unit. If this assumption is correct, the corresponding sites may not be dated earlier than 4200–4100 BC, depending on the specific region of their location (see Mantu, 1998; Rassamakin, 2012; Tkachuk 2005).

The absolute chronology of the Trypillia CII sites is also problematic. The suggested schemes are quite different, depending on whether they consider or consciously ignore the dates that were obtained by the Kiev Laboratory of Radiocarbon Analysis after 1998 (cf. Rassamakin, 2004; Manzura, 2005; Kadrow, 2013; Videiko, 2013). Taking into account the Funnel Beaker culture and the Funnel Beaker-Baden imports and 'influences' on Trypillia, as well as new series of ^{14}C dates for the Baden complex in Slovakia and Funnel Beaker-Baden sites in southeastern Poland (Włodarczak, 2006; Horváthová, 2015; Zastawny, 2015), it would be reasonable to limit the youngest dates for the Late Trypillia to 2950/2900 BC, as suggested by Rassamakin (2004) and Manzura (2005). The mega-sites phenomenon, specifically, fills the interval of 4200/4100–3450/3400 BC. One should note that the date 3450–3400 BC is the result of a combination of the relative and absolute chronologies. The accurate ^{14}C-dates for the second phase of the Kosenivka group were not yet received as an alternative to the extremely young dates obtained by the Kiev Laboratory of Radiocarbon Analysis for the settlement of Vilkhovets 1 (Rassamakin, 2012; Videiko, 2013).

The chronology of the WTC settlements in the Southern Buh and Dnipro interfluve, which is based on Ryzhov's (1993, 1999, 2000, 2002, 2007, 2012), is briefly discussed in the chapter focused on demography (see Diachenko, 2016). The Volodymyrivsko–Tomashivska line of development of the WTC includes settlements of the Volodymyrivska, Nebelivska, and Tomashivska groups. It is important to note that settlements of the Spatial Variant 2 (SV-2) of the second phase of the Nebelevskaya group, located at the northeastern periphery of the region,

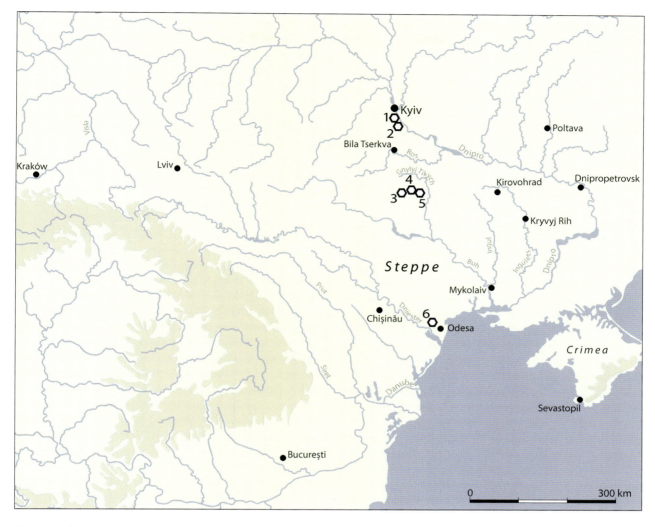

Figure 2. The ETC settlements (1–5) and the Western Trypillia sites outside the Southern Bug and Dnipro interfluve (6) that were considered in this study. (1) Chapaivka, (2) Trypillia, ur. Lypove, (3) Veselyj Kut, (4) Onopriivka, (5) Vilkhovets 2, and (6) Mayaky. Graphic: Institute UFG Kiel, Karin Winter

were the basis for the formation of the Kanivska local group of the WTC in the Dnieper region (Videiko, 2002a; Diachenko & Menotti, 2012; Ryzhov, 2012). The latest WTC mega-site in the region belongs to the second phase of the Kosenivska group that replaced the Tomashivska group after a chronological hiatus of fifty to one-hundred years. The size of the settlements from the third phase of the Kosenivska group, which are also known as sites of the Kocherzhyntsi-Shulgivka type, did not exceed 12 ha (Diachenko, 2010: appendix Г).

Ceramic complexes of the Kocherzhyntsi–Shulgivka type in the Southern Buh and Dnipro interfluve do not include pottery forms or ornamentation typical for Trypillia CII/2 (Ryzhov, 2002). Hence, the youngest Trypillian sites in the given area could be dated to c. 3350–3300 BC.

According to the 'traditional' Trypillian typo-chronologies, the ETC populations moved East to the Dnipro region, abandoning the northern part of the Southern Buh and Dnipro interfluve before the WTC peoples migrated to this area, while some part of the ETC populations mixed with the 'Western Trypillians' resulting in the formation of syncretic sites and 'ETC' influences on the WTC pottery (Kruts, 1989, 2012a; Tsvek, 2006; Ryzhov, 2007). However, considering some delay in the peripheral development (e.g. Kadrow, 2001: 29–49; Diachenko & Menotti, 2015;), the settlement of Veselyj Kut, belonging to the 'second half of Tripolye BI-II', could be synchronous with the Volodymyrivska group sites, while the 'Late Tripolye BI' site Onopriivka could foreshadow or be contemporaneous with the mega-site of Volodymyrivka; the earliest WTC settlement in the entire region (for the 'traditional' relative chronology of Onopriivka and Veselyj Kut (see: Tsvek, 2006). In this respect, the early ETC sites in this area could be synchronous with the Volodymyrivska group settlements.

Now, let us consider terminology, augmenting the notions of 'small', 'medium', and 'large settlements' with specific values.

What is 'Large' and What is 'Small'?

The Trypillia mega-sites are widely known for their size, which exceeds the corresponding values for any other 'huge' settlement of Chalcolithic Europe. Since the CTCC, covering the territory from the Carpathians to the Dnieper, was not internally unified, regional and micro-regional approaches are required for ranking the sites by their size. The Volodymyrivsko–Tomashivska line settlements of the WTC in the Southern Buh and Dnipro interfluve are grouped into three categories with internal subdivisions: 'small' (S): up to 30 ha; 'medium' (M): 35–80 ha; and 'large', (L): 100–320 ha. The 'small' group is divided into three subgroups: S-1: up to 10 ha; S-2: 10–20 ha; and S-3: 20–30 ha. The 'medium' group also includes three subgroups: M-1: 35–40 ha; M-2: 50–60 ha; and M-3: 70–80 ha, whereas the 'large' group includes just two subgroups: L-1: 100–150 ha and L-2: 210–320/340 ha (Diachenko, 2010 with updates from recently obtained data; Kruts et al., 2011, 2013; Müller et al., 2014; Rassmann, et al., 2016; Rassmann et al., 2014). The size of the Kosenivska group sites of the WTC corresponds to this scheme, but it does not exceed the upper limit of the L-1 group. Thus, the WTC mega-sites or large settlements reached the size of 100–320/340 ha.

It should be noted that the population values for the Volodymyrivsko–Tomashivska line, and probably the Kosenivka group sites, are not linearly dependent upon the settlement size, because of the different density of houses. For instance, the density of dwellings in Nebelivka and Taljanky is about half the corresponding values for other large settlements, e.g. Fedorivka, Glybochok, Dobrovody, and Maidanetske (Diachenko, 2016: table 6).

Several sites of the ETC in the Southern Buh and Dnipro interfluve that, according to recent publications (Tsvek, 2006; Videiko, 2013: 19–106, tables 1–4), covered an area of 60–120 (200?) ha are also known as giant-settlements, e.g. Onopriivka, Trypillia-ur, Lypove, Veselyj Kut, and Vilkhovets-2. Meanwhile, the values suggested for their size are overestimated. Similar to some examples of 'measurement' in other parts of the world (e.g. Smith, 2005: 409), the Trypillia settlement size was estimated as using length multiplied by width (Masson, 1980; Diachenko, 2010). This was the case even for those sites that were measured via geomagnetic prospections (cf. Kruts, 1989; Videiko, 2002b; Diachenko, 2010; Chapman et al., 2014; Rassmann et al., 2014). Therefore, the values from such publications should be multiplied by the coefficient of 0.785 to transform the 'rectangles' into 'ellipses' according to the 2D shapes of the sites. The obtained results, however, should be taken as approximations due to the lack of geomagnetic plans and rough working measurements from the field surveys (see, for instance, Hirth, 1978).

Thus, after c. 3450–3400 BC, the Trypillia populations abandoned the tradition that they followed for 700 or 800 years, and stopped building these large settlements. The question is, why?

Different Scales–Different Endings: Collapse, Decline, or Transformation?

Both the 'collapse' and 'decline' were suggested as explanations for the end of the Trypillia mega-sites. As might be expected, 'collapse' was rather typical for culture history approach, while 'decline' was the case in studies focused on the environment. 'Collapse' of the Trypillia as the result of invasion by the Steppe populations was assumed as early as the 1930s and later summarized in Passek's idea regarding the kurgans on Trypillia sites representing the conquest of this territory by the Yamnaya culture populations (Passek, 1949). The idea of conflicts between the Chalcolithic farmers and pastoralists was later elaborated and turned into one of the most influential concepts of Eurasian archaeology (Gimbutas, 1961, 1991; Kruts, 1989, 2012a, 2012b; Dergachev, 2000, 2007; Rassamakin, 2004; cf. Manzura, 2005; Anthony, 2007, 2010).

Kruts raised the issue of population pressure on the local environment in combination with the concept of conflicts between agriculturalists and pastoralists (1989; 2012a). Somewhat similar to Kruk (1973), who explained the transition from an agricultural to transhumance economy in southeastern Poland through deforestation and creating open landscapes, Kruts suggested that the Trypillia populations turned the forest-steppes of the Southern Buh and Dnipro interfluve into steppe and, in this way, made this territory available for the later invasions of pastoralists (Kruts, 1989). He noted that the Trypillia economy was not shifted towards improvements in production, and therefore could exist only because through exploration of new territories until each separate group faced a lack of available lands in a given area (Kruts, 2012b).

Criticizing the idea of conflicts between the Trypillia populations and people of the Nyzhnomykhailivska and Kvitianska Steppe cultures, Zbenovich (1990) and Videiko (2002b) assumed tensions between different Trypillia groups. Videiko includes this assumption in the list of factors that stimulated the high increase of social complexity in the Trypillia societies (Videiko 2002b, 2013). He stated the decline of the Trypillia 'proto-cities' as a fact, but did not explain the reasons for it; most probably following the Kruts' idea of ecological crises caused by human impact on the local environment (Videiko, 2002b, 2013).

In traditional explanations, the abandonment of every single large settlement is related to the rotational movement of populations. Deforestation of the surrounding areas is claimed to be the main reason for these cycles. This could be confirmed by the fact that the catchment areas of the large sites did not overlap (Markevich, 1981; Kruts, 1989, 2012a; Harper, 2013). Abandonment of settlements at the lowest order of the spatial hierarchy does not, of course, explain the decline of the mega-sites after *c.* 3450–3400 BC as a general phenomenon. However, let us scale this issue to an intermediate spatio-temporal tier.

Neither the ETC populations nor the people of the Kanivska group of the WTC built mega-sites in the Dnipro region. Some corresponding values published previously seem to be the result of overestimated settlements size. Moreover, the size of settlements from the Volodymyrivska and Nebelivska groups, which were located in the eastern part of the Southern Buh and Dnipro interfluve, labelled as sites of SV-2 (Diachenko, 2010), did not exceed 80 ha. Only two settlements of SV-2, Chychyrkozivka and Vasylkiv, which belong to the Tomashivska group, exceeded 100 ha (Diachenko 2010).

Given that different habitats are never of the same quality (Dias, 1996), the correlation between settlement size and landscapes seems to be a good explanation for the limited spatial distribution of the mega-sites (Figure 1). All of them are located in meadow-steppe upland dissected landscapes and terrace forest-steppe landscapes that probably had the highest potential for agricultural activities. This trend is also notable for the sites of the Chechelnytska local group, while the largest settlements of the Serednobuzka local group are located in forest-steppe upland dissected landscapes (Diachenko & Zubrow, 2015). Forest-steppe upland dissected landscapes and pine forest terraces probably limited the productivity of the Trypillia catchment areas, at least compared with meadow-steppe upland dissected and terrace forest-steppe landscapes of the Southern Buh and Dnipro interfluve (Figure 1).

Trends in the spatial distribution of populations over time are different for the ETC and certain local groups of the WTC (see Diachenko & Menotti, 2012; Diachenko, 2016). Former inhabitants of the Volodymyrivska, Nebelivska, and Kosenivska group megasites that were formed as a result of interregional (e.g. Fedorivka and Nebelivka) or intraregional (e.g. Chychyrkozivka and Vilkhovets 1) population movement over time, lived in increasingly less-populated settlements and built a set of small villages in the Southern Buh and Dnipro interfluve. Most probably, this trend in the development of large settlements was also typical for the ETC in this region. The suggested correlation between long-distance migrations within the CTCC and aridification events leads to the conclusion regarding the cessation of migrations and, consequently, the surceasing formation of giant-settlements when the climate became more humid in Trypillia CII/2 (Diachenko, 2012). Since the Kosenivska group settlement of Vilkhovets 1 was the latest WTC mega-site, this is also the explanation for the ending of mega-sites as a general phenomenon.

Conversely, the population size of the Tomashivska group increased and stabilized at a relatively high level, reflecting the slight increase in carrying capacity (Diachenko, 2016; Diachenko & Zubrow, 2015). Significant population growth in the largest settlements is also notable for other areas of the CTCC during Trypillia CI–the timespan of the Tomashivska local group (Tarapata, forthcoming; Videiko, 2013). It is still difficult to explain the further decline of the giant-settlements of this group. Was it impacted by overpopulation at Maidanetske, where the number of inhabitants exceeded the 'stabilization limit' of half the carrying capacity (Diachenko, 2016; Diachenko & Zubrow, 2015; also see Strogatz, 1994: 21–24), or acidification of climate in Trypillia CII/1 which resulted in a decrease of catchment productivity? Should both of these factors be considered to solve this issue? The question of the decline of the Tomashivska group mega-sites is still open and requires further examination. Meanwhile, if the assumption regarding the slight increase in regional carrying capacity due to the climate change is correct, then why did the Trypillia CII/2 populations not built mega-sites? Let us consider the socio-economic organization and demographic development of this timespan more precisely.

BECOMING SMALL: A DEMOCRATIC PERSPECTIVE?

As already noted, the settlement hierarchy is one of the cornerstones in reconstructions of WTC social complexity (e.g. Ellis, 1984; Diachenko, 2012; Videiko, 2013). Populations of the Kosenivska group were even claimed to be 'the last Trypillia chiefdom' (Videiko, 2013). However, even taking into account numerous ethno-archaeological cases regarding the fall of chiefdoms (Tainter, 1988; Yoffee & Cowgill, 1988; Semenov, 1993), does the decrease in settlement hierarchy mean decline in social complexity?

The timespan of *c.* 3500–2800 BC is characterized by Trans-European socio-environmental and economic shifts, with retardation in some areas of course. It is still not clear if the extension of open landscapes at the beginning of this period was impacted by climate change or preceding human impact on environment, or caused by both of these factors (*final discussion at the session 'Records of Neolithic transformation process–social and/or environmental crisis?' Kiel, 26 March* 2015, see Menke, 2015: 118–23). According to the indirect evidence, aridification in the timespan of 3600–3400 BC was replaced by a more humid climate *c.* 3400–3350 BC (Diachenko, 2012; Harper, 2013). Deforestation increased the importance of sheep and goat in European economies, in both the steppe and forest-steppe (Dergachev, 2012). The bones of sheep and goat dominate the assemblages from some Late Trypillia settlements, e.g. Sverdlikove in the Southern Buh and Dnipro interfluve, Mayaky at the northwestern coast of the Black Sea and Chapaivka in the Middle Dnipro region (Kruts, 2002; Zhuravlev, 2008), confirming that the economic shifts in the CTCC probably followed general European trends. Agricultural activities at Late Trypillia settlements are also evident (Pashkevych, 2006). Therefore, one may assume a transition from sedentary agriculture to a complex economy, consisting of agriculture and pastoralism, in the forest-steppe and southern part of the forest zone in Trypillia CII/2; as suggested by Videiko (2011) regarding the sites in the Middle Dnipro region.

The shifts in the subsistence strategies of the Trypillia populations are not as evident as the transition to complex economies in Central Europe; for instance, the Bronocice region in southeastern Poland (Kruk & Milisauskas, 1999; Milisauskas *et al.*, 2012; Pipes *et al.*, 2014). Therefore, the related transformations in demographic development, spatial organization, and social structure could be traced to solve this issue (Khazanov, 1984; Milisauskas & Kruk, 1989; Greenfield, 1991; Di Cosmo, 1994; 2002; Bunyatyan, 2003; Anthony, 2007; Kohl, 2007; Gavrylyuk, 2013; Sherratt, 1981).

According to Bunyatyan (2003), the contradiction between mobile transhumance and sedentary agriculture was resolved by the territorial determination of these activities and subdivision of labour within the community that resulted in the formation of settlements of different types. Such subdivision of labour was not strictly determined. Different kinds of work in different seasons could involve different numbers of people; the task of arranging available work resources was decided not only within the community, but also within each family (Bunyatyan, 2003). The transhumance component made the economy unstable, while at the same time allowing the accumulation of wealth–the herd and its products (Pipes *et al.*, 2014; Sherratt, 1981). The economic and demographic risks for the populations could be resolved through the constant increase of economic potential (Bunyatyan, 2003: 270); however, the steady state of the economy was exclusively possible in case of the decreased population pressure enabled by permanent emigration (Diachenko, 2013).

The spatial distribution of the fortified Horodişte-Folteşti–Late Trypillia settlements notably corresponds to the proportion of sheep and goat in herds, allowing for assumptions regarding the similar locations of wealth and fortifications (Figure 3). According to Dergachev (2007: 36–49), the ratio of fortified and unfortified settlements in the northern part of the Prut and Dniester region and Volyn is valued at 1:3.1. Sheep and goat dominated in the former region and reached second place after cattle in the latter area; the corresponding values are fifty-seven and twenty-eight per cent (Kruts, 2002: tables 5 and 6). The portion of sheep and goat in the Dnipro region, estimated to thirty-seven per cent, was even greater than in Volyn, but settlements in this area were also characterized by a high amount of wild fauna (Kruts, 2002). Meanwhile, evident camps related to stock-breeding are still not known, despite the location of sites at different altitudes. Corresponding interpretations of several small settlements (Videiko, 2011) remain a working hypothesis that should be examined in further studies.

Relatively low population estimates for the Trypillia CII/2 sites, especially compared with values for the preceding periods, also correspond to the idea of socio-economic transformations. The related changes in ideology could be confirmed by the appearance of cemeteries that are not archaeologically identified for most of regions in earlier periods of the Trypillia development, and the spread of corded ornamentation on ceramics (see Kruts, 1977; Dergachev, 1978, 1980; Kośko, 1995; Patokova, 1979; Patokova & Petrenko, 1989; Kośko & Szmyt, 2010).

The assumed transformation of the Trypillia economy could be also reflected in the reorganization of social life. On the one hand, agriculture and house construction required the organization of community labour. On the other hand, stock-breeding suggests the labour of families and concentration of products at the same level of social organization (Earle & Kristiansen, 2010). Social stratification is confirmed by the data from cemeteries. Besides sex–age differentiation of the buried, a strata of 'elite' graves was identified (e.g. Dergachev, 1978; Kolesnikov, 1993). Meanwhile, the Trypillia cemeteries lack really 'rich' graves in terms of mortuary inventory, suggesting that wealth inequality was still poorly developed and increased later in this territory–during the Bronze Age (Bunyatyan, 2003). Hence, the Late Trypillia chiefs could be responsible for the organization of community labour related to agricultural activities, control over pastures, and the daily life of populations. According to the finds of imported metal and flint artefacts, the chiefs could control the interregional

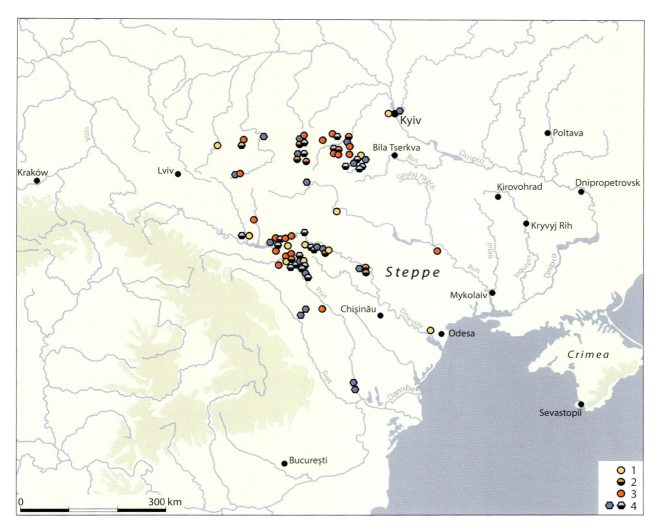

Figure 3. The Horodişte-Folteşti–Tripolye CII sites (after Dergachev, 2000). (1) Fortified settlements, (2) probably fortified settlements, (3) settlements with toponymy related to fortifications, and (4) fortified and probably fortified settlements with toponymy related to fortifications. Graphic: Institute UFG Kiel, Karin Winter.

prestige exchange (Earle, 1997; Earle & Kristiansen, 2010). Commodities made of wool could be also involved in the exchange system (Earle & Kristiansen, 2010; Pipers et al., 2014).

The proposed hypotheses still include numerous open questions. What was the ratio of agriculture to stock-breeding in economies of the Late Trypillia populations, and what was the impact of this ratio on settlement systems? What were the particular types of stock-breeding in different areas? A timespan of c. 400 years of practising the new subsistence strategy suggests that it was sustainable, but what amount of surplus was obtained by chiefs and households? Finally, how did the Late Trypillia transformation impact cultural change, i.e. the decline of Trypillia? Let us concern ourselves with the latter issue.

Studies that were based upon a culture history approach related the collapse of Trypillia to invasions of the Globular Amphora populations from the West to the East and Yamnaya culture peoples from the East to the West. Some evidence for the increased violence that seemed to correspond with the preceding decline of giant-settlements was viewed as an argument for the assimilation of the 'Trypillians' by newcomers (e.g. Kruts, 1989, 2012b). An alternative concept of the 'Badenization' of the Trypillia was recently proposed by Videiko (2008). However, despite the increasing data regarding the Baden complex influences on Trypillia, those were not as significant as, for instance, Baden influences on the Funnel Beaker culture in Poland, which resulted in the formation of the Funnel-Beaker-Baden horizon.

Transformation processes in Trypillia CII/2 somehow remind us of the transition from the late Soviet period to the early years of post-soviet independent countries (incidentally, leaders of the Communist party of the USSR were notably called 'chiefs'–'вожди'–in Russian). The example of the more effective 'Western' economy also made 'Western' movies, music, clothes, and haircuts prestigious. Meanwhile, the post-soviet culture was not absolutely 'westernized' that time as a result of simple adoption of some elements from outside. In the Trypillia case, the seeds of changes were sown, and the latest sites in the forest-steppe probably became the basis for the formation of the eastern group of the Globular Amphora culture. This hypothesis is confirmed by recent radiocarbon dates for the eastern group (Szmyt, 2010). However, the cultural change seems to be caused by internal Trypillia development rather than the impact of immigrants on the local population (cf. Gimbutas, 1980).

Following the concept of Kristiansen and Earle, the economic transformations in the CTCC after c. 3450–3400 BC were most likely accompanied by the transition from centralized chiefdoms to dispersed chiefdoms. The economic reality of semi-autonomous households contradicted the more centralized socio-political organization based upon the agglomeration of people focused on agriculture. Decentralized staple production and a network-based exchange system made political control over large areas impossible (Earle & Kristiansen, 2010: 247–9). There was no place for mega-sites anymore, when the Trypillia populations stepped over the threshold of a new epoch.

Does the Trypillia CII/2 transformation therefore mean a path towards a democratic perspective? It probably does not. Leaving aside 'democracy' as a form of political organization in the modern world, and concerning the issue of 'equality/inequality' (see Ivin, 2006), we cannot recognize a certain type of balance between 'vertical' and 'horizontal' relations in Late Trypillia societies. An 'individual' was still lost in kinship ties and responsibilities caused by their sex and age. Social hierarchy shaped the form, but remained a hierarchy; most likely contributed to by the increase in wealth inequality.

Conclusion and Discussion

Examination of the transitional periods and cultural change in the remote past often results in more questions than answers. This is also the case for the Late Trypillia studies, including the issue related to the end of mega-sites. The ETC settlements that exceeded 48 ha in size and the WTC mega-sites of 100–320/340 ha were built from c. 4200/4100–3450/3400 BC, but later this tradition was abandoned.

Different reasons for the end of giant-settlements could be found at different spatio-temporal scales. Large settlements tend to concentrate in meadow-steppe upland dissected landscapes and terrace forest-steppe landscapes that probably had the highest potential for agricultural activities. Moving from these regions to areas with different landscape types, populations did not build mega-sites. There is also a strong correlation between indirect evidence for climate change and the formation of the largest settlements of the Volodymyrivska, Nebelivska, and Kosenivska local groups. According to further decreases of these mega-sites in size and number of dwellings, those long-distance population movements probably decreased the population pressure in the Dniester region.

The end of the Tomashivska group mega-sites remains an issue because of different trends in the demographic development of their populations. It cannot be excluded that the decline in the size of Tomashivska group giant-settlements, i.e. Maidanetske-Tomashivka, was caused by exceeding the 'limit' of half of the carrying capacity in Maidanetske. However, a significant increase in the size of the Trypillia CI settlements was also typical for other regions of the CTCC, and the ratio of population size to carrying capacity should therefore be clarified in further studies.

The abandonment of the tradition of building giant-settlements after c. 3450–3400 BC was probably caused by crucial transformations in the Trypillia political economies. Most likely, the new subsistence strategy combined sedentary agriculture and transhumance with a highly increased number of sheep and goat, compared with preceding periods, into a complex economic system. Centralized chiefdoms were shifted into dispersed chiefdoms. However, this transformation in socio-political structure should not be recognized as an argument for placing the mega-sites on a path to state formation. The Trypillia giant-settlements seem to be one of many alternative forms of settlement organization in prehistory. At the same time, the decline in settlement hierarchy after c. 3450–3400 BC did not correspond to decline in social complexity. Lack of spatial orders, hence, does not always mean social equality, and this reminds us of Flannery's (1998) notion regarding the necessity of a set of evidence in addition to the settlement hierarchy when arguing for an increase in social complexity.

Finally, the small settlements that preceded or replaced the mega-sites, as well as the small villages in the hinterland of the giant-settlements, are also noteworthy. Only the examination of the full range of sites of different sizes may result in complete understanding of the remote past.

Acknowledgements

I am grateful to Johannes Müller for the invitation to contribute to this volume and his suggested title for the chapter.

References

Anthony, D.W. 2007. *The Horse, the Wheel and Language. How Bronze-Age Riders from Eurasian Steppe Shaped the Modern World*. Princeton: Princeton University Press.

Anthony, D.W. 2010. The Rise and Fall of Old Europe. In: D. Anthony & J. Y. Chi, eds. *The Lost World of Old Europe: The Danube Valley, 5000–3500 BC*. Princeton: Princeton University Press, pp. 29–74.

Anthony, D.W. 2013 (review). F. Menotti & A. Korvin-Piotrovskiy (ed.). The Tripolye Culture Giant-Settlements in Ukraine: Formation, Development and Decline. *Antiquity* 87(335):1233–35.

Bunyatyan, K.P. 2003. Correlations between Agriculture and Pastoralism in the Northern Pontic Steppe Area during the Bronze Age. In: M. Levine, C. Renfrew & K. Boyle, eds. *Prehistoric Steppe Adaptation and the Horse*. Cambridge: McDonald Institute for Archaeological Research, pp. 269–86.

Chapman, J., Videiko, M., Hale, D., Gaydarska, B., Burdo, N., Rassmann, K., Mischka, C., Müller, J., Korvin-Piotrovskiy, A. & Kruts, V. 2014. The Second Phase of the Trypillia Mega-Site Methodological Revolution: A New Research Agenda. *European Journal of Archaeology*, 17(3):369–406.

Dergachev, V.A. 1978. *Vykhvatinskij mogilnik*. Kishinev: Shtiintsa. Дергачев, В.А. 1978. *Выхватинский могильник*. Кишинев: Штиинца.

Dergachev, V.A. 1980. *Pamiatniki pozdnego Tripolja*. Kishinev: Shtiintsa. Дергачев, В.А. 1980. *Памятники позднего Триполья*. Кишинев: Штиинца.

Dergachev, V.A. 2000. Dva etuda v zashchitu migratsionnoj kontseptsii. K probleme vzaimodejstviya ranneskotovod-cheskih i dervnezemledelcheskih obshchestv eneolita – rannej bronzy Vostochnoj i Yugo-Vostochnoj Evropy. *Stratum Plus*, 2:188–236. Дергачев, В.А. 2000. Два этюда в защиту миграционной концепции. К проблеме взаимодействия раннескотоводческих и древнеземледельческих обществ энеолита – ранней бронзы Восточной и Юго-Восточной Европы. *Stratum Plus* 2:188–236.

Dergachev, V.A. 2007. *O skipetrah, o loshadiah i o voine. V zashchitu migratsioonoj kontseptsii M. Gimbutas*. Sankt-Peterburg: Nestor-Istoriya. Дергачев, В.А. 2007. *О скипетрах, о лошадях и о войне. В защиту миграционной концепции М. Гимбутас*. Санкт-Петербург: Нестор-История.

Dergachev, V.A. 2012. Dinamika razvitiya domashnego stada neolita-bronzy yuga Vostochnoj Evropy kak vozmozhnyj indikator klimaticheskih izmenenij proshlogo. In: V. V. Otroshchenko, ed. *Zemledeltsy i skotovody drevnej Evropy: problemy, novye otkrytiya, gipotezy*. Kiev-Sankt-Peterburg: Institute of Archaeology of the NASU and IMCS of the RAS, pp. 26–43. Дергачев, В.А. 2012. Динамика развития домашнего стада неолита-бронзы юга Восточной Европы как возможный фактор климатических изменений прошлого. В сб.: В.В. Отрощенко, ред. *Земледельцы и скотоводы древней Европы: проблемы, новые открытия, гипотезы*. Киев – Санкт-Петербург: Институт археологии НАНУ и ИИМК РАН, с. 26–43.

Diachenko, A. 2010. *Tripolskoe naselenie Bugo-Dneprovkogo mezhdurechya: prostranstvenno-vremennoj analiz*, Unpublished PhD Thesis. Kiev: Institute of Archaeology of the NASU. Дяченко, А. 2010. Трипольское население Буго-Днепровского междуречья: пространственно-временной анализ (рукопись дис. канд. истор. наук). Киев: Институт археологии НАНУ.

Diachenko, A. 2012. Settlement System of West Tripolye culture in the Southern Bug and Dnieper Interfluve: Formation Problems. In: F. Menotti & A. G. Korvin-Piotrovskiy, eds. *The Tripolye Culture Giant-Settlements in Ukraine: Formation, Development and Decline*. Oxford: Oxbow Books, pp. 116–38.

Diachenko, A. 2013. The Mechanics of Semi-Nomadic Economy. In: S. Kadrow & P. Włodarczak, eds. *Environment and Subsistence – Forty Years after Janusz Kruk's 'Settlement Studies…' (= Studien zur Archäologie in Ostmitteleuropa/Studia nad Pradziejami Europy Środkowej)*. Rzeszów, Bonn: Mitel & Verlag Dr. Rudolf Habelt GmbH, pp. 303–10.

Diachenko, A. & Menotti, F. 2012. The Gravity Model: Monitoring the Formation and Development of the Tripolye Culture Giant-Settlements in Ukraine. *Journal of Archaeological Science*, 39(4):2810–17.

Diachenko, A. 2016. Demography Reloaded. In: J. Müller, K. Rassmann & M. Videiko, eds. *Trypillia Mega-Sites and European Prehistory: 4100-3400 BCE*. London and New York: Routledge, pp. 181–194.

Diachenko, A. & Menotti, F. 2015. Cucuteni-Tripolye Contact Networks: Cultural Transmission and Chronology. In: A. Diachenko, F. Menotti, S. Ryzhov, K. Bunyatyan & S. Kadrow, eds. *The Cucuteni-Tripolye Cultural Complex and Its Neighbours: Essays in Memory of Volodymyr Kruts*. Lviv: Astrolabe, pp. 131–52.

Diachenko, A. & Zubrow, E.B.W. 2015. Stabilization Points in Carrying Capacity: Population Growth and Migrations. *Journal of Neolithic Archaeology*, 17:1–15.

Dias, P.C. 1996. Sources and Sinks in Population Biology. *Trends in Ecology and Evolution*, 11(8):326–30.

Di Cosmo, N. 1994. Ancient Inner Asian Nomads: Their Economic Base and its Significance in Chinese History. *The Journal of Asian Studies*, 53(4):1092–126.

Di Cosmo, N. 2002. *Ancient China and its Enemies. The Rise of Nomadic Power in East Asian History*. Cambridge: Cambridge University Press.

Earle, T. 1997. *How Chiefs Came to Power: The Political Economy in Prehistory*. Stanford, CA: Stanford University Press.

Earle, T. & Kristiansen, K. 2010. Organizing Bronze Age Societies: Concluding Thoughts. In: T. Earle & K. Kristiansen, eds. *Organizing Bronze Age Societies: The Mediterranean, Central Europe and Scandinavia Compared*. Cambridge: Cambridge University Press.

Ellis, L. 1984. *The Cucuteni-Tripolye culture. A Study of Technology and Origins of Complex Society*. Oxford: BAR International Series 217.

Flannery, K.V. 1998. The Ground Plans of Archaic States. In: G. M. Feinman & J. Marcus, eds. *Archaic States*. Santa Fe: School of American Research Press, pp. 15–58.

Gavrylyuk, N.A. 2013. *Ekonomika Stepnoj Skifii VI – III vv. do n.e.* Kyiv: Vydavets Oleh Filyuk. Гаврилюк, Н.А. 2013. *Экономика Степной Скифии VI – III вв. до н. э.* Киев: Видавець Олег Філюк.

Gimbutas, M. 1961. Notes on the Chronology and Expansion of the Pit-Grave Culture. In: J. Bohm & S. J. De Laet, eds. *L'Europe à la fin de 1'Age de la pierre*. Prague: Czechoslovak Academy of Sciences, pp. 193–200.

Gimbutas, M. 1980. The Kurgan Wave # 2 (c. 3400–3200 BC) into Europe and the Following Transformation of Culture. *Journal of Indo-European Studies*, 8:273–85.

Gimbutas, M. 1991. *The Civilization of the Goddess*. San Francisco: Harper.

Greenfield, H.J. 1991. Fauna from the Late Neolithic of the Central Balkans. Issues in Subsistence and Land Use. *Journal of Field Archaeology*, 18(2):161–86.

Harper, T.K. 2013. The Effect of Climate Variability on Population Dynamics of the Cucuteni-Tripolye Cultural Complex and the Rise of the Western Tripolye Giant-Settlements. *Chronika*, 3:28–46.

Hirth, K.G. 1978. Problems in Data Recovery and Measurement in Settlement Archaeology. *Journal of Field Archaeology*, 5(2):125–31.

Horváthová, E. 2015. The Current State of Research on the Baden Culture at Slovakian Areas in the Northern Basin of the Tisza River. In: M. Nowak & A. Zastawny, eds. *The Baden Culture around the Western Carpathians*. Krakow: Ekodruk, pp. 151–74.

Ivin, A.A. 2006. Demokratiya. In: A. A. Ivin, ed. *Filosofiya. Entsyklopedicheskij slovar*. Moskva: Gadariki, pp. 218–20. . Ивин, А.А. 2006. Демократия. В кн.: А.А. Ивин, ред. *Философия. Энциклопедический словарь*. Москва: Гадарики, с. 218–20.

Kadrow, S. 2001. *U progu nowej epoki: Gospodarka i społeczeństwo wczesnego okresu epoki brązu w Europie Środkowej*. Kraków: Instytut Archeologii i Etnologii PAN.

Kadrow, S. 2013. Werteba Site in Bilcze Złote: Resent Research and Analyses. In: S. Kadrow, ed. *Bilcze Złote: Materials of the Tripolye Culture from the Werteba and the Ogród sites*. Kraków: Muzeum Archeologiczne w Krakowie, pp. 13–22.

Khazanov, A. 1984. *Nomads and the Outside World*. Cambridge: Cambridge University Press.

Kohl, Ph. 2007. *The Making of Bronze Age Eurasia*. Cambridge: Cambridge University Press.

Kolesnikov, A.G. 1993. *Tripolskoe obshchestvo Srednego Podneprovya: opyt sotsialnyh rekonstruktsij v archeologii*. Kiev: Naukova Dumka. Колесников, А.Г. 1993. *Трипольское общество Среднего Поднепровья: опыт социальных реконструкций в археологии*. Киев: Наукова думка.

Kośko, A., ed. 1995. Cemeteries of the Sofievka Type: 2950–2750 BC. Baltic-Pontic Studies 3.

Kośko, A. & Szmyt, M., eds. 2010. *'Cord' ornaments on pottery in the Vistula and Dnieper interfluvial region: 5th – 4th mill. BC*. Baltic-Pontic Studies 15.

Kruk, J. 1973. *Studia osadnicze nad neolitem wyżyn lessowych*. Wroclaw: Ossolineum.

Kruk, J. & Milisauskas, S. 1999. *Rozkwit i upadek społeczeństw rolniczych Neolitu*. Krakow: Instytut Archeologii i Etnologii Polskiej Akademii Nauk.

Kruts, V.A. 1977. *Pozdnetripolskie pamyatniki Srednego Podneprovya*. Kiev: Naukova Dumka. Круц, В.А. 1977. *Позднетрипольские памятники Среднего Поднепровья*. Киев: Наукова думка.

Kruts, V.A. 1989. K istorii naseleniya tripolskoj kultury v mezhdurechye Uzhnogo Buga i Dnepra. In: S. S. Berezanskaya, ed. *Pervobytnaya archeologiya: Materialy i issledovaniya*. Kiev: Naukova Dumka, pp. 117–32. Круц, В.А. 1989. К истории населения трипольской культуры в междуречье Южного Буга и Днепра. В сб.: С.С. Березанская, ред. *Первобытная археология: материалы и исследования*. Киев: Наукова думка, с. 117–32.

Kruts, V.A. 2002. Zhivotnovodstvo v ekonomike tripolskoj kultury. *Stratum Plus*, 2:179–86. Круц, В.А. 2002. Животноводство в экономике трипольской культуры. Stratum Plus 2:179–86.

Kruts, V.A. 2012a. Giant-settlements of Tripolye culture. In: F. Menotti & A. Korvin-Piotrovskiy, eds. *The Tripolye Culture Giant-Settlements in Ukraine. Formation, Development and Decline*. Oxford: Oxbow Books, pp. 70–78.

Kruts, V.A. 2012b. The Latest Stage of Development of the Tripolye Culture. In: F. Menotti & A. Korvin-Piotrovskiy, eds. *The Tripolye Culture Giant-Settlements in Ukraine. Formation, Development and Decline*. Oxford: Oxbow Books, pp. 230–53.

Kruts, V.A., Korvin-Piotrovkiy, A.G., Mischka, C., Ohlrau, R., Windler, A. & Rassmann, K. 2013. Talianki-2012. The Geomagnetic Prospection. In: A. G. Korvin-Piotrovskiy & K. Rassmann, eds. *Talianki – Settlement-Giant of the Tripolian Culture. Investigations in 2012*. Kiev: Institute of Archaeology of the NASU, pp. 85–103.

Kruts, V.A., Korvin-Piotrovskiy, A.G., Rassmann, K. & Peters, D. 2011. Talianki: Reloaded. Geomagnetic Prospection Three Decades after V.P. Dudkin's Work. In: A. G. Korvin-Piotrovkiy & F. Menotti, eds. *Talianki – Settlement-Giant of the Tripolian Culture. Investigations in 2011*. pp. 60–85.

Mantu, C.-M. 1998. *Cultura Cucuteni. Evoluție, Cronologie, Legături (Bibliotheca Memoriae Antiquitatis V)*. Piatra-Neamț: Muzeul Istorie Piatra-Neamț.

Manzura, I.V. 2005. Severnoe Prichernomorye v eneolite i nachale bronzovogo veka: stupeni kolonizatsii. *Stratum Plus*, 2:63–85. Манзура, И.В. 2005. Северное Причерноморье в энеолите и начале бронзового века: ступени колонизации. *Stratum Plus* 2:63–85.

Markevich, V.I. 1981. *Pozdnetripolskie plemena Severnoj Moldavii*. Kishinev: Shtiintsa. Маркевич, В.И. 1981. *Позднетрипольские племена Северной Молдавии*. Кишинев: Штиинца.

Masson, V.M. 1980. Dinamika razvitiya tripolskogo obshchestva v svete paleodemograficheskih otsenok. In: I. I. Artemenko, ed. *Pervobytnaya archeologiya: Poiski i nakhodki*. Kiev: Naukova Dumka, pp. 204–12. Массон, В.М. 1980. Динамика развития трипольского общества в свете палеодемографических оценок. В сб.: И.И. Артеменко, ред. *Первобытная археология: поиски и находки*. Киев: Наукова думка, с. 204–12.

McAnany, P.A. & Yoffee, N. 2010. Why We Question Collapse and Study Human Resilience, Ecological Vulnerability, and the Aftermath of Empire. In: P. A. McAnany & N. Yoffee, eds. *Questioning Collapse: Human Resilience, Ecological Vulnerability, and the Aftermath of Empire*. Cambridge: Cambridge University Press, pp. 1–17.

Menke, J.N., ed. 2015. *Socio-Environmental Dynamics over the Last 12,000 Years: The Creation of Landscapes IV*.

Milisauskas, S. & Kruk, J. 1989. Neolithic Economy in Central Europe. *Journal of World Prehistory*, 3(4):403–45.

Milisauskas, S., Kruk, J., Pipes, M.-L. & Makowicz-Poliszot, D. 2012. *Butchering and Meat Consumption in the Neolithic. The Exploitation of Animals at Bronocice*. Krakow: Ekodruk.

Müller, J., Hofmann, R., Rassmann, K., Mischka, C., Videiko, M.Yu. & Burdo, N.B. 2014. Maidanetskoe:

issledovaniya po obnovlennomu planu poseleniya. *Stratum Plus*, 2:285–302.

Ohlrau, R. 2014. Tripolje Großsiedlungen. Geomagnetische Prospektion und architektursoziologische Perspektiven, *Unpublished MA Thesis*. Kiel: CAU.

Pashkevych, G.O. 2006. Kulturni roslyny Trypilsko-Kukutenskoi spilnosti. In: G. O. Pashkevych & M. Yu. Videiko, eds. *Rilnytsvo plemen trypilskoi kultury*. Kyiv: Institute of Archaeology of the NASU, pp. 41–80. Пашкевич, Г.О. 2006. Культурні рослини Кукутень-Трипільської спільності. В кн.: Г.О. Пашкевич і М. Ю. Відейко. Рільництво племен трипільської культури. Київ: Інститут археології НАНУ, с. 41–80.

Passek, T.S. 1949. *Periodozatsiya tripolskikh poselenij III – II tys. do n.e.. Materialy i issledovaniya po archeologii SSSR* 10. Пассек, Т.С. 1949. *ериодизация трипольских поселений III – II тыс. до н.э. Материалы и исследования по археологии СССР* 10.

Patokova, E.F. 1979. *Usatovskoe poselenie i mogilniki*. Kiev: Naukova Dumka. Патокова, Э.Ф. 1979. *Усатовское поселение и могильники*. Киев: Наукова думка.

Patokova, E.F. & Petrenko, V.G. 1989. Usatovskij mogilnik Mayaki. In: E. F. Patakova, V. G. Petrenko, N. B. Burdo & L. Yu. Polishchuk, eds. *Pamyatniki tripolskoj kultury v Severo-Zapadnom Prichernomorye*. Kiev: Naukova Dumka, pp. 81–124. Патокова, Э.Ф. и Петренко, В.Г. 1989. Усатовский могильник Маяки. В кн.: Э.Ф. Патокова, В.Г. Петренко, Н.Б. Бурдо и Л.Ю. Полищук. Памятники трипольской культуры в Северо-Западном Причерноморье. Киев: Наукова думка, с. 81–124.

Pipes, M.-L., Kruk, J. & Milisauskas, S. 2014. Assessing the Archaeological Data for Wool-Weaving Sheep during the Middle to Late Neolithic in Bronocice, Poland. In: H. J. Greenfield, ed. *Animal Secondary Products: Archaeological Perspectives on Domestic Animal Exploitation in the Neolithic and Bronze Age*. Oxford & Philadelphia: Oxbow Books, pp. 80–102.

Rassamakin, Yu. 2004. Stepy Prychornomorya v konteksti rozvytku pershyh zemlerobskyh suspilstv. *Archeologiya*, 2:3–26. Рассамакін, Ю.Я. 2004. Степи Причорномор'я в контексті розвитку перших землеробських суспільств. Археологія 2: 3–26.

Rassamakin, Yu. 2012. Absolute Chronology of Ukrainian Tripolian Settlements. In: F. Menotti & A. Korvin-Piotrovskiy, eds. *The Tripolye Culture Giant-Settlements in Ukraine. Formation, Development and Decline*. Oxford: Oxbow Books, pp. 19–69.

Rassmann, K., Ohlrau, R., Hofmann, R., Mischka, C., Burdo, N., Videiko, M. & Müller, J. 2014. High Precision Tripolye Settlement Plans, Demographic Estimations and Settlement Organization. *Journal of Neolithic Archaeology*, 16:63–95.

Rassmann, K., Korvin-Piotrovskiy, A., Videiko, M. & Müller, J. 2016. The New Challenge for Site Plans and Geophysics: Revealing the Settlement Structure of Giant Settlements by Means of Geomagnetic Survey. In: J. Müller, K. Rassmann & M. Videiko, eds. *Trypillia Mega-Sites and European Prehistory: 4100–3400 BCE*. London and New York: Routledge, pp. 29–54.

Ryzhov, S.M. 1993. Nebelivska grupa pamjatok trypilskoi kultury. *Archeologiya*, 3:101–14. Рижов, С.М. 1993. Небелівська група пам'яток трипільської культури. Археологія 3:101–114.

Ryzhov, S.M. 1999. *Keramika poselen trypilskoi kultury Bugo-Dniprovskogo mezhyruzhzhia yak istorychne dzerelo, Unpublished PhD Thesis*. Kyiv: Institute of Archaeology of the NASU. Рижов, С.М. 1999. *Кераміка поселень трипільської культури Буго-Дніпровського межиріччя як історичне джерело (рукопис дис. канд. істор. наук)*. Київ: Інститут археології НАНУ.

Ryzhov, S.M. 2007. Suchasnyj stan vyvchennia kulturno-istorychnoi spilnosti Cucuteni–Trypillya. In: Yu. Ya. Rassamakin & S. M. Ryzhov, eds. *O. Olzhych. Archeologiya*. Kyiv: Vydavnytstvo im. Oleny Teligy, pp. 437–77. Рижов, С.М. 2007. Сучасний стан вивчення культурно-історичної спільності Кукутень-Трипілля. У зб.: Ю.Я. Рассамакін і С.М. Рижов, ред. О. Ольжич. Археологія. Київ: Видавництво ім. Олени Теліги.

Ryzhov, S.N. 2000. Raspisnaya keramika tomashovskoj localno-khronologicheskoj gruppy tripolskoj kultury. *Stratum Plus*, 2:459–73. Рыжов, С.Н. 2000. Расписная керамика томашовской локально-хронологической группы трипольской культуры. Stratum Plus 2: 459–73.

Ryzhov, S.N. 2002. Pozdnetripolskie pamyatniki Bugo-Dneprovskogo mezhdurechya. *Stratum Plus*, 2:187–95. Рыжов, С.Н. 2002. Позднетрипольские памятники Буго-Днепровского междуречья. Stratum Plus 2: 187–95.

Ryzhov, S.N. 2012. Relative Chronology of the Giant-Settlement Period BII—CI. In: F. Menotti & A. G. Korvin-Piotrovskiy, eds. *The Tripolye Culture Giant-Settlements in Ukraine: Formation, Development and Decline*. Oxford: Oxbow Books, pp. 79–115.

Semenov, Yu. I. 1993. Perehod ot pervobytnogo obshchestva k klassovomu: puti i varianty razvitiya (chast 1). *Etnographicheskoe obozrenie*, 1:52–70. Семенов, Ю.И. 1993. Переход от первобытного общества к классовому: пути и варианты развития (часть 1). Этнографическое обозрение 1: 52–70.

Sherratt, A. 1981. Plough and Pastoralism: Aspects of the Secondary Products Revolution. In: I. Hodder, G. Isaak & N. Hammond, eds. *Pattern of the Past: Studies in Honour of David Clarke*. Cambridge: Cambridge University Press, pp. 261–305.

Smith, M.E. 2005. City size in Late Postclassic Mesoamerica. *Journal of Urban History*, 31(4):403–34.

Strogatz, S.H. 1994. *Nonlinear Dynamics and Chaos with Applications to Physics, Biology, Chemistry, and Engineering*. Cambridge, MA: Perseus Publishing.

Szmyt, M. 2010. *Between West and East: People of the Globular Amphora culture in Eastern Europe: 2950–2350 BC*. Baltic-Pontic Studies 8.

Tainter, J.A. 1988. *The Collapse of Complex Societies*. Cambridge: Cambridge University Press.

Tarapata, forthcoming. Trends in demographic development as a tool for relative dating (with application to settlements of the Chechelnitskaya local group). *Acta Archaeologia Conservativa* 1.

Tkachuk, T.M. 2005. *Znakovi systemy Trypilsko-Cucutenskoi kulturno-istorychnoi spilnosti (maliovanyj posud), ch. 2: Semiotychnyj analiz Trypilsko-Kukutenskyh znakovyh system (maliovanyj posud)*. Vinnytsia: Nova Knyga. Ткачук, Т.М. 2005. *Знакові системи Трипільсько-Кукутенської культурно-історичної спільності (мальований посуд), ч. 2: семіотичний аналіз Трипільсько-Кукутенських знакових систем (мальований посуд)*. Вінниця: Нова книга.

Tsvek, O.V. 2006. *Poselennia skhidnotrypilskoi kultury: korotkyi narys*. Kyiv: Institute of Archaeology of the NASU.

Цвек, О.В. 2006. *Поселення східнотрипільської культури: короткий нарис*. Київ: Інститут археології НАНУ.

Videiko, M. 2013. *Kompleksnoe izuchenie krupnykh poselenij Tripolskoj kultury V – IV tys. do n.e.* Saarbrücken: Lambert Academic Publishing. Видейко, М.Ю., 2013. Комплексное изучение крупных поселений Трипольской культуры V – IV тыс. до н.э. Saarbrücken: Lambert Academic Publishing.

Videiko, M.Yu. 2002a. Localnye gruppy tripoloskoj kultury na Sredndem Dnepre. In: E. V. Yarovoj, ed. *Drevnejshie obshchnosti zemledeltsev i skotovodov Severnogo Prichernomorja (V tys. do n.e. – V v. n.e.).* Tiraspol: NIL «Archeologija» PGU im. T. Shevchenko, pp. 60–62. Видейко, М.Ю. 2002а. Локальные группы трипольской культуры на Среднем Днестре. В сб.: Е.В. Яровой, ред. Древнейшие общности земледельцев и скотоводов Северного Причерноморья (V тыс. до н.э. – V в. н.э.). Тирасполь: НИЛ «Археология» ПГУ им. Т. Шевченко, с. 60–62.

Videiko, M.Yu. 2002b. *Trypilski protomista: Istoriya doslidzen.* Kyiv: Institute of Archaeology of the NASU. Відейко, М.Ю. 2002b. *Трипільські протоміста: історія досліджень.* Київ: Інститут археології НАНУ.

Videiko, M.Yu. 2008. Baden Culture Influences to the East of the Carpathian Mountains. In: M. Furholt, M. Szmyt & A. Zastawny, eds. *The Baden Complex and the Outside World.* Bonn: Dr. Rudolf Habelt GmbH, pp. 289–98.

Videiko, M.Yu. 2011. Trypilska kultura u Seredniomy Podniprovyi. *Pereyaslavika. Naukovi zapysky*, 5(7):109–27. Відейко, М.Ю. 2011. Трипільська культура у Середньому Подніпров'ї. Переяславпка. Наукові записки 5(7):109–27.

Włodarczak, P. 2006. Chronologia grupy Południowo-Wschodniej kultury Pucharów Łejkowatych w świetle dat radiowęglowych. In: J. Libera & K. Tunia, eds. *Idea Megalityczna w Obrządku Pogrzebowym Kultury Pucharów Lejkowatych.* Lublin-Krakow: Standruk, pp. 27–66.

Yoffee, N. & Cowgill, G.L., eds. 1988. *The Collapse of Ancient States and Civilizations.* Tucson: University of Arizona Press.

Zastawny, A. 2015. Absolute Chronology of the Baden Culture in Lesser Poland – New Radiocarbon Dates. In: M. Nowak & A. Zastawny, eds. *The Baden Culture around the Western Carpathians.* Krakow: Ekodruk, pp. 191–220.

Zbenovich, V.G. 1990. K porbleme krupnyh tripolskih poselenij. In: V. G. Zbenovich, ed. *Rannezemledelcheskie poseleniya-giganty Tripolskoj kultury na Ukraine: Tezisy dokladov pervogo polevogo seminara.* Taljanki: Institute of Archaeology of the AS of the USSR, pp. 10–12. Збенович, В.Г. 1990. К проблеме крупных трипольских поселений. В сб.: В.Г. Збенович, ред. Раннеземледельческие поселения-гиганты на Украине. Тезисы докладов первого полевого семинара. Тальянки: Институт археологии АН СССР.

Zhuravlev, O.P. 2008. *Tvarynnytstvo ta myslyvstvo u trypilskih plemen na terytorii Ukrainy.* Kyiv: Shlyah. Журавльов, О.П. 2008. Тваринництво та мисливство у трипільських племен на території України. Київ: Шлях.

CHAPTER 16

Trypillia and Uruk

JOHANNES MÜLLER AND SUSAN POLLOCK

Dealing with the largest settlements of European prehistory, Trypillia mega-sites and the Late Trypillia development should be compared with population agglomerations that took place contemporarily in Southern Mesopotamia: the development of 'agricultural towns' and first cities during the Uruk-period. The only two phenomena of such huge population agglomerations worldwide at that time, within the Southern Buh and Dnipro interfluve and Southern Mesopotamia, display quite marked differences in historical outcome and consequences. While Trypillian mega-sites remained a chronologically short phenomenon of individual site durations no longer than 150 years, with the whole mega-site phenomenon restricted to about four centuries (c. 4000–3600 BCE), the Uruk development created 'urban landscapes' not only for a few centuries, but as a constant achievement for hundreds of years (starting around the beginning of the 4th millennium BCE). In Uruk, the 'urban revolution' began, while in Late Trypillia prehistoric small stratified societies continued (e.g. Kolesnikov, 1993; Kośko, 1995).

Thus, a structural comparison between both regions and developments might help to answer different questions: Where are similarities and differences in the development of population agglomerations? Which role did the development of public buildings and the development of political institutions play? Which kinds of dependencies are visible between different settlements or subgroups within the population? In both areas, we might also discuss the aspect of ruralization and urbanization, of management patterns within the mega-sites and cities, and of non-tributary and tributary systems. In a holistic approach, we observe that one society continues an egalitarian way of life without class differences, while the other develops a stratified society with a repressive state administration. A comparison of the settlement systems, demography, and the development of asymmetric relations may be starting points.

URUK

The beginnings of settlement in the alluvial lowlands of Southern Mesopotamia go back to at least the start of the 6th millennium BCE (Figure 1). However, settlement was sparse until the late fifth or early fourth millennium. Most sites were small, only occasionally exceeding 2 or 3 ha, although a handful of sites began to appear in the second half of the 5th millennium that reached sizes of 10–12 ha. These larger settlements, including Ur, Eridu, Nippur, and Uruk, differed from smaller communities in having a temple, in some cases a cemetery, and, presumably, a substantially larger population.

It was only in the Uruk period (c. 4200–3100 BCE)[1] that the settled population density, as well as the sizes of communities, exploded. Although the chronological resolution is quite coarse, relying as it does on regional settlement surveys carried out in the 1950s, 1960s, and 1970s, it is clear that during the first two-thirds of the Uruk period (LC 2–4) substantial portions of the alluvial lowlands in proximity to the multiple, braided channels of the Euphrates and Tigris rivers were settled in densities that far exceeded anything previously witnessed. Within the surveyed portion of the alluvial lowlands, Robert McCormick Adams identified two distinct sub-regions, which he named the Nippur-Adab and the Uruk regions, to the North and South, respectively, after their major settlements (Adams & Nissen, 1972; Adams 1981; Wright, 1981).

Both the total settled area and the sizes of some sites increased dramatically in the Uruk period, although most settlements remained small. The result was a marked hierarchy of site sizes.[2] In LC 2–4 (c. 4200–3400 BCE), the Nippur-Adab region is characterized by the presence of several large settlements, all of a more or less similar size (25–50 ha), and a range of small to medium sites, of which nearly seventy per cent are 1 ha or less. In the Uruk region, in contrast, one single site, Uruk itself, grew to a size of approximately 100 ha, dominating all others. Here, too, well over half of the remaining sites are 1 ha or less.

---

[1] The Uruk period is conventionally divided into Early, Middle, and Late Uruk. More recent reconsiderations have led to an alternative terminology of Late Chalcolithic (LC) 2–5, with Early Uruk corresponding to LC 2, Middle Uruk to LC 3–4, and Late Uruk equivalent to LC 5 (Rothman, 2001).

[2] Adams differentiates between sites less than 10 ha ('villages') and those 10 ha and more ('urban'), Johnson argues for a quadripartite division (< 3 ha, 3–7 ha, 8–15 ha, 19 or more ha), and I have used the categories of 8 ha or less, 8.1–15 ha, and 20 ha or more (Adams, 1981: 71–75; Pollock, 2001: 187).

© European Association of Archaeologists 2016

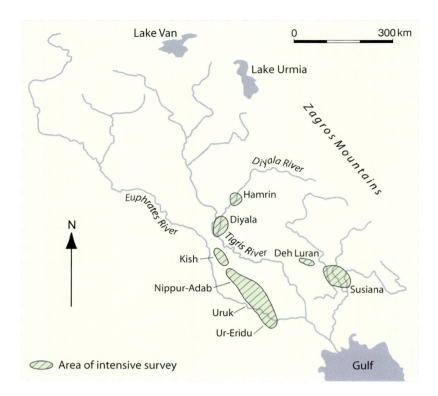

Figure 1. Areas of intensive settlement surveys in Southern Mesopotamia and neighbouring regions (from Pollock, 1999: 55, figure 3.8).

The massive growth in settlement in the earlier part of the Uruk period, although probably partly an artefact of the poor chronological resolution of the survey material, is nonetheless so great that it is very unlikely that it can be attributed to biological growth alone. Rather, the explosive increase in settled population probably had multiple sources: immigration from other regions, coming together of people who had previously resided in very small villages or hamlets that were too ephemeral to be archaeologically visible,[3] and/or settling down of (partially) mobile elements of the population in villages, towns, and cities, particularly in Uruk.

The subsequent LC 5 (c. 3400–3100 BCE) development makes it clear that the two sub-regions moved only partially on a parallel track. In the Nippur-Adab area, the medium-sized and large sites (those larger than 8 ha) remained similar to their LC 2–4 size, although their number was reduced by half. In almost all cases, this reduction was not the result of abandonment but rather of a shrinkage in size (see Pollock, 2001: 189, table 6.1). In the Uruk region, the site of Uruk ballooned to 230 ha, making it home to a population of at least 23,000 people, if not closer to 45,000. The tendency of Uruk to grow massively continued into the third millennium, at which point it reached 400 ha (Finkbeiner, 1991). Interestingly, Uruk's exponential growth did not prevent the continuation of settlement in small communities: In LC 5, the proportion of sites less than 1 ha declined but still constituted nearly forty per cent of the total. Uruk's huge size, as well as its economic and probably political clout, does seem to have prevented the emergence of other large sites. In LC 5, only one other settlement reaches the large category, and at 24 ha it was barely more than ten per cent of the size of Uruk.

Characteristic of both regions is a trend towards ruralization–the proliferation of small sites–that accompanied urbanization (Schwartz & Falconer, 1994; Pollock, 2001: 215). However, the proportion of people living in larger sites, assuming that population numbers are directly related to site size, is high in both regions; accounting for seventy to eighty-two per cent of the total (Pollock, 2001: 215–216).[4] Indeed, Mesopotamia remains a largely urbanized landscape through the Bronze Age (Wilkinson, 2004).

A striking feature of urbanization is that many of the larger communities–those that we generally refer to as cities–remain inhabited for centuries and in some cases millennia. This contrasts with a substantially greater

---

[3]Massive alluviation has certainly obscured short-lived settlements in many parts of the alluvial lowlands. How much has been missed is difficult to estimate, but there is little doubt that it is primarily the smallest sites (Adams, 1981: 39–42; Wilkinson, 2004: 56–57).

[4]These results are substantially different from Adams' (1981: 75, table 4), because I have attempted to account for the "contemporaneity problem" (see Pollock, 1999: chapter 3, 2001).

volatility of small sites, which tended to be settled, abandoned, and refounded more frequently. Overall, however, the rates at which sites were abandoned and others founded are much higher in the Uruk region than in the Nippur-Adab region, suggesting that the former area was more volatile in comparison with a more stable northerly area (Pollock, 2001: 213–4).

The connections between urban and rural settlements were complex and dynamic. One crucial element of their relationship was the dependence of some communities on tribute in the form of labour and goods, especially agricultural and animal products, produced by those living in rural areas. The degree of tribute levied can be indirectly assessed in terms of the area of land available to each settlement, as well as the density of bevelled rim bowls; a coarse, mass-produced pottery vessel that has been argued to have been used as a ration container for corvée labourers (Nissen, 1988: 83–85). It can be shown that already by LC2–4 the city of Uruk was too large to be provisioned by its inhabitants alone, and it must therefore have been dependent on tribute from people living outside it. In contrast, even the two largest sites in the Nippur-Adab region might have been able to meet the food requirements of their populace without rural input, although this does not imply that tribute demands were not levied. Owing to their proportionally greater access to land, as well as indications of substantial involvement in agricultural pursuits, it may be appropriate to envision the larger communities in the Nippur-Adab region as 'agricultural towns' rather than settlements whose residents were primarily engaged in non-subsistence pursuits (Pollock, 2001: 194–210; see also Steinkeller, 2007).

The internal structures of large Uruk-period sites in Southern Mesopotamia are, for the most part, not well known because few have been excavated. Most of the available evidence comes from the later (LC 4–5) part of the period. At Uruk itself, nearly forty seasons of excavations by German teams concentrated almost exclusively on the civic ('public') area of the city, which consisted of massive, highly elaborate buildings. Many have been referred to as temples, but it is by no means certain that all of them were religious or cultic structures; what is clear is that they were not domestic buildings. Regardless of their intended or actual uses, these buildings share several important features. The central area in which many of them were constructed, the so-called Eanna district, was elevated above the surrounding area. After what may have been a relatively short use-life, the buildings were meticulously cleaned before being demolished down to the lowest courses of the walls (Nissen, 2002). Many of the structures exhibit unique or nearly unique features, ranging from the use of particular building materials such as limestone to the exceptional plans of many of the buildings, which were not continued in subsequent centuries (Bernbeck and Pollock, 2002: 184–5).

At Abu Salabikh, the LC 5 occupation of the Uruk Mound was walled on two sides and surrounded by water channels on the remainder. The construction of the wall took place at a time when the settlement had shrunk from 10 ha to approximately half that size. Sometime between LC 3 and LC 5, a large mud-brick platform was built in the northern portion of the site, probably serving as a base on which to construct a major building(s) (Pollock et al., 1996: 689; Pollock, 2015: 272–3).

Uruk-period temple structures developed out of Ubaid prototypes. They were built on a tripartite plan, with a central hall flanked by rows of smaller rooms on the two long sides. Typically, they are distinguished by a niched and buttressed façade, as well as the presence of mud or mud-brick 'altars' and other features (Heinrich, 1982). Their general similarity in ground-plan to houses, as well as linguistic evidence from the 3rd millennium BCE, points to the likelihood that temples began as special houses that over time became more and more differentiated.

The Uruk period also saw an enormous increase in material objects associated with administration that are in turn indicative of complex management of sectors of the economy. These include cylinder seals which rapidly replaced stamp seals in the latter part of the Uruk period; sealings made by stamping or rolling a seal on moist clay to close or mark a pottery vessel, basket, bale, door or clay tablet; clay tokens, made and used for millennia but which became more differentiated in form and decoration in Uruk times; clay bullae or hollow balls with tokens inside and seal impressions and numerical signs on the outside; and finally numerical and then written ('proto-cuneiform') tablets (Pollock, 1999: chapter 6). All of these artefacts, some of which appeared for the first time in the Uruk period, whereas others became more common and/or more differentiated, seem to have been used principally to record economic transactions, in particular, the circulation of goods and information about them. How much of this circulation was local or intraregional and how much extended over substantial geographic extents remains a subject for further research.

At least some of the many changes observable in 4th millennium Mesopotamia can be described as 'exploratory.' During that time, and perhaps especially in LC 5, urban populations searched for possible ways to deal with radically new modes of living. The adoption of novel institutions, technologies, and the like always brings with them dangers of failure. Many of the new forms–including the use of calcareous stone for construction, the decoration of public buildings with coloured wall cones, and building plans that seem never to have been repeated–do seem to have 'failed' in the sense that they were not perpetuated. Nonetheless, Late Uruk society seems to have been flexible enough in other respects to adjust to rapid changes. While the end of the Late Chalcolithic brought substantial transformations in its wake, especially in the regions surrounding Mesopotamia, urban systems were sustained for many centuries to come.

Trypillia

In addition to the huge North Pontic distribution area that the whole Trypillia phenomenon covered, as well as regional differences, a clear chronological and spatial development of site sizes was described by several authors (Tsvek, 2006; Diachenko and Menotti, 2012; Kruts, 1989, 2012; Videiko, 2006, 2013). Especially the introduction of geophysical surveys in the 1970s and the use of elaborated geomagnetic devices for the surveys in the 2010s enabled a reconstruction of house numbers, settlement plans, etc. (Videiko, 2013; Rassmann et al., 2014; Rassmann et al., 2016). Combined with excavation results, a reconstruction of detailed processes in Trypillian settlement patterns and the organization of social space is possible.

Early sites (Trypillia A, c. 4800–4600 BCE) usually have a size of up to 10 ha, often with no more than fifteen dwellings; middle Trypillia sites (BI–BI/II, 4500–4000 BCE) expand to 20–50 ha with up to two-hundred dwellings. In Trypillia BII and Late Trypillia CI (4000–3600 BCE) the mega-sites, with up to 3000 dwellings and settled areas of 350 ha, are known; while in Late Trypillia CII (3600–2900 BCE) a reduction of site sizes to less than 20 ha after 3350 BCE is detected again.

In principle, the domestic settlements look very similar. While in Trypillia A, most of the sites are composed of more or less linear rows of houses, usually on the first water terrace edge, already at some sites (like Bernashivka) the principle of a circular or ellipsoid house ring is present (Zbenovich, 1996a). This kind of settlement planning is typical for most middle and late Trypillia sites, especially in the eastern distribution region, now the sites are located primarily on promontories or plateaus.

Concentrating on the main area of the Trypillia mega-sites, the Southern Buh and Dnipro interfluve with the settlements of the Volodymyrivsko-Tomashivska local group, an increase in population is visible around 4000 BCE and a decrease around 3400 BCE (cf. Diachenko, 2012: 126, figure 5.6). We observe the contemporaneity of different settlement categories (small: <30 ha; medium-sized: 35–80 ha; and large: 100–350 ha) at different stages of the development. Nevertheless, the bigger one site gets in the region, the fewer other smaller sites are observed within the vicinity of, for example, a mega-site. Extensive field surveys around Nebelivka proved the non-existence of smaller, contemporary sites for the Trypillia BII phase (4000–3800 BCE) (Chapman et al., 2014: 136, figure 2). In the cases of Taljanky and Maidanetske, only two sites existed contemporarily in the vicinity of each of these mega-sites during the CI/T3 phase (3900–3700 BCE).

In spite of the marked hierarchy of site sizes, c. ninety-five per cent or even more of the population agglomerated in the mega-sites of the settlement area of the Volodymyrivsko-Tomashivska local group. Even if these smaller sites like Talne 2 and 3 existed, no forms of asymmetric dependencies between the few small settlements and the giant ones can be detected. Both categories of domestic sites were able to gain their subsistence needs from their local vicinity (see Ohlrau et al., 2016). Cooperation might have existed in aspects of cattle herding and woodland use, but not with regard to arable land, as the modelled land-use patterns indicate some degree of overlap in respect to these activities (Ohlrau et al., 2016, figures 2–4).

When the mega-sites disappeared, small- and medium-sized sites existed once again in a more balanced way. Yet, the denser settlement pattern in the Southern Buh and Dnipro interfluve still developed around 4100 BCE and showed a steady population increase until 3700 BCE, which is followed until 3400 BCE by a reduction of the population. Obviously, the phenomena of mega-sites enabled social groups to grow and develop positively until a certain point of departure. During the Trypillia BII/CI phase, the nearly complete absence of fortifications within the whole Trypillia/Cucuteni area was noted (Dergachev, 2007, 36–41; Diachenko, 2012, 128). Even the ditches at mega-sites seem not to reflect any kind of military defensive purpose, as the excavations in Nebelivka seem to indicate (Chapman et al., 2016).

In the most vivid phases of the mega-sites, population agglomerations of about ±15,000 inhabitants existed, e.g. in Maidanetske (Ohlrau, 2014; Müller et al., 2016a). As already described, the reconstruction of land-use patterns showed that the carrying capacity of the fertile Chenorzem plateaus was not reached. Furthermore, data on the subsistence economy do not indicate any severe changes (except in location and settlement size) during several hundred years from early to late Trypillia (4800–3400 BCE) in respect to crops and animal usage, which also points to a stable constitution of the communities (cf. Kirleis and Dal Corso, 2016). Nevertheless, changes appeared, for example, in the transport technology: terracotta models from the Trypillia BII/CI phase indicate the introduction of sledges, which were pulled by oxen; latest until around 4000 BCE (cf. Balabina, 2004; Maran 2004, 436–8). They probably also enabled transport for agrarian purposes, for example, from more distant arable land to the dwellings. The synchronous appearance of sledge models and the mega-sites clearly demonstrates that, from c. 4000 BCE, with the new traction technique, more massive agglomerations of populations were made possible in a self-sustaining system. Mega-sites existed without any kind of ruralized landscape in their surroundings, from which the supply of food, for example, would have been necessary.

In consequence, the contrast to late Uruk is obvious: no tributary system with dependencies between surrounding smaller sites and the main city was necessary. As such, no ruralization, but also no urbanization, took place in Late Trypillia. In contrast, the label 'agricultural towns', as used for the Nippur-Adab Mesopotamian area, might be applicable. However, since not only most of the population, but also most of the economic, social, and political differences, were concentrated within the Trypillian mega-sites. Thus, a comparison of the internal mega-site organization is important before developing a characterization of Late Trypillia mega-sites in respect to the Uruk development.

First of all, the classical layout of the mega-site settlement plans, with concentric house rings around an open space, different avenues within the site, and defined residential quarters, indicates an overall plan; thus, also the existence of at least some kind of collective decision-making institution.

Second, differences in economic activities between the domestic houses, and differences in house sizes, might indicate not only specializations within the settlement, but also asymmetric relations between household groups (cf. Müller *et al.*, 2016b). Nevertheless, the spatial distribution patterns of ceramic designs indicate an open, not restricted, communication within mega-sites such as Maidanetske, which stands in contrast to an accentuation of social differences.

Third, the specialized production of pottery in (communal?) kilns suggests, besides the household-bound production and distribution of primary and secondary aspects of the subsistence economy, a specialized craft on a supra-household level (cf. Korvin-Piotrovskiy *et al.*, 2016). On the one hand, technological progress exemplifies the increasing needs on craft products–in respect to ceramic production, with the introduction of the primitive potter's wheel in the Trypillia B phase (Markevich, 1981; Ellis, 1984), and in respect to weaving as indicated by the concentration of loom-weights in some houses in the Trypillia C1 phase (Zbenovich, 1996b, 236; Müller *et al.*, 2016b)–on the other hand, no craftsmen's quarters were identified at Trypillia sites.

Fourth, within the mega-sites huge, obviously non-domestic, buildings were discovered (cf. Chapman *et al.*, 2016; Chapman *et al.*, 2014). Located in the most visible, and thus 'public', areas of the mega-sites or at crucial nodes on public track ways, these mega-structures seem to indicate some kind of public houses for assemblies or other purposes. The excavation of such a mega-structure in Nebelivka did, on the one hand, indicate the special purpose of the place, probably also for ritual activities, and on the other hand discovered just the enlargement of the usual house architecture and installations to a 'mega-complex'. Even if these mega-structures are at visible places within the settlement, and in this sense also comparable with the most visible Eanna district with public buildings in Uruk, in general no concentration of mega-structures exists within one area of the settlement. For example, in Maidanetske the distribution pattern shows a strategic positioning of these mega-structures every 200 m on the main public ring within the site or at the radial track ways that lead into the centre of the site. Again, the difference from the Mesopotamian early towns and cities is obvious: not a spatial concentration of the public buildings like temples at one place within the settlement, but a diverse spatial distribution is observed.

Here, the main political difference between the Mesopotamian and the Trypillia development seems to be visible. The mega-sites stay in a state of organization that seems to be divided into autonomous internal groups, in contrast to huge population agglomeration and the clearly structured layout of settlement planning. Neither the distribution of kilns, for example, nor the distribution of mega-structures indicates a concentration of economic or social power in a clearly developed hierarchical system. As no economic or social pressure existed to develop such a kind of hierarchical system as known from Uruk, mega-sites could be seen as loose cooperations that split up again under different circumstances–and that did happen. Meanwhile in Uruk, the tendency towards a more and more centralized ruling system continued.

Consequences

In summary, even if the existence of public buildings and specialized craft production is very probable for Trypillia BII/CI mega-sites, clear hints for a complex stratified society are missing. Within the mega-sites, the areas that could be associated with the mega-structures are comparable in size with small and medium Trypillia sites of the preceding and following phase. As no tributary system of an urbanized and ruralized landscape and no elaborated urban management, e.g. with seals[5] and property declarations,

---

[5]The so-called 'seals' from Cucuteni-Trypillia had probably a different function as Uruk seals.

developed as in South Mesopotamia, the sustainability of these mega-sites was not necessary from an economic, political, or social point view. They were a kind of social experiment, triggered perhaps by changes in the transport system and the then new possibility of demographic agglomerations even within a predominantly agrarian subsistence system. In this sense, they are still rural settlements.

REFERENCES

Adams, R.M. & Nissen, H. 1972. *The Uruk Countryside*. Chicago: University of Chicago Press.

Adams, R.M. 1981. *Heartland of Cities*. Chicago: University of Chicago Press.

Balabina, I.V. 2004. Glinianye modeli sanej tripolskoj kultury i tema puti. In: A. N. Gej, ed. *Pamiatniki archeologii i drevnego iskusstva Evrazii. Pamiati Vitalija Vasiljevicha Volkova*. Moscow: Institute of Archaeology of the RAN, pp. 180–213. Балабина, В.И. 2004. Глиняные модели саней трипольской культуры и тема пути. В сб.: А.Н. Гей, ред. Памятники археологии и древнего искусства Евразии. Памяти Виталия Васильевича Волкова. Москва: Институт археологии РАН, с. 180–213.

Bernbeck, R. & Pollock, S. 2002. Reflections on the Historiography of 4th Millennium Mesopotamia. In: A. Hausleiter, S. Kerner & B. Müller-Neuhof, eds. *Material Culture and Mental Spheres. Rezeption archäologischer Denkrichtungen in der Vorderasiatischen Altertumskunde. Internationales Symposium für Hans J. Nissen, Berlin, 23.-24. Juni 2000*. Münster: Ugarit, pp. 171–204.

Chapman, J., Videiko, M.Y., Gaydarska, B., Burdo, N. & Hale, D. 2014. Architectural Differentiation on a Trypillia Mega-Site: Preliminary Report on the Excavation of a Mega-Structure at Nebelivka, Ukraine. *Journal of Neolithic Archaeology*, 16: 135–57.

Chapman, J., Gaydarska, B. & Hale, D. 2016. Nebelivka: Assembly Houses, Ditches, and Social Structure. In: J. Müller, K. Rassmann & M. Videiko, eds. *Trypillia Mega-Sites and European Prehistory: 4100–3400 BCE*. London and New York: Routledge, pp. 117–132.

Dergachev, V.A. 2007. *O skipetrah, o loshadiah i o voine. V zashchitu migratsioonoj kontseptsii M. Gimbutas*. Sankt-Peterburg: Nestor-Istoriya. Дергачев, В.А. 2007. О скипетрах, о лошадях и о войне. В защиту миграционной концепции М. Гимбутас. Санкт-Петербург: Нестор-История.

Diachenko, A. 2012. Settlement System of West Tripolye Culture in the Southern Bug and Dnieper Interfluve. Formation Problems. In: F. Menotti & A. Korvin-Piotrovskiy, eds. *The Tripolye Culture Giant-Settlements in Ukraine: Formation, Development and Decline*. Oxford: Oxbow Books, pp. 116–38.

Diachenko, A. & Menotti, F. 2012. The Gravity Model: Monitoring the Formation and Development of the Tripolye Culture Giant-Settlements in Ukraine. *Journal of Archaeological Science*, 39: 2810–17.

Ellis, L. 1984. *The Cucuteni-Tripolye Culture: A Study in Technology and the Origins of Complex Society*, BAR International Series 217. Oxford: BAR.

Finkbeiner, U. 1991. *Uruk. Kampagne 35–37, 1982–1984. Die archäologische Oberflächenuntersuchung (Survey). Ausgrabungen in Uruk-Warka Endberichte 4*. Mainz: Philipp von Zabern.

Heinrich, E. 1982. *Die Tempel und Heiligtumer im alten Mesopotamien: Typologie, Morphologie und Geschichte*. Berlin: De Gruyter.

Kirleis, W. & Dal Corso, M. 2016. Trypillian Subsistence Economy: Animal and Plant Exploitation. In: J. Müller, K. Rassmann & M. Videiko, eds. *Trypillia Mega-Sites and European Prehistory: 4100–3400 BCE*. London and New York: Routledge, pp. 195–205.

Kolesnikov, A.G. 1993. *Tripolskoe obshchestvo Srednego Podneprovya: opyt sotsialnyh rekonstruktsij v archeologii*. Kiev: Naukova Dumka. Колесников, А.Г. 1993. Трипольское общество Среднего Поднепровья: опыт социальных реконструкций в археологии. Киев: Наукова думка.

Korvin-Piotrovskiy, A., Hofmann, R., Rassmann, K., Videiko, M. & Brandtstätter, L. 2016. Pottery Kilns in Trypillian Settlements. Tracing the Division of Labour and the Social Organization of Copper Age Communities. In: J. Müller, K. Rassmann & M. Videiko, eds. *Trypillia Mega-Sites and European Prehistory: 4100–3400 BCE*. London and New York: Routledge, pp. 221–252.

Kośko, A., ed. 1995. *Cemeteries of the Sofievka Type: 2950–2750 BC. Baltic-Pontic Studies* 3.

Kruts, V.A. 1989. K istorii naseleniya Tripolskoj kultury v mezhdurechye Yuzhnogo Buga i Dnepra. In: S. S. Berezanskaya, ed. *Pervobytnaya archeologiya: Materialy i issledovaniya*. Kiev: Naukova Dumka, pp. 117–32. Круц, В.А. 1989. К истории населения трипольской культуры в междуречье Южного Буга и Днепра. В сб.: С.С. Березанская, ред. Первобытная археология: материалы и исследования. Киев: Наукова думка, с. 117–132.

Kruts, V.A. 2012. Giant-Settlements of Tripolye Culture. In: F. Menotti & A. Korvin-Piotrovskiy, eds. *The Tripolye Culture Giant-Settlements in Ukraine. Formation, Development and Decline*. Oxford: Oxbow Books, pp. 70–78.

Maran, J. 2004. Kulturkontakte und Wege der Ausbreitung der Wagentechnologie im 4. Jahrtausend v. Chr. In: M. Fansa & S. Burmeister, eds. *Rad und Wagen. Der Ursprung einer Innovation. Wagen im Vorderen Orient und Europa*. Mainz: Philipp von Zabern, pp. 429–42.

Markevich, V.I. 1981. *Pozdnetripolskiye plemena Severnoi Moldavii*. Kishinev: Shtiintsa. Маркевич, В.И. 1981. Позднетрипольские племена Северной Молдавии. Кишинев: Штиинца.

Müller, J., Hofmann, R., Brandtstätter, L., Ohlrau, R. & Videiko, M. 2016a. Chronology and Demography: How Many People Lived in a Mega-Site? In: J. Müller, K. Rassmann & M. Videiko, eds. *Trypillia Mega-Sites and European Prehistory: 4100–3400 BCE*. London and New York: Routledge, pp. 133–169.

Müller, J., Hofmann, R. & Ohlrau, R. 2016b. From Domestic Households to Mega-Structures: Proto-Urbanism? In: J. Müller, K. Rassmann & M. Videiko, eds. *Trypillia Mega-Sites and European Prehistory: 4100–3400 BCE*. London and New York: Routledge, pp. 253–268.

Nissen, H. 1988. *The Early History of the Ancient Near East, 9000–2000 B.C*. Translated by Elizabeth Lutzeier. Chicago: University of Chicago Press.

Nissen, H. 2002. Uruk: Key Site of the Period and Key Site of the Problem. In: J. N. Postgate, ed. *Artefacts of Complexity: Tracking the Uruk in the Near East*. British School of Archaeology in Iraq. Warminster: Aris and Phillips, pp. 1–16.

Ohlrau, R. 2014. Tripolje Großsiedlungen. Geomagnetische Prospektion und architektursoziologische Perspektiven (unpublished Master's thesis, Kiel University).

Ohlrau, R., Dal Corso, M., Kirleis, W. & Müller, J. 2016. Living on the Edge? Carrying Capacities of Trypillian Settlements in the Buh-Dnipro Interfluve. In: J. Müller, K. Rassmann & M. Videiko, eds. *Trypillia Mega-Sites and European Prehistory: 4100–3400 BCE*. London and New York: Routledge, pp. 207–220.

Pollock, S. 1999. *Ancient Mesopotamia: The Eden That Never Was*. Cambridge: Cambridge University Press.

Pollock, S. 2001. The Uruk Period in Southern Mesopotamia. In: M. Rothman, ed. *Uruk Mesopotamia and Its Neighbors: Cross-Cultural Interactions in the Era of State Formation*. Santa Fe: School of Advanced Research, pp. 181–231.

Pollock, S. 2015. Abu Salabikh: History of a Southern Mesopotamian Town. In: R. Dittmann & G. Selz, eds. *It's a Long Way to a Historiography of the Early Dynastic Period(s)*. Münster: Ugarit. pp. 267–87.

Pollock, S., Pope, M. & Coursey, C. 1996. Household Production at the Uruk Mound, Abu Salabikh, Iraq. *American Journal of Archaeology*, 100: 683–98.

Rassmann, K., Ohlrau, R., Hofmann, R., Mischka, C., Burdo, N., Videjko, M.Y. & Müller, J. 2014. High precision Tripolye Settlement Plans, Demographic Estimations and Settlement Organization. *Journal of Neolithic Archaeology*, 16: 96–134.

Rassmann, K., Korvin-Piotrovskiy, A., Videiko, M. & Müller, J. 2016. The New Challenge for Site Plans and Geophysics: Revealing the Settlement Structure of Giant Settlements by Means of Geomagnetic Survey. In: J. Müller, K. Rassmann & M. Videiko, eds. *Trypillia Mega-Sites and European Prehistory: 4100–3400 BCE*. London and New York: Routledge, pp. 29–54.

Rothman, M. ed. 2001. *Uruk Mesopotamia and Its Neighbors: Cross-cultural Interactions in the Era of State Formation*. Santa Fe: School of Advanced Research.

Schwartz, G. & Falconer, S. 1994. Rural Approaches to Social Complexity. In: G. Schwartz & S. Falconer, eds. *Archaeological Views from the Countryside*. Washington DC.: Smithsonian Institution Press, pp. 1–9.

Steinkeller, P. 2007. City and Countryside in Third-Millennium Southern Babylonia. In: E. Stone, ed. *Settlement and Society: Essays Dedicated to Robert McCormick Adams*. Los Angeles: Cotsen Institute of Archaeology, pp. 185–211.

Tsvek, O.V. 2006. *Poselennia Skhodnotrypilskoi kultury: korotkyi narys*. Kyiv: Institute of Archaeology of the NAS of Ukraine. Цвек, О.В. 2006. *Поселення Східнотрипільської культури: короткий нарис*. Київ: Інститут археології НАНУ.

Videiko, M.Yu. 2006. Hliborobstvo trypilskyh plemen. In: G. O. Pashkevych & M. Yu. Videiko, eds. *Rilnytsvo plemen trypilskoi kultury*. Kyiv: Institute of Archaeology of the NASU, pp. 81–122. Відейко, М.Ю. 2006. Хліборобство трипільських племен. У кн.: Г.О. Пашкевич і М.Ю. Відейко. Рільництво племен трипільської культури. Київ: Інститут археології НАНУ, с. 81–122.

Videiko, M. 2013. *Kompleksnoe izuchenie krupnykh poselenij Tripolskoj kultury V–IV tys. do n.e.* Saarbrücken: Lambert Academic Publishing. Видейко, М.Ю., 2013. *Комплексное изучение крупных поселений Трипольской культуры V–IV тыс. до н.э.* Saarbrücken: Lambert Academic Publishing.

Wilkinson, T. 2004. The Disjunction Between Mediterranean and Near Eastern Survey: Is It Real? In: E. Athanassopoulos & L. Wandsnider, eds. *Mediterranean Archaeological Landscapes: Current Issues*. Philadelphia: University of Pennsylvania Museum of Archaeology and Anthropology, pp. 55–67.

Wright, H. 1981. The Southern Margins of Sumer: Archaeological Survey of the Area of Eridu and Ur. In: R. M. Adams. *Heartland of Cities*. Chicago: University of Chicago Press, pp. 295–345.

Zbenovich, V.G. 1996a. *Siedlungen der frühen Tripol'e-Kultur zwischen Dnestr und Südlichem Bug*. Leidorf: Espelkamp.

Zbenovich, V.G. 1996b. The Tripolye Culture: Centenary of Research. *Journal of World Prehistory*, 10: 199–241.

CHAPTER 17

Low-density Agrarian Cities: A Principle of the Past and the Present

JOHN CHAPMAN AND BISSERKA GAYDARSKA

INTRODUCTION

The topic of urbanism constitutes one of the central questions in human evolution. The topic has attracted a massive literature in archaeology (e.g. Mumford, 1961; Blanton, 1976; Fox, 1977; Cowgill, 2004), with no sign of the flow of books and articles being stemmed and no sign of any consensus as to the meaning of the term 'urbanism' and the origins of the process of urbanization (Gaydarska, in press). In this chapter, we shall be examining early examples of the emergence of what we call 'Big Weird Sites'[1]–settlements that are unusually large for their local and regional cultural context and which pose questions about the evolutionary model of settlement growth (e.g. Birch, 2013).

Urbanism is one of the most complex of terms and there is no prospect of agreement on its meaning and content. Recent trends in Eurasian archaeology have expanded the content of what an urban site means to include small sites (e.g. 0.8-ha Balkan tells such as Provadia (Nikolov, 2008) and densely packed 2 ha. Late Iron Age sites in Southern France (Dietler, 1997), as well as large sites (e.g. the Trypillia mega-sites: Videiko, 2007). It is deeply ironic that a theme so fully colonized by processual archaeologists has become so devoid of meaning as to make researchers question: 'Does anything go?'. We do not have the space here to pursue this irony and shall be content ourselves with an approach to one specific form of urbanism that has some relevance to the Trypillia problem, as well as other urban debates.

In two meetings–an SAA 2013 conference symposium entitled 'Cities, large villages, or neither? The conundrum of Cahokia, the *oppida*, the Yoruba towns and others' and a follow-up seminar at the Amerind conference centre, near Tucson, Arizona in May 2014, entitled 'Cities or Big Villages? New Approaches to Great, Anomalous Places'–a group of scholars 'assembled' by Roland Fletcher has been studying these sites and trying to define what they may have had in common. We have been stimulated by one of Roland Fletcher's key insights–the low-density pathways to urbanism that form alternatives to Vere Gordon Childe's classic, concentrated, high-density urbanism of the kind typified by Early Bronze Age Ur or Uruk, classical Rome, Early Byzantine Constantinople, and Classic Teotihuacan.

Fletcher (2009) has postulated that a common urban trajectory began with high-density cities with a size of up to 100 ha and a population density of up to 1000 per ha, but these cities morphed into increasingly large but also increasingly low-density settlements of 1–40 km^2 (Fletcher, n.d.) (Figure 1). While the most noteworthy modern example is Mega-lopolis on the east coast of North America, there are also many ancient examples that have been transformed from high-density precursors into huge low-density centres (e.g. Angkor, Cahokia, Great Zimbabwe, Co Loa, and some of the Late Iron Age oppida in Europe) (Figure 2). The neologism 'rurban' (Smith, 1972) captures the flavour of these places, which are, in one sense, dominated by unbuilt space more akin to farm territories than urban quarters. These places are clearly very different from the Childean high-density norm and deserve consideration on their own terms. In this chapter, we have three aims: (1) to introduce the cultural background of the earliest known set of examples of low-density urbanism in the world; (2) to characterize the social space of these so-called Trypillia mega-sites; and (3) to place the mega-sites in the wider context of the development of low-density urbanism.

LOW-DENSITY URBAN SITES IN GLOBAL PERSPECTIVE

Fletcher (2009: n.d.) has characterized 'low-density urban' sites in opposition to the compact, high-density imperial capitals such as Rome and Istanbul, as a different kind of urbanism–one in which the urban centre moved outward and colonized the rural areas to produce a patchwork of monumental foci, residential

---
[1] Roland Fletcher's term for these sites is 'Great, Anomalous Sites' (Fletcher, n.d.).

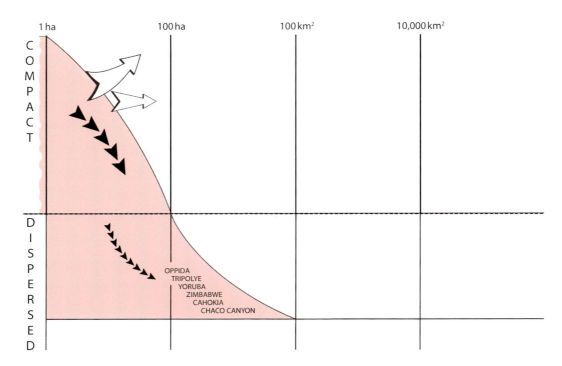

Figure 1. Trajectories of high-density to low-density urban sites (source: Fletcher, n.d.).

houses, and agro-pastoral areas. The global distribution of low-density urban sites is currently patchy, owing to variable research but covers the temperate zone in Europe (Stonehenge, Trypillia, Iron Age oppida), North America (Cahokia, Chaco Canyon), and East Asia (Longshan group, China), the savannah zone in Africa (Great Zimbabwe), as well as the tropical zone in Africa (Yoruba towns), East Asia (Co Loa, Angkor Wat), and South America (Amazonia) (Figure 2). Current areas without obvious low-density urban sites include much of the Near East and North Africa.

These sites clearly comprised immensely varied landscapes, architectural and social complexity, and trajectories of development, peak and decline. Yet there are five overlapping characteristics which most, but rarely all, low-density urban sites shared which came out of the Arizona discussions of low-density urban sites in May 2014.[2]

First, the importance of major building projects, which transformed the 'low-density urban sites' at each new phase. There was a sense, at major monumental foci such as Stonehenge (Barrett, 1994) and Cahokia (Pauketat, 2009: n.d.), that the world was created anew each time a new temple or monument was constructed. Equally, the creation of a second, slightly larger wall in the Late Phase at the Chinese 3rd millennium BCE Shanxi site of Taosi allowed the expanded importance of commoner houses at the expense of the middle phase palatial area–re-structuring the entire settlement (Nu, 2013; White, n.d.). The foundation of each new stone compound by a different Shona king at Great Zimbabwe (Pikirayi, n.d.) also re-formulated royal interactions, creating new foci of elite attention for the entire population. As Parker Pearson (n.d.) observed, what was more important than the design and its future orientation was the actual 'doing'–the construction itself. If we think, together with McAnany (n.d.), of building projects as 'experiments' in agglomeration, we can avoid the dangers of anachronism and teleological reasoning.

Second, there was a strong modular component of kinship-base, house-oriented planning practices in the low-density urban sites. This element was especially significant in the emergence of Yoruba towns, where, from a starting position (AD 500–800) of houses linked to mega-houses, with a loose alliance of mega-houses, each with a corporate head, under an overall ruler, the mega-houses were dismantled and replaced (AD 11th–12th) by an urban component of multiple corporate groups under a centralized government and a divine king (Ogundiran, 2013: n.d.). Pauketat (2009) has also identified a Cahokia architectural module at the residential Neighbourhood level, consisting of rectangular and circular buildings linked to plazas, while Neves (n.d.) recognized a modular principle of plazas, mounds, and fields in a 12-km-long site in French Guiana.

---

[2]We wish to acknowledge all of the participants, but especially the group chair Roland Fletcher, in the Dragoon, Arizona workshop on 'Cities or big villages? New approaches to great, anomalous places'. This section of the paper owes much to our collective discussions of inspiring individual inputs.

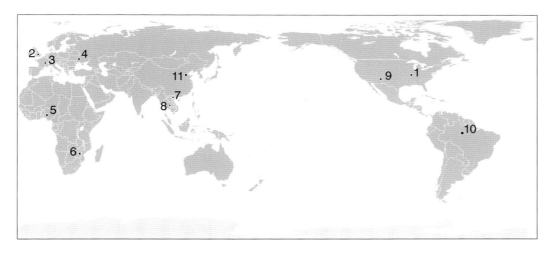

Figure 2. Worldwide distribution of low-density urban sites: (1) Cahokia; (2) Stonehenge; (3) Mont Beuvray; (4) Trypillia mega-sites (Nebelivka); (5) Ile Ife; (6) Great Zimbabwe; (7) Co Loa; (8) Angkor Wat; (9) Chaco Canyon; (10) Manaus (Amazonia); (11) Longshan group (source: Bisserka Gaydarska).

Third, many of the low-density urban sites had seasonal components in their populations. The most extreme example may be the Solomonic Empire of Ethiopia (AD 1270–1529), which moved its capital of some 40,000 residents, with a standing army of a further 40,000 soldiers, every few weeks and left their low-density urban site centre for months at a time (Marcus, 1994; Fletcher, n.d.). Fletcher has indeed provocatively suggested that all low-density urban sites may have had a seasonal component that had the perhaps unintended consequence of weakening household ties.

Fourth, most low-density urban sites downplayed the mortuary domain. Although the Early Shang period of China and Stonehenge at its peak were major exceptions to this tendency, there were many other low-density urban sites with very little burial evidence (Cahokia, many European oppida, Amazonian low-density urban sites, Yoruba towns, and Great Zimbabwe). The concentration of ideological power in the hands of the ruling elites would have created tensions between households and the centre, especially at the time of deaths in the family.

Fifth, there was rarely an obvious successor to the low-density urban site, whether on the same site or in the same region. Regional capitals such as post-Han Co Loa were abandoned in the AD *c.* 150 BCE, not to be re-settled again (Kim, 2013). After the great house-burning events at Cahokia, depopulation took the form of sub-group out-migration with no monumental centres left (Pauketat, n.d.). Although the capital of Ile Ife continued to host Yoruba deities long after its decline, the urban features characterizing its peak period were never rebuilt (Ogundrian n.d.). Pauketat (n.d.) has made the ontological contrast between mud-brick cities, which last millennia, and wattle-and-daub cities, which last centuries if not mere decades.

There are many other interesting aspects of the global pool of low-density urban sites but these five characteristics provide a picture of dynamic, changing settlements whose population may have been more mobile than we may have expected and whose building projects created a succession of 'new worlds' in which successive generations of residents made their lives. We now turn to the Trypillia mega-sites to investigate how they fit into this global pattern of low-density urban sites.

Mega-Site Distribution in Time and Place

Turning now to settlements and site sizes, the Trypillia mega-sites' transcendence of the global communication, limit of 100 ha for mixed farming settlements (Fletcher, 1995) was one of the key elements of interest about these settlements, which constituted the largest sites in fourth millennium Europe and grew to sizes comparable with those of the Early Bronze Age city of Uruk (Mesopotamia) (Liverani, 2006). The sheer size of these mega-sites not only prompts questions of the complexity of social structure(s) necessary to sustain such settlements, and the logistics and long-term planning needed to provision them, but also makes them very hard to investigate.

Thirty years ago, Ellis (1984: map 26) used old settlement data and the discovery of the mega-sites in the Uman area to posit a three-level settlement hierarchy, based on site size: (1) an upper level of 250–400 ha; (2) a middle level of 25–75 ha; and (3) a lower level smaller than 25 ha, with a fourth (lowest)

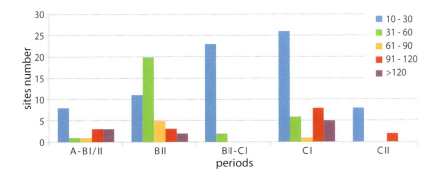

Figure 3. Settlement sizes by Trypillia phase (source: J. Chapman).

level consisting of small ceramic scatters with no recorded size data. However, the absence of chronological data reduces the usefulness of Ellis' map. Recent ground truthing of sites on the Trypillia database (Videiko, 2004) by Nebbia (Nebbia, n.d.) shows that there has been a systematic overestimation of site sizes, with often large areas of ceramic scatters outside the boundary of settlement structures. The same was true of the German fieldwork at Apolianka, which showed a settlement size of 19 ha in comparison with a ceramic scatter previously claimed to cover 90–100 ha (cf. Videiko, 2007; Rassmann et al., 2014). Nonetheless, Diachenko & Menotti (2015; cf. Diachenko, 2012) have used graph theory to show that there was a significant element of hierarchical structuring in some regional Trypillia settlement patterns at the time of the mega-sites.

The re-assessment of the Nebelivka micro-region shows, intriguingly, that there are relatively few settlements within a 25-km radius of Nebelivka coeval with the BII phase of the mega-site (Nebbia, n.d.). These more recent data offer little or no support for a three-level hierarchy at this spatial scale; however, a consideration of settlements within a 50-km radius may produce a stronger size variation. The most significant aspect of the micro-regional site distribution is the seeming lack of a developed, or even an incipient, hinterland around the central site of Nebelivka.

The chronological attribution of each mega-sites to one, and one only, of the main phases of the Trypillia group (A, B, or C; sub-divisions = BI, BI-II, BII, BII-CI transition; CI, CI-II, CII) shows the limited time-depth of mega-sites, as confirmed by the total absence of stratigraphic superpositioning of burnt house floors on any mega-site. There are currently only two mega-sites with a sufficiently large range of AMS dates to posit the time-span of dwelling activities at a mega-site: Nebelivka and Maidanetske. The chronological range of dwelling practices on each site falls within a period of two centuries and perhaps much less.

What is unusual for low-density urban trajectories is the repeated episodes of mega-site dwelling, albeit in different places. Accepting the Trypillia ceramic typo-chronology, there appear to be at least three Trypillia sub-phases—each thought to last several centuries—in which mega-sites (viz., sites larger than 100 ha) have been identified (Figure 3). In between these three sub-phases are periods, also thought by Ukrainian specialists to last several centuries, with no evidence for sites larger than 30 ha. This complex sequence implies potentially major changes in settlement strategies, with one trajectory being environmental overexploitation followed by ecological renewal and the relocation of mega-sites to new areas with their resource potential largely untapped by earlier dwelling phases. However, this sequence makes the assumption of a fully permanent settlement structure at the mega-sites—an assumption that has hardly been challenged in mega-site research so far.

In summary, Trypillia mega-sites larger than 100 ha are known from several sub-phases of the period, interspersed with periods with sites much smaller than 100 ha. In all sub-phases, the settlement pattern comprised a majority of sites far smaller than 100 ha but the three-level settlement hierarchy posited by Ellis (1984) cannot be supported using more recent evidence. The only region with long-term evidence for mega-sites of over 100 ha is the Southern Buh catchment.

Mega-Site Settlement Planning

In a previous chapter, we have summarized the current Durham view on the Nebelivka settlement plan (see Chapman et al., 2016). Taking into account the previous Ukrainian investigations of mega-sites and the recent Ukrainian–German research,[3] the Nebelivka results can contribute to a complex narrative

---
[3] The plans on which these analyses have been based can be found in this volume at p. 33 (Taljanky), p. 118 (Nebelivka), p. 73 (Maidanetske), and p. 50 (Dobrovody).

Figure 4. The Nebelivka house-burning experiment: the two-storeyed house, showing the south wall and door after 1 hour 30 minutes of burning (photo: M. Nebbia).

about Trypillia mega-sites. This narrative is based on the important similarities between the four sites, the variations on shared design principles or elements found at each site, and the equally interesting differences between the mega-sites.

The most obvious similarity is the overall design concept of a central unbuilt space which was separated from concentric rings of houses by radial streets which 'infringed' the unbuilt space (Chapman et al., 2014c). We challenge the traditional account of long-term continuity in concentric planning from Trypillia phase A, on the basis of the ambiguous plan of Mogylna III[4] and suggest that concentric planning may well have been an innovation in Phase BII.

The Neighbourhoods that comprised the most intimate supra-household social unit were also, inevitably, prominent at each mega-site. These plans show that the same degree of variability of size and complexity of the Neighbourhoods were found at each mega-site—a sign of the improvisation and flexibility shown by residents at each mega-site. It is also not surprising that the basic elements of the Trypillia world–burnt houses, unburnt houses, and pits–were found at all mega-sites. A final shared inference is the existence of 'gateways' at points along the concentric house circuits. Although Rassmann et al. (2014: 125) claim that the radial streets at Dobrovody were pathways leading through the outer circuit into the site, this was not always true at the other mega-sites.[5] The naturally occurring water-courses shown at Taljanky (Rassmann et al., 2014: figure 9a) may also have functioned as access passages, not least for stock.

There are two negative traits that are shared by all of the mega-sites so far excavated: a lack of monumental architecture beyond the small number of Assembly houses and the extreme rarity of metal finds, whether gold or copper, or other potential prestige goods (e.g. *Spondylus* shells, polished stone mace-heads or so-called 'sceptres'). The discovery of one of the earliest gold finds of the Trypillia group in the mega-structure at Nebelivka was a tiny hair-ornament, weighing less than 5 g. The debate continues over whether all, most or a few Trypillia Assembly Houses and dwelling houses were built as two-storeyed structures. The recent house-construction and–burning experiment at Nebelivka (Johnston et al., in prep.) showed that a clear separation between the remains of one- and two-storied constructions was possible (Figure 4). The existence of a small number of two-storied houses, and perhaps also Assembly Houses, in the midst of a sea of one-storeyed houses showed the materialization of social differences at the Neighbourhood level.

Variability was the norm in prehistory, since no group had the power to make another community follow the same practices. However, in the supposedly more complex mega-sites, one may expect a greater degree of homogeneity in design and in the execution of building projects. A consideration of some of the basic shared elements of mega-site layout shows little homogeneity (Table 1).

Each mega-site shows a different implementation of the basic shared design concepts, despite the almost identical size of the final picture of built-up areas on Taljanky, Nebelivka, and Maidanetske. The huge difference in size at Taljanky compared with the other sites was made up of a much larger open inner area. (Chapman & Gaydarska, in press). The main practice for the construction of new houses at Nebelivka was the creation of inner radial streets, while at (the later Phase CI) Maidanetske, the expansion of the settled area was first achieved with inner radial streets, especially at the North end and inwards from the third concentric ring, and later through the creation of four to six more concentric house circuits (Rassmann et al., 2014: figure 22a). This led to the reduction of the inner unbuilt space at Maidanetske to the smallest area by ratio of all the mega-sites. The Taljanky practice was to maintain the sanctity of the inner unbuilt space and the same number (three) of concentric circuits, together with a modest expansion through the

---

[4]As in Mogylna III, relatively dated to the Trypillia A phase (Videiko 2007: figure 3)

[5]It did not even seem to be the case at Dobrovody (see figure 33a).

Table 1. Basic quantitative variables for four Trypillia mega-sites

Variable	Taljanky	Nebelivka	Maidanetske	Dobrovody
Overall size (ha)	320	238	200	150 (estimated)
Size of built-up area (ha)	180	173	174	???
Size of inner unbuilt area (ha)	140	65	26	???
Ratio of size of unbuilt area: total area	1: 2.3	1: 3.7	1: 7.7	N/A
No. of house circuits	3	2	3–9	4
No. of radial streets	26 (estimated)	50	12–18 (estimated)	???
No. of Assembly Houses	?1	22 (often paired)	15 (estimated)	15 (estimated)
Maximum ratio of houses: Assembly Houses	2100: 1	96: 1	198: 1 (estimated)	120: 1 (estimated)
Maximum no. of houses	2100 (estimated)	1,357	2970 (estimated)	1800 (estimated)
Maximum density of houses/ha (total size)	6.6 (estimated)	5.7	14.9 (estimated)	12 (estimated)

creation of inner radial streets. These variations in building projects led to the differences in the maximum mean density of houses per ha–lower at Nebelivka and Taljanky, higher at Maidanetske and Dobrovody.[6]

If the variations between the building projects of these four sites seem extreme, there were also qualitative differences between the four sites. The first difference is in the presence/absence of a perimeter ditch or ditches (see Chapman et al., 2016). There is no sign of a perimeter ditch at either Dobrovody or Taljanky, while a ditch with a palisade has been claimed for Maidanetske (Rassmann et al., 2014) and a shallow, narrow ditch without a palisade has been excavated at Nebelivka (Chapman et al., 2014b). There can be no pretence that these sites were fortified in any conventional usage of the term, since there were many apparently unprotected 'gateways' and a number of areas with no sign of a complete perimeter ditch at both Nebelivka and Maidanetske.

The most striking difference between Taljanky and the other mega-sites lies in the almost complete absence of Assembly Houses at the former. If this finding is confirmed by geophysical prospection of the remainder of the site, this would represent a dramatic transformation of the basic social structure of the mega-sites. At the earliest of the investigated mega-sites–Nebelivka (Phase BII: currently modelled date-range of 3950–3800 BCE)–the building of either pairs of Assembly Houses or single examples can be taken as a guide to the formation of some fourteen Quarters, with a variety of sizes and containing a vast range of Neighbourhoods (see Chapman et al., 2016; Chapman et al. 2014a). This basic social module was also re-created a century or two later at Maidanetske, with an estimated total of fifteen Assembly houses and a maximum mean ratio of almost 200 houses per Quarter (Ohlrau, 2014), as well as at Dobrovody. The abandonment of this community structure at Taljanky in effect removed the middle layer of the social structure, resulting in several possibilities: the dispersion of social power to the Neighbourhood level; a greater concentration of social power in the hands of a currently scarcely visible elite, perhaps based in new Corporate Houses;[7] or the collapse of a ritually based social system, materialized in the Assembly Houses, in favour of a more politically focussed structure. It will be an important future research goal to account for this dramatic transformation at Taljanky.

A recent development in mega-site archaeology concerns the discovery of industrial features at the mega-sites, with identical geophysical anomalies on the other two. The excavation of kilns at Taljanky (see Korvin-Piotrovskiy et al., 2016) has prompted the search for similar structures at Nebelivka. Despite the discovery of modern material culture (especially ironwork) during the excavation of two promising magnetic anomalies, M. Yu. Videiko continued with the excavation of a third feature that he interpreted as a kiln, drawing the implication of craft specialization into a discussion of one of Childe's (1950) ten criteria for urban life. However, it must be emphasized that the complex fired clay structure has no means of separating the fuel from the pottery and has no traces of a domed or any other kind of roof (Figure 5). This structure may well have been an oven, used for large-scale cooking and perhaps feasting, but the Durham view is that it was not a pottery kiln.

The principal difference between the mega-sites is the ways in which it can be demonstrated that they were all multi-phase sites. At Nebelivka, there is no implementation of the building project that shows categorically that the mega-site was multi-period,

---

[6]The term 'maximum mean density' refers to the mega-assumption that all of the houses were occupied at the same time (see below, p. 295).

[7]Following the model of the transformation of Yoruba towns from 'Assembly Houses' to 'Corporate Houses' (Ogundiran, 2013).

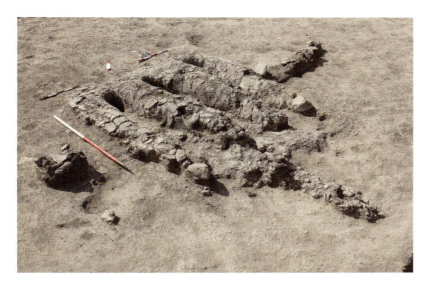

Figure 5. A possible communal cooking feature, from the South (photo: M. Yu. Videiko).

although this is what is strongly suspected. At Taljanky, the only suggestion of a multi-phase settlement was the presence of pit-alignments unconnected to house lines, which Rassmann *et al.* (2014: 109) link to a different dwelling phase, perhaps linked to unburnt houses. The multi-phase aspect of Dobrovody is suggested by different forms of houses and the overlap of inner radial streets in the northern part of the site (Rassmann *et al.*, 2014: 124). It is at Maidanetske that the most obvious evidence for multi-phase developments can be seen. The peripheral two lines of houses outside the northern outer perimeter ditch suggest a different phase, while there are multiple overlaps between both inner and outer ditches and presumably earlier pits (Rassmann *et al.*, 2014: figure 22a). Finally, the change in building practice from inner radial streets to additional house circuits could be an indication of different phases of building activity. It thus becomes impossible to make estimates of house numbers and population size without AMS dating only on the assumption that all of the structures on the site were coeval. Nevertheless, the AMS dates of the house-circuits from the site indicate there is a high probability that the nine house circuits, which represented *c* 2300 burnt houses, were all in contemporary use around 3750 BCE. But in addition, AMS dates from the pits indicate a possible earlier phase of the site that started around 3900 BCE (cf. Müller *et al.*, 2016). The range of population size estimates at Maidanetske of between 12,000 people and 46,000 people should be treated for what they represent: an estimate based on coeval dwelling in a minimum of *c.* 2300 houses and a maximum of all documented houses–viz., 3000 (Rassmann *et al.*, 2014; cf. Müller *et al.*, 2016).

Trypillia Mega-Sites in the Evolution of Low-Density Urbanism

If there is a single key element of the model of low-density urbanism, it is the transformation from high-density precursors, with more than 300–600 people per ha., into huge low-density centres of often fewer than fifty people per ha. This transformation is encapsulated in the relationship between site size and density of dwellings: the more space surrounding each dwelling, the larger the site and the lower the overall population density. As noted above, Smith's (1972) term 'rurban' captures the flavour of the domination of the sites by unbuilt space more akin to farm territories than urban quarters. How do the Trypillia mega-sites fit into this general pattern?

It is in the form of the Trypillia mega-sites that the most obvious similarity is found between mega-sites and other low-density sites. The form of the mega-sites is based on an overall structure of five key planning principles which provide a framework for myriad local decisions about where to build (and when to burn) a dwelling house. The structure creates three internal unbuilt spaces–outer, middle, and inner, with high potential for garden cultivation, animal keeping, and public ceremonial (see Chapman *et al.*, 2016, figure 1).

This settlement form is closely correlated with the estimated population density of the mega-sites in which clear-cut similarities emerge between Trypillia and other low-density examples. The assumption of six to eight people per household shows that the mean frequency of six to seven houses per ha. equates with thirty-six to fifty-six people per ha–a relatively low-density comparable with sites such as Co Loa (Kim,

2013), Cahokia (Pauketat, 2009), Yoruba towns (Ogundiran, 2013), or Great Zimbabwe (Chirikure & Pikirayi, 2008). The key question for the mega-sites concerns the number of houses in coeval occupation; indeed, this question masks the widespread assumption of permanence residence.

But these similarities between mega-sites and other low-density settlements are only part of the story. There is little sign of the key transformation from high-density to low-density dwelling in the ancestral Trypillia (or even pre-Trypillia) sites—only a small decline from ten structures per ha. to six to seven structures (cf. Diachenko, 2012). All of this discussion is predicated on the questionable assumption that all houses were in coeval occupation. Site size analysis of Trypillia settlements shows that early villages such as Mogylna III (Videiko 2007: figure 3) showed a possible shift towards irregular concentricity, with a size of 10 ha. There is no evidence for high-density dwelling at Mogylna III, any more than at other Trypillia or Cucuteni settlements. Given the assumption of contemporaneity of all houses, the earlier geophysical plan of Mogylna III suggests a range of 90–110 dwellings in the 10 ha area, amounting to an estimated ten buildings per ha, perhaps sixty people per ha. One of the highest-density Trypillia sites is Petreni, a tightly packed site with eleven concentric house circuits, dated to the Trypillia B phase (Popa et al., 2010). Moreover, high-density dwelling is noticeably absent in the settlements of those cultural groups ancestral to Trypillia and Cucuteni-the Linearbandkeramik, the Boian, and the Hamangia. It is thus difficult to detect in the eastern Balkans and the North Pontic zone any trend towards high-density dwelling prior to the Trypillia sites. There are hints from Masson's (1980) article about Trypillia settlement in Moldova that earlier, smaller sites had higher population densities than later, larger sites but the statistical basis of this paper has been criticized as inappropriate for large sites (Korvin-Piotrovsky, 2003: 7). We may be dealing with a case of emergent low-density dwelling in which size increases but the population density does not fall. This puts Trypillia BII and later settlements into a category of agglutinative low-density sites which have grown to urban size by the late 4th Millennium BCE.

The other variable in which Trypillia mega-sites matches other low-density urban trajectories is in the length of time by which low-density urbanism is preceded by agro-pastoral developments (Feinman, 2011, 2013; Fletcher, in prep). Both Feinman and Fletcher make the case that low-density urban sites arose sooner after the onset of farming in their region than high-density compact sites and lasted a shorter time. In the Trypillia case, the earliest Trypillia sites East of the Dnistro were, in effect, pioneer agro-pastoral sites, whose inhabitants moved into areas sparsely populated by pottery-using 'Forest Neolithic' groups with few domestic resources and a mobile lifestyle (Kotova, 2003). In other words, the time between the onset of farming and low-density mega-sites was less than a millennium and probably less than 500 years. We do not have a clear internal AMS-based chronology yet for any single mega-site but early dates suggest occupation spans no greater than two hundred years. This dwelling period may well be shorter than that of some classic compact high-density cities of the Near East (e.g. EBA Uruk: Liverani, 2006). However, historical records purport to show a duration of 181–227 years for the 3rd millennium BCE Akkadian dynasty of Agade at Uruk (Kuhrt, 1995),[8] indicating that duration of high-density cities is variable.

Another trait common in low-density urban sites is the emergence of defence at sites surrounded by high-quality arable soils (e.g. Great Zimbabwe, Ile Ife, some of the European *oppida*). It is only in the last three years that geophysical prospection has detected the presence of perimeter ditches on mega-sites (e.g. at Nebelivka and Maidanetske). However, excavations in the 2014 season at Nebelivka showed that the perimeter ditch was too shallow for serious defence and lacked any palisade. Moreover, the width of the so-called 'entrances' at Nebelivka—at 70–100 m—makes defence impractical. At Maidanetske, Videiko made a case for the defensive capabilities of a row of houses sharing party walls and whose outer walls created a defensive barrier (Shmaglij & Videiko, 2003). This may well have been a 'local' defensive obstacle, but there are relatively few examples of such closely spaced houses in either of the house circuits at Nebelivka or, indeed, Maidanetske. Thus, it is currently difficult to support the idea that mega-sites are defended settlements. On the grid of bounded/unbounded vs. monumental/non-monumental features, Nebelivka falls in the category of symbolically bounded sites with modest monumentality in the form of Assembly Houses but lacking in the dramatic monuments found at Angkor, Cahokia, or Stonehenge.

How do the mega-sites compare with the five supplementary characteristics of low-density urban sites discussed above (pp. 290–292)? While there were few individual large-scale, transformative building projects, the construction of an Assembly House would have reshaped the local cultural geography of the Quarter and its Neighbourhoods, shaping future choices as to where and what to construct. The notion of modular

---

[8] Estimates for the duration of the dynasty of Agade (i.e. the Akkadians) (Kuhrt, 1995): it extends from 2340 to 2159 BC (181 years) if you simply use the reigns of the kings (Sargon to Shudurul), but if you extend it to the beginning of the Ur 3 period (2113 BC), then it extends to c. 227 years.

house-based social structures is obviously very familiar from Trypillia settlements, as is the restrained materialization of mortuary rituals, with the exception of house-burning (Chapman, 2015) (Figure 4). The question of seasonality is being actively considered for the mega-sites (Chapman & Gaydarska, in prep.), while the local successors to any specific mega-site have been identified in the Taljanky–Maidanetske micro-region but not so far in the Nebelivka macro-territory.

The picture that emerges from the most recent investigations of Trypillia mega-sites is that many of their features–size, building density, and boundedness–are consistent with a widespread group of large low-density sites in many parts of the world. There are two major differences between the mega-sites and other low-density urban settlements. The first is in the ancestry of these unusual agglomerations. There is no current evidence to suggest that smaller, more compact, higher-density settlements preceded the emergence of the mega-site, which occurred relatively soon after the onset of farming on the North Pontic forest steppe. The second is that, while almost all other low-density complexes are characterized by classic forms of monumentality which give a visual definition to elite practices at the heart of the cities, the Trypillia mega-sites show very few monumental features other than the occasional two-storeyed Assembly Houses and domestic houses. Taken together with the general absence of prestige goods, especially of metal, on the mega-sites but in view of their extreme size, we suggest that Trypillia mega-sites were an egalitarian, pre-state form of early, low-density urban settlement.

Conclusions

The current research on low-density urban sites has provided a realistic alternative to the Childean model of high-density urban centres. The concentration of fifty per cent of the world's entire population in low-density urban settlements (Fletcher, n.d.) means that it is imperative to understand their origins and development. The roots of low-density urbanism remain unclear but one of the candidates for an early form of low-density urban sites is the class of 100+-ha Trypillia mega-sites of Ukraine and Moldova. These sites are concentrated in the Southern Buh catchment in three distinct phases: Phase BII, Phase BII-CI, and Phase CI.

Recent research on the Trypillia mega-sites shows the extent of differences between the three well-explored sites (Taljanky, Nebelivka, and Maidanetske) in the transformation of shared design concepts into building projects. Three key differences concerned the far greater size of the inner unbuilt area at Taljanky, the preference for inner radial streets for inward settlement expansion at Nebelivka in contrast to building perhaps additional concentric house circuits at Maidanetske and the almost complete absence of Assembly Houses at Taljanky in contrast to their frequent construction at the other mega-sites.

To what extent do the Trypillia mega-sites compare with low-density urban sites in global perspective? The size, residential density, and boundedness link the mega-sites to a number of low-density urban sites, as does the timespan after the initial regional emergence of agro-pastoralism, the lack of a clearly materialized mortuary domain and the modular form, and house-based nature of social space. What is not so similar is the lack of high-density precursors to the mega-sites and the smaller scale of Trypillia building projects. The juxtaposition of these traits with the almost complete absence of metal objects and other prestige goods suggests that the best characterization of Trypillia mega-sites is currently an egalitarian, pre-state form of early, low-density urban settlement.

Acknowledgements

This chapter could not have been written without the Kyiv-Durham research team of the AHRC-funded project 'Early urbanism in Europe?: the case of the Ukrainian Trypillia mega-sites' (Grant No. AH/I025867/1). We thank the National Geographic Society for their much appreciated financial support for the mega-structure excavation (Grant No. 2012/211). We thank Durham University, and especially the successive Chairs of Archaeology, Profs Chris Scarre and Chris Gerrard, for their support of the project. Our thanks are also due to the many friends and colleagues who continue to discuss 'Eurasian urbanism' with us–in particular, Roland Fletcher and the Hawaii/Tucson 'Big Sites' group.

References

Barrett, J. 1994. *Fragments from Antiquity: An Archaeology of Social Life in Britain, 2900–1200 BC*. Oxford: Blackwell.

Birch, J. (ed.) 2013. *From Prehistoric Villages to Cities: Settlement Aggregation and Community Transformation*. London: Routledge.

Blanton, R.E. 1976. Anthropological Studies of Cities. *Annual Review of Anthropology*, 5:249–64.

Chapman, J. 2015. Burn or Bury? Mortuary Alternatives in the Neolithic and Chalcolithic of Central and Eastern Europe. In: A. Diachenko, F. Menotti, S. Ryzhov, K. Bunyatyan & S. Kadrow, eds. *The

Cucuteni-Trypillia Cultural Complex and its Neighbours. Essays in Memory of Vlodomyr Kruts. Lviv: Astrolyabia, pp. 259–78.

Chapman, J. & Gaydarska, B., in press. Low-Density Urbanism: The Case of the Trypillia Group of Ukraine. In: M. Fernández-Götz & D. Krausse eds. *Individualization, Urbanization and Social Differentiation: Eurasia at the Dawn of History*. Edinburgh: Edinburgh University Press.

Chapman, J. & Gaydarska, B., in prep. *Seasonality in the Trypillia Mega-sites: the Forbidden Question*.

Chapman, J., Videiko, M.Y., Gaydarska, B., Burdo, N. & Hale, D. 2014a. An Answer to Roland Fletcher's Conundrum?: Preliminary Report on the Excavation of a Trypillia Mega-Structure at Nebelivka, Ukraine. *Journal of Neolithic Archaeology*, 16:135–57 (http://www.jungsteinsite.de/).

Chapman, J., Videiko, M., Gaydarska, B., Burdo, N., Hale, D., Villis, R., Swann, N., Thomas, N., Edwards, P., Blair, A., Hayes, A., Nebbia, M. & Rud, V. 2014b. The Planning of the Earliest European Proto-Towns: A New Geophysical Plan of the Trypillia Mega-Site of Nebelivka, Kirovograd Domain, Ukraine. *Antiquity Gallery*: http://antiquity.ac.uk.ezphost.dur.ac.uk/projgall/chapman339/.

Chapman, J., Videiko, M. Yu., Hale, D., Gaydarska, B., Burdo, N., Rassmann, K., Mischka, C., Müller, J., Korvin-Piotrovskiy, A. & Kruts, V. 2014c. The Second Phase of the Trypillia Mega-site Methodological Revolution—A New Research Agenda. *European Journal of Archaeology*, 17/3:369–406.

Chapman, J., Gaydarska, B. & Hale, D. 2016. Nebelivka: Assembly Houses, Ditches, and Social Structure, in: J. Müller, K. Rassmann & M. Videiko (Eds.), *Trypillia Mega-Sites and European Prehistory: 4100–3400 BCE*. London and New York: Routledge, pp. 117–132.

Childe, V.G. 1950. The Urban Revolution. *The Town Planning Review*, 21(1):3–17.

Chirikure, Sh. & Pikirayi, I. 2008. Inside and Outside the Dry Stone Walls: Revisiting the Material Culture of Great Zimbabwe. *Antiquity*, 82:976–993.

Cowgill, G.L. 2004. Origins and Development of Urbanism. Archaeological Perspectives. *Annual Review of Anthropology*, 33:525–49.

Diachenko, A. 2012. Settlement System of West Tripolye Culture in the Southern Bug and Dnieper Interfluves: Formation Problems. In: F. Menotti & A. G. Korvin-Piotrovskiy, eds. *The Tripolye Culture Giant-Settlements in Ukraine. Formation, Development and Decline*. Oxford: Oxbow Books, pp. 116–38.

Diachenko, A. & Menotti, F. 2015. Cucuteni-Tripolye Contact Networks: Cultural Transmission and Chronology. In: A. Diachenko, F. Menotti, S. Ryzhov, K. Bunyatyan & S. Kadrow, eds. *The Cucuteni-Trypillia Cultural Complex and its Neighbours. Essays in Memory of Vlodomyr Kruts*. Lviv: Astrolyabia, pp. 131–52.

Dietler, M. 1997. *The Iron Age in Mediterranean France: Colonial Encounters, Entanglements, and Transformations*. New York: Kluwer/Plenum.

Ellis, L. 1984. *The Cucuteni-Tripolye Culture: Study in Technology and the Origins of Complex Society*. British Archaeological Reports International Series 217. Oxford: Archaeopress.

Feinman, G. 2011. Size, Complexity, and Organizational Variation: A Comparative Approach. *Cross-Cultural Research*, 45(1):37–58.

Feinman, G. 2013. The Emergence of Social Complexity: Why More Than Population Size Matters. In: D. M. Carballo, ed. *Cooperation & Collective Action. Archaeological Perspectives*. Boulder: University Press of Colorado, pp. 35–56.

Fletcher, R. 1995. *The Limits to Settlement Growth*. Cambridge: Cambridge University Press.

Fletcher, R. 2009. Low-Density Agrarian-Based Urbanism: A Comparative View. *Durham University Institute of Advanced Study Insights*, 2/4:2–19.

Fletcher, R. n.d. Overview. Paper presented at Amerind Foundation Workshop, "Cities or Big villages?'. New approaches to great, anomalous places', Dragoon, AZ, May 2014.

Fox, R.G. 1977. *Urban Anthropology: Cities in Their Cultural Settings*. Englewood Cliffs, NJ: Prentice-Hall.

Gaydarska, B. in press (submitted). The city is dead! – long live the city! *Norwegian Archaeological Review*.

Johnston, S., Litkevych, V., Gaydarska, B., Voke, P., Nebbia, M. & Chapman, J., in prep. The Nebelivka Experimental House-Construction and House-Burning. In: Spasić, M., ed. Housing in archaeological perspective. Beograd: Muzej Grada Beograda.

Kim, N.C. 2013. Lasting Monuments and Durable Institutions: Labor, Urbanism, and Statehood in Northern Vietnam and Beyond. *Journal of Archaeological Research*, 21/3:217–67.

Korvin-Piotrovsky, A.G. 2003. Theoretical Problems of Researches of Settlement-Giants. In: A.G. Korvin-Piotrovsky, V.O. Kruts & S.M. Ryzhov, eds. *Tripolian Settlement-Giants. The International Symposium Materials*. Kyiv: Institute of Archaeology, pp. 5–7.

Korvin-Piotrovskiy, A. G., Hofmann, R., Rassmann, K., Videiko, M. Y. & Brandtstätter, L. 2016. Pottery Kilns in Trypillian settlements. Tracing the division of labour and the social organisation of Copper Age communities. In: J. Müller, K. Rassmann & M. Videiko (Eds.), *Trypillia Mega-Sites and European Prehistory: 4100–3400 BCE*. London and New York: Routledge, pp. 221–252.

Kotova, N. 2003. *Neolithization in Ukraine*. International Series 1109. Oxford: BAR.

Kuhrt, A. 1995. *The Ancient Near East c. 3000–330 BC*. London: Routledge.

Liverani, M. 2006. *Uruk: la prima città*. (English translation). London: Equinox.

MacAnany, P.A. n.d. Discussion paper. Paper presented at Amerind Foundation Workshop, "Cities or Big villages?'. New approaches to great, anomalous places', Dragoon, AZ, May 2014.

Marcus, H. 1994. *A History of Ethiopia*. Berkeley, CA: University of California Press.

Masson, V.M. 1980. Dinamika razvitya tripolskogo obshchestva v svete paleodemograficheskih otsenok. In: I.I. Artemenko, ed. *Pervobitnaya arkheologiya. Poiski i nahodki*. Kiev: Naukova Dumka, pp. 204–12. Массон, В.М. 1980. Динамика развития трипольского общества в свете палеодемографических оценок. В сб.: И.И. Артеменко, ред. Первобытная археология. Поиски и находки. Киев: Наукова думка, с. 204–12.

Müller, J., Hofmann, R., Brandstätter, L., Ohlrau, R. & Videiko, M. 2016. Chronology and Demography: How Many People Lived in a Mega-Site?, in: J. Müller, K. Rassmann & M. Videiko (Eds.), *Trypillia Mega-Sites and European Prehistory: 4100–3400 BCE*. London and New York: Routledge, pp. 133–169.

Mumford, L. 1961. *The City in History: Its Origins, Its Transformations, and Its Prospects*. New York: Harcourt, Brace & World, Inc.

Nebbia, M. n.d. Investigating Trypillia *off-megasites*: the case of Nebelivka, Ukraine. (Paper presented at the Kirovograd Conference, 'At the edges of Old Europe', 13th–14th May 2015).

Neves, E. n.d. Amazonian sites, Brazil. Paper presented at Amerind Foundation Workshop, "Cities or Big villages?'. New approaches to great, anomalous places', Dragoon, AZ, May 2014.

Nikolov, V. 2008. *Praistoricheski solodobiven tsenter Provadia–Solnitsata. Razkopki 2005–2007g*. Sofia: Bulgarska Akademiya na Naukite, Natsionalen Arheologicheski Institut i Muzei.

Nu, H. 2013. The Longshan Period Site of Taosi in Southern Shanxi Province. In: A.P. Underhill, ed. *A Companion to Chinese Archaeology*, 1st ed. Oxford: Blackwell, pp. 256–77.

Ogundiran, A. 2013. Towns and States in the West African Forest Belt. In: P. Mitchell & P. Lane, eds. *The Oxford Handbook of African Archaeology*. Oxford: Oxford University Press, pp. 861–73.

Ogundiran, A. n.d. Ile Ife, Nigeria. Paper presented at Amerind Foundation Workshop, "Cities or Big villages?'. New approaches to great, anomalous places', Dragoon, AZ, May 2014.

Ohlrau, R. 2014. *Tripolje Großsiedlungen. Geomagnetische Prospektion und architektursoziologische Perspektiven*. CAU Kiel, unpub. MA Thesis.

Parker Pearson, M. n.d. Greater Stonehenge, Southern UK. Paper presented at Amerind Foundation Workshop, "Cities or Big villages?'. New approaches to great, anomalous places', Dragoon, AZ, May 2014.

Pauketat, T. 2009. *Cahokia: Ancient America's Great City on the Mississippi*. London: Viking Penguin.

Pauketat, T. n.d. Cahokia, Mississippi Basin, USA. Paper presented at Amerind Foundation Workshop, "Cities or Big villages?'. New approaches to great, anomalous places', Dragoon, AZ, May 2014.

Pikirayi, I. n.d. Great Zimbabwe, Southern Africa. Paper presented at Amerind Foundation Workshop, "Cities or Big villages?'. New approaches to great, anomalous places', Dragoon, AZ, May 2014.

Popa, A., Musteață, S., Rassmann, K., Bicbaev, V., Munteanu, O., Postică, G. & Sîrbu, G. 2010. Rezultate preliminare privind sondajele geofizice din anul 2009 şi perspectivele folosirii magnetometriei în Republica Moldova. In: S. Musteață, A. Popa & J-P. Abraham, eds. *Arheologia intre ştiință, politică şi economia de piată*. Chişinău: Pontos, pp. 145–57.

Rassmann, K., Ohlrau, R., Hofmann, R., Mischka, C., Burdo, N., Videjko, M. Yu. & Müller, J. 2014. High Precision Tripolye Settlement Plans, Demographic Estimates and Settlement Organization. *Journal of Neolithic Archaeology*, 16:96–134. (http://www.jungsteinsite.de/).

Shmaglij, N. & Videjko, M. 2003. Maidanetskoe–tripolskij protogorod. *Stratum Plus*, 2:44–136. Шмаглий, Н.М. и Видейко, М.Ю. 2003. Майданецкое–трипольский протогород. *Stratum plus* 2: 44–136.

Smith, M.G. 1972. Complexity, size and urbanization. In: P. Ucko, R. Tringham & G.W. Dimbleby, eds. *Man, Settlement and Urbanism: Proceedings of a Meeting of the Research Seminar in Archaeology and Related Subjects held at the Institute of Archaeology, London University*. London: Duckworth, pp. 567–74.

Videiko, M.Yu. (ed.) 2004. *Encyclopaedia Tripilskoi cyvilizacii*. Vol. 1. Kyiv: Ukrpoligrafmedia. Відейко, М.Ю., ред. 2004. *Енциклопедія трипільської цивілізації*, Том 1. Київ: Укрполіграфмедіа.

Videiko, M.Yu. 2007. Contours and Contents of the Ghost: Trypillia Culture Proto-cities. *Memoria Antiquitatis*, XXIV:251–276.

White, K. n.d. Neolithic China. Paper presented at Amerind Foundation Workshop, "Cities or Big villages?'. New approaches to great, anomalous places', Dragoon, AZ, May 2014.

CHAPTER 18

Humans Structure Social Space: What We Can Learn From Trypillia

Johannes Müller

Besides the manifold aspects of economic, social, and cultural developments, which are visible in the long-lasting Trypillia history, the most striking aspects of this phenomenon are the construction of extremely well laid out settlements with their concentric house rings and the immense size of the population agglomerations, especially in comparison with other prehistoric and historic cases. As already pronounced by different authors within this book, Trypillia research is able to identify these mega-sites staring around 4000/3900 BCE and lasting especially in the Southern Buh Dnipro region until *c.* 3700/3600 BCE. Within the mentioned time horizon, we can characterize these sites on three different levels.

Planning

The sites are well-planned in the sense that a general idea about an empty central area, different concentric rings of houses, and the principle of tracks and open rings is followed up in each mega-site. This principle is not new, being already visible in early southeast European as well as Trypillia sites from latest 4800 BCE onwards. In such a sense, the principle of organizing social space in such a way is not new, but reflects a general idea that could be applied to both smaller as well as larger sites. Nevertheless, the theme of applying the 'concentric house ring principle' to domestic space within the frame of local variation (and with this, also local decision processes) implies structured approaches of clearly defined institutions.

Short Duration

The sites are of relatively short duration in comparison to, for example, many tell sites of Southeast Europe. As both the radiometric dating and the typochronological considerations (linked to a ^{14}C-chronology within the separated phases) imply that mega-sites never existed for longer than 150 years, they do not differ socially from other Trypillia sites. Again, applying the 'few generations principle' to domestic space within the frame of local variation does not imply a general change of social institutions with the appearance of mega-sites.

Technological Change and Specialization

The appearance of mega-sites is linked to a few technological changes which made the agglomeration of greater numbers of people possible. On the one hand, a better transportation system (the development of animal-traction sledges) reduced the effort necessary for transportation between domestic sites and their vicinity. On the other hand, the development of new pottery kiln firing techniques, for example, enabled much easier mass production of standardized but also sophisticated products.

Population Agglomerations

Besides differences in population estimates between different authors, the general size of mega-sites is indisputable. Both early and more recent population estimations result in a figure of more than 10,000 people living contemporarily within one mega-site. These population agglomerations affected a whole region, since only a few other smaller contemporary domestic sites could be detected in the vicinity of mega-sites.

Separations and Mega-Structures

Within the mega-sites a separation into different spatial units is visible, marked by mega-structures (structures larger than the usual houses) or other divisions of space. While mega-structures were linked to mega-sites as a result of the concentration of geomagnetic research, these structures were also present in some, chronologically earlier smaller sites (cp. Ursu & Terna,

© European Association of Archaeologists 2016

2014). Again, a principle that was already known was transferred to a bigger site.

SUBSISTENCE TRADITIONS

Subsistence economy did not change with the appearance of the mega-sites. Similar animals and plants were used, but most likely the organization of the means of production changed. A differentiation of households between those that concentrate on primary subsistence products, and those which are also engaged in secondary products, is visible within mega-sites.

Summarizing the Late Trypillia evidence, the development of mega-sites in one specific region of the Trypillia distribution represents agglomeration processes which are not linked to an archaeologically visible 'extra-hierarchy' within the society as, for example, represented in the clustering of public buildings and administrative centres at Uruk urban sites. While on the one hand, equally sized mega-structures are distributed all over the area at certain important public junctions in most of the Late Trypillia mega-sites, on the other hand no further kind of hierachization is visible.

Therefore, the Trypillia case of population agglomerations should be separated clearly from other developments in prehistoric Europe. For example, the dense concentration of houses in tell sites, which are nevertheless in many cases associated with quarters with a lower density of structures, and even the Late Iron Age oppida with their concentrations of power in acropolis-like central parts of the settlements, reflect different forms of continuous development that are not present in the Trypillia mega-sites. As such, the social component is neither comparable with the Near Eastern type of urbanization nor other forms of agglomeration within the power structures of prehistoric Europe. Quite clearly none of the various definitions of the oriental, the 'classical' Greek, or the medieval European city are applicable, as in all these cases a certain, quarter-oriented specialization within the sites and a kind of administrative hierachization is a part of the definition.

Obviously, life in Trypillia mega-sites was still rural. Most of the population was engaged in agricultural activities, but a certain amount of specialization and organization indicated social structures that were not only dependent on lineage-based relations, but mainly on residential constraints. The agglomeration to sites in which not everyone knew everybody else by name or even on sight, was only possible once the technical limitations that Gordon Childe made responsible for the low demographic figures of Neolithic sites (Childe 1950: 6) were no longer valid in the steppe area. 'In the absence of wheeled vehicles and roads for the transport of bulky crops men had to live within easy walking distance of their cultivations' (Childe 1950: 6). Certainly, with the introduction of the new sledge system this was no longer valid for the North Pontic landscape. Clearly, at the boundary between the patchy forest steppe and the forest the ecological potential was also present to allow people to agglomerate at certain sites.

In principle, the enlargement of settlement sizes is a tendency already observable in the history of early to middle Trypillia, but the main change to mega-sites could be labelled as a new quality of agglomeration that first became possible with the development of new transportation techniques. While our models of the organizational units that are visible on different spatial scales within the settlement are nevertheless still descriptive, in principle we could label the new development as a *social experiment* within a rural landscape: To unite most of the population living in an area of 100 km^2 within one site changed the efforts required for the spatial organization of economies, political and social institutions, and livelihood. The social experiment included, on the one hand, the house place and household principle, with a house-oriented waste management in huge pits associated with each house, for example. On the other hand, a form of collective management at a supra-household level existed for the management of crops, animals, the production of tools, and means of representation like fine pottery. The social experiment included a new dimension of 'living together': residential principles that no longer depended mainly on lineage ties linked people in a social unit where people no longer knew everyone within their community. Production and consumption were organized between households and quarters, where kilns, for example, were used communally and some items were probably exchanged by means of tokens. In the realm of mega-site development, socio-environmental changes were observed which resulted from the impact of the population agglomeration on the environment: deforestation within the vicinity of the site catchment areas (a result of the huge demand for wood for building purposes, fires, and as a tool for the new sophisticated kilns) shifted the boundary between steppe and forest steppe further to the North.

The reasons for these social experiments could be manifold. As signs of violence are absent in the realm of Trypillia development, from an archaeological point of view it would be quite difficult to associate the agglomeration of many communities at one site with a kind of protection effort as the main trigger of change. Instead, economic reasons for a closer processing, distribution and consumption of primary and secondary products in a demarcated space (made

Figure 1. Pit 50 from the mega-site Maidanetske. Two cattle skulls, many bones, and various pots were deposited before the infilling of huge masses of daub began. The assemblage perhaps displays the remains of a feast with a subsequent ritual deposition, as is also known from other areas of Europe in the 38th century BCE (photograph: Institute UFG).

possible by the changing transportation technology) and a closer cooperation in animal husbandry and field management might together form one reason for the observed 'coming together'. There is little doubt that the management of such large groups of people required a great deal of effort: house clusters and individual houses that could be associated with 'public' or 'ritual' mega-structures, as well as those serving both purposes, correlate in size with group sizes which are optimal for reducing scalar stress between social actors (Johnson, 1982). As such, Late Trypillia societies were able to manage c. 12,000 people and 24,000 animals living together in one place. While each mega-site existed for around two to eight generations, the whole mega-site principle spanned c. three-hundred years; twelve generations in all. From an emic perspective, an 'experiment' which lasted c. three-hundred years and was attractive for many others who entered the group or maintained relationships with the mega-site populations could in principle be called sustainable. It is especially fascinating that a non-literate society was able to keep the process going without producing archaeological signs of violence.

What kind of ideologies kept this 'system' going? We should bear in mind that no mythical aggrandizement of any 'warrior' practice is visible in the archaeological record. Instead, the small number of, for example, arrowheads or other tools which could be used for killing, supports the generally accepted mood envisioned for Trypillia societies, which is linked to a kind of open neighbourhood without the application of force. In principle, the practice of ritual communal feasting, which we might observe in pits with the remains of disarticulated cattle, ceramic vessels, and the possibly symbolic deposition of parts of other items (including houses), indicates a ritual practice that is observed in the 38th century BCE in many areas of Europe (Figure 1). The linkage to this traditional understanding of the world, which was obvious in many non-literate societies at that time, might indicate a long established pattern of the 'world'.

Furthermore, the ability to structure public space by probable public buildings (like mega-structures) and to keep the symbolic system (observable on pots and figurines) accessible for almost everyone indicates social

Figure 2. A vision of the deliberate destruction of a mega-site, archaeological excavations, and a modern city (photograph: Johannes Müller, wall painting/photograph in the Legedzine museum).

practices designed to avoid hierarchies like those which developed with comparable population figures, for example in South Mesopotamia. From a socio-environmental point of view, the missing ecological pressure in the Southern Buh Dnipro region shows no sign that the carrying capacity was overstepped until a certain stage of the development, enabled an agency which did not construct unnecessary social pyramids. In any case, the environmental scenario is difficult to assess. On the one hand, the elaborated organization of social space, especially within the huge inner space of each mega-site and the track system, might also reflect practices for managing and sustaining the extensive crop processing and animal keeping. On the other hand, local deforestation might result in a scenario where the effort involved in moving the population of large sites to different locations in the vicinity becomes too enormous for keeping the 'floating' demographic spatial principle between the mega-sites active any longer.

The new and unique character of spatial organization in Late Trypillia mega-sites displays some insights into human and group behaviour which might still be relevant for us today. Both the ability of non-literate societies to agglomerate in huge population groups under rural conditions of production, distribution, and consumption and their ability to avoid unnecessary social pyramids and instead practice a more public structure of decision making, reminds us of our own possibilities and abilities. In such a sense, the archaeological interpretation of societies that are far removed from what we can observe today, and which might reflect 'other worlds' of human behaviour, is valid for a more general anthropological point of view (Figure 2).

REFERENCES

Childe, V.G. 1950. The Urban Revolution. *The Town Planning Review*, 21:3–17.

Johnson, G.A. 1982. Organizational Structure and Scalar Stress. In: R. Renfrew, M. Rowlands & B.A. Segraves, eds. *Theory and Explanation in Archaeology: the Southampton Conference*. London: Academic Press, pp. 389–421.

Ursu, C.-E. & Terna, S. 2014. Building No. 3/2013 Discovered at Baia—In Muchie (Suceava County), Initial Data. In: G. Dumitroaia, C. Preoteasa & N. Ciprian-Dorin, eds. *Cucuteni Culture within the European Neo-Eneolthic Context*. Piatra-Neamt: Editura Constantin Matasa, pp. 98–104.

Index of Places

René Ohlrau

Aleksandrovka: 147
Andriivka: 212, 214, 216–217
Angkor: 289–291, 296
Apolianka: 10, 29–30, 32, 37, 51–52, 72, 165, 183–187, 292
Ariuşd: 223

Babshin: 148
Balta Sarata-Cîmpul lui Posta: 223
Bălţaţi: 223
Belovode: 4, 8
Berezivka: 25
Berezovskaya GES: 148
Bernadea: 223
Bernashivka 1: 1, 148, 196–198, 284
Bernashivka 2: 183
Bernove-Luka: 196
Bilshivtsy: 143
Bilyj Kamin: 17
Bodeşti-Frumuşica: 223
Bondarka 2: 211, 213, 215, 218
Brenzeni IV: 148, 196, 200
Brenzeni VIII: 19, 21, 30, 148
Buda Orlovetska: 211, 213, 215, 217

Cahokia: 289–291, 296
Cainara: 145
Cernica I-III-Mănăstirea Iezărul: 223
Chaco Canyon: 290–291
Chapaivka: 19, 151, 271, 274
Chechelnik: 196
Cherpovody 2: 211, 213, 215, 218
Chervony khutor: 151
Chirileni III: 223
Chychyrkozivka: 8, 20, 23, 211, 214, 216–217, 270, 273
Cifer-Pác: 223
Circea-La Viaduct, 'Hanuri': 223
Co Loa: 289–291, 295
Cobani: 30, 37, 46, 52, 55, 64–66
Constantinople: 289
Cuconestii Vechi: 147
Cucuteni-Cetăţuia: 146, 223

Danku 2: 147
Deh Luran: 282
Diyala: 282
Dobrovody: 7–8, 10, 19–20, 23, 30, 32, 37, 39, 41, 44, 46, 49–53, 56, 58, 61, 63–64, 71–72, 74, 113, 117, 119, 129, 133, 164–166, 168, 172, 183–188, 211, 213, 215, 217, 270, 272, 292–295
Dovzhok swamp: 172
Drăguşeni-Ostrov: 147, 223
Drutsy 1: 147

Eridu: 281–282
Evminka 1: 151
Fedorivka: 10, 20, 22, 24, 30, 165, 184–188, 211, 213, 215, 217, 270, 272–273

Gălibovtsi: 223
Glavan 1: 30
Glăvăneştii Vechi - Malul Jijiei: 223
Glybochok: 10, 19, 22, 24, 30, 165, 184–186, 188, 211, 213, 215, 218, 270, 272
Gordashivka 1: 211, 213, 215, 217
Gorodnytsya: 146, 211, 213, 215, 218
Gorods'k: 151
Great Zimbabwe: 289–291, 296
Vynogradne (Grebeni): 30, 151
Grebenjukiv Yar: 149
Grenovka: 148
Grumezoaia: 143
Grygorivka: 30, 143
Grygorivka-Ignatenkova Gora: 143–144

Hăbăşeşti-Holm: 146, 223
Hamrin: 282
Hancăuţi-I La Frasin: 143, 223
Hangu: 223
Heuneburg: 8, 12, 15
Horné Lefantovce: 223
Horodistea: 150
Horodka: 30, 55–56
Hotărani, Hotarani-La scoala: 223

Iablona 1: 147
Ile Ife: 291, 296
Ivanovka: 30

Jancha: 30
Jilava, Magura Jilavei: 223
Jushky: 30

Kamnik: 223
Karbuna: 3, 196–198
Kardashinski swamp: 172
Khomyne: 144
Khrystynivka 1: 10, 165, 211, 213, 215, 217
Khutir Nezamoznyk: 150
Kish: 282
Klishchev: 150
Kocherzhyntsi-Pankivka 187, 211, 213, 215, 218
Kolodyste: 17, 211, 213, 215 218
Kolomyjshchyna: 30
Komarivka: 211, 21, 216–217
Konovka: 30
Korman': 148
Korzhova Slobidka: 211, 213, 215, 217

Kosenivka: 8, 19–20, 22–24, 165, 187, 196, 198, 200, 270, 272
Kostešty 9: 223
Koszyłowce Oboz: 223
Kramolín: 223
Krasnostavka: 150
Kryvi Kolina: 10, 165, 186, 211, 213, 215, 217
Ksaverove: 211, 214, 216–217
Kuriache Polé: 30
Kvitky 2: 211, 214, 216–217

Lake Balkhash: 176
Lamojna: 30
Lazo XI - Tăurele: 223
Lebedyn: 211, 214, 216, 218
Leca-Ungureni: 145
Leshchivka: 186, 211, 213, 215, 217
Leu - La Tei: 223
Likareve: 212, 214, 216–217
Longshan: 290–291
Luka Vrublevetskaya: 149, 196, 223

Maidanetske: 7–8, 10, 17, 19–20, 22–26, 29–32, 34, 37–53, 56, 58, 61, 63–64, 71–92, 98, 105, 111, 113, 117, 119, 128–129, 133–136, 148–149, 161, 163–168, 172–178, 182–189, 196, 198, 200–204, 207–208, 210–211, 213, 215, 218, 221–223, 225, 237, 243–250, 253–254, 258–259, 261, 263–268, 270, 272–273, 276, 284–285, 292–297, 303
Malnas-Bai: 144–145
Manaus: 291
Margineni-Cetatuia: 145
Mayaki: 145–146
Mayaky: 271, 274
Mihoveni-Cahla Morii: 147
Miropole: 150, 221
Mogylna III: 30, 293, 296
Mont Beuvray: 291
Moshuriv: 22, 30, 186, 211, 213, 215, 218

Nebelivka: 7–8, 10, 19, 30, 61, 74, 91, 95–113, 117–130, 133, 165–168, 183–188, 196–198, 200, 211, 213, 215, 217, 221, 224–225, 245, 253, 263, 267, 270, 272–273, 284–285, 291–297
Nemorozh: 211, 213, 215, 217
Nezamozhnyk: 211, 213, 215, 217
Nezvisko 2: 148
Nippur: 281–283, 285
Novo-Ukrainka: 211, 214, 216, 217

Ochiul Alb: 30, 37, 52, 55, 65, 67–68
Okolište: 8–12, 15, 250
Okopi: 149
Onopriivka: 269–272
Ostrovets: 211, 213, 215, 217
Ozheve: 196–197

Parța I: 224
Pekari 2: 151
Peregoiovka: 211, 215, 217

Peremozhyntsi: 211, 213, 215, 217
Petreni: 17–19, 21, 30, 37–39, 43, 46, 49, 52–53, 55–56, 59–63, 65, 67–68, 74, 113, 225, 245, 248–250, 296
Pishchana: 22, 186, 211, 214, 216–217
Plocnik: 4
Poduri-Dealul Ghindaru: 145
Polivanov Yar 3: 148
Polonyste: 211, 213, 215, 217
Popova Levada: 30
Popudnia: 17, 211, 213, 215, 217
Preutesti-Halta: 147
Prohezesti: 30, 37
Provadia: 289
Putineshty 3: 30, 147

Rapa Morii: 30
Ripnica 6: 144
Rogozhany 1: 147
Romanivka: 186, 211, 213, 215, 217
Rome: 289
Rozsokhuvatka: 8, 211, 213, 215, 217
Ruginoasa: 30
Ruseștii Noi: 147, 196–197
Rzhyschev-Ripnitsa: 30, 152

Sabatinovka 1: 148
Sabatinovka 2: 148
Sandraky: 151
Sarata Monteoru: 144
Scanteia: 146
Sharyn: 151–152
Shkarivka: 150, 196–197
Sinešty: 224
Sîngerei: 30, 37, 52–53, 55–61, 65
Slavonski Brod-Galovo: 224
Sofievka: 151
Sophia II le Gavan: 19
Sophia V: 19
Sophia VIII: 144
Soroki-Ozero: 147
Stajky: 30
Stara Buda: 211, 213, 215, 217
Stari Kukoneshty=Shcherbaky: 196
Starye Raduliani II: 30
Stoicani: 224
Stolnicheni I: 19, 21
Stonehenge: 291
Suceveni (Galati)-Stoborani: 224
Sushkivka: 8, 10, 17, 20, 165, 211, 213, 215, 217, 259–260
Susiana: 282
Sváby: 224
Sverdlikove: 274
Syrets: 196

Taljanky: 7–8, 10, 19, 22–26, 29–58, 61, 64, 71–72, 86, 91, 96–98, 117, 119–120, 129, 133, 149, 164–168, 172–173, 176, 178, 182–188, 196, 198, 200, 207–208, 211, 218, 221–222, 224–250, 253, 256, 260, 267, 272, 284, 292–295, 297

Talne 1: 211, 213, 215, 217
Talne 2: 22–23, 183, 186, 211, 218, 284
Talne 3: 23, 183, 186, 211, 218, 284
Targu Frumos: 146
Tarpesti: 146
Tărtăria-Gura Luncii: 224
Techirghiol: 224
Teotihuacan: 289
Timkovo: 148
Tîrgu Bereşti: 223
Tomashivka: 8, 10, 165, 211, 213, 215, 218, 270, 276
Trifaneshty: 30
Trinca-Izvorul lui Luca: 224
Trostyanchyk: 221
Troyaniv: 151
Trusesti, Tuguieta: 224
Trypillia-ur. Lypove: 272
Tsipleshty 1: 147
Tsviklovtsy: 148
Tsyurupy: 211, 213, 215, 217

Uivar-Gomilă: 224
Ur: 281
Uruk: 248, 250, 281–285
Usatovo: 145

Vădastra-Măgura Fetelor: 224
Valea Lupului: 146, 224
Valencina de la Concepción: 8–9
Valiava: 211, 214, 216–217

Vărăşti A-Grădiştea Ulmilor: 224
Vărvăreuca: 224
Varvarivka 8: 147, 197, 224
Varvarivka 15: 147
Vasylkiv: 211, 214, 216, 218, 270, 273
Vasylyshyn Jar: 30
Velen Piatra Neamt: 196, 198, 200
Veselyj Kut: 23, 149, 221, 271, 272
Vidra-Măgura Jidovilor: 224
Vilkhovets 1: 10, 24–25, 149–150, 165, 184–186, 269, 273
Vilkhovets 2: 272
Vilshana Slobidka: 150, 186, 211, 214, 216–217
Volodymyrivka: 8, 10, 17–19, 111, 165, 211, 213, 215, 217, 271
Voronovitsy: 148
Vučedol-Vinograd: 224
Vykhvatyntsi cemetery: 182, 189

Yampil: 10, 22, 24, 165, 184–185, 211, 213, 215, 217
Yatranivka: 10, 19, 22, 24, 165, 184–186, 211, 213, 215, 217
Yoruba: 289–291, 294, 296

Zavadivka: 186
Zavalovka: 151
Zelena Dibrova: 150, 211, 213, 215, 217
Zhvanets'-Shchovb: 148
Žvanec: 224

Index of Subjects

RENÉ OHLRAU

activity zone: 91, 256–259
administrative hierarchization: 302
aerial photography: 19, 21, 31, 39, 45, 64, 71
agent-based modelling: 32, 38
agglomeration: 1, 3–5, 7, 9–10, 12–13, 15, 195, 253, 267, 276, 281, 284–286, 290, 297, 301–302
agricultural towns: 281, 283, 285
altars: 76, 91, 99–100, 102–103, 105–107, 109–113, 256, 258–260, 283
anachronism: 290
ancient diet: 209
animal bones: 76, 80, 86, 90–91, 97–98, 105, 111–112, 119, 226, 258–259
animal husbandry: 196–197, 204, 209, 303
archaeomagnetic dating: 23, 25
architecture: 17, 20–21, 25, 32–33, 71, 91, 113, 117, 121, 125–127, 253, 263, 285, 290, 293
artefact density: 76, 259
asymmetric relations: 281, 285

barley: 197–204
biconical vessel: 76, 228, 259
bitter vetch: 197–200, 204
bowl: 76, 86, 92, 103, 108, 111–112, 228, 240, 255, 258–259, 283
building density: 32, 36, 38–39, 265, 297
built space: 50, 71, 208, 263, 289, 293
burnt clay slabs: 245
burnt floor layer: 135, 256
burnt houses: 17, 19, 21, 23, 25, 32–33, 35, 40, 44, 62–64, 72, 76, 86, 96, 99, 102–103, 105–105, 110, 120, 134, 163–154, 183, 207, 246, 253, 292–293, 295
burnt pottery: 86

cambisol: 176–178, 208
canopy regeneration: 208
carrying capacity: 10, 12, 133, 164, 188–189, 195, 207, 212 273, 276, 284, 304
cattle skulls: 79–80, 303
cattle: 3, 10, 173, 195–197, 204, 209–210, 212, 259, 267, 274, 284, 303
causewayed enclosure: 118–119
centralization: 13, 15, 36, 53
centralized chiefdom: 276
ceramic distribution: 55, 127
channels (kiln): 86, 97–98, 100, 227, 232, 234, 236–237, 240–243, 245–246, 250
charcoal: 112, 134, 136–140, 143–151, 162, 173–174, 200, 208
chernozem: 32, 39, 44, 51, 59, 64, 66, 71, 86, 112, 120, 124–125, 176–178, 208, 238
chronological uncertainties: 53
chronology: 1–2, 5, 7, 10, 17, 20, 23, 25–26, 39, 43, 55, 58, 64, 71, 91, 133–135, 161–168, 183, 185, 187, 207, 210, 245, 263, 269–271, 281–282, 284, 292, 296, 301

circulation of goods: 283
clay bench: 76–77
clay tablet: 283
clay token: 128, 283, 302
climate change: 176, 187, 273–274, 276
collapse: 12, 269, 272, 275, 294
collapsed wall: 25, 76, 79, 124, 229, 236, 258
combustion chamber: 227, 232, 234, 242, 250
communal cooking feature: 295
communication limit: 291
complexity: 4, 13, 189, 269, 272–273, 276, 290–291, 293
contemporaneity: 5, 7, 9, 23, 25, 43, 50, 64, 86, 91, 98, 107, 110, 112, 133–135, 163–166, 168, 200, 207–212, 237, 250, 257, 259, 269, 271, 281–282, 284, 295–296, 301
cooperation: 284–285, 303
corvée labourers: 283
cylinder seals: 283

decision performance: 265
decision-making: 13, 265, 267, 285
deforestation: 188, 207, 213–218, 272–274, 302, 304
dehusking: 201, 204, 259
deliberate destruction: 163, 257, 303
demographic development: 12–13, 15, 181, 186, 188, 273–274, 276
depositional processes: 41, 71, 76, 92, 135, 162, 242, 253, 257
disperse settlement pattern: 15
dispersed chiefdom: 276
ditches: 42, 47, 58, 60–66, 68, 71–75, 95–98, 113, 117–121, 128–129, 146, 284, 294–296
division of labour: 4, 36, 222, 245, 250, 274
documentation technique: 79, 253
dogs: 196
domestic animals: 195–197
domestic buildings: 283, 285
dual chamber furnace: 250

eanna district: 283, 285
economic unit: 263, 265
economy: 10, 13, 25–26, 71, 113, 181, 195, 197, 204, 207, 209, 211, 259–260, 268, 272, 274, 276, 283–285, 302
entrance room: 256, 258–259
entrances: 63, 111–112, 129, 296
ethnographic analogy: 15, 134, 164, 181–182, 188, 209, 212, 218, 246, 259
exponential growth: 13, 282

feather grass: 173–174, 178
figurines: 10, 17, 86, 97–98, 100–101, 108, 112, 127, 209, 255, 258–259, 303
fine-ware: 127, 267

fired clay cones: 127, 128
fireplace: 76, 86, 89, 97, 99, 102–103, 106, 109, 111–112, 145, 151, 164, 225, 256, 258–259
fireproof clay: 86
firing chamber: 229–230, 232–236, 243, 250
fish: 196
flint tools: 98, 112, 257, 259
food processing: 76, 259
forest steppe: 1, 171–174, 178, 208, 210, 212, 267–268, 270, 272–274, 276, 297, 302
freestanding updraft kilns: 243

geomagnetic survey: 1, 7, 19–22, 24, 26, 29–33, 39–53, 55, 57–59, 64, 67, 71, 183, 189, 207, 221–222, 225, 237–238, 240, 245, 245, 255, 263
goblet: 76, 78, 80, 88, 91, 96, 103, 108, 125, 258–259
gold objects: 126–128, 263, 293
graph theory: 292
group size: 7, 265, 303

high-density urbanism: 289–290, 296–297
hillfort: 64
hoe: 90
horses: 195–197, 209
house clusters: 31, 64, 261–263, 265, 267, 303
house inventory: 257
house models: 17, 103, 111, 259–260
house place: 55, 72, 74, 76, 79, 91, 253, 255–257, 259–21, 263, 267, 302
house size: 36–39, 52–53, 65, 164, 249, 256, 251, 285
house-burning: 124, 293, 297
household activities: 257, 260
household organization: 253
household-units: 253
houses of the dead: 17
hulled wheats: 197–200
hunting: 12, 196–197, 204

imprints: 21, 74–76, 79, 82, 84, 86, 87, 99, 102, 106, 110–111, 135, 173, 197, 200, 208, 218, 253, 256
incised decoration: 76, 111
industrial features: 294
institutions: 5, 7, 13, 189, 245, 263, 265, 267–268, 281, 283, 285, 301–302
interior: 75–76, 99, 106, 108, 110, 112, 123, 182–183, 228, 236

kiln batteries: 222
kiln construction: 222, 238, 246
kitchen-ware: 103–104, 108, 234, 255, 259
kurgans: 23, 32, 34, 272

land-use models: 209
low-density urbanism: 289–297

malthusian catastrophe: 181
marxism: 181
material culture: 26, 71, 92, 253, 294
meat: 196, 209
mega-complex: 285

mega-structure: 5, 95, 255, 260, 263–268, 285, 293, 301–303
metallurgy: 1, 4
migration: 185, 187–189, 207, 273–274, 282, 291
monumental architecture: 113, 123, 126–127, 129, 181, 269, 289–291, 293, 296–297
mortuary domain: 291, 297
mud-brick cities: 291

naked wheat: 197–200, 204
neighbourhood: 10, 12, 42, 61, 64, 120, 128, 163, 221, 258, 265, 267, 290, 293–294, 296, 303

organizational limits: 265
ornamentation: 1, 134, 166- 168, 261, 271, 274

painted pottery: 3, 17, 86, 104, 166
palaeo-channel: 128
palaeoclimate: 176
palaeo-ecology: 171, 174–175, 208
palisade: 71, 95–96, 109, 113, 119, 294, 296
partition wall: 240–242, 246, 256
pasture: 209–212, 217–218, 267, 274
pea: 197–200, 203–204, 209
perimeter boundary: 117–119, 129
permanent settlement: 292
photogrammetry: 253
phytoliths: 200–204
pigs: 195–196
pits: 25, 31–35, 40–42, 44–46, 49–53, 56–61, 63, 66, 71–77, 79, 86–87, 89–92, 96–98, 100–101, 105, 107–113, 117, 134–135, 161–164, 168, 173–174, 177, 184, 197, 200–204, 221–222, 225, 228, 236–238, 240, 243, 248, 250, 253, 256, 259, 263, 267, 293, 295, 302–303
plant admixture: 76, 86
plant imprints: 197–200, 204
plaster: 76, 86, 97, 99, 110–111, 113, 226–227, 229, 236, 242
platform: 21, 76–79, 86, 97, 99, 102–103, 108, 110–113, 183, 227–236, 250, 283
ploshchadki: 74, 76, 92, 125, 134, 253–254, 256
podium: 83, 85, 107, 109–112, 122–128, 254, 256–260
pollen analysis: 172–173, 200
pontic plant region: 171–172
population densities: 5, 7, 11, 13, 133, 186–188, 281, 289, 295–296
population pressure: 181, 188–189, 272, 274, 276
population size: 4, 7, 10, 13, 15, 31–32, 39, 43, 51, 53, 58, 64, 133, 164, 186–189, 207–208, 267, 273, 276, 295
pottery furnace: 225–228, 233, 236, 250
pottery kiln: 3, 32, 38, 40, 42, 48, 58, 61, 71, 86, 95–98, 221–222, 225, 227–250, 294, 301
pottery production: 91, 221–222, 245, 250
preservation: 33, 35, 41, 43, 46, 51, 56, 61, 99, 119, 173, 183, 201, 208, 221, 258
primary subsistence: 259, 302
private space: 32, 264

production groups: 250
proto-urbanism: 5, 7, 9, 13, 253, 267, 272
public buildings: 113, 129, 281, 283, 285, 302–303
public space: 32, 263–264, 303

quarter-oriented specialization: 302
quarters: 10, 12, 72, 117–119, 128–129, 185, 258, 263, 265–267, 285, 289, 294–296, 302

radiocarbon dates: 22, 39, 53, 76, 86, 91–92, 134–161, 163–164, 167, 175, 185, 188, 245, 250, 269, 276
red paint: 76, 99–100, 112, 123
ruralization: 4, 281–282, 285

scalar stress: 265, 303
secondary products: 259–260, 263, 265, 267, 302
settlement phases: 34, 58, 64–65, 178
settlement planning: 253, 260, 284–285, 292
settlement size: 4, 9–10, 188, 208, 217–218, 272–273, 284, 292
settlement structure: 12, 29, 48, 164, 173, 292
sheep/goat: 196
shells: 196
silica skeletons: 201–202
single-chamber furnace: 250
single-room dwelling: 91
sledge models: 3–4, 14, 209, 268, 284–285, 301–302
snail-rich bulk samples: 119
social agglomeration-control ('agglo-control'): 7, 13, 15, 267–268
social change: 9, 14
social differentiation: 39
social evolution: 13
social experiment: 286, 302
social inequality: 12
social organization: 7, 14, 32, 53, 133, 181, 195, 221, 253, 269, 274
social space: 5, 9, 14, 264 284, 289, 297, 301, 304
social structure: 5, 7, 117, 129, 253, 274, 291, 294, 297, 302
socio-architectural principles: 253
soil formation: 125, 175–177
spatial analysis: 31–32, 38–39, 53–54, 263
special deposits: 123
specialization: 7, 10, 12–13, 221, 250, 265, 267, 285, 294, 301–302
stamp seals: 283
steppe: 1, 3, 30, 171–178, 195–196, 200, 208, 210, 212, 267–268, 270, 272–274, 276, 302
stone fruits: 197–199, 201

stone lintels: 231
storage vessels: 105, 108, 111–112, 240, 255, 258–259
stratification: 12, 274
supra-household organization: 5, 258, 263, 265, 267, 285, 293, 302
sustainability: 209, 286

taphonomy: 257
target excavations: 71, 135, 161–162
technological change: 3, 13, 15, 301
teleological reasoning: 290
temper: 135, 197 200–204, 210, 256
temples: 98, 106, 109, 110, 112, 127, 129, 263, 281, 283, 285, 290
three-level hierarchy: 292
threshing: 197, 200, 204
tool production: 12, 76, 257, 259
transformation: 5, 17, 178, 210, 269–272, 274–276, 284, 294–297
transport technology: 284
trestle: 227, 250
tributary system: 281, 285
trough: 254, 254, 257
two-room dwelling: 91
two-storeyed house: 79, 120, 293, 296
typo-chronology: 26, 133, 165–166, 182, 185, 257, 269, 292
typology: 164, 208, 248

unburnt houses: 32–33, 35, 40, 45, 61, 72–73, 96, 99, 104, 107, 163–164, 183–185, 189, 207, 293, 295
urban landscapes: 5, 281
urban revolution: 281
urbanization: 4, 113, 188–189, 281–282, 285, 289, 302

view-shed analysis: 263–264
vitis: 197
vitrification: 123, 228, 238

wall foundations: 45
wall-painting: 99, 103
waste management: 79, 86, 91, 100, 112–113, 162, 201, 204, 222, 248, 253, 257–260, 267, 302
wattle-and-daub cities: 291
weeds: 197, 201, 204
wild animals: 195–196, 204
wild fruits: 197–200, 204
woodland: 171–178, 195, 197, 200, 208, 210–218, 284
workshops: 23, 31, 38, 221, 248